Lecture Notes in Computer Science 9855

Commenced Publication in 1973
Founding and Former Series Editors:
Gerhard Goos, Juris Hartmanis, and Jan van Leeuwen

More information about this series at http://www.springer.com/series/7407

Ana Paias · Mario Ruthmair · Stefan Voß (Eds.)

Computational Logistics

7th International Conference, ICCL 2016
Lisbon, Portugal, September 7–9, 2016
Proceedings

 Springer

Editors
Ana Paias
Faculdade de Ciências
   da Universidade de Lisboa
Lisbon
Portugal

Mario Ruthmair
University of Vienna
Vienna
Austria

Stefan Voß
University of Hamburg
Hamburg
Germany

ISSN 0302-9743   ISSN 1611-3349 (electronic)
Lecture Notes in Computer Science
ISBN 978-3-319-44895-4   ISBN 978-3-319-44896-1   (eBook)
DOI 10.1007/978-3-319-44896-1

Library of Congress Control Number: 2016948224

LNCS Sublibrary: SL1 – Theoretical Computer Science and General Issues

Printed on acid-free paper

This Springer imprint is published by Springer Nature
The registered company is Springer International Publishing AG Switzerland

Preface

Computational logistics comprises the planning and implementation of large and complex logistics tasks using modern information and communication technology (ICT) and advanced decision support systems. It is applied in various areas, such as the movement of freight and people. More and more it also touches on issues of digital transformation. Optimization models and algorithms are combined with advanced computer technology for obtaining good-quality solutions in a reasonable time as well as for providing/allowing interactivity and visualization for a better understanding of the problem and corresponding solutions. The use of information systems and modern ICT for the design, planning, and control of large-scale logistics networks as well as the complex tasks within them also belongs to the essential options for advancing computational logistics.

The International Conference on Computational Logistics (ICCL) provides an opportunity for academia, industry, and governmental agencies to share solutions, address new challenges, and discuss future research directions in the application of information, communication, optimization, and control technologies to logistic activities. The 7th International Conference on Computational Logistics was organized by the Center for Mathematics Fundamental Applications and Operations Research (CMAF-CIO), and was held at the University of Lisbon, Portugal, September 7–9, 2016.

CMAF-CIO appeared in 2015 as a result of the merging of two former units, the Center for Mathematics and Fundamental Applications and the Operations Research Center. The CMAF-CIO has a solid optimization group that has been working on the modeling and resolution of numerous real-world problems, several of them arising in the field of logistics/routing. Despite the existence of several protocols with governmental agencies and private companies, CMAF-CIO still has the challenge to reduce the gap between academic real-life-based projects and real-life applications. Thus, for this conference, the company Wide Scope was invited as a partner. Wide Scope has been working successfully in many real-life applications in Portugal and even abroad. The Department of Statistics and Operations Research of the University of Lisbon was also closely related to organizing the conference with some of its members being part of the Organizing Committee of the conference. The ICCL conference provides an opportunity to spread, to PhD and master's students of the department, the knowledge and information concerning the bridge between academia and industry.

The special theme of ICCL 2016 was "Road to Logistics Excellence." Despite what has already been achieved in the field of logistics, a proactive look ahead to refinement, improvement, and advancement toward excellence is demanded. Decision analytics and business intelligence are increasingly becoming the key drivers toward solving logistics problems. While this allows us to have a better and advanced integration of logistics processes within supply chains and supply chain networks, the road also opens up for new opportunities. One of the grand challenges in logistics is the question of how to cope with disturbances. While we perform optimization along the supply chain, the vulnerability against errors, failures, and the like becomes even more severe. Logistics excellence not only has to optimize every single part but it also has to think about how to be proactive in avoiding disturbances, or—in case they still happen—how to anticipate proper reactions.

This volume of *Lecture Notes in Computer Science* consists of 29 selected papers presented at the conference. The contributors are from over 30 countries and all the papers were accepted after a thorough review process. The papers were grouped into the following themes:

- Container Terminals and Maritime Transportation
- Intermodal Transport
- Location and Routing
- (General) Logistics and Supply Chain Management

While we believe that these proceedings provide insight into the state-of-the-art of the field, we expect that the development of these themes will continue to grow in the near future, pointing to new research opportunities and paving the road to logistics excellence. Also, a few critical areas have been recognized as the frontier where the links between practical needs, policy requirements, and innovative academic contributions are needed more than ever. These include further integration and/or synchronization in all areas of logistics from warehouse design and operations to multimodal transportation; fostering usage of large-scale computational techniques to tackle the complexity of coordination; the increasing use of greener vehicles such as electric cars or bicycles; and finally efficient ways to deal with disruptions or uncertainty that characterize, for instance, maritime transportation.

Organizing a conference and publishing the proceedings comprise a significant effort, for which we are grateful to the support of a large group of people. The greatest thanks go to the authors, who kept the scientific debate open and at a high-quality standard. We greatly appreciate the valuable cooperation of the reviewers who made a substantial effort in evaluating the papers to achieve a high scientific standard. A special thank you goes to our conference partner Wide Scope and especially Ana Pereira, the Program Committee, and the local organizers in Lisbon.

ICCL 2016 in Lisbon was the seventh of its kind, after Shanghai (2010, 2012), Hamburg (2011), Copenhagen (2013), Valparaíso (2014), and Delft (2015). The contributions presented at ICCL 2016 and the papers in these proceedings show that computational logistics has been spreading among different areas and businesses and we are looking forward to the next developments!

September 2016

Ana Paias
Mario Ruthmair
Stefan Voß

Organization

Organizing Committee

Raquel Bernardino	University of Lisbon and CMAF-CIO, Lisbon, Portugal
Filipe Carvalho	Wide Scope, Portugal
Luis Gouveia	University of Lisbon and CMAF-CIO, Lisbon, Portugal
Miriam Lobato	Wide Scope, Portugal
Rodrigo Marques	CMAF-CIO, Lisbon, Portugal
Ana Paias	University of Lisbon and CMAF-CIO, Lisbon, Portugal
Ana Pereira	Wide Scope, Portugal
Mario Ruthmair	University of Vienna, Austria
Daniel Santos	University of Lisbon and CMAF-CIO, Portugal
Stefan Voß	Institute of Information Systems, University of Hamburg, Germany

Program Committee and Reviewers

Panagiotis Angeloudis	Imperial College London, UK
Mai Ajspur	IT-University of Copenhagen, Denmark
Julia Bachale	University of Hamburg, Germany
Behzad Behdani	Wageningen University, The Netherlands
Khalid Bichou	Imperial College London, UK
Miguel Ayala Botto	Instituto Superior Técnico, Portugal
Jürgen Böse	TU Hamburg-Harburg, Germany
Iris Cagatay	Technical University of Denmark, Denmark
Buyang Cao	Tongji University, Shanghai, China and ESRI, USA
Rafael Carmona	Universidad Anahuac Mexico Norte, Mexico
Pedro Castro	University of Lisbon, Portugal
Jose Ceroni	Pontificia Universidad Catolica de Valparaiso, Chile
Jonas Christensen	Technical University of Denmark, Denmark
Marielle Christiansen	Norwegian University of Science and Technology, Norway
Francesco Corman	Delft University of Technology, The Netherlands
Joachim Daduna	University of Economics and Law, Germany
René De Koster	Erasmus University, The Netherlands
Rommert Dekker	Erasmus University, The Netherlands
Karl Doerner	University of Vienna, Austria
Wolfgang Domschke	TU Darmstadt, Germany
Roberto Domínguez	University of Seville, Spain
Mark Duinkerken	Delft University of Technology, The Netherlands

Kjetil Fagerholt   Norwegian University of Science and Technology,
                              Norway
Maria Conceição   University of Lisbon, Portugal
  Fonseca
Enzo Frazzon   Universidade Federal de Santa Catarina, Brazil
Monica Gentili   University of Salerno, Italy
Rosa Gonzalez   Universidad de Los Andes, Santiago, Chile
Luis Gouveia   University of Lisbon, Portugal
Peter Greistorfer   Karl-Franzens-Universität Graz, Austria
Hans-Otto Guenther   Technical University Berlin, Germany
Richard Hartl   University of Vienna, Austria
Geir Hasle   Sintef, Norway
Leonard Heilig   University of Hamburg, Germany
Sin Ho   Aarhus University, Denmark
Tobias Ibach   University of Hamburg, Germany
Patrick Jaillet   Massachusetts Institute of Technology (MIT), USA
Rune Jensen   IT-University of Copenhagen, Denmark
Herbert Kopfer   University of Bremen, Germany
David Lai   University of Amsterdam, The Netherlands
Ioannis Lagoudis   Malaysia Institute for Supply Chain Innovation, Malaysia
Jasmine Siu Lee Lam   Nanyang Technological University, Singapore
Gilbert Laporte   HEC Montreal and Cirrelt, Canada
Janny Leung   Chinese University, SAR China
Le Li   Delft University of Technology, The Netherlands
Shijie Li   Delft University of Technology, The Netherlands
Andre Ludwig   Kühne Logistics University, Germany
Jose Maestre   University of Seville, Spain
Vittorio Maniezzo   University of Bologna, Italy
Marta Mesquita   University of Lisbon, Portugal
Margarida Moz   University of Lisbon, Portugal
Joao Nabais   Escola Superior de Tecnologia de Setúbal, Portugal
Rudy Negenborn   Delft University of Technology, The Netherlands
Markos Jose Negreiros   Ceara State University, Brazil
  Gomes
Jens Neumann   University of Hamburg, Germany
Carlos Ocampo-   Technical University of Catalonia, Spain
  Martinez
Dario Pacino   Technical University of Denmark, Denmark
Ana Paias   University of Lisbon, Portugal
Margarida Pato   University of Lisbon, Portugal
Günther Raidl   Vienna University of Technology, Austria
Jana Ries   Portsmouth University, UK
Mario Ruthmair   University of Vienna, Austria
Simona Sacone   University of Genoa, Italy
Juan Jose Salazar   University of La Laguna, Spain
Frederik Schulte   University of Hamburg, Germany

Xiaoning Shi	University of Hamburg, Germany and Jiaotong University, China
Douglas Smith	University of Missouri, USA
Matthijs T.J. Spaan	Delft University of Technology, The Netherlands
Fiyyaz Tahir	University of Hamburg, Germany
L.A. Tavasszy	Delft University of Technology, The Netherlands
Philippe Tiede	University of Hamburg, Germany
Kevin Tierney	Paderborn University, Germany
Bart van Riessen	Erasmus University Rotterdam, The Netherlands
Pablo Velarde Rueda	University of Seville, Spain
Jaap Vleugel	Delft University of Technology, The Netherlands
Stefan Voß	Institute of Information Systems, University of Hamburg, Germany
Bart Wiegmans	Delft University of Technology, The Netherlands
David Woodruff	University of California Davis, USA
Tsz Leung Yip	Hong Kong Polytechnic University, SAR China
Shiyuan Zheng	Shanghai Maritime University, China

Contents

Intermodal Transport

Location and Routing

(General) Logistics and Supply Chain Management

Container Terminals and Maritime Transportation

A Multi-product Maritime Inventory Routing Problem with Undedicated Compartments

Elise Foss, Trine N. Myklebust, Henrik Andersson[✉],
and Marielle Christiansen

Department of Industrial Economics and Technology Management,
Norwegian University of Science and Technology, Trondheim, Norway
henrik.andersson@iot.ntnu.no

Abstract. This paper considers the problem of routing bulk tankers to minimize cost while managing the inventory in ports. Multiple non-mixable products are transported and the allocation of products to undedicated compartments onboard the ships is an important aspect of the problem. A mixed integer programming formulation of the problem is proposed, and the model is strengthened by including several valid inequalities. Computational results are reported for an evaluation of the model and the valid inequalities. Results are also reported for two simplified models where either the compartments are dedicated or the products are mixable.

1 Introduction

Maritime transportation has long taken a dominant role in global trade. According to AON (2012), 90 % of all goods traded across boarders are moved by the maritime shipping industry. Remarkable improvements in the efficiency of maritime transportation have been seen in the last 50 years, but still significant improvements can be made by improving the routing and scheduling of ships through the use of operations research.

A maritime inventory routing problem (MIRP) is a planning problem where the problem owner has the responsibility for both the inventory management at one or both ends of the maritime transportation legs and for the ship routing and scheduling. MIRPs are considered to belong to the industrial shipping segment where the mainstay is liquid or dry bulk cargoes that is shipped in large quantities. When transporting liquid bulk, the products are stored in large compartments onboard the ship. As of 2014, tankers have the second largest market share with 29 % of the number of vessels in the markets (UNCTAD 2015).

The purpose of this paper is to give further attention to MIRPs handling multiple non-mixable products with allocation to undedicated compartments. Most of the literature on MIRPs with multiple products simplifies the allocation of products by assigning them to dedicated compartments. Our goal is to develop a model for a MIRP with allocation of products to undedicated compartments

© Springer International Publishing Switzerland 2016
A. Paias et al. (Eds.): ICCL 2016, LNCS 9855, pp. 3–17, 2016.
DOI: 10.1007/978-3-319-44896-1_1

and to explore the behavior of this model. The trade-off between the increased realism of the model and the increase in complexity is evaluated by considering two simplified models with dedicated compartments and mixable products.

The remainder of this paper is organized as follows. In Sect. 2 related literature on MIRPs and the handling of multiple products are reviewed. In Sect. 3, the problem is described in detail. The mathematical formulation and valid inequalities are presented in Sect. 4. The computational results for the undedicated compartment model and the simplified models are reported and discussed in Sect. 5. Finally, concluding remarks are given in Sect. 6.

2   Related Literature

Here, we review relevant literature on MIRPs addressing the transportation of multiple products and the allocation of these. Two recent surveys on the area of maritime transport optimization are Christiansen et al. (2012) and Andersson et al. (2010).

Ronen (2002) was the first to study the transportation of multiple products rather than a single product. Multiple products introduce new challenges like the handling of different products in different ports and ship/product compatibility. Similarly to the problem proposed in this paper, Hemmati et al. (2016) have chosen not to enforce any restrictions on the combinations of products and ports, i.e. each product can be consumed or produced in any number of ports. Al-Khayyal and Hwang (2007), Siswanto et al. (2011), and Agra et al. (2014) have a set of production ports and a set of consumption ports for each product which in a greater degree limits the flow of products. In both Hemmati et al. (2016) and Al-Khayyal and Hwang (2007), a ship is allowed to (un)load different products at the same time, but a port cannot handle the same product by different ships simultaneously. Agra et al. (2014) have solved this issue by restricting the ports to only have one ship operating at a time.

In the context of multi-product MIRPs, the bulk products that are considered often need to be transported in different compartments due to their non-mixable nature. Up until now, little research has addressed the issue of how these products are to be loaded onboard the ship. Ronen (2002), Persson and Göthe-Lundgren (2005), Dauzére-Pérès et al. (2007), and Hemmati et al. (2016) all have models with multiple products, but disregard the allocation of products into compartments onboard the ship. Agra et al. (2014), Al-Khayyal and Hwang (2007), and Li et al. (2010) assume the products to be non-mixable and are thus forced to address the problem of allocating products to compartments. They define each compartment to be dedicated to a specific product, introducing a limitation on which products that can be carried by each compartment of a ship. The use of dedicated compartments is the most used method of solving the problem of allocating products to compartments.

Siswanto et al. (2011) introduce undedicated compartments which they define to be a compartment that can take any product, however it can only store one product at a time. In the event of an empty compartment, any product can be loaded to that compartment. However, Siswanto et al. (2011) assume that only a ship with empty compartments returns to the production ports and thus the danger of mixing products in the same compartment during the shipment is removed.

3   Problem Description

The multi-product MIRP in this paper considers the transportation of multiple non-mixable products and the allocation of the products to undedicated compartments onboard the ship. For maritime transportation this is especially relevant for the shipping of liquid bulk products. Given the nature of the products that are carried, the compartments must be washed regularly, and often before they can be loaded with a different product. This is necessary to avoid pollution of the products, e.g. to avoid a deposition of crude oil in the tankers. Since the time used washing a compartment between switching products is insignificant compared with the time used in port, it is disregarded.

We consider a short-sea transportation problem with a planning horizon that spans a few weeks. It is solved with respect to the ship routing and scheduling, inventory management in ports, and the allocation of products to compartments on each ship. The objective is to minimize the costs consisting of four components; sailing costs between ports, waiting costs outside a port, operating costs in port, and (un)loading unit costs in port. One actor, which is the producer, consumer of the shipping company, is responsible for both the inventory in ports and the routing and scheduling of the ships, and for that reason the inventory holding costs are ignored.

The problem deals with the transportation of multiple products in a many-to-many distribution network. Each port has a berth capacity restricting the number of ships operating in the port simultaneously.

Each ship has an initial start position either at a port or a point at sea. The sailing time between all ports is known for all ships. A ship is not allowed to visit a port without operating in that port. When a ship arrives at a port, it may wait outside the port before starting to operate. Operate is the activity of (un)loading products during a ship's port visit. Waiting outside a port may be necessary if e.g. there is no available berth at the port, or to better time the start of operation with the inventory levels in the port. However, after a ship has started to operate in a port, the ship is not allowed to wait and then continue to operate. When a ship has finished all operating activities in a port, it must immediately sail to its next destination port without waiting.

Over the course of the planning period, a port either consumes or produces a set of products. All ports have one separate storage for each of the products it handles and fixed lower and upper inventory limits are specified for each product in each port. The initial inventory for each product in all ports is known. If a port neither produces or consumes a given product during the planning horizon, it does not handle that product and it does not have a storage of that product.

Each ship can carry a selection of products, possibly all. In addition, each ship has a given number of undedicated compartments where products can be allocated. The compartments can vary in size and each have a maximum capacity. The products that are transported cannot be mixed and thus a compartment can only contain one product at a time. The capacity of a compartment in a ship is often large compared with the quantity that is (un)loaded in a given port, and hence it is natural to allow partial (un)loading. If a compartment has available capacity it can be loaded with more of the same product which it currently contains. However, if a compartment is emptied at a port, any product can now be loaded into the compartment. Allocation of products, (un)loading in port and the possibility of partial unloading are illustrated in Fig. 1.

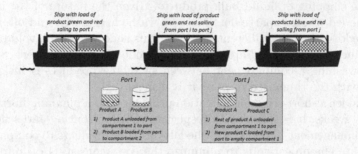

Fig. 1. An example of allocation of three products to a ship with two compartments

At the start of each schedule, the initial load of a product in every compartment in each ship is known. When a ship visits a port, the binding loading capacity under operation is the lowest of the ship's and the port's loading capacity. When a product is loaded into a compartment, it continues to stay in that compartment during sailing and waiting outside ports, until it is unloaded in a different port. Hence, no reallocation of products between compartments can take place between operating times in the ports. However, a product can be reallocated to a different compartment via the storage of that product in the port.

4   Model Description

The model is originally based on the work of Agra et al. (2013), but significant modifications have been made to account for multiple products and undedicated compartments. A time-discrete model is proposed to handle varying production and consumption rates.

4.1   Mathematical Formulation

The formulation of the problem is described in four parts: flow conservation, loading and unloading, inventory management, and objective function.

Flow Conservation Constraints. Let $\mathcal{V}$ be the set of ships to be routed and scheduled. Each ship v has a starting position either in port or a point at sea, $o(v)$, and an artificial point of destination $d(v)$. The ships are routed to serve a set of ports $\mathcal{N}$ and each ship will have one schedule over the planning horizon. $\mathcal{T}$ defines the set of time periods and $\overline{T}$ is the total number of time periods in the planning horizon. The number of time periods needed for each ship to sail between two ports is assumed to be known, and the travel time for ship v between port i and j is defined as T_{ijv}.

B_{it} is the berth capacity in port i in time period t and limits the number of ships simultaneously operating in the port. Each ship is assumed to have three types of possible modes; sailing, waiting, and operating. To design the routing constraints with these modes, three binary variables are needed. x_{ijvt} equals 1 if ship v sails from port i directly to port j starting at the beginning of period t, and 0 otherwise. o_{ivt} equals 1 if ship v operates in port i in period t, and 0 otherwise. Finally, the waiting variable w_{ivt} equals 1 if ship v is waiting outside port i in period t, and 0 otherwise. Figure 3 illustrates all the variables.

$$\sum_{j\in\mathcal{N}\cup d(v)} x_{o(v)jv1} + o_{o(v)v1} + w_{o(v)v1} = 1 \qquad\qquad v\in\mathcal{V} \qquad (1)$$

$$\sum_{i\in\mathcal{N}\cup o(v)}\sum_{t\in\mathcal{T}} x_{id(v)vt} = 1 \qquad\qquad v\in\mathcal{V} \qquad (2)$$

$$\sum_{j\in\mathcal{N}\cup o(v)} x_{jiv(t-T_{jiv})} + w_{iv(t-1)} + o_{iv(t-1)}$$

$$= \sum_{j\in\mathcal{N}\cup d(v)} x_{ijvt} + w_{ivt} + o_{ivt} \qquad\qquad i\in\mathcal{N}, v\in\mathcal{V}, t\in\mathcal{T} \qquad (3)$$

$$o_{iv(t-1)} \leq \sum_{j\in\mathcal{N}\cup d(v)} x_{ijvt} + o_{ivt} \qquad\qquad i\in\mathcal{N}, v\in\mathcal{V}, t\in\mathcal{T} \qquad (4)$$

$$o_{iv(t-1)} \geq \sum_{j\in\mathcal{N}\cup d(v)} x_{ijvt} \qquad\qquad i\in\mathcal{N}, v\in\mathcal{V}, t\in\mathcal{T} \qquad (5)$$

$$\sum_{v\in\mathcal{V}} o_{ivt} \leq B_{it} \qquad\qquad i\in\mathcal{N}, t\in\mathcal{T} \qquad (6)$$

$$x_{ijvt}\in\{0,1\} \qquad i\in\mathcal{N}\cup o(v), j\in\mathcal{N}\cup d(v), v\in\mathcal{V}, t\in\mathcal{T} \qquad (7)$$

$$w_{ivt}, o_{ivt}\in\{0,1\} \qquad\qquad i\in\mathcal{N}, v\in\mathcal{V}, t\in\mathcal{T} \qquad (8)$$

Constraints (1) and (2) ensure that the ships' schedules have a beginning and an end. If a ship travels directly from $o(v)$ to $d(v)$, the ship is not used and is idle during the entire planning horizon. Constraints (3) are the ship flow conservation constraints. Constraints (4) restrict the ships to only be able to wait prior to operation. Constraints (5) enforce operations in a port, i.e. a ship cannot leave a port prior to operating, while constraints (6) are the berth capacity constraints. Constraints (7) and (8) are the binary restrictions.

Figure 2 shows an example of a ship's route. As can be seen, at time period one, $t = 1$, the ship sails directly from its origin node, o, and arrives in *Port 2*

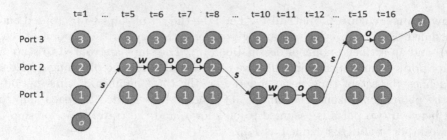

Fig. 2. Example of a ship route consisting of sailing s, waiting w, and operating o

at $t = 5$. Then, the ship waits at $t = 6$, operates in two time periods and sails to *Port 1* at $t = 8$. The ship waits outside *Port 1* at $t = 11$ and operates at $t = 12$. Finally, the ship sails to *Port 3* and operates in one time period before the schedule ends at $t = 16$ when the ship sails to the destination node, d.

Loading and Unloading Constraints. Let $\mathcal{K}$ be the set of all products, $\mathcal{K}_v$ the set of products ship v can transport, and $\mathcal{V}_k$ the set of ships that can transport product k. $\overline{Q}_v^V$ and $\overline{Q}_i^P$ define the upper (un)loading capacity of ship v and port i in each time period. Thus, each ship can (un)load as many products or as much of a product within one time period as long as it does not exceed the (un)loading capacity of the port or the ship. A ship v has a set of compartments, defined as $\mathcal{C}_v$, and each compartment c has a capacity $\overline{K}_{vc}$. Each ship v starts with an initial load in each compartment c of product k, defined as L_{vck}^0. Variable l_{vckt} denotes the load onboard ship v of product k in compartment c at the end of time period t. Variables q_{ivckt}^L and q_{ivckt}^U represent the quantity loaded and unloaded of product k to/from compartment c by ship v from/to port i in time period t. Finally, to handle the allocation of products, variable y_{vckt} equals 1 if compartment c in ship v contains product k at the end of time period t, and 0 otherwise.

$$\sum_{k \in \mathcal{K}_v} \sum_{c \in \mathcal{C}_v} (q_{ivckt}^L + q_{ivckt}^U) \le min\{\overline{Q}_v^V, \overline{Q}_i^P\} o_{ivt} \qquad i \in \mathcal{N}, v \in \mathcal{V}, t \in \mathcal{T} \qquad (9)$$

$$\begin{aligned} l_{vck(t-1)} + \sum_{i \in \mathcal{N}} q_{ivckt}^L \\ = \sum_{i \in \mathcal{N}} q_{ivckt}^U + l_{vckt} \end{aligned} \qquad v \in \mathcal{V}, c \in \mathcal{C}_v, k \in \mathcal{K}_v, t \in \mathcal{T} \quad (10)$$

$$l_{vck0} = L_{vck}^0 \qquad\qquad v \in \mathcal{V}, c \in \mathcal{C}_v, k \in \mathcal{K}_v \quad (11)$$

$$\sum_{k \in \mathcal{K}_v} y_{vckt} \le 1 \qquad\qquad v \in \mathcal{V}, c \in \mathcal{C}_v, t \in \mathcal{T} \quad (12)$$

$$l_{vckt} \le \overline{K}_{vc} y_{vckt} \qquad\qquad v \in \mathcal{V}, c \in \mathcal{C}_v, k \in \mathcal{K}_v, t \in \mathcal{T} \quad (13)$$

$$q_{ivckt}^L, q_{ivckt}^U \ge 0 \qquad i \in \mathcal{N}, v \in \mathcal{V}, c \in \mathcal{C}_v, k \in \mathcal{K}_v, t \in \mathcal{T} \quad (14)$$

$$l_{vckt} \ge 0 \qquad\qquad v \in \mathcal{V}, c \in \mathcal{C}_v, k \in \mathcal{K}_v, t \in \mathcal{T} \quad (15)$$

$$y_{vckt} \in \{0,1\} \qquad\qquad v \in \mathcal{V}, c \in \mathcal{C}_v, k \in \mathcal{K}_v, t \in \mathcal{T} \quad (16)$$

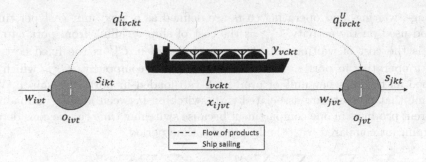

Fig. 3. Illustration of variables

Constraints (9) ensure that a ship can only (un)load when it is operating in a port and define the upper limit on the total quantity (un)loaded by a ship in a time period. Constraints (10) represent the load balance for each ship, while constraints (11) define the initial load of every product in every compartment for each ship. Constraints (12) ensure that only one product can be in each compartment at any time. The load capacity of each compartment is given in constraints (13), which also enforce the binary variable y_{vckt} to be 1 when there is a load in a compartment. Constraints (14) and (15) define the non-negativity constraints, while constraints (16) define the binary restrictions.

Inventory Management Constraints. The production/consumption quantities of a product k in port i in time period t are denoted P_{ikt} and D_{ikt}, respectively, and can vary over the planning horizon. Each port has a storage for each product it handles, and the initial inventory of product k in port i is called S_{ik}^0. $\overline{S}_{ik}$ and $\underline{S}_{ik}$ define the upper and lower inventory limit in port i for product k, respectively. Variable s_{ikt} gives the inventory level in port i of product k at the end of time period t.

$$
\begin{aligned}
s_{ik(t-1)} + \sum_{v\in\mathcal{V}}\sum_{c\in\mathcal{C}_v} q_{ivckt}^U + P_{ikt} \\
= D_{ikt} + \sum_{v\in\mathcal{V}}\sum_{c\in\mathcal{C}_v} q_{ivckt}^L + s_{ikt}
\end{aligned}
\qquad i\in\mathcal{N}, k\in\mathcal{K}, t\in\mathcal{T} \qquad (17)
$$

$$
\underline{S}_{ik} \le s_{ikt} \le \overline{S}_{ik} \qquad\qquad i\in\mathcal{N}, k\in\mathcal{K}, t\in\mathcal{T} \qquad (18)
$$

$$
s_{ik0} = S_{ik}^0 \qquad\qquad\qquad i\in\mathcal{N}, k\in\mathcal{K} \qquad (19)
$$

Constraints (17) are the inventory balance for all ports and products. Constraints (18) state lower and upper inventory limits for each product in every port. Lastly, constraints (19) define the initial inventory of each product.

Objective Function. The objective function, presented in (20), minimizes the sailing-, waiting-, and operation costs as well as the variable (un)loading costs.

Sailing-, waiting- and operating costs are defined as a fixed unit cost per time period used on the activity. C_{ijv}^T is the cost of ship v sailing from port i to j. C_v^W is the cost of waiting outside a port for ship v. C_{iv}^O is the fixed cost of ship v operating in port i. There is also a variable component, C_{ivk}^Q, which is defined as the cost per unit of product k (un)loaded in port i by ship v. We assume that no costs are associated with switching between loading/unloading different products in one compartment because switching time can be considered insignificant compared with the length of a time period.

$$\min \sum_{v\in\mathcal{V}} \sum_{i\in\mathcal{N}\cup o(v)} \sum_{j\in\mathcal{N}\cup d(v)} \sum_{t\in\mathcal{T}} C_{ijv}^T x_{ijvt} + \sum_{i\in\mathcal{N}} \sum_{v\in\mathcal{V}} \sum_{t\in\mathcal{T}} C_v^W w_{ivt}$$

$$+ \sum_{i\in\mathcal{N}} \sum_{v\in\mathcal{V}} \sum_{t\in\mathcal{T}} C_{iv}^O o_{ivt} + \sum_{i\in\mathcal{N}} \sum_{v\in\mathcal{V}} \sum_{c\in\mathcal{C}_v} \sum_{k\in\mathcal{K}_v} \sum_{t\in\mathcal{T}} C_{ivk}^P (q_{ivckt}^L + q_{ivckt}^U) \qquad (20)$$

4.2 Valid Inequalities and Tightening Constraints

By exploiting the structure of the problem, valid inequalities have been developed to strengthen the LP-relaxation of the problem and in turn reduce the solution time. In this paper, only the most promising valid inequalities from our studies have been included.

Minimum Number of Visits with Ship Capacity Sequence (MV). MV is inspired by similar valid inequalities addressed by Andersson et al. (2015). Here, a ship capacity sequence is introduced to avoid the generalization done when the maximum ship capacity is used to calculate the lower bound for the entire planning horizon.

The ship capacity sequence is defined over a subinterval of the planning horizon and is built upon the maximum number of times each ship can visit a port. To be able to define a maximum number of visits of each ship, two assumptions are made, (1) each ship will only travel back and forth from port i to its nearest port after the initial visit to port i and (2) each ship will only operate one period in each port visit. With this, the maximum number of visits ship v can make to port i in time interval $\mathcal{T}' = \{\underline{T}', \ldots, \overline{T}'\}$ is V_{iv}^{MAX}:

$$V_{iv}^{MAX} = \left\lceil \frac{T' - T_{jiv}}{2 \cdot T_i^{MIN} + 2} \right\rceil \qquad\qquad i \in \mathcal{N}, v \in \mathcal{V} \qquad (21)$$

T' is the length of time interval $\mathcal{T}'$, and T_i^{MIN} is the sailing time for ship v from port i to its nearest port. j denotes the ship's position at the beginning of the time interval.

Ship Capacity Sequence. The ship capacity sequence, defined for each port i, gives the maximum amount of products that can be (un)loaded in a port in m visits during a time interval. First, the highest ship capacity is added cumulatively to the capacity sequence a number of times equal to the maximum number of visits defined in (21). The same follows for the rest of the ships, in descending order based on capacity. The length of the ship capacity sequence is equal to the total number of visits to port i in the time interval, from all ships. The ship capacity sequence of port i is denoted $\overline{\mathcal{K}}_i^V = \{\overline{K}_{i0}^V, \overline{K}_{i1}^V, \ldots, \overline{K}_{im}^V\}$ for $i \in \mathcal{N}$.

Assume a fleet of two ships where the largest ship has a capacity of 200 and can visit port i at most three times in time interval $\mathcal{T}'$. The other ship has a capacity of 100 and can visit port i a maximum of two times. The ship capacity sequence of port i, with $\overline{K}_{i0}^V = 0$ for the case of no loading, is then equal to $\overline{\mathcal{K}}_i^V = \{0, 200, 400, 600, 700, 800\}$ for the given time interval.

Excess Production and Consumption. The excess production of product k in port i, $e_{ikT'}^P$ and the excess consumption of product k in port i, $e_{ikT'}^D$, during time interval $\mathcal{T}'$ is defined in (22) and (23), respectively.

$$e_{ikT'}^P = \sum_{t \in T'} P_{ikt} + s_{ik(\underline{T}'-1)} - \overline{S}_{ik} \qquad i \in \mathcal{N}, k \in \mathcal{K} \qquad (22)$$

$$e_{ikT'}^D = \sum_{t \in T'} D_{ikt} - s_{ik(\underline{T}'-1)} + \underline{S}_{ik} \qquad i \in \mathcal{N}, k \in \mathcal{K} \qquad (23)$$

Since a ship can handle both excess consumption and production in the same visit, the lower bounds on visits for produced and consumed products cannot be added together. On this note, the maximum of $e_{ikT'}^P$ and $e_{ikT'}^D$ aggregated over product, $e_{iT'} = max\{\sum_{k \in \mathcal{K}} e_{ikT'}^P, \sum_{k \in \mathcal{K}} e_{ikT'}^D\}$, is used as the restricting quantity in the inequalities.

If time interval $\mathcal{T}'$ starts at $t = 1$, then the incoming inventory level of product k, $s_{ik(\underline{T}'-1)}$ is equal to the initial inventory of that product, S_{ik}^0. By this, the minimum number of visits needed to serve the excess level can be calculated a priori. Let p_i be the first position in the ship capacity sequence corresponding to a capacity high enough to cover $e_{iT'}$. Hence, p_i corresponds to the minimum number of visits needed. In all other cases, the incoming inventory is a variable and this simplification is impossible. The valid inequalities for time interval $\mathcal{T}'$ are defined by (24) or (25) depending on the starting period of the time interval.

$$\sum_{j \in \mathcal{N}} \sum_{v \in V} \sum_{t \in T'} x_{jivt} \geq p_i \qquad\qquad i \in \mathcal{N} \qquad (24)$$

$$\sum_{j \in \mathcal{N}} \sum_{v \in V} \sum_{t \in T'} x_{jivt} \geq$$

$$\frac{e_{iT'} + (m-1)\overline{K}_{im}^V - m\overline{K}_{i(m-1)}^V}{\overline{K}_{im}^V - \overline{K}_{i(m-1)}^V} \qquad i \in \mathcal{N}, 1 < m < |\overline{\mathcal{K}}_i^V| \qquad (25)$$

Valid inequalities (24) and (25) give a lower bound on the number of visits to port i in time interval $\mathcal{T}'$.

Minimum Number of Compartments per Product with Compartment Capacity Sequence (MCP). MCP is an extension of a valid inequality presented by Andersson et al. (2015) adapted to account for both multiple products and a heterogeneous set of tanks on the ships. A compartment capacity sequence is designed equivalently to the ship capacity sequence, using compartment capacities. The sequence is created for all products k and ports i and is written as $\overline{\mathcal{C}}_{ik}^V$ = $\{\overline{C}_{ik0}^V, \overline{C}_{ik1}^V, .., \overline{C}_{ikm}^V\}$. The excess production, $e_{ik\mathcal{T}'}^P$, and consumption, $e_{ik\mathcal{T}'}^D$, are calculated in (22) and (23) respectively, and $e_{ik\mathcal{T}'}$ is the maximum of excess production and consumption. Let p_{ik} represent the first position in the ship compartment capacity sequence sufficient to cover $e_{ik\mathcal{T}'}$. p_{ik} is then the minimum number of compartments needed for each port and product combination. When N_v^C is the number of compartments in ship v, the valid inequalities MCP for time interval $\mathcal{T}'$ are presented in (26) and (27).

$$\sum_{j \in \mathcal{N}} \sum_{v \in \mathcal{V}_k} \sum_{t \in \mathcal{T}'} N_v^C x_{jivt} \geq p_{ik} \qquad\qquad i \in \mathcal{N}, k \in \mathcal{K} \quad (26)$$

$$\sum_{j \in \mathcal{N}} \sum_{v \in \mathcal{V}_k} \sum_{t \in \mathcal{T}'} N_v^C x_{jivt}$$

$$\geq \frac{e_{ik\mathcal{T}'} + (m-1)\overline{C}_{ikm}^V - m\overline{C}_{ik(m-1)}^V}{\overline{C}_{ikm}^V - \overline{C}_{ik(m-1)}^V} \qquad i \in \mathcal{N}, k \in \mathcal{K}, 1 < m < |\overline{\mathcal{C}}_{ik}^V| \quad (27)$$

Minimum Number of Operation Periods (MO). The idea of imposing a lower bound on the minimum number of operation periods has been introduced by e.g. Agra et al. (2013) for a single-product inventory routing problem. Here, it is extended to account for multiple products. Excess production, e_{ik}^P, and consumption, e_{ik}^D are calculated by (22) and (23) respectively, but for the entire planning horizon and thus the initial stock level is S_{ik}^0. Under the assumption that each product is either produced or consumed, only e_{ik}^P or e_{ik}^D is positive. The minimum number of operation periods required by each port is equal to the sum of operation periods required by each product. The valid inequalities (28) enforce a lower bound on the number of operation periods needed in each port.

$$\sum_{v \in \mathcal{V}} \sum_{t \in \mathcal{T}} o_{ivt} \geq \left\lceil \sum_{k \in \mathcal{K}} \frac{e_{ik}^P + e_{ik}^D}{min\{\overline{Q}_i^P, max\{\overline{Q}_v^V ; v \in \mathcal{V}\}\}} \right\rceil \qquad i \in \mathcal{N} \qquad (28)$$

5   Computational Study

All instances of our mathematical programming models are solved using Mosel Xpress-MP. Mosel Xpress-MP is run on a Hewlett Packard 64-bit Windows 7 Enterprise PC with Intel(R) Core(TM) i7-3770 3.40 GHz processor and 16.0 GB (15.9 GB usable) RAM. Note that Xpress solves LP problems integrated with the IP solution procedure. Due to the use of Presolve in Xpress, the LP bounds that are reported in this chapter may be higher than if the LP relaxation of the IP problem was solved explicitly.

5.1   Instances and Data

The name of each instance is built up of two components; which case is used and which valid inequality that has been added. The small case consists of two ships with two compartments each, four ports, and three products and is denoted by S. The medium case have three ships, with two or three compartments each, six ports, and four products and is denoted M. Finally, the large case is equivalently denoted L and consists of four ships, with two or three compartments each, eight ports, and four products. To represent which of the three valid inequalities that has been added, the notation introduced in Sect. 4.2 is used, namely MV for valid inequalities defined in (24) and (25), MCP for valid inequalities in (26) and (27) and MO for valid inequalities in (28). UC is used to refer to the instance where no valid inequalities have been added.

MV and MCP use a time interval when deciding the binding capacity of a ship or a compartment in the ship/compartment capacity sequence. Preliminary testing showed that using the entire length of the time horizon as the length of the time interval gives the tightest formulation. Thus, all succeeding tests employ the full planning horizon as time interval. Andersson et al. (2015) present results that indicate that starting the time interval in the first time period is most beneficial. Thus, here the incoming inventory level of the time interval, $s_{ik(\underline{T}'-1)}$, is always equal to the initial inventory, S_{ik}^0.

5.2   Exact Solution Method and Valid Inequalities

In this section, the results from the testing of the model and the valid inequalities are presented. We have tested the valid inequalities independently, as well as other interesting combinations. Table 1 shows the results from testing the model alone, and with the different valid inequalities. We use bold font to identify the best solution and best lower bounds in Table 1. Note that the LP bounds presented below corresponds to results obtained from Xpress when it solves the LP problem integrated with the IP solution procedure. This can lead to different results than if the LP relaxation was solved explicitly.

As can be seen, MV tightens the formulation and increases the LP bound, resulting in a more efficient branch-and-bound procedure. This is evident in S_MV as the time to optimality is improved from S_UC. MCP gives an even tighter formulation and higher LP bound than MV. S_MCP gives a significantly better time to optimality and has the best performance over all test cases, in terms of both the highest bound and the lowest gap. MCP reduced the gap between the LP solution and the optimal integer solution from 45.6 % to 15.9 % in the small test case, and it is reasonable to believe that this reduction can explain the high efficiency of this inequality. MV and MCP are the two best performing valid inequalities, however, a combination of the two is not efficient. The combination of the two increases the complexity more than it manages to reduce the search space, and the time to optimality is higher than without any valid inequalities.

Table 1. Results of small-, medium- and large-sized test cases with different valid inequalities. Running time 5000 s

Test case	Info	UC	MV	MCP	MO	MCP_MV
S	LP bound	16 257	18 975	**25 199**	16 419	20 395
	Best solution	29 883	29 883	29 883	29 883	29 883
	Best bound	29 883	29 883	29 883	29 883	29 883
	Time to optimality	2 100 s	1 783 s	**1 012 s**	3 928s	3 463s
M	LP bound	19 016	21 589	**25 198**	19 547	19 779
	Best solution	35 633	42 415	36 673	35 233	**35 153**
	Best bound	26 065	25 742	**27 582**	26 183	24 518
	Gap	26.9 %	39.3 %	**24.8 %**	25.7 %	30.3 %
L	LP bound	24 473	28 293	**34 391**	24 592	29 377
	Best solution	64 930	**57 252**	61 310	61 673	-
	Best bound	31 017	30 718	**34 933**	30 782	30 443
	Gap	52.2 %	46.3 %	**43.0 %**	50.1 %	-

Even though the LP bound is improved, S_MO has the highest running time to optimality. While MO has one of the highest running times to optimality in the small test case, M_MO finds a good integer solution and thus achieves one of the best bounds. Even though MO showed a slight improvement from the small- to the medium-sized test case, it did not show any improvement in the large-sized test case.

5.3 Model Simplifications

To use undedicated compartments (UC) to model the handling of multiple non-mixable products is a highly realistic approach to real life applications. However, alternative approaches do exist, namely either employing dedicated compartments (DC), or assuming the products to be mixable and thus no separate compartments are needed (NC). Only minor changes are needed to the UC model introduced to employ either DC or NC, and explicit formulations for these models are not included. In this section, we report and compare the performance of the three models. To be able to compare the models, no valid inequalities have been added to the test instances. UC, DC, and NC are used to denote which model is tested.

The UC model has the freedom to change which products that are loaded in which compartments and can thus choose an optimal allocation of each product, while DC must always adhere the capacity constraints of each product's dedicated compartment(s). This is a restriction of the UC model; less variables are needed and the complexity of the model is reduced. In NC models, the only capacity limit is the ship capacity, and NC is thus a relaxation of the UC model. NC is an even greater simplification than DC. Compared with NC, the number of variables and constraints in UC increases approximately 30 % and 20 % respectively. The results of the test instances can be found in Table 2.

S_NC is the first to prove optimality, followed by S_DC and last S_UC, as expected. The optimal objective value in S_DC is higher than those of S_NC and S_UC, which illustrates that NC and UC utilize a degree of freedom not applicable in DC. S_NC did not, however, find a better solution than the optimal solution of S_UC. Note that the underlying flexibility on quantity (un)loaded of all MIRP models in general, often makes it possible for a model with compart-ments to adapt and replicate the solution of a model without compartments. This would, however, not be possible in cases of tramp shipping where the ship only (un)load fixed sized cargoes. For the medium-sized test case, the same pat-tern is seen in the solutions and the size of the gaps as in the small test case. However, due to the large gaps the results in the large-sized test case deviate from the expected pattern.

Table 2. Model simplification results of the three test cases. Running time 5 000 s.

Test case	Info	NC	UC	DC
S	Best solution	29 883	29 883	30 303
	Best bound	29 883	29 883	30 303
	Time to optimality	737 s	2 100 s	1 519 s
M	Best solution	35 463	35 633	36 400
	Best bound	26 296	26 065	26 803
	Gap	25.8 %	26.9 %	26.4 %
L	Best solution	57 713	64 930	52 500
	Best bound	32 905	31 017	32 957
	Gap	43.0 %	52.2 %	37.2 %

5.4 Comparison of the Model and Model Simplifications

We have chosen to compare the solutions of the model and the model simpli-fications on the small-sized instances since he optimal solution is known for all models. The focus is on the comparison of models with UC and DC results, since the solutions of UC and NC proved to be equal for the tested case.

Figure 4 shows how the routing of the ships differ between UC and DC. The UC model manages to find a shorter feasible route compared with the DC model. Often the reason is that in UC the ships have the flexibility of loading a compartment with any product the ship can carry after it is emptied. Emptying a compartment of a product will thus free up capacity that can now be available to all products. Another aspect of the flexibility contained in UC is the ability to reallocate products in order to obtain the optimal allocation of products to compartments. In DC, the dedication of products to compartments is not necessarily optimal, but it cannot be improved. For example, in the optimal solution of DC, *Product* 3 is dedicated/fixed to the smallest compartment. In contrast, *Product* 3 ends up using the largest compartment available in the fleet in UC. Thus, in DC the compartment capacity of *Product* 3 is binding and the fact that *Product* 3 is fixed to the smallest compartment prevents DC from finding the optimal solution found by UC. This lack of flexibility is reflected in the costs, and the possibility of saving economical values by using UC exists.

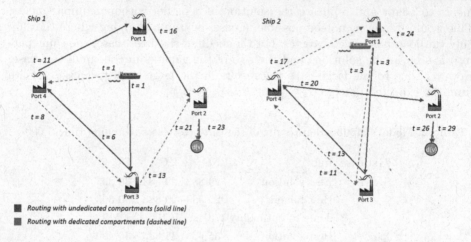

Fig. 4. Comparison of routing of ships with undedicated and dedicated compartments

When compartments are dedicated, the given capacities for each product must remain the same through the planning horizon. This implies that the DC model can be vulnerable to varying production rates while UC can more easily adapt to a high variation in supply and demand during the planning horizon by reallocating its products. UC handles the allocation of products in a more realistic way than both NC and DC, however using undedicated compartments come with the drawback of adding more complexity. The greater the number of compartments in an UC model, the less capacity is locked to a product at a time and the flexibility increases. As a result, the performance of a UC model moves toward the performance of the NC model. In a DC model, however, the performance is not dependent on the number of compartments due to the fact that it always has one fixed capacity per product.

6   Concluding Remarks

In this paper, we developed a mathematical formulation for a maritime inventory routing problem addressing the allocation of multiple products to undedicated compartments onboard the ships. Three different types of valid inequalities were developed and tested, the most promising using a capacity sequence to define the minimum number of compartment visits required in a port. Computational results were also given for two simplified models to compare different ways of handling the allocation of products. Employing undedicated compartments is the most realistic approach to real life applications but it comes with the drawback of added complexity. However, comparison with models employing dedicated compartments or mixable products indicate a potential for economical savings by using undedicated compartments.

References

Agra, A., Andersson, H., Christiansen, M., Wolsey, L.: A maritime inventory routing problem: discrete time formulations and valid inequalities. Networks **62**(4), 297–314 (2013)

Agra, A., Christiansen, M., Delgado, A., Simonetti, L.: Hybrid heuristics for a short sea inventory routing problem. Eur. J. Oper. Res. **236**(3), 924–935 (2014)

Al-Khayyal, F., Hwang, S.J.: Inventory constrained maritime routing and scheduling for multi-commodity liquid bulk, Part I: applications and model. Eur. J. Oper. Res. **176**(1), 106–130 (2007)

Andersson, H., Christiansen, M., Desaulniers, G.: A new decomposition algorithm for a liquefied natural gas inventory routing problem. Int. J. Prod. Res. **54**(2), 564–578 (2015)

Andersson, H., Hoff, A., Christiansen, M., Hasle, G., Lokketangen, A.: Industrial aspects and literature survey: combined inventory management and routing. Comput. Oper. Res. **37**(9), 1515–1536 (2010)

AON: Industry analysis: maritime transportation. White Paper, Advisen Ltd. (2012)

Christiansen, M., Fagerholt, K., Nygreen, B., Ronen, D.: Ship routing and scheduling in the new millennium. Eur. J. Oper. Res. **228**(3), 467–483 (2012)

Dauzère-Pérès, S., Nordli, A., Olstad, A., Haugen, K., Koester, U., Myrstad, P.O., Teistklub, G., Reistad, A.: Omya Hustadmarmor optimizes its supply chain for delivering calcium carbonate slurry to European paper manufacturers. Interfaces **37**(1), 39–51 (2007)

Hemmati, A., Hvattum, L.M., Christiansen, M., Laporte, G.: An iterative two-phase hybrid matheuristic for a multi-product short sea inventory-routing problem. Eur. J. Oper. Res. **252**(3), 775–788 (2016)

Li, J., Karimi, I., Srinivasan, R.: Efficient bulk maritime logistics for the supply and delivery of multiple chemicals. Comput. Chem. Eng. **34**(12), 2118–2128 (2010)

Persson, J.A., Göthe-Lundgren, M.: Shipment planning at oil refineries using column generation and valid inequalities. Eur. J. Oper. Res. **163**(3), 631–652 (2005)

Ronen, D.: Marine inventory routing: shipments planning. J. Oper. Res. Soc. **53**(1), 108–114 (2002)

Siswanto, N., Essam, D., Sarker, R.: Solving the ship inventory routing and scheduling problem with undedicated compartments. Comput. Ind. Eng. **61**(2), 289–299 (2011)

UNCTAD: Review of maritime transport 2015. UNCTAD/RMT 2015 (2015)

A MIP Based Local Search Heuristic for a Stochastic Maritime Inventory Routing Problem

Agostinho Agra[1][(⊠)], Marielle Christiansen[2], Lars Magnus Hvattum[3], and Filipe Rodrigues[1][(⊠)]

[1] Department of Mathematics, CIDMA, University of Aveiro, Aveiro, Portugal
{aagra,fmgrodrigues}@ua.pt
[2] Department of Industrial Economics and Technology Management,
Norwegian University of Science and Technology, Trondheim, Norway
mc@iot.ntnu.no
[3] Molde University College, Molde, Norway
hvattum@himolde.no

Abstract. We consider a single product maritime inventory routing problem in which the production and consumption rates are constant over the planning horizon. The problem involves a heterogeneous fleet of ships and multiple production and consumption ports with limited storage capacity. In spite of being one of the most common ways to transport goods, maritime transportation is characterized by high levels of uncertainty. The principal source of uncertainty is the weather conditions, since they have a great influence on sailing times. The travel time between any pair of ports is assumed to be random and to follow a log-logistic distribution. To deal with random sailing times we propose a two-stage stochastic programming problem with recourse. The routing, the order in which the ports are visited, as well as the quantities to load and unload are fixed before the uncertainty is revealed, while the time of the visit to ports and the inventory levels can be adjusted to the scenario. To solve the problem, a MIP based local search heuristic is developed. This new approach is compared with a decomposition algorithm in a computational study.

Keywords: Maritime transportation · Stochastic programming · Uncertainty · Matheuristic

1 Introduction

We consider a maritime inventory routing problem (MIRP) where a heterogeneous fleet of ships is transporting a single product between ports. There exists one type of ports where the product is produced, and in the other ports the product is consumed. The production and consumption rates are constant over the planning horizon. At all ports, there exists an inventory for storing the product,

© Springer International Publishing Switzerland 2016
A. Paias et al. (Eds.): ICCL 2016, LNCS 9855, pp. 18–34, 2016.
DOI: 10.1007/978-3-319-44896-1_2

and lower and upper limits are given for each port. Each port can be visited one or several times during the planning horizon depending on the size of the storage, the production or consumption rate, and the quantity loaded or unloaded at each port visit. The MIRP consists of designing routes and schedules for a fleet of ships in order to minimize the transportation and port costs, and to determine the quantities handled at each port call without exceeding the storage limits. The MIRP is a very important and common problem in maritime shipping and is relevant when the actors involved in a maritime supply chain have the responsibility for both the transportation of the cargoes and the inventories at the ports. The shipping industry is capital intensive, so a modest improvement in fleet utilization can imply a large increase in profit. Therefore, the ability of ship operators to make good decisions is crucial. However, the MIRPs are very complex to solve due to the high degree of freedom in the routing, scheduling, number of port visits, and the quantity loaded or unloaded at each port visit.

There exists a solid amount of research and resulting publications within MIRPs, and these have formed the basis of several surveys: Papageorgiou et al. [18], Christiansen et al. [10], and Christiansen and Fagerholt [8,9]. In addition, Coelho et al. [12] and Andersson et al. [4] surveyed both land-based and maritime inventory routing problems. Maritime transportation is characterized by high levels of uncertainty, and one of the most common uncertainties is the sailing times that are affected by heavily changing weather conditions. In practice, unpredictable delays may affect the execution of an optimal deterministic plan. In order to compensate for such delays, it is possible for the ships to speed up when necessary. However, in practice it will most often be beneficial to consider the uncertainty explicitly when finding the optimal plan.

Even though maritime transportation is heavily influenced by uncertainty, most of the research reported in the literature on maritime routing and scheduling consider static and deterministic problems. However, some contributions exist, and we describe the ones that are closest to the MIRP with stochastic travel times studied here. For a ship routing and scheduling problem with predefined cargoes, Christiansen and Fagerholt [7] design ship schedules that are less likely to result in ships staying idle at ports during weekends by imposing penalty costs for arrivals at risky times (i.e. close to weekends). The resulting schedule needs to be more robust with respect to delays from bad weather and time in port due to the restricted operating hours in port during weekends. Agra et al. [3] solved a full-load ship routing and scheduling problem with uncertain travel times using robust optimization. Furthermore, Halvorsen-Weare and Fagerholt [14] analysed various heuristic strategies to achieve robust weekly voyages and schedules for off-shore supply vessels working under tough weather conditions. Heuristic strategies for obtaining robust solutions with uncertain sailing times and production rate were also discussed by Halvorsen-Weare et al. [15] for the delivery of liquefied natural gas. For a crude oil transportation and inventory problem, Cheng and Duran [6] developed a decision support system that takes into account uncertainty in sailing time and demand. The problem is formulated as a discrete time Markov decision process and solved by using discrete event simulation and optimal control theory. Rakke et al. [19] and Sherali and Al-Yakoob [20,21] introduced penalty functions for deviating from the customer contracts and the storage limits, respectively, for their MIRPs. Christiansen and Nygreen [11] used soft inventory levels to handle uncertainties in sailing time and time in port, and these levels were transformed into soft time windows for a single product MIRP. Agra et al. [2] were the first to use stochastic programming to model uncertain sailing and port times for a MIRP with several products and inventory management at the consumption ports only. A two-stage stochastic programming model with recourse was developed where the first-stage consists of routing, and loading/unloading decisions, and the second stage consists of scheduling decisions. The model was solved by a decomposition approach similar to an L-shaped algorithm where optimality cuts were added dynamically, and the solution process was embedded within the sample average approximation method.

The objective of this paper is to present a general single product MIRP with stochastic sailing times and a heuristic method to solve the problem. As in the work by Agra et al. [2], we have developed a two-stage stochastic programming model with recourse where the first-stage consists of routing and loading/unloading decisions, and the second stage consists of scheduling decisions. Although the two problems have several differences (the number of products considered, management inventory at supply ports, and random aspects of uncertainty), this work was also motivated by the stability problems reported for the approach followed by Agra et al. [2]. When the instances become harder, the objective function values obtained by the heuristic approach had large levels of variance. As in previous work we assume the inventory limits can be violated with a penalty. Here we discuss in more detail the impact of the value of such penalties on the stability of the solution procedure, since different penalty values may correspond to different decision maker strategies, and may influence the efficiency of branch and cut based procedures. Low penalty values will be used when backlogged consumption and excess of production are less important than the routing cost, and generate low transportation cost solutions. High penalty values create solutions that are averse to inventory limit violations. Since the fractional solutions obtained by linear relaxations will present, in general, no violation of the inventory limits, the integrality linear gaps tend to be much higher when the penalty values are higher, which deteriorates the performance of branch and cut based procedures. Additionally, in order to circumvent the stability problems, we propose a new heuristic procedure which is based on a local search heuristic that uses the solution from a corresponding deterministic problem as a starting solution.

The remainder of this paper is organized as follows: The mathematical model of the deterministic problem is presented in Sect. 2, while the stochastic model is presented in Sect. 3. Section 4 presents the heuristic stochastic solution approaches. Extensive computational results are reported and discussed in Sect. 5, followed by some concluding remarks in Sect. 6.

2 Mathematical Model for the Deterministic Problem

In this section we introduce a mathematical formulation for the deterministic problem.

Routing Constraints. Let V denote the set of ships and N denote the set of ports. Each ship $v \in V$ must depart from its initial position, that can be a point at sea. For each port we consider an ordering of the visits accordingly to the time of the visit.

The ship paths are defined on a network where the nodes are represented by a pair (i, m), where i indicates the port and m indicates the visit number to port i. Direct ship movements (arcs) from node (i, m) to node (j, n) are represented by (i, m, j, n). For ease of notation, if a ship departs from a point at sea, an artificial port is created and a single visit is associated with it.

We define S^A as the set of possible nodes (i, m), S^A_v as the set of nodes that may be visited by ship v, and set S^X_v as the set of all possible movements (i, m, j, n) of ship v.

For the routing we define the following binary variables: x_{imjnv} is 1 if ship v travels from node (i, m) directly to node (j, n), and 0 otherwise; w_{imv} is 1 if ship v visits node (i, m), and 0 otherwise; z_{imv} is equal to 1 if ship v ends its route at node (i, m), and 0 otherwise; y_{im} indicates whether a ship is making the mth visit to port i, (i, m), or not. The parameter $\underline{\mu}_i$ denotes the minimum number of visits at port i and the parameter $\overline{\mu}_i$ denotes an upper bound on the number of visits at port i.

$$w_{imv} - \sum_{(j,n) \in S^A_v} x_{jnimv} = 0, \qquad \forall v \in V, (i,m) \in S^A_v, \tag{1}$$

$$w_{imv} - \sum_{(j,n) \in S^A_v} x_{imjnv} - z_{imv} = 0, \qquad \forall v \in V, (i,m) \in S^A_v, \tag{2}$$

$$\sum_{v \in V} w_{imv} = y_{im}, \qquad \forall (i,m) \in S^A, \tag{3}$$

$$y_{im} = 1, \qquad \forall (i,m) \in S^A : m \in \{1, \cdots, \underline{\mu}_i\}, \tag{4}$$

$$y_{i(m-1)} - y_{im} \geq 0, \qquad \forall (i,m) \in S^A : \underline{\mu}_i + 1 < m \leq \overline{\mu}_i, \tag{5}$$

$$x_{imjnv} \in \{0,1\}, \qquad \forall v \in V, (i,m,j,n) \in S^X_v, \tag{6}$$

$$w_{imv}, z_{imv} \in \{0,1\}, \qquad \forall v \in V, (i,m) \in S^A_v \tag{7}$$

$$y_{im} \in \{0,1\}, \qquad \forall (i,m) \in S^A. \tag{8}$$

Equations (1) and (2) are the flow conservation constraints, ensuring that a ship arriving at a node also leaves that node or ends its route. Constraints (3) ensure that a ship can visit node (i, m) only if y_{im} is equal to one. Equations (4) fix y_{im} to 1 for the mandatory visits. Constraints (5) state that if port i is visited m times, then it must also have been visited $m - 1$ times. Constraints (6)–(8) define the variables as binary.

Loading and Unloading Constraints. Parameter J_i is 1 if port i is a producer; -1 if port i is a consumer. C_v is the capacity of ship v. The minimum and maximum loading and unloading quantities at port i are given by $\underline{Q}_i$ and $\overline{Q}_i$, respectively.

In order to model the loading and unloading constraints, we define the following continuous variables: q_{imv} is the amount loaded or unloaded from ship v at node (i, m); f_{imjnv} denotes the amount that ship v transports from node (i, m) to node (j, n). The loading and unloading constraints are given by:

$$\sum_{(j,n)\in S_v^A} f_{jnimv} + J_i q_{imv} = \sum_{(j,n)\in S_v^A} f_{imjnv}, \qquad \forall v \in V, (i, m) \in S_v^A, \quad (9)$$

$$f_{imjnv} \leq C_v x_{imjnv}, \qquad \forall v \in V, (i, m, j, n) \in S_v^X, \tag{10}$$

$$\underline{Q}_i w_{imv} \leq q_{imv} \leq min\{C_v, \overline{Q}_i\} w_{imv}, \qquad \forall v \in V, (i, m) \in S_v^A, \tag{11}$$

$$f_{imjnv} \geq 0, \qquad \forall v \in V, (i, m, j, n) \in S_v^X, \tag{12}$$

$$q_{imv} \geq 0, \qquad \forall v \in V, (i, m) \in S_v^A. \tag{13}$$

Equations (9) are the flow conservation constraints at node (i, m). Constraints (10) require that the ship capacity is obeyed. Constraints (11) impose lower and upper limits on the loading and unloading quantities. Constraints (12) and (13) are the non-negativity constraints.

Time Constraints. We define the following parameters: T_i^Q is the time required to load/unload one unit of product at port i; T_{ijv} is the travel time between port i and j by ship v. It includes also any set-up time required to operate at port j. T_i^B is the minimum time between two consecutive visits to port i. T is the length of the time horizon, and A_{im} and B_{im} are the time windows for starting the mth visit to port i. To ease the presentation we also define, for each node (i, m), the following upper bound for the end time of the visit: $T'_{im} = min\{T, B_{im} + T_i^Q \overline{Q}_i\}$. Given time variables t_{im} that indicate the start time of the mth visit to port i, the time constraints can be written as:

$$t_{im} + \sum_{v\in V} T_i^Q q_{imv} - t_{jn} + \sum_{v\in V|(i,m,j,n)\in S_v^X} \max\{T'_{im} + T_{ijv} - A_{jn}, 0\} x_{imjnv}$$

$$\leq T'_{im} - A_{jn}, \qquad \forall (i, m), (j, n) \in S^A, \tag{14}$$

$$t_{im} - t_{i,m-1} - \sum_{v\in V} T_i^Q q_{i,m-1,v} - T_i^B y_{im} \geq 0, \qquad \forall (i, m) \in S_A : m > 1, \quad (15)$$

$$A_{im} \leq t_{im} \leq B_{im}, \qquad \forall (i, m) \in S^A. \tag{16}$$

Constraints (14) relate the start time associated with node (i, m) to the start time associated with node (j, n) when ship v travels directly from (i, m) to (j, n). Constraints (15) impose a minimum interval between two consecutive visits at port i. Time windows for the start time of visits are given by (16).

Inventory Constraints. The inventory constraints are considered for each port. They ensure that the stock levels are within the corresponding limits and link the stock levels to the loading or unloading quantities. For each port i, the consumption/production rate, R_i, the minimum $\underline{S}_i$, the maximum $\overline{S}_i$ and the initial S_i^0 stock levels, are given. We define the nonnegative continuous variables s_{im} indicating the stock levels at the start of the mth visit to port i.

The inventory constraints are as follows:

$$s_{i1} = S_i^0 + J_i R_i t_{i1}, \qquad \forall i \in N, \tag{17}$$

$$s_{im} = s_{i,m-1} - J_i \sum_{v \in V} q_{i,m-1,v} + J_i R_i (t_{im} - t_{i,m-1}), \qquad \forall (i,m) \in S^A : m > 1, \tag{18}$$

$$s_{im} + \sum_{v \in V} q_{imv} - R_i \sum_{v \in V} T_i^Q q_{imv} \leq \overline{S}_i, \qquad \forall (i,m) \in S^A | J_i = -1, \tag{19}$$

$$s_{im} - \sum_{v \in V} q_{imv} + R_i \sum_{v \in V} T_i^Q q_{imv} \geq \underline{S}_i, \qquad \forall (i,m) \in S^A | J_i = 1, \tag{20}$$

$$s_{i\overline{\mu}_i} + \sum_{v \in V} q_{i,\overline{\mu}_i,v} - R_i (T - t_{i\overline{\mu}_i}) \geq \underline{S}_i, \qquad \forall i \in N | J_i = -1, \tag{21}$$

$$s_{i\overline{\mu}_i} - \sum_{v \in V} q_{i,\overline{\mu}_i,v} + R_i (T - t_{i\overline{\mu}_i}) \leq \overline{S}_i, \qquad \forall i \in N | J_i = 1, \tag{22}$$

$$s_{im} \geq \underline{S}_i, \qquad \forall (i,m) \in S^A | J_i = -1, \tag{23}$$

$$s_{im} \leq \overline{S}_i, \qquad \forall (i,m) \in S^A | J_i = 1. \tag{24}$$

Equations (17) calculate the stock level at the start time of the first visit to a port, and Eq. (18) relate the stock level at the start time of mth visit to the stock level at the start time of the previous visit. Constraints (19) and (20) ensure that the stock levels are within their limits at the end of each visit. Constrains (21) impose a lower bound on the inventory level at time T for consumption ports, while constrains (22) impose an upper bound on the inventory level at time T for production ports. Constraints (23) and (24) ensure that the stock levels are within their limits at the start of each visit.

Objective Function. The objective is to minimize the total routing costs, including traveling and operating costs. The traveling cost of ship v from port i to port j is denoted by C_{ijv}^T and it includes the set-up costs. The objective function is defined as follows:

$$Min \qquad C(X) = \sum_{v \in V} \sum_{(i,m,j,n) \in S_v^X} C_{ijv}^T x_{imjnv}. \tag{25}$$

3   Mathematical Model for the Stochastic Problem

In the stochastic approach, the sailing times between ports are assumed to be independent and random, following a known probability distribution (a log-logistic probability distribution which is discussed in Sect. 5). As in the work by Agra et al. [2], the model introduced here is a recourse model with two levels of decisions. The first-stage decisions are the routing, the port visits sequence, and the load/unload quantities. These decisions must be taken before the scenario is revealed. The corresponding first-stage variables are $x_{imjnv}, z_{imv}, w_{imv}, y_{im}$, and q_{imv}. The adjustable variables are the time of visits and the inventory levels. In the stochastic approach we allow the inventory limits to be violated by including a penalty P_i for each unit of violation of the inventory limits at each port i. In addition to the variables $t_{im}(\xi)$, and $s_{im}(\xi)$ indicating the time and the stock level at node (i, m), when scenario ξ is revealed, new variables $r_{im}(\xi)$ are introduced to denote the inventory limit violation at node (i, m). If i is a consumption port, $r_{im}(\xi)$ denotes the backlogged consumption, that is the amount of demand satisfied with delay. If i is a production port, $r_{im}(\xi)$ denotes the demand in excess to the capacity. We assume the quantity in excess is not lost but a penalty is incurred.

The main goal of the stochastic approach is to find the solution that minimizes the routing cost $C(X)$ plus the expected penalty value for inventory deviation to the limits, $E_\xi(Q(X, \xi))$, where $Q(X, \xi)$ denotes the minimum penalty for the inventory deviations when scenario ξ with a particular sailing times vector is considered and a set of first stage decisions, denoted by X, is fixed. In order to avoid using the theoretical joint probability distribution of the travel times, we follow the common Sample Average Approximation (SAA) method, and replace the true expected penalty value $E_\xi(Q(X, \xi))$ by the mean value of a large random sample $\Omega = \{\xi^1, \ldots, \xi^k\}$ of ξ, obtained by the Monte Carlo method. This larger set of k scenarios is regarded as a benchmark scenario set representing the true distribution [17].

The objective function of the SAA model becomes as follows:

$$Min \qquad C(X) + \frac{1}{|\Omega|} \sum_{\xi \in \Omega} \sum_{(i,m) \in S^A} P_i r_{im}(\xi). \tag{26}$$

In addition to the routing and loading and unloading constraints (1)–(13), the SAA problem has the following time and inventory constraints.
Time constraints:

$$t_{im}(\xi) + \sum_{v \in V} T_i^Q q_{imv} - t_{jn}(\xi) + \sum_{v \in V | (i,m,j,n) \in S_v^X} T^M x_{imjnv},$$

$$\leq T^M, \qquad \forall (i, m), (j, n) \in S^A, \xi \in \Omega, \tag{27}$$

$$t_{im}(\xi) - t_{i,m-1}(\xi) - \sum_{v \in V} T_i^Q q_{i,m-1,v} - T_i^B y_{im} \geq 0, \qquad \forall (i, m) \in S_A : m > 1, \xi \in \Omega, \tag{28}$$

$$A_{im} \leq t_{im}(\xi) \leq B_{im}^M, \qquad \forall (i, m) \in S^A, \xi \in \Omega. \tag{29}$$

The inventory constraints are similar to the constraints for the deterministic problem, but now including the possible violation of the inventory limits. The big constant T^M is now set to $2T$ since the visits to ports can now occur after time period T. Similarly, B_{im}^M is set to $2T$. The inventory constraints are as follows:

$$s_{i1}(\xi) = S_i^0 + J_i R_i t_{i1}(\xi) - J_i r_{i1}(\xi), \qquad \forall i \in N, \xi \in \Omega, \tag{30}$$

$$s_{im}(\xi) - J_i r_{i,m-1}(\xi) = s_{i,m-1}(\xi) - J_i r_{im}(\xi) - J_i \sum_{v \in V} q_{i,m-1,v} + J_i R_i(t_{im}(\xi) - t_{i,m-1}(\xi)),$$

$$\forall(i,m) \in S^A : m > 1, \xi \in \Omega, \tag{31}$$

$$s_{im}(\xi) + \sum_{v \in V} q_{imv} - R_i \sum_{v \in V} T_i^Q q_{imv} \leq \overline{S}_i, \qquad \forall(i,m) \in S^A | J_i = -1, \ \xi \in \Omega, \tag{32}$$

$$s_{im}(\xi) - \sum_{v \in V} q_{imv} + R_i \sum_{v \in V} T_i^Q q_{imv} \geq \underline{S}_i, \qquad \forall(i,m) \in S^A | J_i = 1, \ \xi \in \Omega, \tag{33}$$

$$s_{i\overline{\mu}_i}(\xi) + \sum_{v \in V} q_{i,\overline{\mu}_i,v} - R_i(T - t_{i\overline{\mu}_i}(\xi)) + r_{i\overline{\mu}_i}(\xi) \geq \underline{S}_i, \qquad \forall i \in N | J_i = -1, \xi \in \Omega, \tag{34}$$

$$s_{i\overline{\mu}_i}(\xi) - \sum_{v \in V} q_{i,\overline{\mu}_i,v} + R_i(T - t_{i\overline{\mu}_i}(\xi)) - r_{i\overline{\mu}_i}(\xi) \leq \overline{S}_i, \qquad \forall i \in N | J_i = 1, \xi \in \Omega, \tag{35}$$

$$s_{im}(\xi), r_{im}(\xi) \geq 0 \qquad \forall(i,m) \in S^A : m > 1, \xi \in \Omega. \tag{36}$$

For brevity we omit the description of the constraints as their meaning is similar to the meaning of the corresponding constraints for the deterministic problem. The stochastic SAA model is defined by (26) and the constraints (1)–(13), (27)–(36), and will be denoted by SAA-MIRP.

Next we make two important remarks.

Remark 1. The SAA-MIRP model has relatively complete recourse, since for each feasible solution to the first stage, the inclusion of r variables ensures that the second stage has always a feasible solution.

Remark 2. When a first stage solution X is known, the second stage variables can easily be obtained by solving k separate linear subproblems.

4   Solution Methods

While the deterministic model can be solved to optimality for small size instances, the SAA-MIRP model becomes much harder with the inclusion of the inventory violation variables r, and cannot consistently be solved to optimality for large sample sizes. We consider M separate sets $\Omega_i, i \in \{1, \ldots, M\}$ each one containing $\ell \ll k$ scenarios. The SAA-MIRP model is solved for each set of scenarios Ω_i, (replacing Ω by Ω_i in model SAA-MIRP) giving M candidate solutions. Let us denote by $X^1, \ldots, X^M$, the first stage solutions of those candidate solutions. Then, for each candidate solution the value of the objective function for the large sample $z_k(X^i) = C(X^i) + \frac{1}{k} \sum_{\xi \in \Omega} Q(X^i, \xi)$ is computed and the best solution is determined by $X^* = argmin\{z_k(X^i) : i \in \{1, \ldots, M\}\}$. The average value over all sets of scenarios, $\overline{z}_\ell = \frac{1}{M} \sum_{i=1}^M z_\ell^i$ is a statistical estimate for a lower bound on the optimal value of the true problem and $z_k(X^*)$, is a statistical estimate for an upper bound on the optimal value.

Henceforward we discuss two procedures for solving the SAA-MIRP model for the small sets Ω_i. When employing scenario generation solution procedures it is desirable that no matter which set of scenarios is used, one obtains approximately the same objective function value. This is referred to as stability requirement conditions [17]. Agra et al. [2] used a decomposition scheme for a stochastic MIRP that was shown to be insufficient to reach stability for hard instances. Here we revisit this procedure and introduce an alternative method.

4.1   Decomposition Procedure

A common approach to solve stochastic problems is to decompose the model into a master problem and one subproblem for each scenario, following the idea of the L-shaped algorithm [5]. The master problem consists of the first stage variables and constraints (constraints (1)–(13)), and recourse variables and constraints (27)–(36) defined for a restricted set of scenarios. The subproblems consider fixed first stage decisions, and are solved for each scenario to supply new variables and constraints to the master problem. Since the problem has relatively complete recourse, the resulting subproblems are feasible.

We first solve the master problem including only one scenario to optimality. Then for each disregarded scenario we check whether a penalty for inventory limit violations is incurred when the first stage decision is fixed. If such a scenario is found, we add to the master problem additional variables and constraints enforcing that deviation to be penalized in the objective function. Then the revised master problem is solved again, and the process is repeated until all the recourse constraints are satisfied. Hence, as in the L-shaped method, the master problem initially disregards the recourse penalty, and an improved estimation of the recourse penalty is gradually added to the master problem by solving subproblems and adding the corresponding constraints. A formal description of this process is given below.

Algorithm 1. Decomposition procedure.

1: Consider the master problem with the scenario corresponding to the deterministic problem
2: Solve the master problem
3: **while** There is a scenario $\xi \in \Omega_i$ leading to an increase of the objective function cost **do**
4:     Add constraints (27)–(36) for scenario ξ
5:     Reoptimize the master problem with the new constraints using a solver for α seconds
6: **end while**

To check whether there is a scenario $\xi \in \Omega_i$ leading to an increase of the objective function cost, one can use a simple combinatorial algorithm that, for each scenario, determines the earliest arrival time based on the computation of a longest path in an acyclic network [2].

4.2 MIP Based Local Search Procedure

In order to circumvent some possible stability problems resulting from the previous procedure, which is based on a truncated branch and cut procedure, we propose a heuristic approach that iteratively searches in the neighborhood of a solution. The procedure starts with the optimal solution from a deterministic model, and ends when no improvement is observed. For the starting solution we either use the deterministic model (1)–(25), with no inventory violations allowed, or the stochastic model containing only one scenario where all travelling times are set to their expected value. To define the neighborhood of a solution, let $\overline{w}$ denote the solution vector of w variables. Following the local branching idea of Fischetti and Lodi [13], we consider as the neighborhood of a solution, the set of solutions that can differ in at most Δ variables, focusing only on the ship visit variables w_{imv}. This local search can be done by adding the following inequality,

$$\sum_{(i,m)\in S_v^A, v\in V|\overline{w}_{imv}=0} w_{imv} + \sum_{(i,m)\in S_v^A, v\in V|\overline{w}_{imv}=1} (1 - w_{imv}) \leq \Delta. \qquad (37)$$

Inequality (37) counts the number of variables w_{imv} that are allowed to flip their value from the value taken in the solution. Note that the routing variables as well as the quantities to load and unload can be changed freely.

In each iteration of the heuristic procedure, the SAA-MIR model restricted with the inclusion of (37) is solved in its extensive form (without the decomposition procedure), since preliminary tests have not shown clear benefits in using the decomposition technique in the restricted model. The procedure is described in Algorithm 2.

Algorithm 2. MIP based Local Search procedure

1: Solve either model (1)–(25), or the SAA-MIRP with a single scenario consisting of expected travel times
2: Set $\overline{w}$ to the optimal value of w
3: **repeat**
4:     Add constraint (37) to the model defined for ℓ scenarios
5:     Solve the model for α seconds
6:     Update the solution $\overline{w}$
7: **until** No improvement in the objective function is observed

---

5 Computational Tests

This section presents some of the computational experiments carried out to test the two solution approaches for a set of instances of a maritime inventory routing problem. The instances are based on real data, and come from the short sea shipping segment with long loading and discharge times relative to the sailing times. These instances result from those presented in [1], with two main differences. One is the computation of the traveling times, which we discuss in detail below, and the other is the production and consumption which we assume here to be constant, where the rates are given by the average of the corresponding values given in the original set of instances. The number of ports and ships of each instance is given in the second column of Table 2. The time horizon is 30 days. Operating and waiting costs are time invariant.

Distribution of Travel Times and Scenario Generation

Here we describe the sailing times probability distribution as well as how scenarios are generated. We assume that the sailing times $T_{ijv}(\xi)$ are random and follow a three-parameter log-logistic probability distribution. The cumulative probability distribution can be written as

$$F(T_{ijv}(\xi)) = \frac{1}{1 + (\frac{1}{t})^{\alpha}},$$

where $t = \frac{T_{ijv}(\xi) - \gamma}{\beta}$.

This type of distribution was used in [15] for an LNG (liquefied natural gas) tanker transportation problem, and was motivated by the sailing times calculated for a gas tanker between Rome (Italy) and Bergen (Norway), as reported in [16]. In the three-parameter log-logistic probability distribution, the minimum travel time is equal to γ, and the expected travel time is equal to $E[T_{ijv}(\xi)] = \frac{\beta\pi}{\alpha \sin(\pi/\alpha)} + \gamma$. The three parameters, in [15], were set to $\alpha = 2.24$, $\beta = 9.79$, and $\gamma = 134.47$. In our settings, the deterministic travel time T_{ijv}, given in [1], is set to the expected travel time value, that is, $T_{ijv} = E[T_{ijv}(\xi)]$. In addition, we let $\gamma = 0.9 \times T_{ijv}$, $\alpha = 2.24$ (the same value as in [15], since α is a form parameter), and β is obtained from the equation $T_{ijv} = E[T_{ijv}(\xi)] = \frac{\beta\pi}{\alpha \sin(\pi/\alpha)} + \gamma$. In order to draw a sample, each travel time is randomly generated as follows. First a random number r from $(0, 1]$ is generated. Then the travel time $T_{ijv}(\xi)$ can be found by setting $r = \frac{1}{1 + (\frac{1}{t})^{\alpha}}$, which gives $T_{ijv}(\xi) = \gamma + \beta \left(\frac{1-r}{r}\right)^{-\frac{1}{\alpha}}$.

Computational Results

All tests were run on a computer with an Intel Core i5-2410M processor, having a 2.30GHz CPU and 8GB of RAM, using the optimization software Xpress Optimizer Version 21.01.00 with Xpress Mosel Version 3.2.0.

The number of ports and ships of each instance is given in the second column of Table 1. The following three columns give the size of the deterministic model (1)–(25), and the last three columns give the size for the complete stochastic model SAA-MIRP with $\ell = 25$.

Table 2 gives the optimal values of several instances for the deterministic model. Columns "No violations" give the optimal value (column $C(X)$) and running time in seconds (column $Time$) for the model (1)–(25) with no inventory limit violations allowed. The following columns consider the stochastic model

Table 1. Summary statistics for the seven instances

Inst.	$(|N|, |V|)$	Deterministic model			Stochastic model		
		# Rows	# Col	# Int. var.	# Rows	# Col	# Int. var.
A	(4,1)	765	545	273	8413	1713	273
B	(3,2)	767	590	302	5303	1466	302
C	(4,2)	1214	1042	530	8798	2210	530
D	(5,2)	1757	1622	822	13157	3082	822
E	(5,2)	1757	1622	822	13157	3082	822
F	(4,3)	1663	1539	787	9183	2707	787
G	(6,5)	4991	5717	2909	20687	7469	2909

with the expected travel times scenario only. For three different penalty values for inventory limit violations ($P_i = 1 \times \ell$, $P_i = 10 \times \ell$ and $P_i = 100 \times \ell$, where the ℓ is omitted for ease of notation) we provide the routing cost $C(X)$, the value of the inventory violation (columns *Viol*) and the running time (columns *Time*).

Table 2. Instances and the corresponding routing costs and inventory violations for the expected value scenario

Inst.	No violations		$P_i = 1$			$P_i = 10$			$P_i = 100$		
	C(X)	Time	C(X)	Viol	Time	C(X)	Viol	Time	C(X)	Viol	Time
A	130.7	1	6.7	60.0	0	130.7	0.0	0	130.7	0.0	0
B	364.8	6	5.2	235.0	0	364.8	0.0	13	364.8	0.0	19
C	391.5	15	14.7	172.0	0	290.5	3.0	4	324.5	0.5	10
D	347.1	3	55.9	177.0	4	347.1	0.0	42	347.1	0.0	52
E	344.9	343	55.8	184.0	4	344.9	0.0	194	344.9	0.0	181
F	460.9	290	182.0	110.0	3	460.9	0.0	437	460.9	0.0	442
G	645.8	2962	336.3	176.5	17	645.8	0.0	6947	645.8	0.0	16296

Table 2 shows the influence of the penalty on the solution value and instance hardness. The running times are small when $P_i = 1$ and tend to increase with the increase of the penalty. For small penalty values the instances become easier to solve than for the case with hard inventory bounds. When the penalty increases, the integrality gaps also increase (as fractional solutions contain, in general, no violation of the inventory limits) making the instances harder to solve. For $P_i = 10$, $P_i = 100$ and for the case where violations are not allowed, the solutions coincide for all instances except instance C.

Next we report the results using both procedures following the solution approach described in Sect. 4 with $M = 10$ sets of scenarios with size $\ell = 25$, and a large sample of size $k = 1000$. In Tables 3, 4, and 5, we present the computational results for the decomposition procedure using branch and cut to solve each master problem with a running time limit of $t = 1$, $t = 2$, and $t = 5$ min. After this time limit, if no feasible solution is found, then the running time is extended until the first feasible solution is found. For each table we give the results for the three considered cases of penalties, denoted by $P_i = 1$, $P_i = 10$, and $P_i = 100$. For each penalty we report the following values: the routing cost $C(X)$ of the best solution X^* obtained with the procedure described in Sect. 4; the average number of violations (columns $Viol$) for solution X^*; the variance between samples $\hat{\sigma}_B^2 = \dfrac{1}{(M-1)M} \sum_{i=1}^{M} (z_\ell^i - \bar{z}_\ell)^2$; the variance in the larger sample $\hat{\sigma}_L^2 = \dfrac{1}{(k-1)k} \sum_{\xi \in \Omega} (C(X^*) + Q(X^*, \xi) - z_k(X^*))^2$; and the running time, in seconds, of the complete solution procedure. The running time includes solving the M stochastic problems, and for each solution, computing the penalty value for the large set of k samples.

Variances $\hat{\sigma}_B^2$ and $\hat{\sigma}_L^2$ are used to evaluate the stability of the procedure. One can observe that when the penalties increase, the variance for the large sample, $\hat{\sigma}_L^2$, increases as expected. For the variance between samples, $\hat{\sigma}_B^2$, the value also increases when we compare $P_i = 1$ against the other values. Such behavior can be explained by the fact that each master problem is solved by a branch and cut procedure and as explained above, when the penalty increases, the integrality gaps also increase making the instances harder to solve. For those harder instances the branch and cut algorithm acts as a heuristic since the search tree is truncated when the time limit is reached. Thus, the variance tends to increase when we compare those cases where the instances are solved to optimality (some instances with $P_i = 1$) against those cases where the solution procedure acts, in general, as a heuristic (most instances with $P_i = 10$ and $P_i = 100$). However between the cases $P_i = 10$ and $P_i = 100$ there is no obvious trend. There are instances where the decomposition procedure had a better degree of in-sample stability for $P_i = 100$ than for $P_i = 10$. Perhaps as the penalty cost is so high, for some instances the solver identifies the same solution (a solution which is *robust* in relation to inventory bounds violation and minimizes the routing cost) for most of the small samples Ω_i considered. In general, we may state that the decomposition procedure tends to be less stable with the increase of the penalties. There is no clear decrease in the variances when the running time limit is increased.

In Table 6, we report the computational results for the MIP based local search heuristic, starting with a solution obtained by using a single scenario consisting of expected travel times in the SAA-MIRP model. Based on preliminary results, not reported here, we chose $\Delta = 2$. The running time limit is set to 5 min, however for most iterations the restricted problem is solved to optimality quickly. In Table 7, we report the corresponding results for the same heuristic but starting with a solution obtained using the model (1)–(25), that is, the model where no deviations to the inventory limits are allowed. We can see that using hard inventory limits for the starting solution leads to a better solution for six instances and worse for two instances.

Table 3. Computational results using the decomposition procedure with a running time limit for each master problem set to 1 min

Inst.	$P_i = 1$					$P_i = 10$					$P_i = 100$				
	$C(X)$	Viol	$\hat{\sigma}_B^2$	$\hat{\sigma}_L^2$	Time	$C(X)$	Viol	$\hat{\sigma}_B^2$	$\hat{\sigma}_L^2$	Time	$C(X)$	Viol	$\hat{\sigma}_B^2$	$\hat{\sigma}_L^2$	Time
A	130.7	0.0	4	0	105	130.7	0.0	27	0	116	130.7	0.0	27	0	118
B	364.8	1.4	13	0	492	364.8	1.4	64	5	3654	364.8	1.3	57	413	4965
C	263.5	3.0	73	0	151	343.9	2.5	91	0	292	411.5	0.0	36	2	749
D	347.1	2.0	190	0	1627	347.1	2.1	2463	5	3975	347.1	2.2	205	514	3524
E	344.9	3.2	358	0	2277	344.9	5.8	5830	13	5394	260.4	18.4	1945	698	4262
F	501.1	0.1	145	0	327	460.9	0.0	451450	0	5361	460.9	0.0	44413	0	4993
G	433.0	133.9	2136	1	1115	484.8	213.6	71357	151	6962	457.6	212.1	2121500	6	7696

Table 4. Computational results using the decomposition procedure with a running time limit for each master problem set to 2 min

Inst.	$P_i = 1$					$P_i = 10$					$P_i = 100$				
	$C(X)$	Viol	$\hat{\sigma}_B^2$	$\hat{\sigma}_L^2$	Time	$C(X)$	Viol	$\hat{\sigma}_B^2$	$\hat{\sigma}_L^2$	Time	$C(X)$	Viol	$\hat{\sigma}_B^2$	$\hat{\sigma}_L^2$	Time
A	130.7	0.0	4	0	102	130.7	0.0	27	0	114	130.7	0.0	27	0	109
B	364.8	1.4	13	0	583	364.8	1.4	1368	5	6143	364.8	1.3	7539	413	8413
C	263.5	3.0	73	0	150	343.9	2.5	91	0	301	391.5	0.0	54	2	928
D	347.1	2.0	190	0	2367	363.2	0.2	792	0	7133	347.1	2.1	314	486	6602
E	344.9	3.2	358	0	2716	363.9	3.2	8839	7	8637	352.9	0.2	1809	40	9032
F	501.1	0.1	145	0	333	460.9	0.0	7025	0	7368	460.9	0.0	4024	0	7824
G	433.0	133.9	2136	1	3260	543.7	154.5	95489	135	10837	442.3	121.9	746118	9670	13003

When comparing the variances with those observed for the decomposition procedure one can observe that the variances between samples are in general lower, meaning that the local search procedure presents a higher degree of in-sample stability than the classical decomposition approach. For the larger sample, both procedures present similar variance values, except for the harder instance (G with $P_i = 100$) where the new heuristic procedure provides better out-of-sample stability. The running times of the local search heuristic are also lower than those for the decomposition procedure.

Table 5. Computational results using the decomposition procedure with a running time limit for each master problem set to 5 min

Inst.	$P_i = 1$					$P_i = 10$					$P_i = 100$				
	$C(X)$	Viol	$\hat{\sigma}_B^2$	$\hat{\sigma}_L^2$	Time	$C(X)$	Viol	$\hat{\sigma}_B^2$	$\hat{\sigma}_L^2$	Time	$C(X)$	Viol	$\hat{\sigma}_B^2$	$\hat{\sigma}_L^2$	Time
A	130.7	0.0	4	0	102	130.7	0.0	27	0	116	130.7	0.0	27	0	121
B	364.8	1.4	13	0	602	364.8	1.4	1350	5	11781	364.8	1.3	76	413	17530
C	263.5	3.0	73	0	148	343.9	2.5	91	0	277	391.5	0.0	31	2	1611
D	347.1	2.0	190	0	4120	347.1	2.0	590	5	15130	430.3	1.1	395	127	16889
E	344.9	3.2	358	0	6827	352.9	0.2	1791	1	21592	360.9	3.4	5474	768	25769
F	501.1	0.1	145	0	321	460.9	0.0	36	0	11118	460.9	0.0	11200	0	13218
G	433.0	133.9	2136	1	6421	534.0	57.3	54937	4	20462	517.0	107.3	43724	23544	21564

Table 6. Computational results using the MIP based local search heuristic

Inst.	$P_i = 1$					$P_i = 10$					$P_i = 100$				
	$C(X)$	Viol	$\hat{\sigma}_B^2$	$\hat{\sigma}_L^2$	Time	$C(X)$	Viol	$\hat{\sigma}_B^2$	$\hat{\sigma}_L^2$	Time	$C(X)$	Viol	$\hat{\sigma}_B^2$	$\hat{\sigma}_L^2$	Time
A	130.7	0	4	0	205	130.7	0.0	54	0	210	130.7	0.0	54	0	210
B	260.7	32.7	74	0	406	364.8	1.3	22	4	698	364.8	1.3	44	400	769
C	263.5	3.0	87	0	388	391.5	0.0	11	0	704	411.5	0.0	131	0	944
D	377.2	6.2	28	0	2729	347.1	2.0	1	5	2768	347.1	2.0	48	490	2610
E	405.3	5.6	0	0	3731	344.9	3.1	0	7	3728	344.9	3.1	63	718	3694
F	460.9	0.0	46	0	1484	460.9	0.0	197	0	3438	460.9	0.0	197	0	3118
G	711.9	4.8	239	3	5174	679.5	1.6	602	5	6116	798.9	13.3	731	3246	9686

Table 7. Computational results using the MIP based local search heuristic with the starting solution obtained for the deterministic model with hard inventory constraints

Inst.	$P_i = 1$					$P_i = 10$					$P_i = 100$				
	$C(X)$	Viol	$\hat{\sigma}_B^2$	$\hat{\sigma}_L^2$	Time	$C(X)$	Viol	$\hat{\sigma}_B^2$	$\hat{\sigma}_L^2$	Time	$C(X)$	Viol	$\hat{\sigma}_B^2$	$\hat{\sigma}_L^2$	Time
A	130.7	0	4	0	72	130.7	0.0	54	0	89	130.7	0.0	54	0	96
B	345.2	3.8	24	0	383	364.8	1.3	22	4	722	364.8	1.3	44	400	719
C	263.5	3.0	87	0	266	354.5	0.5	38	0	533	391.5	0.0	57	0	630
D	347.2	2.0	28	0	1097	347.1	2.0	1	5	2992	347.1	2.0	48	490	3675
E	344.9	3.1	0	0	1214	344.9	3.1	0	7	3227	344.9	3.1	63	718	5822
F	460.9	0.0	46	0	941	460.9	0.0	460	0	1670	460.9	0.0	197	0	1388
G	654.9	1.8	138	0	4592	679.5	1.6	994	5	8130	912.5	0.6	402	112	10332

Table 8. Cost $z_k(X)$ of the best solution obtained with each one of the solution procedures

Inst.	$P_i = 1$		$P_i = 10$		$P_i = 100$	
	Decomp.	MIPLS	Decomp.	MIPLS	Decomp.	MIPLS
A	130.7	130.7	130.7	130.7	130.7	130.7
B	441.0	441.0	725.6	**696.0**	3707.2	**3632.3**
C	338.5	338.5	968.9	**479.5**	454.1	**391.5**
D	397.7	397.7	857.0	**853.9**	**3261.5**	5414.2
E	422.0	422.0	**405.1**	1115.2	8804.7	**8047.7**
F	502.9	**460.9**	460.9	460.9	460.9	460.9
G	3780.8	**692.4**	14861.1	**1085.8**	268712.0	**2359.6**

Finally, in Table 8 we present the overall cost $z_k(X)$ for the best solution obtained with the two solution procedures. Columns *Decomp.* give the cost value for the decomposition procedure using a time limit of 5 min, and columns *MIPLS* give the corresponding value for the MIP based local search heuristic using the starting solution with no inventory deviations. The best result from the two approaches is highlighted in bold.

We can see that the new MIP based local search procedure is better than the decomposition procedure in ten instances and worse in two. The decomposition procedure performs well when instances can be solved to optimality.

Overall, we may conclude that the local search heuristic is more attractive than the decomposition procedure based on the branch and cut when the instances are not solved to optimality, since the local search heuristic is faster, presents better levels of in-sample stability for almost all instances and better levels of out-of-sample stability for the hardest instance, and provides good quality solutions. On the other hand, for the instances that can be solved to optimality, the decomposition procedure is the best option.

6 Conclusions

We consider a maritime inventory routing problem where the travel times are stochastic. The problem is modeled as a two-stage stochastic programming problem with recourse, where violations of inventory limits are penalized. A decomposition procedure that solves the master problem using a commercial solver and a MIP based local search algorithm, are proposed. For several instances the master problem is not solved to optimality within reasonable running times. Hence both procedures can be regarded as heuristics. The two procedures are tested for stability using different values for the penalties. A computational study based on a small set of benchmark instances shows that when the penalties are low, the instances are easier to solve by exact methods, and the decomposition procedure can be used efficiently. On the other hand, when penalties are high, the integrality gaps tend to increase making the decomposition procedure, that uses the branch and cut to solve the master problem, less stable than the MIP based local search heuristic. Additionally, the new proposed heuristic is in general faster than the decomposition procedure.

Aknowledgements. The work of the first author was funded by FCT (Fundação para a Ciência e a Tecnologia) and CIDMA (Centro de Investigação e Desenvolvimento em Matemática e Aplicações) within project UID/MAT/04106/2013. The work or the fourth author was funded by FCT under Grant PD/BD/114185/2016.

References

1. Agra, A., Andersson, H., Christiansen, M., Wolsey, L.: A maritime inventory routing problem: discrete time formulations and valid inequalities. Networks **64**, 297–314 (2013)
2. Agra, A., Christiansen, M., Delgado, A., Hvattum, L.M.: A maritime inventory routing problem with stochastic sailing and port times. Comput. Oper. Res. **61**, 18–30 (2015)
3. Agra, A., Christiansen, M., Figueiredo, R., Hvattum, L.M., Poss, M., Requejo, C.: The robust vehicle routing problem with time windows. Comput. Oper. Res. **40**, 856–866 (2013)
4. Andersson, H., Hoff, A., Christiansen, M., Hasle, G., Løkketangen, A.: Industrial aspects and literature survey: combined inventory management and routing. Comput. Oper. Res. **37**, 1515–1536 (2010)

5. Birge, J.R., Louveaux, F.: Introduction to Stochastic Programming. Springer Series in Operations Research and Financial Engineering, 2nd edn. Springer, New York (2011)
6. Cheng, L., Duran, M.A.: Logistics for world-wide crude oil transportation using discrete event simulation and optimal control. Comput. Chem. Eng. **28**, 897–911 (2004)
7. Christiansen, M., Fagerholt, K.: Robust ship scheduling with multiple time windows. Naval Res. logistics **49**, 611–625 (2002)
8. Christiansen, M., Fagerholt, K.: Maritime inventory routing problems. In: Floudas, C.A., Pardalos, P.M. (eds.) Encyclopedia of Optimization, pp. 1947–1955. Springer, New York (2009)
9. Christiansen, M., Fagerholt, K.: Ship routing and scheduling in industrial and tramp shipping. In: Toth, P., Vigo, D. (eds.) Vehicle Routing: Problems, Methods, and Applications. MOS-SIAM Series on Optimization, pp. 381–408. SIAM, Philadelphia (2014)
10. Christiansen, M., Fagerholt, K., Nygreen, B., Ronen, D.: Ship routing and scheduling in the new millennium. Eur. J. Oper. Res. **228**, 467–483 (2013)
11. Christiansen, M., Nygreen, B.: Robust inventory ship routing by column generation. In: Desrosiers, G., Solomon, M.M. (eds.) Column Generation, pp. 197–224. Springer, New York (2005)
12. Coelho, L.C., Cordeau, J.-F., Laporte, G.: Thirty years of inventory routing. transp. sci. **48**, 1–19 (2014)
13. Fischetti, M., Lodi, A.: Local branching. Math. Program. Ser. B **98**, 23–47 (2003)
14. Halvorsen-Weare, E.E., Fagerholt, K.: Robust supply vessel planning. In: Pahl, J., Reiners, T., Voß, S. (eds.) INOC 2011. LNCS, vol. 6701, pp. 559–573. Springer, Heidelberg (2011)
15. Halvorsen-Weare, E.E., Fagerholt, K., Rönnqvist, M.: Vessel routing and scheduling under uncertainty in the liquefied natural gas business. Comput. Ind. Eng. **64**, 290–301 (2013)
16. Kauczynkski, W.: Study of the reliability of the ship transportation. In: Proceedings of the International Conference on Ship and Marine Research (1994). 15p
17. Kaut, M., Wallace, S.: Evaluation of scenario-generation methods for stochastic programming. Pac. J. Optim. **3**, 257–271 (2007)
18. Papageorgiou, D.J., Nemhauser, G.L., Sokol, J., Cheo, M.-S., Keha, A.B.: MIRPLib - a library of maritime inventory routing problem instances: survey, core model, and benchmark results. Eur. J. Oper. Res. **234**, 350–366 (2014)
19. Rakke, J.G., Stålhane, M., Moe, C.R., Andersson, H., Christiansen, M., Fagerholt, K., Norstad, I.: A rolling horizon heuristic for creating a liquefied natural gas annual delivery program. Transp. Res. Part C **19**, 896–911 (2011)
20. Sherali, H.D., Al-Yakoob, S.M.: Determining an optimal fleet mix and schedules: Part I - single source and destination. In: Karlof, J.K. (ed.) Integer Programming Theory and Practice, pp. 137–166. CRC Press, Boca Raton (2006)
21. Sherali, H.D., Al-Yakoob, S.M.: Determining an optimal fleet mix and schedules: Part II - multiple sources and destinations, and the option of leasing transshipment depots. In: Karlof, J.K. (ed.) Integer Programming Theory and Practice, pp. 167–194. CRC Press, Boca Raton (2006)

2D-Packing with an Application to Stowage in Roll-On Roll-Off Liner Shipping

Jone R. Hansen[1]([✉]), Ivar Hukkelberg[1], Kjetil Fagerholt[1,2],
Magnus Stålhane[1], and Jørgen G. Rakke[3]

[1] Department of Industrial Economics and Technology Management,
Norwegian University of Science and Technology, Trondheim, Norway
hansenjone90@gmail.com
[2] Marine Technology Research Institute (MARINTEK), Trondheim, Norway
[3] Wallenius Wilhelmsen Logistics, Lysaker, Norway

Abstract. Roll-on/Roll-off (RoRo) ships represent the primary source for transporting vehicles and other types of rolling material over long distances. In this paper we focus on operational decisions related to stowage of cargoes for a RoRo ship voyage visiting a given set of loading and unloading ports. By focusing on stowage on one deck on board the ship, this can be viewed as a special version of a 2-dimensional packing problem with a number of additional considerations, such as one wants to place vehicles that belong to the same shipment close to each other to ease the loading and unloading. Another important aspect of this problem is shifting, which means temporarily moving some vehicles to make an entry/exit route for the vehicles that are to be loaded/unloaded at the given port. We present several versions of a new mixed integer programming (MIP) formulation for the problem. Computational results show that the model provides good solutions on small sized problem instances.

Keywords: Maritime transportation · 2D-packing · Roll-on Roll-off

1 Introduction

Roll-on/Roll-off (RoRo) vessels are the preferred choice when transporting vehicles and other types of rolling material around the globe. However, due to more efficient short sea feeder traffic in and out of main ports, the containerized fleets are becoming more and more of a threat to the RoRo segment. Therefore, it is important for the RoRo industry to continuously improve and become more effective, maintaining the position as the leading maritime transportation method for this type of cargo.

A RoRo ship transports different types of vehicles, such as cars, trucks, heavy rolling machinery, and trains, as illustrated in Fig. 1. During loading, the vehicles typically enter the ship through a ramp placed at the stern or the side and from there they are placed in one of several decks on the ship. A major problem that occurs when loading/unloading the cargo is shifting, which means temporarily

© Springer International Publishing Switzerland 2016
A. Paias et al. (Eds.): ICCL 2016, LNCS 9855, pp. 35–49, 2016.
DOI: 10.1007/978-3-319-44896-1_3

moving some vehicles to make an entry/exit route for the vehicles that are to be loaded/unloaded at a given port. This forces the ship to stay longer in the port and increase the cost of workers. Therefore, it is important to develop a good stowage plan that brings as much cargo as possible, utilizing the available space on the decks, while at the same time keeps the cost and time spent on shifting as low as possible.

Fig. 1. RoRo vessel. Source: WWL

In the field of RoRo-transportation, strategic planning is concerned with a time horizon of several years, and typically involves decisions such as determining the fleet size and mix, see for example [11]. In [2] the authors consider fleet deployment in RoRo-shipping on a tactical level. At the operational level of planning, the greater part of research regarding RoRo-ships focuses on safety and stability, such as [8]. Despite its importance, research within stowage on RoRo-ships is scarce, and to the authors' knowledge, only the research conducted in [9,10] exists on stowage on board RoRo-ships.

In other fields of maritime transportation, stowage problems are more common, as e.g. tank allocation problems in maritime bulk shipping [7]. However, the vast majority of literature regarding stowage in maritime transportation focuses on stowage problems for container ships. The containers are stacked on top of one another, and when dispatching a certain container, containers stacked on top of it needs to be removed. The objective in container stowage problems is therefore often to minimize the loading/unloading time of all containers [1] or the number of container movements [3]. Where a container is lifted straight up from its position, a vehicle's entry/exit route needs to be calculated for each vehicle in the RoRo ship stowage problem (RSSP). This is a complicating factor, considering the deck layout and ramp placement, which makes the stowage plans difficult to evaluate. The RSSP presented in [9] aims at deciding a deck configuration with respect to height, which optional/spot cargos to carry, and how to stow the vehicles carried during the voyage, given a predefined route. The authors in [9] propose a mixed integer programming (MIP) model and a heuristic method for solving this problem, where the objective is to maximize the sum of revenue from optional cargoes, minus the penalty costs incurred when having to move cargoes when performing the stowage along the route. For modeling purposes, the authors in [9] divide each deck into several logical lanes into which the vehicles are lined. The vehicles enter the ship at the stern, and are unloaded according to the last in-first out (LIFO) principle. However, dividing the decks into lanes may be too restricting, limiting the possibilities of finding good solutions. Therefore, the models presented in this paper does not rely upon this assumption.

As stowing vehicles on a deck may be seen as packing problem, a short review of cutting and packing problems is now presented. The authors in [13] present a typology of cutting and packing problems, partially based on the original ideas in [4]. According to this typology, the RoRo ship stowage problem is classified as either a two-dimensional knapsack problem (2KP) or a multiple heterogeneous large object placement problem (MHLOPP). Here, a fixed number of small items have to be allocated on a smaller number of large objects, where each item increase the profit by a specified value, if placed. This is transferable to the RSSP, where all vehicles (small items) from the mandatory cargoes and the carried spot cargoes have to be allocated on one of the ships decks (large objects). The authors in [5] present an exact tree-search procedure for solving the 2KP, where the algorithm limits the size of the tree search using a bound derived from a Lagrangean relaxation of a binary formulation of the problem. In [6] two types of hybrid algorithms to solve the 2KP are suggested. Recently, in [12] a heuristic for solving a pickup and delivery allocation problem for offshore supply vessels is proposed. In terms of mathematical modeling, the resulting problem is seen as a rich variant of the 2KP, using a grid representation of the deck. Several constraints are evaluated, many of them comparable to the RSSP, such as packing constraints, weight limitations, adjacency of delivery/pick-up cargoes, positioning of dangerous and refrigerated cargoes.

The objective of this paper is to propose a new and more realistic mathematical model for the RoRo ship stowage problem. We focus on stowage of a single deck, which is an essential building block in solving the problem for multiple decks, i.e. for the whole ship.

The outline of the remaining of the paper is as follows: Sect. 2 describes the RoRo ship stowage and the shifting problems in detail. The proposed mathematical model is presented in Sect. 3. Computational results are reported in Sect. 4, while concluding remarks are provided in Sect. 5.

2 Problem Description

In this section, the stowage challenges for a RoRo ship are presented. First, the general RoRo ship stowage problem (RSSP) is presented. Then, a detailed description of the two-dimensional RoRo ship stowage problem for one deck (2DRSSP) is given, which is the problem we aim to solve in this paper. Finally, the shifting problem is presented. This research is based on a collaboration with one of the world's largest RoRo-shipping companies, operating more than 50 RoRo ships all over the world.

The RSSP focuses on how to utilize the ships decks, carrying a number of cargoes along a voyage with a predefined given set of loading and unloading ports to visit. A cargo (or a shipment) is defined as a set of vehicles or units of some other rolling material that are to be loaded and unloaded at the same ports. In this work, the term vehicle is used to describe the content of the cargo. The cargoes are divided into two categories, mandatory cargoes and optional cargoes. Mandatory cargoes have to be transported due contractual terms, while optional cargoes are only desirable to transport if they can increase the profit on the voyage given available capacity on the deck. For every vehicle and deck, the weight, width, height and length are known. At each port, a fixed number of mandatory cargoes are present. There is also a given upper limit of optional cargoes the ship may take at each loading port. The objective is to maximize the revenue from optional cargoes while keeping the shifting cost to a minimum. Different factors complicate the problem, such as weight limits on the deck, stability considerations, and placement of vehicles.

In this paper, a simplification of the RSSP is addressed, namely the two-dimensional RoRo ship stowage problem (2DRSSP) that arises if we consider only one deck. The problem may then be reduced to a two-dimensional packing problem, where one has to stow all mandatory cargoes and then stow as much optional cargo as possible in the space that is left, and at the same time keep the shifting costs to a minimum. It is assumed that each vehicle is placed longitudinal to the deck, i.e. with its front facing the bow, which is most common. Stability constraints are not included in the model, as considering the stability of a single deck gives no real value. However, in the case where all decks are considered, the stability calculation becomes an essential part of the problem. Height and weight limitations are implicitly taken care of in the pregeneration of feasible areas of the deck for stowing each cargo.

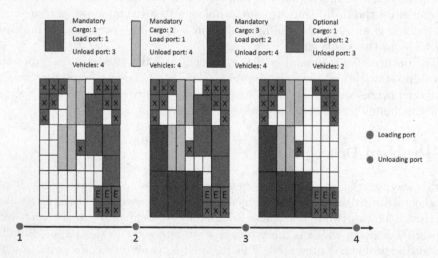

Fig. 2. A possible solution to the packing problem for each sailing leg during the voyage. Grey squares marked X is unavailable space, and squares marked E is the entry/exit point.

To illustrate the problem, a small example is shown in Fig. 2. Here, there are three mandatory cargoes, with four vehicles of different sizes. There is also one optional cargo, with two vehicles. It is assumed that no flexibility is allowed for the cargoes, meaning that one have to bring all or none of the vehicles of the optional cargo and all vehicles of the mandatory cargoes. There are four ports along the voyage, first two loading and then two unloading ports. The four ports indicate that the problem has a total of three sailing legs, where a leg is defined as the part of the voyage between two subsequent ports. The figure shows a feasible stowage plan for each sailing leg. It should be noted that a given cargo cannot be moved from one sailing leg to the next. From the solution one can also see that even though it is enough area on the deck to bring the optional cargo, the outline of the deck makes it impossible to include it. This example illustrates that allocating vehicles based only on a deck's area capacity, could give infeasible solutions.

Given a feasible solution from the 2DRSSP, as illustrated in Fig. 2, the shifting costs associated with the stowage plan must be evaluated. The shifting costs reflect the costs and/or time used to move cargoes in order to access other cargoes that are to be unloaded at a given port. For each vehicle, both an entry and exit route needs to be calculated. The total shifting cost of a voyage, is given by the sum of shifting costs for each entry/exit route for all vehicles along the voyage. The shifting model discussed in Sect. 3.3 is used to evaluate the total shifting cost for a stowage plan along a voyage.

3 Mathematical Models

In this section, we propose a MIP model for the 2DRSSP. First, some modeling choices and definitions that are used in the mathematical model are introduced. Then, the objective functions and the constraints of the mathematical model are presented. Finally, the evaluation of the shifting is discussed.

3.1 Assumptions and Modeling Approach

Our approach to solve the 2DRSSP splits the problem in two phases. First, we solve the stowage problem for a given deck. Then, we evaluate the number of shifts needed when applying the resulting stowage plan for the voyage. This results in two models: A stowage model and a shifting model. It is a reasonable approach to deal with these two problems in sequence, since the results of the stowage, i.e. the extra revenue from optional cargoes that can be transported, is assumed more important than the shifting costs.

Still the results from the stowage influence the shifting costs. Therefore, to implicitly take into account the shifting when determining a stowage plan, different objective functions are proposed and tested. Two concepts are introduced with expectation to reduce the shifting costs, namely *grouping* and *placement*. Placing vehicles from the same cargo next to each other is denoted as grouping. By grouping vehicles together, the shifting costs may decrease, as vehicles from the same cargo can use the same entry/exit route. The example in Fig. 2 shows how vehicles from the same cargo are grouped together. Placing cargoes which are on the ship for the most number of sailing legs farther away from the entry/exit than cargoes with shorter time on the vessel, is known as placement. This is introduced based on the expectation that vehicles placed farthest away from the entry/exit, is probably less exposed to shifting, and those squares should therefore be more costly to use.

Instead of dividing the deck into lanes such as [9], we suggest a grid representation of the deck, as illustrated in Fig. 3. This enables us to represent real deck layouts in a better way, and the resulting stowage plan becomes more realistic. This is done by defining a set of rows $\mathcal{I}$ and columns $\mathcal{J}$. Square $(1,1)$ is defined as the square located at stern, on the ship's port side (bottom left corner in Fig. 3). All squares are assumed to be of the same size.

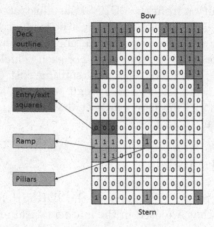

Fig. 3. Illustration of the grid representation of a deck. The 1's indicate that the corresponding square is unusable.

Each cargo $c \in \mathcal{C}$ consists of N_c identical vehicles. If, in practice, one is to carry a cargo consisting of heterogeneous vehicles, this cargo is split into several cargoes consisting of identical vehicles. When all vehicles in a cargo are identical, the number of squares needed to place a vehicle from that cargo is equal for all vehicles in the cargo. For a given grid representation of the deck, each vehicle in a cargo needs S_c^L length squares, and S_c^W width squares to be placed on the deck. These parameters will vary with the grid resolution chosen, given by the number of rows times the number of columns ($|\mathcal{I}||\mathcal{J}|$). The area of the resulting square usage always gives an overestimation of the actual area usage. Increased resolution will give a more detailed representation of the deck and the vehicles, but increases the number of variables in the model.

The ports are assumed to be separated into two regions, one supply region and one demand region, where the loading ports are visited before the unloading ports. This is how most voyages are in RoRo-shipping. Also following common practice, it is assumed that once a vehicle is placed, it stays in the same location during the whole voyage. From this it follows that all carried vehicles are to be placed on the deck on the sailing leg between the last loading port and the first unloading port. Hence, by generating a stowage plan for this sailing leg, the vehicle placements for all other sailing legs can be derived from this stowage plan.

3.2   2DRSSP Stowage Model

Indices

c :   cargo
i :   row
j :   column

Sets

$\mathcal{C}$:   set of all cargoes
$\mathcal{C}^{\mathcal{O}}$:   set of all optional cargoes
$\mathcal{C}^{\mathcal{M}}$:   set of all mandatory cargoes
$\mathcal{I}_c$:   set of all rows where the corner of a vehicle in cargo c can be placed
      $\mathcal{I}_c = \{1, ... |\mathcal{I}| - S_c^L + 1\}$
$\mathcal{J}_c$:   set of all columns where the corner of a vehicle in cargo c can be placed
      $\mathcal{J}_c = \{1, ..., |\mathcal{J}| - S_c^W + 1\}$

Parameters

L^D :   length of deck
W^D :   width of deck
C_c^L :   length of one vehicle in cargo c
C_c^W :   width of one vehicle in cargo c
B :   minimum clearance between vehicles
N_c :   number of vehicles in cargo c
S_c^L :   number of length squares needed to place one vehicle from cargo c
      $S_c^L = \lceil \frac{(C_c^L + B)|\mathcal{I}|}{L^D} \rceil$
S_c^W :   number of width squares needed to place one vehicle from cargo c
      $S_c^W = \lceil \frac{(C_c^W + B)|\mathcal{J}|}{W^D} \rceil$
P_c^L :   loading port of cargo c
P_c^U :   unloading port of cargo c, $P_c^U > P_c^L$
R_c :   revenue earned if optional cargo c is taken
U_{ij} :   1 if square (i,j) is unusable, 0 otherwise
E_{ij} :   1 if square (i,j) is an exit square, 0 otherwise
D :   A small positive number that will increase the value of the objective function if vehicles from the same cargo are grouped together
C_{ij}^S :   The artificial cost of using square (i,j) for a vehicle

Decision Variables

x_{ijc} :   1 if the lower left corner of a vehicle from cargo c is placed in square (i, j), 0 otherwise

y_c :   1 if optional cargo c is taken, 0 otherwise

u_{ijc} :   Number of vehicles from the same cargo c placed next to square (i, j), if a vehicle from cargo c is placed in (i, j)

Objective Functions. The objective of the 2DRSSP is to maximize the revenue from optional cargoes, minus the penalty costs incurred when shifting vehicles. Since the stowage model does not explicitly evaluate shifting cost, four objective functions are proposed and tested in an effort to place vehicles in a way that reduce the need for shifting.

$$\max z = \sum_{c \in C^O} R_c y_c \tag{1}$$

$$\max z = \sum_{c \in C^O} R_c y_c + \sum_{c \in C} \sum_{i \in \mathcal{I}_c} \sum_{j \in \mathcal{J}_c} D u_{ijc} \tag{2}$$

$$\max z = \sum_{c \in C^O} R_c y_c - \sum_{c \in C} \sum_{i \in \mathcal{I}_c} \sum_{j \in \mathcal{J}_c} \sum_{i'=i}^{i+S_c^L-1} \sum_{j'=j}^{j+S_c^W-1} (P_c^U - P_c^L) \frac{C_{i'j'}^S x_{ijc}}{S_c^L S_c^W} \tag{3}$$

$$\max z = \sum_{c \in C^O} R_c y_c + \sum_{c \in C} \sum_{i \in \mathcal{I}_c} \sum_{j \in \mathcal{J}_c} (D u_{ijc} - \sum_{i'=i}^{i+S_c^L-1} \sum_{j'=j}^{j+S_c^W-1} (P_c^U - P_c^L) \frac{C_{i'j'}^S x_{ijc}}{S_c^L S_c^W}) \tag{4}$$

The objective function (1) maximizes the revenues from optional cargoes. The objective function (2) maximizes the revenues from optional cargoes and the artificial value of placing vehicles from the same cargo together. The objective function (3) maximizes the sum of revenues from optional cargoes minus the placement cost of each vehicle in all carried cargoes. The placement cost for each vehicle is a function of the number of sailing legs a vehicle is placed on the ship, multiplied with the cost of using the chosen square placement. The cost of using a square should reflect the square's probability of being exposed to shifting. The objective function (4) combines objectives (2) and (3).

Unusable Space and Entry/Exit Squares. Some squares are unusable due to ramp placement, deck outline, pillars, etc. These constraints are handled in the variable declaration of the model. For all squares (i, j), if the corner of a vehicle from cargo c cannot be placed in that square due to unusable space ($U_{ij} = 1$) or entry/exit squares ($E_{ij} = 1$), then x_{ijc} is fixed to zero for the given cargo and square.

Common Constraints

$$\sum_{i \in \mathcal{I}_c} \sum_{j \in \mathcal{J}_c} x_{ijc} = N_c, \qquad\qquad c \in \mathcal{C}^{\mathcal{M}} \tag{5}$$

$$\sum_{i \in \mathcal{I}_c} \sum_{j \in \mathcal{J}_c} x_{ijc} = N_c y_c, \qquad\qquad c \in \mathcal{C}^{\mathcal{O}} \tag{6}$$

$$\sum_{i'=i}^{i+S_c^L-1} \sum_{j'=j}^{j+S_c^W-1} x_{i'j'c} \le 1, \qquad c \in \mathcal{C}, i \in \mathcal{I}_c, j \in \mathcal{J}_c \tag{7}$$

$$\sum_{i'=max(i-S_{c'}^L+1,1)}^{min(i+S_c^L-1,|\mathcal{I}_{c'}|)} \sum_{j'=max(j-S_{c'}^W+1,1)}^{min(j+S_c^W-1,|\mathcal{J}_{c'}|)} x_{i'j'c'} \le M_{cc'}(1 - x_{ijc}),$$

$$c \in \mathcal{C}, c' \in \mathcal{C}\backslash\{c\}, i \in \mathcal{I}_c, j \in \mathcal{J}_c \tag{8}$$

$$x_{ijc} \in \{0,1\}, \qquad\qquad c \in \mathcal{C}, i \in \mathcal{I}_c, j \in \mathcal{J}_c \tag{9}$$
$$y_c \in \{0,1\}, \qquad\qquad c \in \mathcal{C}^{\mathcal{O}} \tag{10}$$

Constraints (5) guarantee that all the mandatory cargoes are placed on the deck. Constraints (6) ensure that all vehicles in an optional cargo are placed on the deck, if the optional cargo is taken. Constraints (7) guarantee that at most one vehicle from the same cargo uses the same place on the deck. Constraints (8) make sure that different cargoes do not .use the same place on the deck. Min and max expressions are included to ensure that the constraints do not include squares outside the deck area. An upper bound on $M_{cc'}$ is given by $(S_c^L + S_{c'}^L - 1)(S_c^W + S_{c'}^W - 1)$. Constraints (9) and (10) force the variables to take binary values.

Grouping Constraints

$$u_{ijc} \le x_{i+S_c^L,jc} + x_{i-S_c^L,jc} + x_{i,j+S_c^W,c} + x_{i,j-S_c^W,c}, \quad c \in \mathcal{C}, i \in \mathcal{I}_c, j \in \mathcal{J}_c \tag{11}$$

$$u_{ijc} \le M x_{ijc}, \qquad\qquad c \in \mathcal{C}, i \in \mathcal{I}_c, j \in \mathcal{J}_c \tag{12}$$

$$\sum_{i \in \mathcal{I}_c} \sum_{j \in \mathcal{J}_c} u_{ijc} \ge 2N_c - 2, \qquad\qquad c \in \mathcal{C}^{\mathcal{M}} \tag{13}$$

$$\sum_{i \in \mathcal{I}_c} \sum_{j \in \mathcal{J}_c} u_{ijc} \ge (2N_c - 2)y_c, \qquad\qquad c \in \mathcal{C}^{\mathcal{O}} \tag{14}$$

$$u_{ijc} \ge 0, \qquad\qquad c \in \mathcal{C}, i \in \mathcal{I}_c, j \in \mathcal{J}_c \tag{15}$$

Constraints (11) force u_{ijc} to take a value equal to the number of vehicles from the same cargo placed next to the vehicle in square (i, j). Constraints (12) ensure that the number of neighboring vehicles is only calculated for the squares where a vehicle is placed. The upper bound on M is 4, which is the maximum number of neighboring vehicles, defined as a vehicle placed exactly in front, behind, left or right of a vehicle. Thus, a vehicle placed in $x_{i+S_c^L,j+1,c} = 1$ is not defined as a neighbor, even though it could be interpreted as a neighbor in practice. This modeling choice is made to reward practical stowage solutions. Constraints (13) and (14), in addition to (11) and (12) enforce vehicles from same cargo to have a total number of neighbors greater than or equal to the weakest form of compactness. Given that every vehicle is placed next to a vehicle from the same cargo, the weakest form of compactness is a line. In this case, all vehicles would have two neighbors, except the vehicles at each end of the line, which will only have one neighbor. The lower bound on the total number of neighboring vehicles for a cargo in this case is given by: $2N_c - 2$. Finally, non-negativity requirements for the variables related to grouping are given in (15).

3.3   2DRSSP Shifting Model

Based on a given feasible solution from the stowage model described in Sect. 3.2, we want to evaluate the solution with respect to the shifting cost. The cost of shifting a given vehicle is set as a function of the area of the vehicle, since the cost of moving a large vehicle, e.g. a semi-trailer, is assumed higher than the cost of moving a small vehicle, e.g. a 3-door car. The shifting cost could also be based on other considerations than the area, e.g. expected time usage or shifting distance. It is assumed that a vehicle that is shifted is moved out of the deck during the port call and returned to the exact same square when the loading/unloading is done. We assume that each vehicle can move one square horizontally or vertically. In practice, vehicles have a given turning radius and can therefore not move sideways. However, sideways movement is assumed possible, as the inclusion of turning radius would drastically increase the modeling complexity of the shifting evaluation.

The most apparent shifting evaluation method is to treat the stowage solution as a node network, and solve it as a shortest path problem (SPP). For each port, an entry or exit route for all vehicles in every loaded or unloaded cargo could be calculated. However, this approach would only give an upper bound on the number of shifts, since it does not take into account the shifts made for other entering/exiting vehicles. In order to determine the entry/exit routes for all exiting vehicles simultaneously, a shifting model for the 2DRSSP has been developed. As the shifting model only evaluates a given stowage solution, the model is only briefly discussed in the following paragraph.

The objective of the shifting model is to find an optimal entry and exit path for each vehicle v in cargo c for the related loading and unloading ports of the cargoes, in order to minimize the total shifting cost. The problem is solved for every port, and the sum of the shifting cost for all ports along the given voyage is reported as the objective value. A small example for a given port is given in Fig. 4. An exit path for both of the vehicles V1 and V2 is to be decided. The shortest path problem gives a shifting cost of 6 for V1, and 2 for V2, which gives a total shifting cost of 8. The 2DRSSP shifting model provides a better

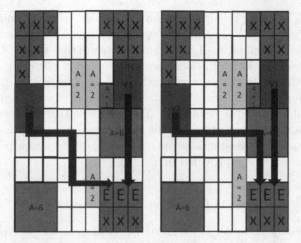

Fig. 4. Solution to the SPP for each vehicle to the left, and the optimal solution from the shifting model to the right. V1 and V2 indicates the vehicles that are to be unloaded, while A is the number of squares the other vehicles are occupying and indicate the cost to move those vehicles.

result. By taking into account that each vehicle only is shifted once, both V1 and V2 could use the squares where the shifted vehicle were placed. This gives an optimal solution of shifting cost equal to 6.

4 Computational Study

This section presents a computational study performed on a number of test instances generated from real data from the case company. The mathematical models are implemented in Mosel and solved using the commercial optimization software Xpress. The test instances were run on a computer with Intel Core i7-3770 (3.40 GHz) CPU and 16 GB RAM, running on Windows 7 Enterprise 64-bit Operating System. Section 4.1 describes the test instances, while the computational results are presented and discussed in Sect. 4.2

4.1 Test Instances

The test instances are generated based on cargo data provided by the company. A typical real-sized deck has a length greater than $100m$ and width greater than 40 m. Using decks with areas of this size and a practical grid resolution, the stowage model is most likely not going to provide a solution within a reasonable amount of time. Hence, two smaller deck layouts are used to test the model. These layouts are created based on a scaled outline of a typical real sized deck. A deck measuring 45 m × 20 m and a deck measuring 20 m × 10 m are used, named decks 1 and 2, respectively. The cargo sets are randomly generated subsets of a real cargo list provided by the company. For each cargo set, the number of mandatory cargoes is low enough to ensure a feasible solution, and the number of optional cargoes is set such that the total area usage for all cargoes at least exceeds the decks area capacity. This is done to ensure that the 2DRSSP stowage model has to evaluate which optional cargoes to carry. For each instance, the number of length and width squares needed for each vehicle is pre-calculated, based on the vehicles length, width and the minimum clearance required between the cars, as well as the grid resolution. The discretization process from a real deck layout to a grid representation reduces the available area, due to an over-estimated area usage of the unusable space. The resulting area available of total area and test instances are provided in Table 1.

Table 1. Test instances characteristics.

Test instance	Deck #	Length of deck (m)	Width of deck (m)	Grid resolution	Cargo set	Area available of total area
$i10j10c1d1$	1	45	20	10×10	1	80%
$i15j15c1d1$	1	45	20	15×15	1	88%
$i20j20c1d1$	1	45	20	20×20	1	96%
$i10j10c2d1$	1	45	20	10×10	2	80%
$i15j15c2d1$	1	45	20	15×15	2	88%
$i20j20c2d1$	1	45	20	20×20	2	96%
$i10j10c3d2$	2	20	10	10×10	3	90%
$i20j20c3d2$	2	20	10	20×20	3	95%
$i10j10c4d2$	2	20	10	10×10	4	90%
$i20j20c4d2$	2	20	10	20×20	4	95%
$i10j10c5d2$	2	20	10	10×10	5	90%
$i20j20c5d2$	2	20	10	20×20	5	95%

4.2   Results 2D Stowage Model

A goal in this computational study is to evaluate the performance of different model versions with regard to revenue generated, shifting cost and solution time. Even though the instances used is a scaled down version of real sized decks, the provided examples give valuable information of the performance of the different objectives for further study on the RoRo stowage problem.

The different objectives presented in Sect. 3.2 aim at influencing the vehicle placements so that the shifting cost is reduced. From this, five versions of the stowage model are presented in Table 2. Common for all the model versions is that the objective is to maximize the revenue generated from optional cargoes. For the basic model version N, this is the only objective. Model version P additionally influences the vehicles placement by introducing square costs.

Table 2. Model versions

Model version	Objective	Constraints
Normal (N)	(1)	(5)–(10)
Placement (P)	(3)	(5)–(10)
Hard grouping (H)	(1)	(5)–(10), (11)–(15)
Soft grouping (S)	(2)	(5)–(10), (11)–(12), (15)
Placement + Soft grouping (SP)	(4)	(5)–(10), (11)–(12), (15)

This results in placing vehicles carried for the most sailing legs furthest away from the exit, where the probability of being exposed to shifting is less. Model version H enforces a weak form of compactness to each cargo, placing the vehicles together. Model version S rewards grouping of vehicles. For each vehicle in a cargo, a higher number of neighboring vehicles from the same cargo increases the objective value. Finally, model version SP penalizes placement and rewards grouping.

Each of the 12 instances from Table 1 was tested on the following versions of the MIP model: N, P, H, and S and SP. A maximum running time of 7200 s was set for the MIP model. If optimality was not proven within that time, the best solution is reported together with the gap from the upper bound. If the absolute gap between best bound and best solution was less than 0.01 % the search was terminated. The clearance between vehicles was set to 0.15 m, $D = 0.001$, and the square cost, C_{ij}^S, was set to one thousand of the minimum number of squares to reach an exit for each square (i, j). Table 3 shows the average results over all instances, obtained within the time limit of 7200 s.

Table 3. Average results for all test instances for the stowage model.

Extension	Gap (%)	Time (s)	# optional cargo	Revenue optional	Area used (%)	# of shifts
N	59.72	3600	1.33	17.67	78.53	9.91
P	24.03	3075	1.58	20.33	81.23	7.42
H[1]	35.34	3212	1.42	18.08	65.32	11.10
S	17.38	3432	1.58	20.50	81.75	8.36
SP	0.01	1778	1.58	20.50	81.75	5.64

[1]Two instances did not provide a feasible solution.

The main objective of this problem is to maximize the revenue from the optional cargoes, while minimizing the shifting cost can be considered as a secondary objective. Since the extra terms in the objective functions (2)–(4) have a minor contribution to the objective value, the revenue of bringing an extra cargo always exceeds the cost of where to place or/and group the vehicles. The model versions N, P, S, and SP would therefore generate the same optional revenue in their optimal solutions, but the vehicles' placement could differ. The H-version is a bit different, as constraints (13)–(14) reduce the solution space. This model could therefore give an optimal solution which generates less revenue than the optimal solution for the other four models, or even give infeasible solutions, as for the two instances. The infeasible solutions may indicate that constraints (13)–(14) are too strict, excluding possible good stowage solutions.

Without evaluating the shifting cost of the solutions, there are some interesting findings regarding the performance of the different model versions. Model versions S and SP provide the best average revenue generated within the time limit. The stowage plans are not necessarily identical, but they do at least carry the same set of optional cargoes for every instance. The average gap for model version SP is 0.01, which implies that the optimal set of optional cargoes is carried for every instance. Based on the average gap, and the solution time, we conclude that version SP performs best on the given test instances.

For each model version and each instance, the shifting costs for the resulting stowage plans are calculated, using the 2DRSSP shifting model, briefly described in Sect. 3.3. This is done in order to evaluate the placement strategies used by the different versions of the stowage model. In Table 3, the average number of shifts for each model version is reported instead of the shifting costs. The two measures have a high correlation, and number of shifts is chosen for readability purposes. When evaluating the solutions it is important to consider the number of optional cargoes carried. As the revenues generated using the different model versions vary, the number of vehicles on the deck differ. With more vehicles on the deck, the number of shifts is expected to be higher. The computational results from the stowage model showed that the SP version of the model achieved the highest optional revenue on average. This implies that the resulting stowage plans from SP carry the largest number of vehicles. Despite this, the stowage plans from SP actually give the best results with regards to the total number of shifts. On average, model version SP gives the stowage solutions with the lowest number of shifts, lowest computational time, and carries the most optional cargoes. From this, it is reasonable to conclude that both grouping and placement modifications is preferable to incorporate in a RoRo stowage model.

5   Concluding Remarks

The RoRo stowage problem is an essential part of the operational decisions for RoRo-operators in order to maintain their competitive position in the vehicle transportation market. We have proposed a mixed integer programming model for the two-dimensional RoRo ship stowage problem for one deck (2DRSSP).

Five alternative version of the 2DRSSP stowage model have been evaluated using 12 test instances. Test results showed that the inclusion of both grouping and placement objectives in the stowage model was preferable. This model version provided the overall best results, both regarding the revenue generated from optional cargoes, and the number of shifts.

However, the complexity of the problem limits the use of the models for real-life problems. We believe, however, that the research presented in this paper provide both important insights and modeling components that can be used in future research. A heuristic solution method is currently being tested, and preliminary results show that it provides feasible solutions to realistically sized problem instances for one deck. The natural extension to multiple decks is a promising venue for future research.

Acknowledgments. We would like to thank an anonymous referee for many valuable comments and suggestions that led to improvements in the paper.

References

1. Ambrosino, D., Sciomachen, A., Tanfani, E.: Stowing a containership: the master bay plan problem. Transp. Res. Part A Policy Pract. **38**(2), 81–99 (2004)
2. Andersson, H., Fagerholt, K., Hobbesland, K.: Integrated maritime fleet deployment and speed optimization: case study from roro shipping. Comput. Oper. Res. **55**, 233–240 (2015)
3. Avriel, M., Penn, M., Shpirer, N., Witteboon, S.: Stowage planning for container ships to reduce the number of shifts. Ann. Oper. Res. **76**, 55–71 (1998)
4. Dyckhoff, H.: A typology of cutting and packing problems. Eur. J. Oper. Res. **44**(2), 145–159 (1990)
5. Hadjiconstantinou, E., Christofides, N.: An exact algorithm for general, orthogonal, two-dimensional knapsack problems. Eur. J. Oper. Res. **83**(1), 39–56 (1995)
6. Hopper, E., Turton, B.C.: An empirical investigation of meta-heuristic and heuristic algorithms for a 2D packing problem. Eur. J. Oper. Res. **128**(1), 34–57 (2001)
7. Hvattum, L.M., Fagerholt, K., Armentano, V.A.: Tank allocation problems in maritime bulk shipping. Comput. Oper. Res. **36**(11), 3051–3060 (2009)
8. Kreuzer, E., Schlegel, V., Stache, F.: Multibody simulation tool for the calculation of lashing loads on roro ships. Multibody Sys.Dyn. **18**(1), 73–80 (2007)
9. Øvstebø, B.O., Hvattum, L.M., Fagerholt, K.: Optimization of stowage plans for roro ships. Comput. Oper. Res. **38**(10), 1425–1434 (2011)
10. Øvstebø, B.O., Hvattum, L.M., Fagerholt, K.: Routing and scheduling of roro ships with stowage constraints. Transp. Res. Part C Emerg. Technol. **19**(6), 1225–1242 (2011)
11. Pantuso, G., Fagerholt, K., Wallace, S.W.: Uncertainty in fleet renewal: a case from maritime transportation. Transp. Sci. **50**(2), 390–407 (2015)
12. Seixas, M.P., Mendes, A.B., Pereira Barretto, M.R., Da Cunha, C.B., Brinati, M.A., Cruz, R.E., Wu, Y., Wilson, P.A.: A heuristic approach to stowing general cargo into platform supply vessels. J. Oper. Res. Soc. **67**(1), 148–158 (2016)
13. Wäscher, G., Haußner, H., Schumann, H.: An improved typology of cutting and packing problems. Eur. J. Oper. Res. **183**(3), 1109–1130 (2007)

A Vessel Pickup and Delivery Problem from the Disruption Management in Offshore Supply Vessel Operations

Nils Albjerk[1], Teodor Danielsen[1], Stian Krey[1], Magnus Stålhane[1(✉)], and Kjetil Fagerholt[1,2]

[1] Department of Industrial Economics and Technology Management, Norwegian University of Science and Technology, Trondheim, Norway
magnus.staalhane@iot.ntnu.no
[2] Norwegian Marine Technology Research Institute (MARINTEK), Otto Nielsens veg 10, 7052 Trondheim, Norway

Abstract. This paper considers a vessel pickup and delivery problem that arises in the case of disruptions in the supply vessel logistics in the offshore oil and gas industry. The problem can be modelled as a multi-vehicle pickup and delivery problem where delivery orders are transported by supply vessels from an onshore supply base (depot) to a set of offshore oil and gas installations, while pickup orders are to be transported from the installations back to the supply base (i.e. backload). We present both an arc-flow and a path-flow formulation for the problem. For the path-flow formulation we also propose an efficient dynamic programming algorithm for generating the paths, which represent feasible vessel voyages. It is shown through a computational study on various realistic test instances provided by a major oil and gas company that the path-flow model is superior with respect to computational performance.

Keywords: Disruption management · Offshore supply · Vehicle routing

1 Introduction

Norway is a major oil and gas producer with a total petroleum production of about 230 million Sm^3 (standard cubic meters) in 2015 [8]. This production takes place from offshore installations on the Norwegian continental shelf with about 60 oil and gas fields. To ensure continuous production, the offshore installations are supplied with different equipment and material by specialized offshore supply vessels (OSVs). The OSVs represent one of the largest cost elements in the upstream supply chain, where the annual costs of one OSV amount to millions of USDs.

The oil and gas companies operating on the Norwegian continental shelf usually have a long-term plan for supplying its offshore installations, where a set of voyages are to be sailed on a weekly basis by a given chartered fleet of OSVs.

A. Paias et al. (Eds.): ICCL 2016, LNCS 9855, pp. 50–64, 2016.
DOI: 10.1007/978-3-319-44896-1_4

A voyage performed by an OSV starts at the onshore supply base, then the OSV visits and services a set of offshore installations in a pre-determined sequence, before returning to the supply base. In addition to bringing all types of products that are needed to the offshore installations, the OSVs also carry backload from the installations to the supply base. Each voyage is scheduled to take two or three days and each OSV usually completes two or three voyages each week. Figure 1 illustrates a weekly plan where three OSVs are scheduled to visit five installations.

	Monday			Tuesday			Wednesday			Thursday			Friday			Saturday			Sunday		
	8	16	24	32	40	48	56	64	72	80	88	96	104	112	120	128	136	144	152	160	168
Star		GRA			BID	DSD		BRA			GRA			BID		BRA					
Symphony					GRA	HDA			BID	DSD	BRA				BID	DSD	BRA				
Foresight	DSD	BRA						GRA			BID		DSD				GRA	HDA			BID

Fig. 1. Illustration of a weekly plan including three OSVs (Star, Symphony and Foresight) and five offshore installations (GRA, BID, DSD, BRA, HAD). Each voyage is represented by a rectangle, where the shaded area represents the time at the supply base [10].

The offshore installations are located in a part of the world where weather conditions can be harsh, especially during the winter season. Sometimes wave heights may limit both an OSV's sailing speed and its ability to perform unloading/loading operations at the installations. Another major source of disruptions to the plan comes from unexpected orders or extra high demand from the offshore installations, which especially occurs after periods with bad weather where the installations have not been serviced for some days. To mitigate the effects of these disruptions, the planners may have to deviate from the planned voyages and re-route the OSVs. They also have the possibility to charter an extra OSV from the spot market to handle the disruptions, though at a very high cost.

In this paper we study the problem of how to determine the OSV voyages for the next days after a disruption has occurred. The goal is to return to the long-term plan before the next voyage is planned to start for each OSV. Using the example from Fig. 1, suppose that the planner on Monday morning receive reports saying that the weather will be bad for the next two days, resulting in increased sailing and service times at the offshore installations. The planner then needs to determine how to adjust the next voyage for the OSVs Star (starting on Monday) and Symphony (starting on Tuesday) so that they hopefully can start on their next voyages on Thursday and Friday, respectively. These decisions affect both the service level perceived by the offshore installations, in case of delays in their services, and the sailing and chartering costs. Hence, the objective of the problem is to minimize these costs, while at the same time maintain a sufficient service level to the offshore installations and avoid delays of the OSVs that cause knock-on effects to the long-term plan.

Several papers address routing in the upstream supply chain for the offshore oil and gas industry. [5] study a pickup and delivery problem that arises in the service of offshore installations in the Norwegian Sea. Unlike the problem studied in this paper, they consider the routing of only one OSV. [11] extend the problem by taking into account demands for multiple commodities and the stowage of these commodities in dedicated compartments onboard the OSVs. They present a mathematical model of the problem and a heuristic to provide high quality solutions in a short amount of time.

As we can see in Sect. 2, the problem studied in this paper can be modelled as a multi-vehicle pickup and delivery problem where the delivery orders are transported from the supply base and the pickup orders (i.e. backload) are returned to the depot. The offshore installations might be visited once or twice, either conducting pickup and delivery simultaneously or at different points in time, possibly by different OSVs. Using the classification proposed by [1], our problem can be viewed as a special version of the 1-M-1|P-D|m, i.e. a one-to-many-to-one pickup and delivery problem with multiple vehicles. Problems of this type have been studied in the literature, though in very different contexts than ours. [3] studies a problem arising in reverse logistics, and, as this paper, propose both an arc-flow and path-flow model for the problem. [9] studies the same problem, but also takes into account time limits on the vehicles. However, in contrast to our problem neither allow customers to be visited twice and they do not consider the possibility of chartering an extra vessel/vehicle.

Relatively few studies regarding disruption management in ship routing exist, and to the authors' knowledge there exist no publications on disruption management in offshore supply logistics. However, in container liner shipping there exist a few studies, such as [2], which consider the vessel schedule recovery problem. Different recovery actions are proposed in the case of disruptions, such as increasing speed, canceling deliveries, and swapping port visits. A model considering sailing costs, delays, and misplaced cargo is presented, and it is run with data from real life cases. [7] proposes a mathematical model for simultaneous rescheduling of ships and cargo in a container liner network. Poor weather conditions, port congestion, low port productivity, towage, tidal windows, and several other sources of disruptions are mentioned. The model's suggested recovery actions include changing the departure or arrival time at ports, transshipment of cargo between ports, and speed adjustments. The possible measures to handle disruptions in [2,7] are to some extent the same as the ones available in our problem, such as canceling orders and re-routing. However, increasing speed to reduce delays will be less effective in our problem due to shorter sailing distances and is therefore not included, while the possibility of chartering additional OSVs from the spot market is an additional option available in offshore supply.

The contribution of this paper is to propose and test two mathematical models of the problem, i.e. an arc-flow and a path-flow model. For the path-flow model we also propose an efficient dynamic programming algorithm for generating the paths (feasible OSV voyages). It is shown that the path-flow model is superior to the arc-flow model with regards to computational performance.

Section 2 provides a formal description of the problem together with an arc-flow and a path-flow model of the problem. The dynamic programming algorithm for generating all feasible paths are presented in Sect. 3, while computational experiments are shown in Sect. 4. Finally, some concluding remarks are given in Sect. 5.

2 Problem Description and Mathematical Models

The problem studied in this paper can be formulated on a graph $G = (\mathcal{N}, \mathcal{A})$. At a given point in time there are n cargoes that must be transported from the onshore depot to different offshore installations, while at the same time m cargoes need to be transported from (possibly different) installations and back to the onshore depot. The set of nodes $\mathcal{N} = \{0, ..., n+m+1\}$ contains two nodes representing the onshore supply depot (nodes 0 and $n+1$) and one node for each cargo to be picked up or delivered. The set $\mathcal{N}$ can be divided into the set $\mathcal{N}^P = \{1, ..., n\}$ containing all pickup nodes, and the set $\mathcal{N}^D = \{n+2, ..., n+m+1\}$ containing all delivery nodes. We use the term *sibling nodes* to denote a pickup and a delivery node that is associated with the same offshore installation. The set of arcs $\mathcal{A}$ consists of arcs between all node pairs, with the following exceptions: there are no arcs entering node 0, no arcs leaving node $n+1$, and for sibling nodes there are no arcs from the pickup node to the delivery node since it is always preferable to deliver before picking up at an installation.

Each cargo occupies a given number of square meters on the deck of an OSV, and for each node $i \in \mathcal{N}^D$ we denote this area D_i, while for each node $i \in \mathcal{N}^P$ we denote it P_i. In addition, a penalty cost C_i^R is incurred if node $i \in \mathcal{N}$ cannot be serviced on the planned upcoming set of voyages and must be postponed. This penalty can be set differently for each cargo depending on the importance of its delivery or pickup.

To transport the cargoes, a set of OSVs is available. Let $\mathcal{V} = \{1, ..., k+1\}$ denote the set of OSVs, where $k+1$ represents an OSV chartered from the spot market. Each OSV v has a total deck capacity Q_v measured in square meters, and a cost C_{vij}^S and time T_{vij} associated with sailing from node i to node j, and servicing node j. Note that both of these parameters are weather dependent, however, we assume that they are known at the time of planning. Since we are only planning the next voyage, i.e. the next couple of days, this is a reasonable assumption. For example, if we know that the weather will be bad in the next couple of days we adjust C_{vij}^S and T_{vij} accordingly. Further, let T_v^{MIN} be the time OSV v is available to begin the next voyage, and let T_v^{MAX} be the planned departure time of the subsequent voyage for OSV v. However, we do allow the OSV to return back to the depot up to Γ hours after T_v^{MAX}, but at a cost of C_v^D per hour. The OSV $k+1$ must be chartered for a whole number of time periods (days), where the length of a time period is denoted by the parameter H, and the daily time charter rate is represented by C^{TC}.

2.1 Arc-Flow Model

The variable x_{vij} equals 1 if OSV v sails arc (i, j), and 0 otherwise. The auxiliary variable y_{vi} equals 1 if OSV v visits node i, and 0 otherwise. If the visit to node i

is postponed (i.e. not serviced on the voyage of any of the OSVs), the variable u_i equals 1, and 0 otherwise. The cargo load variables l_{vij} equal the load measured in square meters on OSV v when sailing arc (i, j). If the arc is not traversed, the corresponding load variable is equal to 0. The number of hours OSV v arrives at the depot after T_v^{MAX} is represented by the variable t_v^D. The number of whole days that the OSV $k + 1$ from the spot market needs to be chartered is denoted by t^{TC}. To simplify the notation, the constraints are defined using sets of nodes, even though some constraints may contain combinations of the indices v, i, and j for which the corresponding variable x_{vij} does not exist. In these cases the missing variable can be assumed to take the value 0. The operational planning and disruption management problem can be formulated as follows:

Objective

$$\min \sum_{v \in \mathcal{V}} \sum_{(i,j) \in \mathcal{A}} C_{vij}^S x_{vij} + C^{TC} t^{TC} + \sum_{i \in \mathcal{N}} C_i^R u_i + \sum_{v \in \mathcal{V} \backslash \{k+1\}} C_v^D t_v^D \qquad (1)$$

subject to:

$$\sum_{i \in \mathcal{N} \backslash \{0\}} x_{v0i} = 1 \qquad\qquad v \in \mathcal{V} \qquad (2)$$

$$\sum_{i \in \mathcal{N} \backslash \{n+1\}} x_{vi(n+1)} = 1 \qquad\qquad v \in \mathcal{V} \qquad (3)$$

$$\sum_{j \in \mathcal{N}} x_{vji} - \sum_{j \in \mathcal{N}} x_{vij} = 0 \qquad\qquad v \in \mathcal{V}, i \in \mathcal{N} \backslash \{0, n+1\} \qquad (4)$$

$$y_{vi} - \sum_{j \in \mathcal{N} \backslash \{i\}} x_{vij} = 0 \qquad\qquad v \in \mathcal{V}, i \in \mathcal{N} \qquad (5)$$

$$\sum_{v \in \mathcal{V}} y_{vi} + u_i = 1 \qquad\qquad i \in \mathcal{N} \backslash \{0, n+1\} \qquad (6)$$

$$l_{vij} \leq (Q_v - P_j) x_{vij} \qquad\qquad v \in \mathcal{V}, i \in \mathcal{N}, j \in \mathcal{N}^P \qquad (7)$$

$$l_{vij} \leq Q_v x_{vij} \qquad\qquad v \in \mathcal{V}, i \in \mathcal{N}, j \in \mathcal{N}^D \qquad (8)$$

$$l_{vij} \geq P_i x_{vij} \qquad\qquad v \in \mathcal{V}, i \in \mathcal{N}, j \in \mathcal{N}^P \qquad (9)$$

$$l_{vij} \geq D_j x_{vij} \qquad\qquad v \in \mathcal{V}, i \in \mathcal{N}^D, j \in \mathcal{N}^D \qquad (10)$$

$$l_{vij} \geq (P_i + D_j) x_{vij} \qquad\qquad v \in \mathcal{V}, i \in \mathcal{N}^P, j \in \mathcal{N}^D \qquad (11)$$

$$\sum_{i \in \mathcal{N}} l_{vij} + P_j x_{vjh} - l_{vjh} + Q_v x_{vjh} \leq Q_v \qquad v \in \mathcal{V}, j \in \mathcal{N}^P, h \in \mathcal{N} \qquad (12)$$

$$\sum_{i \in \mathcal{N}} l_{vij} - D_j x_{vjh} - l_{vjh} + Q_v x_{vjh} \leq Q_v \qquad v \in \mathcal{V}, j \in \mathcal{N}^D, h \in \mathcal{N} \qquad (13)$$

$$\sum_{j \in \mathcal{N}^D} D_j y_{vj} - l_{v0i} + Q_v x_{v0i} \leq Q_v \qquad v \in \mathcal{V}, i \in \mathcal{N} \qquad (14)$$

$$l_{vi(n+1)} - \sum_{j \in \mathcal{N}^P} P_j y_{vj} + Q_v x_{vi(n+1)} \leq Q_v \qquad v \in \mathcal{V}, i \in \mathcal{N} \tag{15}$$

$$t^{TC} \geq \left(\sum_{(i,j) \in \mathcal{A}} T_{(k+1)ij} x_{(k+1)ij} \right) \frac{1}{H} \tag{16}$$

$$T_v^{MIN} + \sum_{(i,j) \in \mathcal{A}} T_{vij} x_{vij} - T_v^{MAX} \leq t_v^D \qquad v \in \mathcal{V} \backslash \{k+1\} \tag{17}$$

$$t_v^D \leq \Gamma \qquad v \in \mathcal{V} \backslash \{k+1\} \tag{18}$$

$$\sum_{i \in \mathcal{S}} \sum_{j \in \mathcal{S}} x_{vij} \leq |\mathcal{S}| - 1 \qquad v \in \mathcal{V}, \mathcal{S} \subset \mathcal{N}, |\mathcal{S}| \geq 2 \tag{19}$$

$$x_{vij} \in \{0,1\} \qquad v \in \mathcal{V}, (i,j) \in \mathcal{A}, \tag{20}$$

$$y_{vi} \in \{0,1\} \qquad v \in \mathcal{V}, i \in \mathcal{N} \tag{21}$$

$$u_i \in \{0,1\} \qquad i \in \mathcal{N} \tag{22}$$

$$t_v^D \geq 0 \qquad v \in \mathcal{V} \backslash \{k+1\} \tag{23}$$

$$t^{TC} \in \mathbb{Z}^+ \tag{24}$$

The objective function (1) consists of four parts. The first term summarizes the costs related to sailing and servicing nodes for all OSVs, while the second term expresses the cost related to chartering an OSV from the spot market. The third and fourth terms are artificial costs that penalize orders that are postponed and OSVs that return to the onshore supply depot later than planned. Constraints (2) and (3) ensure that all voyages begin and end at the depot, while constraints (4) conserve the flow through the problem defining network. The auxiliary variables are set by constraints (5), and constraints (6) ensure that all nodes are either serviced by an OSV or the visit is postponed until a later voyage. Further, constraints (7)–(11) ensure that the capacity of each OSV is not violated on any arc along its route, while constraints (12) and (13) are the cargo flow conservation constraints. Since the model does not distinguish between cargo that is to be delivered to an installation and backload, constraints (14) ensure that the total amount of cargo to be delivered to installations on a voyage equals the load on-board when the OSV leaves the depot. Similarly, constraints (15), together with constraints (7) and (8), ensure that the load on-board, when the OSV arrives at the depot, equals the total amount of picked up cargo on a voyage. If an OSV is chartered from the spot market, constraint (16) calculates the time it is used, and rounds up to the nearest whole day. Constraints (17) calculate the delay of each OSV when returning to the depot, while constraints (18) assure that the delay is not more than Γ hours for each OSV in the long-term fleet. Finally, constraints (19) are the subtour eliminating constraints, and constraints (20)–(24) define the domain of each set of variables.

2.2 Path-Flow Model

Arc-flow models are well suited to describe a problem, however, they often perform inferior to path-flow models due to the large number of constraints and a relatively weak linear programming bound. In this section we describe a path-flow model obtained by applying Dantzig-Wolfe decomposition to the Arc-flow model presented above. A path through the graph G for vessel v is considered feasible if it satisfies constraints (2)–(5), (7)–(21), (23) and (24).

Let the set $\mathcal{R}_v$ contain all feasible paths for OSV v, and let the parameter A_{ri} be equal to 1 f node i is included on path r, and 0 otherwise. The cost associated with sailing and servicing all nodes on path r for OSV v is denoted by C_{vr}^S. This includes the sailing costs (C_{vij}^S) and any penalty costs from returning to the depot late (C_v^D). In addition, let $C_{(k+1)r}^S$ for all paths r associated with the OSV chartered from the spot market include the time charter costs C^{TC}, in addition to the fixed charter costs. Further, let variable λ_{vr} equal 1 if OSV v use path r, and 0 otherwise. As for the arc-flow model, if the visit to node i is postponed, the variable u_i equals 1, and 0 otherwise. Using this notation the path-flow model can be formulated as follows:

$$min \sum_{v \in \mathcal{V}} \sum_{r \in \mathcal{R}_v} C_{vr}^S \lambda_{vr} + \sum_{i \in \mathcal{N}} C_i^R u_i \tag{25}$$

subject to:

$$\sum_{v \in \mathcal{V}} \sum_{r \in \mathcal{R}_v} A_{ri} \lambda_{vr} + u_i = 1 \qquad i \in \mathcal{N} \setminus \{0, n+1\} \tag{26}$$

$$\sum_{r \in \mathcal{R}_v} \lambda_{vr} \leq 1 \qquad v \in \mathcal{V} \tag{27}$$

$$\lambda_{vr} \in \{0,1\} \qquad v \in \mathcal{V}, r \in \mathcal{R}_v \tag{28}$$

$$u_i \in \{0,1\} \qquad i \in \mathcal{N} \tag{29}$$

The objective function (25) corresponds to (1) for the arc-flow model, and sums the costs related to the voyages for all OSVs and the costs associated with nodes that are postponed until a later voyage. Constraints (26) ensure that all nodes are either serviced by an OSV or postponed until a later voyage, while constraints (27) ensure that each OSV sails at most one voyage. Finally, constraints (28) and (29) put binary restrictions on the variables.

3   Path Generation Using Dynamic Programming

In this section we describe how we generate all feasible paths through graph G which are needed to solve the path-flow model described in Sect. 2.2. All paths are generated for each OSV v through $|\mathcal{N}|$ *stages*, where $|\mathcal{N}|$ is the number of nodes in the network. The chosen approach applies full enumeration of possible paths with removal of infeasible and dominated paths.

Algorithm 1 shows the pseudocode for the generation of paths, and is based on the labeling algorithm described in [6]. In this approach all partial paths are encoded using labels which stores each (partial) path and the accumulation of resources along the path. Let M_p be the set of all labels representing paths of length p. The algorithm begins by creating an initial label representing a path starting at the depot node, and an empty set of labels representing complete feasible paths $\mathcal{R}$. Then, while p is less than or equal to the number of nodes in G, we create new labels L' by extending all labels L representing a path of length p to all nodes $i \in \mathcal{N}$. If the label L' is feasible it is added to the set M_{p+1}, unless it is extended to the depot node, in which case it is added to the set $\mathcal{R}$. Once all labels in M_p have been extended to labels in M_{p+1} we check all pairs of labels in M_{p+1} to see whether we can remove some labels due to dominance, and the counter p is updated. Finally, all labels in $\mathcal{R}$ are returned, and their corresponding paths are added to the path-flow model.

In the following we explain what data is stored in a label, how a label is extended, what constitutes a feasible extension of a label, and under what circumstances we can say that one label dominates another.

Algorithm 1. Pseudocode for dynamic voyage generation

```
 1: procedure VOYAGEGENERATOR
 2:     Create initial label
 3:     Add initial label to initial stage M₁
 4:     R = ∅
 5:     p = 1
 6:     while p ≤ |N| do
 7:         for all labels L in stage Mₚ do
 8:             for all nodes i in N do
 9:                 Create new label L' by extending label L to node i
10:                 if L' is feasible then
11:                     if i = n + 1 then
12:                         Add L' to R
13:                     else
14:                         Add L' to Mₚ₊₁
15:                     end if
16:                 end if
17:             end for
18:         end for
19:         Remove all dominated states from Mₚ₊₁
20:         p = p + 1
21:     end while
22:     Return R
23: end procedure
```

3.1 Label Data

In each stage, new labels are created containing the following data:

- i - The current node
- R - The predecessor label
- V - The set of nodes visited
- C - The sailing and service cost
- T - The sailing and service time
- π^D - The maximum deck capacity occupied at any point along the path
- π^P - The deck capacity needed for backload

In the following we use $i(L)$ to denote the current node i for label L and similarly use $R(L)$, $V(L)$, $C(L)$, $T(L)$, $\pi^D(L)$ and $\pi^P(L)$ for the rest of the label data.

The initial label represents an OSV starting at the depot pickup node. The initial state has no predecessor, which is denoted by *null*.

$$L_0 = \{0, \; null, \; \emptyset, \; 0, \; 0, \; 0, \; 0\},$$

3.2 Label Extension

When extending a label along an arc $(i(L), \; j)$, a new label L' is created at node j. The label data are updated as follows:

$$i(L') = j \tag{30}$$
$$R(L') = L \tag{31}$$
$$V(L') = V(L) \bigcup \{j\} \tag{32}$$
$$T(L') = T(L) + T^S_{vi(L)j} \tag{33}$$
$$C(L') = C(L) + C^S_{vi(L)j} + \begin{cases} max\{C^D_v * (T(L') + T^{MIN}_v - T^{MAX}_v), 0\}, & \text{if } j = n+1 \\ 0, & \text{otherwise} \end{cases} \tag{34}$$
$$\pi^D(L') = \begin{cases} max\{\pi^D(L) + D_j, \pi^P(L)\}, \text{ if } j \in \mathcal{N}^D \\ max\{\pi^D(L), \pi^P(L) + P_j\}, \text{ if } j \in \mathcal{N}^P \end{cases} \tag{35}$$
$$\pi^P(L') = \begin{cases} \pi^P(L), \text{ if } j \in \mathcal{N}^D \\ \pi^P(L) + P_j, \text{ if } j \in \mathcal{N}^P \end{cases} \tag{36}$$

Equations (30) and (31) update the current node and the predecessor for L'. The new current node is marked as visited in Eq. (32). The time and cost data are updated in Eqs. (33) and (34). The capacity data are updated in Eqs. (35) and (36) according to whether node j is a delivery or a pickup node. Figure 2 illustrates how the capacity data are updated along a path.

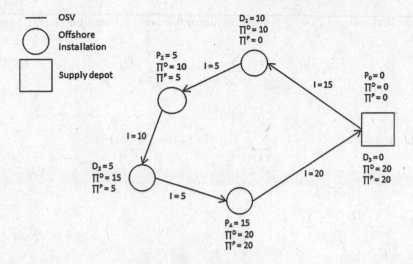

Fig. 2. Illustration showing how capacity data are updated during label extension. Requested delivery and backload size is given for each delivery and pickup node, respectively. The current amount of cargo carried on deck of the OSV is given for each arc.

Proposition 1. *Let L_f be the final label associated with a path r. Then $\pi^D(L_f)$ equals the maximum load onboard the OSV on path r.*

Proof. Let the maximum load on path r be carried on arc (i^*, j^*). Then the maximum load on r is

$$l_{i^*j^*} = \sum_{j \in \Omega^P} P_j + \sum_{j \in \Theta^D} D_j,$$

where $\Omega^P \subseteq \mathcal{N}^P$ is the set of pickup nodes already visited and $\Theta^D \subseteq \mathcal{N}^D$ is the set of delivery nodes not yet visited.

Consider the labels L_1 and L_2 with current nodes i_1 and i_2, respectively. L_1 is the predecessor of L_2, and both labels are predecessors of L_f. Let $\mathcal{N}_f^D$ denote the set of delivery nodes in the path of L_f. Assume, without the loss of generality, that the nodes visited on path r are numbered in the sequence they are visited. Then, the load on deck after visiting node i_1 and i_2, denoted by l_{i_1} and l_{i_2}, respectively, is

$$l_{i_1} = \sum_{j \in \mathcal{N}_f^D} D_j - \sum_{0 \leq j \leq i_1} D_j + \sum_{0 \leq j \leq i_1} P_j, \text{ and} \tag{37}$$

$$l_{i_2} = \sum_{j \in \mathcal{N}_f^D} D_j - \sum_{0 \leq j \leq i_2} D_j + \sum_{0 \leq j \leq i_2} P_j. \tag{38}$$

Assume that either l_{i_1} or l_{i_2} is the maximum load on r. The difference in load is

$$l_{i_1} - l_{i_2} = \sum_{i_1 < j \leq i_2} P_j - \sum_{i_1 \leq j \leq i_2} D_j \tag{39}$$

If $l_{i_1} > l_{i_2}$, then

$$\pi^D(L_2) = max\{\pi^D(L_1) + \sum_{i_1 \leq j \leq i_2} D_j, \pi^P(L_1) + \sum_{i_1 < j \leq i_2} P_j\}$$

$$= \pi^D(L_1) + \sum_{i_1 \leq j \leq i_2} D_j, \text{ and}$$

$$l_{i^*j^*} = \sum_{j \in \mathcal{N}_f^D} D_j - \sum_{0 \leq j \leq i_1} D_j + \sum_{0 \leq j \leq i_1} P_j$$

If $l_{i_2} > l_{i_1}$, then

$$\pi^D(L_2) = max\{\pi^D(L_1) + \sum_{i_1 \leq j \leq i_2} D_j, \pi^P(L_1) + \sum_{i_1 < j \leq i_2} P_j\}$$

$$= \pi^P(L_1) + \sum_{i_1 < j \leq i_2} P_j, \text{ and}$$

$$l_{i^*j^*} = \sum_{j \in \mathcal{N}_f^D} D_j - \sum_{0 \leq j \leq i_2} D_j + \sum_{0 \leq j \leq i_2} P_j$$

Not depending on which of l_{i_1} and l_{i_2} is greatest, the maximum load can be expressed as

$$l_{i^*j^*} = \sum_{j \in \Omega^P} P_j + \sum_{j \in \Theta^D} D_j = \pi^D(L_f).$$

Thus, Proposition 1 is correct.

Additional remark: if node i^* were a delivery node, then the load on board before visiting i^* would be greater than $l_{i^*j^*}$. Thus, i^* is a pickup node. Similar, if j^* were a pickup node, then the load on board after visiting j^* would be greater than $l_{i^*j^*}$. Thus, j^* is a delivery node.

3.3 Feasible Extension

An extension of state L to state L' along an arc $(i(L),\ j)$ is feasible if the following hold:

$$j \notin V(L) \tag{40}$$

$$k \notin V(L), \text{ if } j \in \mathcal{N}^D \text{ and } j \text{ and } k \text{ are siblings.} \tag{41}$$

$$T(L) + T_{vi(L)j}^S \leq T_v^{MAX} + \Gamma - T_v^{MIN}, \text{ if } j = n+1 \tag{42}$$

$$T(L) + T_{vi(L)j}^S + T_{vj(n+1)}^S \leq T_v^{MAX} + \Gamma - T_v^{MIN}, \text{ if } j \neq n+1 \tag{43}$$

$$max\{\pi^D(L) + D_j, \pi^P(L)\} \leq Q_v, \text{ if } j \in \mathcal{N}^D \tag{44}$$

$$max\{\pi^D(L), \pi^P(L) + P_j\} \leq Q_v, \text{ if } j \in \mathcal{N}^P \tag{45}$$

If the inequality (40) holds, node j is not already visited in path in label L. Inequality (41) assures that the pickup node should never be visited before the delivery node for the same installation. A *sibling* of a delivery node is defined as the corresponding pickup node of the installation, if one exists. Likewise, the sibling of a pickup node is the delivery node of the installation. As stated in inequality (42), the time needed to service the nodes in a path sailed by OSV v should not exceed the time available to v, where τ is the maximum allowed delay on a voyage. If node j is not the depot delivery node, there should also be enough time available to sail back to the onshore supply depot. This is assured by inequality (43). The inequalities (44) and (45) hold if the load on deck at any point of the path does not exceed the available deck capacity of the OSV.

3.4   Label Domination

At each stage, all labels dominated by anoter label are identified and removed. The label dominance criteria are:

Proposition 2. *The label L_1 dominates L_2 if*

$$V(L_1) = V(L_2), \tag{46}$$
$$i(L_1) = i(L_2), \tag{47}$$
$$C(L_1) \leq C(L_2), \tag{48}$$
$$T(L_1) \leq T(L_2). \tag{49}$$

Note that $V(L_1) = V(L_2)$ also implies that $\pi^P(L_1) = \pi^P(L_2)$ and $\pi^D(L_1) = \pi^D(L_2)$. Because the cost and time and non-decreasing and separable resources, it can easily be shown that Proposition 2 is a valid dominance criterion.

4   Computational Study

In this section we present a comparison of the computational performance of the two models. In Sect. 4.1 we describe the test instances used, while in Sect. 4.2 we present the computational results.

4.1   Test Instances

The test instances are based on data supplied by Statoil, the major Norwegian oil and gas company, and consist of an onshore supply depot and a set of offshore installations. As of today, each onshore supply depot services up to 13 offshore installations (28 nodes). However, when looking at recovery planning, it is rare that all the installations are to be visited within the short planning horizon. We have thus created instances with 4 to 8 installations (10 to 18 nodes). These instances are summarized in Table 1, which gives the id of each instance (ID), the name of the associated depot (Depot), the number of nodes (# Nodes), and the number of OSVs (# OSVs).

Three versions of each instance are tested:

- **No disruptions** All vessels have normal sailing speeds and all cargoes are of (roughly) normal size. These instances are denoted using the standard IDs from Table 1.
- **Reduced sailing speed** due to adverse weather conditions. This is done by reducing the speed of each vessel from ten to five knots, and thus, increasing the sailing time. The increase in sailing time will also affect the sailing costs. The ID for these instances have a superscript "S" for speed, e.g. M_{12}^S.
- **Large cargo sizes**, which often is the case after periods where adverse weather conditions have made supplying the offshore installations impossible or too costly. This is done by setting the demand and backload amount to the triple of the size used in the non-disrupted case to ensure that deck capacity becomes a binding constraint. The ID for these instances have a superscript "L" for load, e.g. M_{12}^L.

The reason for these choices of disruptions is that both speed reductions and more cargo to transport are the most common consequences of bad weather conditions. Either the speed of each vessel is reduced for a period of time, or the cargo has piled up both at the depot and at the installations because the OSVs have been prevented from sailing for a few days.

Table 1. Test instances used to compare the arc-flow and the path-flow models. #OSVs includes one spot vessel.

ID	Depot	# Nodes	# OSVs
M_{10}	Mongstad	10	2
M_{12}	Mongstad	12	2
$Å_{14}$	Ågotnes	14	2
F_{16}	Florø	16	2
$Å_{18}$	Ågotnes	18	3

4.2 Test Results

The arc-flow and path-flow models have been tested on a computer running Windows 7 with an Intel i7-3770 3.40 GHz CPU and 16 GB of RAM. The dynamic programming algorithm for the apriori generation of paths for the path-flow model is implemented in Java, while the arc-flow and path-flow models are implemented in Xpress-IVE 1.24.04 with Xpress-Mosel 3.6.0 and solved with Xpress-Optimizer 21.01.04 [4]. For both models we set an upper time limit of one hour (3,600 s).

The results of the computational tests can be seen in Table 2. For the arc-flow model the optimality gap (Opt. gap) and the computational time (Time) are given, while for the path-flow model we only give the computing time (Time).

Table 2. Comparison of the arc-flow and path-flow solution methods. For the arc-flow model the optimality gap (Opt. gap) and the solution time is presented and for the path-flow model the total solution time, including the time it takes to generate all paths, is presented.

ID	Arc-flow		Path-flow
	Opt. gap	Time [s]	Time [s]
M_{10}	0.0 %	0.1	0.13
M_{10}^S	0.0 %	7.2	0.06
M_{10}^L	0.0 %	3.0	0.03
M_{12}	0.0 %	0.4	0.51
M_{12}^S	68.9 %	>3 600	0.38
M_{12}^L	0.0 %	709	0.04
$Å_{14}$	0.0 %	0.6	13.1
$Å_{14}^S$	63.3 %	>3 600	13.0
$Å_{14}^L$	38.7 %	>3 600	0.56
F_{16}	0.0 %	0.4	529.3
F_{16}^S	77.0 %	>3 600	553.4
F_{16}^L	46.4 %	>3 600	101.3
$Å_{18}$	69.6 %	>3 600	>3 600
$Å_{18}^S$	94.8 %	>3 600	>3 600
$Å_{18}^L$	68.6 %	>3 600	1 222

The reason for this, is that in the instances where the path-flow model exceeds the time limit it does so while generating paths, and thus we do not have any optimality gap in those instances. As can be seen from the results, except for the two instances $Å_{14}$ and F_{16}, the path-flow model finds the optimal solution in less time than the arc-flow model. The path-flow model is also able to find the optimal solution in six instances where the arc-flow model cannot within the given time limit. This shows that the path-flow model is superior to the arc-flow model with respect to the computational performance for this problem.

5 Concluding Remarks

In this paper we have studied a vessel pickup and delivery problem that arises in the case of disruptions in the supply vessel logistics in the offshore oil and gas industry. We have shown that the problem can be modelled as a multi-vehicle pickup and delivery problem and proposed two alternative formulations for the problem, i.e. an arc-flow and a path-flow formulation. For the path-flow formulation we have also proposed an efficient dynamic programming algorithm for generating the paths, which represent feasible vessel voyages. It was shown through a computational study on various realistic test instances provided by a major oil and gas company that the path-flow model was superior with respect to computational performance.

Even though the path-flow model presented in this paper can solve many instances to optimality, there is a need for methods that can provide high quality solution to even larger instances in a short amount of time. An interesting extension of this work would therefore be to look either at more advanced exact solution methods, such as branch-and-price, or to develop heuristic solution methods for the problem.

References

1. Berbeglia, G., Cordeau, J.F., Gribkovskaia, I., Laporte, G.: Static pickup and delivery problems: a classification scheme and survey. TOP **15**(1), 1–31 (2007)
2. Brouer, B.D., Dirksen, J., Pisinger, D., Plum, C.E., Vaaben, B.: The vessel schedule recovery problem (VSRP) - a MIP model for handling disruptions in liner shipping. Eur. J. Oper. Res. **224**(2), 362–374 (2013)
3. Dell'Amico, M., Righini, G., Salani, M.: A branch-and-price approach to the vehicle routing problem with simultaneous distribution and collection. Transp. Sci. **40**(2), 235–247 (2006)
4. Fico.com: FICO Xpress Optimization Suite (2016). http://www.fico.com/en/products/fico-xpress-optimization-suite
5. Gribkovskaia, I., Laporte, G., Shlopak, A.: A tabu search heuristic for a routing problem arising in servicing of offshore oil and gas platforms. J. Oper. Res. Soc. **59**(11), 1449–1459 (2007)
6. Irnich, S., Desaulniers, G.: Shortest path problems with resource constraints. In: Desaulniers, G., Desrosiers, J., Solomon, M.M. (eds.) Column Generation. GERAD 25th Anniversary Series, pp. 33–65. Springer, New York (2005)
7. Kjeldsen, K.H.: Routing and scheduling in liner shipping. Ph.D. thesis, Aarhus University, p. 166 (2012)
8. Norwegian Petroleum Directorate: Petroleum figures (2015). http://www.npd.no/en/news/Production-figures/2015/December-2015/
9. Polat, O., Kalayci, C.B., Kulak, O., Günther, H.O.: A perturbation based variable neighborhood search heuristic for solving the vehicle routing problem with simultaneous pickup and delivery with time limit. Eur. J. Oper. Res. **242**(2), 369–382 (2015)
10. Shyshou, A., Gribkovskaia, I., Laporte, G., Fagerholt, K.: A large neighbourhood search heuristic for a periodic supply vessel planning problem arising in offshore oil and gas operations. INFOR: Inf. Syst. Oper. Res. **50**(4), 195–204 (2012)
11. Sopot, E., Gribkovskaia, I.: Routing of supply vessels to with deliveries and pickups of multiple commodities. Procedia Comput. Sci. **31**, 910–917 (2014)

Path Planning for Autonomous Inland Vessels Using A*BG

Linying Chen[✉], Rudy R. Negenborn, and Gabriel Lodewijks

Department of Maritime and Transport Technology,
Delft University of Technology, Delft, The Netherlands
L.chen-2@tudelft.nl

Abstract. To meet the transportation demand and maintain sustainable development, many countries are aiming to promote the competitive position of inland waterway shipping in the transport system. Autonomous transport is seen as a possibility for maritime transport to meet today's and tomorrow's challenges. In realizing autonomous navigation, path planning plays an important role. Being the most widely used path planning algorithm for robotics and land-based vehicles, in this paper we analyze A* and its extensions for waterborne applications. We hereby exploit the fact that for vessels optimal paths typically have heading changes only at the corners of obstacles to propose a more efficient modified A* algorithm, A*BG, for autonomous inland vessels. Two locations where ship accidents frequently occur are considered in simulation experiments, in which the performance of A*, A*PS, Theta* and A*BG are compared.

1 Introduction

Currently, economic development is putting enormous pressure on transport systems. Freight transport is likely to grow over the next decades [7]. If roads and railways are the major means of transport for handling the growth, they will face frequent congestion. Inland waterway shipping still have the capability of transporting large additional volumes. It offers an environment-friendly alternative to road and rail transport in terms of both energy consumption and gas emissions [6]. To meet the transportation demand and maintain sustainable development, many countries are aiming to promote and strengthen the competitive position of inland waterway shipping in the transport system.

Research has proposed many measures to improve the position of inland shipping, such as optimizing ship dimensions [10], removing bottlenecks [5], improving utilization of ports [8] and locks [25]. Among these measures, employing autonomous vessels has recently drawn much attention [13,27]. Autonomous vehicles are already state-of-the-art in the land-based transport domain. There exist several examples of self-driving and automated guided vehicles in modern container terminals [26]. Consequently, applying autonomous vessels is seen as a way to improve the safety and efficiency of inland shipping.

© Springer International Publishing Switzerland 2016
A. Paias et al. (Eds.): ICCL 2016, LNCS 9855, pp. 65–79, 2016.
DOI: 10.1007/978-3-319-44896-1_5

Safety can be improved as human error is one of the main causes of ship accidents. Figure 1 shows the mains causes of ship accidents between 2005 and 2014 in Dutch inland waterways [14]. The category operation error includes alcohol/drug use, wrong estimation, fatigue, etc.; the category communication error indicates not maintaining watch on correct VHF channel, unclear explanation, etc.; the category environmental error includes disturbances caused by wind, wave and current, poor visibility, etc.; the category equipment error indicates the failure of engine, rudder or other navigation equipments. For autonomous vessels, detection of obstacles, estimation of the risk, communication between vessels and infrastructure can be done without humans. Thus, applying autonomous vessels could be an efficient measure to reduce the number of accidents.

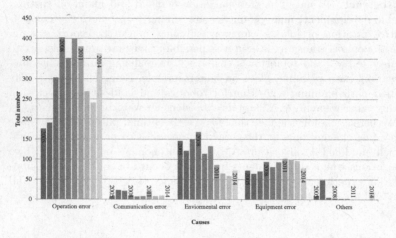

Fig. 1. The causes of the shipping accidents (based on [17]).

Efficiency can be improved by autonomous vessels due to the intelligent path planning and better control of vessel motion. Communication and coordination with infrastructures also make it possible for autonomous vessels to minimize the waiting time at ports, locks, etc.

The overall architecture of an autonomous vessel is shown in Fig. 2. To realize autonomous navigation, a vessel controller uses sensors to get self-state information (e.g., position, speed and heading), environmental information (e.g., wind speed, current velocity) and information of obstacles. Based on the obtained information, optimal paths to follow and desired speed and heading with specified objectives and constraints can be determined. The commands are sent to actuators for autonomous navigation.

In Fig. 2, the module 'Path planning' plays an important role in autonomous navigation. It describes how the autonomous vessel make decisions regarding its course to sail. The path planning problem can be subdivided into a global and a local planning task: an approximate global planner computes paths ignoring the kinematic and dynamic constraints; an accurate local planner accounts for the

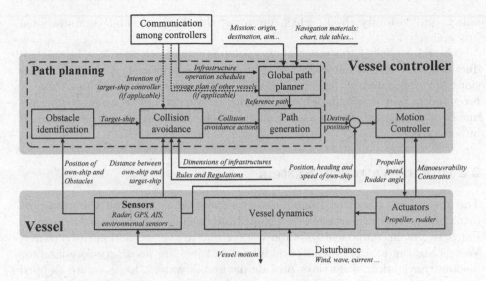

Fig. 2. The overall architecture of autonomous vessels.

constraints and generates feasible local trajectories [20]. The final path are determined on the basis of reference path provided by the global planner according to the transport mission, known stationary obstacles (e.g., islands, shallow waters) and infrastructure operation schedules, and the collision avoidance actions taking into account the regulations and the limitation of infrastructures (e.g., width and depth of waterways). Communication between vessel controllers will help the controller make better path planning decision. As a starting point, this paper focuses on the global path planning problem.

Many path planning algorithms have been developed for the navigation of unmanned surface vehicles as well as robots, such as Artificial Potential Field methods [23], Evolutionary Algorithms [12], and Heuristic Search Algorithms [4,19]. For a detailed review of path planning and collision avoidance technologies and techniques, see [2,21]. Among these methods, the group of heuristic search algorithms, especially A* and its extensions, are commonly used to determine the path from an origin to a destination for land-based vehicles [18,22].

Compared with mobile robotics path planning, the static obstacles in inland waterway networks are usually larger and continuous. Clear passages (waterways) can be found in the map. Moreover, when autonomous vessels are in a hybrid environment where exist vessels operated by humans. In order to ensure safety it is necessary that autonomous vessels comply with navigation rules throughout their missions [2]. Several recent efforts have been made to integrate rules into path planning algorithms [11,19].

In order to find a suitable global path planning algorithm for inland autonomous vessels, in this paper we carry out a comparison among A* and its extensions. We moreover propose a new algorithm called A*BG for autonomous inland vessels. Based on the existing algorithms, A*BG takes advantage of grid search and visibility check, which improves the searching and computational properties.

The remainder of this paper is organized as follows. In Sect. 2, a brief introduction of the inland waterway transport system is provided. A* and its extensions are elaborated on in Sect. 3. Based on this, the new algorithm A*BG is proposed in Sect. 4. Simulation experiments are carried out to assess the performance of the algorithms in Sect. 5. Conclusions and future research are presented in Section 6.

2   Inland Waterway System

The main function of an inland waterway system is to fulfill the transport demand, i.e., to transport goods or people from one place to another. As shown in Fig. 3, two main components in waterway systems are vessels and infrastructures. Vessels are the means of transport. Infrastructures are necessary to guarantee a sound navigation: waterways provide navigable waters; locks create stepped navigational pools with reliable depths; bridges balance the road traffic and the waterborne traffic.

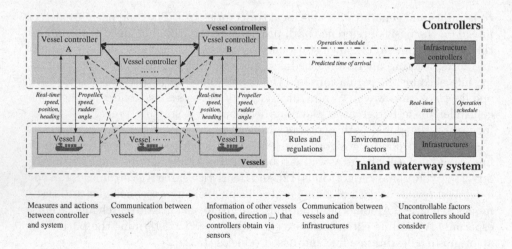

Fig. 3. Inland waterway system.

Rules and regulations provide suggestions to the skippers. These "rules of the road" specify the types of maneuvers that should be taken in situations where there is a risk of collision. Vessels navigating in waterways are also influenced by the external environment (e.g., wind, current and waves).

The architecture of an autonomous vessel in Fig. 2 can be regarded as the detail explanation of the relation of a vessel controller and a vessel in Fig. 3. When vessels navigating between the origins and destinations, controllers control the propeller and rudder to let the vessel move to desired position. The sensors measure the practical speed and headings of the vessel and provide them to the controllers as feedbacks. Vessel controller can obtain the position and direction of other vessels via sensors. When there is a risk of collision, actions that should be taken to avoid the collision are decided by the controllers. The communication between vessel controllers can help controllers to cooperate with each other.

Infrastructure controllers making schedules with the predicted time of arrival reported by vessel controllers and also keep an eye on the state of the infrastructures (e.g., availability, waiting time and length of the line). In return, the operation schedules also have impacts on vessel controllers decision making on the route, departure time and speed choices.

3 Existing Path Planning Algorithms

In this section, A* and its improved extensions and their characteristics are introduced. The method to apply the algorithms to inland autonomous vessels considering rules and regulations is explained as well.

3.1 A*

A* is the most widely used path planning algorithm, which can be applied on metric or topological map [4]. This algorithm uses a combination of heuristic searching and searching based on the shortest path. A* is defined as best-first algorithm, because each node in the map is evaluated by the function:

$$f(s_{\text{start}}, s, s_{\text{goal}}) = g(s_{\text{start}}, s) + h(s, s_{\text{goal}}) \tag{1}$$

where $g(s_{\text{start}}, s)$ provides the length of the shortest path from a start node s_{start} to node s found so far, $h(s, s_{\text{goal}})$ provides an estimate of the distance from node s to goal node s_{goal}, $f(s_{\text{start}}, s, s_{\text{goal}})$ provides an estimate of the length of a shortest path from the start node s_{start} via node s to the goal node s_{goal}.

A* uses a priority queue *Open* to perform the repeated selection of minimum $f(s_{\text{start}}, s, s_{\text{goal}})$ nodes to expand (expanding a node means this node is a candidate in the shortest path). At each step, the node s with the minimum $f(s_{\text{start}}, s, s_{\text{goal}})$ is removed from *Open*. The unblocked neighbor nodes which are in the line-of-sight of node s are recorded in the set $nbr_{los}(s)$. For each s' in $nbr_{los}(s)$, its related values are updated: $parent(s') = s$, $g(s_{\text{start}}, s') = g(s_{\text{start}}, s) + distance(s, s')$. If s' is already included in *Open*, A* compares the two $g(s_{\text{start}}, s')$ in $nbr_{los}(s)$ and *Open*, and updates the s' with lower $g(s_{\text{start}}, s')$. If not, s' is added to *Open*. The algorithm then repeats this procedure until s is s_{goal}. The length of the path that A* finds is then $f(s_{\text{start}}, s_{\text{goal}}, s_{\text{goal}})$.

The basic A* is restricted to a so-called 8-connectivity grid. This means that the path it finds is based on the connection between the closest possible nodes. The turning angle of each movement is restricted to multiples of 45°, which makes the path linked in a zigzag style. Consequently, the path A* finds is not guaranteed to be the optimal path.

3.2   A* with Larger Neighborhood

The length and smoothness of the paths A* finds are influenced by the connectivity of possible nodes which is determined by so-called '*neighborhood*'. The term '*neighborhood*' indicates the area that A* algorithm explores in a single step, which determines the successor nodes that can be reached from a source node.

One method to improve A* is to enlarge the neighborhood. As shown in Fig. 4, when *neighborhood* = 1 is considered, the algorithm can search 8 successor nodes. This is the most frequently used A*. 8 directions are possible to move into in a single step. When the *neighborhood* increases to 2, 16 more grids and 8 more directions can be searched in each step. Thus, the larger the neighborhood is, the more successor nodes the algorithm can reach, and the more directions are possible to be explored in a single step.

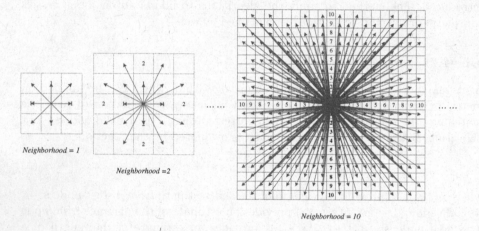

Fig. 4. Neighborhood in A* algorithm.

It is considered that a larger neighborhood results in the discovery of a shorter path due to the increased fineness of possible directions. However, the computation time will also increase since more nodes need to be explored at each step. The trade-off must be made between the optimality of the path and the computation time in terms of requirements during for implementation.

3.3   A* with Post-smoothing

A* with Post-smoothing (A*PS) runs A* on grids and then smooths the resulting path, which often shortens it at the cost of an increase in computation time. Denote by $[s_0, s_1, ..., s_n]$ the path that A* finds on grids, with $s_0 = s_{\text{start}}$ and $s_n = s_{\text{goal}}$. A*PS firstly uses s_0 as the current node. It then find out the farthest node s_i that is in line-of-sight with s_0 on the path from s_n to s_1. Then, A*PS removes the intermediate nodes s_1 to s_{i-1} from the path, thus shortening it. Then s_i becomes the current node and A*PS repeats this procedure until it reaches the end of the path.

A*PS typically finds shorter paths than A* on grids, but is not guaranteed to find the optimal path [3,22]. The reason for this is that it only considers resulting paths and thus cannot make informed decisions regarding other paths during the A* search, which motivates the idea of interleaving smoothing [3].

3.4   Theta*

Theta* is an extension of the A*, which resides in the visibility test between successor nodes and the parent nodes. The main difference between A* and Theta* is that Theta* considers the path from the $parent(s)$ to node s'. In each step, when s (the node with the lowest $f(s_{\text{start}}, s, s_{\text{goal}})$ in $Open$) expanding its successors s' in $nbr_{los}(s)$, the visibility between s' and $parent(s)$ is checked. If $parent(s)$ is visible to s', $parent(s')$ becomes $parent(s)$, and $g(s', s_{\text{start}})$, $h(s', s_{\text{goal}})$ and $f(s_{\text{start}}, s', s_{\text{goal}})$ are updated correspondingly. Thus, $parent(s)$ and s' are directly connected. A detailed description of Theta* can be found in [3].

Theta* reduces some unnecessary heading changes taking advantage of the visibility test. Since Theta* carry out line-of-sight checks between a source node and its neighbor nodes, the computation time of Theta* is longer than A* and A*PS. However, Theta* is not guaranteed to find optimal paths. The parent of a node should be a visible neighbor of the node or a parent of a visible neighbor, which lead to a limitation of expanding nodes [3,22].

3.5   A* Adaptation Considering Navigation Regulations

As mentioned, it is necessary to take the navigation rules and regulations into account when planning paths for inland autonomous vessels. Thus, adaption should be made when applying A* and its extensions to inland vessels.

The main regulations in Dutch inland waterways are the RPR (Rijnvaart-politiereglement, Rhine Navigation Police Regulations) and the BPR (Binnen-vaartpolitiereglement, Inland Waterways Police Regulations). One important item related to global path planning in these two regulations is: 'if two vessels encounter each other with the risk of collision, the vessel not following the starboard side of the waterway must give way to the ship following the starboard side' [15]. Accordingly, vessel controllers generally choose the path on the starboard side of the waterway as preferred path. To reflect this circumstance, the middle line of a waterway is applied to separate the vessel traffic from different directions when implementing the path planning algorithms for autonomous inland vessels.

The paths that the planning algorithms compute are usually close to the border of obstacles. Because of ship-bank interaction, sailing closer to the obstacles will increase the risk of collision [20,24]. For the sake of safety, vessels usually keep a certain distance from the obstacles. Therefore, buffer areas are set around the obstacles. When planning the path, the paths via the buffer areas are still available to vessels with a penalty in path length. In this way, when implementing A* and its extensions, $f(s_{\text{start}}, s, s_{\text{goal}})$ of a grid in a buffer area is larger than its original value when there is no buffer areas.

4   A* on Border Grids

The algorithms presented in Sect. 3 are not guaranteed to find the optimal paths. An algorithm named A* on Visibility Graphs (A*VG) has been proven to be able to find the optimal paths on a map with disjoint polygonal obstacles [1,3]. In A*VG, visibility graphs are constructed before the A* search. If two locations do not pass through any obstacle, an edge is drawn between them to represent the visibility connection. The paths A*VG finds are along the edge and have heading changes only at the border of obstacles. However, A*VG can be slow. Visibility checks need to be performed for every pair of blocked nodes to determine whether or not there should be a visibility edge between them.

The above mentioned algorithms have different advantages and disadvantages. The characteristics of each algorithm are concluded in Table 1. A* on grid maps are simple and with relatively low computation time. However, the path it calculates is usually the longest. Theta* and A*VG take the advantage of the visibility check, and the paths these two algorithm find are relatively shorter. At the same time, their computation times are longer. Based on the comparison, a new algorithm for inland autonomous vessels is proposed next.

Table 1. Summary of the characteristics of the algorithms.

Algorithm	Description	Typical path length	Computation time	Advantage	Disadvantage
A*	A*	Longest	Shortest	Simple; Modifiable	Not any angle; Zigzag style path
A*PS	A* + Post process visibility test	Shorter than A*	Longer than A*	Any angle	Rely on the path found by A*
Theta*	A* + Resides in visibility test	Shorter than A*PS	Longer than A*PS	Any angle	Long computation time
A*VG	A*+Visibility graph	Optimal (with polygonal obstacles)	Longest	Any angle	Long computation time

Inspired by A*VG, in the new algorithm, the border of the obstacles are decomposed into grids. The grids in the line-of-sight of a source node are its successor nodes. This algorithm is represented as A* on Border Grids (A*BG).

Algorithm 1 shows the pseudo code of A*BG. s is the node with the lowest $f(s_{\text{start}}, s, s_{\text{goal}})$ in *Open*. Line-of-sight checks are carried out between the source node s and all border grids. The nodes visible to s are included in the set *Candidates* as the candidate successors to be expanded. For each node s' in *Candidates*, if it is visible to *parent(s)*, its *parent(s')* and other related values will be updated. Then, the node with lowest $f(s_{\text{start}}, s, s_{\text{goal}})$ in *Open* is assigned to s again. This procedure is repeated until s is s_{goal}.

Algorithm 1. A*BG

---

1   **while** $s \neq s_{\text{goal}}$ **do**
2 | $s \leftarrow$ node with the smallest $f(s_{\text{start}}, s, s_{\text{goal}})$ in $Open$;
3 | $Candidates = \emptyset$;
4 | **foreach** $n \in BorderGrids$ **do**
5 | | **if** $lineofsight(n, s)$ **then**
6 | | | $parent(n) = s$;
7 | | | $g(n) = g(s) + distance(n, s)$; $h(n) = distance(n, s_{\text{goal}})$;
8 | | | $Candidates.Insert(n, parent(n), g(s_{\text{start}}, n), h(n, s_{\text{goal}}), f(s_{\text{start}}, n, s_{\text{goal}}))$

9 | **foreach** $s' \in Candidates$ **do**
10 | | **if** $lineofsight(s', parent(s))$ **then**
11 | | | **if** $g(s_{\text{start}}, parent(s)) + distance(parent(s), s') < g(s_{\text{start}}, s')$ **then**
12 | | | | $parent(s') = parent(s)$;
13 | | | | $g(s_{\text{start}}, s') = g(s_{\text{start}}, parent(s)) + distance(parent(s), s')$;

14 | | **if** $s' \in Open$ **then**
15 | | | **if** $g(s_{\text{start}}, s')$ in $Candidates < g(s_{\text{start}}, s')$ in $Open$ **then**
16 | | | | Remove the item s' from $Open$
17 | | **else** continue;   `// Do not execute line 18`
18 | | $Open.Insert(s', parent(s'), g(s_{\text{start}}, s'), h(s', s_{\text{goal}}), f(s_{\text{start}}, s', s_{\text{goal}}))$

Inspired by Theta* and A*VG, A*BG considers the connection of $parent(s)$ and s', and the paths A*BG calculated only have heading changes at where line-of-sight is blocked, which reduces unnecessary heading changes and the path length. Applying border grids instead of visibility graph can greatly reduce the number of visibility test. Using border grids instead of transferring the whole map into grids reduces the amount of nodes the algorithm need to search, which makes the algorithm faster. Moreover, regarding all visible border grids as candidates when expanding successors, A*BG does not influenced by the size of neighborhood and it is able to search in every direction.

5 Simulation Experiments

To test the performance of the algorithms, in this section, we compare A*, A*PS, Theta* and A*BG with respect to their path length and computation time.

5.1 Case Study Areas

Safety is one of the main factors that should be kept in mind when planning for autonomous vessels. Consequently, we choose for our experimental areas inland waterway regions where relatively many accidents have taken place in the past.

    The locations of ship accidents occurred in Dutch inland waterways during 2008–2015 are shown in Fig. 5. The places where accidents frequently occur are ports and intersections. Accordingly, we choose an intersection and a port area for carrying out the experiments. Case Study 1 is the area of the Oude Maas.

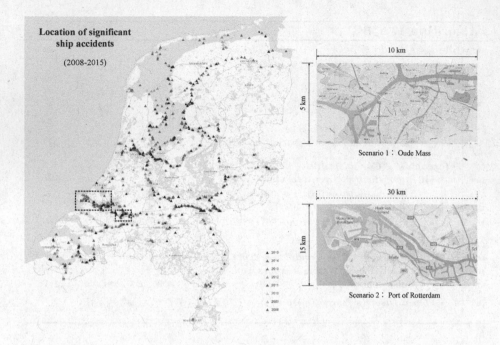

Fig. 5. Location of ship accidents [16] and case study areas (maps taken from [9]).

Table 2. Experimental results.

Neighbor-hood	A*		A*PS		Theta*		A*BG	
	Computation time (s)	Path length (unit)	Computation time (s)	Path length (unit)	Computation time (s)	Path length (unit)	Computation time (s)	Path length (unit)
Case Study 1								
1	45.86	514.99	45.93	497.98	46.09	495.63	93.23	494.39
2	112.48	501.63	112.54	497.04	121.57	494.95		
3	210.09	497.32	210.13	495.29	226.37	494.85		
4	333.05	496.06	333.09	494.94	364.32	494.58		
5	485.30	495.45	485.33	494.68	532.33	494.57		
6	660.84	495.07	660.86	494.56	722.57	494.49		
7	862.00	494.84	862.02	494.49	975.32	494.47		
8	1083.59	494.70	1083.61	494.48	1198.15	494.42		
9	1333.76	494.61	1333.79	494.45	1473.00	494.42		
10	1611.61	494.56	1611.63	494.44	1791.48	494.41		
Case Study 2								
1	87.67	540.78	87.77	514.14	94.50	514.24	502.15	510.32
2	241.38	517.98	241.45	512.23	262.70	511.52		
3	468.63	512.68	468.67	511.57	510.03	511.12		
4	771.08	511.49	771.12	511.22	833.87	510.97		
5	1143.20	511.22	1143.25	511.07	1236.45	510.58		
6	1591.53	510.85	1591.57	510.68	1713.21	510.58		
7	2118.28	510.76	2118.32	510.67	2262.04	510.49		
8	2721.35	510.73	2721.39	510.66	2903.01	510.34		
9	3390.31	510.71	3390.35	510.66	3615.47	510.33		
10	4143.80	510.71	4143.84	510.66	4380.30	510.33		

It is an intersection near the Port of Rotterdam, where is the convergent place of river Noord, Benede-Merwede, Dordsche Kil and Oude Maas. Case Study 2 is Port of Rotterdam. It is the largest port in Europe and the place accidents most frequently occurred.

5.2   Setup

All algorithms tested in our experiments are grid-based. Thus, the maps of our case study areas are transfered into 500×250 grids. The length of 1 grid is 1 unit. The buffer area in Case study 1 is two grids near the obstacles and in Case study 2 is 1 grid. Vessels can sail in the buffer area, but with a penalty length. We use middle lines to take the regulations into consideration. To study the influence of the size of neighborhood, the algorithms are carried out with increasing neighborhood (from $neighborhood = 1$ to $neighborhood = 10$).

The algorithms tested in our experiments maintain three values for every node: $g(s_{start}, s)$ is the length of the path from s_{start} to s; $h(s, s_{goal})$ is the

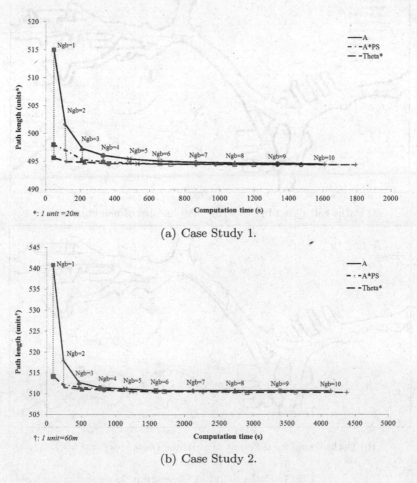

(a) Case Study 1.

(b) Case Study 2.

Fig. 6. Experiment results (Ngb: Neighborhood of the algorithms).

straight-line distance of s and s_goal; $f(s_\text{start}, s, s_\text{goal}$ is the sum of $g(s_\text{start}, s)$ and $h(s, s_\text{goal})$. We use the Euclidean distance in the experiments. The distance between two nodes $N(x, y)$ and $N'(x', y')$ is $\sqrt{(x - x')^2 + (y - y')^2}$. That is, the distance from one grid to an adjacent left\right\up\down node is 1 unit, and to an adjacent diagonal node is $\sqrt{2}$ units.

The experiments are run on a PC with a dual-core 3.2GHz Intel(R) Core(TM) i5-3470U CPU and 8GB of RAM. Each case has been repeated for 5 times.

5.3 Experiment Results

The results of the simulation experiments are shown in Table 2 and Fig. 6. The path length and average computation time over 5 repetitions are provided.

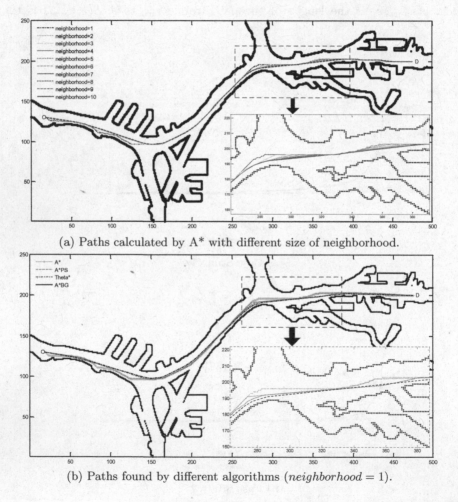

(a) Paths calculated by A* with different size of neighborhood.

(b) Paths found by different algorithms ($neighborhood = 1$).

Fig. 7. Paths found in Case study 1.

As shown in Table 2, two case studies show similar relations between the path length, computation time and the size of neighborhood. For A*, A*PS and Theta*, with the increase of neighborhood, the length of the paths becomes shorter, but the computation time increase dramatically as well. When the neighborhood is small, the length of the paths that the three algorithms found differs greatly. The difference decreases when the neighborhood is enlarged (Fig. 6). The path length of the three algorithms then approaches to a certain value.

With respect to A*BG, the size of neighborhood does not influence the results of A*BG. In the two case studies, A*BG shows the best performance. The path it computed is shorter than the shortest path the other three algorithms find, and the computation time is much shorter. Similar to other three algorithms, when the planning area becomes larger, the computation time of A*BG increases.

Figure 7 shows the path found in Case study 1. The paths calculated by A* with different size of neighborhood are shown in Fig. 7(a) as an example to show the impacts of the neighborhood size. Because the length of paths that the tested algorithms find differs greatly when $neighborhood = 1$, this situation is chosen as an example to present the difference of the paths found by different algorithms in Fig. 7(b). The main difference among the paths lies in the bend segments. The algorithms which find the shorter paths, A* when $neighborhood = 10$ and A*BG, find smoother paths at the bend segments.

6 Conclusions and Future Research

Autonomy is seen as a possibility for maritime transport to meet today's and tomorrow's challenges. In realizing autonomous navigation, path planning plays an important role. As a starting point of path planning for inland autonomous vessels, a modified A* algorithm (A*GB) is proposed to solve the global path planning problem. In this paper, we carry out experiments to compare the performance of A*, A*PS, Theta* and A*GB. Two places where ship accidents frequently occurred in the past are chosen as case study areas. The path length and computation time of each algorithms is analyzed. Trading off the path length and computation time, the performance of A*GB is more satisfying for inland autonomous vessels'path planning.

There are several directions in which this research will be extended. Firstly, when the planning area is larger, the computation time increases and the fineness of the grids also decreases, which affect the performance of the algorithm. The principle of Model Predictive Control can then be used to solve this problem. Long voyages are divided into smaller segments, after which a vessel updates its path at subsequence decision steps. Secondly, in this paper, the impact of infrastructures is not included. As important components in inland waterway system, infrastructures such as locks and bridges have great impact on inland shipping. Most delays are caused by operation of locks and bridges. Global path planning should also consider these influences. Finally, real-time information should also be taken into account. If preplanned paths are blocked due to accidents, or if there is a long waiting time at a certain lock, it is important that the vessel can replan its path according to real-time information.

Moreover, the global path planner considered here only provides reference paths considering static obstacles for an autonomous vessel. Algorithms for local path planning, i.e., collision avoidance, are needed to deal with the moving obstacles. These moving obstacles not only include other autonomous vessels, but also vessels operated by humans. With different obstacles, the information available is different. Besides, the actions controllers take and the resulting trajectories of the vessels operated by humans are uncertain. How the autonomous vessel communicates and coordinates with others using different sources of information and deals with uncertainties are future research problems.

Acknowledgment. This research is supported by the China Scholarship Council under Grant 201426950041.

References

1. de Berg, M., Cheong, O., van Kreveld, M., Overmars, M.: Computational Geometry: Algorithms and Applications, pp. 323–333. Springer, New York (2008)
2. Campbell, S., Naeem, W., Irwin, G.: A review on improving the autonomy of unmanned surface vehicles through intelligent collision avoidance manoeuvres. Ann. Rev. Control **36**(2), 267–283 (2012)
3. Daniel, K., Nash, A., Koenig, S., Felner, A.: Theta*: any-angle path planning on grids. J. Artif. Intell. Res. **39**(2010), 533–579 (2010)
4. Duchoň, F., Babinec, A., Kajan, M., Beňo, P., Florek, M., Fico, T., Jurišica, L.: Path planning with modified a star algorithm for a mobile robot. Procedia Eng. **96**, 59–69 (2014)
5. Economic commission for Europe: inventory of most important bottlenecks and missing links in the E waterway network. Technical report. ECE/TRANS/SC.3/159/Rev.1, Economic Commission for Europe, Inland Transport Committee, United Nations (2013)
6. European Commission: Naiades II: Towards quality inland waterway transport. Technical report COM 623, European Commission (2013)
7. European Commission: The European Union explained: Transport. Technical report European Commission (2014)
8. Froese, J.: Safe and efficient port approach by vessel traffic management in waterways. In: Ocampo-Martinez, C., Negenborn, R.R. (eds.) Transport of Water versus Transport over Water. Operations Research/Computer Science Interfaces Series, vol. 58, pp. 281–296. Springer, New York (2015)
9. Google Maps: Port of Rotterdam, Street map (2016). https://www.google.nl/maps/@51.8820487,4.4343202,10.75z
10. Hekkenberg, R.: Technological challenges and developments in European inland waterway transport. In: Ocampo-Martinez, C., Negenborn, R.R. (eds.) Transport of Water versus Transport over Water. Operations Research/Computer Science Interfaces Series, vol. 58, pp. 297–313. Springer, New York (2015)
11. Kuwata, Y., Wolf, M., Zarzhitsky, D., Huntsberger, T.: Safe maritime autonomous navigation with COLREGS using velocity obstacles. IEEE J. Oceanic Eng. **39**(1), 110–119 (2014)
12. Lazarowska, A.: Ship's trajectory planning for collision avoidance at sea based on ant colony optimisation. J. Navig. **68**(2), 291–307 (2015)

13. Li, S., Negenborn, R.R., Lodewijks, G.: Distributed constraint optimization for addressing vessel rotation planning problems. Eng. Appl. Artif. Intell. **48**(2016), 159–172 (2016)
14. Movares Projectteam MNV'13: Monitoring nautische veiligheid 2013. Technical report, Rijkswaterstaat Water, Verkeer en Leefomgeving, Afdeling Veiligheidsmanagement en Verkeersveiligheid (2013)
15. Rijkswaterstaat: Binnenvaartpolitiereglement (1983). http://wetten.overheid.nl/BWBR0003628/2016-01-01#DeelI_Hoofdstuk6_AfdelingI_Artikel6.01
16. Rijkswaterstaat: Scheepsongevallen significant (2016). https://geoweb.rijkswaterstaat.nl/westnederlandnoord/GeoWeb41/?Viewer=WNN_Scheepsongevallen
17. Rijkswaterstaat: Scheepsongevallendatabase (2016). https://www.rijkswaterstaat.nl/zakelijk/verkeersmanagement/scheepvaart/scheepsongevallenregistratie/index.aspx
18. Sariff, N., Buniyamin, N.: An overview of autonomous mobile robot path planning algorithms. In: Proceedings of the 4th Student Conference on Research and Development, pp. 183–188. Selangor, Malaysia (2006)
19. Shah, B.C., Švec, P., Bertaska, I.R., Sinisterra, A.J., Klinger, W., Ellenrieder, K., Dhanak, M., Gupta, S.K.: Resolution-adaptive risk-aware trajectory planning for surface vehicles operating in congested civilian traffic. Autonomous Robots, first Online (2015)
20. Siegwart, R., Nourbakhsh, I.R., Scaramuzza, D.: Introduction to Autonomous Mobile Robots, 2nd edn. MIT Press, Cambridge (2011)
21. Statheros, T., Howells, G., Maier, K.M.: Autonomous ship collision avoidance navigation concepts, technologies and techniques. J. Navig. **61**(1), 129–142 (2008)
22. Uras, T., Koenig, S.: An empirical comparison of any-angle path-planning algorithms. In: Proceedings of the 8th Annual Symposium on Combinatorial Search, pp. 206–210. Ein Gedi, Israel (2015)
23. Vaneck, T.W.: Fuzzy guidance controller for an autonomous boat. IEEE Control Syst. Mag. **17**(2), 43–51 (1997)
24. Vantorre, M., Delefortrie, G., Eloot, K., Laforce, E.: Experimental investigation of ship-bank interaction forces. In: Proceedings of International Conference on Marine Simulation and Ship Maneuverability, pp. 1–9. Kanazawa, Japan (2003)
25. Verstichel, J., Causmaecker, P.D., Spieksma, F., Berghe, G.V.: The generalized lock scheduling problem: an exact approach. Trans. Res. Part E: Logistics Transp. Rev. **65**, 16–34 (2014)
26. Xin, J., Negenborn, R.R., Corman, F., Lodewijks, G.: Control of interacting machines in automated container terminals using a sequential planning approach for collision avoidance. Transp. Res. Part C: Emerg. Technol. **60**(2015), 377–396 (2015)
27. Zheng, H., Negenborn, R.R., Lodewijks, G.: Predictive path following with arrival time awareness for waterborne AGVs. Transportation Research Part C: Emerging Technologies (2015). http://dx.doi.org/10.1016/j.trc.2015.11.004

Agent-Based Support for Container Terminals to Make Appointments with Barges

Martijn Mes[✉] and Albert Douma

Department of Industrial Engineering and Business Information Systems,
University of Twente, P.O. Box 217, 7500 AE Enschede, The Netherlands
m.r.k.mes@utwente.nl

Abstract. We consider a container terminal that has to make appointments with barges dynamically with only limited knowledge about future arriving barges, and in the view of uncertainty and disturbances. We study this problem using a case study at the Port of Rotterdam, considering a proposed multi-agent system for aligning barge rotations and terminal quay schedules. We take the perspective of a single terminal participating in this system and focus on the decision making capabilities of its intelligent agent. Using simulation, with input settings based on characteristics of the larger terminals within the Port of Rotterdam, we analyze the benefits of our approach. We conclude that a terminal can increase its utilization significantly by using various sources of flexibility in the operational planning.

Keywords: Terminal planning · Quay scheduling · Dynamic assignment · Multi-agent system · Simulation

1 Introduction

The Port of Rotterdam, located in the Netherlands, is the largest port in Europe and the world's tenth-largest container port in terms of twenty-foot equivalent units (TEU) handled. Over the past years there has been a tremendous growth in container transportation, going from less then 0.4 TEU in 1970 to over 12 million TEU in 2015. During these years, the quality and accessibility of hinterland transportation has become increasingly important. The number of transported containers to the hinterland has grown tremendously, and nowadays the hinterland services form a large share in the total transportation bill [11]. To reduce the pressure on the current road infrastructure as well as to reduce greenhouse gas emissions, the port aims for a modal shift from road to barge or train. Here we focus on barge hinterland container transportation. Specifically, we take the perspective of a terminal operator on how it can improve its operational performance when making appointments with barges dynamically and in real-time.

A major problem in the port is the poor alignment of barge and terminal operations. This poor alignment results in uncertain dwell times of barges and a significant loss of capacity for terminal operators. Typically, barges have to visit about eight terminals when visiting the port. The sequence in which the terminals are visited, determines to a large extent the time a barge needs to complete all its loading and unloading activities. An additional problem is that a delay at one terminal propagates quickly to the other terminals. The alignment of barge and terminal operations, the so-called barge handling problem, is considered to be the most urgent problem in hinterland barge container transportation by the Port of Rotterdam. Solving this problem improves the hinterland connectivity and thereby the attractiveness of the port significantly, and stimulates a modal shift towards barge transportation.

To provide a solution for the barge handling problem, an agent-based decision support system has been proposed [5,6]. The reason to use a multi-agent (or distributed planning) system is that players are reluctant to share information with their competitors and prefer to have control over their own operations. In earlier research, the focus was on decision support for barge operators. However, the new way of working will have a major impact on the way terminal operators make appointments with barge operators. Opposed to the old situation, where appointments were made manually and the terminal planning was made off-line, the new situation requires real-time (partly) automated decision making.

The objective of this paper is to come up with operational planning rules for terminals to efficiently utilize their capacity given the changed setting in which they have to operate, i.e., a setting in which they have to make reliable appointments with barges taking into account future events and disturbances, e.g., delayed arrivals of container vessels. To support the operational planning rules, we present various sources of flexibility and provide numerical results on the impact of using them on quay utilization and barge waiting times.

The remainder of this paper is structured as follows. In Sect. 2, we give a brief overview of the relevant literature. In Sect. 3, we present our model, the decisions involved, and our solution approach. We present our simulation model, with corresponding numerical results, in Sects. 4 and 5. We close with conclusions in Sect. 6.

2 Literature Review

During the last decade, a substantial amount of research has been conducted to increase the efficiency of container terminal operations. Different subjects within this area include the berth allocation problem, quay and yard cranes assignment and scheduling, and yard storage management and container stacking. Extensive literature reviews on these subjects can be found in [1,24,28].

A closely related problem is the berth allocation problem (BAP), which concerns the assignment of berths to ships such that berth utilization is maximized or the waiting time for ships are minimized. Extensive literature reviews on this subject can be found in [2,23,24,26]. The literature on the BAP makes assumptions which do not hold for the barge handling problem. First, the arrival times of vessels are generally assumed to be known [1,19,26]. This assumption is made for the so-called static BAP, where ships are waiting at the start of the planning horizon, but also for the dynamic BAP where ships arrive during the planning horizon [2, 10], as also considered in this paper. The planning of quay cranes is called the quay crane assignment problem (QCAP) and the quay crane scheduling problem (QCSP). A recent trend in the BAP literature is to combine these three problems, see, e.g., [1, 9, 14, 20, 21] for an overview.

Although our focus is on a terminal as a single decision maker, research on multi-agent systems is relevant since we aim at an implementation environment where the single terminal participates in such a system. In the area of road transportation, many examples of agent-based approaches can be found [16]. However, applications of agents in transportation via water are scarce and most papers have focused on the alignment of activities at a single terminal [3]. Examples include the optimal placement of containers in the yard [7], strategies for the cranes to minimize the trucks' wait time [27], simulation of ships and their allocation [25], and simulation of various strategies regarding the movement of containers from the ship into the yard [8]. A multi-agent cooperative planning system between multiple intermodal transport operators is considered in [13].

Agent-based or distributed planning approaches for inland barge traffic in the port of Rotterdam have been suggested by various authors. Initially, the focus was on creating an off-line planning system, where barge rotations were planned one day in advance [22]. From this work it became clear that a decentralized control structure offers an acceptable solution for the parties involved [18]. Next, the focus was on real-time agent-based planning [6]. Based on these agent-based systems, two multi-player games have been developed [5, 17] that contributed to the acceptance among barge operators of the proposed multi-agent system.

In this paper, we contribute to the existing literature by studying how to schedule ships (barges and container vessels) such that a high quay utilization is realized. We take the perspective of a single terminal that operates within a port-wide multi-agent system for the barge handling problem as described in [6]. A consequence of using this system is that the terminal agent has to respond to barge handling requests dynamically, in real-time, and partly automatic.

3   Model Description

First, we describe the environment within which the terminal operates (Sect. 3.1). Next, we present our modeling assumptions and notation (Sect. 3.2), our objective (Sect. 3.3), and the decisions we have to make (Sect. 3.4).

3.1   Multi-agent Environment

We illustrate our approach using the multi-agent system from [6]. In the remainder of this section, we briefly explain this system to understand the decisions a terminal has to make in this specific case.

Starting point of the distributed planning approach is improving the reliability of appointments. The basic idea of the proposed system is that terminal and barge operators get a software agent that act on their behalf. This planning approach is preferred by the operators, because it enables them to stay in control of their own operations and share only limited information. The crucial information shared by the terminal agents are the so-called service-time profiles. A service-time profile (STP) is issued on request of a barge operator and denotes a guaranteed maximum service time given a certain arrival time at the terminal, where service time is defined as the sum of the waiting and handling time at this terminal. Hence, an STP is barge and time specific. Barge operators can use the STPs to optimize their rotation (sequence of terminals visits). Terminal operators in turn can use the STPs to indicate preferred handling times thereby optimizing their capacity utilization.

Barges arrive in the port over time. On arrival in the port, the barge operator requests STPs at all terminals he has to visit. A terminal has to reply instantaneously and has to do so with only limited knowledge about future arriving barges. After receiving all STPs, the barge operator determines its best rotation and announces its preferred arrival time at the terminal. The terminal operator makes an appointment by confirming the barge's latest arrival time and a guaranteed maximum service time. By making the appointment, the barge commits to a latest arrival time and the terminal commits to a latest departure time (namely the latest arrival time plus the guaranteed maximum service time). When barges arrive after their latest arrival time, the appointment will be canceled, regardless of the reason for the delay. During the whole process from planning to execution, the terminal has to deal with uncertainty and disturbances, such as uncertain arrival times and handling times of barges and container vessels, as well as cancellations and no-shows.

3.2   Assumptions and Notation

As stated earlier, we take the perspective of a single terminal. We assume that the activities at other terminals are reflected in the arrival process of barges at the terminal of interest. This assumption is not unrealistic, since terminals do not share their operational information with each other for competitive reasons. As point of reference, we consider the large terminals within the Port of Rotterdam. These terminals are characterized by high volumes, large numbers of quay resources, and high utilization rates. Our focus is on the operational planning level of the terminal. This means that decisions made at the tactical level (such as the amount of capacity deployed) are considered fixed.

The planning process starts with a barge $n \in \mathcal{N}$ requesting an appointment at the terminal. We assume that this barge has a preferred (or earliest) arrival time e_n. When the barge cannot be scheduled within a given planning period, it will be rejected ($r_n = 1$). Obviously, rejection is often not possible in practice and the terminal has to assign additional capacity to handle these requests. However, using the number of rejected requests, we can gain insight in the amount of additional capacity that needs to be assigned. If the barge is not rejected, ($r_n = 0$), we provide the barge an STP. This STP gives for each possible latest arrival time l_n a service-time $s_n = d_n - l_n$, with d_n being the latest departure time.

The latest departure time d_n is guaranteed by the terminal when the barge arrives on time $(a_n \leq l_n)$, with a_n being the actual arrival time. When the barge arrives too late $(a_n > l_n)$, the appointment will be canceled $(r_n = 1)$. We further introduce a handling time h_n for the time required to load/unload the containers from barge n, and a planned starting time b_n, with $l_n \leq b_n \leq d_n - h_n$. The actual starting time might take place before l_n in case of an early arrival. We illustrate the notation using the example schedule of Fig. 1. Here, the first ship arrives earlier than its latest arrival time $(a_1 < l_1)$ and handling of the ship is started earlier than its latest arrival time $(b_1 < l_1)$. The other ships have a planned starting time b_n equal to their latest arrival time l_n. For ship 3, we have the possibility to postpone the starting time b_3 by two time units because the service time s_3 is two time units longer than the handling time $h_3 = 3$.

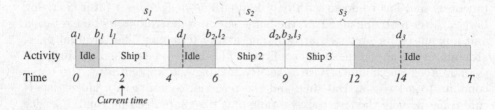

Fig. 1. Illustration of a schedule

3.3 Objective

The objective of the terminal operators we interviewed in the Port of Rotterdam is to maximize the utilization of their quay resources. More specifically, to maximize the utilization of crew, crane(s), and berthing position(s), and in this sequence. We make two comments regarding the utilization rate as terminal objective. First, maximizing the utilization of quay resources cannot be done without keeping an eye on the waiting time of barges. Given the variability in barge arrivals, a utilization rate of 100 % will definitely lead to infinite waiting times for the barges. Second, if the capacity of the terminal is fixed during a certain time period by decisions made at the tactical level, as we assume in this paper, then the utilization rate of a terminal only depends on the barges we accept to handle within this period. Therefore, the main objective is to make appointments, in such a way that the utilization rate of the terminal within a given time period is maximized. Since we assume the capacity to be fixed, this results in the maximization of the sum of the handling times of all accepted barges within the given time period, i.e., $\max(\sum_{\forall n \in \mathcal{N}} (1 - r_n)h_n)$, subject to having an average waiting time for the accepted barges below a reasonable bound.

3.4 Decisions

The main decision of the terminal is to set the service-times $s_n = d_n - l_n$, for all possible latest arrival times l_n, as part of the STP. To create the STP in real-time, we assume that the terminal starts with a list of intervals in which barges can be handled. These intervals depend on, e.g., opening times, scheduled ships, and resource capacities, and do not depend on a specific barge. Without loss of generality, we assume that the intervals are given by the maximum length of the idle periods between planned ships as shown in Fig. 1. Since the terminal has some flexibility in choosing the planned starting times (see Sect. 3.5), the interval between ship n and ship $n + 1$ is given by planning the starting times of ships before ship $n + 1$ as early as possible and for ships after ship n as late as possible, resulting in an interval $[b_n + h_n, b_{n+1}]$. These intervals are determined for each possible insertion position. Upon a barge request, the terminal (i) makes a selection of intervals to offer to the barge operator and (ii) constructs the STP using these intervals, see [6]. These two decisions are based on the amount of buffer and slack to be used respectively (see Sect. 3.5). After an appointment has been made, the terminal has to schedule the starting times b_n and has the option to re-schedule barges (see Sect. 4).

3.5   Sources of Flexibility

We approach the problem from a practical point of view by considering various sources of flexibility. We define a source of flexibility as a factor that offers planning flexibility in the terminal schedule. From multiple interviews with barge and terminal operators within the Port of Rotterdam, we conclude that sources of flexibility are used frequently to deal with real-time decision making under uncertainty. With this approach, we aim to provide insight into the benefits of deploying these sources of flexibility to improve terminal performance.

There are several factors in the planning and execution of barges that potentially improve the planning flexibility of the terminal. We mention the following instruments terminals might use:

- *Buffer.* The terminal might only consider intervals that are at least a buffer w_n longer then the required handling time h_n, i.e., intervals shorter then $h_n + w_n$ are not offered to the barge.
- *Slack.* The terminal can add slack v_n to an appointment with a barge, such that the latest departure time becomes $d_n = l_n + h_n + v_n$. This way, the terminal has flexibility in choosing the planned starting time b_n and postpone it up to $l_n + v_n$.
- *Re-scheduling.* The terminal may reschedule barge appointments thereby improving its quay schedules.
- *Cancellation.* The terminal can cancel appointments, e.g., when a schedule becomes infeasible.

Even though the terminal as no (or little) influence on it, the characteristics of barges might also provide a potential source of flexibility. We mention the following:

- *Early arrival.* A barge arrives earlier than its latest arrival time $(a_n < l_n)$.
- *Cancellation.* A barge cancels an appointment at the terminal, meaning that the terminal can use the time that comes free for other purposes.
- *Deviation in handling time.* The handling time distribution of a barge may impact the flexibility of the terminal to fill an interval.

Note that not all of these sources of flexibility are desired by the terminal. For instance, a cancellation by a barge is usually a disturbance in the schedule, although it can sometimes be welcomed when the terminal deals with delays. Here we assume that cancellations just take place and therefore consider it as a potential source of flexibility.

4   Simulation Model

To investigate the impact of the different sources of flexibility, we use discrete event simulation. To provide realistic insights, we use the large terminals within the Port of Rotterdam as point of reference. The simulation settings are based on these terminals and on interviews with barge operators as reported in [4]. An overview of our simulation model is given in Fig. 2.

We determine the arrival rate of barges and container vessels using a desired utilization rate (instead of the other way around). The desired quay utilization rate in the simulation is set to 85 %, with a share of 45 % for barges and 40 % for container vessels. These numbers are based on 2006 figures from two large terminals within the Port of Rotterdam, see [4]. The 85 % is also close to the average utilisation of 86.6 % for North European deep seaports [15] and in line with the Drewry Maritime Research forecasts for average container terminal utilization world wide. We choose to control the utilization rate and derive from that the mean interarrival time for both barges and container vessels:

$$\text{mean interarr. time} = \frac{\text{mean handling time} \cdot (1 - \text{cancellation rate})}{\text{terminal capacity} \cdot \text{desired utilization rate}}, \quad (1)$$

where the terminal capacity is given by the amount of time this terminal is open multiplied with the number of quays.

Barges arrive with exponentially distributed interarrival times upon which a preferred arrival time is determined and announced to the terminal. The preferred arrival time is drawn uniformly between the current time and 48 h later. This way, we mimic a realistic arrival process, i.e., a barge that arrives later may be processed earlier than another barge that arrived earlier. The number of containers to load/unload, announced by a barge, is distributed according to a Weibull distribution (parameters shown in Table 1). The handling time per container is assumed to be 3 min. We assume that the exact number of containers to load/unload is known at the start of handling a barge.

Container vessels arrive according to a Poisson process. They announce their arrival time and total number of containers to load and unload three weeks prior to their initial planned arrival time. The handling of a container vessel has

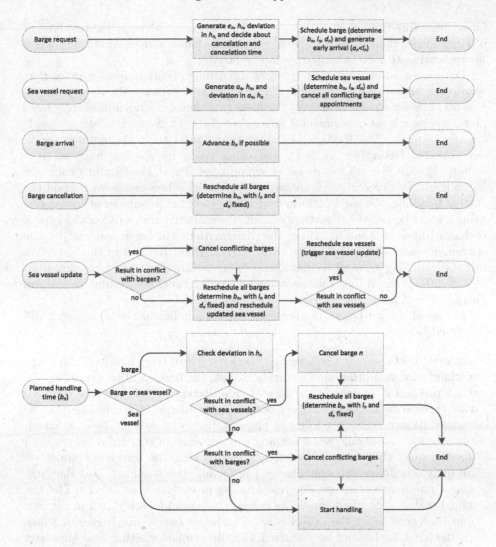

Fig. 2. Overview of the simulation model

priority over the handling of barges. The handing time, in minutes, is drawn from the Beta distribution with $\alpha = 1.14$, $\beta = 8.3$, multiplied by 6400.

Without loss of generality, we assume the terminal is open 24 h per day and has 4 quays. A quay is a combination of resources that are all necessary to handle a ship; both sea vessels and barges are handled at one quay. The schedule of the terminal will consist of several gaps (intervals), since it is not likely that barges are scheduled directly after one another. When the terminal receives an announcement of the barge preferred arrival time e_n at the terminal, it schedules the latest arrival time l_n of this barge at the first possible starting time after e_n. Initially, the terminal schedules each barge with starting time $b_n = l_n$ and latest departure time $d_n = a_n + h_n + v_n$. The terminal can start the handling of a barge earlier than its latest arrival time if the barge arrives earlier and when no appointments with other barges are violated.

During the simulation, four types of disturbing events may take place that require an action of the terminal. First, a barge arrives earlier than planned, this becomes known upon arrival. Earliness in minutes is drawn uniformly from $[0, x]$, where x is an experimental factor (see Table 1). Second, a barge cancels its appointment. The fraction of barges that cancel their appointment is an experimental factor (see Table 1), and cancellation by a barge happens at a uniform time $[0, 5]$ h prior to its latest arrival time. Third, the handling time of a barge might be different than announced before, this becomes known upon the start of handling. We use a uniform deviation $[-4, 5]$ in the number of containers, using a lower bound of 1. Fourth, a container vessel arrives at a different moment or has a different handling time, this information will be announced by the container vessel 48 h prior to its latest arrival time. Regarding the deviation in total handling time of a container vessel, we assume a uniform deviation $[-20\%, 20\%]$. Regarding the deviation in arrival time, we assume a uniform delay $[-8, 8]$ h, using the current time as lower bound.

In case of a disturbance, the terminal applies a policy as shown in Fig. 2 and described below.

- *On arrival of a barge.* The terminal checks if it can start handling the barge without violating other appointments. If not, the barge will be cancelled.
- *On cancellation of a barge.* In case of cancellation by a barge, the terminal can perform two actions, namely not to reschedule or to reschedule. Not to reschedule means that the terminal plans all barges in one specific quay schedule as early as possible while keeping the sequence of scheduled barges on a specific quay the same. To reschedule means that the terminal reconsiders all quay schedules, and may change the timing, the sequence, and the quay where barges are planned. The rescheduling procedure is as follows. The terminal makes a list of all candidate barges that could be scheduled in the new gap that arose after the cancellation. Candidate barges are barges of which (i) the handling has not been started, (ii) the planned starting time is greater than the start of the new gap, and (iii) that fit into the new gap. The barge with the lowest latest arrival time of all candidate barges is scheduled in the new gap. If this barge does not fill the gap completely, then the terminal looks for the next candidate barge until either the gap is filled or the list of candidate barges is empty. The same procedure is then applied for all gaps that arise after moving the barges to the new gap until all gaps are filled or no candidate barges for rescheduling are available anymore.
- *On handling a barge.* Upon the start of handling a barge, it might appear that the handling time will be longer then planned. As a result, other appointments might become infeasible. The terminal will not cancel the barge currently in process. Instead, the terminal will check for each barge and container vessel planned after this barge whether the appointment is going to be violated. If an appointment with a barge is violated, then this appointment is cancelled.

Table 1. Experimental factors with their corresponding low and high values

No.	Factor	Low	High	Comment
1	Early arrival	120	0	The barge arrives in the low scenario a uniformly distributed time between 0 and 120 min earlier, and in the high scenario at its latest arrival time
2	Handling time	−	+	Weibull distribution for the number of containers to load and unload, with parameters $\lambda = 2.1$ and $\kappa = 33.9$ for the low value and with parameters $\lambda = 1$ and $\kappa = 30$ for the high value (corresponding with a mean of 30 min and standard deviation of 15 and 30 min)
3	Cancellations	0	0.2	Fraction of barges that cancel an appointment
4	Re-scheduling	No	Yes	Re-schedule on cancellation of a barge, see the policy for 'on cancellation of a barge'
5	Slack	0	40	Minutes slack to add to appointments
6	Buffer	0	30	Minutes buffer to use between appointments

If an appointment with a container vessel is violated due to a scheduled barge, then the barge appointment is cancelled.
- *On receiving an update from a container vessel.* When a container vessel announces its real arrival time and the required handling time, then the terminal updates the quay schedules. In case the container vessel appointment conflicts with scheduled barges, then the barge appointments are cancelled. If the appointment conflicts with an earlier scheduled container vessel, then the arrival time of the container vessel is updated with the completion time of the earlier scheduled container vessel. If the appointment conflicts with later scheduled container vessels, then the appointments with later scheduled container vessels are postponed.

To analyze the effects of the different sources of flexibility, without considering the computationally intractable full-factorial design, we split our analysis in two parts. In the first part, we use a $2k$ factorial design [12], where we choose two levels (high and low) for each of the six factors (sources of flexibility), which means that we have $2^6 = 64$ possible factor-level combinations. Table 1 denotes the six sources of flexibility that are considered, with their respective high and low values. The values 120 min early arrival, 40 min slack, and 30 min buffer correspond with roughly the 95th, 87th, and 86th percentiles of the distribution in handling time deviations of all ships, respectively. In the second part of our analysis, we perform a full factorial experiment using the most promising factors found in the first part.

We validated our model by comparing it with [4] under similar conditions without using the various sources of flexibility. To provide accurate results, we replicate each experiment five times, where each replication has a warm-up period of 10 days and a run length of 365 days.

5 Numerical Results

In this section, we present the results from the simulation experiments described in the previous section.

Factorial Analysis. The results (averaged over all replications) of each scenario considered with respect to both, the utilization rate and the average barge waiting time, are shown in Fig. 3. The design points follow the logic from [12]; using '−' and '+' to denote the low and high level respectively, the first five design points are given by: $(-,-,-,-,-,-)$, $(+,-,-,-,-,-)$, $(-,+,-,-,-,-)$, $(+,+,-,-,-,-)$, and $(-,-,+,-,-,-)$.

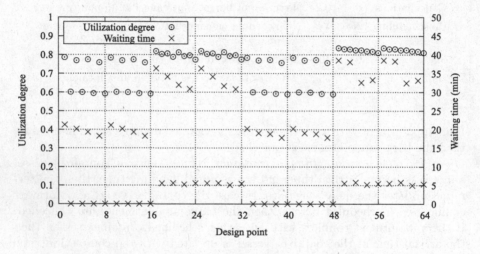

Fig. 3. Results for the 2k factorial design

We draw the following conclusions. First, scenarios with slack (scenarios 17–32 and 49–64) result in the highest average quay utilization rate. Clearly, a relatively low amount of slack provides enough flexibility to deal with disturbances; a slightly lower value for the buffer and a much higher value for earliness have a much lower impact on the utilization rate. Second, in scenarios where barges arrive early (the uneven scenarios), we observe a higher utilization rate than the corresponding scenarios in which barges arrive at their latest arrival time. This is different when also slack is added to appointments (compare, e.g., scenarios 1–16 with 17–32). Third, if barges arrive early, they usually have more waiting time. When also slack is added to the appointments, then the waiting time increases even further (compare, e.g., scenarios 1–16 with 17–32). Fourth, a buffer seems to have effect only when also slack is used in the appointments (small differences between scenarios 49–64 and 17–32 with slack and almost no differences between scenarios 33–48 and 1–16 without slack). Finally, re-planning on cancellations seems to have no visible impact (compare, e.g., scenarios 1–8 with 9–16, or scenarios 49–56 with 57–64).

The above mentioned observations are confirmed by the main effects and the two-way interaction effects (results not shown). The two sources of flexibility with the largest positive impact on the terminal performance are early arrivals and slack. The buffer has a much lower impact, but may be interesting to have a closer look at. The factors 2 (handling time distribution), 3 (fraction of cancellations), and 4 (re-scheduling on cancellation), have hardly any impact on the utilization rate of the terminal or on the average barge waiting time. This explains why there are many scenarios with almost similar results.

Zooming in on Three Sources of Flexibility. In this section we focus on three sources of flexibility that have the highest impact on the terminal performance, namely slack, early arrivals, and the buffer. We evaluate these factors in all combinations using broader ranges then considered in the $2k$ factorial analysis: slack $\in \{0, 40, 80, 120\}$, early arrival $\in \{0, 30, 60, 120\}$, and buffer $\in \{0, 20, 40, 60\}$. For clarity of presentation, we fix one parameter at a time to its second lowest value while varying the other two (the remaining combinations exhibit similar patterns).

Figure 4 shows, for a given buffer of 20 min, the impact of early arrival and slack on the utilization rate and the waiting time of the barge respectively. We draw the following conclusions. First, early arrival of barges positively impacts the utilization rate of the terminal, but worsens the average waiting time of barges. Second, the extent to which early arrivals contribute to an improvement of the quay utilization rate depends on the amount of slack used. If slack is being used (≥ 40), then early arrivals only have a limited effect on the utilization. Third, if 40 min slack is used (in case no barge arrives early), then the quay utilization rate improves from about 60 % to more than 80 %, whereas the average waiting of barges increases with less than 10 min.

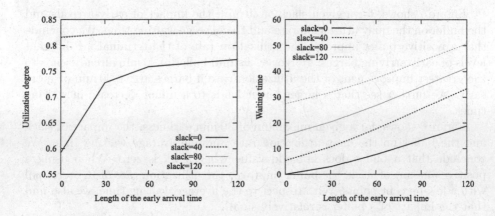

Fig. 4. Varying length of early arrival time for given buffer of 20 min

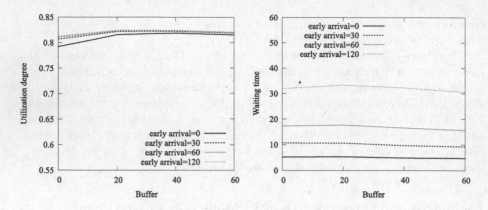

Fig. 5. Varying buffer for given slack of 40 min

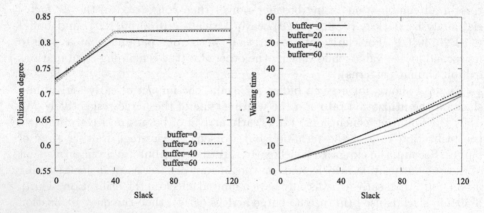

Fig. 6. Varying slack for given length of 30 min early arrival time

Figure 5 shows, for a given slack of 40 min, the impact of early arrivals and the buffer on the quay utilization rate and the average waiting time. We conclude that a positive buffer improves the utilization rate of the terminal for different levels of early arriving barges. Moreover, a small buffer of 20 min already leads to the greatest improvement of the utilization rate if barges arrive 30 min or more early. We further see that a larger buffer leads to a minor decrease in waiting times.

Figure 6 shows, for a given maximum of 30 min earliness, the impact of slack and the buffer on the quay utilization rate and the average waiting time. We conclude that a buffer does not add value when slack is zero. When using a positive amount of slack, the buffer improves the utilization rate of the terminal with a few percent points. With respect to the average waiting time, we also find that the impact of a buffer is relatively small.

Summarizing we conclude that, within the experimental setting considered, a quay utilization rate of 82 % can be realized with a minimum use of three sources of flexibility, namely slack (40 min), a buffer (20 min), and early arrivals (uniformly between 0 and 30 min). Without the use of these sources of flexibility, the quay utilization rate is as low as 60 %. Note that the maximum utilization rate that could be realized in our experimental setting is 85 %. The main takeaway from these results is that in environments with uncertainty and disturbances, dynamic appointment making can be supported by the relatively simple concepts of slack and buffers. We belief that these insights also apply to other settings, such as dynamic appointment scheduling in hospitals.

6   Conclusions

We focused on the operational planning of a terminal operator that has to plan dynamically and partly automatic. As a case of reference, we assumed that the terminal has to make appointments by means of an intelligent software agent that is part of the multi-agent system as described in [6]. The main challenge for the terminal agent is to make appointments with barges dynamically with only limited knowledge about future arriving barges. During the whole process from planning to execution, the terminal has to deal with uncertainty and disturbances, such as uncertain arrival and handling times of barges and container vessels, as well as cancellations and no-shows.

Using simulation, we explored the deployment of various sources of flexibility that are naturally available to the terminal. To give realistic insights, we used the large terminals within the Port of Rotterdam as point of reference for our experimental setup. From our numerical results, we found three major sources of flexibility, namely (i) early arrivals of barges, (ii) the use of slack in appointments, and (iii) the use of a buffer between appointments. For the instances considered, we found that a terminal, with a target utilization of 85 %, could significantly increase its performance using these sources of flexibility. Specifically, an increase in utilization rate from 60 % to 82 % can be realized with a minimum use of the two sources of flexibility (slack of 40 min and a buffer of 20 min). This major increase in utilization is achieved under a minor increase in barge waiting times (5 min).

References

1. Bierwirth, C., Meisel, F.: A survey of berth allocation and quay crane scheduling problems in container terminals. Eur. J. Oper. Res. **202**(3), 615–627 (2010)
2. Cordeau, J., Laporte, G., Legato, P., Moccia, L.: Models and tabu search heuristics for the berth-allocation problem. Transp. Sci. **39**(4), 526–538 (2005)
3. Davidsson, P., Henesey, L., Ramstedt, L., Törnquist, J., Wernstedt, F.: An analysis of agent-based approaches to transport logistics. Transp. Res. Part C **13**(4), 255–271 (2005)
4. Douma, A.M.: Aligning the operations of barges and terminals through distributed planning. Ph.D. thesis, University of Twente, Enschede, December 2008

5. Douma, A., van Hillegersberg, J., Schuur, P.: Design and evaluation of a simulation game to introduce a multi-agent system for barge handling in a seaport. Decis. Support Syst. **53**(3), 465–472 (2012)
6. Douma, A., Schuur, P., Schutten, J.: Aligning barge and terminal operations using service-time profiles. Flexible Serv. Manuf. J. **23**, 385–421 (2011)
7. Gambardella, L.M., Rizzoli, A.E., Zaffalon, M.: Simulation and planning of an intermodal container terminal. Simulation **71**(2), 107–116 (1998)
8. Henesey, L., Davidsson, P., Persson, J.A.: Evaluation of automated guided vehicle systems for container terminals using multi agent based simulation. In: David, N., Sichman, J.S. (eds.) MAPS 2008. LNCS, vol. 5269, pp. 85–96. Springer, Heidelberg (2009)
9. Imai, A., Chen, H., Nishimura, E., Papadimitriou, S.: The simultaneous berth and quay crane allocation problem. Transp. Res. Part E **44**(5), 900–920 (2008)
10. Imai, A., Nishimura, E., Papadimitriou, S.: The dynamic berth allocation problem for a container port. Transp. Res. Part B **35**(4), 401–417 (2001)
11. Konings, R.: Opportunities to improve container barge handling in the port of rotterdam from a transport network perspective. J. Transp. Geogr. **15**, 443–454 (2007)
12. Law, A.: Simulation Modeling and Analysis. McGraw-Hill Series in Industrial Engineering and Management Science. McGraw-Hill, Boston (2007)
13. Li, L., Negenborn, R.R., Schutter, B.D.: Multi-agent cooperative transport planning of intermodal freight transport. In: 2014 IEEE 17th International Conference on Intelligent Transportation Systems (ITSC), pp. 2465–2471 (2014)
14. Lokuge, P., Alahakoon, D.: Improving the adaptability in automated vessel scheduling in container ports using intelligent software agents. Eur. J. Oper. Res. **177**(3), 1985–2015 (2007)
15. Meersman, H., de Voorde, E.V., Vanelslander, T.: Port congestion and implications to maritime logistics. In: Song, D., Panayides, P. (eds.) Maritime Logistics: Contemporary Issues, Chap. 4, pp. 49–68. Bingley, Emerald (2012)
16. Mes, M., van der Heijden, M., Schuur, P.: Interaction between intelligent agent strategies for real-time transportation planning. CEJOR **21**(2), 337–358 (2013)
17. Mes, M., Iacob, M.-E., van Hillegersberg, J.: A distributed barge planning game. In: Meijer, S.A., Smeds, R. (eds.) ISAGA 2013. LNCS, vol. 8264, pp. 214–221. Springer, Heidelberg (2014)
18. Moonen, H., Van de Rakt, B., Miller, I., Van Nunen, J., Van Hillegersberg, J.: Agent technology supports inter-organizational planning in the port. In: de Koster, R., Delfmann, W. (eds.) Managing Supply Chains-Challenges and Opportunities, pp. 1–21. Copenhagen Business School Press, Copenhagen (2007)
19. de Oliveira, R.M., Mauri, G.R., Lorena, L.A.N.: Clustering search for the berth allocation problem. Expert Syst. Appl. **39**(5), 5499–5505 (2012)
20. Park, Y., Kim, K.: A scheduling method for berth and quay cranes. OR Spectr. **25**(1), 1–23 (2003)
21. Raa, B., Dullaert, W., Schaeren, R.V.: An enriched model for the integrated berth allocation and quay crane assignment problem. Expert Syst. Appl. **38**(11), 14136–14147 (2011)
22. Schut, M.C., Kentrop, M., Leenaarts, M., Melis, M., Miller, I.: Approach: decentralised rotation planning for container barges. In: de Mántaras, R.L., Saitta, L. (eds.) Proceedings of the 16th Eureopean Conference on Artificial Intelligence, ECAI 2004, pp. 755–759. IOS Press (2004)
23. Stahlbock, R., Voß, S.: Operations research at container terminals: a literature update. OR Spectr. **30**, 1–52 (2008)

24. Steenken, D., Voß, S., Stahlbock, R.: Container terminal operation and operations research-a classification and literature review. OR Spectr. **26**(1), 3–49 (2004)
25. Thurston, T., Hu, H.: Distributed agent architecture for port automation. In: Proceedings of the 26th International Computer Software and Applications Conference on Prolonging Software Life: Development and Redevelopment, COMPSAC 2002, pp. 81–90. IEEE Computer Society, Washington, D.C. (2002)
26. Ting, C.J., Wu, K.C., Chou, H.: Particle swarm optimization algorithm for the berth allocation problem. Expert Syst. Appl. **41**(4), 1543–1550 (2014)
27. Vidal, J.M., Huynh, N.: Building agent-based models of seaport container terminals. In: Proceedings of the 6th Workshop on Agents in Traffic and Transportation, Toronto, Canada (2010)
28. Vis, I., Koster, R.: Transshipment of containers at a container terminal: an overview. Eur. J. Oper. Res. **147**(1), 1–16 (2003)

A Logic-Based Benders Decomposition Approach to Improve Coordination of Inland Vessels for Inter-Terminal Transport

Shijie Li[✉], Rudy R. Negenborn, and Gabriel Lodewijks

Department of Maritime and Transport Technology, Delft University of Technology,
Mekelweg 2, 2628 CD Delft, The Netherlands
{s.li-2,R.R.Negenborn,G.Lodewijks}@tudelft.nl

Abstract. Large seaports usually contain multiple terminals serving container vessels, railways, trucks and other modes of hinterland transportation. Every time an inland vessel enters a seaport, it visits several terminals for loading and unloading containers. A vessel rotation is the sequence in which a vessel visits the different terminals in a large seaport. Currently, in a seaport like the port of Rotterdam, around 40 % of the inland vessels have to spend a longer time in the port area than originally planned, due to the low utilization of terminal quay resources and uncertainty of waiting times at different terminals. To better utilize the terminal resources in the ports, as well as to reduce the amount of time inland vessels spend in the port area, this paper first proposes a new model in which inland vessels coordinate with each other with respect to the arrival, departure time and the number of inter-terminal containers carried, besides their conventional hinterland containers, with the aim to prevent possible conflicts of their rotations. Then, a logic-based Benders' decomposition approach is proposed to minimize the total time the inland vessels spent in the port. We compare the performance of the proposed approach with the performance of a centralized approach on the aspects of the runtime, solution quality, and three logistical performance indicators. Simulation results show that the proposed approach generates both faster optimal and faster high-quality solutions than the centralized approach in both small and large problem instance.

1 Introduction

Nowadays, larger ports are being constructed to keep up with the growth of containerized shipping. Large ports usually consist of multiple terminals serving container vessels, railways, and other forms of hinterland transportation. Figure 1 shows the main terminals in the port of Rotterdam. As we can see, there are several clusters of terminals in a port. Containers are often transferred between terminals when they are transshipped between different modes of transportation. This type of movement is called inter-terminal transportation (ITT) [5,10,13,14]. There is a range of types of vehicles for ITT, including railway, truck, and container ships, each coming with its advantages and disadvantages. Comparing with

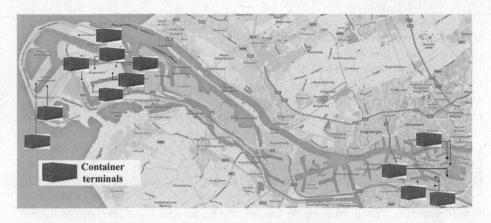

Fig. 1. Container terminals in Port of Rotterdam (adapted from [11])

land-based vehicles, container vessels have shorter connecting distances, as well as higher capacity for containers. In this paper we mainly focus on the container vessels for inter-terminal transport and investigate from a logistical perspective the possibility of using inland vessels for ITT.

On a typical day, around 25 inland vessels visit the port of Rotterdam, with each vessel visiting on average 8 different container terminals [9]. In earlier papers [3,4], a vessel rotation is defined as the sequence in which the vessel visits different terminals in a large seaport. In this paper, we consider other more advanced features in a vessel's rotation, including the arrival and departure time at different terminals, as well as the number of containers to load and unload at each terminal. As there may be some extra space on inland vessels for carrying containers when they travel between terminals, we investigate in this paper the possibility of using inland vessels also for ITT, which could provide a extra income for the inland vessel operators and also alleviate the congestion of land-based vehicles. Thus, we consider two types of containers: optional inter-terminal containers and the mandatory conventional hinterland containers that need to be loaded and unloaded at different terminals.

The goal of this paper is to improve the coordination among the inland vessels traveling between terminals in the port area, so that they can transport their mandatory hinterland containers, as well as inter-terminal containers that need to be transported from one terminal to another in an automatic and efficient way. This concerns finding the optimal rotations for the inland vessels so that they can finish the transport task in the port area with shorter time. We first propose a model in which the inland vessels coordinate with each other both the transport of inter-terminal containers besides their mandatory hinterland containers. Since the complexity of the problem increases substantially with the increase of the number of vessels and terminals considered, an exact approach would be unable to handle larger problem instances with more vessels and terminals. Therefore, we propose a logic-based Benders decomposition approach with the aim to minimize the total time of stay of inland vessels in the port area.

The planning of vessel rotations involves many equalities and logical conditions between inland vessels. For example, the waiting time that a vessel spends at a terminal not only depends on the departure times of the other vessels that are currently being handled at the same terminal, but also depends on the sequences how the other vessels visit the previous terminals on their rotations. This means that the calculation of the waiting time of a inland vessel at a terminal involves a sequence of variables representing how this vessel visit the previous terminals, as well as a sequence of variables how the other vessels visit the previous terminals on their rotations. As this type of relation is difficult to be represented using mathematical equations, we make use of the logical operators in constraint programming to formulate the coordination problem of inland vessels.

Benders decomposition has been originally proposed for solving large mixed-integer programming problems by [1]. The classical Benders decomposition solves a problem by partitioning it into a mixed-integer master problem and linear sub-problems. The solution process iterates between solving the master problem and the linear subproblems [6]. Benders decomposition can profitably combine mathematical programming and constraint programming, since one approach can be applied to solve the master problem and the other to solve the subproblem, depending which is the most suitable for the particular problem structure. This sort of combination has yielded substantial speedups in the computation [12].

Conventional Benders decomposition assumes that the master problem be mixed-integer and the subproblems be linear. In our case, however, we face a problem that involves logical relations between vessel operators and is most suitable for constraint programming techniques. Therefore, we use a generalized Benders decomposition, defined as logic-based Benders decomposition to solver the problem. Logic-based Benders decomposition was introduced by [8] and further developed by [7]. A major advantage of the logic-based Benders decomposition is that the subproblem does not need to have a specific form: it can be an optimization problem, a constraint program, or a simple feasibility problem [15]. We make use of the logic-based Benders decomposition framework by decomposing the problem into a rotation generation master problem and a rotation evaluation sub-problem, both formulated as constraint programming problems. The master problem is formulated as optimization problem, and the sub-problem is formulated as a satisfaction problem.

This paper is organized as follows. In Sect. 2, we introduce the formulation of the rotation generation master problem and the rotation evaluation problem, respectively. Solution approaches are presented in Sect. 3. Simulation results are given in Sect. 4. Conclusions and future work are provided in Sect. 5.

2   Mathematical Problem Formulation

In practice, inland vessel operators already have the information of the set of terminals to be visited, the number of containers to load and unload at each terminal, and the distance between any two terminals before they enter the port area. We also consider that due to the capacity limits of terminal quay resources, a limited number of vessels can be served simultaneously at the same terminal. In addition, we assume that each terminal should be visited exactly once and that every vessel enters and leaves the port via a port entrance and exit point.

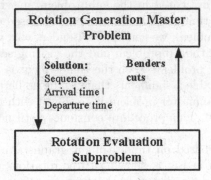

Fig. 2. Benders decomposition approach

To make the model formulation more realistic, we also consider the following three practical constraints in inter-terminal transport of inland vessels in large seaports:

- Restricted opening times of terminals: terminals can be closed during a certain period of the day;
- Priority of sea-going vessels: sea-going vessels have priority over inland vessels, and their rotations have been decided days ahead and cannot be changed;
- Different terminal capacities and sizes: in practice the terminals in the port have different numbers of quays and can serve different numbers of vessels simultaneously.

It is important to consider these factors in the mathematical formulation from an application perspective. Taking into account restricted opening times of terminals means that the loading and unloading process of a inland vessel can be interrupted by the closing time. Consequently, the closing times of terminals would affect the service time and waiting time of the vessels in the terminal. Considering the priority of sea-going vessels means that during the service time window of the sea-going vessels, the inland vessels cannot be served. This also affects the service time and waiting time of the vessels. In addition, in practice different terminals have different capacities, opening times, and other characteristics (number of quays, berths, cranes, ..., etc.). For example, certain terminals will be closed during the night, and this would increase the waiting time of the vessels that arrive during the night, or this could cause the vessels to visit other terminals that are open. These aspects have not been taken into account in the formulations of the vessel rotation planning in earlier works.

We make use of the logic-based Benders decomposition framework to decompose the problem into a rotation generation master problem and a rotation evaluation subproblem, as shown in Fig. 2. During a iteration, the master problem decides on the sequences of vessels' visits to terminals, as well as the number of inter-terminal containers the involved inland vessels transport from one terminal to another, this thus generates initial rotations for the inland vessels. The resulting rotations are evaluated in the subproblem, in which we calculate for each vessel the waiting times at different terminals. Based on the waiting times calculated in the subproblem, we generate a Benders cut, which is a constraint on the waiting times in the subproblem and the visiting sequences of vessels to terminals in the master problem. Then the Benders cut is added to the master problem to exclude variable assignments that can be no better than the previous solution. After that, the master problem is re-solved with the new Benders cut to find a better solution. This procedure continues until no better solution can be found.

Our formulation is based on time-segment graphs. An example of a time-segment graph is given in Fig. 3, showing three rotations of three vessels. For example, as vessel 1 and 2 visit terminal 1 first, therefore, we also refer to this situation as terminal 1 is on the first segment of vessel 1 and 2's rotations.

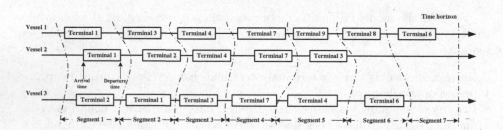

Fig. 3. Time-segment graph for instance with 3 vessels

The parameters that will be used below in our formulation are shown in Table 1. Since we also aim to investigate the potential of making use of the extra space on the inland vessels when they are traveling between two terminals, we consider two types of containers in this phase: besides the mandatory hinterland containers that need to be loaded and unloaded from different terminals (represented by u_i^m and l_i^m), we also consider inter-terminal containers R_{ij} that need to be transported between terminals in the port.

Table 1. Parameters used in problem formulation

Symbols	Definitions
M	The number of vessels entering the port
N_m	The set of terminals that vessel m needs to visit
Q_i	The set of quays in terminal i
R_{ij}	The number of inter-terminal containers that need to be transported from terminal i to j
$K_m^{\max}$	The number of segments on the rotation of vessel m
$t_i^{\text{load}}/t_i^{\text{unload}}$	The average loading/unloading time, per loaded container at terminal i
T_i^{entrance}	The traveling time from the entrance/exit of the port to terminal i
$T_{jq}^{\text{departure}}$	The latest departure time of the vessels being served in terminal j at quay q
T_{ij}^{travel}	The traveling time between terminal i to j
l_i^m/u_i^m	The numbers of hinterland containers that need to be loaded/unloaded by vessel m at terminal i
C_m^{capacity}	The carrying capacity of vessel m in TEU
C_m^{original}	The original number of containers on of vessel m before entering the port in TEU
$[W_s^j, W_e^j]$	The closing time period of terminal j
$[S_q^j, E_q^j]$	The service time period of the sea vessel at quay q of terminal j

2.1 Rotation Generation Master Problem

As most of the constraints we consider are logical constrains, we formulate both the master problem and sub problem based on constraint programming. The following constraint programming problem defines the master problem. It uses several sets of variables. Table 2 shows the decision variables used in the master problem. In addition, we also introduce auxiliary variables, $e_{mm'k}, g_{jkr}^q, f_{jkr}^q$ and h_{jk}^q to determine variables r_{mk} and w_{mk}. Variable $e_{mm'k}$ is used to determine the ranking of the arrival time of vessel m at segment k. Variables λ_{jkr}, ξ_{jk} and η_{jkr}^q are used to determine the waiting time of vessel m at segment k. Variable λ_{jkr} represents the possible starting time for vessels that will visit terminal j on segment k with the ranking of r. Variable η_{jkr}^q represents the departure time of terminal j on segment k of the vessel with rank r. Variable ξ_{jk} represents the latest departure time of terminal j on segment k.

The aim of the master problem is to generate initial rotations for the vessels, and we therefore formulate the objective as minimizing the sum of the vessels spending in the port area:

Table 2. Decision variables in the master problem

Symbols	Definitions
z_{jk}^m	1 if terminal j is on segment k of vessel m's rotation
$\tau_{k-1,k}^m$	Traveling time between segment $k-1$ and segment k for vessel m
α_i^m	Arrival time of vessel m at terminal i
β_i^m	Departure time of vessel m at terminal i
γ_i^m	Service time of vessel m at terminal i
v_{ij}^m	The number of inter-terminal containers from terminal i to j carried by vessel m
b_i^m	The number of containers on vessel m when it leaves terminal i
W_m^{wait}	The sum of waiting time of vessel m
a_{mk}^{master}	Arrival time of vessel m at segment k
d_{mk}^{master}	Departure time of vessel m at segment k
s_{mk}^{master}	Service time of vessel m at segment k
w_{mk}^{master}	Waiting time of vessel m at segment k
t_{mk}^{master}	The terminal vessel m visits on segment k
r_{mk}^{master}	Ranking of the arrival time of vessel m at segment k

$$\min \quad \sum_{m=1}^M \left(d_{mK_m^{\max}}^{\text{master}} + T_{t_{mK_m^{\max}}^{\text{master}}}^{\text{entrance}} + W_m^{\text{wait}} \right),$$

where $d_{mK_m}^{\text{master}}$ is the departure time of vessel m when it leaves the last terminal on its rotation, and $T_{t_{mk}^{\text{master}}}^{\text{entrance}}$ is the traveling time from the last terminal to the port entrance/exit point, taking into account the following constraints:

$$\left(\tau_{k,k+1}^m - T_{ij}^{\text{travel}} \right) z_{ik}^m z_{j,k+1}^m = 0 \quad \forall i,j \in N_m, \forall m \in M, k \in \{1,2,\ldots,K_m^{\max}\} \quad (1)$$

$$\sum_{k=1}^{K_m^{\max}} z_{jk}^m = 1, \ \sum_{j \in N_m} z_{jk}^m = 1 \qquad \forall j \in N_m, \forall k \in \{1,2,\ldots,K_m^{\max}\} \quad (2)$$

$$\sum_{m \in M} v_{ij}^m = R_{ij} \qquad \forall i,j \in N_m, \forall m \in M \quad (3)$$

$$\sum_{k'=1}^k v_{ij}^m z_{ik}^m z_{jk'}^m = 0 \qquad \forall i,j \in N_m, \forall m \in M, \forall k' < k \leq K_m^{\max} \quad (4)$$

$$v_{ij}^m \neq 0 \rightarrow \alpha_j^m \leq T_j^{\text{deadline}} \qquad \forall i,j \in N_m, \forall m \in M \quad (5)$$

$$b_i^m = \left(C_m^{\text{original}} + l_i^m - u_i^m + \sum_{p \in N_m} v_{ip}^m \right) z_{i1}^m$$

$$+ \left(l_i^m - u_i^m + \sum_{k=2}^{K_{\max}^m} \sum_{p \in N_m} \left(b_p^m z_{p,k-1}^m z_{ik}^m \right) + \sum_{p \in N_m} v_{ip}^m - \sum_{p \in N_m} v_{pi}^m \right) (1 - z_{i1}^m) \tag{6}$$

$$\forall i, p \in N_m, m \in M$$

$$b_i^m \leq C_m^{\text{capacity}} \qquad\qquad i \in N_m, m \in M \tag{7}$$

$$\alpha_i^m = T_i^{\text{entrance}} z_{i1}^m + \left(\sum_{k=2}^{K_m^{\max}} \left(\sum_{p \in N_m} (\beta_p^m + T_{pi}^{\text{travel}}) z_{p,k-1}^m \right) z_{ik}^m \right) (1 - z_{i1}^m) \tag{8}$$

$$\forall i, p \in N_m, \forall m \in M$$

$$\beta_i^m = \alpha_i^m + \gamma_i^m \qquad\qquad \forall i \in N_m, \forall m \in M \tag{9}$$

$$\gamma_i^m = l_i^m t^{\text{load}} + u_i^m t^{\text{unload}} + \sum_{p \in N_m} v_{ip}^m t^{\text{load}} + \sum_{p \in N_m} v_{pi}^m t^{\text{unload}} \tag{10}$$

$$\forall i, p \in N_m, \forall m \in M$$

$$element(\sum_{j \in N_m} j z_{jk}^m, N_m, t_{mk}^{\text{master}}) \tag{11}$$

$$\forall j \in N_m, \forall m \in M, \forall k \in \{1, 2, \ldots, K_m^{\max}\}$$

$$element(t_{mk}^{\text{mater}}, (\gamma_1^m, \gamma_2^m, \ldots, \gamma_{|N_m|}^m), s_{mk}^{\text{mater}}) \tag{12}$$

$$\forall j \in N_m, \forall m \in M, \forall k \in \{1, 2, \ldots, K_m^{\max}\}$$

$$element(t_{m1}^{\text{mater}}, (\alpha_1^m, \alpha_2^m, \ldots, \alpha_{|N_m|}^m), a_{m1}^{\text{mater}}) \tag{13}$$

$$\forall j \in N_m, \forall m \in M, \forall k \in \{1, 2, \ldots, K_m^{\max}\}$$

$$a_{mk}^{\text{master}} = d_{mk-1} + \tau_{k-1,k}^m \qquad \forall j \in N_m, \forall m \in M, \forall k \in \{2, \ldots, K_m^{\max}\} \tag{14}$$

$$a_{mk}^{\text{master}} (1 - e_{mm'k}) z_{jk}^m z_{jk}^{m'} < a_{m'k}^{\text{master}}$$
$$\forall m, m' \in M, \forall j \in \{N_m \cap N_{m'}\}, \forall k \in \{1, 2, \ldots, K_m^{\max}\} \tag{15}$$

$$a_{mk}^{\text{master}} \geq a_{m'k}^{\text{master}} e_{mm'k} z_{jk}^m z_{jk}^{m'}$$
$$\forall m, m' \in M, \forall j \in \{N_m \cap N_{m'}\} \forall k \in \{1, 2, \ldots, K_m^{\max}\} \tag{16}$$

$$r_{mk}^{\text{master}} = \sum_{m=1}^{M} e_{mm'k} \qquad\qquad \forall m, m' \in M, \forall k \in \{1, 2, \ldots, K_m^{\max}\} \quad (17)$$

$$w_{mk}^{\text{master}} = \max\left(a_{mk}, \lambda_{t_{mk}kr_{mk}}\right) - a_{mk} \qquad \forall m \in M, \forall k \in \{1, 2, \ldots, K_m^{\max}\} \quad (18)$$

$$d_{mk}^{\text{master}} = a_{mk}^{\text{master}} + s_{mk}^{\text{master}} + w_{mk}^{\text{master}} \qquad \forall m \in M, \forall k \in \{1, 2, \ldots, K_m^{\max}\} \quad (19)$$

$$\lambda_{j11} = T_j^{\text{departure}} \qquad\qquad\qquad\qquad \forall j \in N_m \quad (20)$$

$$\lambda_{jk1} = \xi_{jk-1} \qquad\qquad\qquad \forall j \in N_m, \forall k \in \{1, 2, \ldots, K_m^{\max}\} \quad (21)$$

$$\xi_{jk} = \eta_{jkr_j^{\max}} \qquad\qquad\qquad \forall j \in N_m, \forall k \in \{1, 2, \ldots, K_m^{\max}\} \quad (22)$$

$$\lambda_{t_{m'k}kr_{mk+1}} = \eta_{t_{mk}kr_{mk}} \qquad\qquad \forall m, m' \in M, \forall k \in \{1, 2, \ldots, K_m^{\max}\} \quad (23)$$

$$\eta_{t_{mk}kr_{mk}} = \max\left(a_{mk}^{\text{master}}, \lambda_{t_{mk}kr_{mk}}\right) + s_{mk}^{\text{master}}$$
$$\forall m \in M, \forall j \in N_m, \forall k \in \{1, 2, \ldots, K_m^{\max}\} \quad (24)$$

Constraints (1) state that if terminal i and terminal j are on segment K and segment $K + 1$ of vessel m's rotation, the traveling time of vessel m between segment K and segment $K + 1$ equals T_{ij}^{travel}. Constraints (2) ensure that each terminal will only be visited once. Constraints (3) ensure that the inter-terminal containers that need to be transported from terminal i to terminal j will be transported by the M vessels. Constraints (4) state that at terminal i vessel m will not carry the inter-terminal containers that need to be transported from i to already visited terminals. Constraints (5) ensure that the inter-terminal containers need to be transported to the destination before the deadline.

Constraints (6) state that the number of containers on vessel m when it leaves the first terminal equals the initial number of containers on-board, plus the number of hinterland containers that need to be loaded at terminal i and inter-terminal containers that need to be transported from terminal i, minus the number of hinterland containers that need to be unloaded at terminal j. Additionally, the number of containers on vessel m when it leaves terminal i that is not the first visited terminal is equal to the number of containers on-board at the previous terminal, plus the number of inter-terminal and hinterland containers that need to be loaded at terminal i, minus the number of inter-terminal and hinterland containers that need to be unloaded at terminal i. Constraints (7) ensure that the number of containers on-board will not exceed the capacity of each vessel.

Constraints (8) state that if vessel m will visit terminal i as the first terminal, then the arrival time at i equals the traveling time from the port entrance point to terminal i, and that the arrival time at terminal i equals the departure time from the previous terminal plus the traveling time. Constraints (9) state that the departure time equals the arrival time plus the service time. Constraints (10) ensure that the service time at terminal i equals the sum of the loading and unloading time for the inter-terminal containers and hinterland containers. Constraints (11) state the that if $z_{jk}^m = 1$, vessel m will visit terminal j on the k-th segment of its rotation. Constraints (12) state that the service time of vessel m at segment k equals to the service time of vessel m at terminal t_{mk}^{mater} it visits at segment k. Similarly, Constraints (13) ensure that the arrival time of vessel m at its first segment of its rotation equals to the arrival time of vessel m at terminal t_{mk}^{mater}. Constraints (14) establish the arrival time at segment k of vessel m's rotation. Constraints (15), (16) and (17) establish the calculation of the ranking of the arrival times of vessels that arrive at the same terminals at the same segment. Constraints (18) and (19) state the calculation of waiting and departure time of vessel m on segment k, respectively.

Constraints (20) state that the possible starting time for the first vessel arriving at terminal j on its first segment equals $T_j^{\text{departure}}$, which is the latest departure time of the vessels that have already be served before the upcoming vessels. Constraints (21) ensure that in the subsequent segments ($k > 1$), the possible starting time for the first vessel arriving at terminal j on segment k equals the latest departure time of the vessels that arrived earlier at terminal j on segment $k - 1$. Constraints (22) state that the latest departure time of terminal j on segment k equals the maximum departure time of the vessels that arrive at terminal j at segment k. Constraints (23) state that for the next vessel that will arrive at terminal $t_{m'k}$ on segment k with ranking $r_{mk} + 1$, the possible start time will then be the departure time of the vessel m that arrived earlier with ranking r_{mk}. Constraints (24) ensure that the latest departure time of terminal j on segment k will be updated accordingly each time when a vessel has been loaded and unloaded.

2.2   Rotation Evaluation Subproblem

Once the master problem has determined the sequence of vessels to different terminals, the waiting time of these rotations needs to be evaluated. The solutions from the master problem include the arrival, departure time at different terminals, and the number of inter-terminal containers to load and unload at each terminal. Based on the optimal solution from the master problem, which consists of the optimal rotations for each vessel, we calculate the respective waiting times. Therefore, the subproblem is a satisfaction problem using the CP formulation.

Table 3. Decision variables in the sub-problem

Symbols	Definitions
a_{mk}^{sub}	Arrival time of vessel m at segment k
d_{mk}^{sub}	Departure time of vessel m at segment k
s_{mk}^{sub}	Service time of vessel m at segment k
w_{mk}^{sub}	Waiting time of vessel m at segment k
t_{mk}^{sub}	The terminal vessel m visits on segment k
r_{mk}^{sub}	Ranking of the arrival time of vessel m at segment k

The decision variables in the subproblem are shown in Table 3. We also introduce auxiliary variables, $e_{mm'k}$, g^q_{jkr}, f^q_{jkr} and h^q_{jk} to calculate variable r^{sub}_{mk} and w^{sub}_{mk}. Variable $\delta_{mm'k}$ is used to calculate the ranking of the arrival time of vessel m at segment k. Variables g^q_{jkr}, h^q_{jk} and f^q_{jkr} are used to calculate the waiting time of vessel m at segment k. Variable g^q_{jkr} represents the possible starting time at quay q for vessels that will visit terminal j on segment k with the ranking of r. Variable f^q_{jkr} represents the departure time at quay q of terminal j on segment k of the vessel with rank r. Variable h^q_{jk} represents the latest departure time at q of terminal j on segment k.

Given the solutions α^{m*}_i, β^{m*}_i, γ^{m*}_i and k^{m*}_{ij} from the master problem, we introduce the following constraints:

$$t^{\text{sub}}_{mk} = t^{\text{sub}}_{m'k} \rightarrow a^{\text{sub}}_{mk}(1 - \delta_{mm'k}) < a^{\text{sub}}_{m'k} \qquad \forall m, m' \in M, \forall k \in \{1, 2, \ldots, K^{\max}_m\} \tag{25}$$

$$t^{\text{sub}}_{mk} = t^{\text{sub}}_{m'k} \rightarrow a^{\text{sub}}_{m'k}\delta_{mm'k} < a^{\text{sub}}_{mk} \qquad \forall m, m' \in M, \forall k \in \{1, 2, \ldots, K^{\max}_m\} \tag{26}$$

$$r^{\text{sub}}_{mk} = \sum_{m=1}^{M} \delta_{mm'k} \qquad \forall m, m' \in M, \forall k \in \{1, 2, \ldots, K^{\max}_m\} \tag{27}$$

$$g^q_{j11} = T^{\text{departure}}_{jq} \qquad \forall j \in N_m, \forall q \in Q_j \tag{28}$$

$$g^q_{jk'1} = h^1_{jk'-1} \qquad \forall j \in N_m, \forall k' \in \{2, \ldots, K^{\max}_m\} \tag{29}$$

$$h^q_{jk} = f^q_{jkr^{\max}_j} \qquad \forall j \in N_m, \forall k \in \{1, 2, \ldots, K^{\max}_m\} \tag{30}$$

$$g^q_{t_{m'k}kr_{mk}+1} = f^q_{t_{mk}kr_{mk}} \qquad \forall m, m' \in M, \forall k \in \{1, 2, \ldots, K^{\max}_m\} \tag{31}$$

$$g^q_{t_{mk}kr} \neq \min\left(g^1_{t_{mk}kr_{mk}}, \ldots, g^{Q_{t_{mk}}}_{t_{mk}kr_{mk}}\right) \rightarrow h^q_{t_{mk}k} = g^q_{t_{mk}kr_{mk}}$$
$$\forall m \in M, \forall k \in \{1, 2, \ldots, K^{\max}_m\} \tag{32}$$

For $g^q_{t_{mk}kr_{mk}} = \min(g^1_{t_{mk}kr_{mk}}, g^2_{jkr_{mk}}, \ldots, g^{Q_{t_{mk}}}_{t_{mk}kr_{mk}})$, and to make the formulation concise, we defines $\theta = \max\left(a^{\text{sub}}_{mk}, g^q_{t_{mk}kr_{mk}}\right)$. We can then introduce the following constraints:

$$\theta \leq W^{t^{\text{sub}}_{mk}}_s \wedge \theta \leq W^{t^{\text{sub}}_{mk}}_e \wedge \theta + s^{\text{sub}}_{mk} \geq W^{t^{\text{sub}}_{mk}}_s$$
$$\rightarrow w^{\text{sub}}_{mk} = W^{t^{\text{sub}}_{mk}}_e + \theta - W^{t^{\text{sub}}_{mk}}_s - a^{\text{sub}}_{mk} \tag{33}$$
$$\forall m \in M, \forall k \in \{1, 2, \ldots, K^{\max}_m\}, \forall q \in Q_{t_{mk}}$$

$$\theta \leq W_s^{t_{mk}^{\text{sub}}} \wedge \theta \leq W_e^{t_{mk}^{\text{sub}}} \wedge \theta + s_{mk}^{\text{sub}} \geq W_s^{t_{mk}^{\text{sub}}}$$

$$\rightarrow f_{t_{mk}kr_{mk}}^q = W_e^{t_{mk}^{\text{sub}}} + s_{mk}^{\text{sub}} + \theta - W_s^{t_{mk}^{\text{sub}}}; \tag{34}$$

$$\forall m \in M, \forall k \in \{1, 2, \ldots, K_m^{\max}\}, \forall q \in Q_{t_{mk}}$$

$$\theta > W_s^{t_{mk}^{\text{sub}}} \wedge \theta < W_e^{t_{mk}^{\text{sub}}} \wedge \theta + s_{mk}^{\text{sub}} > W_s^{t_{mk}^{\text{sub}}}$$

$$\rightarrow w_{mk}^{\text{sub}} = W_e^{t_{mk}^{\text{sub}}} - a_{mk}^{\text{sub}}; \tag{35}$$

$$\forall m \in M, \forall k \in \{1, 2, \ldots, K_m^{\max}\}, \forall q \in Q_{t_{mk}}$$

$$\theta > W_s^{t_{mk}^{\text{sub}}} \wedge \theta < W_e^{t_{mk}^{\text{sub}}} \wedge \theta + s_{mk}^{\text{sub}} > W_s^{t_{mk}^{\text{sub}}}$$

$$\rightarrow f_{t_{mk}kr_{mk}}^q = W_e^{t_{mk}^{\text{sub}}} + s_{mk}^{\text{sub}}; \tag{36}$$

$$\forall m \in M, \forall k \in \{1, 2, \ldots, K_m^{\max}\}, \forall q \in Q_{t_{mk}}$$

$$\theta > W_e^{t_{mk}^{\text{sub}}} \vee \theta + s_{mk}^{\text{sub}} < W_s^{t_{mk}^{\text{sub}}} \rightarrow w_{mk}^{\text{sub}} = \theta - a_{mk}^{\text{sub}} \tag{37}$$

$$\forall m \in M, \forall k \in \{1, 2, \ldots, K_m^{\max}\}, \forall q \in Q_{t_{mk}} \tag{38}$$

$$\theta > W_e^{t_{mk}^{\text{sub}}} \vee \theta + s_{mk}^{\text{sub}} < W_s^{t_{mk}^{\text{sub}}} \rightarrow f_{t_{mk}kr_{mk}}^q = \theta + s_{mk}^{\text{sub}} \tag{39}$$

$$\forall m \in M, \forall k \in \{1, 2, \ldots, K_m^{\max}\}, \forall q \in Q_{t_{mk}}. \tag{40}$$

Constraints (25) and (26) show the comparison of the arrival time of the vessels that arrive at the same terminal on the same segments in order to calculate the ranking of vessel m on segment k in constraints (27). Constraints (28)–(31) determine the calculation of waiting time of vessel m at segment k. Constraints (28) state that the possible starting time for the first vessel arriving at terminal j on its first segment at quay q equals $T_{jq}^{\text{departure}}$, which is the latest departure time of the vessels already being served before the upcoming vessels. Constraints (29) state that in the subsequent segments ($k' > 1$), the possible starting time for the first vessel arriving at quay q of terminal j on segment k' equals the latest departure time of the vessels arrived earlier at terminal j on their segment $k'-1$. Constraints (30) ensure that the latest departure time at quay q of terminal j on segment k equals maximum departure time of the vessels that arrive at terminal j on segment k. Constraints (31) state that for the next vessel that will arrive at terminal t_{mk} on segment k with ranking $r_{mk}+1$, the possible starting time is the departure time of the vessel that arrived earlier with ranking r_{mk}.

Constraints (32)–(39) ensure that for vessel m that will arrive at terminal t_{mk} on segment k with ranking r_{mk}, it will be served at quay q if q has the closest possible starting time, and q updates its latest departure time $f_{kt_{mk}}^q$ accordingly. If q does not have the closest possible starting time, then the latest departure time will not be updated, as shown in Constraints (32). We also consider the

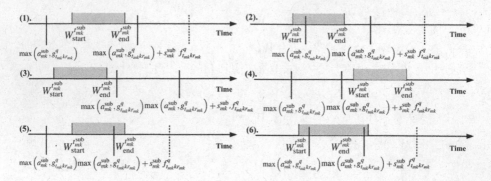

Fig. 4. Six possible relations between a vessel's arrival, departure time window and closing of the terminal (adapted from [4])

closing times of certain terminals in Constraints (33)–(39). Figure 4 shows six possible relations of a vessel's arrival, departure time window and the closing of a terminal. When a vessel is assigned to a quay of a terminal, it has to wait until the other vessel that is being served at the quay has left. Thus, the actual starting time for vessel m with arrival time a_{mk} is $\max(a_{mk}, g^q_{t_{mk}kr_{mk}})$, and the updated departure time is $\max(a_{mk}, g^q_{t_{mk}kr_{mk}}) + s_{m,t_{mk}}$. Then the updated arrival and departure time window $(\max(a_{mk}, g^q_{t_{mk}kr_{mk}}), \max(a_{mk}, g^q_{t_{mk}kr_{mk}}) + s_{m,t_{mk}})$ is compared with the closing time of the terminal. The waiting time of the vessel, as well as and the updated departure time from the quay (when the vessel has left) caused by situation (1) and (5) in Fig. 4 are represented by Constraints (33) and constraints (34), respectively. Similarly, the waiting time of the vessel and the updated departure time from the quay caused by situation (2) and (6), are represented by Constraints (35) and (36). In addition, the waiting time of the vessel and the updated departure time from the quay caused by situation (3) and (4), are represented by Constraints (37) and (39).

We also consider sea-going vessels, which always have priority over inland vessels. The calculation of the waiting time caused by sea-going vessels is similar to the calculation of the waiting time caused by closing of terminals in Constraints (33)–(39). The difference is that the time windows of the sea-going vessels are more specific regarding the quay assigned. The start and end time window $[S^j_q, E^j_q]$ represents the estimated start and end time of the sea-going vessel at quay q of terminal j.

3   Solution Approach

The basic steps of the logic-based decomposition approach are shown in Algorithm 1. During one iteration, the algorithm first solves the master problem and generates initial solution z^{m*}_{jk}, α^{m*}_i, β^{m*}_i, and γ^{m*}_i. Based on the initial solution, the subproblems is solved to determine the waiting time $w^{\text{sub}*}_{mk}$ for each vessel m. Then we create Benders cuts based on $w^{\text{sub}*}_{mk}$ and master problem variable z^m_{jk}.

Algorithm 1. Basic steps of the Benders decomposition approach

1: Solve rotation generation master problem
   (a): generate initial solution using CP solver;
2: Solve rotation evaluation subproblem
   (b): use solution $z_{jk}^{m*}, \alpha_i^{m*}, \beta_i^{m*}$, and γ_i^{m*} from master problem as the input;
   (c): calculate waiting time $w_{mk}^{\mathrm{sub}*}$ for each vessel m;
3: Derive Benders cut
   (e): create a Benders cut with subproblem solution $w_{mk}^{\mathrm{sub}*}$ and master problem variable z_{jk}^m;
4: **while** termination criteria not reached **do**
   (f): add new Benders cut to the master problem;
   (g): re-solve the master problem and then subproblem;
5: return s_{best} and obj(s_{best})

According to [2], a valid Benders cut as a logical expression should adhere to two conditions: (1) the cut removes the current solution from the master problem; (2) the cut does not eliminate any global optimal solution. As a result, the cut should remove the current solution from the master problem since using the same assignment requires an increase in the sum of round-trip time.

The cut from subproblem in iteration h is therefore:

$$W_m^{\mathrm{wait}} \geq \sum_{k=1}^{K_m^{\max}} w_{mkh}^{\mathrm{sub}*} - \sum_{j=1}^{N_m} \sum_{k=1}^{K_m^{\max}} (1 - z_{jk}^m) w_{mkh}^{\mathrm{sub}*}. \tag{41}$$

Here, W_m^{wait} is a master problem variable representing the sum of vessel m's waiting time at different terminals, and $w_{mkh}^{\mathrm{sub}*}$ is the waiting time for vessel m found in iteration h when solving the rotation evaluation subproblem. This cut states that the future solution of the master problem can only decreases the total round-trip time if another sequence of a vessel's visits to terminals is given. That is, if the same assignment is given to the subproblem, the z_{jk}^m variables that are part of this cut will all equal to 1. If this is the case, then $(1 - z_{jk}^m) = 0$ for all m and the waiting time of the subproblem becomes a lower bound on W_m. When a different visiting sequence of a vessel is made and at least one of the z_{jk}^m variables that previously had a value of 1 turns to 0, the waiting time of vessel m at that terminal j is removed from the subproblem. This would result in a smaller lower bound for W_m, which consists of the sum of waiting time with waiting at terminal j removed. This cut follows the 2 conditions defined by [2] to be a valid cut: the cut removes the current solution from the master problem and does not eliminate any global optimal solutions.

4   Experimental Results

Simulation experiments are carried out to assess and analyze the effectiveness of the proposed approach. In this section, we first describe the experimental setting. To evaluate the performance of the proposed method, we compare the runtime, quality of solutions, and three logistical performance indicators with a centralized CP approach in which the master problem and sub problem are considered at the same time as a CP model. The three performance indicators include: total round-trip time (i.e., the sum of the round-trip time of all vessels), total waiting time (i.e., the sum of the waiting time of all vessels) and departure time of the last vessel (i.e., the time when the last vessel leaves the port area).

4.1   Experimental Settings

Our experiments are performed on an Intel Core i5-2400 CPU with 4GB of RAM using a Windows 7 system. As a CP solver we use the CPLEX 12.6 CP solver. The Benders decomposition approach is implemented in C++. In the experiments, we assume that the terminals are open 12 h a day (6:00 am–6:00 pm). The number of inter-terminal containers that need to be transported ranges from 20 TEU to 60 TEU, and the capacity of the inland vessels ranges from 150 TEU to 250 TEU. In addition, we consider the arrival times of the vessels at the port entrance point are within a range of four hour's length, which means that we coordinate the inland vessels every four hours. To evaluate the performance of the proposed approach, we use a centralized formulation for comparison, in which the master problem and the sub problem are considered as a large CP problem.

We set up two cases, a small case, and a large case. In Case 1, we consider 3 vessels, in which each vessel visits 3 terminals. We set up this small instance because this is the largest instance the centralized approach can handle with a one hour runtime limit.

In Case 2, we consider 8 vessels, in which each vessel visits 8 terminals. As the complexity of the problem increases substantially in Case 2, the centralized approach is not able to solve the problem to optimality with a reasonable time. Therefore, to compare with proposed approach, we impose 4 different run time limits, including 180 s, 360 s, 720 s, and 1800 s on the proposed approach and the centralized approach in Case 2. We do not set up longer time limits because in practice, the vessels are entering the port area every now and then, therefore rotations being generated for more than 1 h would be unsuitable for application.

For each case, we set up 10 different instances with vessels that arrive within a 4-h time range. In each instance, we vary the required number of containers the vessels need to transport and the ID of the terminals the vessels need to visit. For each instance, we run 10 repetitions of experiments after which the average values are generated.

4.2   With Coordination and Without Coordination

Figures 5 and 6 illustrate the implemented rotations before and after coordination, respectively. Those rotations are the implemented considering the practical situations, including the closing time of terminals, the terminal capacities, as well as the priority of sea-going vessels. The waiting time at different terminals

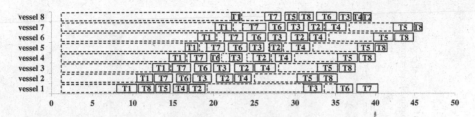

Fig. 5. An example of implemented of rotations generated without coordination

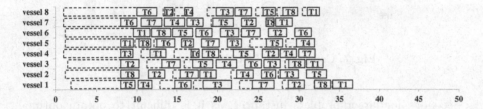

Fig. 6. An example of implemented of rotations generated with coordination

are included, represented as the blocks in dots. Here we use the results from one of the experiments in Case 2, as an example to visualize the rotations and show the differences. The numbers in the block represent the terminal each vessel has visited. The length of the block in bold line with numbers represents the length of the times of stay in each terminal. The block in dots are the waiting time of each vessel at different terminals. As we can see, the implemented rotations with coordination have shorter round-trip time, as well as shorter waiting time. A more extensive analysis on the quality and logistical performance of the rotations generated with the proposed coordination approach is given in the subsequent sections.

4.3   Quality of Solutions

Firstly, we compare the runtime of the proposed approach with a centralized formulation. Figure 7 shows the comparison of the proposed logical Bender's cut approach to the centralized formulation with respect to the CPU runtime in Case 1. The values reported in the figure are the ratio of CPU runtimes[1] between the proposed approach and the centralized approach. We can see that in 90 % of the instances, Benders decomposition method obtains the optimal solution faster than the centralized formulation. In addition, the Benders decomposition method is on average 50 % faster than the centralized formulation among the 10 instances. It is clear that the Benders decomposition approach is capable of solving smaller problem instances in significantly shorter times.

---

[1] Ratio of CPU runtime $= \dfrac{\text{total CPU runtime from proposed approach}}{\text{total round-trip time from centralized approach}}$.

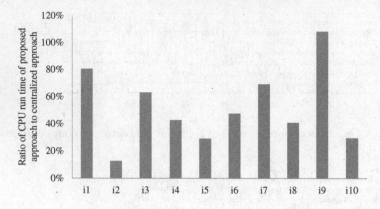

Fig. 7. Comparison of CPU runtime in Case 1

Secondly, for larger problem instances, as it is difficult to obtain optimal solutions in a reasonable time, we therefore impose 4 different run time limits for the 10 instances in Case 2. Figure 8 presents the results that are obtained with 180 s, 360 s, 720 s, and 1800 s. Similar to Fig. 7, the values in the figure are the ratio of objective values[2] between proposed approach and the centralized approach. As we can see, in 99 % of the experiments we carried out for the 10 instances in Case 2, the Benders method obtains better solutions than the centralized approach with the same runtime limits. In addition, in instances 6, 7 and 9, the centralized approach cannot generate even feasible solutions within 180 s, and in instances 6, it cannot generate feasible solutions within 360 s. The complexity of the constraints make is hard for the centralized approach to find initial solutions. In addition, as the Benders cut generated could effectively prevent the master problem from revisiting similar areas of the search space, we can also see that with the increase of run time, the Benders decomposition approach has even better solutions than the centralized approach.

Table 4. Comparison of logistical performance indicators in Case 2

Time limits	Total round-trip time			Total waiting time			Departure time[a]		
	Max(%)	Min(%)	Avg.(%)	Max(%)	Min(%)	Avg.(%)	Max(%)	Min(%)	Avg.(%)
180 s	103.13	83.85	94.05	108.84	70.50	88.30	99.08	88.22	93.14
360 s	103.36	69.77	90.63	109.40	42.26	80.63	98.86	61.85	86.98
720 s	98.39	68.93	85.76	91.16	41.27	64.58	94.28	61.19	70.77
1800 s	100.30	71.97	86.81	97.68	45.82	68.37	94.48	62.71	73.49

[a]The time when the last vessel leaves the port area.

---

[2] Ratio of objective value $= \dfrac{\text{objective value from proposed approach}}{\text{objective value from centralized approach}}$.

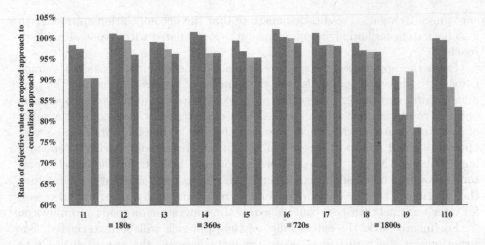

Fig. 8. Comparison of objective values with run time limits in Case 2

4.4   Logistical Performances

We also compare the proposed approach with respect to logistical performance indicators, as shown in Table 4. Table 4 shows the maximum, minimum, and average ratio between the proposed approach and the centralized approach with respect to the total round-trip time, total waiting time and the departure time of the last vessel. These ratios equal to the values of the total round-trip time, total waiting time, departure time of the last vessels from the proposed approach, divided by the values of the total round-trip time, total waiting time, departure time of the last vessels from the centralized approach, respectively.

As can be seen in the table, in most experiments, the proposed approach has better solutions than the centralized approach. In relatively shorter runtime like 180 s, the proposed approach does not show significant improvement comparing with the centralized approach, with on average 5 % less total round-trip time, 12 % less total waiting time and 7 % less the latest departure time. With the increase of runtime limits, the improvements of the proposed approach on the three logistical performance indicators increase substantially. With a 1800 seconds' runtime limits, the Benders decomposition approach finds better solutions with on average 15 % less shorter total round-trip time, 32 % less total waiting time, and 27 % less departure time.

5   Conclusions and Future Work

With the growth of container transport volume in large seaports, this paper investigates how inland vessels could be used for inter-terminal transportation in a larger seaport in an efficient way. We propose a logic-based Benders decomposition approach to generate optimal rotations for a set of inland vessels in a large seaport that coordinate among each other also the transport of inter-terminal containers. Simulation results demonstrate that the decomposition approach can lead both to faster and higher-quality solutions compared with a centralized approach.

From the application perspective, provided the required container volume transported between terminals, and the number of vessels coming into the port area within a certain time range, the proposed approach can give vessel operators optimal rotations with which these vessels can transport the required number of containers with shortest time. The contribution is threefold: firstly, the vessel operators could transport inter-terminal containers without having to spend a longer time in the port, this could bring economic benefits for the vessel operators; secondly, the terminals could serve the vessels in an efficient way, in which the idle time of terminal resources could be reduced; thirdly, using inland vessels for inter-terminal transport could alleviate the congestion on roads and railways.

For future work, the extensibility of the approach will be investigated. For situations in which disturbances or accidents happen, the approach needs to react to the disturbances in a quick manner. In addition, though we are able to solve problem instances for practical settings in this paper, future work will investigate possible heuristics based on the Benders decomposition approach for even larger port instances.

Acknowledgment. This research is supported by the China Scholarship Council under Grant 201206680009.

References

1. Benders, J.: Partitioning procedures for solving mixed-variables programming problems. Numer. Math. **4**(1), 238–252 (1962)
2. Chu, Y., Xia, Q.: Generating benders cuts for a general class of integer programming problems. In: Régin, J.-C., Rueher, M. (eds.) CPAIOR 2004. LNCS, vol. 3011, pp. 127–141. Springer, Heidelberg (2004)
3. Douma, A., Schutten, M., Schuur, P.: Waiting profiles: an efficient protocol for enabling distributed planning of container barge rotations along terminals in the port of Rotterdam. Transp. Res. Part C Emerg. Technol. **17**(2), 133–148 (2009)
4. Douma, A.M.: Aligning the operations of barges and terminals through distributed planning. Ph.D. thesis, University of Twente, Enschede, The Netherlands, December 2008
5. Duinkerken, M., Dekker, R., Kurstjens, S., Ottjes, J., Dellaert, N.: Comparing transportation systems for inter-terminal transport at the maasvlakte container terminals. In: Kim, K., Gunther, H.O. (eds.) Container Terminals and Cargo Systems, pp. 37–61. Springer, Heidelberg (2007)
6. Fazel-Zarandi, M.M., Beck, J.C.: Using logic-based benders decomposition to solve the capacity- and distance-constrained plant location problem. INFORMS J. Comput. **24**(3), 387–398 (2012)
7. Hooker, J., Ottosson, G.: Logic-based benders decomposition. Math. Program. **96**(1), 33–60 (2003)
8. Hooker, J.: Logic-Based Methods for Optimization: Combining Optimization and Constraint Satisfaction. Wiley, New York (2000)

9. Moonen, H., Van de Rakt, B., Miller, I., Van Nunen, J., Van Hillegersberg, J.: Agent technology supports inter-organizational planning in the port. Technical report, ERIM Report Series Reference No. ERS-2005-027-LIS (2005)

10. Nieuwkoop, F., Corman, F., Negenborn, R., Duinkerken, M., van Schuylenburg, M., Lodewijks, G.: Decision support for vehicle configuration determination in inter terminal transport system design. In: Proceedings of the 2014 IEEE International Conference on Networking, Sensing, and Control (ICNSC 2014), Miami, Florida, pp. 613–618, April 2014

11. Port of Rotterdam Authority: Container terminals and depots in port of Rotterdam (2011). http://www.portofrotterdam.com/nl/Business/containers/Documents

12. Rossi, F., Beek, P.V., Walsh, T.: Handbook of Constraint Programming. Elsevier (2006)

13. Schroer, H., Corman, F., Duinkerken, M., Negenborn, R., Lodewijks, G.: Evaluation of inter terminal transport configurations at Rotterdam Maasvlakte using discrete event simulation. In: Proceedings of the Winter Simulation Conference 2014 (WSC 2014), Savannah, Georgia, pp. 1771–1782, December 2014

14. Tierney, K., Voß, S., Stahlbock, R.: A mathematical model of inter-terminal transportation. Eur. J. Oper. Res. **235**(2), 448–460 (2014)

15. Wheatley, D., Fatma, G., Jewkes, E.: Logic-based benders decomposition for an inventory-location problem with service constraints. Omega **55**, 10–23 (2015)

Scenarios for Collaborative Planning
of Inter-Terminal Transportation

Herbert Kopfer[✉], Dong-Won Jang, and Benedikt Vornhusen

Chair of Logistics, University of Bremen, 28359 Bremen, Germany
{kopfer,dwjang,bvornhusen}@uni-bremen.de
http://www.logistik.uni-bremen.de

Abstract. The immense growth of containerized transport and the increasing frequency of calls of mega-vessels at terminals, serving as transshipment points, require powerful planning methods for the efficient fulfillment of inter-terminal transportation tasks. Collaborative planning, and in particular the exchange of tasks among carriers, is a promising instrument for increasing the efficiency of inter-terminal transportation. The exchange of tasks can be organized by auctions performed by the carriers. Three different collaborative planning scenarios are presented in this paper. These scenarios are evaluated by computational experiments. Based on the preferences of terminal operators and the outcome of computational experiments, recommendations for collaborative inter-terminal transportation are derived.

Keywords: Inter-terminal transportation · Collaborative transportation planning · First-price auction · Forwarding profit · Collaboration profit

1 General Scenario for Inter-Terminal Transportation

Inter-Terminal Transportation (ITT) refers to the transportation of transshipment containers between different terminals in a port or between terminals of neighboring ports. At first glance, ITT might seem avoidable, either through scheduling container vessels that will transship containers to arrive at the same terminal, or by placing key logistics components of a port all in the same location. However, in nearly every mid to large sized port some amount of ITT is required, due to the fact that avoiding ITT would involve building rail, barge, and container ship connections all in one place, and there simply is not enough space [10]. The importance and amount of ITT is growing due to the increasing frequency of calls of mega-vessels which are using ports as transshipment points. Table 1 shows the recent and expected amounts of ITT at the ports of Busan (in Korea), which is one of the major container transshipment points in the world. There are several ports in the Busan area which are used as terminals for the Korean hinterland transport and as important transshipment points within the transportation net for international container flows. Many of the incoming

© Springer International Publishing Switzerland 2016
A. Paias et al. (Eds.): ICCL 2016, LNCS 9855, pp. 116–130, 2016.
DOI: 10.1007/978-3-319-44896-1_8

transshipment containers pass more than one container terminal in the Busan area since their point of origin and their point of destination are served by ship routes which are assigned to different terminals. Consequently, there are many containers which have to be carried from their incoming terminal to their outgoing terminal. For providing transportation links, which are connecting ingoing container flows with outgoing container flows, a collaborative transportation planning system generates transportation tasks and assigns these tasks to trucking companies, which are paid for the tasks and are responsible for the fulfillment of all tasks which have been assigned to them. In the Busan area, ITT has suffered from decreasing operation profits during the last few years. That is why the Busan Port Authority (BPA) has initiated a project for surveying and analyzing the efficiency and quality of ITT processes. An outcome of this project is the proposal to implement an ITT platform which is intended to improve ITT processes [9]. This platform should enable the exchange of tasks among carriers to take advantage of collaborative transportation strategies. For the operation of the platform, a resource and profit sharing concept is needed.

Research related to collaborative planning in the direction of ITT is scarce, but becomes increasingly important for coordinating ITT flows [4,7,8]. In particular, using software platforms in combination with vehicle routing is a promising remedy for inefficient ITT [3]. This paper presents and evaluates collaborative approaches for ITT, which refer to the ITT platform intended by the BPA [9]. The assignment of tasks to trucking companies (carriers) is predefined and considered as given data in this paper. The task assignments identify carriers as owners of their tasks. The freight payments (shipper-freights) made to the owners of tasks are specified in advance. Moreover, we assume that the shipper-freight of a task is not only known to the owner of the task but also to all other carriers. Carriers expect to reduce their transportation costs through forwarding some of their own ITT tasks to other carriers; i.e., tasks are allowed to be arbitrarily exchanged among carriers.

In the following sections, we analyze planning scenarios for carriers which are involved in ITT. First, the isolated planning situation of each single carrier is considered. Second, the scenario for central planning of ITT is discussed. Then, three different collaborative scenarios are presented. The presented collaborative scenarios are an elementary approach for task exchange and two extended approaches with an enlarged potential for resource sharing. All scenarios are described as IP (Integer Programming) models and are evaluated by computational experiments.

Table 1. The latest and expected amounts of ITT at Pusan Ports [6]

	2010	2020	2030
Total amounts of containers	262,072 RT	416,721 RT	629,382 RT
ITT containers	236,636 RT	376,954 RT	584,628 RT
	14,194 TEU (100 %)	22,354 TEU (157 %)	34,630 TEU (244 %)

RT: Revenue Tons; TEU: Twenty-foot equivalent unit

2 Isolated Planning Scenario and Central Planning Scenario

There are several carriers $c \in C = \{1, ..., m\}$ which have been entrusted with ITT tasks. The carriers have own homogeneous fleets K_c which are positioned at carrier-individual depots O_c. Consider $K = K_1... \cup ...K_m$ to be the set of all available vehicles of the coalition and $O = \{O_1, ..., O_m\}$ to be the set of all carrier depots. All routes of a carrier's vehicles start and end at the carrier's depot O_c. An ITT task consists of carrying one container or a pair of two containers as a full-truckload from a pickup location (terminal for arrival) to a delivery (terminal for departure) location. Additionally, time windows are specified for the ITT tasks. That is why the ITT problem can be perceived as a Full-Truckload Pickup and Delivery Problem with Time Windows (FTL-PDPTW) including several carriers with different depots.

Assume that $LOC = (O_1, ..., O_m, loc_1, ..., loc_{2n})$ is the list consisting of all carrier depots followed by all pickup and delivery locations of the FTL-PDPTW. Let each $loc_j \in \{loc_1, ..., loc_n\}$ denote a pickup location, and let $\{loc_{n+1}, ..., loc_{2n}\}$ consist of all delivery locations. Consider J to be the set which is composed of all carrier depots O_c ($c = 1, ..., m$) and of all pickup and delivery transportation tasks $j = (loc_j, loc_{j+n})$ with $1 \le j \le n$. Let J_c denote the set containing the depot O_c and all ITT tasks which are owned by carrier c. Each task has assigned a shipper-freight $F_j (1 \le j \le n)$. Further on, the operation time of a task j (including time for waiting and service at the locations as well as time for traveling from the pickup to the delivery location) amounts to t_j. Each task j has to be performed within a given time window $[a_j, b_j]$. Finally, the distance matrix for locations in LOC is denoted by $DIST(loc_i, loc_j)$.

An FTL-PDP can be considered as an asymmetric multiple traveling salesman problem with time windows (amTSPTW) [1] if the depot respectively the set of transportation tasks of the FTL-PDP are taken as the salesman's starting point respectively the set of customer locations of the amTSP. The ITT problem for central planning can be transformed to an amTSPTW with several depots (several starting points of the salesmen). The transportation distance d_j^f of task j (i.e., the full traveling distance) is equal to $DIST(j, j + n)$. The empty traveling distance d_{ij}^e from a depot O_c to a task j can be calculated as $DIST(O_c, j)$ and, reversely, the empty traveling distance from j to the depot is equal to $DIST(j + n, O_c)$. The empty traveling distance d_{ij}^e between two tasks i and j is given by $DIST(i + n, j)$ for all $i, j \in J$. We assume a constant average travel speed v. Consequently, the time needed for traveling from i to j is equal to d_{ij}^e / v. The traveling time of drivers and their vehicles $k \in K$ is limited to a maximum duration T. Let f_c denote the transportation costs per travel unit for loaded traveling of vehicles of carrier c; and let e_c denote the costs per empty travel distance unit for vehicles of carrier c. The variable z_{jc}^o indicates whether a task j is owned by a carrier c ($z_{jc}^o = 1$) or not ($z_{jc}^o = 0$). The binary variable $y_{jk} = 1$ if task j is fulfilled by vehicle k, otherwise $y_{jk} = 0$. The variable x_{ijk} is one if vehicle k is fulfilling task j straight after task i, and otherwise x_{ijk} is zero. The decision variable w_ik represents the departure time of vehicle k after the service operation at customer location i.

First, we consider the Central Planning for ITT. All assignments of tasks to carriers are completely ignored; i.e., any vehicle of any carrier can fulfill any transportation task independently of the assignments made by the a collaborative transportation planning system. This planning situation can be formally described by the following basic ITT-model (1)–(12):

$$\max \sum_{i \in J \setminus O} F_i - \left[\sum_{i \in J \setminus O} \sum_{k \in K} \left(f_c \cdot d_i^f \cdot y_{ik} \right) + \sum_{i \in J} \sum_{j \in J} \sum_{k \in K} \left(e_c \cdot d_{ij}^e \cdot x_{ijk} \right) \right] \quad (1)$$

s.t.

$$\sum_{i \in J} x_{ijk} = \sum_{i \in J} x_{jik} \qquad\qquad \forall j \in J, \forall k \in K \quad (2)$$

$$\sum_{i \in J} x_{ijk} = y_{jk} \qquad\qquad \forall j \in J \setminus O, \forall k \in K \quad (3)$$

$$\sum_{k \in K} y_{jk} = 1 \qquad\qquad \forall j \in J \setminus O \quad (4)$$

$$\sum_{j \in J \setminus O} x_{O_c jk} \leq 1 \qquad\qquad \forall c \in C, \forall k \in K \quad (5)$$

$$\sum_{j \in J \setminus O} x_{O_c jk} = 0 \qquad\qquad \forall c \in C, \forall k \notin K_c \quad (6)$$

$$\sum_{j \in J} x_{O_c jk} = \sum_{i \in J} x_{iO_c k} \qquad\qquad \forall c \in C, \forall k \in K \quad (7)$$

$$\sum_{i \in J \setminus O} (t_i \cdot y_{ik}) + \sum_{i \in J} \sum_{j \in J} \left(d_{ij}^e / v \cdot x_{ijk} \right) \leq T \quad \forall k \in K \quad (8)$$

$$w_{ik} + d_{ij}^e / v + t_j - M \cdot (1 - x_{ijk}) \leq w_{jk} \quad \forall i \in J, \forall j \in J \setminus O, \forall k \in K \quad (9)$$

$$a_j \leq w_{jk} \leq b_j \qquad\qquad \forall j \in J, \forall k \in K \quad (10)$$

$$x_{ijk} \in \{0,1\} \qquad\qquad \forall i \in J, \forall j \in J, \forall k \in K \quad (11)$$

$$y_{jk} \in \{0,1\} \qquad\qquad \forall j \in J, \forall k \in K \quad (12)$$

The objective function (1) maximizes the total profit contribution (revenue) of the collectivity of all carriers. The total revenue is the difference between the sum of all shipper-freights and the traveling costs for the routes serving all transportation tasks. Equation (2) guarantees the balance of flow for the vehicles. Equation (3) establishes the connections between vehicles and transportation tasks served by them. Equation (4) ensures that each task is served exactly once. Constraints (5) require that each vehicle is used at most once. Constraints (6) are responsible for assigning a carrier's vehicles to the carrier's depot. Constraints (7) ensure that each vehicle which is leaving its depot O_c will come back to that depot. All vehicles are irrevocably assigned to drivers. The duration of the vehicles' routes are limited by Constraints (8). Constraints (9) and (10) are needed for modeling the time windows and are guaranteeing sub-tour elimination. Finally, Constraints (11) and (12) specify the integral conditions for the variables x_{ijk} and y_{jk}.

Second, we consider Isolated Planning for ITT. Now, each carrier is planning independently from all other carriers and is fulfilling all own transportation tasks with own vehicles. Isolated planning can be performed by solving the basic model (1)–(12) separately for each individual carrier. Solving the model separately for a carrier c means restricting the set of carriers C to $\{c\}$, O to $\{O_c\}$, K to K_c, and J to J_c. Equation (7) is not needed for the isolated planning and thus can be omitted. The revenue (profit) R_c gained by a single carrier c is equal to the optimal solution of the separately solved model (1)–(12). The entire optimal transportation plan for all carriers is composed of the individual transportation plans of all carriers. It can alternatively be derived simultaneously by one holistic model. In this case, the basic model (1)–(12) has to be extended by the following restriction (13).

$$\sum_{k \in K_c} y_{jk} = z_{jc}^o \qquad\qquad \forall j \in J \setminus O, \forall c \in C \qquad (13)$$

3   The Bidding Process for Collaborative ITT

In collaborative scenarios, carriers form a coalition and agree to exchange transportation tasks within the coalition in order to enhance their transportation efficiency. Most approaches presented in literature for collaborative transportation planning [11, 12] are based on combinatorial auctions [2]. However, since the ITT-players in Busan wish to have a direct and transparent influence on the task exchange and on the amount of profits generated by their own ITT tasks, a first-price sealed bid auction [5] is applied. In addition to this auction type, this paper investigates the effects of manually released limits for bidding prices (freight payments). These limits reflect the requirements of the coalition partners for profits gained by their own tasks and the freight payments obtained for tasks which they receive from other coalition partners.

The collaborative planning scenarios considered in this paper are based on the following assumptions. All transportation tasks as well as the amount of the shipper-freight for these tasks are known to all carriers. Any transportation task which has been assigned by a collaborative transportation planning system to a carrier can be offered for exchange by that carrier. The exchange of tasks actually has the effect of a reallocation of tasks to carriers. The outcome of the reallocation determines which carrier will actually fulfill which task. Independently of any possible task exchange, the shipper-freight for a task is paid to the owner of the task. In case that a task is transferred, the owner of the task will make a freight payment (carrier-freight) to that carrier who has actually fulfilled the task.

For each ITT task j offered for exchange within the coalition, the owner of the task requires a minimum relative profit p_j (a percentage rate of the original shipper-freight) for transferring task j to a coalition partner. This means, the owner is willing to accept a reallocation of task j to any other carrier if the freight which has to be paid to this carrier is below $F_j \cdot (1 - p_j)$. Additionally to offering own tasks for exchange, carriers c can bid for any task j by announcing a maximum rebate (discount) r_{jc} that they are willing to grant on the original shipper-freight; i.e., the bidder is willing to take over task j if the carrier-freight is above $F_j \cdot (1 - r_{jc})$. The announcement of the carrier-freight corresponds to specifying the price in a first bid auction.

Transferring a transportation task j to carrier c fulfills the requirement for minimum forwarding profit of the task owner if and only if $p_j \leq r_{jc}$. In this case the bid r_{jc} is called acceptable; and the corresponding task reallocation is called admissible. If there are no acceptable bids (i.e., there is no carrier c offering a bid with $r_{jc} \geq p_j$), then task j will not be transferred and will have to be fulfilled by the task owner. For uniformity reasons we consider the announced minimum relative profit p_j as a bid given by the task owner for an own task j.

The revenue R_c ($= R_c^1 + R_c^2$) of a single carrier is composed of the revenue R_c^1 drawn from fulfilling tasks by own vehicles and the revenue R_c^2 that has been realized by transferring own tasks to coalition partners. The transportation revenue R_c^1 is equal to the total freight paid to carrier c minus the transportation costs of carrier c. The total freight paid to c is composed of the shipper-freights for own tasks which have not been transferred to other carriers and the carrier-freights for tasks which have been received from other carriers. The transportation costs of c are equal to the costs for fulfilling all tasks which have been reallocated to c, including own tasks which are not transferred. The forwarding revenue R_c^2 of a carrier c is equal to the sum of the forwarding profits of all forwarded own tasks. The forwarding profit of a single task emanates from the difference between the shipper-freight and the carrier-freight. The revenue R of the coalition of all carriers can be determined by summing up the individual revenues R_c of all carriers.

4 Collaborative Planning Scenarios

We assume that the following data is given for each ITT task j: the shipper-freight F_j, the owner c_j of task j, and all bids r_{jc} made by any coalition partner c. The collaborative planning process is realized by an auction with bids for ITT tasks. The outcome of the auction depends on the auction type and the bidding made by the coalition partners. The partners are bidding for single tasks and they are allowed to specify arbitrary values for their bids.

Scenario A (*first-price auction*). In Scenario A, a sealed first-price auction [5] takes place. The best acceptable bid for a task is taken as winning bid; i.e., a task j is transferred to that carrier c who has announced the highest rebate r_{jc} for task j. The binary variable z_{jc}^r is used for indicating whether a task j is reallocated to carrier c ($z_{jc}^r = 1$) or not ($z_{jc}^r = 0$). Thus, $z_{jc}^r = 1$ if and only if $r_{ic} = max\{r_{ic'}|c' \in C\}$. In case of ties, one of the best bids is selected randomly. The optimal transportation plans of individual carriers can be generated by separately solving for each carrier the isolated planning problem under the assumption that all tasks have been reassigned according to the outcome of the sealed first-price auction; i.e., the values of z_{jc}^o in Eq. (13) have to be replaced by the values of z_{jc}^r. Alternatively, the Scenario A can be solved holistically in one single step by employing the basic ITT-model (1)–(12) for the entire coalition (like in the central planning scenario) and additionally fixing the values of y_{ik} and z_{jc}^r by the following restrictions:

$$\sum_{k \in K_c} y_{jk} = z_{jc}^r \qquad\qquad \forall j \in J \setminus O, \forall c \in C \qquad (14)$$

$$z_{jc}^r \leq \left(r_{jc} - \max_{c' \in C}\{r_{jc'}\} \right) + 1 \qquad\qquad \forall j \in J \setminus O, \forall c \in C \qquad (14')$$

Constraints (14) constitute the link between z_{jc}^r and y_{jk}. Constraints (14') guarantee that $z_{jc}^r = 1$ if and only if r_{jc} is a best bid. As a consequence of strictly reallocating tasks to carriers according to the first-price strategy, it is possible that some partners will have more reallocated tasks than they can fulfill with their own vehicles. That is why we assume that the carrier fleets will be big enough for any outcome of the auction in Scenario A or additional vehicles of subcontractors will be hired if necessary.

Scenario B (*freight margins*). The reallocation strategy of Scenario B is exploiting the flexibility for task exchange which is provided by the relative margins $m_{jc} = max((r_{jc} - p_j), 0)$ for possible freight payments. Not only the best bids are considered as winning bids, but all acceptable bids are candidates for being selected as winning bids; i.e., all bids with $m_{jc} > 0$. The decision on the allocation of tasks (by determining winning bids) and the transportation planning are carried out simultaneously. This can be done by solving the basic model (1)–(12) for the entire coalition under the condition that only admissible reallocations (i.e., those which are corresponding to acceptable bids) are allowed. This condition can be implemented in the model by adding the following restrictions:

$$\sum_{k \in K_c} y_{jk} \leq M \cdot m_{jc} + z_{jc}^o \qquad\qquad \forall j \in J \setminus O, \forall c \in C \qquad (15)$$

Equation (15) ensures that a task j can only be reallocated to a carrier c if it has originally been assigned to c ($z_{jc}^o = 1$) or if the reallocation to another carrier is admissible. An admissible reallocation generates a forwarding profit which complies with the task owner's requirement for minimum relative profit (i.e., $p_j < r_{jc}$). Otherwise, the right side of Eq. (15) becomes zero and forces $y_{jk} = 0$. Consequently, the requirements (defined by p_j) for minimum forwarding profits are fulfilled for each single task j.

Scenario C (*positive forwarding profits*). In Scenario C, as a kind of relaxation of Scenario B, the task owners' requirements for minimum relative profits are not fulfilled for each single task but only in an aggregated way for all tasks owned by a single carrier. Equation (16) guarantees for each carrier c that the aggregated absolute amount of discounts granted by carriers which are fulfilling the tasks owned by carrier c exceeds the amount of forwarding profits which are at least required by carrier c for all transferred own tasks, including the tasks that carrier c has not transferred. This practically means that $R_c^2 \geq 0$ for all carriers c. Note that Eq. (16) is linear since z_{ic}^o is a predefined constant value.

$$\sum_{i \in J \setminus O} \sum_{c' \in C} F_i \cdot r_{ic'} \cdot z_{ic}^o \cdot z_{ic'}^r \geq \sum_{i \in J \setminus O} F_i \cdot p_i \cdot z_{ic}^o \qquad \forall c \in C \qquad (16)$$

5   A Problem Instance for ITT

In this section, the reallocation of tasks and the resulting revenues for different scenarios are demonstrated for an ITT example. There are three terminals and three carriers. At each terminal there is one carrier located. Each carrier has three own vehicles (including optional vehicles of subcontractors). The distance between a terminal and the carrier depot which is attached to this terminal is zero. The distances between all locations (i.e., the terminals 1, 2, and 3) are given by the symmetric matrix $DIST(loc_1, loc_2)$ with $DIST(1,2) = 20\,\mathrm{km}$, $DIST(1,3) = 12\,\mathrm{km}$ and $DIST(2,3) = 9\,\mathrm{km}$. There are nine transportation tasks $j = (loc_1, loc_2)_j$ with loc_1 respectively loc_2 as pickup respectively delivery location: $(3,1)_1$, $(3,2)_2$, $(1,2)_3$, $(2,1)_4$, $(1,3)_5$, $(3,2)_6$, $(2,3)_7$, $(1,3)_8$, $(2,1)_9$. Carriers $C = \{1,2,3\}$ are located at the terminals 1, 2, 3; and they are the owners of the sets of tasks $\{1,2\}$, $\{3,4,5,7\}$, $\{6,8,9\}$ respectively. The loaded traveling distances d_j^f and the empty traveling distances d_{ij}^e are derived from the matrix $DIST$. The shipper-freights F_j ($j = 1, ..., 9$) are 200, 200, 120, 120, 120, 200, 220, 90, 220, respectively. All tasks have to be fulfilled within 8 h. The operation time t_j uniformly amounts to 2.0 h for any tasks and the average traveling speed is set to 20 km/h. The unit costs for loaded traveling amounts to $f_c = \$4$ for all carriers c; and their unit cost for empty travel distance amounts consistently to $e_c = \$3.5$. The traveling costs are that high since they cover the costs for waiting at the pickup and delivery locations. Table 2 shows the bids for tasks. Bids for own tasks are marked by italic and underlined typeset.

Table 2. Bids r_{jc} for transportation tasks ($j \in J \setminus O$ and $c \in C$)

	1	2	3	4	5	6	7	8	9
c_1	*0.2*	*0.2*	0.2	0.2	0.2	0.15	0.2	0.15	0.15
c_2	0.18	0.18	*0.15*	*0.15*	*0.15*	0.1	*0.15*	0.1	0.1
c_3	0.25	0.25	0.12	0.12	0.12	*0.3*	0.12	*0.3*	*0.3*

Table 3. Reallocation of tasks and revenues for different scenarios

	Isolated Planning	Scenario A	Scenario B	Scenario C	Central Planning
R	788	851	872	935	935
A_1	{1,2}	{3,4,5,7}	{1,5}	{3,4}	{}
R_1	242	247	250	118	100
$(R_1^1 + R_1^2)$	(242 + 0)	(147 + 100)	(200 + 50)	(32 + 86)	(0 + 100)
A_2	{3,4,5,7}	{}	{3,4,7}	{2,7}	{3,4,8,9}
R_2	263	116	257	375	250
$(R_2^1 + R_2^2)$	(263 + 0)	(0 + 116)	(233 + 24)	(312 + 63)	(200 + 50)
A_3	{6,8,9}	{1,2,6,8,9}	{2,6,8,9}	{1,5,6,8,9}	{1,2,5,6,7}
R_3	283	488	365	442	595
$(R_3^1 + R_3^2)$	(283 + 0)	(488 + 0)	(365 + 0)	(442 + 0)	(564 + 31)

Table 3 shows the reallocation of tasks to carriers and the revenues for different scenarios. A_c denotes the set of tasks allocated to carrier c; i.e., $A_c = \{j \in J \setminus O | z_{jc}^r = 1\}$. The entries for one scenario (column) in Table 3 indicate the assignment of revenues to carriers (i.e., the fragmentation of the total profit R to carrier profits R_1, R_2, and R_3).

Based on the set of tasks A_1, A_2, and A_3 shown in Table 3 for allocating tasks to carriers, the routes performed by the carriers 1, 2, and 3 can be generated for the different scenarios. Figure 1 illustrates the empty trips within these routes in case of Isolated Planning (Fig. 1a) and in case of Central Planning (Fig. 1b). In Fig. 1 the terminals 1, 2 respectively 3 are denoted by T1, T2 respectively T3. The depot O_c of a carrier c whose empty trips are illustrated in a graph of Fig. 1 is marked by a square around the circle. Each arc (i, j) in Fig. 1 represents an empty trip of length d_{ij}^e which accrues when one of carrier's c vehicles is traveling empty between two terminals. An arc (i, j) denotes either an empty trip from a carrier's depot (O_1, O_2 or O_3 in Fig. 1) to a pickup location of task j, a trip from the delivery location of transportation task i to the pickup location of transportation task j or a vehicle's trip back to its depot after it has finished task j.

6   Computational Analysis

Several computational experiments have been performed for ITT on problem instances with randomly generated transportation tasks. More precisely, small problem instances with 16 transportation tasks have been solved with a commercial solver (CPLEX) for Integer Programming. Consider the set LOC of all locations (pickup locations, delivery locations and carrier depots) of the PDPTW which is describing the ITT problem. For all instances generated for our experiments, there are five terminals $(1, ..., 5)$ and three carriers with own depots at the terminals 1, 2, and 3. Each carrier has three vehicles. The distances between the terminals 1, 2, 3 are the same as in the example of Sect. 5. Additionally,

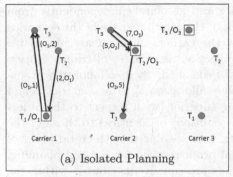 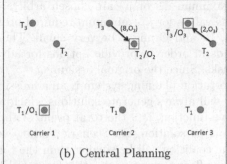

(a) Isolated Planning   (b) Central Planning

Fig. 1. Empty trips of carriers

the distances between Terminal 4 and the terminals 1, 2, 3 are 21 km, 2 km, and 10 km, respectively. The distances between Terminal 5 and the terminals 1, 2, 3, 4 are 22 km, 2 km, 11 km, and 2 km, respectively. All distances between relevant locations are stored in the matrix $DIST(loc_i, loc_j)$. For each transportation task two terminals, one as pickup location and the other as delivery location, are randomly selected. Since the vehicles are partly traveling over publicly accessible roads in an area with much traffic, the average traveling speed v is relatively low and is set to 20 km/h in our experiments. The loaded traveling distances d_j^f and empty traveling distances d_{ij}^e are derived from $DIST(loc_i, loc_j)$ according to the description in Sect. 2. The values for the shipper-freight F_j depend on the transportation distance and on the number (e.g., one 20-foot container, one 40-foot container, or two 20-foot containers) as well as the type (e.g., standard container, high cube container, 45-foot container) of the transported container. In our experiments, the shipper-freights are randomly determined between $(7 \cdot d_j^f)$ and $(9 \cdot d_j^f)$. The traveling costs f_c and e_c amount to the same values as in the example in Sect. 5. The planning horizon is one day (24 h for the time interval $[0, 24]$). The maximal operation time T of a driver and a vehicle is 8 h. The operation time t_j of a task j is composed of the time for loaded traveling as well as an estimated service time of 0.2 h and an expected waiting time of 0.5 h at each pickup or delivery location. Thus, the operation time t_j assumed in our experiments amounts to $t_j = d_{ij}^f/v + 2 \cdot (0.2 + 0.5)$, which means that operation times can vary between 110 min and 140 min for a single transportation task. There are experiments on tight time-windows with a length of 6 h and wide time windows with a length of 12 h. The time windows $[a_j, b_j]$ for transportation tasks j are equally distributed over the entire planning horizon. Traveling to the first pickup location or traveling home from the last delivery location can last up to one hour. That is why for tight time windows with $b_j = a_j + 6$, the values for a_j can vary between $[1, 17]$. For wide time windows with $b_j = a_j + 12$, the values for a_j can vary between $[1, 11]$.

We have randomly generated and tested 30 problem instances. The bids are also randomly generated. Since the bids for tasks (i.e., the values r_{jc} for the maximum discount) are chosen arbitrarily and absolutely independently from the values for p_j (minimum required profits), the solution space of the scenarios A, B, and C might be very small. Thus, the carriers must release reasonable bids in order to provide options for advantageous exchanges of transportation tasks. Since the original assignment z_{jc}^o of tasks made by a collaborative transportation planning system is an admissible reallocation z_{jc}^r, the scenarios B and C will always generate solutions which are superior (with respect to the objective function, i.e., the total profit of the coalition) or identical to those of the isolated solution. For Scenario A, however, it is possible that the total profit of the coalition will be smaller than the total profit reached for isolated planning. For all our experiments, the generated bids are equally distributed within the intervals $[0, 20]$ for p_j and $[10, 30]$ for r_{jc}. All problem instances have successfully been solved for each scenario without any optimality gap. Table 4 summarizes the averaged values for the revenues achieved by the carriers for the different scenarios. A comparison of the revenues for isolated planning with those for central planning quantifies the collaboration potential (maximal reachable profit increase by collaboration). The collaboration potential for our experiments averagely amounts to 144 %, which is rather high compared to other scenarios for collaborative transportation planning. ITT problems generally provide a high potential for collaboration since there usually are only few locations and many transportation tasks which can be efficiently combined to round trips between the few existing locations.

Table 4. Averaged revenues for different scenarios

	Isolated Planning	Scenario A	Scenario B	Scenario C	Central Planning
R	209	221	500	510	510
R_1	10	27	167	177	195
$(R_1^1 + R_1^2)$	$(10 + 0)$	$(-81 + 108)$	$(115 + 52)$	$(120 + 57)$	$(145 + 50)$
R_2	105	114	188	185	167
$(R_2^1 + R_2^2)$	$(105 + 0)$	$(6 + 108)$	$(128 + 60)$	$(122 + 63)$	$(107 + 60)$
R_3	94	81	145	148	150
$(R_3^1 + R_3^2)$	$(94 + 0)$	$(-26 + 107)$	$(77 + 68)$	$(78 + 70)$	$(75 + 75)$

Comparing the averaged revenues achieved by the different collaborative scenarios shows that Scenario A can only slightly increase the total profit of the isolated planning. Scenario B comes very close to the results of central planning. This demonstrates the positive effect which can be realized by exploiting the given freight margins defined by the bids instead of strictly applying a first-price auction. Scenario C reaches the optimal value of central planning. This means that the potential for collaboration has fully been exploited while simultaneously the aggregated carrier requirements for minimum forwarding profits of their own tasks are fulfilled. The results of Table 4 further show that the profit allocation (i.e., the fragmentation of the total profit R) to collaborating carriers differs a

Table 5. Averaged collaboration profits (CP) and portion of test cases with profit decrease

	Scenario A	Scenario B	Scenario C	Central Planning
CP	12 (41/90)	291 (14/90)	301 (9/90)	301 (13/90)
CP_1	16 (13/30)	156 (0/30)	166 (0/30)	184 (0/30)
CP_2	10 (12/30)	83 (5/30)	81 (2/30)	62 (6/30)
CP_3	−14 (16/30)	52 (9/30)	54 (7/30)	55 (7/30)

lot for different scenarios. The collaboration profit of a scenario is defined as the difference of the revenue for isolated planning and the revenue achieved for that scenario. Table 5 summarizes the averaged collaboration profit CP for the whole coalition and the averaged collaboration profits CP_1, CP_2, and CP_3 for single carriers 1, 2, and 3. Reallocations of tasks which are based on the bidding of carriers may cause greatly imbalanced revenues with high values for the profit increase for some carriers and low values for other carriers. The collaboration profits may even be negative for some carriers (see e.g., CP_3 for Scenario A). The values in brackets in Table 5 refer to reallocations which have caused a profit reduction for any coalition partner in any of the 30 problem instances. The values indicate the quotient of the number of reallocations with profit reductions in relation to the number of all 90 reallocations performed for a given scenario. These values show that even for Scenario C and the Central scenario, which have a high amount of additional profit to share between the partners, there is a probability of more than 10 % that an individual partner will suffer from a decrease of the own profit due to reallocation. That is

$$
\sum_{i \in J \setminus O} F_i \cdot (1 - \bar{r}_{ic}) \cdot z_{ic}^r + \sum_{i \in J \setminus O} F_i \cdot \bar{r}_{ic} \cdot z_{ic}^o \cdot z_{ic}^r
$$

$$
+ \sum_{i \in J \setminus O} F_i \cdot (\bar{r}_{ic} - p_i) \cdot z_{ic}^o \cdot (1 - z_{ic}^r)
$$

$$
- \left[\sum_{i \in J \setminus O} \sum_{k \in K} \left(f_c \cdot d_i^f \cdot y_{ik} \right) + \sum_{i \in J} \sum_{j \in J} \sum_{k \in K} \left(e_c \cdot d_{ij}^e \cdot x_{ijk} \right) \right] \geq R_c(I) \quad \forall c \in C
$$

$$(17)$$

why an additional restriction for the alignment of collaboration profits is added to the optimization models of the different planning scenarios. Let $R_c(I)$ denote the revenue of carrier c for the Isolated Scenario. For a given ITT problem instance, $R_c(I)$ is a constant which can be determined by solving the model (1)–(12) separately for each carrier. The profit alignment caused by the Eq. (17) guarantees that no carrier will have a negative collaboration profit in any problem instance.

Table 6 summarizes the averaged values for the revenues achieved by the carriers for the different scenarios in case that Eq. (17) is added to the central model (1)–(12) in order to guarantee that none of the carriers will ever have

Table 6. Averaged revenues for different scenarios with Eq. (17)

	Isolated Planning	Scenario A with (17)	Scenario B with (17)	Scenario C with (17)	Central Planning
R	209	-	470	485	
R_1	10	-	134	140	195
$(R_1^1 + R_1^2)$	$(10 + 0)$	-	$(89 + 45)$	$(94 + 46)$	$(145 + 50)$
R_2	105	-	174	177	167
$(R_2^1 + R_2^2)$	$(105 + 0)$	-	$(132 + 42)$	$(138 + 39)$	$(107 + 60)$
R_3	94	-	162	169	150
$(R_3^1 + R_3^2)$	$(94 + 0)$	-	$(121 + 41)$	$(124 + 45)$	$(75 + 75)$

Table 7. Averaged collaboration profits (CP) for scenarios with (17) and portion of test cases with profit decrease

	CP	CP_1	CP_2	CP_3
Scenario A	-	-	-	-
Scenario B	261 (0/90)	123 (0/30)	69 (0/30)	69 (0/30)
Scenario C	276 (0/90)	128 (0/30)	73 (0/30)	75 (0/30)

a negative collaboration profit caused by the reallocation of tasks of a given problem instance. Based on the results of Tables 6 and 7 summarizes the averaged collaboration profit CP for the whole coalition and the averaged collaboration profits $CP1$, $CP2$, and $CP3$ for single carriers 1, 2, and 3. Additionally, like in Table 5, the values in brackets show the quotient $(n/90)$ of reallocations for which any of the three carriers in any of the 30 problem instances had a decrease of own revenue due to collaboration.

Adding Eq. (17) to the model for Scenario A yields that none of the 30 test instances has a feasible solution; i.e., all sealed first-price auctions performed on our test set result in reallocations with at least one carrier having a negative collaboration profit. For Scenario B respectively Scenario C, Eq. (17) has the effect that the total revenue of the whole coalition is averagely reduced by 6 % respectively 5 % and that the distribution of the collaboration profit among the individual partners is adjusted. Without applying Eq. (17) the collaboration profit for Scenario B respectively Scenario C is divided in portions of 54 % (for Carrier 1), 28 % (for Carrier 2) and 18 % (for Carrier 3) respectively 55 %, 27 %, 18 %. Adding Eq. (17) yields the following results: 46 %, 27 %, 27 % respectively 47 %, 26 %, 27 % for Scenario B respectively Scenario C.

7   Conclusions

ITT problems are characterized by the existence of many transportation tasks combining a relatively low number of different locations (the terminals). That is why ITT tasks which have been more or less randomly assigned to different carriers provide great potential for improving the transportation efficiency by reallocating tasks within collaborative approaches. The experiments in Sect. 6 have shown that a reallocation of tasks based on a sealed first-price auction was not even able to exploit a small part of this collaboration potential, even if we assume reasonable and meaningful bids for ITT tasks. If we extend the options for reallocation by accepting all bids which meet the freight margins (requirements given by the carriers for the minimum forwarding profits and maximum discounts of transportation tasks), the planning situation improves dramatically. By this kind of relaxation for task reallocation (Scenario B), averagely 98 % of the collaboration potential could be realized in our experiments. In a further relaxation the price announcements postulated for single bids are aggregated for each carrier. By this kind of relaxation for task reallocation (Scenario C), 100 % of the collaboration potential could be realized in our experiments.

The above computational results show that there are great discrepancies with respect to the collaboration profits of individual carriers. Up to a certain degree, this has to be accepted since, due to diverse isolated planning situations, some carriers are in privileged positions from scratch (carrier 1 in our experiments) and some other carriers are in worse positions (carrier 3 in our experiments). However, there is reason to exclude reallocations of tasks which will worsen the situation of some carriers since such reallocations would raise incentives for carriers to leave the coalition. That is why it could be required that no carrier should have a negative collaboration profit caused by the exchange of ITT tasks. According to the above experiments, this requirement will reduce the total profit of the coalition by 6 % for Scenario B and 5 % for Scenario C.

If the carriers insist that their limits for forwarding profits and discounts are strictly observed for each single task and if they do not want to accept that the situation of single carriers will be worsened by collaboration, then they should choose Scenario B with the additional Eq. (17) for profit alignment. In this case 86 % of the collaboration potential of the entire coalition has been reached while all expectations of the coalition partners will be measured up. If carriers want to increase their collaboration profit, they can choose Scenario C with Eq. (17). In this case 95 % of the collaboration potential has been reached in our experiments. The collaborative approaches presented in this paper exploit the full information transparency within the coalition. In particular, all tasks and their freights are known to all carriers. This could be a drawback which actually reduces the acceptance of the approaches unless there is a strong port authority prescribing the rules for collaboration. In future research, approaches with less information exchange will be developed.

Acknowledgment. This research was supported by Basic Science Research Program through the National Research Foundation of Korea (NRF) funded by the Ministry of Education, Science and Technology (2015R1A6A3A03019652)

References

1. Bektaş, T.: The multiple traveling salesman problem: an overview of formulations and solution procedures. OMEGA: Int. J. Manag. Sci. **34**(3), 209–219 (2006)
2. Cramton, P.C., Shoham, Y., Steinberg, R. (eds.): Combinatorial Auctions. MIT press, Cambridge (2006)
3. Heilig, L., Lalla-Ruiz, E., Voß, S.: Port-IO: a mobile cloud platform supporting context-aware inter-terminal truck routing. In: Proceedings of the 24th European Conference on Information Systems (in press)
4. Heilig, L., Voß, S.: Inter-terminal transportation: an annotated bibliography and research agenda. Flex. Serv. Manufact. J., 1–29 (2016). doi:10.1007/s10696-016-9237-7
5. Klemperer, P.: Auction theory: a guide to the literature. J. Econ. Surv. **13**(3), 227–286 (1999)
6. Korea Railroad Research Institute: Research and development of inter-terminal transhipment transportation system. Korea Institute of Marine Science & Technology Promotion Final Report (2012)
7. Li, S., Negenborn, R.R., Lodewijks, G.: A two phase approach for inter-terminal transport of inland vessels using preference-based and utility-based coordination rules. In: Corman, F. (ed.) ICCL 2015. LNCS, vol. 9335, pp. 281–297. Springer, Heidelberg (2015). doi:10.1007/978-3-319-24264-4_20
8. Nabais, J.L., Negenborn, R.R., Carmona Benítez, R.B., Botto, M.A.: Setting cooperative relations among terminals at seaports using a multi-agent system. In: Proceedings of the 16th IEEE Conference on Intelligent Transportation Systems (IEEE ITSC 2013), pp. 1731–1736 (2013)
9. Park, N.G., Gong, Y.D.: Collaborative study for designing and operation of an ITT platform at the Pusan New Port. Busan Port Authority, Final Report (2014)
10. Tierney, K., Voß, S., Stahlbock, R.: A mathematical model of inter-terminal transportation. Eur. J. Oper. Res. (EJOR) **235**(2), 448–460 (2014)
11. Verdonck, L., Caris, A.N., Ramaekersa, K., Janssens, G.K.: Collaborative logistics from the perspective of road transportation companies. Transp. Rev. **33**(6), 700–719 (2013)
12. Wang, X., Kopfer, H.: Collaborative transportation planning of less-than-truckload freight. OR Spectr. **36**(2), 357–380 (2014)

Solving the Robust Container Pre-Marshalling Problem

Kevin Tierney[1]([⊠]) and Stefan Voß[2]

[1] Decision Support and Operations Research Lab, University of Paderborn,
Paderborn, Germany
`tierney@dsor.de`
[2] Institute of Information Systems, University of Hamburg, Hamburg, Germany
`stefan.voss@uni-hamburg.de`

Abstract. Container terminals across the world sort the containers in the stacks in their yard in a process called pre-marshalling to ensure their efficient retrieval for onward transport. The container pre-marshalling problem (CPMP) has mainly been considered from a deterministic perspective, with containers being assigned an exact exit time from the yard. However, exact exit times are rarely known, and most containers can at best be assigned a time interval in which they are expected to leave. We propose a method for solving the robust CPMP (RCPMP) to optimality that computes a relaxation of the robust problem and leverages this within a solution procedure for the deterministic CPMP. Our method outperforms the state-of-the-art approach on a dataset of 900 RCPMP instances, finding solutions in many cases in under a second.

1 Introduction

The container trade is an increasingly important component of the global economy. Roughly 182 million twenty-foot equivalent units (TEU) of containers were transported by sea in 2014, with the total throughput at the world's ports being "more than two and a half times that number" [23]. The world's largest port, Shanghai, China, handled over 35 million TEU in 2014, and the largest port in Europe, Rotterdam, the Netherlands, transferred over 12 million TEU. With more and more containers being shipped around the world, ensuring efficient transportation of containers through terminals is becoming increasingly challenging.

Container terminals wish to avoid delays in loading/unloading and transshipping containers, as shippers are especially sensitive to lateness [24]. There are a number of sources of delay within container ports, such as moving containers between terminals [21], internal container handling and vehicle dispatching operations [6], and delays due to improper stacking in the yard. We focus on this last source of delay, as quickly and efficiently removing containers from the yard is critical for ensuring ships, trains and trucks can depart the terminal on time.

When containers enter the yard, it is often not clear exactly when they will leave, meaning it is not possible to optimally arrange the containers according

© Springer International Publishing Switzerland 2016
A. Paias et al. (Eds.): ICCL 2016, LNCS 9855, pp. 131–145, 2016.
DOI: 10.1007/978-3-319-44896-1_9

to their exit time. Thus, some containers with early exit times may be blocked by containers with later exit times stacked above them. We call this situation a *misoverlay*. When containers are misoverlaid, blocking containers must be first moved out of the way to retrieve a container below them, thus wasting time. Given that vessels can load thousands of containers in a single port, retrieval delays can quickly accumulate, resulting in a postponed departure of a vessel. Ideally, containers would be already correctly sorted when vessels berth at a port, ensuring their efficient retrieval during busy periods.

We focus on solving the robust version of the pre-marshalling problem, in which containers in stacks are rearranged during off-peak times. We assume that the exact time containers will leave the stacks is not known, but can be estimated within some time interval. The goal is to sort the containers in a minimal number of container moves such that no containers are misoverlaying any other containers.

Although there has been much work on the deterministic pre-marshalling problem in recent years (e.g., [4,12,13,20]) both for optimal and heuristic approaches, the robust container pre-marshalling problem (RCPMP) has only been addressed in a single article [17]. We introduce a novel relaxation of the RCPMP that allows the problem to be solved to optimality using the iterative deepening A* (IDA*) technique for the CPMP from [20]. We experimentally analyze several different options for using this relaxation and show that our approach outperforms the state-of-the-art constraint programming technique from [17] on a dataset of 900 RCPMP instances. In fact, our IDA* based approach solves 349 instances to optimality in under a second compared to 11 instances for the CP model, and overall solves 546 instances compared to 61 for CP within an hour.

We first formally describe the RCPMP in Sect. 2, then present related work in Sect. 3. Next, we describe our solution approach for the RCPMP in Sect. 4. Computational results are given in Sect. 5, and we conclude and discuss future research opportunities in Sect. 6.

2 Robust Container Pre-marshalling

In the yard of a container terminal, containers are usually stored in *blocks* that contain several rows of container stacks (see Fig. 1). In many ports, rail mounted gantry cranes (RMGCs) perform the movement or shuffling of containers. A row of stacks in a block is referred to as a *bay*, as seen in Fig. 2. A bay has a maximum height restriction on how many containers may be stacked on top of one another, defined by a number of *tiers*. The yard acts as a buffer for containers being transferred between ships, trucks and trains.

The goal of the CPMP is to sort the containers of a single bay based on the departure times of the containers from the bay. The departure times are referred to as *groups*.[1] In the RCPMP, we assume that the departure times of the containers are not known exactly. This is a realistic assumption, as trucks, ships and

---

[1] A group is called a priority in [4,5] and referred to as an exit time in [19].

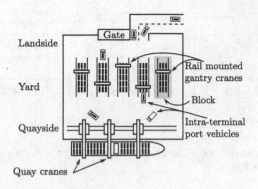

Fig. 1. The layout of a container terminal.

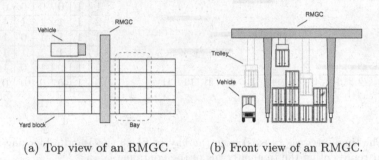

(a) Top view of an RMGC.   (b) Front view of an RMGC.

Fig. 2. A rail-mounted gantry crane over a yard block, from [20].

trains often do not arrive in ports exactly as scheduled. In the robust version of pre-marshalling presented in [17], containers are assigned time intervals in which they will depart the stacks. We generalize this notion and replace the time intervals of containers with a *blocking matrix*, in which it is explicitly specified which containers may be stacked on other containers. This allows terminal operators to not only perform robust pre-marshalling, but also to incorporate other stacking rules into the final layouts of the bays.

Formally, a bay is defined by a number of stacks S and a maximum number of tiers T. There are C containers that must be re-ordered within the bay. The function $c(s, t)$ returns the container in stack s, tier t, if there is one, otherwise it returns the value 0. The blocking matrix is defined with the function

$$b(i, j) \in \begin{cases} 0 & \text{if container } i \text{ may be placed above container } j, \\ 1 & \text{if container } i \text{ blocks container } j. \end{cases}$$

A bay is considered sorted if $b(c(s, t'), c(s, t)) = 0$ for all $1 \leq s \leq S$, $1 \leq t < t' \leq T$. In other words, in every stack there should not be any container placed above another container if doing so would cause a misoverlay. Given a specified configuration of a bay, the goal of the RCPMP is to find a minimal set of moves

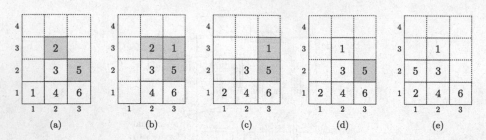

Fig. 3. A bay being sorted, with blocking containers shown in gray; the corresponding blocking matrix is in Fig. 4.

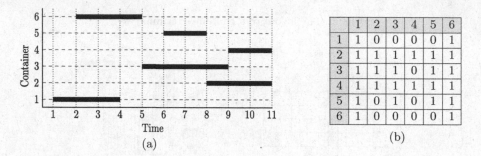

Fig. 4. The time intervals (x-axis) from the bay in Fig. 3 (left) and a blocking matrix (right) for representing the time intervals of the containers.

to sort the bay, where a single move consists of taking a container from the top of one stack and moving it to the top of another stack.

Figure 3 shows an example RCPMP where containers are labeled with an ID. The blocking matrix for the containers is given in Fig. 4, along with the time intervals for each container used to generate the matrix. We build a blocking matrix out of time intervals for containers as follows. When the time intervals for containers i and j overlap, we let $b(i,j) = b(j,i) = 1$. When the intervals are non-overlapping, we set $b(i,j) = 1$ if the earliest exit time of container i is greater than the latest exit time of container j. If neither one of these is the case, we let $b(i,j) = 0$.

We make several assumptions regarding the RCPMP. First, we assume we are operating a crane on a single bay. This assumption is standard in the pre-marshalling and container relocation literature [3,13]. This assumption is based on the fact that moving containers within a bay is quick and easy for a RMGC, but moving the RMGC between bays takes significantly longer. Furthermore, there are safety considerations in systems with multiple cranes or in which trucks are loaded at the side of the stacks, rather than in front or back of the block. We also assume that all container moves within a bay have the same cost. This means that we do not consider that some moves might take slightly more time than other moves, again because moves within a single bay tend to be cheap. Finally, we assume that time intervals for containers can be estimated with some precision. We believe that with the amount of data available to container terminals today, this can be done in a reasonable fashion.

3   Related Work

The container relocation literature is quite rich. We distinguish between problems involving intra-bay and inter-bay exchanges of containers. Besides the CPMP there are also problems assuming that containers must be moved outside of the terminal, implying some reshuffling. This can be motivated by means of loading sequences for vessels [2] as well as requiring time windows given by a truck appointment system [11]. Note that the CPMP is also closely related to blocks world planning; see, e.g., [7].

It has been shown that the CPMP is NP-hard [2], and a comprehensive survey on the CPMP and related problems is provided in [2,14]. There are quite a few papers proposing solution approaches for solving the CPMP. A heuristic tree search algorithm is given in [1], and the corridor method paradigm is introduced in [4]. An explicit optimization model is defined in [13]. Some comments on logical observations leading to a lower bound are provided in [25]. Algorithms with direct heuristics have been developed by [9]; a neighborhood search heuristic is given in [12]. More recent heuristics are those by [5,10,26]. A metaheuristic using a biased random key genetic algorithm has been proposed by [8]. Moreover, [5] incorporates a simple A* algorithm that was later improved and appended with some symmetry breaking rules and an IDA* approach by [20], which is a central component in our work. An approach similar to [20] with less general versions of the branching rules is described in [27]. A version of the CPMP is addressed in [22] in which reach stackers can access containers from the side of the stacks.

Regarding the RCPMP, there is only the work of [17], which proposes a constraint programming approach as indicated above.

4   Solution Procedure

We base our solution method on the iterative deepening A* (IDA*) search introduced in [20]. However, we note that any optimal search procedure for the CPMP could be used with our proposed relaxation of the RCPMP. Briefly described, we use a constraint program to assign groups as in the deterministic CPMP to the containers of the RCPMP. We use the relaxation to compute a lower bound on the number of moves necessary to sort the bay, and use this as guidance for the IDA* search.

4.1   RCPMP Relaxation

We define a binary constraint satisfaction problem that converts an RCPMP bay into a CPMP bay. The goal is to make a CPMP bay in which the blocking relations match those of the RCPMP as closely as possible. We note that if any containers in the RCPMP are mutually blocking, i.e., $b(i,j) = b(j,i) = 1$, then the relaxation will likely underestimate the true number of moves necessary to solve the problem, as the CPMP has no mechanism to model mutually blocking containers. Let the decision variable $x_i \in \{1, \ldots, C\}$ define the container group for container i. We model the following objective and constraints to relax the RCPMP into the CPMP.

$$\min \sum_{1 \leq i \leq C} x_i \tag{1}$$

$$x_i < x_j \quad \forall 1 \leq i < j \leq C \text{ such that } b(i,j) = 0 \land b(j,i) = 1 \tag{2}$$

$$x_j < x_i \quad \forall 1 \leq i < j \leq C \text{ such that } b(i,j) = 1 \land b(j,i) = 0 \tag{3}$$

$$x_i \neq x_j \quad \forall 1 \leq i < j \leq C \text{ such that } b(i,j) = 1 \land b(j,i) = 1 \tag{4}$$

$$x_i \in \{1, \ldots, C\} \qquad\qquad\qquad\qquad\qquad\quad \forall 1 \leq i \leq C \tag{5}$$

The objective function (1) minimizes the values of the groups to try to force the relaxation to place as many containers as possible into similar groups. We note that the objective function is not strictly necessary; in fact, sometimes leaving it out results in a stronger relaxation. We explore this experimentally in the following section. Constraints (2) and (3) ensure that if a container blocks some other container, it receives a higher group value, thus also blocking that container in the relaxation. Constraints (4) prevent containers that block each other from being in the same group. We leave the order of these containers open for the solver to determine, as either ordering of the containers could be used.

The IDA* approach used with this relaxation, which we describe in more detail in the following subsection, requires that the lower bound on the number of moves necessary to solve the problem be valid, i.e., given an unsorted bay the lower bound never overestimates the number of moves needed to sort the bay. Let LB return the number of moves in a valid lower bound procedure for the CPMP. Example lower bounds are the lower bound proposed by Bortfeldt and Forster in [1] (BFLB) or the "direct" lower bound discussed in [20]. Furthermore, let $Relax(bay)$ compute the mapping of the RCPMP to the CPMP presented in the previous model on a given bay. Finally, let $opt(bay)$ indicate the minimal number of moves necessary for sorting the bay. We now show that applying a lower bound heuristic for the CPMP on the relaxation of the RCPMP is also a lower bound for the RCPMP. For the following proof, we say that two containers are *mutually blocking* if for containers i and j, $b(i,j) = b(j,i) = 1$.

Proposition 1. $LB(Relax(bay)) \leq opt(bay)$

Proof. Any container that must be moved in the RCPMP will also have to be moved in the relaxation. Consider a container c that blocks a container c', i.e., $b(c,c') = 1$. In the case where $b(c',c) = 0$, inequalities (2) and (3) ensure that the group of c is greater than the group of c', guaranteeing that it will block c' in the relaxation. Should $b(c',c) = 1$, the group of c could be smaller than the one assigned to c'. However, this does not matter because in the relaxation either c

blocks c' or c' blocks c, meaning that either c must be moved away from c' (or c' away from c) or no move is required in the relaxation, which is not more moves than would be required in the RCPMP.   □

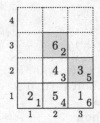

Fig. 5. The relaxation of the bay shown in Fig. 3, with the original container IDs shown in the bottom right corner of each container.

Figure 5 shows the relaxation of the bay given in Fig. 3. Instead of being labeled with its ID, each container is now labeled with the group assigned by the binary constraint satisfaction problem. Several pairs of containers are mutually blocking, and this cannot be captured in the relaxation. For example, containers 3 and 5 (groups 4 and 3, respectively) are mutually blocking, so in the RCPMP container 5 may not be placed on top of container 3, however in the relaxation placing a container with group 3 on top of one with group 4 is valid. Nonetheless, the lower bound provided is still useful for the RCPMP. In this case, the Bortfeldt &Forster lower bound returns a value of 3. The optimal number of moves is actually 4, although the gap in this lower bound turns out to be due to a weakness in the lower bound, rather than due to the relaxation.

4.2 IDA* for the CPMP

IDA* is a so-called "heuristic search" algorithm for finding solutions to path planning problems in graphs (see, e.g. [18]). We note that the term "heuristic search" comes from the field of AI and refers to the use of a heuristic in the algorithm for guiding the search. In contrast to the meaning of a heuristic search in Operations Research, IDA* is guaranteed to find an optimal solution to a problem or prove that none exists, given that the guiding heuristic is *admissible*, i.e., it never overestimates the number of steps required to reach a goal state. IDA* is given a root node of a graph where it begins its search, and it attempts to find a goal node by expanding the nodes along a search fringe.

The IDA* algorithm successively performs a depth-limited depth first search in the search graph. The objective function of a graph node, x, is given by $f(x) = g(x) + h(x)$, where $g(x)$ is the number of nodes in the path from the root node to the node x and $h(x)$ is a heuristic that estimates the number of nodes necessary to reach the goal node from x. As mentioned above, IDA* will always find the optimal solution or indicate that no solution can be found when

Algorithm 1. An IDA* algorithm for the CPMP, from [20].

1: **function** CPMP-IDA*(n, g, h, k, k^{max})
2:    **if** $k \geq k^{max}$ **then return** *no solution*
3:    $m \leftarrow$ CPMP-IDA*-RECUR(n, g, h, k)
4:    **if** $m \neq \emptyset$ **then**
5:       **return** m
6:    **else**
7:       **return** CPMP-IDA*$(n, g, h, k + 1, k^{max})$

8: **function** CPMP-IDA*-RECUR(n, g, h, k)
9:    **if** MISOVERLAYS$(n) = 0$ **then return** n
10:   **for** $m \in$ BRANCHES(n) **do**
11:      **if** $g(m) + h(m) \leq k$ **then**
12:         $r \leftarrow$ CPMP-IDA*-RECUR(m, g, h, k)
13:         **if** $r \neq \emptyset$ **then return** r
14:   **return** $\emptyset$

$h(x)$ is admissible. Thus, $h(x)$ is a lower bound on the number of nodes left to explore. When $h(x)$ is *consistent* (*monotone*), meaning that $h(x') \geq h(x)$ holds for any successor node x' of x, no node in the graph must be explored more than once. IDA* differs from its well-known variant, A*, in that it has a low memory footprint, but requires more CPU time. A* can run out of memory on even small problems because the entire search fringe must be saved. IDA* avoids this problem by repeating itself in each iteration. We refer to [20] for a more detailed discussion of IDA* versus A* for the CPMP.

The CPMP (and RCPMP) can be solved using IDA* by the following graph model. Each node in the graph represents a configuration of containers in the bay. The root node is the starting configuration of the bay, and the goal is represented by any bay configuration in which the containers are sorted. An arc between nodes i and j exists if moving a single container in configuration i from the top of a stack to the top of another stack results in the configuration j.

Algorithm 1 provides the pseudocode for the IDA* approach for solving the CPMP. The input to the algorithm is given by the parameters n, g, h, k and k^{max}, which are the initial solution, the functions g and h as previously described, the current IDA* depth, and the maximum depth allowed, respectively. When the maximum depth is exceeded, then no solution exists and the algorithm immediately exits. Otherwise, a depth first search is started with the given depth limit k. When this search finds a solution, m, it is returned on line 5, otherwise the IDA* is called again and k is incremented by one.

The function CPMP-IDA*-RECUR in Algorithm 1 performs the depth limited search. The function first checks whether the bay configuration provided (parameter n) is a valid solution. If it is, this is returned. Otherwise, all configurations that can be reached from configuration n are explored if their lower bound is less than k. In [20] several symmetry breaking and branching rules are introduced for the BRANCHES function to reduce the number of nodes explored in each iteration. We refer to [20] for the full details about these rules, but note that they are all also applicable for solving the RCPMP.

4.3 Extending IDA* to the RCPMP

We now present our approach for solving the RCPMP building off of the previous two subsections. We first compute a relaxation of the RCPMP using the previously defined binary constraint satisfaction problem. The relaxation can be computed with or without the objective function (1). When computed with the objective function, we sometimes do not find a relaxation within a given timeout. When this happens, we remove the objective function and resolve the constraint program. If the relaxation is solved without the objective function, then the user can choose how many solutions to examine. The relaxation with the best root node lower bound is chosen for the rest of the search.

Once a relaxation is found, for each container i, let r_i indicate the group value of the container as computed in the relaxation and $R(n)$ be the configuration specified by the relaxation for RCPMP configuration n. First, we modify CPMP-IDA* and CPMP-IDA*-RECUR to accept the function R. Second, we change the condition of the if statement in line 11 to be $g(m) + h(R(m)) \leq k$. In other words, instead of checking the lower bound of the RCPMP configuration, we examine its relaxation. If the relaxation's lower bound is less than k, we explore the configuration m, otherwise we throw the configuration away. No further changes are necessary and any RCPMP instance with a blocking matrix can now be solved to optimality.

5 Computational Results

We now evaluate our proposed method. We use Intel Xeon E5506 CPUs at 2.13 GHz for all experiments. We allow a single process to use up to 3.5 GB of RAM. We implement our IDA* approach in C++ and interface with the solver G12 with lazy constraints through the MiniZinc language [15]. We conduct three sets of experiments. First, we analyze options for computing the relaxation of the RCPMP. Second, we investigate the quality of the relaxation in comparison to the optimal number of moves for several categories of RCPMP instances. Finally, we compare our approach to the state-of-the-art CP model from [17].

5.1 Dataset

We made a robust CPMP problem generator that can generate problem instances with varying numbers of stacks, tiers, containers, time horizons, and container exit time intervals. The generator and instances we have generated for this paper are available at https://bitbucket.org/eusorpb/rcpmp-as. We note that we did not have any real data from a container terminal to base our generator on; however, its probability distributions could be easily changed to model real data.

Given a number of stacks, tiers and a *fill percentage*, from which the number of containers is derived, an instance is generated as follows. A maximum time t is specified and containers are assigned a discrete time interval beginning in the range $[1, t]$ uniformly at random. The duration of each container's time interval is chosen uniformly at random within the range $[1, s]$, where s is a specified maximum interval time. We then make a list of the containers, shuffle it, and place containers into a random non-full stack until all containers are in the bay.

Table 1 provides the parameters we used for generating our dataset. We set the maximum time of an instance to ten times the number of stacks times the number of tiers times the fill percentage. We note that there is no guarantee that the instances we generate are feasible, especially when the fill percentage is 0.8. We orient the sizes of the instances we generate on the sizes of bays in real terminals. To the best of our knowledge, very few bays are larger than 10 stacks by 5 tiers, due to the physical limitations of the RMGCs.

Table 1. Instance generation parameters for our dataset.

Tiers	$\{3, 4, 5, 6, 10\}$
Stacks	$\{5, 8, 10\}$
Fill percent	$\{0.4, 0.6, 0.8\}$
Max. interval duration	$\{4, 8\}$

5.2   Relaxation Model Solutions

We first assess the quality of the relaxation model with and without the objective function across our dataset. Usually when solving the relaxation with an objective function there is only a single solution returned by the solver. However, removing the objective function value allows for multiple solutions on most instances in our dataset. Furthermore, some of these instances have different lower bounds, meaning there is the potential for strengthening the problem relaxation by analyzing multiple solutions.

Objective Function Quality. We generated as many relaxation solutions as possible for each instance for 10 s and compared this with the optimal values found using the objective function. In all cases, we found at least one relaxation mapping within 10 s that was as good as the value found using the objective function. In 29 cases, we could not find a relaxation using the objective function within the time limit, and using an objective function finds worse relaxations on 194 instances. On these instances, the median gap between using an objective function and not using one is only 1 move, with an average of 1.46 moves, meaning usually the objective function finds a good value. Ten instances had a gap of 3 moves, seven a gap of 4 moves, and one instance a gap of 5 moves. Note that these high gaps are only on instances with a fill percentage of larger than 0.6 and mostly have 24 slots or more.

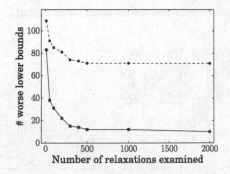

Fig. 6. We examine all relaxations found within 10 s and take the best one as a reference value. This figure shows the number of times using a timeout of 1 s (dashed) or 10 s (solid) finds worse values when examining a given number of relaxations.

Number of Solutions. We examine the quality of the relaxation compared to how many solutions are examined and for how much time in Fig. 6. The y-axis shows the number of instances in which the best root node relaxation found had less moves than when we examine all solutions for 10 s. While only observing 10 relaxations leads to a large number of instances with a gap for both a 10 s and 1 s timeout, observing 50 solutions with a 10 s timeout is already enough to lower the gap to 38 instances. We note that when we only allow a 1 s timeout of our constraint programming solver, it is unable to find many solutions; hence we do not improve significantly even when allowing more and more relaxations to be examined. Nonetheless, these results are promising as in most cases we can find good solutions with the relaxation quickly. We therefore use a 1 s timeout with up to 500 relaxations for the rest of this work.

5.3   Relaxation Quality

Given that the Bortfeldt &Forster lower bound can often have a gap of several moves on the deterministic version of pre-marshalling, we provide an analysis of its gap on the RCPMP to ensure that the gap using the relaxation is not unreasonable. Table 2 provides the average gaps over all instances of a given number of stacks and tiers in (a) and grouped by fill percentage in (b) for using the objective function in the relaxation (R-Obj), as well as checking up to 500 solutions with a 1 s (R-1s-500) and 10 s timeout (R-10s-500). We provide the average over instances that were solved and over all instances. In the cases where the instance could not be solved, the best bound proven is used to compute the gap. Surprisingly, even some large instances have rather small gaps, such as those with 6 or 10 stacks. Of course, this only holds for instances that are solved – gaps for all instances might seem low in these categories, but really this just means the solver could not prove a higher bound. On smaller instances, we see that sometimes the gap can be rather large, with 3 stacks and 10 tiers having gaps of upwards of 8 moves even on instances that were solved. When grouping instances

Table 2. Average gap of the relaxation root node lower bound to the final solution or highest bound proven.

(a) Grouped by stacks and tiers.

S	T	R-Obj Solved	R-Obj All	R-1s-500 Solved	R-1s-500 All	R-10s-500 Solved	R-10s-500 All
3	5	2.3	9.9	2.1	9.7	2.1	9.7
	8	6.4	10.9	6.1	10.8	6.1	10.8
	10	8.4	12.7	8.0	12.5	8.0	12.5
4	5	1.8	5.3	1.6	5.2	1.6	5.2
	8	4.8	7.3	4.5	7.2	4.5	7.2
	10	5.9	7.6	5.9	7.6	5.9	7.6
5	5	2.7	2.7	2.5	2.5	2.5	2.5
	8	3.3	5.0	3.2	5.0	3.2	5.0
	10	4.1	5.7	4.2	5.7	4.2	5.7
6	5	2.3	2.3	2.1	2.1	2.1	2.1
	8	3.0	4.1	3.0	4.0	3.0	4.0
	10	2.8	4.6	2.7	4.5	2.7	4.5
10	5	1.2	1.3	1.1	1.1	1.1	1.1
	8	1.0	2.0	1.1	2.0	1.1	2.0
	10	1.5	2.3	1.3	2.3	1.3	2.3

(b) Grouped by fill percentage.

Fill	R-Obj Solved	R-Obj All	R-1s-500 Solved	R-1s-500 All	R-10s-500 Solved	R-10s-500 All
0.4	2.4	2.4	2.2	2.2	2.2	2.2
0.6	4.3	4.9	4.2	4.8	4.2	4.8
0.8	4.6	9.5	4.3	9.4	4.3	9.4

by their fill percentage, we observe, unsurprisingly, that the fill percentage has a strong impact on the quality of the relaxation lower bound. Dense instances have rather high gaps, and indeed, these instances are very difficult to solve. In summary, these results show that while the relaxation provides a reasonable starting point for solving the RCPMP, there is still significant room for improving the lower bound.

5.4   Comparison to the State-of-the-Art

We compare our approach to an implementation of the state-of-the-art constraint programming model presented in [17]. We note that the CP model does not support a blocking matrix, but rather accepts intervals in which the containers will leave the bay. Since our instance generation assigns containers time intervals before computing the blocking matrix, this poses no problems for comparability. Furthermore, we acknowledge that our implementation of the CP model is not the same as the original. Unfortunately, the original could not be provided for comparison. We use a different variable and value selection scheme, but note that we are also using a newer version of the Choco solver (3.3.3) [16].

In Table 3 we show the number of instances solved and the average CPU time required for each category of stacks, tiers and fill percentage. We use a timeout of 3600 s (1 h) of CPU time for execution of the IDA* and CP approaches. Each instance category has 20 instances, 10 of which have container time intervals between 1 and 4 time units (inclusive) and 10 instances with time intervals between 1 and 8 time units (inclusive). Our approach outperforms the CP model across all instances, both when using the objective function in the relaxation, and when checking the first 500 relaxation solutions found in a second. We note that extending this time to 10 s provided practically no performance increase,

Table 3. Number of instances solved and average CPU time required for the IDA* with two parameterizations and the CP model from [17].

S	T	Fill	IDA* 1s-Obj. #	CPU	1s-500 #	CPU	CP [17] Default #	CPU
		0.4	20	0.0	20	0.0	18	17.1
	5	0.6	19	180.0	19	180.0	10	2312.0
		0.8	0	3600.0	0	3600.0	0	3600.0
		0.4	20	0.0	20	0.0	4	3071.2
3	8	0.6	19	243.5	19	185.9	0	3600.0
		0.8	0	3600.0	0	3600.0	0	3600.0
		0.4	20	3.1	20	0.6	0	3600.0
	10	0.6	7	2527.6	7	2527.8	0	3600.0
		0.8	0	3600.0	0	3600.0	0	3600.0
		0.4	20	0.0	20	0.0	17	855.5
	5	0.6	20	0.0	20	0.0	2	3409.9
		0.8	1	3420.0	1	3420.0	0	3600.0
		0.4	20	0.0	20	0.0	0	3600.0
4	8	0.6	19	303.0	19	241.7	0	3600.0
		0.8	0	3600.0	0	3600.0	0	3600.0
		0.4	20	5.8	20	5.8	0	3600.0
	10	0.6	10	2283.3	11	2160.6	0	3600.0
		0.8	0	3600.0	0	3600.0	0	3600.0
		0.4	20	0.0	20	0.0	9	2329.2
	5	0.6	20	0.0	20	0.0	0	3600.0
		0.8	20	120.6	20	101.7	0	3600.0
		0.4	20	0.1	20	0.1	0	3600.0
5	8	0.6	15	1238.9	16	1079.3	0	3600.0
		0.8	0	3600.0	0	3600.0	0	3600.0
		0.4	20	85.9	20	85.8	0	3600.0
	10	0.6	5	3008.5	6	2885.7	0	3600.0
		0.8	0	3600.0	0	3600.0	0	3600.0

S	T	Fill	IDA* 1s-Obj. #	CPU	1s-500 #	CPU	CP [17] Default #	CPU
		0.4	20	0.0	20	0.0	1	3410.6
	5	0.6	20	0.0	20	0.0	0	3600.0
		0.8	20	178.4	20	126.5	0	3600.0
		0.4	20	0.4	20	0.4	0	3600.0
6	8	0.6	17	1515.9	18	1409.1	0	3600.0
		0.8	0	3600.0	0	3600.0	0	3600.0
		0.4	18	434.0	18	412.6	0	3600.0
	10	0.6	1	3521.4	1	3521.4	0	3600.0
		0.8	0	3600.0	0	3600.0	0	3600.0
		0.4	20	4.0	20	4.0	0	3600.0
	5	0.6	19	332.7	20	132.7	0	3600.0
		0.8	16	992.4	19	486.5	0	3600.0
		0.4	18	428.1	18	428.2	0	3600.0
10	8	0.6	4	2979.8	5	2975.8	0	3600.0
		0.8	0	3600.0	0	3600.0	0	3600.0
		0.4	8	2446.2	9	2263.1	0	3600.0
	10	0.6	0	3600.0	0	3600.0	0	3600.0
		0.8	0	3600.0	0	3600.0	0	3600.0

even though we previously showed that slightly better lower bounds for the root node can be achieved.

Analyzing the performance of the IDA* approach by fill rate, we see that as long as bays are not too full, we can solve most RCPMP instances. The IDA* can solve instances with a fill rate of 40 % in nearly all combinations of tiers and stacks, with the only exceptions being 6 stacks/10 tiers and 10 stacks with 8 and 10 tiers. Furthermore, bays with a 60 % fill rate are in most cases solvable, with only a few exceptions in low stack/tier instances. Finally, 80 % filled bays show an interesting property. While small instances are quite difficult, and we cannot solve them,[2] nonetheless, the IDA* solves all instances with 5 or 6 stacks and 5 tiers with an 80 % fill, indicating that more time may just be necessary on other

---

[2] We note that it may be possible that some of these instances do not have a solution in which there are absolutely no misoverlays.

instances. Note that these instances are particularly difficult as the lower bound is not very tight, and several containers must be handled multiple times.

6   Conclusion and Future Work

We presented an IDA* approach for solving the RCPMP that harnesses a relaxation of the RCPMP to compute lower bounds on the solution quality. We investigated several options for using the relaxation within the IDA* from [20], determining that reasonable lower bounds can be found on the RCPMP even using a lower bound for the CPMP. We further showed that our approach dominates the state-of-the-art across a large dataset of instances with various sizes and properties.

A number of avenues for future work remain open. First, higher quality lower bound computations are necessary to further close the gap between the root bound node and the final solution of the model for both the CPMP and RCPMP. Second, the IDA* approach could be extended to entire yard blocks with a cost function for inter-bay container movements. Third, algorithm selection approaches were successfully applied to the CPMP in [19] and would likely result in improved performance for the RCPMP as well. Finally, infeasible instances for the RCPMP can occur when many containers cannot be stacked on top of each other. In these cases, a version of the RCPMP that seeks to minimize the number of misoverlays in the final bay configuration would provide more useful solutions to terminal operators.

Acknowledgements. We thank the Paderborn Center for Parallel Computing (PC^2) for the use of their high-throughput cluster. We also thank the anonymous referees for their valuable comments.

References

1. Bortfeldt, A., Forster, F.: A tree search procedure for the container pre-marshalling problem. Eur. J. Oper. Res. **217**(3), 531–540 (2012)
2. Caserta, M., Schwarze, S., Voß, S.: Container rehandling at maritime container terminals. In: Böse, J.W. (ed.) Handbook of Terminal Planning. Operations Research/Computer Science Interfaces Series, vol. 49, pp. 247–269. Springer, New York (2011)
3. Caserta, M., Schwarze, S., Voß, S.: A mathematical formulation and complexity considerations for the blocks relocation problem. Eur. J. Oper. Res. **219**(1), 96–104 (2012)
4. Caserta, M., Voß, S.: A corridor method-based algorithm for the pre-marshalling problem. In: Giacobini, M., et al. (eds.) EvoWorkshops 2009. LNCS, vol. 5484, pp. 788–797. Springer, Heidelberg (2009)
5. Expósito-Izquierdo, C., Melián-Batista, B., Moreno-Vega, M.: Pre-marshalling problem: heuristic solution method and instances generator. Expert Syst. Appl. **39**(9), 8337–8349 (2012)
6. Grunow, M., Günther, H.-O., Lehmann, M.: Strategies for dispatching AGVs at automated seaport container terminals. OR Spectr. **28**(4), 587–610 (2006)

7. Gupta, N., Nau, D.S.: On the complexity of blocks-world planning. Artif. Intell. **56**(2–3), 223–254 (1992)

8. Hottung, A., Tierney, K.: A biased random-key genetic algorithm for the container pre-marshalling problem. Comput. Oper. Res. **75**, 83–102 (2016)

9. Huang, S.-H., Lin, T.-H.: Heuristic algorithms for container pre-marshalling problems. Comput. Indus. Eng. **62**(1), 13–20 (2012)

10. Jovanovic, R., Tuba, M., Voß, S.: A multi-heuristic approach for solving the pre-marshalling problem. Cent. Eur. J. Oper. Res. (2015)

11. Ku, D., Arthanari, T.S.: Container relocation problem with time windows for container departure. Eur. J. Oper. Res. **252**(3), 1031–1039 (2016)

12. Lee, Y., Chao, S.L.: A neighborhood search heuristic for pre-marshalling export containers. Eur. J. Oper. Res. **196**(2), 468–475 (2009)

13. Lee, Y., Hsu, N.Y.: An optimization model for the container pre-marshalling problem. Comput. Oper. Res. **34**(11), 3295–3313 (2007)

14. Lehnfeld, J., Knust, S.: Loading, unloading and premarshalling of stacks in storage areas: survey and classification. Eur. J. Oper. Res. **239**(2), 297–312 (2014)

15. Nethercote, N., Stuckey, P.J., Becket, R., Brand, S., Duck, G.J., Tack, G.R.: MiniZinc: towards a standard CP modelling language. In: Bessière, C. (ed.) CP 2007. LNCS, vol. 4741, pp. 529–543. Springer, Heidelberg (2007)

16. Prud'homme, C., Fages, J., Lorca, X.: Choco Documentation. TASC, INRIA Rennes, LINA CNRS UMR 6241, COSLING S.A.S (2015)

17. Rendl, A., Prandtstetter, M.: Constraint models for the container pre-marshaling problem. In: Katsirelos, G., Quimper, C.-G. (eds.) ModRef 2013: 12th International Workshop on Constraint Modelling and Reformulation, pp. 44–56 (2013)

18. Russell, S.J., Norvig, P.: Artificial Intelligence: A Modern Approach. Prentice Hall, Upper Saddle River (2010)

19. Tierney, K., Malitsky, Y.: An algorithm selection benchmark of the container pre-marshalling problem. In: Jourdan, L., Dhaenens, C., Marmion, M.-E. (eds.) LION 9 2015. LNCS, vol. 8994, pp. 17–22. Springer, Heidelberg (2015)

20. Tierney, K., Pacino, D., Voß, S.: Solving the pre-marshalling problem to optimality with A* and IDA*. Flexible Services and Manufacturing (2016, in Press)

21. Tierney, K., Voß, S., Stahlbock, R.: A mathematical model of inter-terminal transportation. Eur. J. Oper. Res. **235**(2), 448–460 (2014)

22. Tus, A., Rendl, A., Raidl, G.R.: Metaheuristics for the two-dimensional container pre-marshalling problem. In: Jourdan, L., Dhaenens, C., Marmion, M.-E. (eds.) LION 9 2015. LNCS, vol. 8994, pp. 186–201. Springer, Heidelberg (2015)

23. UNCTAD: United Nations Conference on Trade and Development (UNCTAD), Review of maritime transport (2015)

24. Vernimmen, B., Dullàert, W., Engelen, S.: Schedule unreliability in liner shipping: origins and consequences for the hinterland supply chain. Marit. Econ. Logistics **9**(3), 193–213 (2007)

25. Voß, S.: Extended mis-overlay calculation for pre-marshalling containers. In: Hu, H., Shi, X., Stahlbock, R., Voß, S. (eds.) ICCL 2012. LNCS, vol. 7555, pp. 86–91. Springer, Heidelberg (2012)

26. Wang, N., Jin, B., Lim, A.: Target-guided algorithms for the container pre-marshalling problem. Omega **53**, 67–77 (2015)

27. Zhang, R., Jiang, Z., Yun, W.: Stack pre-marshalling problem: a heuristic-guided branch-and bound algorithm. Int. J. Ind. Eng. Theor. Appl. Pract. **22**(5), 509–523 (2015)

A Cooperative Approach to Dispatching and Scheduling Twin-Yard Cranes in Container Terminals

Shell Ying Huang[(✉)] and Ya Li

School of Computer Science and Engineering,
Nanyang Technological University, Singapore 639798, Singapore
{assyhuang,LIYA}@ntu.edu.sg

Abstract. To increase the productivity of the storage yard of a container terminal, two identical yard cranes are often deployed in a yard block. In theory, the productivity of a yard block may be doubled with twin-cranes. However, crane interference may severely lower the combined productivity of the twin-cranes. In this paper, we propose an online job dispatching method for twin yard cranes when side loading is used. The method adopts the non-zero-sum game approach to induce the cooperative behaviour in the dispatching and scheduling of jobs for the two cranes to minimize the total job completion time. A one-step lookahead algorithm and a two-step lookahead algorithm are proposed. We evaluate our algorithms against Ng's lower bound of total completion time for twin-cranes and against the greedy heuristic Smallest Completion Time-First. Our experiments showed that our dispatching and scheduling algorithm performs very well.

Keywords: Yard crane dispatching and scheduling · Optimization · Container terminal

1 Introduction

The storage yard of a container terminal is for the temporary storage of containers. After containers are unloaded from a vessel, they are stored in the yard before being loaded onto another vessel or before being collected by external trucks/trains/barges to deliver to other inland places later (and vice versa). In-terminal vehicles transport containers between the vessels and the yard, and between the yard and the truck holding area(s)/railyard/barge handling positions. External trucks may also directly transport containers to/from the yard from/to places outside the terminal. Previous studies have pointed out that yard crane (YC) operations are of great importance and likely to be a potential bottleneck to the overall terminal performance (Li et al. 2009).

The storage yard is organized in a number of yard blocks. In many terminals, containers are arranged in a number of rows and slots in a yard block as shown in Fig. 1. Vehicles travel along lanes to load/unload containers at the side of a yard block. Side loading is the common practice in most transshipment-intensive terminals. Yard Cranes (YCs) need to move among different slot locations to serve vehicle jobs. To increase the productivity of a storage yard in a high-throughput terminal, two identical

© Springer International Publishing Switzerland 2016
A. Paias et al. (Eds.): ICCL 2016, LNCS 9855, pp. 146–158, 2016.
DOI: 10.1007/978-3-319-44896-1_10

YCs (twin-YCs) are often deployed in one yard block. It is intended that these two YCs work simultaneously as much as possible to increase the yard productivity. In theory, the productivity of the yard block may be doubled. However, when these two YCs run along the same track, the two YCs cannot pass each other and have to maintain a safe separation distance at all times. There is another fact about this kind of YC system in a yard block. We assume that the YCs do not move beyond either end of a yard block. Otherwise the vehicle traffic between the blocks will be disrupted by the YCs. Therefore a few slots at each end of the block will be the exclusive zone for one YC where the other YC cannot access. For such a yard block, given a list of incoming storage and retrieval jobs, the scheduling and dispatching of YCs is the deciding factor of how much productivity can be achieved. We consider the problem of scheduling and dispatching two identical cranes (twin cranes) when side loading is used.

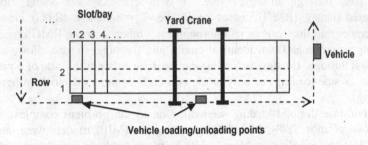

Fig. 1. A yard block with twin-yard cranes

The scheduling and dispatching algorithm will assign jobs that are coming to the yard block to the two YCs. It will also schedule the operations of the two YCs such that crane interferences are minimized and handled properly. Interference between YCs happens when one YC wants to access a slot which is on the other side of the other YC or is too close to the other YC. Interference causes delay in YC's operation and reduces productivity. This means the objective of the algorithm is not a single YC's productivity but the combined efficiency of the twin YCs. To achieve good combined efficiency of the two YCs, cooperation between the YCs is very important.

In many works presented in the past, the objective is to minimize the total (average) vehicle waiting time (Ng and Mak 2005a, b; Kumar and Omkar 2008; Guo et al. 2011); or to minimize the makespan (Jung and Kim 2006; Lee et al. 2007), that is, the total time taken to finish a set of jobs by the YC. An objective equivalent to minimizing total vehicle waiting time is to minimize total job completion time (NG 2005). This is because under the assumption that job arrival times are known and the time taken by a YC to move a container between a vehicle and a yard stack (job processing time) is almost constant, total job completion time minus the sum of job arrival times and the sum of the job processing times is the total vehicle waiting time.

In this paper, we present two twin-YC dispatching and scheduling algorithms based on the non-zero-sum game approach where a YC exhibits cooperative behavior in selecting the next job to do. The objective of the algorithms is to minimize total job completion time. In order to evaluate the performance of the algorithm, we use an algorithm proposed by Ng (2005) that computes the lower bound to the total job completion time. Experiments with two different yard block sizes, tree different YC utilization rates and three different planning window sizes are used.

The rest of the paper is structured as follows. We review the related studies in Sect. 2. Our twin-YC dispatching and scheduling algorithms are presented in Sect. 3. The experimental evaluations are presented in Sect. 4. Conclusion is drawn in the last section.

2 Related Work

There are a number of different types of crane systems. A Double-Rail-Mounted-Gantry (DRMG) crane system for a yard block has two rail tracks and a smaller crane that can pass through a bigger one. A twin crane system using either two Rail-Mounted-Gantry (RMG) cranes or Rubber-Tyred-Gantry (RTG) cranes have identical cranes and they cannot pass through each other. A triple RMG crane system has one bigger crane and two identical cranes and the bigger crane allows a smaller crane to pass through. Loading/unloading can be done either at the side of a yard block (referred to as side-loading) or only at the two ends of the yard block (referred to as end-loading).

First, consider the end-loading scenario. Due to the problem complexity in dispatching two or more YCs, Mixed Integer Program (MIP) models were commonly employed just to formulate problems while heuristic methods were proposed to find near-optimal solutions. Cao et al. (2008) used a combined greedy and Simulated Annealing (SA) algorithm to minimize the loading time of containers for a DRMG crane system. Vis and Carlo (2010) proposed a SA based algorithm for a DRMG crane system to minimize the makespan, i.e. the period between the starting time of the first YC operation and the finishing time of the last YC operation. Stahlbock and Voss (2010) evaluated different online algorithms for sequencing and scheduling of jobs for automated DRMGs serving a yard block. They showed that under high workload, the SA approach performed better than the priority rule-based heuristics.

Dorndorf and Schneider (2010) considered scheduling triple RMGs with end-loading in automated terminals. They used beam search to assign jobs to YCs and a crane routing method that minimized crane waiting times.

Park et al. (2010) studied heuristic methods and local search methods for scheduling twin RMGs in an automated container terminal. Different from others, they considered the need to reshuffle containers when a container to be retrieved is not on top of stack. The reshuffling work was treated as independent jobs. Choe et al. (2012) proposed Genetic Algorithm to schedule twin YC operations in an automated terminal with end-loading. Gharehgozli et al. (2015) used an adaptive large neighborhood search heuristic to schedule twin RMGs to minimize the makespan.

There are only a few studies on the side-loading scenario, which is the one considered by this paper. Ng (2005) studied the problem of scheduling multiple YCs to handle jobs with different ready times within a yard zone with MIP and heuristics. Guo and Huang (2012) proposed space and time partitioning methods to manage the workload among multiple YCs working in a row of yard blocks. Huang et al. (2015)

proposed a job dispatching algorithm with lookahead to minimize total job tardiness for twin YCs.

3 The YC Dispatching and Scheduling Algorithm

3.1 The Problem

For each job i that will come to a yard block to be processed by the twin YCs, it has a ready time (r_i) which is the time the vehicle is expected to arrive at the yard block. The time for gantry movement by one of the YC from the position of job j to that of job i (s_{ji}) is also provided. The YC dispatching and scheduling algorithm will plan the jobs with a lookahead window that consists of n jobs. s_{0i} is the YC gantry time from its position at the start of the lookahead window to the position of job i. The time for gantry movement by the other YC from the position of job j $(j = 1, 2, ..., n)$ to that of job i is the same since the two YCs are identical. The job service time (p_i) by the YC is the time for a YC to load/unload a container. We assume that all jobs involve the top of the stack in a yard block. This is also the assumption in Ng (2005) and more justifi-cations for this are given in the next section. Therefore all p_i are the same. Due to the uncertainty of the terminal operations, job ready time (r_i) are only known for jobs in the near future. In other words, the size of the lookahead window, n, cannot be a very large value.

Our objective of the YC dispatching and scheduling algorithm is to assign the jobs to one of the two YCs and sequence the jobs for both YCs so as to

$$minimize \ \Sigma_{i=1}^{n} C_i \tag{1}$$

If there is only one crane in the yard block, the completion time for job i is equal to its start time + process time, that is, $C_i = max(C_j + s_{ji}, r_i) + p_i$, if job j is the job handled before job i by the YC. When there are two cranes in the block, delays may be incurred due to crane interference which may cause two changes to crane schedule. The first one happens when YC A wants to move to a slot which is blocked by the other YC B. YC A has to wait until B completes its operation and moves away. Then $C_i = max(C_j + s_{ji} + w_i, r_i) + p_i$, where w_i is the waiting time of the crane before it can proceeds to the job location. The second change to the crane schedule due to interference is when YC B completes its operation and has to move enough distance so that crane A can proceed to its job location. Due to this move, B's starting position and available time for its next operation change accordingly. Obviously, if a job is within the safety zone of B so A cannot access (the end portion of the block only B can access), YC B has to handle this job. C_0 is the time a YC is available to start to move to the position of its first job in the lookahead window. C_0 may be different for different YCs.

3.2 The Twin-Crane Dispatching and Scheduling Algorithm

We propose an approach to assign jobs in a lookahead window of n jobs one at a time to one of the two YCs in the twin YC yard block. This is done every time a YC is about to complete its current operation. We call this YC the *current YC*. It is a two-step procedure to assign a job to the current YC and work out the work schedule for the current YC to complete this job. The first step is to get the YC to examine its own interests and prioritize the next few jobs that serve the interests of this YC. In order not to be serving its own interests only, prioritization of the next few jobs for the other YC based on the other YC's interests is also done. In other words, the high priority jobs from each single YC's perspective are identified. These are the jobs the YC would choose without consideration of the impact of their choice on the other YC. The second step is to introduce the cooperative behaviour to the current YC by playing a non-zero-sum game. The objective is to choose the next job which leads to a win-win situation. So the YC selects its next job in order to achieve the best combined efficiency of the two YCs. In doing so, it may select a lower priority job in place of a higher priority job if it is in the common interests of the two YCs. The idea is a YC should choose the job which helps maximize its own productivity but at the same time, this choice would have minimum adverse impact on the other YC's productivity. In this way the two YCs will finish all the jobs with good efficiency. Figure 2 presents the outline of the approach.

---

1. *currentYC* = YC that has the earlier completion time for its current job;
2. *otherYC* = YC that has the later completion time for its current job;
3. *JobSet* = set of x jobs that are already in the yard block or are coming to the yard block;
4. A priority based selection of h jobs from *JobSet* for the current YC and h' jobs for the other YC. ($h=h'$ if there is no overlap in the two selected groups of jobs)
5. Construct the payoff matrix of the non-zero-sum game between the current YC and the other YC;
6. Assign job r to the *currentYC* that gives the best payoff.

Fig. 2. Outline of the cooperative approach.

In the first step of the online algorithm (line 3), it starts by gathering information like arrival time and job position for the next x jobs that are coming to the yard block. These jobs form the current lookahead window. In line 4, some heuristic rules can be used to evaluate these jobs' priorities *with respect to the current YC*. The priorities of these x jobs *with respect to the other YC* are also evaluated. Based on the priority values, h jobs with the highest priority values are selected as the current YC's and the other YC's strategies respectively in the non-zero-sum game.

The second step of the approach (line 5 and line 6) tries to choose a job from its highest priority h jobs such that its choice will have minimum adverse effect on the future operations of the other crane. We propose two variations: a one-step lookahead algorithm and a two-step lookahead algorithm. One-step lookahead algorithm means the current YC will examine the h possible choices for its next job. The benefits of each choice and the impact of this choice on the other YC will be evaluated. Two-step lookahead algorithm means the current YC will examine the possible choices of its next two jobs among the h jobs. There are $h(h-1)$ choices of the next two jobs. Each choice (of two jobs) is evaluated by the benefits of scheduling the first job in the choice as the current YC's next job and the effect of scheduling this job on the other YC and on its own second job in the choice.

In the one-step lookahead algorithm, two jobs with the highest priority values for the current YC and three jobs with the highest priority values for the other YC are considered. The payoff matrix representing the non-zero-sum game is shown in Table 1.

Table 1. One-step lookahead game.

		Other YC		
		othBest1	othBest2	othBest3
Current YC	curBest1	(curP, othP)		
	curBest2			

In Table 1 the two rows for the current YC represent its 2 highest priority valued jobs and the three columns for the other YC represent its 3 highest priority valued jobs. Each cell represents the scenario where the current YC takes the job labelled by the row and the other YC takes the job labelled by the column of the matrix as their next jobs. For example, cell(curBest1, othBest1) represents a lookahead scenario where job curBest1 is assigned to the current YC and othBest1 will be assigned to the other YC later. In this scenario, the payoff of the current YC is represented by curP and the payoff of the other YC by othP in the cell. In general, a cell in the matrix is calculated by

$$
\begin{aligned}
C(m, n) &= (999999, 999999) \text{ if } (\text{job } m == \text{job } n) \\
&= (C_m + C_{m'}, C_n) \qquad \text{otherwise}
\end{aligned}
\tag{2}
$$

where C_m is the completion time of job m if m is the current YC's next job and C_n is the completion of job n if n is the other YC's next job after the other YC completes its own current job. Job m' is the other job in the two highest priority valued jobs for the current YC. $C_{m'}$ is the completion time of job m' if m' was done after m by the current YC. $C_{m'}$ is used as a penalty for not choosing m' as the current YC's next job. Therefore possible clashing of m' with the other YC is not considered. The scenario $m == n$ will happen when the set of two highest priority jobs for the current YC intersects with the set of three highest priority jobs for the other YC. If $m' == n$, set $T_{m'}$ to zero.

When C_m the completion time of job m is computed, its possible interference with the current operation of the other YC is taken into consideration. When there is crane interference, a crane cannot move to the location of its target job but has to wait in its current location. Therefore

$$
C_m = \max(C_i + s_{im} + w_m, r_m) + P_m
\tag{3}
$$

where w_m is the waiting time of the crane (if any) before it proceeds to the location of job m. C_i is the YC available time before job m. The waiting time w_m of the crane is computed by

$$w_m = C'_{current} - C_i \tag{4}$$

where $C'_{current}$ is the completion time of the current job of the other YC. When this other YC completes its current operation, it has to move away so that the current YC can move to its new job location. The gantry time of this YC to the nearest slot which is safe from the current YC is added to $C'_{current}$ after the computation of w_m to indicate its available time for its next operation.

Similarly, when the completion time of job n is computed, its possible interference with the current YC doing job m is taken into consideration. C_n is calculated in the same way as C_m. Column "othBest3" in a row for job m is by default (999999, 999999) and is only computed if $m ==$ othBest1 or $m ==$ othBest2.

After the cell values are computed for the matrix, the cell with the lowest curT + othT will be identified. Suppose this cell is from row r and column c. This means that assigning job r to the current YC will allow the other YC to have a chance to take job c and the sum of the job completion times is the best among other combinations of job assignments. In other words, this is the best choice for the current YC when it chooses one of its own highest priority jobs while bringing minimum adverse effect on the other YC's next job. Note that only the current YC will be assigned the job r. Job c is not assigned to the other YC at this point. When the other crane finishes its own current job, it will become 'the current YC' in the algorithm to get a job assigned. At that point, a job will be selected which causes minimum adverse effect on the other YC's next job. 'The other YC' at that point will be the current YC now.

In the two-step lookahead algorithm three jobs with the highest priority values for the current YC and three jobs with the highest priority values for the other YC are considered. The matrix representing the game is shown in Table 2. The three jobs with the highest priority values for the current YC are labelled by curBest1, curBest2 and curBest3. The three jobs with the highest priority values for the other YC are labelled by othBest1, othBest2 and othBest3.

Each row labeled by (job1, job2) for the current YC in the matrix means that the next job for the current YC will be job1 and the job after that will be job2. Each column

Table 2. Two-step lookahead game.

		Other YC		
		othBest1	othBest2	othBest3
Current YC	curBest1, curBest2	(curT, othT)		
	curBest2, curBest1			
	curBest1, curBest3			
	curBest3, curBest1			
	curBest2, curBest3			
	curBest3, curBest2			

for the other YC in the matrix means the next job for the other YC. For example, cell ((curBest1, curBest2), othBest1) represents the scenario where the current YC will do job curBest1 and then job curBest2 while the other YC will do job othBest1 after it finishes its own current job. The cell will store the payoff for the current YC and that for the other YC. The value of the cell will be computed by

$$C((m1, m2), n) = (999999, 999999) \quad \text{if } (m1 == n) \text{ or } (m2 == n)$$
$$= (C_{(m1,m2)}, C_n) \quad \text{otherwise.} \tag{5}$$

$C_{(m1, m2)}$ is the payoff of the current YC and C_n is the payoff of the other YC. $C_{(m1, m2)}$ is defined as

$$C_{(m1,m2)} = C_{m1} + C_{m2} \quad \text{if } (m3 == n)$$
$$= C_{m1} + C_{m2} + C_{m3} \quad \text{otherwise.} \tag{6}$$

C_{m1} is the completion time of job $m1$ if $m1$ is the current YC's next job, C_{m2} is the completion time of job $m2$ if $m2$ is the job after $m1$. Job $m3$ is the job that is not included in $(m1, m2)$ among the three highest priority valued jobs for the current YC. C_{m3} is the completion time of job $m3$ if $m3$ is done after $m2$. C_{m3} is used as a penalty for not choosing $m3$ in the tentative plan. Therefore possible clashing of $m3$ with the other YC is not considered. It is called a tentative plan because only one job will be assigned to the current YC even though we are examining the scenarios of the next two jobs for the crane. C_n is the completion time of job n if n is the other YC's next job after its own current job. C_{m1}, C_{m2} and C_n are calculated by (3). C_{m3} is calculated by (3) but w_m is zero. To save computational time, the computation of the cell values $C((m1, m2), n)$ in each row will stop after the first column where $(m1 \neq n)$ and $(m2 \neq n)$.

In the same way as the one-step lookahead algorithm, the cell with the lowest curT + othT will be identified. Suppose this cell is $C((m1*, m2*), n*)$. Job $m1*$ will be assigned to the current YC. It is an assignment which, after giving $m1*$ to the current YC, allows the other YC to take $n*$ after its own current job and the current YC to take $m2*$ after $m1*$, and this lookahead scenario yields better/equally good total completion time results up to $m2*$ and n in the job sequences of the current YC and the other YC respectively.

4 Performance Evaluation

To evaluate the performance of the proposed YC dispatching and scheduling algorithm, simulation experiments were carried out. The YC dispatching models are programmed in C ++ language under Microsoft Visual Studio 2010 using Dell Precision T3500, Windows 7 64-bit OS, Intel(R) Xeon(R) CPU with 3.2 GHz and 6 GB RAM.

We evaluate our algorithms against Ng's lower bound (LB) for total completion time for a 2-YC yard block (NG 2005). Our twin-crane dispatching and scheduling algorithms include the one-step lookahead (LA1) and two-step lookahead (LA2) algorithms. Our implementation of the integer program in Ng's LB algorithm is done using MATLAB. Since the objective of YC dispatching and scheduling in this study is to minimize total completion time, we also include a greedy heuristic the Smallest Completion Time-First (SCF) algorithm in the evaluation. In this heuristic method, after a YC completes a job, it will select the next job based on which job it can finish earliest among the remaining jobs without the consideration of crane interference. The finishing time of a job is based on the current position of the YC, gantry movement time to the location of the job, the job's arrival time and the container move time between the stack and the vehicle. Forty independent runs are done for each experimental setting.

First we use the same setting as Ng's experiments when he compared his heuristic algorithm with the lower bound (NG 2005). A yard block has 40 slots. A YC takes 4 min to do one container move between a yard location and a vehicle. The constant 4 min of YC storage and retrieval time represents the scenario where the majority containers are transshipment containers (for a transshipment intensive terminal). They have better predicted storage and retrieval times than import/export containers with external trucks. Due to this, the container allocation system is able to allocate the containers in such a way that most of the times they are on top of the stack with no reshuffling need when their storage/retrieval operation comes. The YC gantry movement time is 3 s per slot. YC separation distance is 1 slot/bay. The inter-arrival time for jobs has the mean of 2 min. We use three different sizes of lookahead window: 10 jobs, 20 jobs and 30 jobs. The results are shown in Table 3. We cannot compare our heuristic algorithms with Ng's heuristic because we do not know what distribution he used for inter-arrival time. We use an exponential distribution.

Table 3 shows the minimum, mean and maximum of

$$\frac{total\ completion\ time\ of\ algorithm\ x - Ng's\ LB\ of\ total\ completion\ time}{Ng's\ LB\ of\ total\ completion\ time}100\%$$

LAP1 has a mean total completion time which is 12.73 % – 16.41 % from the lower bound of total completion time. LAP2 has a mean total completion time which is 8.90 % – 14.55 % from the lower bound of total completion time. SCF has a mean total completion time which is 16.02 % – 17.27 % from the lower bound of total completion time. LAP1 is better than SCF and LAP2 is much better than SCF. When it takes 4 min to complete one container move and jobs are coming one every 2 min, the 2 YCs have a 100 % utilization rate. Even under this condition, the algorithms are performing reasonably well.

Table 3. Total completion time (TCT) performance: $(TCT_x - TCT_{LB})/TCT_{LB}*100\ \%$

Number of jobs	10			20			30		
Algorithm	LAP1	LAP2	SCF	LAP1	LAP2	SCF	LAP1	LAP2	SCF
Minimum	0.94	1.05	1.43	5.95	3.10	3.14	4.69	2.33	4.78
Mean	15.04	9.82	16.83	16.41	14.55	17.27	12.73	8.90	16.02
Maximum	39.37	44.03	44.97	39.43	28.43	43.70	23.16	19.05	37.86

We then use two sizes of yard blocks to evaluate our lookahead algorithms against Ng's lower bound. The two sizes are 40 slots and 50 slots. The time a YC takes to move a container is set to be 75 s. The average of inter-arrival time of jobs is 75 s and 100 s respectively. This creates test conditions of 90 % and 67.5 % utilization of YCs respectively without including the waiting time of YC due to crane interference. The other settings are the same as the previous experiment. For the 40-slot yard block, Tables 4 and 5 show the mean, the median, the 75 percentile, the 90 percentile and the maximum from the 40 runs for the 90 % YC utilization scenario and Tables 6 and 7 show the results for the 67.5 % YC utilization scenario.

Table 4. Total completion time (TCT) performance (90 % YC utilization, 40-slot block): $(TCT_x - TCT_{LB})/TCT_{LB}*100$ %

Number of jobs	10			20			30		
Algorithm	LAP1	LAP2	SCF	LAP1	LAP2	SCF	LAP1	LAP2	SCF
Mean	9.58	7.52	12.41	8.02	6.87	8.96	6.09	4.96	7.82
Median	7.95	6.68	11.32	7.20	5.12	8.29	6.00	4.42	6.73
75 percentile	11.39	9.73	14.27	9.09	7.50	9.61	7.14	5.72	9.14
90 percentile	16.03	11.96	19.35	11.24	11.60	11.13	8.33	6.83	9.06
Maximum	14.28	10.24	14.39	14.01	14.41	20.79	11.35	9.77	18.89

Tables 4 and 5 show that our LA1 and LA2 algorithms are able to produce results which are close to the lower bound value of the total completion time for jobs. The mean total completion time of LA1 is 6 % – 12 % from the lower bound. The mean total completion time of LA2 is 5 % – 8 % from the lower bound. The mean total completion time of SCF is 8 % – 15 % from the lower bound. We presented the percentage differences of mean, median, 75 percentile, 90 percentile and the maximum between LAP1/LAP2/SCF and the lower bound value to show the profiles. It can be seen that LAP1 is better than the simple SCF in many of these statistical indicators and LAP2 is better than SCF in all these indicators. At worst (maximum), LAP2 is about 7.7 % – 14.4 % from the lower bound while SCF is about 12.4 % – 25.9 % from the lower bound.

Table 5. Total completion time (TCT) performance (90 % YC utilization, 50-slot block): $(TCT_x - TCT_{LB})/TCT_{LB}*100$ %

Number of jobs	10			20			30		
Algorithm	LAP1	LAP2	SCF	LAP1	LAP2	SCF	LAP1	LAP2	SCF
Mean	12.18	8.10	14.86	8.93	7.46	11.05	6.82	5.24	8.32
Median	11.81	8.65	15.16	7.75	5.80	10.20	6.23	5.36	7.81
75 percentile	13.98	10.72	21.92	11.75	10.47	12.72	7.30	5.78	9.68
90 percentile	22.01	12.05	21.13	13.80	11.51	13.38	8.46	6.80	8.87
Maximum	20.60	13.72	25.87	13.79	11.54	17.77	9.23	7.74	12.40

Tables 6 and 7 show the results when the YC utilization rate is at around 67.5 %. In this condition, the YCs are less busy than the previous two utilization levels. The mean total completion time of LA1 is 3.23 % – 7.82 % from the lower bound. The mean total completion time of LA2 is 2.53 % – 6.77 % from the lower bound. The mean total completion time of SCF is 4.14 % – 11.20 % from the lower bound. Generally, a bigger lookahead window produces better results. At this YC utilization level, even the SCF can be said to produce acceptable results. However LAP2 still leads to better results and the computational time consumed is very little, as shown in Table 8. Table 8 shows the computational time for the 90 % YC utilization level for the 40-slot yard block. The amounts of computational time for other experimental setting are very similar.

Table 6. Total completion time (TCT) performance (67.5 % YC utilization, 40-slot block): $(TCT_x - TCT_{LB})/TCT_{LB}*100$ %

Number of jobs	10			20			30		
Algorithm	LAP1	LAP2	SCF	LAP1	LAP2	SCF	LAP1	LAP2	SCF
Mean	5.89	4.36	7.81	3.96	3.20	5.05	3.23	2.53	4.14
Median	4.55	3.21	6.39	3.71	2.40	4.75	2.97	1.92	4.29
75 percentile	6.24	5.04	8.53	4.23	4.24	5.10	3.45	2.73	4.51
90 percentile	12.42	7.68	10.89	5.55	5.52	6.22	4.96	4.10	5.42
Maximum	10.83	8.03	12.10	12.15	5.31	9.40	6.16	8.55	6.39

Table 7. Total completion time (TCT) performance (67.5 % YC utilization, 50-slot block): $(TCT_x - TCT_{LB})/TCT_{LB}*100$ %

Number of jobs	10			20			30		
Algorithm	LAP1	LAP2	SCF	LAP1	LAP2	SCF	LAP1	LAP2	SCF
Mean	7.82	6.77	11.20	4.72	4.19	6.01	3.50	2.83	4.29
Median	7.23	6.28	10.33	4.54	4.23	5.88	3.19	2.89	4.48
75 percentile	9.33	8.40	15.30	5.46	5.03	6.65	3.81	3.17	4.82
90 percentile	14.73	11.60	18.74	7.14	6.68	7.23	4.75	3.38	4.61
Maximum	12.77	11.90	18.11	7.81	6.56	8.77	5.60	4.33	5.42

Table 8. Computational time of LAP1, LAP2 and SCF (seconds).

		LAP1	LAP2	SCF
40-slot block (90 % YC utilization)	10	0.004	0.006	0.001
	20	0.014	0.019	0.004
	30	0.028	0.036	0.010

With these results, we see that LAP2 is better than LAP1 in producing smaller total completion time. The computational time of LAP2 is also not excessive. So it may be worthwhile to investigate whether it is beneficial to look ahead more jobs. This will be left for future studies.

5 Conclusions

We propose two algorithms based on the cooperative approach of the non-zero-sum game for solving the twin-YC scheduling and dispatching problem. Simulation experiments are conducted to evaluate all algorithms proposed, together with the Smallest Completion time First heuristic, against a lower bound of total completion time. The results show that the two-step lookahead algorithm performs well.

In real operations, the safe/practical separation distance is 3 slots for RMGs and 8 slots for RTGs. We use 1 slot separation distance in order to have the same setting as the lower bound algorithm. More experiments will be conducted to evaluate the performance of our algorithms using various settings in practice.

References

Cao, Z., Lee, D.H., Meng, Q.: Deployment strategies of double-rail-mounted gantry crane systems for loading outbound containers in container terminals. Int. J. Prod. Econ. **115**, 221–228 (2008)

Choe, R., Yuan, H., Yang, Y. Ryu, K.R.: Real-time scheduling of twin stacking cranes in an automated container terminal using a genetic algorithm. In: Symposium of Applied Computing, pp. 238–243 (2012)

Dorndorf, U., Schneider, F.: Scheduling automated triple cross-over stacking cranes in a container yard. OR Spectr. **32**(3), 617–632 (2010)

Gharehgozli, A.H., Laporte, G., Yu, Y., de Koster, R.: Scheduling twin yard cranes in a container block. Transp. Sci. **9**(3), 706–719 (2015)

Guo, X., Huang, S.Y., Hsu, W.J., Low, M.Y.H.: Dynamic yard crane dispatching in container terminals with predicted vehicle arrival information. Adv. Eng. Inform. **25**(3), 472–484 (2011)

Guo, X., Huang, S.Y.: Dynamic space and time partitioning for yard crane workload management in container terminals. Transp. Sci. **46**(1), 134–148 (2012)

Huang, S.Y., Li, Y., Fan, F.: TwinCrane-ATCRSS-game: job dispatching with lookahead for twin yard cranes. In: The 5th International Conference on Logistics and Maritime Systems (2015)

Jung, S.H., Kim, K.H.: Load scheduling for multiple quay cranes in port container terminals. J. Intell. Manuf. **17**, 479–492 (2006)

Kumar, M.M., Omkar, S.N.: Optimization of yard crane scheduling using particle swarm optimization with genetic algorithm operators (PSOGAO). J. Sci. Ind. Res. **67**, 335–339 (2008)

Lee, D.H., Cao, Z., Meng, Q.: Scheduling of two-transtainer systems for loading outbound containers in port container terminals with simulated annealing algorithm. Int. J. Prod. Econ. **107**, 115–124 (2007)

Li, W., Wu, Y., Petering, M., Goh, M., de Souza, R.: Discrete time model and algorithms for container yard crane scheduling. Eur. J. Oper. Res. **198**, 165–172 (2009)

Ng, W.C.: Crane scheduling in container yards with intercrane interference. Eur. J. Oper. Res. **164**, 64–78 (2005)

Ng, W.C., Mak, K.L.: An effective heuristic for scheduling a yard crane to handle jobs with different ready times. Eng. Optim. **37**(8), 867–877 (2005a)

Ng, W.C., Mak, K.L.: Yard crane scheduling in port container terminals. Appl. Math. Model. **29** (3), 263–276 (2005b)

Park, T., Choe, R., Ok, S.M., Ryu, K.R.: Real-time scheduling for twin RMGs in an automated container yard. OR Spectr. **32**, 593–615 (2010)

Stahlbock, R., Voss, S.: Efficiency consideration for sequencing and scheduling of double-rail-mounted gantry cranes at maritime container terminals. Int. J. Shipping Transp. Logistics **2**(1), 95–123 (2010)

Vis, I.F.A., Carlo, H.J.: Sequencing two cooperating automated stacking cranes in a container terminal. Transp. Sci. **44**(2), 169–182 (2010)

Online and Offline Container Purchasing and Repositioning Problem

Neil Jami$^{(\boxtimes)}$, Michael Schröder, and Karl-Heinz Küfer

Fraunhofer Institute for Industrial Mathematics (ITWM),
67663 Kaiserslautern, Germany
neil.jami@itwm.fraunhofer.de

Abstract. We study the management of containers in a logistic chain between a supplier and a manufacturer in a ramp-up scenario where the demand is stochastic and expected to increase. This paper extends our previous study with deterministic demand. We consider a periodic review system with T periods of R time steps. The supplier sends full containers at every step and receives empty containers every period. We consider positive lead times. To face demand increase, the manufacturer can purchase reusable containers at a setup cost while the supplier can buy single-use disposables. Using a dynamic programming framework, we develop an online exact algorithm and an offline heuristic.

1 Introduction

We consider a closed-loop supply chain between a manufacturer and its supplier in which the items are transported in packages. A package is either a returnable container or a one-way disposable. In our application from the research project "Visual Logistics Management (VILOMA)", the supplier sends items to the manufacturer on a daily basis, and orders empty containers back on a weekly basis. Disposables like cardboard boxes are directly available by the supplier and are used whenever no container is available. In our scenario, the demand is expected to increase, so we need an efficient purchasing plan of containers. In particular, purchasing new containers incurs a setup cost and should hence only be done occasionally. Moreover, it takes a few days to transport the packages to their destination. This paper extends the container purchasing and repositioning problem from Jami et al. [1] to stochastic demands.

This paper builds up on three streams of research, namely the stochastic inventory control, the stochastic lot-sizing and the empty container repositioning. Among stochastic inventory control systems, we are particularly interested in a lost-sales behavior where unmet demand is lost, as it is equivalent to our use of disposables. It is well-known in the literature that lost-sales models are very complex. Janakiraman and Muckstadt [2] derive properties of optimal policies in a stochastic inventory control with lost-sales and fractional lead time. Fractional lead times correspond in our case to transportation times shorter than one week. Contrary to them, holding costs in our setting are incurred not only at the end

© Springer International Publishing Switzerland 2016
A. Paias et al. (Eds.): ICCL 2016, LNCS 9855, pp. 159–174, 2016.
DOI: 10.1007/978-3-319-44896-1_11

of each week, but also every day. Halman et al. [3] solve a stochastic inventory control problem using dynamic programming. Moreover, they prove the convexity of the cost functions and derive a fully-polynomial time approximation scheme (FPTAS). Our paper uses $L^\natural$-convexity (L-natural convexity), which is a generalization of convexity introduced by Murota [4]. Zipkin [5] applies it to characterize optimal inventory control policies in a system with lost-sales and lead times. Simchi-Levi et al. [6] summary some results we use in this paper. Chen et al. [7] use the $L^\natural$-convexity properties from [5] and deduce a pseudo-polynomial approximation scheme similar to the FPTAS in [3].

Lot-sizing usually consists in purchasing non-returnable items given a purchasing setup cost and a holding cost. A fundamental study has been proposed by Wagner and Within [8] when the demand is deterministic. They solve the problem using dynamic programming. Lot-sizing problems with stochastic demands are very challenging. Bookbinder and Tan [9] describe three alternative generalizations of the lot-sizing problem: a *dynamic* strategy, a *static* strategy and a *static-dynamic* strategy. In the dynamic strategy, every decision is taken online. In the static approach, the purchasing quantities are decided at the beginning of the time horizon. In the static-dynamic strategy, purchasing times are chosen at the start, but the actual quantities are dynamically decided. Levi and Shi [10] consider the dynamic strategy and develop a randomized cost-balancing policy that is at most three times as expensive as the optimal policy. Vargas [11] solves the static stochastic lot-sizing problem when unmet demand is backlogged. Özen et al. [12] compute a static-dynamic strategy using a dynamic program similar to ours.

Finally, empty container repositioning processes (ECR) manage container flows to ensure that demands are satisfied. This stream of research usually does not include container purchasing. Erera et al. [13,14] consider ECR in the chemical industry, and extend their deterministic model to stochastic demand using a robust optimization approach with budget. Li et al. [15] study a ECR over multiple ports with immediate lead times and stationary demands. They use a Markov decision process framework and prove that the cost functions are convex. They deduce that the optimal solution has a threshold-control structure, represented by a minimum and a maximum stock level at each port. Lam et al. [16] use approximate dynamic programming to solve the multi-period ECR.

Our paper is structured as follows. Section 2 describes our container purchasing management problem. In Sect. 3, we model a Markov decision process for the online strategy. In Sect. 4, we show that the cost function are $L^\natural$-convex if we remove the setup costs. In Sect. 5, we propose an heuristic for the offline strategy using dynamic programming and $L^\natural$-convexity. Simulations in Sect. 6 test the performance of the heuristic. Finally, we discuss future research directions.

2   Problem Description

We use the interval notation $[x, y]$ to denote the set of integral values between x and y. We consider a time horizon of T periods, where each period is divided into R time steps. We denote by $(t,r) \in [0, T-1] \times [0, R-1]$ the point in time defined by the time step r of period t. For convenience, we sometimes write time (t, R) instead of $(t+1, 0)$. At time (t, r) the supplier must fulfill a demand $d_{t,r}$, realization of the random variable $D_{t,r}$. We assume that the demand cannot exceed a value $D_{\max}$. We denote by L_{ord} (resp. L_{del}) the ordering (resp. delivery) delay, i.e. number of time steps required to send empty containers (resp. full containers) from the manufacturer to the supplier (resp. from the supplier to the manufacturer). These lead times are assumed short, but not negligible:

$$0 < L_{ord} + L_{del} \leq R \qquad (1)$$

We call *order size* β_t the number of empty containers sent from the manufacturer to the supplier at time $(t, 0)$, and denote by α_t the number of containers purchased before ordering. At time (t, r), the sequence of events is:

1. If $r = 0$, the manufacturer purchases α_t containers, then the supplier orders β_t empty containers.
2. Demand $D_{t,r}$ occurs and is fulfilled using the available packages.
3. Outgoing containers arrive to their respective locations:
   – The containers used for demand at time $(t, r) - (L_{del} - 1)$ are added to the manufacturer stock.
   – If $r = L_{ord} - 1$, β_t containers are added to the supplier stock.

A consequence of positive delivery times is that full containers sent to the manufacturer during period t after time step $r = R - L_{del}$ will arrive after the ordering of empty containers at period $t+1$ and can only be ordered again starting from period $t+2$. We call a time step r *early* if $r \leq R - L_{del}$ and late otherwise.

At the beginning of each period t, we denote by X_t the supplier stock, by Y_t the manufacturer stock and by Z_t the number of outgoing full containers. We call *container fleet size* U_t the number of containers in the system before purchasing. By (1), there is no outgoing order at time $(t, 0)$ and thus:

$$U_t = X_t + Y_t + Z_t. \qquad (2)$$

We consider the following costs. At time (t, r), a disposable costs $C_{dis}(t, r)$. Container holding costs are $C_{man}(t, r)$ for the manufacturer and $C_{sup}(t, r)$ for the supplier. We assume a non-speculative cost structure so that we rather let unused containers in the manufacturer stock:

$$0 < C_{man}(t, r) < C_{sup}(t', r') \quad \forall t, r, t', r' \qquad (3)$$

At period t, container purchasing incurs a setup cost of $C_{setup}(t)$ plus an additional cost $C_{cont}(t)$ per container. We suppose that it is always more profitable for the supplier to fulfill the earliest demand with the containers at disposal. Thus, the supplier will never hold containers while buying disposables.

Our objective is to find a purchasing and ordering policy minimizing the expected costs over the whole time horizon. Container ordering is an operational decision, because it has to be done dynamically depending on the supplier stock.

Therefore, we take the order decision β_t during period t Meanwhile, we see container purchasing as a tactical decision where at purchasing decision should look into the future to avoid additional purchasing in the near future, due to the setup costs. We consider two different strategies:

1. An *online strategy*, where the purchasing size α_t is decided at period t.
2. An *offline strategy*, where α_t is decided at $t = 0$.

Our online strategy extends the dynamic strategy from Bookbinder and Tan [9] and our offline strategy extends their static strategy. We do not consider in this paper an extension of the static-dynamic strategy, where the purchasing times are fixed first and the quantities are dynamically chosen. We believe that this third strategy is less impactful in a container management problem than in a lot-sizing without containers due to the stability of the container stocks. However, this strategy is a meaningful future research direction as we would like to quantify the impact of dynamically deciding on the exact purchasing quantities on the expected costs of the system in the context of container management.

We conclude this section with an NP-hardness result using a similar reduction as in Halman et al. [3].

Lemma 1 *(Halman et al. [3]). The problem of computing the convolution of N independent random variables is NP-hard with respect to N. In particular, this problem is equivalent to computing the distribution of the sum of N independent random variables.*

Proposition 1. *Even under stationary cost functions, the container production planning problem is NP-hard with respect to R for each of the three strategies.*

Proof. Suppose that the container purchasing costs $C_{setup}(t)$ and $C_{cont}(t)$ are null and the time horizon consists in a single period: $T = 1$. Thus, every decision is taken at the beginning of the time horizon, so any policy is at the same time online and offline. The objective is to find an ordering quantity minimizing the costs over R time steps of demand, which is equivalent to computing the distribution of the sum of R independent random variables. By Lemma 1 this problem is NP-hard with respect to R.   □

3   Online Strategy

We model the online problem as a Markov decision process over $R \cdot T$ time steps, where the state at time (t, r) is noted $\boldsymbol{S_{t,r}}$. The decision $\boldsymbol{\gamma_t}$ at period t is:

$$\boldsymbol{\gamma_t} := [\alpha_t, \beta_t] \tag{4}$$

In this paper, we use capital letters for random variables and lower case letters for their realization. The realizations of $\boldsymbol{S_{t,r}}$, $X_{t,r}$, $Y_{t,r}$, $Z_{t,r}$ are thus denoted by $\boldsymbol{s_{t,r}}$, $x_{t,r}$, $y_{t,r}$, $z_{t,r}$. We denote by $\mathbb{P}_{t,r}(d) := \mathbb{P}(D_{t,r} = d)$ the probability that variable $D_{t,r}$ takes value d. We only need three parameters in $\boldsymbol{S_{t,r}}$:

$$S_{t,r} := [X_{t,r},\ Y_{t,r},\ Z_{t,r}]. \tag{5}$$

Since the decisions are only taken at times $(t,0)$, we define $S_{t,0} := [X_t, Y_t, Z_t]$ as our main states, while states $S_{t,r}$ for $r > 0$ are only transition states used to avoid the computation of R simultaneous demand variables, which would take a lot of time as shown by Lemma 1. Consider $t \in [0, T-1]$ and $r > 0$. We define $X_{t,r}$ as the supplier stock at time (t, r). We define $Y_{t,r}$ as the *ensured manufacturer stock* at time (t, r) for time $(t+1, 0)$, that is the current manufacturer stock plus the number of full containers which left the supplier before time (t, r) and arriving between times $(t, 1)$ and $(t+1, 0)$. We define $Z_{t,r}$ as the *ensured outgoing fleet* at time (t, r) for time $(t+1, 0)$ plus the outgoing order size. Thus, for $r \in [1, L_{ord}-1]$, $Z_{t,r}$ equals β_t; for $r \in [L_{ord}, R-L_{del}]$ we have $Z_{t,r} = 0$; and for $r > R-L_{del}$, $Z_{t,r}$ is the number of full containers which left the supplier before time (t, r) and will arrive to the manufacturer after time $(t+1, 0)$. Note that X_t, Y_t, Z_t correspond to the definition of $X_{t-1,R}, Y_{t-1,R}, Z_{t-1,R}$, so our notations are consistent. Let $\Delta_{t,r}$ be the number of containers used for demand $D_{t,r}$:

$$\Delta_{t,r} := \min\{D_{t,r}, X_{t,r}\} \tag{6}$$

Consider state $s_{t,r} = [x_{t,r}, y_{t,r}, z_{t,r}]$, demand realization $d_{t,r}$ inducing $\delta_{t,r} := \min\{d_{t,r}, x_{t,r}\}$ full containers sent at time (t, r), and possibly decision $\gamma_t = [\alpha_t, \beta_t]$. The next state at time $(t, r+1)$ is then:

- For $r = 0$:

$$s_{t,1}[s_{t,0}, \gamma_t, d_{t,0}] = [x_{t,0} - \delta_{t,0};\ y_{t,0} + \alpha_t - \beta_t + z_{t,0} + \delta_{t,0};\ \beta_t] \tag{7}$$

- For $r \in [1, L_{ord} - 2]$:

$$s_{t,r+1}[s_{t,r}, d_{t,r}] = [x_{t,r} - \delta_{t,r};\ y_{t,r} + \delta_{t,r};\ z_{t,r}] \tag{8}$$

- For $r = L_{ord} - 1$:

$$s_{t,r+1}[s_{t,r}, d_{t,r}] = [z_{t,r} + x_{t,r} - \delta_{t,r};\ y_{t,r} + \delta_{t,r};\ 0] \tag{9}$$

- For $r \in [L_{ord} + 1, R - L_{del}]$:

$$s_{t,r+1}[s_{t,r}, d_{t,r}] = [x_{t,r} - \delta_{t,r};\ y_{t,r} + \delta_{t,r};\ 0] \tag{10}$$

- For $r > R - L_{del}$:

$$s_{t,r+1}[s_{t,r}, d_{t,r}] = [x_{t,r} - \delta_{t,r};\ y_{t,r};\ z_{t,r} + \delta_{t,r}] \tag{11}$$

Lemma 2. *The state and action parameters at each time (t, r) verify:*

- $0 \le x_{t,r} \le (R + L_{ord}) \cdot D_{\max}$
- $0 \le y_{t,r} \le (R + L_{ord} + L_{del}) \cdot D_{\max}$
- $0 \le z_{t,r} \le L_{del} \cdot D_{\max}$
- $0 \le \alpha_t \le (R + L_{ord} + L_{del}) \cdot D_{\max}$

$- 0 \leq \beta_t \leq R \cdot D_{\max}$

Moreover, an upper bound of the optimal container fleet size is:

$$U_M := (R + L_{ord} + L_{del}) \cdot D_{\max} \leq 2 \cdot R \cdot D_{\max} \tag{12}$$

Proof. The maximum demand between two ordering arrivals is $R \cdot D_{\max}$. Therefore, whenever we order more than $R \cdot D_{\max}$ containers, some containers will be left in the supplier stock before the next order arrival. We deduce: $\forall t, \ \beta_t \leq R \cdot D_{\max}$. Likewise, if the inventory position is above $(R + L_{ord}) \cdot D_{\max}$, the stock before order arrival will not be empty, hence: $x_{t,r} \leq x_t + \beta_t \leq (R + L_{ord}) \cdot D_{\max}$. The maximum container fleet size is so that we can create an ordering policy never buying any disposable. It is thus bounded by the maximum inventory position given that the number of outgoing containers is maximum. The number of outgoing containers at $r = 0$ is bounded by: $z_t \leq L_{del} \cdot D_{\max}$. We hence have the upper bound $U_M := (R + L_{ord} + L_{del}) \cdot D_{\max}$ of the optimal fleet size. Any container over U_M will stay in the manufacturer stock during the whole process, hence only incurring additional purchasing and holding costs. Since we will never have more than U_M containers, we will never purchase more than U_M containers at once and the manufacturer will never have more than U_M containers in stock: $\alpha_t, y_t \leq U_M = (R + L_{ord} + L_{del}) \cdot D_{\max}$.   □

We denote by *EoH* the end of the time horizon, i.e. time $(T, 0)$. Let $\varphi_{t,r}^*(s)$ be the expected cost of an optimal policy starting from state s at time (t, r) up to EoH, and $\varphi_t^*(s) := \varphi_{t,0}^*(s)$. Let $\varphi_t^*(s, \gamma)$ be the minimum expected cost starting from state s and decision γ at time $(t, 0)$ and up to EoH, when future decisions are taken optimally. Then:

$$\varphi_t^*(s) = \min_{\gamma} \varphi_t^*(s, \gamma) \tag{13}$$

We denote by $\psi_{t,r}(s, d)$ the costs incurred at time (t, r) when starting from state s and under demand d, and by $\psi_t(s, \gamma, d)$ the costs at time $(t, 0)$ under state s, decision γ and demand d.

– For $r = 0$:

$$\varphi_t^*(s, \gamma) = \sum_d \mathbb{P}_{t,0}(d) \cdot \left(\psi_t(s, \gamma, d) + \varphi_{t,1}^* (s_{t,1}[s, \gamma, d], \gamma) \right) \tag{14}$$

– For $r \in [1, R - 1]$:

$$\varphi_{t,r}^*(s) = \sum_d \mathbb{P}_{t,r}(d) \cdot \left(\psi_{t,r}(s, d) + \varphi_{t,r+1}^* (s_{t,r+1}[s, d]) \right) \tag{15}$$

The single time step costs $\psi_{t,r}$ must be defined as a function of the current state s, demand d and decision γ. The ensured manufacturer stock $Y_{t,r}$ is greater than the actual manufacturer stock as it contains the full containers which should arrive later in the current period. Therefore, the cost $\psi_{t,r}$ must already include the manufacturer holding cost of the $V_{t,r}$ full containers from their planned arrival (t', r') up to the next ordering time $(t' + 1, 0)$. At time $(t, 0)$, we consider in addition the holding cost for each container which has not been ordered and will thus stay idle in the manufacturer stock up to the next ordering time $(t+1, 0)$. Let $C_{man}(t, r \rightarrow R)$ denote the total manufacturer holding cost of a container from time (t, r) to time $(t+1, 0)$, so that $C_{man}(t, R-1 \rightarrow R) = C_{man}(t, R-1)$ and $C_{man}(t, R \rightarrow R) = 0$. We define the single step cost function $\psi_{t,r}$ as following:

- If $r = 0$:

$$\psi_{t,r}(s, \gamma, d) = (d - \delta) \cdot C_{dis}(t, 0) + \delta \cdot C_{man}(t, L_{del} \rightarrow R)$$
$$+ (x - \delta) \cdot C_{sup}(t, 0) + (y + \alpha - \beta) \cdot C_{man}(t, 0 \rightarrow R) \quad (16)$$

- If $r \in [1, R - L_{del}]$:

$$\psi_{t,r}(s, d) = (d - \delta) \cdot C_{dis}(t, r) + \delta \cdot C_{man}(t, r + L_{del} \rightarrow R)$$
$$+ (x - \delta) \cdot C_{sup}(t, r) \quad (17)$$

- If $r > R - L_{del}$:

$$\psi_{t,r}(s, d) = (d - \delta) \cdot C_{dis}(t, r) + \delta \cdot C_{man}(t + 1, r + L_{del} - R \rightarrow R)$$
$$+ (x - \delta) \cdot C_{sup}(t, r) \quad (18)$$

Algorithm 1 computes an optimal online policy to the container purchasing problem. We note that the optimal policy corresponding to φ_t^* is computed at the same time as its expected cost, so we will equivalently say that we compute an optimal policy or its expected cost.

Algorithm 1. Online Exact Algorithm

$\varphi_T^*(s) := 0$ for all s;
for *period t from $T - 1$ to 0* **do**
    for *step r from $R - 1$ to 1* **do**
        for each *state $s_{t,r}$* **do**
             Compute $\varphi_{t,r}^*(s_{t,r})$ using (14), (17) and (18);

    for each *state s_t* **do**
        for each *decision γ_t* **do**
             Compute $\varphi_t^*(s_t, \gamma_t)$ using (13), (15) and (16);
        $\varphi_t^*(s_t) := \min_\gamma \left[\varphi_t^*(s_t, \gamma) \right]$;
return $\varphi_t^*([0, 0, 0])$;

Theorem 1. *Algorithm 1 computes an optimal online policy in $O(T \cdot R^5 \cdot D_{\max}^6)$ time.*

Proof. By Lemma 2, the state space is $O(R^3 \cdot D_{\max}^3)$, the demand space $O(D_{\max})$ and the decision space $O(R^2 \cdot D_{\max}^2)$. There are T time steps with decision and $(R - 1) \cdot T$ steps without, so the total complexity is $O(T \cdot R^5 \cdot D_{\max}^6)$. $\qquad\square$

4 $L^\natural$-Convexity Under Linear Costs

In this section, we exclude the setup costs $C_{setup}(t)$ from the process, and prove that the cost functions are then $L^\natural$-convex with respect to the decision γ_t. We use alternative states similarly to Zipkin [5].

4.1 Literature Results

We denote by $\mathcal{E}$ a one dimensional space, and by $\mathcal{E}^+$ its restriction to positive values. The vector of '1' is denoted e. Given two vectors $w = [w_1, \ldots, w_n] \in \mathcal{E}^n$ and $w' = [w'_1, \ldots, w'_n] \in \mathcal{E}^n$, we define:

$$w \wedge w' := \big[\min\{w_1, w'_1\}, \ldots, \min\{w_n, w'_n\}\big] \tag{19}$$

$$w \vee w' := \big[\max\{w_1, w'_1\}, \ldots, \max\{w_n, w'_n\}\big] \tag{20}$$

Definition 1. *A space $\mathcal{E}^n$ is lattice if for each $w, w' \in \mathcal{E}^n$ and $\lambda \in \mathcal{E}^+$, the vectors $(w + \lambda \cdot e) \wedge w'$ and $w \vee (w' - \lambda \cdot e)$ are also in $\mathcal{E}^n$.*

Definition 2. *A function $f : \mathcal{E}^n \to \mathbb{R}$ is $L^\natural$-convex if $\mathcal{E}^n$ is lattice and for each $w, w' \in \mathcal{E}^n$ and $\lambda \in \mathcal{E}^+$, we have:*

$$f(w) + f(w') \geq f((w + \lambda \cdot e) \wedge w') + f(w \vee (w' - \lambda \cdot e)) \tag{21}$$

Theorem 2 *[Simchi-Levi et al. 2013]*.

1. *Any set with representation $\{w \in \mathcal{E}^n : l \leq w \leq u, \ w_i - w_j \leq v_{i,j} \ \forall i \neq j\}$ is lattice, where $l, u \in \mathcal{E}^n$ and $v_{i,j} \in \mathcal{E}(i \neq j)$. In fact, any closed lattice set in the space $\mathcal{E}^n$ can have such a representation.*
2. *A function $f : \mathcal{E}^n \to \mathbb{R}$ is $L^\natural$-convex if and only if the function $g(w, \lambda) := f(w - \lambda \cdot e)$ is $L^\natural$-convex.*
3. *If $f_1, f_2 : \mathcal{E}^n \to \mathbb{R}$ are $L^\natural$-convex and $\lambda \in \mathcal{E}^+$, then $\lambda \cdot f_1 + f_2$ is also $L^\natural$-convex.*
4. *If $f(\cdot, \cdot) : \mathcal{E}^n \times \mathcal{E}^m \to \mathbb{R}$ is $L^\natural$-convex with respect to its first parameter, then $g(v) := \mathbb{E}_w[f(v, w)]$ is also $L^\natural$-convex, if it is well defined.*
5. *If $f(\cdot) : \mathcal{E}^n \to \mathbb{R}$ is $L^\natural$-convex, then $g : \mathcal{E}^{n+1} \to \mathbb{R}$ defined by $g(v, \lambda) := f(v - \lambda \cdot e)$ is also $L^\natural$-convex.*
6. *If $f(\cdot, \cdot) : \mathcal{E}^n \times \mathcal{E}^m \to \mathbb{R}$ is $L^\natural$-convex, then the function $g(v) := \inf_w f(v, w)$ is also $L^\natural$-convex.*
7. *The minimum of a $L^\natural$-convex function can be found using a binary search.*

We consider the following two hypothesis used by Chen et al. [7], adapted to our model with T periods of R time steps:

Conjecture 1. For each time (t, r), state s, decision γ, demand d, the functions $\varphi^*_{t,r}(s), \psi_t(s, \gamma, d), \psi_{t,r}(s, d)$ are $L^\natural$-convex and their definition domain is lattice.

Conjecture 2. For each time (t, r), the functions $s_{t,1}[s, \gamma, d]$ and $s_{t,r+1}[s, d]$ computing the next state are $L^\natural$-convex in (s, γ) for every demand realization d.

Chen et al. [7] prove that under Conjectures 1 and 2, the cost functions of the problem are $L^\natural$-convex, so by Theorem 2.(7) we can use a binary search to find the optimal decision in logarithmic time with respect to the decision space.

4.2 Application to Our Case

We set the number of containers $\delta_{t,r} \in [0, d_{t,r}]$ used for demand $d_{t,r}$ as a decision variable. By assumption, the value of $\delta_{t,r}$ minimizing the expected costs is:

$$\delta_{t,r}^* = \min(x_{t,r}, \; d_{t,r}). \tag{22}$$

For time (t,r) t, we define state $\hat{s}_{t,r}$ as following:

– For $r = 0$:
$$\hat{s}_{t,0} := [x_t; \; -y_t - z_t; \; -z_t] \tag{23}$$

– For $r = 1$:
$$\hat{s}_{t,1} := \left[\hat{x}_{t,0} - \delta_{t,0}^*; \; \hat{y}_{t,0} + \hat{z}_{t,0} + \beta_t - \alpha_t - \delta_{t,0}^*; \; \beta_t\right] \tag{24}$$

– For $r \in [2, \; L_{ord} - 1]$:
$$\hat{s}_{t,r} := \left[\hat{x}_{t,r-1} - \delta_{t,r-1}^*; \; \hat{y}_{t,r-1} - \delta_{t,r-1}^*; \; \hat{z}_{t,r-1}\right] \tag{25}$$

– For $r = L_{ord}$:
$$\hat{s}_{t,L_{ord}} := [\hat{x}_{t,L_{ord}-1} + \hat{z}_{t,r-1}; \; \hat{y}_{t,L_{ord}-1}; \; 0] - \delta_{t,L_{ord}-1}^* \cdot e \tag{26}$$

– For $r \in [L_{ord} + 1, \; R - L_{del}]$:
$$\hat{s}_{t,r} := [\hat{x}_{t,r-1}; \; \hat{y}_{t,r-1}; \; 0] - \delta_{t,r-1}^* \cdot e \tag{27}$$

– For $r \in [R - L_{del} + 1, \; R]$:
$$\hat{s}_{t,r} := [\hat{x}_{t,r-1}; \; \hat{y}_{t,r-1}; \; \hat{z}_{t,r-1}] - \delta_{t,r-1}^* \cdot e \tag{28}$$

We easily check using Theorem 2.(1) and Lemma 2 that the definition domain of $\hat{s}_{t,r}$ is lattice for every (t,r). Therefore, the definition domains of $\varphi_t^*(\hat{s})$, $\psi_t(\hat{s}, \gamma, d)$ and $\psi_{t,r}(\hat{s}, d)$ are also lattice. By construction, starting from state s_t, decision γ_t at time $(t,0)$ and with the same demand realizations $d_{t,0}$ to $d_{t,R-1}$, the states $s_{t+1,0}$ and $\hat{s}_{t+1,0}$ generated with (7) to (11) and with (23) to (28) are equivalent. Consequently, we can compute state $s_{t,r}$ from $\hat{s}_{t,r}$ and use the same linear cost functions $\varphi_{t,r}^*$ and $\psi_{t,r}$. We prove by recurrence on time (t,r) using Theorem 2.(2,3,5,6) and starting from the EoH costs $\varphi_{T,0}^* = 0$ that the cost functions $\psi_{t,r}$ and $\varphi_{t,r}^*$ are $L^\natural$-convex. We can thus replace states $s_{t,r}$ by $\hat{s}_{t,r}$ in Algorithm 1 and use a binary search to find the optimal decisions.

Theorem 3. *Without setup costs, Algorithm 1 computes an optimal online policy in* $O\big(T \cdot R^4 \cdot D_{\max}^4 \cdot \log[D_{\max} \cdot R]^2\big)$ *time.*

Proof. We follow the same lead as in Theorem 1, but the decision space size is $O(\log[D_{\max} \cdot R]^2)$. □

5   Offline Heuristic

A naive approach to compute an optimal offline policy is to consider every possible purchasing plan. The time complexity grows then exponentially with R and D_{max}, as will be shown in Sect. 6. In this section, we propose an offline heuristic based on the online algorithm from Sect. 4. We first use the same states $s_{t,r}$ as in Algorithm 1, and show afterward how to efficiently compute the offline policy.

We denote by $\varphi^*[k_1, k_2, u_\alpha](s_{k_1})$ the expected cost of an optimal offline policy from state s_{k_1} at period k_1 to EoH so that k_1 and k_2 are the first two placements and so that the container fleet size after purchasing at period k_1 is u_α. We compute a policy along with its expected cost, so our objective is equivalent to computing the expected cost of the optimal policy. We denote by $\varphi^*[k_2](s_{k_2})$ the optimal offline policy cost from state s_{k_2} at period k_2 to EoH. The policy $\varphi^*[k_2]$ is so that the container fleet size after purchasing at period k_2 is the same for each starting state s_{k_2} at period k_2. We only consider values of u_α lower than the fleet size after purchasing at period k_2, as otherwise there is no purchasing at period k_2 while we pay the unnecessary cost $C_{setup}(k_2)$. Given the costs $\varphi^*[k_2]$, we can compute $\varphi^*[k_1, k_2, u_\alpha]$ using backward dynamic programming.

For a fixed k_1, there are two values $k_2^*(k_1) > k_1$ and $u_\alpha^*(k_1)$ inducing an optimal policy with cost $\varphi^*[k_1] := \varphi^*[k_1, k_2^*(k_1), u_\alpha^*(k_1)]$ from period k_1 to EoH. If a state s_{k_1} at time $(k_1, 0)$ starts with a higher fleet size than $u_\alpha^*(k_1)$, this state is excluded from the search as it can not be attained from an optimal policy.

However, as it will be shown in our simulations, different values of S_{k_1} at period k_1 may lead to different best values of $k_2(k_1)$ and $u_\alpha(k_1)$. When using a Markov decision process, we thus need the probability distribution of S_{k_1} at period k_1 to find $k_2^*(k_1)$. Contrary to [8] and [11], the optimal solution after purchasing period k_1 depends therefore on the optimal solution before purchasing time k_1. The state probability distribution at period k_1 can only be derived from an optimal policy up to period k_1. But in order to get it, we need the expected cost $\varphi[k_1](s_{k_1})$ for each state s_{k_1} at period k_1, which we actually want to compute.

Our heuristic neglects the influence of the state s_{k_1} on the optimal container fleet size after period k_1. Hence, we approximate the optimal container fleet size $u_\alpha^*(k_1)$ after purchasing and the next purchasing time $k_2^*(k_1)$ as the cost minimizing values $u_\alpha'(k_1)$ and $k_2'(k_1)$ when starting from the *reference state* $s_{k_1}' := [0,0,0]$ at time $(k_1, 0)$. We would like $u_\alpha'(k_1)$ and $k_2'(k_1)$ to be close to $u_\alpha^*(k_1)$ and $k_2^*(k_1)$. Then, for each other state s_{k_1}, we set $u_{k_1} := x_{k_1} + y_{k_1} + z_{k_1}$, $\alpha_{k_1}(s_{k_1}) := u_\alpha'(k_1) - u_{k_1}$ and compute the optimal order size β_{k_1} given $u_\alpha'(k_1)$ and $k_2'(k_1)$. Since we are only computing a suboptimal solution, we use the notation φ instead of φ^*. Our hybrid policy computes $\varphi[k_1, k_2]$ from $\varphi[k_2]$, and deduce $k_2'(k_1)$ and $u_\alpha'(k_1)$. The optimal solution is approximated by:

$$\varphi[k_1] := \varphi[k_1, k_2'(k_1), u_\alpha'(k_1)] \tag{29}$$

Our algorithm is initialized with the EoH costs:

$$\forall s, \ \varphi[T](s) = 0 \tag{30}$$

Without loss of generality, we can assume that some containers are purchased at period 0. To relax this assumption, we add a dummy period -1 with zero demand, zero manufacturer holding cost and infinite supplier holding costs. We now explain how to efficiently compute $\varphi[k_1, k_2]$ from $\varphi[k_2]$ using backward programming and the $L^{\natural}$-convexity. For $k_2 \in [1, T]$ and given cost $\varphi[k_2]$, we define $\phi'[k_1, k_2](s)$ as the expected cost of the optimal policy starting from state s at time $(k_1, 1)$ up to EoH without purchasing containers before period k_2 and so that the expected cost from state s_{k_2} at period k_2 up to EoH is $\varphi[k_2](s_{k_2})$.

Lemma 3. *Consider a period k_2 and suppose that the costs $\varphi[k_2]$ are known and $L^{\natural}$-convex. Then, the costs $\phi'[k_1, k_2]$ for all $k_1 \in [0, k_2 - 1]$ are also $L^{\natural}$-convex and can be computed altogether in $O(T \cdot R^4 \cdot D_{max}^4 \cdot \log[R \cdot D_{max}])$ time.*

Proof. For a fixed k_2, all $\phi'[k_1, k_2]$ can be computed altogether with a single backward dynamic program starting from $\varphi[k_2]$ up to time $(k_1, 1)$, with $O(R \cdot T)$ iterations. Since we are not purchasing any container while computing $\phi'[k_1, k_2]$, we prove using the same reasoning and the same states $\hat{s}_{t,r}$ as in Sect. 4, that the cost of all $\phi'[k_1, k_2]$ are $L^{\natural}$-convex. By Lemma 2, the state space is $O(R^3 \cdot D_{max}^3)$ and the decision space is $O(R \cdot D_{max})$. Due to the $L^{\natural}$-convexity, we get the best ordering size in $O(\log[R \cdot D_{max}])$ time. With the same reasoning as Theorems 1 and 3, the total complexity is $O(T \cdot R^4 \cdot D_{max}^4 \cdot \log[R \cdot D_{max}])$. □

Lemma 4. *Consider periods k_1 and k_2 and suppose that the costs $\phi'(k_1, k_2)$ are known and $L^{\natural}$-convex. Then the costs $\varphi[k_1]$ are also $L^{\natural}$-convex and can be computed in $O(T \cdot R^3 \cdot D_{max}^4 \cdot \log[R \cdot D_{max}])$ time.*

Proof. The policy relative to $\varphi[k_1]$ already includes the setup cost $C_{setup}(k_1)$, thus the computation of the costs $\varphi[k_1]$ only consider linear costs and the $L^{\natural}$-convex cost functions $\phi'(k_1, k_2)$. Using the same reasoning as in Lemma 3, the cost $\varphi[k_1, k_2, u_{\alpha}](\hat{s})$ is $L^{\natural}$-convex for each state $\hat{s}$ and every k_1, k_2, u_{α}. We compute $k_2'(k_1)$ and $u_{\alpha}'(k_1)$ using a binary search on the purchasing and ordering decisions over a single time step and a single state, which takes $O(T \cdot D_{max} \cdot \log[R \cdot D_{max}]^2)$ time. We then compute $\varphi[k_1] := \varphi[k_1, k_2'(k_1), u_{\alpha}'(k_1)]$ for $O(R^3 \cdot D_{max}^3)$ states and with a binary search for the order size, which takes $O(R^3 \cdot D_{max}^4 \cdot \log[R \cdot D_{max}])$ time. The total complexity is $O(T \cdot R^3 \cdot D_{max}^4 \cdot \log[R \cdot D_{max}])$. □

Proposition 2. *Every cost $\phi'(k_1, k_2)$ for $0 \leq k_1 < k_2 \leq T$ is $L^{\natural}$-convex and can be computed altogether in $O(T^2 \cdot R^3 \cdot D_{max}^4 \cdot \log[R \cdot D_{max}])$ time.*

Proof. This proposition is proven by recurrence. For $k_2 = T$, the costs $\varphi(T) = 0$ are $L^{\natural}$-convex. Therefore the costs $\phi'(k_1, T)$ for $k_1 \in [0, T-1]$ are $L^{\natural}$-convex and we compute them them $O(T \cdot R^4 \cdot D_{max}^4 \cdot \log[R \cdot D_{max}])$ time. Consider now a value of $k_2 \in [1, T-1]$ and suppose that for all $k_4 \in [k_2 + 1, T]$ and all $k_3 \in [0, k_2]$, the cost $\phi'(k_3, k_4)$ is known and $L^{\natural}$-convex. In particular, the cost $\phi'(k_2, k'(k_2))$ is $L^{\natural}$-convex, and by Lemma 4 $\varphi(k_2)$ is $L^{\natural}$-convex and computed in $O(T \cdot R^4 \cdot D_{max}^4 \cdot \log[R \cdot D_{max}])$ time. By Lemma 3, for all $k_1 \in [0, k_2 - 1]$, the costs $\phi'(k_1, k_2)$ are also $L^\natural$-convex and take $O\left(T \cdot R^4 \cdot D_{\max}^4 \cdot \log[R \cdot D_{\max}]\right)$ time to compute. We conclude that all costs $\phi'(k_1, k_2)$ for $0 \leq k_1 < k_2 \leq T$ can be computed altogether in $O\left(T^2 \cdot R^4 \cdot D_{\max}^4 \cdot \log[R \cdot D_{\max}]\right)$ time.   □

Algorithm 2. Offline Heuristic Algorithm

$\varphi_T^*(s) := 0$ for all s;
for *period k from* $T - 1$ *to 0* **do**
    Compute $\phi'[k, k+1]$ from $\varphi[k+1]$;
    for *period t from* $k - 1$ *to 0* **do**
        Compute $\phi'(t, k+1)$ from $\phi'(t+1, k+1)$;
    Compute $k_2'(k)$ and $u_\alpha'(k)$ from $\{\phi'[k, k_2], \ k_2 > k\}$;
    Compute $\varphi(k)$ from $\phi'[k, k_2'(k)]$ and $u_\alpha'(k)$;

return $\varphi(0)[0, 0, 0]$;

Theorem 4. *Algorithm 2 computes an offline policy with the time complexity* $O\left(T^2 \cdot R^4 \cdot D_{\max}^4 \cdot \log[R \cdot D_{\max}]\right)$.

Proof. This theorem follows directly from Proposition 2 and Lemma 4.   □

6 Computational Study

In this section, we simulate and compare the efficiency of our offline heuristic with several algorithms taken as reference. Our objective is to compare the performance of our heuristic policy to a very slow optimal offline solution and to a fast and simple approximation. We use a virtual data set in order to highlight the strengths and weaknesses of our algorithms.

6.1 Reference Algorithms

First of all, we compute an optimal offline policy as following. For each purchasing plan, the purchasing costs are fixed, so the cost functions are $L^\natural$-convex and the optimal ordering decisions can be found using a binary search as described in Sect. 4. Under fixed purchasing plan, the value of z_t and α_t can be disregarded, so with the same reasoning as in Theorem 3, it then takes $O(T \cdot R^3 \cdot D_{\max}^3 \cdot \log[D_{\max} \cdot R])$ time to compute the optimal ordering policy. We then iterate over every possible purchasing. Since the maximum fleet size is $O(R \cdot D_{\max})$, there are in total $O(R^T \cdot D_{\max}^T)$ possible purchasing plans. In our simulations, we denote this optimal offline algorithm by *Opt-F*. Since the complexity of the optimal offline policy is exponential, we can only compute it for very small test instances. For bigger instances, we consider the optimal online policy from this paper, which is at least as good as the optimal offline policy.

On the other side, we compare the performance of Algorithm 2 to a simple offline heuristic. This simple heuristic computes the best policy while avoiding disposables at all costs. As a consequence, the order size follows immediately from the supplier stock. This simple algorithm is meaningful in our simulation where the support of each demand variable is a small interval. We note that this algorithm can be adapted to a bigger demand space by approximating the largest demand value by a quantile. We use an algorithm similar to the Wagner-Within algorithm [8] to deduce the purchasing plan from these minimum fleets, in $O(T^2)$ time. A forward dynamic program computes the expected cost of the policy. Since the fleet size is known for every period, we only need two state parameters so the complexity is $O(T \cdot R^3 \cdot D_{\max}^3)$. In our simulations, we denote this simple algorithm by *NoDis*.

6.2 Simulations

As pointed out by Özen et al. [12], Markov decision process based algorithms are slow in practice and cannot be used for big test instances. They develop a Markov decision process with a single state parameter, a single time step per period and one ordering decision per period. Using a binary search to find the optimal order, their algorithm already takes a few hours for a time horizon as small as $T = 18$ periods. For this reason, our simulations only consider a short time horizon $T \leq 15$, an aggregation of the time steps $R = 3$ and relatively small demand values. We set transportation delays as $L_{ord} = 1$ and $L_{del} = 2$, so that every period contains a time step before demand arrival and a time step with late demand. The asymmetry $L_{ord} = L_{del} - 1$ of the delays is a consequence of how we defined them. Indeed, suppose that a transport takes a little less that one time step. Empty containers depart at the beginning of a step and arrive before its end, while full packages depart during the step and arrive to the manufacturer during the next time step, hence after container ordering; finally we get $L_{ord} = 1$ but $L_{del} = 2$. We consider stationary costs, and write the vector of costs $C := [C_{man}, C_{sup}, C_{dis}, C_{setup}, C_{cont}]$. We model the demand variability as a binomial distribution $\mathcal{B}(n, p)$.

Table 1 shows the expected costs (rounded to an integer) and the running times (in seconds) of the considered algorithms on very small instances. In this

Table 1. Simulation 1: $C := [2, 6, 30, 200, 50]$, $D(t, r) \rightarrow 3 \cdot t + \mathcal{B}(2, 1/2)$

	$T = 3$	$T = 4$	$T = 5$	$T = 6$	$T = 7$	$T = 8$	$T = 9$	$T = 10$	$T = 15$
Algo.1 cost	1080	1946	2816	3832	5022	6335	7679	9147	-
Algo.1 time	0.4 s	2.5 s	11.0 s	37.6 s	104 s	243 s	521 s	1015 s	-
Opt-F cost	1080	1946	2816	(3832)	-	-	-	(9147)	-
Opt-F time	0.1 s	20.0 s	2514 s	-	-	-	-	-	-
Algo.2 cost	1236	1946	2816	3832	5035	6336	7728	9147	17672
Algo.2 time	0.0 s	0.2 s	0.5 s	1.7 s	3.4 s	6.8 s	12.7 s	22.0 s	208 s
NoDis cost	2244	3300	4482	5880	7280	8822	10366	12052	21352
NoDis time	0. s	0. s	0. s	0. s	0. s	0. s	0. s	0. s	0.1 s

Table 2. Simulation 2: $T = 4$, $D(t, r) \to 2 \cdot t + \mathcal{B}(2, 1/2)$

	Algo.1	Opt-F	Algo.2	NoDis
Running time	0.7 s	53.4 s	0.1 s	0 s
Cost for $C := [3, 6, 50, 100, 50]$	1816	1816	1816	2476
Cost for $C := [3, 6, 150, 10, 50]$	2046	2055	2136	2316
Cost for $C := [3, 6, 1500, 0, 50]$	3510	3547	3639	3636

first simulation the maximum demand value $D_{\max}(T) := 3 \cdot T + 2$ increases linearly with T. As a consequence, even for $T = 5$ it takes more than 40 min to compute the optimal offline policy. We note that the online policy does not scale very well, due to the absence of a convexity structure. Up to now, we did not find any way to accelerate the computation without losing optimality. In this experiment, policies generated by Algorithm 2 are optimal or close to optimal. Moreover, our offline heuristic computes much better solutions than the simple algorithm 'NoDis'. However, the running time of our algorithm still increases much faster, and is not suited for instances where the demand can go above 50. We note that for $T = 3$, Algorithm 2 generates a suboptimal solution. Consequently, the best values u'_{k_1+1} and $k'_2(k_1)$ corresponding to the reference state $[0, 0, 0]$ are not equal to the optimal values $u^*_{k_1+1}$ and $k^*_2(k_1)$.

We believe that our offline heuristic performs well for reasonable system costs. However, Algorithm 2 may perform poorly when the optimal offline policy purchases new containers at nearly every period. Indeed, our reference state $[0, 0, 0]$ deciding on the best fleet size underestimates the required container fleet, because it neglects the value of X_t and Z_t at purchasing time. The approximation error increases when purchasing times get closer to each others. Table 2 presents a simulation with increasing disposable costs and decreasing setup costs, which leads to a worse and worse performance of Algorithm 2. In the last instance of this second simulation, with costs $C = [3, 6, 1500, 0, 50]$, Algorithm 2 gets very high costs when purchasing at consecutive periods, so the generated policy does not purchase containers at period 2, contrary to the other algorithms. We conclude that the reference state should be adapted to the system costs.

7   Conclusion

In this paper, we study the purchasing and repositioning of containers in a closed-loop supply chain with a stochastic demand at every time step and a periodic backward flow of empty containers. This model can be seen as a lot-sizing problem where the purchased items are containers coming back for reuse after a known duration. We state that the flow of empty containers is an operational decision that must be dynamically taken, while container purchasing is a tactical decision that can be decided at the beginning of the time horizon. We extend two of the three strategies described by Bookbinder and Tan [9] to a container management process. Our optimal online algorithm dynamically decides whether to purchase containers or not. Our offline algorithm sets a purchasing plan at the beginning of the time horizon and dynamically sends empty containers to the supplier. This offline heuristic neglects the impact of the state at purchasing time, allowing us to divide the problem into $L^{\natural}$-convex sub-problems without setup cost. The algorithm has been shown to perform well for reasonable costs. The static-dynamic strategy from [9] fixes the purchasing times and decides later on the actual quantities. We estimate that this third strategy is not fundamental in a container management process, so we postpone its analysis to a future study. Another future research is to develop heuristics to make our algorithms fast enough for large test instances. In particular, we are interested into alternatives to our reference state and state space aggregation methods. A last interesting study would be to find efficient myopic ordering policies to get more insight on how the containers should be balanced between consecutive weeks.

References

1. Jami, N., Schroeder, M., Küfer, K.: A model and polynomial algorithm for purchasing and repositioning containers. In: Management and Control of Production and Logistics (upcoming), vol. 7 (accepted 2016)
2. Janakiraman, G., Muckstadt, J.A.: Periodic review inventory control with lost sales and fractional lead times. Cornell University, School of Operations Research and Industrial Engineering (2004)
3. Halman, N., Klabjan, D., Mostagir, M., Orlin, J., Simchi-Levi, D.: A fully polynomial-time approximation scheme for single-item stochastic inventory control with discrete demand. Math. Oper. Res. **34**(3), 674–685 (2009)
4. Murota, K.: Discrete Convex Analysis. SIAM, Philadelphia (2003)
5. Zipkin, P.: On the structure of lost-sales inventory models. Oper. Res. **56**(4), 937–944 (2008)
6. Simchi-Levi, D., Chen, X., Bramel, J.: The Logic of Logistics: Theory, Algorithms, and Applications for Logistics Management. Springer Science & Business Media, New York (2013)
7. Chen, W., Dawande, M., Janakiraman, G.: Fixed-dimensional stochastic dynamic programs: an approximation scheme and an inventory application. Oper. Res. **62**(1), 81–103 (2014)
8. Wagner, H.M., Whitin, T.M.: Dynamic version of the economic lot size model. Manag. Sci. **5**(1), 89–96 (1958)
9. Bookbinder, J.H., Tan, J.Y.: Strategies for the probabilistic lot-sizing problem with service-level constraints. Manag. Sci. **34**(9), 1096–1108 (1988)
10. Levi, R., Shi, C.: Approximation algorithms for the stochastic lot-sizing problem with order lead times. Oper. Res. **61**(3), 593–602 (2013)
11. Vargas, V.: An optimal solution for the stochastic version of the Wagner-Whitin dynamic lot-size model. Eur. J. Oper. Res. **198**(2), 447–451 (2009)
12. Özen, U., Doğru, M.K., Tarim, S.A.: Static-dynamic uncertainty strategy for a single-item stochastic inventory control problem. Omega **40**(3), 348–357 (2012)
13. Erera, A.L., Morales, J.C., Savelsbergh, M.: Global intermodal tank container management for the chemical industry. Transp. Res. Part E Logistics Transp. Rev. **41**(6), 551–566 (2005)

14. Erera, A.L., Morales, J.C., Savelsbergh, M.: Robust optimization for empty repositioning problems. Oper. Res. **57**(2), 468–483 (2009)
15. Li, J.A., Leung, S.C., Wu, Y., Liu, K.: Allocation of empty containers between multi-ports. Eur. J. Oper. Res. **182**(1), 400–412 (2007)
16. Lam, S.W., Lee, L.H., Tang, L.C.: An approximate dynamic programming approach for the empty container allocation problem. Transp. Res. Part C Emerg. Technol. **15**(4), 265–277 (2007)

Towards Real-Time Automated Stowage Planning - Optimizing Constraint Test Ordering

Zhuo Qi Lee[⊠], Rui Fan, and Wen-Jing Hsu

School of Computer Science and Engineering, Nanyang Technological University,
Singapore, Singapore
{zqlee,fanrui,hsu}@ntu.edu.sg

Abstract. Container stowage planning is a complex task in which multiple objectives have to be optimized while ensuring that the stowage rules as well as the safety and balance requirements are observed. Most algorithms for solving the problem are comprised of 2 parts: a container-location selection mechanism and a constraint evaluation engine. The former selects one or more container-location pairs for allocation iteratively and the latter evaluates whether the selected container-location pairs violate any of the constraints. We observe that, using the same selection mechanism, the order in which the constraints are evaluated can have significant impact on the overall efficiency. We propose Sequential Sample Model (SSM) as an improvement over the existing Random Sample Model (RSM) for analysis of the problem. We present and evaluate several strategies in optimizing the constraint evaluation engine. We show how to achieve the optimal constraint ordering with respect to SSM. However, such ordering requires perfect information on the constraint tests which is impractical. We present alternative strategies and show empirically that their efficiencies are close to the optimum. Experiments show that, when compared to an arbitrary ordering, an average of 2.42 times speed up in the evaluation engine can be achieved.

Keywords: Maritime logistics · Stowage plans · Optimization · Heuristic algorithms · Markov model

1 Introduction

Stowage planning is the task of assigning suitable stowage locations to the loading containers such that the profit is maximized while observing the safety and balance requirements. There are multiple factors affecting the overall profit. For instance, uneven distribution of workloads across the bays may cause the ship to stay at the port for an extended period of time. Apart from paying more port charges [1], the ship will have less margin in voyage time to the next port. Hence, the ship has to sail at a greater speed to meet the deadline and thus increases the fuel cost and increases emission [16]. Moreover, additional complex stowage rules, such as *dangerous goods* (DGs) segregation rules [4] as well as ship

© Springer International Publishing Switzerland 2016
A. Paias et al. (Eds.): ICCL 2016, LNCS 9855, pp. 175–189, 2016.
DOI: 10.1007/978-3-319-44896-1_12

strength and stability consideration [14,23], increases the difficulty in achieving an evenly distributed workload.

The problem is conventionally solved manually by the ship planners. The loading lists are usually made available to the ship planners just hours before the ships arrival at the next destination port. An initial plan needs to be sent to the port planners for further optimizations before committing. Thus, the planners are constantly under tremendous pressure to meet the deadlines. The increased deployment of mega-scale vessels with more than 18,000 TEUs (Twenty-foot Equivalent Units) capacity [16] has made the task exceedingly challenging. As a result, automated stowage planning has become a trend. Since computer generated solutions may still require additional manual modifications, it is ideal to generate a plan within a 10-min time bound [17] and as quickly as possible.

While most studies improve the efficiency of the stowage planning algorithm by reducing and pruning the search space, we consider an alternative approach in this paper. We observe that the constraint evaluation engine is the core for most container stowage planning algorithms. By reducing the time spent in evaluating constraints, we can improve the efficiency of a stowage planning algorithm.

The rest of the paper is organized as follows. In Sect. 2, we briefly review existing results on automated stowage planning and constraint test optimization. In Sect. 3, we present Random Sample Model (RSM) and State-based Sequential Sample Model (SSM) to study the problem. We also present how to achieve the optimum efficiency w.r.t. SSM. A window-based approach for estimating the constraint evaluation cost is also presented. In Sect. 4, we present the empirical results on the efficiency of the strategies studied in this paper. We also show the impact of window size on the effectiveness in improving the efficiency. We conclude the paper in Sect. 5.

2   Related Works

The container stowage optimization problem, which is also known as the Master Bay Plan Problem, was shown to be NP-hard in [6]. Since it is computationally challenging to obtain an optimal solution, many studies are conducted to devise *near optimal* solutions, rather than the *optimum*, to the problem. The existing approaches for solving the problem can mainly be divided into the following three categories: (i) mixed integer programming (MIP) based, e.g., [5,9]; (ii) meta-heuristics based, e.g., [2,3,13], and (iii) heuristics based, e.g., [2,21].

For safety concerns, a stowage plan is only feasible when none of the constraint is violated. As such, constraint tests must be present in certain stages of a stowage planning algorithm. From this, we may generalize the structure of most stowage algorithms as a combination of a container-location selection mechanism and a constraint evaluation engine (c.f. Fig. 1). The container-location selection mechanism may select one or more pairs of container-location assignments for considerations and these assignments are checked by the evaluation engine for feasibility. On one extreme, the container-location mechanism does not perform any filtering and hence the algorithm evaluates all possible assignments of the

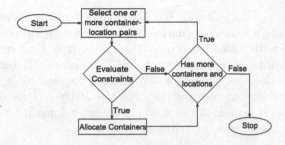

Fig. 1. Flow chart of a stowage planning algorithm. The container-location pair selection mechanism and the constraint evaluation engine form the core of most stowage planning algorithms. Some approaches include the hydrostatic limits in the constraint evaluation engine, while some others do not, and the preliminary solution is modified to meet the hydrostatic limits in a later phase.

containers. On the other extreme, the constraint evaluation engine is fully merged with the selection mechanism to prune out all infeasible assignments from being considered by the algorithm. Nevertheless, when more than one tests need to be run during a certain stage of the algorithm, the order in which the tests are run may have impact on the overall efficiency of the algorithm.

In this paper, we consider an algorithm that employs a 2-phase approach for stowage planning that is comprised of an allocation phase followed by an adjustment phase [12, 14, 15, 23]. In the first phase, only hard-constraints (e.g. slot type match, DG segregations, weight limit, etc.) are considered. In the second phase, the preliminary solution from the first phase is improved by a combination of swapping containers of equivalent classes and ballast tank adjustments to meet the strength and stability constraints (e.g. trim, list, bending moment, shear force, etc.). Through experiments, we find that the time spent in constraint evaluation attributes to 96 % of the overall time spent in the allocation phase. This presents a huge opportunity for optimizing the efficiency of the algorithm.

In the constraint evaluation engine, a container-location pair is evaluated against an ordered set of tests in a sequential manner. Each test is composed of a set of related criteria. For instance, a test could be checking the stack weight limit, or checking the segregation among the DGs. The constraint evaluation returns false if the container-location pair is rejected by at least one of the tests. The order in which the tests are evaluated could have significant impact on the total costs incurred. For instance, suppose that we are given three tests (ϕ_1, ϕ_2, ϕ_3) with evaluation costs of 1000, 100, and 10 respectively. Assume that for the current iteration, both ϕ_1 and ϕ_2 return "True" while ϕ_3 return "False". If we evaluate the sequence in the given order of (ϕ_1, ϕ_2, ϕ_3), then the cost incurred would be 1110. However, if we evaluate ϕ_3 first, then the cost incurred is 10, which is significantly less than the default order. Of course, we may not know in advance which tests would return "False" and hence the problem is usually studied with a probabilistic framework.

The constraint test optimization has been studied under different themes and has been extended for various scenarios, such as tests with precedence requirements [11], tests with one-sided errors [7], etc. In [19], Ünlüyurt presented a survey of the test order optimization problem. Test order optimization has applications in diagnostic based processes like cargoes inspections [8,10,22], regression testing for software engineering [18], and the design of screening procedures [11]. It has also been applied in the machine learning domain for improving the reaction time of classification algorithms [20].

3   Constraint Ordering

Previous studies in optimizing the constraint evaluation order considered the case where the samples (container-location pair) are evaluated in a random order. We observe that, in practice, most existing stowage algorithms will evaluate the samples in certain pre-ordered manner. This leads to a recurring pattern both in the constraint evaluation result and the computational time incurred in evaluating the constraint tests. Hence, we propose the State-based Sequential Sample Model (SSM) as a refinement over the existing Random Sample Model (RSM). We show how to achieve a near-optimal efficiency under SSM. We also present a moving window scheme for capturing the recurrence of the evaluation cost and also estimating the actual cost.

3.1   Preliminaries

A constraint test sequence is comprised of a set of constraint tests, and is denoted by $\Phi = \{\phi_1, \phi_2, \phi_3, ..., \phi_N\}$. A test ϕ_i requires certain *cost* c_i to evaluate, and the cost is the *computational time* to run the test in the case of stowage algorithms. Since the costs may change over time, the average cost is usually used for analysis of the problem. The tests may be evaluated in any permutation. In particular, a strategy X may evaluate the tests in the order $\Phi^X(t) = \left(\phi_1^X(t), \phi_2^X(t), \phi_3^X(t), ..., \phi_N^X(t)\right)$ at time t, where the ordering is a permutation of the set Φ.

Conventionally, the constraint order optimization problem is studied by considering that a randomly selected sample is evaluated at the constraint evaluation engine. A sample in this context refers to a container-location pair. In the following, we describe the *Random Sample Model (RSM)*, and Fig. 2(a) shows the schematic of RSM.

Definition 1. Random Sample Model *describes a scenario in which a randomly selected sample is evaluated by the constraint evaluation engine. Under this model, a constraint test ϕ_i may evaluate to "True" with probability $p(\phi_i)$, and to "False" with probability $1 - p(\phi_i) = f(\phi_i)$.*

Since the costs and probabilities of "False" do not change over time under RSM, we drop the time parameter in the expressions in this section. With RSM, we may calculate the expected cost of evaluating a sequence as follows:

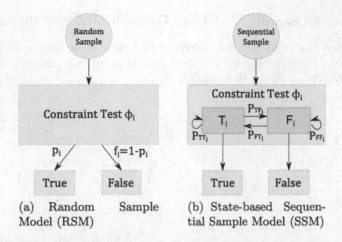

Fig. 2. (a) Schematic of random sample model. A constraint test evaluates to "True" or "False" probabilistically. The constraint test evaluation is oblivious of the container allocation process. (b) Schematic of State-based Sequential Sample Model. The constraint test has inner states composed of T_i and F_i. When the test is in the T_i state, it will always return "True". Similarly, it returns "False" when it is in the F_i state. After evaluating each sample, the test may change state between T_i and F_i with the specified probabilities $p_{TT_i}, p_{TF_i}, p_{FT_i}, p_{FF_i}$.

Definition 2. *The* expected cost *of evaluating a sequence* using a strategy X *is given by*

$$\mathbb{E}[C(\Phi^X)] = c_1^X + p_1^X c_2^X + p_1^X p_2^X c_3^X + p_1^X p_2^X p_3^X c_4^X \qquad (1)$$
$$+ ... + p_1^X p_2^X ... p_{N-1}^X c_N^X$$

where c_i^X is the cost of the constraint test at index i as dictated by the strategy X, and p_i^X is the probability of the constraint test at index i as dictated by the strategy X returning "True".

The goal of constraint test optimization is to order the constraint tests such that the expected computational cost of evaluating a set of container-location pairs against the constraint test sequence is minimized.

Cost-Effective First (CE) Strategy

Definition 3. *The* cost effectiveness *of a constraint test is given by the expression $\theta(\phi_i) = \frac{f(\phi_i)}{cost\phi_i}$, which is the ratio of "False" probability to the cost of evaluating the test.*

It was shown in [7] that, ordering the constraint tests in non-increasing order of cost-effectiveness achieves the lowest expected evaluation cost among all possible permutations w.r.t. RSM, i.e., $\Phi^{CE} = (\phi_1^{CE}, \phi_2^{CE}, \phi_3^{CE}, ..., \phi_N^{CE})$ such that $\theta(\phi_i^{CE}) \geq \theta(\phi_j^{CE})$ for $i < j$.

3.2   Sequential Sample Model and Dynamic Ordering Strategies

RSM assumed that the samples arrive at the evaluation engine in a random order. However, in practice we observed certain recurring patterns in the test evaluation result, as shown in Fig. 3(a).

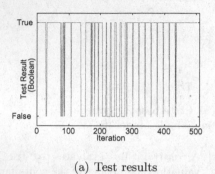
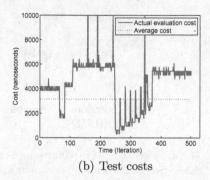

| (a) Test results | (b) Test costs |

Fig. 3. (a) An example of recurring pattern for evaluating multiple samples against a single constraint test from real historical log of constraint evaluations. A "True" result is usually followed by a series of "True" before turning into a series of "False" and vice versa. (b) Comparison of average cost and actual evaluation costs. The average cost is an over- or under-estimation of the true cost most of the times.

The 'recurring' pattern can be explained by considering, for example, the stack weight limit constraint test. The test checks if adding the container to the stack at which candidate location resides will exceed the specified stack weight limit. As the stowage planning algorithm plans on a stack-by-stack basis, when the stack is low, the test result is usually "True". This means that it is safe to place the container at the candidate location without violating the stack weight limit. Testing additional containers at the same location is likely to yield the same "True" result, which leads to a chain of "True". However, as more containers are allocated onto the stack, it becomes much more likely to violate the stack weight limit. Once the limit is exceeded, the test evaluates to "False" until the stowage algorithm moves on to another stack. This leads to the observed repeating pattern of a long chain of "True"s followed by another chain of "False"s. With this observation, we consider reordering the constraint test sequence dynamically.

Recent First (RF) Strategy. An obvious strategy is to move the recently violated constraint test to the front of the sequence at each time step. This is because a test that returned "False" previously is likely to return "False" on the next sample. The RF strategy orders the constraint test sequence in the following manner:

$$\Phi^{RF}(t+1) = (\phi_k^{RF}(t), \phi_1^{RF}(t), \phi_2^{RF}(t), ..., \phi_{k-1}^{RF}(t), \phi_{k+1}^{RF}(t), ..., \phi_N^{RF}(t))$$

where k is the index of the first test that evaluates to "False" at time t.

However, a recently violated constraint test could be very costly to evaluate, leading to a high expected cost despite the high probability of the test returning "False". In addition, repeatedly moving constraint tests to the front may destroy any initial ordering of the sequence very quickly. When combined with the 'recurring' pattern described earlier, this may be detrimental for the case where the tests are pre-sorted in certain manner (such as CE strategy).

State-Based Sequential Sample Model and State-Based (SB) Strategy. While RF strategy does not require much information about the tests, it does not offer guarantees on the expected evaluation cost. Thus, we propose the State-based Sequential Sample Model (SSM) as an alternative to the Random Sample Model to model the test behaviour and to analyse the expected evaluation cost.

Definition 4. State-based Sequential Sample Model *describes a scenario in which the samples from an instance of stowage planning are evaluated sequentially by the constraint evaluation engine. A constraint test ϕ_i is modelled by a Markov Chain with two states, namely T_i and F_i. Only one state can be active at a time. The evaluation result of the constraint test is determined by the currently active state. If the state is T_i, then the evaluation result will be "True", and similarly F_i state for "False". After evaluating each sample, the state may change as follows:*

$$state(\phi_i(t+1)) = \begin{cases} T_i \ with \ prob \ p_{TT_i} \ if \ state(\phi_i(t)) = T_i \\ F_i \ with \ prob \ p_{TF_i} \ if \ state(\phi_i(t)) = T_i \\ T_i \ with \ prob \ p_{FT_i} \ if \ state(\phi_i(t)) = F_i \\ F_i \ with \ prob \ p_{FF_i} \ if \ state(\phi_i(t)) = F_i \end{cases} \tag{2}$$

Figure 2(b) shows a schematic of SSM. The state transition mechanism in SSM is for modelling the strings of repeated "True" or "False" results observed in practice. For instance, in the stack weight limit example described previously, moving from the bottom of a stack to the top of the stack may correspond to a state change from T_i to F_i, and a state change from F_i to T_i occur when the stowage algorithm moves to a different stack.

With the sequential sample model, we can get a more precise estimation of "False" probabilities, and thus enable the ordering of constraint tests dynamically based on their dynamic cost-effectiveness.

Definition 5. *The* dynamic cost-effectiveness *of a constraint test ϕ_i at time t is given by $\hat{\theta}(\phi_i(t)) = \frac{\hat{f}(\phi_i(t))}{cost(\phi_i(t))}$, where $\hat{f}(\phi_i(t))$ denotes the state-dependent probability of constraint test ϕ_i evaluating to "False" at time t, and is given by*

$$\hat{f}(\phi_i(t)) = \begin{cases} p_{TF_i} \ if \ state(\phi_i(t)) = T_i \\ p_{FF_i} \ otherwise \end{cases} \tag{3}$$

At any time t, the SB strategy orders the constraint tests in non-increasing (or decreasing) order of dynamic cost-effectiveness such that $\hat{\theta}(\phi_i^{SB}(t)) \geq \hat{\theta}(\phi_j^{SB}(t))$ for $i < j$. We show that the SB strategy is optimal with respect to SSM.

Proposition 1. *Suppose that we are given a constraint test sequence $\Phi = \{\phi_1,$ $\phi_2, ..., \phi_N\}$ that follows SSM where the states of the constraint tests are known at time t. If the sequence is ordered dynamically using the SB strategy then $\mathbb{E}[C(\Phi^{SB})] \leq \mathbb{E}[C(\Phi^X)]$ for any other strategy X in the next time step.*

Proof. The proposition can be proved by using the technique as shown in [7, 12]. □

State-Estimation-Based (SEB) Strategy. While it is desirable to use the SB strategy since it guarantees optimum expected evaluation cost w.r.t. SSM, it is not always possible to know the real state of the constraint tests. This is because the constraint evaluation engine always stops evaluating the rest of the tests as soon as a "False" test is found, while the real state of a test can be determined only after evaluating the test. Figure 4 shows an example.

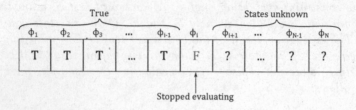

Fig. 4. An example of the states of the constraint tests. The evaluation stops at ϕ_i because the first "False" result has been seen. The states of the remaining tests cannot be determined as they are not evaluated.

In order to tackle this problem, we revise the constraint evaluation engine as follows. To evaluate a given sample (container-location pair), the evaluation engine will proceed as usual and start evaluating the sequence of tests until the first "False" is encountered. After that, instead of stopping immediately, the evaluation engine continues and uses a low cost operation to estimate the "False" probabilities of the remaining tests in the sequence. The estimated state-dependent "False" probabilities for the next time step are calculated as follows:

$$\tilde{f}(\phi_i(t+1)) = \begin{cases} p_{\mathrm{TF}_i} & \text{if } \phi_i \text{ returned "True" at } t \\ p_{\mathrm{FF}_i} & \text{if } \phi_i \text{ returned "False" at } t \\ \tilde{f}(\phi_i(t))p_{\mathrm{FF}_i} + (1 - \tilde{f}(\phi_i(t)))p_{\mathrm{TF}_i} & \text{if } \phi_i \text{ is not evaluated at } t \end{cases} \tag{4}$$

We note that if a constraint test is not evaluated consecutively for a sufficiently large number of rounds, $\tilde{f}(\phi_i(t))$ will converge to a constant $f(\phi_i)$. This also means that, if we lose track of the state of a constraint test, the constraint test model falls back to RSM. In the following, we prove the convergence of $\tilde{f}(\phi_i(t))$.

Proposition 2. *Suppose that we are given the state transitions in the following form,*

$$\begin{bmatrix} \tilde{p}(\phi_i(t+1)) \\ \tilde{f}(\phi_i(t+1)) \end{bmatrix} = \begin{bmatrix} p_{TT_i} & p_{FT_i} \\ p_{TF_i} & p_{FF_i} \end{bmatrix} \begin{bmatrix} \tilde{p}(\phi_i(t)) \\ \tilde{f}(\phi_i(t)) \end{bmatrix} \tag{5}$$

where $\tilde{p}(\phi_i(t)) = 1 - \tilde{f}(\phi_i(t))$. *For sufficiently large* τ, $\tilde{f}(\phi_i(\tau))$ *converges to certain value* $f_i = \frac{p_{TF_i}}{p_{TF_i}+p_{FT_i}}$.

Proof. The proposition can be proved by applying the stationary condition for a Markov chain. □

With the changes in the "False" probabilities, the estimated dynamic cost-effectiveness is then given by $\tilde{\theta}(\phi_i^{SEB}(t)) = \frac{\tilde{f}(\phi_i^{SEB}(t))}{\text{cost}(\phi_i^{SEB}(t))}$.

Similar to the SB strategy, the constraint test sequence is always sorted according to the estimated dynamic cost-effectiveness. Algorithm 1 describes the revised constraint evaluation engine for the SEB strategy. In Line 11, the algorithm updates the $\tilde{f}(\phi_i^{SEB}(t))$ of the constraint tests that are not evaluated in the current round by using Eq. (4).

Algorithm 1. SEB constraint evaluation engine.

Data: Constraint test sequence $\Phi^{SEB}(t)$, container r, location l
Result: TRUE if all constraints are satisfied, FALSE if at least one constraint
  is violated.
1 $i \leftarrow 0$;
2 $violated \leftarrow$ FALSE ;
3 **while** *(i < numConstraint)* ∧ *(!violated)* **do**
4 $result \leftarrow$ evaluate$(\phi_i^{SEB}(t), r, l)$;
5 $i \leftarrow i + 1$;
6 **if** $result = FALSE$ **then**
7   $violated \leftarrow$ TRUE ;

8 **while** $i < numConstraint$ **do**
9 update$(\phi_i^{SEB}(t))$;
10 $i \leftarrow i + 1$;
11 $\Phi^{SEB}(t+1) \leftarrow$ sort $\Phi^{SEB}(t)$ in non-increasing order of $\tilde{\theta}(\phi_i^{SEB}(t))$;
12 **return** $!violated$;

3.3 Dynamic Cost Estimation

Windowed Cost Effectiveness (WCE) Strategy. While the average cost assumption simplifies the analysis and is easier to implement, we notice that in practice, the average cost may be an over- or under- estimation of the true cost incurred in evaluating the constraints. Figure 3(b) shows an example of the actual evaluation cost vs. the average cost. The imprecise estimation may lead to the tests not being evaluated in the ideal order as shown in Proposition 1.

We note that, however, the actual evaluation cost can only be obtained after evaluating the sample. Moreover, we observe that the costs also display similar 'recurring' patterns (despite the presence of spikes) as that of test results (T/F) shown in Fig. 3(a). To capture this, we apply a moving window heuristic to reduce the gap between the estimated cost and actual evaluation cost. For each constrain test ϕ_i, we use two windows $W_{T_i} = \{w_{T_1}, w_{T_2}, ..., w_{T_L}\}$ and $W_{F_i} = \{w_{F_1}, w_{F_2}, ..., w_{F_L}\}$ with length L to store the historical evaluation costs for the T_i and F_i states respectively. Initially, the windows are fully filled with the average cost (or the state-based average cost). Subsequently, after a sample is evaluated, the corresponding window is updated with the new cost. The average of each window can be maintained efficiently with a circular buffer.

The size of the windows may affect the sensitivity of the estimated cost. In the extreme case, a window of infinite length is not reacting to any changes in the costs and is the same as using the average cost; while a window of unit length is too sensitive to the minor changes in the costs and may not be a good indicator of the subsequent costs.

With the moving window cost estimation, we can then compute the *windowed cost-effectiveness* of a test as follows:

$$\bar{\theta}(\phi_i(t)) = \frac{\tilde{f}(\phi_i(t))}{\bar{c}(\phi_i(t))} = \frac{\tilde{f}(\phi_i(t))}{(1 - \tilde{f}(\phi_i(t)))\bar{c}^T(\phi_i(t)) + \tilde{f}(\phi_i(t))\bar{c}^F(\phi_i(t))} \tag{6}$$

where $\bar{c}^T(\phi_i(t))$ and $\bar{c}^F(\phi_i(t))$ denote the average costs from the windows W_{T_i} and W_{F_i} respectively, and the denominator calculates the expected cost of the next iteration.

The expression $\bar{c}(\phi_i(t)) = (1 - \tilde{f}(\phi_i(t)))\bar{c}^T(\phi_i(t)) + \tilde{f}(\phi_i(t))\bar{c}^F(\phi_i(t))$ in Eq. (6) may appear counter-intuitive as the expected cost is used instead of $\bar{c}^F(\phi_i(t))$, the average cost in the F-state. We elaborate in more detail in the following. To simplify the expressions, we write $\bar{c}_i$ as a shorthand of $\bar{c}(\phi_i(t))$, and similarly for $\tilde{f}_i$, $\tilde{p}_i$, $\bar{c}_i^T$, and $\bar{c}_i^F$. As a result of generalizing the costs to T- and F- states specific, the expected cost of evaluating a sequence as given in Eq. (1) is generalized to the following:

$$\mathbb{E}[C(\Phi)] = \tilde{f}_1\bar{c}_1^F + \tilde{p}_1 \left(\bar{c}_1^T + \textbf{Expected cost of } \phi_2 \textbf{ and beyond}\right) \tag{7}$$

$$= \tilde{f}_1\bar{c}_1^F + \tilde{p}_1 \left(\bar{c}_1^T + \tilde{f}_2\bar{c}_2^F + \tilde{p}_2(\bar{c}_2^T\right. \tag{8}$$

$$\left. + \textbf{Expected cost of } \phi_3 \textbf{ and beyond})\right)$$

$$= \tilde{f}_1\bar{c}_1^F + \tilde{p}_1\tilde{f}_2\bar{c}_2^F + \tilde{p}_1\tilde{p}_2\tilde{f}_3\bar{c}_3^F + ... + \tilde{p}_1\tilde{p}_2...\tilde{p}_{N-1}\tilde{f}_N\bar{c}_N^F \tag{9}$$

$$\tilde{p}_1\bar{c}_1^T + \tilde{p}_1\tilde{p}_2\bar{c}_2^T + \tilde{p}_1\tilde{p}_2\tilde{p}_3\bar{c}_3^T + ... + \tilde{p}_1\tilde{p}_2...\tilde{p}_{N-1}\tilde{p}_N\bar{c}_N^T$$

$$= (\tilde{f}_1\bar{c}_1^F + \tilde{p}_1\bar{c}_1^T) + \tilde{p}_1(\tilde{f}_2\bar{c}_2^F + \tilde{p}_2\bar{c}_2^T) + \tilde{p}_1\tilde{p}_2(\tilde{f}_3\bar{c}_3^F + \tilde{p}_3\bar{c}_3^T) + ... \tag{10}$$

$$+ \tilde{p}_1\tilde{p}_2...\tilde{p}_{N-1}(\tilde{f}_N\bar{c}_N^F + \tilde{p}_N\bar{c}_N^T)$$

$$= \bar{c}_1 + \tilde{p}_1(\bar{c}_2) + \tilde{p}_1\tilde{p}_2(\bar{c}_3) + \tilde{p}_1\tilde{p}_2...\tilde{p}_{N-1}(\bar{c}_N) \tag{11}$$

In Eq. (7), the expected cost of evaluating a sequence is defined recursively. If the test ϕ_i returns "False", then only the T-costs of the tests before ϕ_i and the F-cost of ϕ_i are incurred; otherwise, the expected cost is the sum of T-cost of ϕ_i and the expected cost of evaluating test from ϕ_{i+1} onwards. In Eq. (8) we expand the expression in one more layer as an example. In Eq. (9), we show the expressions when they are fully expanded. In Eq. (10), we group the expressions according to the cost terms. In Eq. (11), we replace the expressions $\tilde{f}_i \bar{c}_i^F + \tilde{p}_i \bar{c}_i^T$ with $\bar{c}_i$. At this point, one may observe that the resultant expression is almost the same as Eq. (1). Then the optimality of the tests ordered following the WCE strategy can be proved similarly as shown in [7,12].

4   Experiments

We conducted experiments on data obtained from real stowage planning instances to compare the effectiveness of the test reordering strategies. For each container-location pair evaluated by the constraint evaluation engine, we recorded the computational costs[1] and the outcome of each constraint test without stopping at the first "False". The collected data is then divided into training set and evaluation set respectively. The training set is used to obtain the model parameters p_i, f_i, $cost$, and the transition probabilities. The parameters are used for constructing the test case generator as well as input for the strategies to reorder the test sequence. By using the historical log of all of the constraint evaluation results and computational costs, we can replay the results to simulate the constraint evaluation engine and compare the effectiveness of the strategies in reducing the computational costs.

The simulation results are compared in Fig. 5. The training set and evaluation set are each composed of real data from 244 different instances of stowage planning problem respectively. Each instance is composed of iterations of constraint evaluations. As shown in the figure, the SB and SEB strategies are consistently the best while RF comes next. The dynamic reordering strategies consistently outperform the static CE strategy except in the generated set.

Next, we evaluate the effect of window length on the speed-up achieved by the WCE strategy. The speed-up achieved by a strategy X is defined as the total cost incurred by the RND strategy divided by the total cost incurred by the strategy X. We experimented with window sizes from 10 to 100 with an interval of 10. The results are shown in Fig. 6(a). Two peaks can be observed from the figure at window lengths 30 and 60 respectively. This observation suggests that the constraint tests may have a periodicity of multiples of 30.

We compare the overall speed up achieved by the strategies in Fig. 6(b). Since the best empirical window length is 30 for WCE, we only show the speed up result for WCE(30). The total costs are the sum of the evaluation costs in all instances, including the training set, evaluation set, and generated sets. We note that, as the dynamic strategies also introduce re-ordering overhead after evaluating each sample, we also compare the speed up achieved when taking the overhead into consideration. For SB, SEB, and WCE strategies, the overhead is significant because of the sorting operation introduced at each step (the test sequence is

---

[1] The experiments are written in Java language and conducted on HP Z400 Workstation with Intel(R) Xeon(R) CPU W3565 @3.20 GHz (8CPUs); 12288 MB RAM; 64-bit Windows 7.

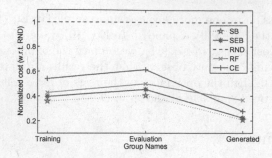

Fig. 5. Comparison of total cost incurred (normalized w.r.t. RND) in the constraint evaluation engine by different reordering strategies. The RND strategy randomly permutes the test sequence once at the beginning. The column labelled 'Generated' are the accumulated cost for evaluating 10,000,000 iterations of constraint tests whose results are generated by using the model parameters learnt from the training set. The SB and SEB strategies are consistently the best while the RF strategy comes next.

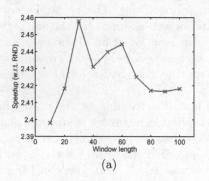   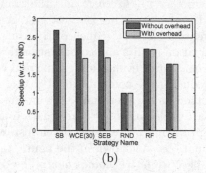

(a)   (b)

Fig. 6. (a) The effect of window lengths on the speedup achieved by WCE strategy. Two peaks can be observed from the figure at window lengths 30 and 60 respectively. (b) Comparison of speed up achieved by the strategies. Dark grey bars represent the speed up achieved by each strategy without considering the logic overhead while the light grey bars represent the speed up with logic overhead introduced. Without considering the logic overhead introduced by the dynamic strategies, SB and WCE(30) achieves the best speed ups, while SEB is very close to WCE(30). With the logic overhead, SB is still the best strategy while SEB is ranked slightly behind RF.

comprised of 29 constraint tests). Without considering the re-ordering overhead introduced by the dynamic strategies, SB and WCE achieves the best speed ups at 2.69 and 2.46 speed up respectively. With the re-ordering overhead, SB is still the best strategy while SEB is ranked slightly behind RF, at 2.30, 1.95, and 2.17 times speed up respectively. While RF appears promising, it does not offer any theoretical guarantee and may be sensitive to the correlation between the costs and "False" probabilities of the tests. Moreover, if the tests have higher evaluation costs, the overhead induced by SB, SEB, and WCE strategies will be insignificant.

5   Conclusion

We have presented the State-based Sequential Sample Model (SSM) which is an improvement over RSM in modelling the constraint test procedure. For SSM, as it is unrealistic to assume full knowledge about the states of the constraint tests, we showed how to modify the optimal strategy SB to produce a near optimal strategy SEB. We showed empirically that SEB performs nearly as well as SB and achieves a speed up of 2.42, as compared to the random ordering strategy.

By improving the efficiency of the constraint evaluation engine, we also improve the efficiency of the stowage planning algorithm. As a result, we may now generate a good feasible stowage plan with comparable quality to that of the human planners in around 3 min time. For detailed descriptions of the stowage algorithm, the reader may refer to [12,14,15,23].

We note that, while the efficiency of the constraint evaluation engine may also be improved by simply running the tests in parallel, there may be cases where the number of tests to be conducted is more than the available parallelism. In such cases, we may still need to determine the order in evaluating the constraint tests.

We focused on describing the constraint test optimization in the theme of automated stowage planning problem. However, the technique described can be applied to problems in other domains as well. Most heuristics for solving combinatorial optimization problem explore the search space in certain manner, which may result in the recurring constraint violation patterns as observed in the stowage algorithm we considered, and thus our results can be applied directly.

Lastly, the evaluation costs need not necessarily be computational cost. For instance, to check if a cargo contains illegal substances, a series of tests (x-ray detectors, gamma-ray detectors, various sensors, etc.) can be conducted [8,10,22]. Each test incurs a different cost and has a different probability of success. The test reordering strategies may be adapted to such scenario to reduce the time and monetary cost to detect violating substance.

Acknowledgements. The authors gratefully acknowledge the grants from the NOL Fellowship programme and the co-funding from the Singapore Maritime Institute (SMI). We also extend our gratitude to the anonymous reviewers for their constructive feedbacks and comments.

References

1. Singapore port marine notice, April 2013. http://www.mpa.gov.sg/sites/circulars_and_notices/pdfs/port_marine_notices/pn13-47.pdf. Accessed 25 Mar 2015
2. Ambrosino, D., Anghinolfi, D., Paolucci, M., Sciomachen, A.: A new three-step heuristic for the master bay plan problem. Marit. Econ. Logistics **11**(1), 98–120 (2009)
3. Ambrosino, D., Anghinolfi, D., Paolucci, M., Sciomachen, A.: An experimental comparison of different heuristics for the master bay plan problem. In: Festa, P. (ed.) SEA 2010. LNCS, vol. 6049, pp. 314–325. Springer, Heidelberg (2010)

4. Ambrosino, D., Sciomachen, A.: Using a bin packing approach for stowing hazardous containers into containerships. In: Fasano, G., Pintér, J.D. (eds.) Optimized Packings with Applications. Springer Optimization ánd Its Applications, pp. 1–18. Springer International Publishing, Cham (2015)
5. Ambrosino, D., Sciomachen, A., Tanfani, E.: A decomposition heuristics for the container ship stowage problem. J. Heuristics **12**(3), 211–233 (2006)
6. Avriel, M., Penn, M., Shpirer, N.: Container ship stowage problem: complexityand connection to the coloring of circle graphs. Discrete Appl. Math. **103**(13), 271–279 (2000)
7. Berend, D., Brafman, R., Cohen, S., Shimony, S., Zucker, S.: Optimal ordering of independent tests with precedence constraints. Discrete Appl. Math. **162**, 115–127 (2014)
8. Boros, E., Elsayed, E., Kantor, P., Roberts, F., Xie, M.: Optimization problems for port-of-entry detection systems. In: Chen, H., Yang, C.C. (eds.) Intelligence and Security Informatics: Techniques and Applications. SCI, pp. 319–335. Springer, Heidelberg (2008)
9. Chen, C., Lee, S., Shen, Q.: An analytical model for the container loading problem. Eur. J. Oper. Res. **80**(1), 68–76 (1995)
10. Elsayed, E.A., Young, C.M., Xie, M., Zhang, H., Zhu, Y.: Port-of-entry inspection: sensor deployment policy optimization. IEEE Trans. Autom. Sci. Eng. **6**(2), 265–276 (2009)
11. Garey, M.: Optimal task sequencing with precedence constraints. Discrete Math. **4**(1), 37–56 (1973)
12. Lee, Z.Q., Fan, R., Hsu, W.-J.: Optimizing constraint test ordering for efficient automated stowage planning. In: Corman, F., Voß, S., Negenborn, R. (eds.) ICCL 2015. LNCS, vol. 9335, pp. 343–357. Springer, Heidelberg (2015). doi:10.1007/978-3-319-24264-4_24
13. Liu, F., Low, M.Y.H., Hsu, W.J., Huang, S.Y., Zeng, M., Win, C.A.: Randomized algorithm with Tabu search for multi-objective optimization of large containership stowage plans. In: Böse, J.W., Hu, H., Jahn, C., Shi, X., Stahlbock, R., Voß, S. (eds.) ICCL 2011. LNCS, vol. 6971, pp. 256–272. Springer, Heidelberg (2011)
14. Liu, F., Low, M.Y.H., Huang, S.Y., Hsu, W.-J., Zeng, M., Win, C.A.: Stowage planning of large containership with tradeoff between crane workload balance and ship stability (2010)
15. Low, M., Zeng, M., Hsu, W., Huang, S.Y., Liu, F., Win, C.A.: Improving safety and stability of large containerships in automated stowage planning. IEEE Syst. J. **5**(1), 50–60 (2011)
16. Monaco, M.F., Sammarra, M., Sorrentino, G.: The terminal-oriented ship stowage planning problem. Eur. J. Oper. Res. **239**(1), 256–265 (2014)
17. Pacino, D., Delgado, A., Jensen, R.M., Bebbington, T.: Fast generation of near-optimal plans for eco-efficient stowage of large container vessels. In: Böse, J.W., Hu, H., Jahn, C., Shi, X., Stahlbock, R., Voß, S. (eds.) ICCL 2011. LNCS, vol. 6971, pp. 286–301. Springer, Heidelberg (2011)
18. Rothermel, G., Untch, R.H., Chu, C., Harrold, M.J.: Prioritizing test cases for regression testing. IEEE Trans. Softw. Eng. **27**(10), 929–948 (2001)
19. Tonguç, U.: Sequential testing of complex systems: a review. Discrete Appl. Math. **142**(13), 189–205 (2004)
20. Viola, P., Jones, M.: Rapid object detection using a boosted cascade of simple features. In: Proceedings of the 2001 IEEE Computer Society Conference on Computer Vision and Pattern Recognition, CVPR 2001, vol. 1, pp. I-511–I-518 (2001)

21. Xiao, X., Low, M.Y.H., Liu, F., Huang, S.Y., Hsu, W.J., Li, Z.: An efficient block-based heuristic method for stowage planning of large containerships with crane split consideration. In: The International Conference on Harbour, Maritime and Multimodel Logistics Modelling and Simulation (2009)
22. Young, C.M., Li, M., Zhu, Y., Xie, M., Elsayed, E.A., Asamov, T.: Multiobjective optimization of a port-of-entry inspection policy. IEEE Trans. Autom. Sci. Eng. **7**(2), 392–400 (2010)
23. Zeng, M., Low, M., Hsu, W., Huang, S.Y., Liu, F., Win, C.A.: Automated stowage planning for large containerships with improved safety and stability. In: Proceedings of the 2010 Winter Simulation Conference (WSC), pp. 1976–1989, December 2010

Intermodal Transport

Optimizing Train Load Planning: Review and Decision Support for Train Planners

Hilde Heggen[1(✉)], Kris Braekers[1,2], and An Caris[1]

[1] Hasselt University, Agoralaan Building D, 3590 Diepenbeek, Belgium
{hilde.heggen,kris.braekers,an.caris}@uhasselt.be
[2] Research Foundation Flanders (FWO), Egmontstraat 5, 1000 Brussels, Belgium

Abstract. Train load planners are confronted with complex practical considerations during the booking and planning process. In order to optimally utilize the available loading space, train capacity is monitored in terms of available length and weight while accounting for the urgency with which load units must be sent. Furthermore, the execution of the load plan by the terminal operator must be performed efficiently to minimize total handling costs. The contribution of this paper is threefold. First, current literature on train load planning is reviewed based on three main groups of factors influencing the load plan composition. Second, a static model is developed to introduce a number of practical constraints from the viewpoint of the network operator. Finally, the model is adapted to reflect the planning environment of a real-life case study.

Keywords: Train load planning · Intermodal transportation · Container terminals · Rail transportation

1 Introduction

Railway transportation is strongly supported by the European Commission [18] as a means to stimulate intermodal transportation. By significantly raising the efficiency and capacity of rail transport over long distances, intermodal rail-road freight transport can be encouraged [9]. One factor determining the railway system capacity concerns the load capacity per train [8]. However, on-train capacity utilization did not receive much research attention yet in comparison to route and network capacity [23]. For a review on service network design, the reader is referred to [17]. Improved capacity utilization per train can increase rail freight volumes, and consequently the overall railway system capacity utilization, without adding expensive network capacity. Therefore, it is important to determine which load units will be loaded, and on which location on the train, to maximize the train's loading degree and minimize costs per load unit.

The train load planning problem is situated at the operational decision level and is related to two types of decision makers, the terminal operator and the network operator. The terminal operator is responsible for transshipment from one mode to another, and focuses on the efficient allocation of resources such

© Springer International Publishing Switzerland 2016
A. Paias et al. (Eds.): ICCL 2016, LNCS 9855, pp. 193–208, 2016.
DOI: 10.1007/978-3-319-44896-1_13

as minimizing handling costs. The transshipment process increases the chain lead time and total transportation cost. Hence, it needs to be executed fast and efficiently [20]. The second decision maker involved is the network operator, who often deals with a large variety of wagon and load unit types. This increases the complexity of train load planning [20]. Given a number of outbound load units, available wagons and their corresponding characteristics, the network operator's train planner typically has to establish a feasible train load plan.

Intermodal transport companies often perform the assignment of load units to a specific location on an intermodal train manually. Automation of this task can assist train planners in their decision process. It results in cost savings by increasing the number of load units assigned and consequently, decreasing costs per load unit, and by avoiding costs for the removal of a wagon and its cargo transfer due to excess axle loads at certain measure points. Moreover, important time savings can be gained in the planning process. Finally, it can have a significant influence on the time and energy spent on handling load units [16].

A lot of research has already been conducted on crane and storage planning in container terminals. An overview of literature on container terminals is provided in [22], and is updated in [21]. Train loading is part of the land-side operations in a container terminal, but has not been discussed extensively so far [16].

The remainder of this paper is organized as follows. In Sect. 2 a literature review of all factors influencing the train load planning problem is provided. Current research is classified to identify the factors considered in each model. In Sect. 3, a train load planning model is presented from the viewpoint of the network operator which owns and manages its own trains, introducing additional characteristics of a real-life train planning environment. The model is able to handle wagons with a third bogie at its center, while previous models only considered two bogies. Next, it is expanded with practical constraints that train planners are confronted with, such as trains stopping at an intermediate terminal before arriving at the final destination terminal. Load units can have flexible destinations. Therefore, preferences for being unloaded at the intermediate or final terminal are determined by the distance between the unload terminal and the load unit's final destination in order to minimize the amount of kilometers traveled on the road. The model including these additional practical constraints is tested for a real-life case study. Preliminary experimental results are presented in Sect. 4. Finally, Sect. 5 identifies opportunities for future research.

To the best of our knowledge, this paper is the first to include weight restrictions in case of wagons with three bogies, and to assign wagons to fixed destinations, with flexible destination terminals for load units depending on the proximity of the unload terminal to the load unit's final destination.

2   Factors Influencing the Load Plan

A major contribution to the development of the train loading problem has been provided by Corry and Kozan [16], who developed a realistic model which can be extended to various specific environments. Furthermore, Bruns and Knust [11] are the first - and currently still the only - to adopt continuous weight restrictions in a train load planning problem. Both works [11,16] laid the groundwork for realistic train load planning problems. Recently, the optimization of train load planning has been integrated with optimization of other operational decisions in an intermodal seaport terminal. It is first introduced by [2], who simultaneously optimize crane and storage planning. The overview in this section discusses both types of problems, namely problems focusing on pure train load planning and problems integrating train load planning with crane and storage planning.

The composition and revision of train load plans is influenced by three groups of factors. Formulations can be distinguished by their defined performance measures (Sect. 2.1). Furthermore, train load planning is restricted due to characteristics inherent to the train components and operational constraints related to the specific environment in which train loading takes place (Sect. 2.2). Section 2.3 introduces the influence of the planning environment on the load plan.

2.1   Performance Indicators

Objectives of train load planning problems in current literature can be divided into four categories. An overview is presented in Table 1. An important measure for the network operator to define its performance is the train utilization or loading degree. It can be expressed in number of load units, total weight or length of the load units, and the urgency for getting each load unit at its destination. This objective can be implemented in two ways. On the one hand, the number of load units assigned can be maximized, where a large number of load units serves as input. On the other hand, a fixed number of load units can be used as input, which all must fit on the train using the least possible number of wagons.

The terminal operator aims at minimizing costs of handling operations at the terminal during execution of the load plan. Corry and Kozan [16] divide handling into three components: double handling, carry travel and pin changes. Double handling occurs when a load unit is not directly transferred from the truck to a wagon, which means that excess handling occurs [14]. It is only considered in cases in which loading and unloading are executed simultaneously. In these cases uncertainty exists about the occurrence of double handling for each load unit, because truck arrivals and move sequences of handling material are uncertain. As inbound load units are unloaded, slots become vacant. Consequently, the probability of double handling for outbound load units which are assigned to these slots but did not arrive yet by truck becomes zero. Another definition of double handling may be unloading a loaded load unit. Carry travel or handling equipment travel corresponds to the transportation cost from the storage position to the assigned location on the train [11]. Uncertainty about this performance indicator exists if not all load units arrive before loading starts. Furthermore, each load unit is fixed on a wagon by means of four pins, which must be aligned with castings located at certain points on load units [16]. Changing the pin positions of a wagon is labor-intensive and occurs when the pin positions from the inbound wagons do not satisfy the pins needed to lock an outbound load unit on the wagon. In that case, set-up costs occur.

A third performance indicator is related to the weight distribution of the train [14]. A good weight distribution may reduce the wear of the brakes. It is optimal if the distance from the center-of-mass to the front of the train is minimized, which implies a minimal amount of empty space between consecutive load units.

The fourth category aims at minimizing two types of unproductive movements. Rehandles or reshuffles are unproductive movements required in multilevel stacking areas when the load unit to be picked up is not on top of the stack. This can be reduced by performing non-sequential or backward empty crane movements when loading the train, which is a second type of unproductive operations [5].

The categories of objectives are combined using a weighted sum in all available train load planning research. To our knowledge, no paper applies multiobjective optimization to the problem. Furthermore, the minimization of unproductive moves is only considered in combination with problems which integrate train load planning optimization with crane and storage planning. Handling cost minimization is mainly aimed at in pure train load planning problems. No further patterns seem to exist with respect to fixed combinations of objectives. However, optimization of the weight distribution has not been considered in recent, realistic problems.

Table 1. Objectives for the train load planning problem

		Train load planning								Integration with crane/storage planning					
		Feo and Gonzalez-Vélarde (1995) [19]	Corry and Kozan (2006) [14]	Corry and Kozan (2004) [13]	Corry and Kozan (2006) [15]	Corry and Kozan (2008) [16]	Aggoun et al. (2011) [1]	Bruns and Knust (2012) [11]	Bruns et al. (2014) [10]	Ambrosino et al. (2011) [2]	Ambrosino et al. (2013) [3]	Ambrosino and Siri (2014) [4]	Anghinolfi and Paolucci (2014) [7]	Anghinolfi et al. (2014) [6]	Ambrosino and Siri (2015) [5]
Utilization	Max number of load units							•	•	•	•	•	•	•	•
	Max number of urgent load units									•	•	•	•	•	•
	Max load unit length							•	•			•		•	•
	Max load unit weight							•	•					•	
	Min number of wagons	•					•	•	•						
Handling costs	Min changes in pin position			•		•		•	•					•	
	Min transportation cost	•	•		•			•	•				•		
	Min double handling	•	•		•										
Opt weight distribution				•	•	•									
Unproductive moves	Min rehandles in storage area									•	•	•	•	•	•
	Min backward empty moves										•	•			•

2.2 Characteristics of Train Components and Other Operational Constraints

Train component characteristics restrict loading possibilities. As defined by Corry and Kozan [14], a load plan provides an assignment of load units to slots on a train, where each slot equals one load unit length. Load units can be divided into three types: trailers, containers and swap bodies [11]. Each load unit is further characterized by its length, commercial value or urgency and loaded weight.

Trains can only carry a limited weight and length. They consist of a number of wagons of a specific length and tare wagon weight. Each wagon has a limited weight, and a limited draw gear capacity, which means that the mass that is allowed to trail behind the wagon is limited [15]. Each wagon is restricted to a finite number of possible loading patterns or configurations [16]. They specify how many and which types of load units can be loaded on a wagon, and the maximum weights per slot and wagon are limited based on the allowed axle loads. Every change in the configuration implies a set-up cost for changing pin positions [11]. Bruns and Knust [11] suggest two options to limit axle loads. The first option models weight distributions discretely. It is based on loading pattern descriptions provided by wagon manufacturers, as is most common in practice. For the second option, axle loads are calculated based on continuous weight distributions instead of using a set of fixed allowed patterns. The authors also mention two ways of categorizing load units into types. The first approach considers length-types, where each length-type corresponds to exactly one load unit length. The second approach is based on fixation-types. Load units with the same fixation-type may have various lengths, as long as they fit the same wagon pin configuration. This implies variable overhangs for load units belonging to one fixation type. Finally, some papers mention the possibility of double stacking, in which more than one load unit can be stacked on a single slot [11,16]. However, in Europe this is not allowed due to the presence of low bridges and tunnels and electrical wires above the rails.

Depending on the operational environment, additional constraints must be satisfied. Certain types of dangerous goods must be separated by a minimum distance, or at least they cannot be located next to each other on the same wagon. A train can have more than one destination. In that case, wagons must be grouped per destination. Load units carrying refrigerated goods must be attached to wagons with power supply. Moreover, the train height may be limited for some routes due to the fact that trains pass low bridges on their route [15]. Finally, incompatibilities between certain load units and wagons may exist [13].

Corry and Kozan [13] mention that some factors might conflict with the minimization of double handling, such as the weight distribution of the train, the wagon axle load, the separation of dangerous goods and the train height limit, as well as aspects related to container handling, such as the travel of equipment and changes in the pin configuration. The authors stress the fact that it may be beneficial to incur carry travel if it results in improvements in double handling or weight distribution [14].

An overview of all train component characteristics and other operational constraints included in problems formulated in current literature is provided in Table 2. Factors influencing the load plan which are related to the train components are now well-established. However, pure train load planning models did not yet focus on a longer planning horizon, accounting for the urgency with which load units must be shipped, whereas models integrating train load planning with crane and storage planning do not add specific operational constraints. Finally, the draw gear capacity is only considered in one paper [15].

Table 2. Train component characteristics and other operational constraints

	Feo and Gonzalez-Vélarde (1995) [19]	Corry and Kozan (2006) [14]	Corry and Kozan (2004) [13]	Corry and Kozan (2006) [15]	Corry and Kozan (2008) [16]	Aggoun et al. (2011) [1]	Bruns and Knust (2012) [11]	Bruns et al. (2014) [10]	Ambrosino et al. (2011) [2]	Ambrosino et al. (2013) [3]	Ambrosino and Siri (2014) [4]	Anghinolfi and Paolucci (2014) [7]	Anghinolfi et al. (2014) [6]	Ambrosino and Siri (2015) [5]
	Train load planning								Integration with crane/storage planning					
Train component characteristics														
Load unit — Type						•	•	•						
Length	•			•	•	•	•	•	•	•	•	•	•	•
Commercial value/urgency									•	•	•	•	•	•
Loaded weight	•	•				•	•	•	•	•	•	•	•	•
Wagon — Configurations	•	•	•	•	•	•	•	•	•	•	•	•	•	•
Load unit length types per configuration	•	•	•	•	•	•	•	•	•	•	•	•	•	•
Pin positions per configuration		•		•		•	•	•			•		•	
Weight limit per slot						•	•	•	•	•	•	•	•	•
Draw gear capacity				•										
Train — Weight limit						•	•	•	•	•	•	•	•	•
Length limit						•								
Double stacking						•								
Other operational constraints														
Dangerous goods separation						(•)	•	•						
Destination grouping						•								
Incompatibilities between wagons and load units						(•)		•						
Refrigerated containers require power supply						•								
Train height limit						•								

(•) = Formulated as a restriction, but not used to solve the model

2.3   The Planning Environment

In practice, train load planning starts with the first booking of a load unit on a train. More load units are assigned to the train until no feasible load plan can be established by adding another load unit, which marks the last booking and the end of the booking process. When the load plan is finalized, it is communicated to the terminal operator and loading starts. In the meantime load units arrive at the terminal until closing time. The process ends just before train departure, when all load units are loaded onto the train.

Train load planning can be categorized into one out of three types of planning environments. An overview is presented in Table 3. Static plans are used when terminals receive all load units before the loading process starts, the train is initially empty and all information is known with certainty. A static load plan can also be used as a guide in the booking process each time a load unit is booked to check if enough capacity is available [15]. Problems integrating train load planning with crane and storage planning are all static, as is more common in seaport terminals, and are not shown in the overview.

However, Caris et al. [12] mention that intermodal transport has grown into a dynamic research field. Uncertain events can occur in the last hours of the planning process and between the moment the load plan is sent to the terminal operator and train departure. They are related to the **train planning environment** and make the load planning a dynamic process. An initial load plan is established before loading starts, after which revisions can occur. These revisions may be necessary whenever certain events arise that change the suitability of the current load plan [14]. More urgent transport orders can emerge, planned load units might not arrive in time at the terminal and information on the type of load unit may be updated. Moreover, the quality of the input data differs depending on the moment of planning [10]. Real weights can differ from the initial data, wagons can be damaged and thus cannot be used temporarily and overhangs can change in comparison with available data. Input data adaptations and the occurrence of unexpected events trigger revisions to the load plan, complicating the load planning process.

Another type of dynamic planning occurs when unloading and loading are performed simultaneously, the train is initially not empty and load units arrive while loading [13]. In that case it is assumed that all load units are booked and known in advance. It is related to the environment in which **terminal operations** are performed to execute the load plan. Arrival times of trucks at the terminal are random (within a predefined time window) and thus uncertain. It is impossible to pre-plan train loading and still minimize handling time, because uncertainty exists about the occurrence of double handling. Outbound load units may arrive faster than inbound load units are unloaded. Consequently, a number of outbound load units must be stored in a temporary storage area. Hence, when a truck arrives to collect or deliver a load unit or a load unit is being unloaded from a train (in which case free space becomes available), the load plan is revised.

In conclusion, automation of the load planning process can support train planners by providing a load plan, and by optimizing the capacity utilization of

Table 3. Static and dynamic train load planning problems

Authors	Static	Dynamic	
		Terminal operations	Train planning operations
		Uncertainty related to loading operations	Uncertainty about information on load units
Feo and Gonzalez-Vélarde (1995)[19]	•		
Corry and Kozan (2006) [14]	•	•	
Corry and Kozan (2004) [13]		•	
Corry and Kozan (2006) [15]	•		
Corry and Kozan (2008) [16]	•	•	
Aggoun et al. (2011) [1]			•
Bruns and Knust (2012) [11]	•		
Bruns et al. (2014) [10]			•

the train. Moreover, automated train load plans can be used in an environment in which load units are all available before loading, as is for example often the case in seaport terminals. Furthermore, load plans can offer the decision maker a support tool incorporating real-time, integrated information in such a way that he can make fast decisions [14]. Moreover, the type of operator deciding on the train load plan determines the way in which a train load plan is constructed and revised. The network operator focuses on optimizing capacity utilization of the available trains and managing dynamics during the booking process, whereas the terminal operator minimizes handling costs with a given number of load units and dynamically revises the load plan with this cost minimization as a driver.

3   Model Formulation

The model in this paper takes the viewpoint of a network operator who owns and manages its own trains. The focus is on the composition of load plans during the planning process, not on its execution by terminal equipment. Consequently, the performance measures will be based on optimizing train utilization with a given number of wagons. A static model is presented, adding factors which are taken into account by train planners of Move Intermodal, an intermodal transportation company with activities throughout Europe. One of its most important activities concerns the intermodal rail-road connection between Belgium and the Netherlands on the one hand, and two unload terminals in the North of Italy on the other hand.

3.1   Base Model

The mathematical formulation builds on the third IP model of Bruns and Knust [11], which is the only train load planning problem considering axle loads as continuous functions. This provides more flexibility as not all weight configurations must explicitly be defined, and has proven to lead to smaller run times. However, our formulation is based on load unit length-type categorizations instead of fixation types. Moreover, realistic elements are added to the model based on observations of a real-life train planning department. The objective function is also adapted. The loading degree is maximized by maximizing the total length of all load units assigned to the train, while priority is given to urgent load units. Only if a load unit requires shipping on that train to arrive in time at its destination, more importance is attached to the load unit than to assigning more load units. Moreover, the model is able to account for wagons with a third bogie at the wagon center. In that case, the tare wagon weight is distributed over all three axes: 50 % over the center bogie, and 25 % over the front and rear bogie. This differs from existing models in which only wagons with two axles are considered. It results in the following formulation:

Sets and indices

$I = \{1, ..., n\}$ = set of load units with index i

$J = \{1, ..., m\}$ = set of wagons with index j

$R = \{1, ..., r\}$ = set of wagon types with index r

τ_j = wagon type of wagon j, where $\tau_j \in R$

κ_r = set of physical configurations for wagons of type r, with index k

S_{jk} = set of all possible slots of configuration k for wagon j, with index s

Parameters

l_i = length of load unit i

g_i = weight of load unit i, tare load unit weight included

p_i = urgency of load unit i

w_j = tare wagon weight of wagon j

G = train weight limit, tare wagon weights w_j included

W_j = wagon weight limit for wagon j

γ_{τ_j} = maximum feasible payload for the bogies of wagon type τ_j,

which is the same for each bogie of a single wagon

d_{τ_j} = distance between two adjacent bogies for wagon type τ_j

$e_{\tau_j}^{ks}$ = distance between the center of the load unit and the front

of the bogie for slot s in configuration k for wagon type τ_j

α_{ijks} $\begin{cases} = 1, & \text{if load unit } i \text{ fits onto slot } s \text{ of wagon } j \text{ in configuration } k \\ = 0, & \text{otherwise} \end{cases}$

z_j $\begin{cases} = 1, & \text{if wagon } j \text{ has two bogies} \\ = 0, & \text{if wagon } j \text{ has three bogies} \end{cases}$

Variables

a_j = payload on bogie a for wagon j

b_j = payload on bogie b for wagon j

c_j = payload on bogie c for wagon j, only if it has three bogies

y_{jk} $\begin{cases} = 1, & \text{if configuration } k \text{ is chosen for wagon } j \\ = 0, & \text{otherwise} \end{cases}$

x_{ijks} $\begin{cases} = 1, & \text{if load unit } i \text{ is assigned to slot } s \text{ in configuration } k \text{ of wagon } j \\ = 0, & \text{otherwise} \end{cases}$

$$\max \sum_{i \in I} \sum_{j \in J} \sum_{k \in \kappa_{\tau_j}} \sum_{s \in S_{jk}} (l_i + p_i) \cdot x_{ijks} \tag{1}$$

subject to

$$\sum_{j \in J} \sum_{k \in \kappa_{\tau_j}} \sum_{s \in S_{jk}} x_{ijks} \leq 1 \qquad\qquad \forall i \in I \tag{2}$$

$$\sum_{i \in I} x_{ijks} \leq 1 \qquad\qquad \forall j \in J, k \in \kappa_{\tau_j}, s \in S_{jk} \tag{3}$$

$$\sum_{k \in \kappa_{\tau_j}} y_{jk} = 1 \qquad\qquad \forall j \in J \tag{4}$$

$$x_{ijks} - \alpha_{ijks} \cdot y_{jk} \leq 0 \qquad\qquad \forall i \in I, j \in J, k \in \kappa_{\tau_j}, s \in S_{jk} \tag{5}$$

$$a_j = \sum_{i \in I} \sum_{k \in \kappa_{\tau_j}} \sum_{s \in S_{jk}} g_i \cdot \frac{d_{\tau_j} - e_{\tau_j}^{ks}}{d_{\tau_j}} \cdot x_{ijks} + \frac{w_j}{2} \quad \forall j \in J, z_j = 1 \tag{6}$$

$$b_j = \sum_{i \in I} \sum_{k \in \kappa_{\tau_j}} \sum_{s \in S_{jk}} g_i \cdot \frac{e_{\tau_j}^{ks}}{d_{\tau_j}} \cdot x_{ijks} + \frac{w_j}{2} \qquad \forall j \in J, z_j = 1 \tag{7}$$

$$a_j = \sum_{i \in I} \sum_{k \in \kappa_{\tau_j}} \sum_{s=1}^{2} g_i \cdot \frac{d_{\tau_j} - e_{\tau_j}^{ks}}{d_{\tau_j}} \cdot x_{ijks} + \frac{w_j}{4} \qquad \forall j \in J, z_j = 0 \tag{8}$$

$$b_j = \sum_{i \in I} \sum_{k \in \kappa_{\tau_j}} \sum_{s=1}^{2} g_i \cdot \frac{e_{\tau_j}^{ks}}{d_{\tau_j}} \cdot x_{ijks}$$

$$+ \sum_{i \in I} \sum_{k \in \kappa_{\tau_j}} \sum_{s=3}^{4} g_i \cdot \frac{d_{\tau_j} - e_{\tau_j}^{ks}}{d_{\tau_j}} \cdot x_{ijks} + \frac{w_j}{2} \quad \forall j \in J, z_j = 0 \tag{9}$$

$$c_j = \sum_{i \in I} \sum_{k \in \kappa_{\tau_j}} \sum_{s=3}^{4} g_i \cdot \frac{e_{\tau_j}^{ks}}{d_{\tau_j}} \cdot x_{ijks} + \frac{w_j}{4} \qquad \forall j \in J, z_j = 0 \tag{10}$$

$$a_j \leq \gamma_{\tau_j} \qquad\qquad \forall j \in J \tag{11}$$

$$b_j \leq \gamma_{\tau_j} \qquad\qquad \forall j \in J \tag{12}$$

$$c_j \leq \gamma_{\tau_j} \qquad\qquad \forall j \in J \tag{13}$$

$$a_j - 3 \cdot b_j \leq 0 \qquad\qquad\qquad \forall j \in J \qquad\qquad (14)$$

$$b_j - 3 \cdot a_j \leq 0 \qquad\qquad\qquad \forall j \in J \qquad\qquad (15)$$

$$b_j - 3 \cdot c_j \leq 0 \qquad\qquad\qquad \forall j \in J \qquad\qquad (16)$$

$$c_j - 3 \cdot b_j \leq 0 \qquad\qquad\qquad \forall j \in J \qquad\qquad (17)$$

$$\sum_{i \in I} \sum_{k \in \tau_j} \sum_{s \in S_{jk}} g_i \cdot x_{ijks} \leq W_j \qquad\qquad \forall j \in J \qquad\qquad (18)$$

$$\sum_{i \in I} \sum_{j \in J} \sum_{k \in \kappa_{\tau_j}} \sum_{s \in S_{jk}} g_i \cdot x_{ijks} + \sum_{j \in J} w_j \leq G \qquad\qquad (19)$$

$$x_{ijks} \in \{0,1\} \qquad\qquad \forall i \in I, j \in J, k \in \kappa_{\tau_j}, s \in S_{jk} \qquad (20)$$

$$y_{jk} \in \{0,1\} \qquad\qquad\qquad \forall j \in J, k \in \kappa_{\tau_j} \qquad\qquad (21)$$

The utilization of the available length is maximized while accounting for the urgency of each load unit (1). Each load unit can be assigned to at most one slot (2), and a slot can only carry one load unit (3). Constraint (4) guarantees that a single configuration per wagon is chosen. Furthermore, a load unit can only be assigned if the slot in a chosen configuration fits its dimensions, as indicated by (5). The payload of each bogie is determined by (6) and (7) for wagons with two bogies, and by (8)–(10) for wagons with three bogies. It is assumed that wagons with three bogies can carry at most four load units, two at each side of the center bogie. In case a configuration with only two slots is chosen, one at each side of the center, indices $s = 1$ and $s = 3$ are used. The payloads are limited in (11)–(13). Constraints (14)–(17) ensure that the payloads on each bogie are balanced relative to the adjacent bogies. Furthermore, the allowed wagon weight is limited by (18). The total train weight is limited by (19). Finally, (20) and (21) define the domain of the decision variables.

3.2   Adding Practical Considerations

In this section, additional practical constraints are added to the model, based on the problem context of the company. Trains leaving Belgium or the Netherlands have two destinations, an intermediate destination and a final destination. The first f wagons of the train are decoupled at terminal u, while the remaining ones continue to terminal v. Because of a weight restriction on the railway path between destination u and v, the total train weight limit is lower for the path between the intermediate rail stop and the final destination. In this case, Eq. (19) must be replaced by two separate restrictions (22) and (23), where the sum of both maximum weights, G_u and G_v, constitutes the overall train weight limit. The destination of each wagon j is indicated with D_j. Consequently, the following restriction is added to the problem, where G_u and G_v are the train weight limit for respectively the first f wagons, unloaded at the intermediate terminal, and all other wagons, unloaded at the final terminal.

$$\sum_{i \in I} \sum_{j \in J, \leq f} \sum_{k \in \tau_j} \sum_{s \in S_{jk}} g_i \cdot x_{ijks} + \sum_{j \in J, j \leq f} w_j \leq G_u \qquad (22)$$

$$\sum_{i \in I} \sum_{j \in J, j > f} \sum_{k \in \tau_j} \sum_{s \in S_{jk}} g_i \cdot x_{ijks} + \sum_{j \in J, j > f} w_j \leq G_v \qquad (23)$$

Due to the destination grouping of wagons, load units should be grouped per destination. This can be accomplished by assigning a destination preference λ_{ij} to each load unit, indicating the preference for assigning the load unit to a wagon j with destination D_j. These preferences can be based on the proximity of the unload terminal to the load unit's final destination. To assign as much load units as possible to their preferred destination, a maximization of the number of load units assigned to wagons unloaded at their preferred location is added to the objective function, as in (24). Clearly, preference values should be carefully weighted against the other elements in the objective function.

$$\max \sum_{i \in I} \sum_{j \in J} \sum_{k \in \tau_j} \sum_{s \in S_{jk}} (l_i + p_i + \lambda_{ij}) \cdot x_{ijks} \qquad (24)$$

4   Experimental Case Study

In current literature, data is produced based on real-life characteristics of load units, wagons and configurations in the United States [19], Australia [13–16], Germany [10,11] or Italy [2–7]. As no benchmark instances are available, in this paper, input data and parameter values are set after analysis of load units transported from Belgium to two locations in Northern Italy. Practical considerations (Sect. 3.2) are added to the base model to perform numerical experiments. Priority parameters indicating the urgency with which each load unit must arrive at its destination split load units into three classes: urgent load units, load units with a one-day margin, and non-urgent load units. As urgent load units must always be assigned to a location on the train, their priority value is set very large. No priority is given to non-urgent load units. Furthermore, priority values (p_i) for load units with one day slack are set equal to the parameter value (λ_{ij}) for load units being assigned to their preferred destination.

The wagon set is fixed to a representative composition, consisting of 3 wagons for the intermediate terminal and 19 wagons for the final terminal. The model is tested for three types of instances, consisting of 50, 75 or 100 load units respectively. It is realistic for train planners to have 50 load units available to assign to one specific train. Instances of 75 and 100 load units are considered to simulate the possibility to add load units available for future trains and account for a longer term planning horizon, if this implies an increased train utilization. For each type of instance, 30 instances are randomly sampled by selecting load units from a pool of load units with their characteristics as they were historically shipped. After discussion with practitioners, it is assumed that on average 44 load units can be assigned to the wagon set, consisting of approximately 25 urgent load units. Load units with a margin of one day on their ultimate departure date constitute around 17 load units. The remaining train slots are filled with other available load units. The absolute numbers are converted to percentages in function of the total number of available load units in each instance type, as shown in Table 4, such that on average 25 urgent load units and 17 less urgent load units are available.

Table 4. Input data

	Instance type		
	1	2	3
Number of load units	50	75	100
Average percentage of urgent load units	50	33	25
Average percentage of load units with 1 day slack	25	23	17
Average percentage of non-urgent load units	25	44	58

The model is solved using CPLEX. In order to reflect the real-time environment in which train planners make decisions, a time limit of 20 min is imposed. Results are presented in Table 5.

Table 5. Results

		Instance type		
		1	2	3
Instances solved to optimality		12	5	1
Solution time (s)	Mean (all)	773.2	1085.8	1166.4
	Std Dev (all)	540.1	303.3	186.8
	Mean (only optimal)	132.6	512.6	177.3
	Std Dev (only optimal)	151.8	417.1	0.0
Number of load units assigned	Mean	43.2	43.7	44.3
A_Total length (ft)	Mean	1,469.8	1,526.8	1,530.7
B_Urgent load units	Mean	51,111	47,203.7	50,716.7
C_Destination preferences	Mean	413	419	424
D_Objective value	Mean	52,994	49,150	52,671

In total, 72 out of 90 instances are not solved to optimality, but all with an optimality gap of less than 0.3 %. If more load units are used as input, the overall average run times become slower and less instances are solved to optimality within the time limit. On average, the instances with 75 load units generate the lowest objective value, which may be explained due to the fact that slightly less urgent load units are available (23.5 load units on average due to randomness) for this instance type. With respect to the total length of all load units assigned, the model performs well on average, taking into account the fact that each train has an available loading length of 1590 ft. Looking at the destination preferences, on average only 1 to 2 load units per instance are not assigned to their preferred destination for the currently used preference values. Furthermore, the aim of 44 load units on each train is reached, with an average between 43 and 44 load units for all instance types, indicating that the model performs equally well as the current manual train load planning in the case study.

Results indicate that the model can be used in practice to compose static load plans, or even on a tactical level to analyze and adapt the ideal wagon set composition. However, a number of instances exists in each category for which the optimal solution is not found within the time limit, whereas train planners in this case study require a train load plan to be generated very fast. They want to know immediately if changes to the load plan provide a feasible train load plan. The findings suggest that the exact model's run times are not always fast enough to provide real-time decision support for train planners. Adding a longer planning horizon with more available load units provides more options for train planners to find a train load plan with a higher utilization, at the cost of larger computation times.

5   Conclusions and Future Work

In this paper, practical considerations are added to the train load planning problem to reflect realistic characteristics of the train load planning task, such as the urgency with which load units must be sent to their destination and the flexible routing of load units to one out of two terminals. The model further deals with wagons with three bogies. In this paper, parameter values assigned to each objective are determined arbitrarily based on preliminary testing and analysis of real data. For example, equal importance is attached to destination preferences as to assigning load units with one day slack. However, the relationship between the load unit urgency and its destination preference should be set carefully. Further research will examine the interaction between the objectives and will focus on fine-tuning priority values and destination preferences, after performing additional experiments and further discussions with practitioners. Finally, for some instances run times are too large to provide a train load plan in a short amount of time, as required by practitioners. Consequently, it may be interesting to further analyze the model to determine factors influencing run times the most and maybe turn to heuristics to solve the problem.

Acknowledgments. This work is supported by the Interuniversity Attraction Poles Programme initiated by the Belgian Science Policy Office (research project COMEX, Combinatorial Optimization: Metaheuristics & Exact Methods).

References

1. Aggoun, A., Rhiat, A., Grassien, J.-P.: Online assignments of containers to trains using constraint programming. In: Sombattheera, C., Agarwal, A., Udgata, S.K., Lavangnananda, K. (eds.) MIWAI 2011. LNCS, vol. 7080, pp. 395–405. Springer, Heidelberg (2011)
2. Ambrosino, D., Bramardi, A., Pucciano, M., Sacone, S., Siri, S.: Modeling and solving the train load planning problem in seaport container terminals. In: Proceedings of the 2011 IEEE Conference on Automation Science and Engineering, pp. 208–213. IEEE (2011)
3. Ambrosino, D., Caballini, C., Siri, S.: A mathematical model to evaluate different train loading and stacking policies in a container terminal. Marit. Econ. Logistics 15(3), 292–308 (2013)
4. Ambrosino, D., Siri, S.: Models for train load planning problems in a container terminal. In: de Sousa, J.F., Rossi, R. (eds.) Computer-Based Modelling and Optimization in Transportation, vol. 262, pp. 15–25. Springer, Cham (2014)
5. Ambrosino, D., Siri, S.: Comparison of solution approaches for the train load planning problem in seaport terminals. Transp. Res. Part E Logistics Transp. Rev. 79, 65–82 (2015)
6. Anghinolfi, D., Caballini, C., Sacone, S.: Optimizing train loading operations in innovative and automated container terminals. In: Proceedings of the 19th International Federation of Automatic Control World Congress, 2014, pp. 9581–9586 (2014)
7. Anghinolfi, D., Paolucci, M.: A general purpose lagrangian heuristic applied to the train loading problem. Procedia Soc. Behav. Sci. 108, 37–46 (2014)
8. Boysen, H.E.: General model of railway transportation capacity. In: 13th International Conference on Design and Operation in Railway Engineering (Comprail), pp. 335–347. Wessex Institute of Technology, New Forest (2012)
9. Boysen, H.E.: Øresund and Fehmarnbelt high-capacity rail corridor standards updated. J. Rail Transp. Plan. Manag. 4(3), 44–58 (2014)
10. Bruns, F., Goerigk, M., Knust, S., Schöbel, A.: Robust load planning of trains in intermodal transportation. OR Spectrum 36(3), 631–668 (2014)
11. Bruns, F., Knust, S.: Optimized load planning of trains in intermodal transportation. OR Spectrum 34(3), 511–533 (2012)
12. Caris, A., Macharis, C., Janssens, G.K.: Planning problems in intermodal freight transport: accomplishments and prospects. Transp. Plan. Technol. 31(3), 277–302 (2008)
13. Corry, P., Kozan, E.: Dynamic container train planning. In: Kozan, E. (ed.) Proceedings of the Fifth Asia Pacific Industrial Engineering and Management Systems Conference 2004, pp. 30.4.1–30.4.20. Queensland University of Technology, Brisbane (2004)
14. Corry, P., Kozan, E.: An assignment model for dynamic load planning of intermodal trains. Comput. Oper. Res. 33(1), 1–17 (2006)
15. Corry, P., Kozan, E.: A decision support system for intermodal train planning. In: Kozan, E. (ed.) Proceedings of the Second International Intelligent Logistics Systems Conference, pp. 13.1–13.17 (2006)
16. Corry, P., Kozan, E.: Optimised loading patterns for intermodal trains. OR Spectrum 30(4), 721–750 (2008)
17. Crainic, T.G.: Service network design in freight transportation. Eur. J. Oper. Res. 122(2), 272–288 (2000)

18. European Commission: White paper: Roadmap to a single European transportarea – Towards a competitive and resource efficient transport system (2011)

19. Feo, T.A., González-Velarde, J.L.: The intermodal trailer assignment problem. Transp. Sci. **29**(4), 330–341 (1995)

20. Macharis, C., Bontekoning, Y.: Opportunities for OR in intermodal freight transport research: a review. Eur. J. Oper. Res. **153**(2), 400–416 (2004)

21. Stahlbock, R., Voß, S.: Operations research at container terminals: a literature update. OR Spectrum **30**(1), 1–52 (2008)

22. Steenken, D., Voß, S., Stahlbock, R.: Container terminal operation and operations research - a classification and literature review. OR Spectrum **26**(1), 3–49 (2004)

23. Woodburn, A.: An empirical study of the variability in the composition of British freight trains. J. Rail Transp. Plan. Manag. **5**(4), 294–308 (2015)

Analysis of Cost Allocation Techniques for Freight Bundling Networks in Intermodal Transport

Katrien Ramaekers[1(✉)], Lotte Verdonck[1,2], An Caris[1], Dries Meers[3], and Cathy Macharis[3]

[1] Universiteit Hasselt, Agoralaan - building D, 3590 Diepenbeek, Belgium
[2] Research Foundation Flanders (FWO), Egmontstraat 5, 1000 Brussels, Belgium
{katrien.ramaekers,lotte.verdonck,an.caris}@uhasselt.be
[3] Research Group MOBI, Vrije Universiteit Brussel,
Pleinlaan 2, 1050 Brussels, Belgium
{Dries.Meers,cathy.macharis}@vub.ac.be

Abstract. In order to improve the competitive position and efficiency level of intermodal transport, consolidation of freight flows is often suggested. Bundling networks require cooperation between multiple partners in the intermodal transport chain. In this context, the question rises how benefits may be allocated fairly among the participants in the cooperation. A great deal of scientific literature reports on the behavior of allocation methods in collaborations between shippers or carriers making use of unimodal road transport. However, research on cost or savings allocation methods in intermodal transport is scarce. Moreover, since various types of vessels with differing price structures may be considered in intermodal barge transport, the application of allocation mechanisms is not so straightforward compared to a unimodal environment. The main contribution of this paper is thus to provide a first insight in the complexity of sharing cost savings fairly amongst shippers who bundle freight flows in order to reach economies of scale in intermodal barge transport. By applying three different allocation methods, a comparison is made between simple and straightforward allocation mechanisms and more advanced techniques based on cooperative game theory. Special attention is also paid to the stability of the found solutions. The situation of three-, four- and five-partner coalitions is investigated, both for partners with an equal and an unequal amount of shipments. For these six situations, the case of a common barge trajectory and a common end terminal are studied.

Keywords: Cost allocation · Consolidation · Intermodal transportation · Shipper collaboration

1 Introduction

Policy makers at European as well as regional levels express the need to stimulate intermodal transport chains [8]. Macharis and Bontekoning [14] define intermodal

© Springer International Publishing Switzerland 2016
A. Paias et al. (Eds.): ICCL 2016, LNCS 9855, pp. 209–226, 2016.
DOI: 10.1007/978-3-319-44896-1_14

transport as the combination of at least two modes of transport in a single transport chain, without a change of container for the goods, with most of the route travelled by rail, inland waterway or ocean-going vessel and with the shortest possible initial and final journeys by road. A growing market share for intermodal transport should mean a shift towards more environmental friendly transport modes, less congestion and a better accessibility of seaports. In order to improve the competitive position and efficiency level of intermodal transport, consolidation of freight flows is often suggested as it creates denser freight flows and leads to economies of scale.

Multiple research efforts have been undertaken to investigate bundling networks in intermodal transport. The basic idea is to consolidate loads for efficient long-haul transportation (e.g. by rail, inland waterway barge or ocean-going vessel), while taking advantage of the efficiency of local pickup and delivery operations by truck [1]. Kreutzberger [11] analyzes in which transport landscape which bundling network types ensure the lowest operational cost and which of the lowest cost bundling networks may be competitive with unimodal road transport. Kreutzberger and Konings [12] propose a new concept to bundle the container hinterland transport flows of the seaports of Rotterdam and Antwerp in order to increase the size of trainloads, the service frequency or the network connectivity and hence to improve the cost performance and quality of rail hinterland transport. Caris et al. [4] point out that the analysis of bundling networks for intermodal barge transport is necessary to further integrate inland waterways in the intermodal supply chain. Bundling networks in intermodal barge transport, which are the focus of our paper, have been studied amongst others by [5,6,10]. Braekers et al. [3] present a decision support tool for bundling freight in a corridor network in intermodal barge transport. Barge operators, logistic service providers or shipping lines that want to offer regular roundtrip barge services between a number of ports located along the same waterway may use this model to determine vessel capacity and frequency of these roundtrips. Van Lier et al. [22] discuss bundling of freight activities at the operational level. Shippers attain scale economies and a better utilization of transport equipment through consolidation of freight inside a loading unit. The cost of freight transport may be decreased by raising the fill rate of loading units. This may on the one hand reduce the costs of pre- and end-haulage by road or on the other hand increase the attractiveness of intermodal freight transport for further continental distribution.

Bundling networks require cooperation between multiple partners in the intermodal transport chain. Questions rise which type of bundling network is manageable and how benefits may be allocated among the participants in the cooperation. While economies of scale are an obvious advantage for the consolidation of freight flows as a whole (as opposed to the sum of the stand-alone costs of the partners), the benefits for a single partner are not always clear. Cruijssen et al. [7] suggest incentive alignment as a crucial facilitator for horizontal cooperation in transport and logistics. Realigning the benefits and burdens among the partners results in an individual responsibility for the attainment of overall coalition profitability. One such realignment mechanism is the fair division of cooperation related costs or savings in such a manner that partners are induced to behave according to the collaborative goal. A great deal of scientific literature reports on the behavior of cost or savings allocation methods in collaborations between shippers or carriers making use of unimodal road transport. A structured overview of allocation mechanisms applied in a unimodal road collaboration context can be found in Verdonck et al. [24]. In intermodal barge transport various types of vessels with differing price structures may be considered for the bundling network. As such, applying the allocation methods which have been thoroughly studied in a unimodal road context is not so straightforward in an intermodal environment. Moreover, research on cost or savings allocation methods in intermodal transport is scarce. To the best of our knowledge, the only scientific contributions which study allocation mechanisms in intermodal transport are [19, 20]. Both papers apply game theoretic methods to allocate costs fairly in a cooperative intermodal project consisting of terminal operating companies bundling freight. No studies have yet been performed on allocation methods for collaboration between shippers making use of intermodal barge transport. In addition, as game theoretic allocation mechanisms may raise questions from partnering companies about mathematical complexity and fairness transparency, this paper applies two additional allocation techniques to the intermodal freight bundling problem. The main contribution of our research is thus to provide a first insight in the complexity of sharing cost savings fairly amongst shippers who bundle freight flows in order to reach economies of scale in intermodal barge transport.

The remainder of this paper is organized as follows. In Sect. 2 the current research field of allocation methods proposed for collaborations in unimodal transport is discussed. Next, Sect. 3 presents a case study in which shippers cooperate to bundle their freight flows and make use of intermodal barge transport. Three different allocation methods are applied to provide clarity in the allocation of cost savings among the participants. In this way, a comparison is made between simple and straightforward allocation methods and more advanced techniques based on cooperative game theory. Finally, conclusions are formulated.

2   Collaborative Cost Allocation

As the goal of a logistics cooperation is to increase the participants' efficiency and since collaboration often results in additional profits or cost savings, a great deal of scientific literature on unimodal collaborative logistics devotes its research attention to the identification of efficient allocation schemes. Dividing the coalition costs or savings in a fair manner constitutes a key issue, since the proposed allocation mechanism should induce partners to behave according to the collaborative goal and may improve cooperation stability.

Verdonck et al. [24] provide a structured review of allocation mechanisms applied in unimodal horizontal collaborations distinguishing between (1) proportional sharing mechanisms, (2) allocation mechanisms using game theory concepts and (3) allocation techniques designed to cope with additional cooperation properties. Firstly, the most commonly used profit or cost division mechanism in practice is the proportional allocation method [13]. In this case, the collaborative profit is allocated to the cooperating organizations equally, on the basis of, among others, their individual cost level or the volume they have to transport as a consequence of their engagement in the cooperation [24]. A detailed description and a numerical application of two proportional allocation methods can be found in Sects. 3.3 and 3.4 respectively. Secondly, a logistics cooperation clearly matches the structure of a cooperative game. Collaborating partners share and consolidate freight and receive or make payments in return. This cooperation process results in an allocation of benefits or costs to each participant that may be considered equivalent to the outcome of a cooperative game. A well-known allocation method based on the foundations of game theory is the Shapley [18] value. This value allocates to each participant the weighted average of his contributions to all (sub)coalitions, assuming the grand coalition is formed one company at a time [24]. A detailed theoretical description and a numerical application of the classic Shapley value to our intermodal freight bundling case can be found in Sects. 3.3 and 3.4 respectively. A more complex allocation mechanism supported by game theory is the nucleolus. This profit or cost sharing procedure, developed by Schmeidler [17], has the distinct property of minimizing the maximal excess, which constitutes the difference between the total cost of a coalition and the sum of the costs allocated to its participants. Finally, several authors have developed distinct, more intuitively clear allocation mechanisms that account for certain specific cooperation characteristics, some of them partly based on game theory ideas [24]. Tijs and Driessen [21] discuss three allocation techniques based on the division of the total collaborative costs in separable and non-separable costs. Frisk et al. [9] and Liu et al. [13] create profit sharing mechanisms with the goal of finding a stable allocation that minimizes the largest relative difference in cost savings between any pair of cooperating partners. Özener and Ergun [16] develop allocation mechanisms ensuring that, among others, existing partners do not loose savings when an additional company joins the collaboration.

The overview provided in the previous paragraph demonstrates that a wide range of possible allocation mechanisms exists. As each method has its specific benefits and drawbacks, it remains ambiguous which technique(s) could guarantee stability and sustainability in an intermodal freight bundling context. Moreover, the only scientific contributions which study allocation mechanisms in intermodal transport are [19,20] applying game theoretic methods to allocate costs fairly in a cooperative intermodal project consisting of terminal operating companies bundling freight. For this reason, a comparative analysis, applying three different allocation mechanisms to a case study, is performed in Sect. 3. A comparison is made between two simple and straightforward cost allocation methods often used in practice and one more advanced technique based on cooperative game theory. In addition, special attention is paid to the stability of the found solutions. In this way, we are the first to provide insight in the complexity of sharing cost savings fairly amongst shippers who bundle freight flows in order to reach economies of scale in intermodal barge transport.

3   Case Study

The case study is carried out within the framework of the Aggregate-Disaggregate-Aggregate (ADA) model of Ben-Akiva and de Jong [2], an activity-based freight transportation model. The ADA-model is originally developed for the Netherlands but the concepts have also been applied to Flanders [15]. In Sect. 3.1 the generation of the freight flows, based on the ADA-model and used in the case study, is illustrated. For clarification purposes, an example of a Total Logistic Cost (TLC) calculation is given in Sect. 3.2. In Sect. 3.3 the selected allocation methods are explained in detail and in Sect. 3.4 numerical results are presented.

3.1   Freight Flows

In the freight transportation model for Flanders, the 308 communities of Flanders are used as zones. The model starts from the production-consumption (PC)-flows per NSTR category between the different zones. The NSTR classification is a standard goods classification for transport statistics, which is often used in Europe. In a first step, the disaggregation step, the PC-flows are disaggregated to firm-to-firm flows, based on the number of producers of the commodity in the first zone, the number of consumers of the commodity in the second zone and the fraction of actually realized links between senders and receivers of the two zones. Next, all possible transport chains for every firm-to-firm flow are built and the Total Logistic Cost (TLC) is calculated for each transport chain. An average shipment size (based on the NSTR category) is used to build the transport chains. The TLC function exists of an ordering cost, an inventory cost, a capital cost of the goods in transport and in inventory and a transport cost. The transport cost is split into several components: a variable cost based on the distance of the links traveled, a transshipment cost between different transport modes and a loading and unloading cost. The TLC is used to determine the optimal transfer points for chains which use several transport modes and to determine the best transport chain(s) for a given firm-to-firm flow. In Sect. 3.2, the TLC calculations and the necessary data are described in more detail.

In the remainder of this paper, all 'road–inland waterways–road' transport chains of the transportation model are considered and the options for bundling are studied. In the terminology of Woxenius [25], our case may be considered a corridor bundling strategy, which appears to be most suited in an intermodal barge context. Two possible bundling options are taken into account: chains which have the entire barge trajectory in common and chains which have one terminal in common. In Sect. 3.4, results of a numerical example are presented. First, the total logistic cost is calculated when several firm-to-firm flows are consolidated. Next, the collaborative cost savings realized by consolidating, as opposed to the sum of the stand-alone costs of the partnering shippers, are divided using the methods described in Sect. 3.3.

3.2   Total Logistic Cost Calculations

In this section, an example of a TLC calculation is given for the transport of goods of NSTR-category 1 (agricultural goods) between Antwerp and Kortrijk, two Belgian cities. As stated earlier, only the road–inland waterways–road transport chains are considered in this paper. The data, necessary for the calculations is shown in Table 1. Using the terminals from Deurne and Wielsbeke leads to the lowest TLC, resulting in a main haulage distance of 128.25 km and a pre- and end-haulage by truck of 9.9 and 14.75 km respectively.

Table 1. Notation and data

Symbol	Description	Value
o	Order cost	55 €
Q	Yearly demand (in ton)	664 tonnes
q	Shipment size (in ton)	68.4 tonnes
D_{ph}	Distance pre-haulage	9.9 km
D_{mh}	Distance main-haulage	128.25 km
D_{eh}	Distance end-haulage	14.75 km
TC_r	Transport cost road	1 €/km
TC_{iww}	Transport cost inland waterways	6 €/km
Cap_{iww}	Capacity inland waterways	1000 tonnes
L_r	Cost to (un)load road	2 €/ton
L_{iww}	Cost to (un)load inland waterways	0.4 €/ton
d	Interest rate (per year)	4 %
v	Value of goods	672 €/ton
w	Warehouse cost	20 %

First the number of shipments per year z is calculated and rounded up to the next integer number. Next, the order cost, the transport cost, the capital cost of goods in transit, the inventory cost and the capital cost of inventory are calculated. For detailed calculations on all cost components, the reader is referred to [15].

3.3   Applied Cost Allocation Methods: Description, Calculation and Properties

This section describes the three cost allocation techniques selected for their application in the case study. Details are provided on their theoretical foundation, calculation approach and fairness properties.

The reasons for choosing the proportional, decomposition and Shapley method are the following. Up to now only game theoretic methods have been applied to allocate costs fairly in a cooperative intermodal network [19,20]. The most prevalent solution concepts within cooperative game theory are the Shapley value and the nucleolus. The preference for the Shapley value may be explained by its ease of calculation. However, basic game theoretic mechanisms may raise questions about mathematical complexity, applicability, fairness transparency and stability in practice. As such, the importance of convenient implementation and interpretation in practice favors the use of the proportional and decomposition methods. In addition, in this way a comparison can be made between simple and straightforward allocation mechanisms and more advanced techniques based on cooperative game theory.

The notation used in this section is explained in Table 2. The grand coalition N coincides with all participating shippers i in the cooperation, while a coalition S denotes a subset of collaborators. When a coalition S collaborates, they realize a certain amount of collaborative costs which can be captured using the function $c(S)$. As such, the benefits or cost savings generated by a coalition $S, \forall S \subseteq N$, denoted by $v(S)$, are equivalently calculated as $\sum_{i \in S} c(i) - c(S)$. Each considered allocation method assigns a cost c_i or a savings amount y_i to coalition participant i [24].

Table 2. Notation

i, j	Individual partner
N	Grand coalition
S	Subcoalition
$c(N), c(S)$	Cost of a coalition
$c(i)$	Stand-alone cost of partner i
$v(N), v(S)$	Cost savings of a coalition
c_i	Cost allocated to partner i
y_i	Savings allocated to partner i

Cost allocations satisfy a variety of properties desirable in the context of a logistics collaboration. Table 3, based on Vanovermeire [23] and Verdonck et al. [24], provides an outline of allocation characteristics satisfied by the Shapley value and the applied proportional mechanisms.

Proportional Allocation Based on Volume. In practice, the most commonly used profit or cost division mechanism is the proportional allocation method [13]. In this case, the collaborative profit is allocated to the cooperating organizations equally, on the basis of their stand-alone cost or the volume they have to transport as a consequence of their engagement in the cooperation. The reason for the widespread use of the proportional allocation technique lies in the fact that it is easy to understand, compute and implement. However, it does not guarantee long-term collaboration stability as it is possible that an

Table 3. Fairness properties satisfied by proportional and Shapley allocations

Property	Proportional (volume & trajectory links)	Shapley
Group rationality (Efficiency) [1]	✓	✓
Individual rationality [2]		✓
Anonymity (Symmetry) [3]		✓
Stability [4]		
Dummy [5]		✓
Additivity [6]		✓

[1] The total cooperative cost is shared as the grand coalition forms: $\sum_{i \in N} c_i = c(N)$
[2] No carrier pays more than his stand-alone cost: $c_i \leq c(\{i\}), \forall i \in N$
[3] The identity of the participants does not change the resulting allocation, each partner gains the same amount when cooperating in the same way with fellow organizations: $c(S \cup i) = c(S \cup j) \rightarrow c_i = c_j$
[4] No single participant or subcoalition of participants of the collaboration would benefit from leaving the grand coalition: $\sum_{i \in S} c_i \leq c(S)$ and $\sum_{i \in N} c_i = c(N)$
[5] Participants, who add zero benefits to the coalition they join, should not be allocated a share of the collaborative savings
[6] The cost allocation of a combination of several separate coalitions is equal to the sum of the separate allocation values of these coalitions: $c(i + j) = c(i) + c(j)$

individual partner leaves the partnership considering the fact that he may gain more when operating on an individual basis [13,24].

The proportional allocations computed in our case study are volume based. This volume is expressed as the number of shipments z_i per year that each coalition partner i requires along the same trajectory. Total collaborative savings are weighted with each participant's volume as follows:

$$y_i = w_i * v(N) \qquad \forall i \in N \tag{1}$$

with $w_i = \frac{z_i}{\sum_{i \in N} z_i}$.

Decomposition Method. A second gain sharing mechanism especially suited for intermodal freight transport is based on a decomposition of the total trajectory in common links of the participants. A volume based proportional allocation, as described in the previous paragraph, is then applied on each of these links separately. For example, in a cooperation between three shippers A, B and C, the total transport chain may be divided in two common links. On the first common link shippers A and B bundle their freight. On the second link, the freight of all three participants is consolidated. The proportional allocation method will share collaborative savings on the first link between shippers A and B according to their number of shipments. Along the second link, coalition savings will be shared proportionally according to the number of shipments of participants A, B and C respectively.

Shapley Value. To allow a comparison of relatively simple and intuitive proportional methods with more complex game-theoretic allocation methods, we chose Shapley as our third allocation mechanism. The Shapley value [18] allocates to each participant the weighted average of his contributions to all (sub)coalitions, assuming the grand coalition is formed one company at a time. The Shapley allocation to participant i can be mathematically expressed as:

$$c_i = \sum_{S \subseteq N \setminus \{i\}} \frac{(|S| - 1)!(|N| - |S|)!}{|N|!} [c(S \cup i) - c(S)] \tag{2}$$

with $|.|$ denoting the number of participants in the considered (sub)coalition. The Shapley value provides a unique allocation with characteristics that are beneficial in the context of a logistics cooperation, as visualized in Table 3. However, the Shapley value has an important disadvantage, namely that this allocation may not lead to a stable collaboration [9,13,24].

3.4 Results

The firm-to-firm flows of Sect. 3.1 are now bundled in order to calculate the collaborative savings of this bundling as opposed to the sum of the stand-alone costs of the partnering shippers. First, the total logistic cost of the bundled situation is determined. Next, the collaborative savings are shared among the participants of the coalition using the three methods described in Sect. 3.3. In the next paragraph, the experimental design is explained. Then, an example is given of how the sharing of the collaborative savings is determined for the three different allocation methods. Finally, the results of the experiment are described.

Experimental Design. In this paper, a first insight is provided in the complexity of sharing collaborative cost savings fairly amongst shippers who bundle freight flows in order to reach economies of scale in intermodal barge transport. The impact of the number of partners, the equality of partners and the common trajectory is examined. The situation of three, four and five partners is investigated, both for partners with an equal and an unequal amount of shipments. For these six situations, the case of a common barge trajectory and a common end terminal are studied.

First, it is assumed that only one type of vessel is available. As a consequence, bundling always leads to a higher fill rate and therefore, to a lower transport cost. In this case, important properties of cost allocation methods as individual rationality and stability are always satisfied. Next, a second type of vessel (with a higher capacity and a higher cost) is introduced, which adds more realistic characteristics of intermodal barge transport to the problem. In this context, attention is paid to the properties of the allocation methods.

Example: Collaborative Gain Sharing Among Partners. In this example, firm-to-firm flows which use the same end terminal for their barge transport are

Table 4. Example: situation before bundling

Firm-to-firm flow	Shipments	Stand-alone TLC
Zaventem-Antwerpen	3	8461€
Mechelen-Antwerpen	17	20792€
Aalst-Antwerpen	7	13112€

bundled. Three flows are used: Zaventem-Antwerpen (partner A), Mechelen-Antwerpen (partner B) and Aalst-Antwerpen (partner C). The barge trajectory that is followed is Brussel-Vilvoorde-Willebroek-Deurne. The goods from Aalst start their barge transport in Brussel, the goods from Zavemtem start their barge transport in Vilvoorde and the goods from Mechelen start their barge transport in Willebroek. All goods end the barge transport in Deurne. The number of shipments and the stand-alone cost for each partner is given in Table 4.

The barge trajectory can be divided in three parts for this example: Brussel-Vilvoorde, Vilvoorde-Willebroek and Willebroek-Deurne. The first part, Brussel-Vilvoorde, is only used by the flow Aalst-Antwerpen and no bundling can take place on that part. The second part, Vilvoorde-Willebroek, is used by two partners: three shipments can be bundled for this part of the trajectory, the four residual shipments of Aalst-Antwerpen cannot be bundled. The third part, Willebroek-Deurne, is used by all three partners: three shipments can be bundled for the three partners, an additional four shipments can be bundled for two partners (Aalst-Antwerpen and Mechelen-Antwerpen) and ten shipments of Mechelen-Antwerpen cannot be bundled. The total logistic cost for this situation equals 40311€ and the total gain is 2055€.

Using the proportional allocation method, the total savings amount is divided over the partners based on the number of shipments of each partner. This results in a benefit of 228€ for partner A, 1294€ for partner B and 533€ for partner C. With the decomposition method, the cost savings amount is calculated for each part of the barge trajectory separately. In this example, the barge trajectory can be divided in three parts: Brussel-Vilvoorde, Vilvoorde-Willebroek and Willebroek-Deurne. The first part, Brussel-Vilvoorde, is only used by the flow Aalst-Antwerpen so no bundling can take place on this part. In the second part, Vilvoorde-Willebroek, two participants can bundle freight. The benefit of 278€ is allocated to these two partners based on their number of shipments. In the last part of the trajectory, Willebroek-Deurne, the shipments of the three partners can be bundled. The benefit of 1777€ earned on this part of the trajectory is again divided over the three partners based on their respective number of shipments. To determine the Shapley value for each partner, Eq. (2) is used. In this way, each participant is allocated the weighted average of his contributions to all possible (sub)coalitions. The results of applying the three cost allocation methods to the example are shown in Table 5.

Table 5. Example: cost allocation results (in €)

Firm-to-firm flow	Stand-alone	Proportional	Decomposition	Shapley
Zaventem-Antwerpen	8461	8233	8180	7967
Mechelen-Antwerpen	20792	19498	19673	20081
Aalst-Antwerpen	13112	12580	12457	12263

Table 6. Results: common barge trajectory, equal partners (in €)

	Firm-to-firm flow	Stand-alone	Proportional	Shapley
3 partners	Gent-Antwerpen	22452	17896	17896
	Aalst-Antwerpen	23695	19139	19139
	Brugge-Antwerpen	24174	19618	19618
4 partners	Gent-Antwerpen	22452	17327	17327
	Aalst-Antwerpen	23695	18570	18570
	Brugge-Antwerpen	24174	19049	19049
	Gent-Antwerpen	22452	17327	17327
5 partners	Gent-Antwerpen	22452	16985	16985
	Aalst-Antwerpen	23695	18228	18228
	Brugge-Antwerpen	24174	18707	18707
	Gent-Antwerpen	22452	16985	16985
	Brugge-Antwerpen	24174	18707	18707

Results. The results of the experiments with only one vessel type are summarized in Tables 6, 7, 8 and 9. Tables 6 and 7 present the results of the case of a common barge trajectory. Tables 8 and 9 visualize the results of the case of a common end terminal. As in the example described above, first the stand-alone cost (the cost without bundling) is given. Next, the results after bundling are provided for each partner using the proportional allocation method, the decomposition method and the Shapley value.

When all partners share the complete barge trajectory, the decomposition method is not applied since the barge trajectory does not have to be split up in separate links. If the partners are equal in size (Table 6), the proportional allocation method and the Shapley value lead to the same results. If the partners are unequal in size (Table 7), the Shapley value favors the smaller partners of the coalition, i.e. more benefit is granted to the smaller partners Aalst-Antwerpen and Brugge-Antwerpen. These conclusions are valid for three, four and five partners.

When the partners only share the same end terminal, the three allocation methods presented in Sect. 3.3 can be applied. If the partners are equal in size, the results of the decomposition method are equal to the results of the Shapley value (Table 8). Compared to the proportional allocation method, decomposition

Table 7. Results: common barge trajectory, unequal partners (in €)

	Firm-to-firm flow	Shipments	Stand-alone	Proportional	Shapley
3 partners	Gent-Antwerpen	23	33330	27972	29344
	Aalst-Antwerpen	7	14573	12942	12295
	Brugge-Antwerpen	14	24174	20912	20188
4 partners	Gent-Antwerpen	23	33330	27268	29100
	Aalst-Antwerpen	27	14573	12728	12051
	Brugge-Antwerpen	14	24174	20484	19943
	Gent-Antwerpen	6	12718	11137	10522
5 partners	Gent-Antwerpen	23	33330	26798	28978
	Aalst-Antwerpen	7	14573	12585	11929
	Brugge-Antwerpen	14	24174	20198	19821
	Gent-Antwerpen	6	12718	11014	10400
	Brugge-Antwerpen	5	12159	10739	10206

Table 8. Results: common end terminal, equal partners (in €)

	Firm-to-firm flow	Stand-alone	Proportional	Decomposition	Shapley
3 partners	Zaventem-Antwerpen	12466	11420	11312	11312
	Mechelen-Antwerpen	11792	10747	10963	10963
	Aalst-Antwerpen	13112	12067	11959	11959
4 partners	Zaventem-Antwerpen	12466	11208	11100	11100
	Mechelen-Antwerpen	11792	10535	10859	10859
	Aalst-Antwerpen	13112	11855	11747	11747
	Zaventem-Antwerpen	12466	11208	11100	11100
5 partners	Zaventem-Antwerpen	12466	11211	11038	11038
	Mechelen-Antwerpen	11792	10538	10797	10797
	Aalst-Antwerpen	13112	11858	11685	11685
	Zaventem-Antwerpen	12466	11211	11038	11038
	Mechelen-Antwerpen	11792	10538	10797	10797

and Shapley favor partners that take part in more links of the barge trajectory, i.e. more benefit is granted to Zaventem-Antwerpen and Aalst-Antwerpen both taking part in two bundled links. If the partners are unequal in size, the three cost allocation methods lead to different results (Table 9). Compared to the proportional allocation method, the decomposition method favors partners that take part in more bundled links. Comparing the results of the Shapley value to those of the decomposition method for three partners, the partners taking part in more bundled parts are even more in favor. However, these participants are coincidentally also the smaller participants in the coalition and previous results already revealed the benefit of Shapley for smaller participants. When an

Table 9. Results: common end terminal, unequal partners (in €)

	Firm-to-firm flow	Shipments	Stand-alone	Proportional	Decomposition	Shapley
3 partners	Zaventem-Antwerpen	3	8461	8233	8180	7967
	Mechelen-Antwerpen	17	20792	19498	19673	20081
	Aalst-Antwerpen	7	13112	12580	12457	12263
4 partners	Zaventem-Antwerpen	3	8461	8102	8033	7876
	Mechelen-Antwerpen	17	20792	18760	19198	19741
	Aalst-Antwerpen	7	13112	12276	12114	11868
	Zaventem-Antwerpen	9	14484	13408	13200	13062
5 partners	Zaventem-Antwerpen	3	8461	8081	8003	7849
	Mechelen-Antwerpen	17	20792	18639	19024	19685
	Aalst-Antwerpen	7	13112	12226	12043	11812
	Zaventem-Antwerpen	9	14484	13344	13108	13005
	Mechelen-Antwerpen	5	9988	9355	9468	9295

analogue comparison is made for coalitions established between 5 partners, we can improve our insights and conclude that the Shapley value especially favors the smaller partners. For example, the two flows from Zaventem to Antwerpen both benefit from the Shapley value compared to the decomposition method but the smaller flow (three shipments) is much more rewarded by the Shapley value than the larger flow (nine shipments). When comparing the results for the two flows from Mechelen to Antwerpen, the results are even more distinct: although this flow only takes part in one bundled link, the Shapley value leads to favoring results compared to the proportional allocation method for the smaller partner (five shipments). For the larger partner (17 shipments) the Shapley value grants the least benefit of all three cost allocation methods to this partner.

Until now, only one vessel type is used in the experiments and as a consequence, bundling always leads to a lower transport cost. Therefore, important properties of cost allocation methods as individual rationality and a stable cooperation are always satisfied. To illustrate the use of the cost allocation methods when more vessel types are available, the same experiments are repeated but with a shipment size of 273.6 tonnes. In this case, four and five partners can only bundle their freight if another type of vessel is used since the initial type of vessel has a capacity of only 1000 tonnes. The second type of vessel that is introduced in the case study has a capacity of 2000 tonnes and a transport cost of 9€ per kilometer. The results for the experiments with two vessel types are summarized in Tables 10, 11, 12 and 13. Tables 10 and 11 present the results of the case of a common barge trajectory. Tables 12 and 13 visualize the results of the case of a common end terminal.

Compared to the results of the experiments with one vessel type, two important differences can be observed. First, when the coalition is extended from three to four partners, all partners have a higher allocated cost due to the use of the second (and more expensive) vessel type. When the coalition is extended from four to five partners, the extra costs of the second vessel type are spread over more partners and thus the cost allocated to each partner is lower than in the case of four partners. When comparing the results of five partners with those of

Table 10. Results: common barge trajectory, equal partners, two vessel types (in €)

	Firm-to-firm flow	Stand-alone	Proportional	Shapley
3 partners	Gent-Antwerpen	34789	33487	33487
	Aalst-Antwerpen	36091	34790	34790
	Brugge-Antwerpen	36593	35291	35291
4 partners	Gent-Antwerpen	34789	33569	33569
	Aalst-Antwerpen	36091	34871	34871
	Brugge-Antwerpen	36593	35373	35373
	Gent-Antwerpen	34789	33569	33569
5 partners	Gent-Antwerpen	34789	33422	33422
	Aalst-Antwerpen	36091	34725	34725
	Brugge-Antwerpen	36593	35226	35226
	Gent-Antwerpen	34789	33422	33422
	Brugge-Antwerpen	36593	35226	35226

Table 11. Results: common barge trajectory, unequal partners, two vessel types (in €)

	Firm-to-firm flow	Shipments	Stand-alone	Proportional	Shapley
3 partners	Gent-Antwerpen	6	41188	39724	40049
	Aalst-Antwerpen	2	29067	28579	28416
	Brugge-Antwerpen	4	36593	35617	35454
4 partners	Gent-Antwerpen	6	41188	40142	40344
	Aalst-Antwerpen	2	29067	28718	28701
	Brugge-Antwerpen	4	36593	35896	35739
	Gent-Antwerpen	2	28388	28040	28022
5 partners	Gent-Antwerpen	6	41188	39907	40310
	Aalst-Antwerpen	2	29067	28640	28554
	Brugge-Antwerpen	4	36593	35739	35592
	Gent-Antwerpen	2	28388	27961	27876
	Brugge-Antwerpen	2	29282	28855	28770

three partners, it depends on the experiment and the partner considered whether the allocated cost is less than in the case with three partners. Therefore, it is important to look at the stability of these results. The second major difference is that the Shapley value now leads to allocation values differing from the decomposition method for the case of a common end terminal with equal partners. This can be explained by the fact that the Shapley value rewards partners that contribute most to the collaborative goal. Since the partner Aalst-Antwerpen has to perform the first part of the barge trajectory alone with the more expensive

Table 12. Results: common end terminal, equal partners, two vessel types (in €)

	Firm-to-firm flow	Stand-alone	Proportional	Decomposition	Shapley
3 partners	Zaventem-Antwerpen	28020	27722	27691	27691
	Mechelen-Antwerpen	27810	27511	27573	27573
	Aalst-Antwerpen	28467	28168	28137	28137
4 partners	Zaventem-Antwerpen	28020	27740	27706	27709
	Mechelen-Antwerpen	27810	27529	27588	27622
	Aalst-Antwerpen	28467	28186	28195	28155
	Zaventem-Antwerpen	28020	27740	27706	27709
5 partners	Zaventem-Antwerpen	28020	27725	27679	27673
	Mechelen-Antwerpen	27810	27514	27561	27586
	Aalst-Antwerpen	28467	28171	28169	28130
	Zaventem-Antwerpen	28020	27725	27679	27673
	Mechelen-Antwerpen	27810	27514	27561	27586

Table 13. Results: common end terminal, unequal partners, two vessel types (in €)

	Firm-to-firm flow	Shipments	Stand-alone	Proportional	Decomposition	Shapley
3 partners	Zaventem-Antwerpen	1	25023	29944	24925	24858
	Mechelen-Antwerpen	5	36432	36040	36098	36224
	Aalst-Antwerpen	2	28467	28310	28272	28213
4 partners	Zaventem-Antwerpen	1	25023	24957	24943	24984
	Mechelen-Antwerpen	5	36432	36105	36149	36248
	Aalst-Antwerpen	2	28467	28336	28351	28264
	Zaventem-Antwerpen	3	30983	30788	30744	30691
5 partners	Zaventem-Antwerpen	1	25023	24940	24924	24931
	Mechelen-Antwerpen	5	36432	36019	36056	36224
	Aalst-Antwerpen	2	28467	28302	28314	28206
	Zaventem-Antwerpen	3	30983	30736	30688	30634
	Mechelen-Antwerpen	2	27790	27625	27640	27627

vessel type, its cost savings compared to the non-collaborative scenario become negative. As such, this partner has to make the most profound changes in its transport activities. The Shapley value accounts for this contribution by rewarding this partner with a higher share in the collaborative savings.

To identify whether the cost allocations defined for the studied cases with two vessel types guarantee cooperation stability, compliance of the proportional, decomposition and Shapley solutions with individual, subgroup and group rationality is verified. Analyzing cost allocations over all cases reveals that stability of the grand coalition is guaranteed in all three-partner collaborations. If the grand coalition is stable, then no subgroup of partner companies has the incentive to leave the grand coalition and be better off acting alone. In contrast, none of the four-partner coalitions are stable. As the shipment sizes considered in our case result in a lot of unused capacity for the more expensive vessel type, collaborating becomes detrimental for the partnering shippers. Stability of the five-partner coalitions depends on the equality of the partners. When collaborating shippers are equal in terms of shipment sizes the grand coalition is stable. The remark needs to be made here, however, that for the case of a common end terminal other allocation mechanisms besides Shapley, proportional and decomposition are needed to define a stable solution. A possible alternative may be the Equal Profit Method, developed by [9]. Collaborations set up between five shippers with different shipment sizes do not guarantee long-term stability in our case study.

4   Conclusions

Policy makers at European as well as regional levels express the need to stimulate intermodal transport chains. In order to improve the competitive position and efficiency level of intermodal transport, consolidation of freight flows is often suggested. Bundling networks requires cooperation between multiple partners in the intermodal transport chain. In this context, question rises how benefits may be allocated fairly among the participants in the cooperation. A great deal of scientific literature reports on the behavior of allocation methods in collaborations between shippers or carriers making use of unimodal road transport. In intermodal barge transport various types of vessels with differing price structures may be considered for the bundling network. As such, applying the allocation methods which have been thoroughly studied in a unimodal road context is not so straightforward in an intermodal environment. Moreover, research on cost or savings allocation methods in intermodal transport is scarce. The main contribution of our paper is thus to provide a first insight in the complexity of sharing cost savings fairly amongst shippers who bundle freight flows in order to reach economies of scale in intermodal barge transport. By applying three different allocation methods, a comparison is made between simple and straightforward allocation mechanisms and more advanced techniques based on cooperative game theory.

First, the situation of one vessel type is studied. When the partners in the coalition share the complete barge trajectory, there is no difference in applying the proportional allocation method and the decomposition method. The Shapley value leads to the same result as the proportional allocation method if the partners of the coalition are equal. If the partners of the coalition are unequal, the Shapley value leads to different results and favors the smaller partners in the coalition. When the partners of the coalition only share a common end terminal, the barge trajectory is divided in minimum three parts with different bundling for each part. In that case, the decomposition method always leads to other results than the proportional allocation method. The decomposition method favors the partners in the coalition that take part in more bundled parts of the barge trajectory. The Shapley value leads to the same results as the decomposition method if the participants in the coalition are equal. If the partners in the coalition are unequal, the Shapley value again favors the smaller partners in the coalition. When only one vessel type is used, bundling always leads to a lower transport cost. Therefore, important properties of cost allocation methods as individual rationality and a stable cooperation are always satisfied.

Next, the experiments are elaborated with a second vessel type. In this situation, bundling does not always lead to a lower transport cost, which makes it important to look at the stability of these results. Analyzing cost allocations over all cases reveals that stability of the grand coalition is guaranteed in all three-partner collaborations. In contrast, none of the four-partner coalitions are stable. Stability of the five-partner coalitions depends on the equality of the partners. When collaborating shippers are equal in terms of shipment sizes the grand coalition is stable. However, for the case of a common end terminal other allocation mechanisms besides Shapley, proportional and decomposition are needed to define a stable solution. Collaborations set up between five shippers with different shipment sizes do not guarantee long-term stability in our case study.

References

1. Bektas, T., Crainic, T.: A brief overview of intermodal transportation. In: Taylor, G. (ed.) Logistics Engineering Handbook, Chap. 28, pp. 1–16. Taylor and Francis Group, Boca Raton (2008)
2. Ben-Akiva, M., de Jong, G.: The aggregate-disaggregate-aggregate (ADA) freight model system. In: Ben-Akiva, M., Meersman, H., Van de Voorde, E. (eds.) Freight Transport Modelling, pp. 69–90. Emerald, Bradford (2013)
3. Braekers, K., Caris, A., Janssens, G.: Optimal shipping routes and vessel size for intermodal barge transport with empty container repositioning. Comput. Ind. **64**(2), 155–164 (2013)
4. Caris, A., Limbourg, S., Macharis, C., Van Lier, T., Cools, M.: Integration of inland waterway transport in the intermodal supply chain: a taxonomy of research challenges. J. Transp. Geogr. **41**, 126–136 (2014)
5. Caris, A., Macharis, C., Janssens, G.: Network analysis of container barge transport in the port of antwerp by means of simulation. J. Transp. Geogr. **19**(1), 125–133 (2011)
6. Caris, A., Macharis, C., Janssens, G.: Corridor network design in hinterland transportation systems. Flex. Serv. Manuf. J. **24**(3), 294–319 (2012)
7. Cruijssen, F., Dullaert, W., Fleuren, H.: Horizontal cooperation in transport and logistics: a literature review. Transp. J. **46**(3), 22–39 (2007)
8. EU: Transport white paper: roadmap to a single european transport area towards a competitive and resource efficient transport system. Technical reports, European Commission (2011)
9. Frisk, M., Göthe-Lundgren, M., Jörnsten, K., Rönnqvist, M.: Cost allocation in collaborative forest transportation. Eur. J. Oper. Res. **205**(2), 448–458 (2010)
10. Konings, R., Kreutzberger, E., Maras, V.: Major considerations in developing a hub-and-spoke network to improve the cost performance of container barge transport in the hinterland: the case of the port of rotterdam. J. Transp. Geogr. **29**, 63–73 (2013)
11. Kreutzberger, E.: Lowest cost intermodal rail freight transport bundling networks: conceptual structuring and identification. Eur. J. Transp. Infrastruct. Res. **10**(2), 158–180 (2010)

12. Kreutzberger, E., Konings, R.: Twin hub network: an innovative concept to boost competitiveness of intermodal rail transport to the hinterland. In: Proceedings of the TRB 92nd Annual Meeting (2013)

13. Liu, P., Wu, Y., Xu, N.: Allocating collaborative profit in less-than-truckload carrier alliance. J. Serv. Sci. Manage. **3**(1), 143–149 (2010)

14. Macharis, C., Bontekoning, Y.: Opportunities for or in intermodal freight transport research: a review. Eur. J. Oper. Res. **153**(2), 400–416 (2004)

15. Maes, T., Ramaekers, K., Caris, A., Janssens, G., Bellemans, T.: Simulation of logistic decisions within a freight transportation model. In: Proceedings of the Industrial Simulation Conference (2011) '

16. Özener, O., Ergun, O.: Allocating costs in a collaborative transportation procurement network. Transp. Sci. **42**(2), 146–165 (2008)

17. Schmeidler, D.: Nucleolus of a characteristic function game. Siam J. Appl. Math. **17**(6), 1163–1170 (1969)

18. Shapley, L.: A value for n-person games. In: Kuhn, H., Tucker, W. (eds.) Contributions to the Theory of Games, pp. 31–40. Princeton University Press, New Jersey (1953)

19. Soons, D.: The determination and division of benefits among partners of a horizontal cooperation in transportation. Master's thesis, TU/e School of industrial engineering (2011)

20. Theys, C., Dullaert, W., Notteboom, T.: Analyzing cooperative networks in intermodal transportation: a game-theoretic approach. In: Nectar Logistics and Freight Cluster Meeting. Delft, The Netherlands (2008)

21. Tijs, S., Driessen, T.: Game theory and cost allocation problems. Manage. Sci. **32**(8), 1015–1028 (1986)

22. Van Lier, T., Caris, A., Macharis, C.: Sustainability SI: bundling of outbound freight flows: analyzing the potential of internal horizontal collaboration to improve sustainability. Netw. Spat. Econ. **16**(1), 277–302 (2016)

23. Vanovermeire, C.: Horizontal collaboration in logistics: Increasing efficiency through flexibility, gain sharing and collaborative planning. Ph.D. thesis, University of Antwerp (2014)

24. Verdonck, L., Beullens, P., Caris, A., Ramaekers, K., Janssens, G.: Analysis of collaborative savings and cost allocation techniques for the cooperative carrier facility location problem. J. Oper. Res. Soc. (2016, in Press)

25. Woxenius, J.: Generic framework for transport network designs: applications and treatment in intermodal freighttransport literature. Transp. Rev. **27**(6), 733–749 (2007)

Service and Transfer Selection for Freights in a Synchromodal Network

Arturo Pérez Rivera[(⊠)] and Martijn Mes

Department of Industrial Engineering and Business Information Systems,
University of Twente, P.O. Box 217, 7500 AE Enschede, The Netherlands
{a.e.perezrivera,m.r.k.mes}@utwente.nl

Abstract. We study the problem of selecting services and transfers in a synchromodal network to transport freights with different characteristics, over a multi-period horizon. The evolution of the network over time is determined by the decisions made, the schedule of the services, and the new freights that arrive each period. Although freights become known gradually over time, the planner has probabilistic knowledge about their arrival. Using this knowledge, the planner balances current and future costs at each period, with the objective of minimizing the expected costs over the entire horizon. To model this stochastic finite horizon optimization problem, we propose a Markov Decision Process (MDP) model. To overcome the computational complexity of solving the MDP, we propose a heuristic approach based on approximate dynamic programming. Using different problem settings, we show that our look-ahead approach has significant benefits compared to a benchmark heuristic.

Keywords: Synchromodal planning · Anticipatory planning · Intermodal transport · Approximate dynamic programming

1 Introduction

We consider the problem of selecting services and transfers in a synchromodal network, to transport freights from their origin to their destination, while minimizing costs over a multi-period horizon. In a synchromodal setting, all freights are booked "mode-free", meaning that there are no restrictions for selecting a transportation mode or deciding the number transfers among the intermodal terminals. The network operator is able to decide over all services in the network even if they are not its own. However, the flexibility in selecting services and transfers is encumbered by various time restrictions, such as service schedules and freight time-windows, and by the variability in the arrival of freights over time. In this paper, we study how these challenges can be tackled, heuristically, in order to solve this stochastic and finite horizon optimization problem.

In synchromodal planning, it is possible to change the transportation plan to bring a freight from its origin to its destination, at any point in time. Even though the planner might have a complete plan at a given moment, only the first part

© Springer International Publishing Switzerland 2016
A. Paias et al. (Eds.): ICCL 2016, LNCS 9855, pp. 227–242, 2016.
DOI: 10.1007/978-3-319-44896-1_15

of such a plan is implemented. The next decision moment, the planner has the flexibility to change the original plan if necessary. Consequently, there are three types of decisions each day: (i) transport a freight to its final destination, (ii) transport a freight to an intermediate terminal, and (iii) postpone the transport of a freight. All types of decisions incur some form of costs. The first and the second type incur *direct* costs, which are costs realized by the services required for the transportation of a freight. The third type has direct costs only in case of holding costs. Since the problem is to minimize costs over a multi-period horizon, the second and third type also incur *future* costs, which are costs that are incurred on a posterior moment within the horizon. Future costs depend on the new arriving freights and their characteristics (which are uncertain) and the known transportation mode characteristics (e.g., schedules, capacity, etc.). The optimal balance between direct and future costs guarantees the best performance over the horizon. However, anticipating future costs is challenging.

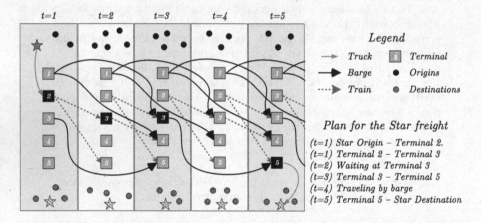

Fig. 1. Time evolution and planning example of service and transfer selection

Decisions are influenced by two types of time restrictions. The first type corresponds to the durations and schedules of services and transfers. As an example, consider Fig. 1, which shows a possible plan spanning 5 days using both train and barge. In this example, barges have a duration of 2 days, and the train between Terminals 3 and 4 departs on even days. The second type corresponds to the time-window of freights, which limit the feasible transportation services and transfers, and thus the feasible decisions. In addition to the time restrictions, the variability in the number of freights that arrive each day and their characteristics (i.e., origin, destination, time-window), also influence the decisions. Although freights and their characteristics are unknown beforehand, there is probabilistic information about their arrival. Every day, the planner must consider all these characteristics and select which freights use the services available that day, balancing direct and future costs.

The objective of this paper is twofold: (i) to design a model and look-ahead solution method that capture all problem characteristics and their effect on the planning objective, and (ii) to explore the use of look-ahead decision methods under several settings. We model the decision problem and the evolution of the network using a Markov Decision Process (MDP) model. With this model, the optimal trade-off between the three types of decisions, over time and under uncertain demand, can be obtained. However, solving MDP models become unmanageable as problem instances grow larger. To overcome this, we use Approximate Dynamic Programming (ADP), a framework that uses parts from the MDP model and iteratively estimates future costs. ADP combines simulation, optimization, and statistical techniques to solve an MDP heuristically.

The remainder of this paper is organized as follows. In Sect. 2, we briefly mention the relevant literature and specify our contribution to it. In Sect. 3, we introduce the MDP model. In Sect. 4, we explain our ADP solution approach. In Sect. 5, we test various designs within the ADP algorithm, and provide a comparison with benchmark heuristics. Finally, we close in Sect. 6 with conclusions and insights for further research.

2   Literature Review

In this section, we focus our attention on the literature about planning problems in dynamic and flexible intermodal transportation networks. It is our goal to provide an overview of the advantages and limitations of related work, i.e. possible solution methods. Extensive literature reviews about this area and thorough explanation of modeling and solution approaches can be found in [2,14].

Synchromodal planning is the proactive organization and control of intermodal transportation services based on the latest information available [14]. In such a planning paradigm, decision methods must balance the demand with all available services and intermodal transfers each time new information becomes known [13]. Although research about synchromodal planning methods is on its infancy, several studies show how existing methods for intermodal transport planning can be extended to such problem settings [16] and how significant gains can be achieved in practice [9,16].

In intermodal transport planning, Dynamic Service Network Design (DSND) problems are the closest to the synchromodal planning problems. DSND involves the selection of transportation services and modes for freights, where at least one feature of the network varies over time [14]. Due to the time-space nature of DSND problems, graph theory and mathematical programming approaches are commonly used in this area. However, these approaches have computational limitations for large and complex time-evolving problem instances [15], which are characteristics common to synchromodality [13]. To overcome these limitations, additional designs, such as decomposition algorithms [5], receding horizons [6], and model predictive control [10], are necessary. These additional designs are less suitable for including probabilistic information in the decisions, which may explain why most DSND studies assume deterministic demand [14] even though the need to incorporate stochastic demand has been recognized [7].

To incorporate stochasticity in DSND approaches, techniques such as scenario generation [3,7], two-stage stochastic programming [1,8], and Approximate Dynamic Programming (ADP) [4,11] have been used. Although these approaches perform better than their deterministic counterpart, they have limitations when considering synchromodal planning. In the scenario generation technique, plans do not change as new information becomes available. In the two-stage stochastic programming approach, explicit probabilistic constraints and high computational requirements limit their applicability to large instances. In ADP, a proper design and validation of the approximation algorithm is crucial and challenging. Nevertheless, ADP allows generic modeling of complex, time-revealing, stochastic networks and a fast response time for updating plans.

To summarize, DSND research provides a useful base for synchromodal planning. Considering all challenges and opportunities mentioned before, we believe that our contribution to the literature about stochastic DSND problems and synchromodal planning has three key points. First, we design an MDP model and solution method based on ADP that capture all problem characteristics and their effect on the planning objective. Second, we explore the use of such a look-ahead approach, under different problem settings, and provide design and validation insights. Third, we compare the ADP approach against an advanced sampling procedure and specify further research directions based on the insights.

3   Optimization Model

In this section, we present our optimization model. Following the DSND convention, we begin presenting the network parameters using a directed graph. Then, we present the MDP model for our stochastic planning problem.

3.1   Input Parameters

We define a directed graph $G_t = (\mathcal{N}_t, \mathcal{A}_t)$, where $t \in \mathcal{T} = \{0, 1, 2, \ldots, T^{\max} - 1\}$ represents the finite planning horizon (i.e., $T^{\max}$ decision periods), $\mathcal{N}_t$ represents the set of all nodes at time t, and $\mathcal{A}_t$ represents the set of all directed arcs at time t. In the remainder of the paper, we refer to a time period t as a day, although it is important to note that time can be discretized in any arbitrary interval. Also in the remainder of the model description, all notation and formulations indexed by t correspond to that day. Nodes $\mathcal{N}_t$ represent physical locations where freight can begin or end transportation, i.e., origins, intermodal terminals, and destinations. We denote the set of origin nodes as $\mathcal{N}_t^O$, the set of destination nodes as $\mathcal{N}_t^D$, and the set of intermodal terminal nodes as $\mathcal{N}_t^I$. These three sets are mutually exclusive, make up the set of all nodes, and are all indexed with i, j and d. Note that this separation of the node sets applies to the model, but not necessarily to the problem instance. For example, an intermodal terminal which receives arriving freights will be modeled both as an origin and terminal node, with all services between these two nodes properly adjusted. Arcs $\mathcal{A}_t$ represent all transportation services in the network. Similar to the node classification, we classify the arcs into three types. The set of arcs between an origin and an intermodal node is denoted as $\mathcal{A}_t^O = \{(i,j)|i \in \mathcal{N}_t^O \text{ and } j \in \mathcal{N}_t^I\}$. The set of arcs between two intermodal terminal nodes is denoted as $\mathcal{A}_t^I = \{(i,j)|i,j \in \mathcal{N}_t^I\}$. The set of arcs between an origin or an intermodal node, and a destination, is denoted as $\mathcal{A}_t^D = \{(i,d)|i \in \mathcal{N}_t^O \cup \mathcal{N}_t^I \text{ and } d \in \mathcal{N}_t^D\}$.

We make three modeling assumptions with respect to the services between different types of locations. First, we assume that services beginning at an origin, i.e., $\mathcal{A}_t^O$, as well as services ending in a destination, i.e., $\mathcal{A}_t^D$, are available every day and are realized by truck. This assumption corresponds to the usual pre- and end-haulage operations in an synchromodal network. Second, we assume that services between two intermodal terminals, i.e., $\mathcal{A}_t^I$, are done by high-capacity modes and never by truck. Although this is a simplification of the network, trucks between intermodal terminals are rarely used. If the problem instance requires it, a truck service between two intermodal terminals can be modeled using "dummy" nodes for the respective terminals, with other arcs properly adjusted. Third, we assume there is at most one service between two intermodal terminal nodes. Just as before, multiple services between two intermodal terminals can be modeled using more than one pair of nodes representing those terminals. Note that the services between two intermodal terminals are not necessarily the same every day to represent the schedules for the high-capacity modes.

Services in the network have their starting and ending location modeled as nodes within G_t. For the service between two intermodal terminals $(i,j) \in \mathcal{A}_t^I$, there is a *maximum capacity* $Q_{i,j,t}$ measured in number of freights. For all services involving an origin or a destination, we assume that there is an unlimited number of trucks. All services $(i,j) \in \mathcal{A}_t$ have a *service duration* of $L_{i,j,t}^A$ days, which lasts at least one day. All transfer and handling operations at each location $i \in \mathcal{N}_t$ have a duration of $L_{i,t}^N$ days. To measure the total time required for the service between two locations, we define the parameter $M_{i,j,t} = L_{i,t}^N + L_{i,j,t}^A + L_{j,t}^N$. We assume that traveling directly to a destination by truck is always faster than going through an intermodal terminal, i.e., $L_{i,d,t}^A < \min_{j \in \mathcal{N}_t^I} \left\{ M_{i,j,t} + L_{j,d,t}^A \right\}, \forall (i,d) \in \mathcal{A}_t^D$. This assumption works in a similar way as the triangle inequality in routing problems. All relevant costs from a service $(i,j) \in \mathcal{A}_t$ are captured in the *cost function* $C_{i,j,t}$. This means that, although pre- and end-haulage decisions, as well as freight handling decisions, are outside the scope of the planner, their costs can be captured with the function $C_{i,j,t}$.

Each day t, freights with different attributes become known to the planner. These freights are characterized by an origin $i \in \mathcal{N}_t^O$, a destination $d \in \mathcal{N}_t^D$, a release day $r \in \mathcal{R}_t = \{0,1,2,\ldots,R_t^{\max}\}$, and a time-window length $k \in \mathcal{K}_t = \{0,1,2,\ldots,K_t^{\max}\}$, where $R_t^{\max}$ and $K_t^{\max}$ are the maximum release day and time-window length, respectively, that a freight can have. Note that the absolute due-day is k days after r. Even though new freights and their characteristics are only known until they arrive, there is probabilistic knowledge about their arrival. In between two consecutive days $t-1$ and t, a total of $f \in \mathbb{N}$ freights arrive into the system with probability $p_{f,t}^F$. A freight that arrives has origin $i \in \mathcal{N}_t^O$ with probability $p_{i,t}^O$, destination $d \in \mathcal{N}_t^D$ with probability $p_{d,t}^D$, release-day $r \in \mathcal{R}_t$ with probability $p_{r,t}^R$, and time-window length $k \in \mathcal{K}_t$ with probability $p_{k,t}^K$.

3.2   MDP Model

In this section, we transform the problem horizon, constraints, and objective into the building blocks of an MDP: stages, state, decision, transition, and optimality equations. The stages of the MDP are defined by $t \in \mathcal{T}$. The state S_t consists of all freights in the network and their characteristics. To model these freights, we introduce the variable $F_{i,d,r,k,t} \in \mathbb{Z}^+$ that represents the number of freights at location $i \in \mathcal{N}_t^O \cup \mathcal{N}_t^I$, that have destination $d \in \mathcal{N}_t^D$, release day $r \in \mathcal{R}_t'$, and time-window length $k \in \mathcal{K}_t$; and define the state S_t as seen in (1). The state space is denoted as $\mathcal{S}$, i.e., $S_t \in \mathcal{S}$.

$$S_t = [F_{i,d,r,k,t}]_{\forall i \in \mathcal{N}_t^O \cup \mathcal{N}_t^I, d \in \mathcal{N}_t^D, r \in \mathcal{R}_t', k \in \mathcal{K}_t} \tag{1}$$

Note that we use a new set $\mathcal{R}_t'$ for the release days. The release day definition at origin nodes remains the same. The release day at an intermodal terminal, however, is now used to represent the days "left" for a freight to arrive at that node. For example, if a released freight is sent to an intermodal terminal j on a barge whose total service duration is four days, this freight will appear the day after it was sent, as a freight with $r = 3$ at location j. This new set, which is defined as $\mathcal{R}_t' = \left\{ 0, 1, 2, \ldots, \max \left\{ R_t^{\max}, \max_{(i,j) \in \mathcal{A}_t^I} M_{i,j,t} \right\} \right\}$, allows us to model multi-day durations of services without the need of remembering decisions from more than one day ago, i.e., to be more computationally efficient. Note that, in case no total service duration is larger than $R_t^{\max}$, then $\mathcal{R}_t = \mathcal{R}_t'$. Time-window lengths k still model the number of days after the release-day r, within which the freight has to be at its final destination. We will elaborate more on the evolution of the network over time later on in this section.

At each stage, the planner must decide how many released freights to transport and to postpone, for all locations. Remind that, in a synchromodal network, only the first part of the plan to transport a freight to its destination is implemented at each decision moment. Consequently, at every stage, the decision to transport a freight can be either to send it directly to its final destination, or to send it to an intermodal terminal. To model this decision, we introduce the variable $x_{i,j,d,k,t} \in \mathbb{Z}^+$, which represents the number of freights having destination $d \in \mathcal{N}_t^D$ and time-window length $k \in \mathcal{K}_t$ that are transported from location i to location j using service $(i,j) \in \mathcal{A}_t$. Thus, the decision vector x_t consists of all transported freights in the network, as seen in (2a).

$$x_t = [x_{i,j,d,k,t}]_{\forall (i,j) \in \mathcal{A}_t, d \in \mathcal{N}_t^D, k \in \mathcal{K}_t} \tag{2a}$$

$$\text{s.t.}$$

$$\sum_{j \in \mathcal{N}_t^I \cup \{d\}} x_{i,j,d,k,t} \leq F_{i,d,0,k,t}, \quad \forall i \in \mathcal{N}_t^O \cup \mathcal{N}_t^I, d \in \mathcal{N}_t^D, k \in \mathcal{K}_t \tag{2b}$$

$$x_{i,d,d,L^A_{i,d,t},t} \geq F_{i,d,0,L^A_{i,d,t},t}, \quad \forall(i,d) \in \mathcal{A}^D_t, k \in \mathcal{K}_t \tag{2c}$$

$$x_{i,j,d,k,t} = 0, \quad \forall(i,j) \in \mathcal{A}_t, d \in \mathcal{N}^D_t, k \in \mathcal{K}_t | k < M_{i,j,t} + M_{j,d,t} \tag{2d}$$

$$\sum_{d \in \mathcal{N}^D_t} \sum_{k \in \mathcal{K}_t} x_{i,j,d,k,t} \leq Q_{i,j,t}, \quad \forall(i,j) \in \mathcal{A}^I_t \tag{2e}$$

The decision x_t depends on the state S_t and the feasible decision space $\mathcal{X}_t$, which has four constraints. First, the number of freights transported from one location to all other locations cannot exceed the number of released freights available at the start location, as seen in (2b). Second, released freights whose time-window length is as long as the duration of direct transport (i.e., trucking) must be transported using this service, as seen in (2c). Third, freights whose time-window length is smaller than the duration of the shortest path between an intermodal terminal and their destination cannot be transported via that terminal, as seen in (2d). Fourth, transport between two intermodal terminals cannot exceed the capacity of the long-haul vehicle, as seen in (2e).

After making a decision x_{t-1}, but before entering the state S_t, new freights become known to the planner. We represent new freights with origin $i \in \mathcal{N}^O_t$, destination $d \in \mathcal{N}^D_t$, release day $r \in \mathcal{R}_t$, and time-window length $k \in \mathcal{K}_t$, by $\widetilde{F}_{i,d,r,k,t}$. We denote the vector of all new freights that arrive between stages $t-1$ and t by W_t, as seen in (3). This vector represents the exogenous information (i.e., new random freights) that became known between stages $t-1$ and t.

$$W_t = \left[\widetilde{F}_{i,d,r,k,t}\right]_{\forall i \in \mathcal{N}^O_t, d \in \mathcal{N}^D_t, r \in \mathcal{R}_t, k \in \mathcal{K}_t} \tag{3}$$

The evolution of the network over time is influenced by decisions, exogenous information, and various time relations. We represent this evolution by using a transition function S^M, as seen in (4a). The general idea of S^M is to define the freights at S_t using only the previous-stage decision x_{t-1} and the exogenous information W_t. Although decisions can span more than one day (i.e., when the duration of a service is longer than a day), we use freight release days (i.e., new set $\mathcal{R}'_t$) and time-window lengths to avoid remembering a decision for more than one stage. When freights are not transported, they remain at the same location and their release days and time-window lengths decrease. However, when freights are transported from a given location i to an intermodal terminal j, they are modeled as freights whose release day increases and their time-window length decreases in line with the total duration of transport $M_{i,j,t}$. To model all these relations, S^M classifies freight variables $F_{t,i,d,r,k}$ into seven categories, as shown in (4b)–(4h). To exemplify in detail the workings of these categories, consider (4c). These constraints apply to released freights at an intermodal terminal i with destination d and time-window length k. These freights are the result of three types of freights: (i) released freights in the same terminal, from the previous stage, that had the same destination, that had one additional day in the time-window, and that were not transported to any other node (i.e., $F_{t-1,i,d,0,k+1} - \sum_{j \in \mathcal{A}_t} x_{t-1,i,j,d,k+1}$); (ii) freights in the same node, from the previous stage, that had the same destination, that had a release-day of one, and that had the same time-window length (i.e., $F_{t-1,i,d,1,k}$); and (iii) freights that arrived from other locations to i, that have the same destination, whose total duration of transportation was one period, and whose time-window length was $k + M_{j,i,t}$ at the moment of the decision x_{t-1} (i.e., $\sum_{j \in \mathcal{A}_t | M_{j,i,t}=1} x_{t-1,j,i,d,k+M_{j,i,t}}$). All other constraints work in a similar fashion.

$$S_t = S^M (S_{t-1}, x_{t-1}, W_t)$$

$$\text{s.t.} \tag{4a}$$

$$F_{t,i,d,0,k} = F_{t-1,i,d,0,k+1} - \sum_{j \in \mathcal{A}_t} x_{t-1,i,j,d,k+1} + F_{t-1,i,d,1,k} + \widetilde{F}_{t,i,d,0,k},$$

$$\forall i \in \mathcal{N}_t^O, d \in \mathcal{N}_t^D, k + 1 \in \mathcal{K}_t \tag{4b}$$

$$F_{t,i,d,0,k} = F_{t-1,i,d,0,k+1} - \sum_{j \in \mathcal{A}_t} x_{t-1,i,j,d,k+1} + F_{t-1,i,d,1,k}$$

$$+ \sum_{j \in \mathcal{A}_t | M_{j,i,t}=1} x_{t-1,j,i,d,k+M_{j,i,t}},$$

$$\forall i \in \mathcal{N}_t^I, d \in \mathcal{N}_t^D, k + 1 \in \mathcal{K}_t \tag{4c}$$

$$F_{t,i,d,0,K_t^{\max}} = F_{t-1,i,d,1,K_t^{\max}} + \widetilde{F}_{t,i,d,0,K_t^{\max}},$$

$$\forall i \in \mathcal{N}_t^O, d \in \mathcal{N}_t^D \tag{4d}$$

$$F_{t,i,d,r,k} = F_{t-1,i,d,r+1,k} + \widetilde{F}_{t,i,d,r,k},$$

$$\forall i \in \mathcal{N}_t^O, d \in \mathcal{N}_t^D, r + 1 \in \mathcal{R}_t | r \geq 1, k \in \mathcal{K}_t \tag{4e}$$

$$F_{t,i,d,r,k} = F_{t-1,i,d,r+1,k} + \sum_{j \in \mathcal{A}_t | M_{j,i,t}=r+1} x_{t-1,j,i,d,k+M_{j,i,t}},$$

$$\forall i \in \mathcal{N}_t^I, d \in \mathcal{N}_t^D, r + 1 \in \mathcal{R}_t' | r \geq 1, k \in \mathcal{K}_t \tag{4f}$$

$$F_{t,i,d,|\mathcal{R}_t'|,k} = \sum_{j \in \mathcal{A}_t | M_{j,i,t}=|\mathcal{R}_t'|+1} x_{t-1,j,i,d,k+M_{j,i,t}}$$

$$\forall i \in \mathcal{N}_t^I, d \in \mathcal{N}_t^D, k \in \mathcal{K}_t, \tag{4g}$$

$$F_{t,i,d,R_t^{\max},k} = \widetilde{F}_{t,i,d,R_t^{\max},k},$$

$$\forall i \in \mathcal{N}_t^O, d \in \mathcal{N}_t^D, k \in \mathcal{K}_t \tag{4h}$$

The goal is to minimize the total costs over a multi-period horizon, considering all possible states that can occur each day, and considering the stochastic arrival of freight. To do so, we define a policy π as a function that maps each possible state $S_t \in \mathcal{S}$ to a decision $x_t^\pi \in \mathcal{X}_t$. Consequently, the objective is to determine the policy π from the set of all policies Π that minimizes the expected costs over the planning horizon, given an initial state S_0, as seen in (5):

$$\min_{\pi \in \Pi} \mathbb{E} \left[\sum_{t \in \mathcal{T}} C_t (x_t^\pi) = \sum_{t \in \mathcal{T}} \sum_{(i,j) \in \mathcal{A}_t} \left(C_{i,j,t} \cdot \sum_{d \in \mathcal{N}_t^D} \sum_{k \in \mathcal{K}_t} x_{i,j,d,k,t}^\pi \right) \Bigg| S_0 \right] \tag{5}$$

To solve this stochastic and sequential optimization problem, we transform (5) into the Bellman's equations (6). In these equations, the expected next-stage cost is computed using the value of the next-stage state S_{t+1} (obtained using S^M), the decision x_t^π, a realization of the exogenous information $\omega \in \Omega_{t+1}$, and the associated probability $p_\omega^{\Omega_{t+1}}$. The solution to all recursive equations of (6), e.g., through backward induction, provide the optimal policy for the MDP.

$$V_t(S_t) = \min_{x_t^\pi \in \mathcal{X}_t} \left(C_t(x_t^\pi) + \sum_{\omega \in \Omega_{t+1}} p_\omega^{\Omega_{t+1}} \cdot V_{t+1}\left(S^M\left(S_t, x_t^\pi, \omega\right)\right) \right), \forall S_t \in \mathcal{S} \quad (6)$$

However, solving the Bellman equations (6) for large problems is computationally challenging. The state space $\mathcal{S}$, decision space $\mathcal{X}_t$, and the realizations of the exogenous information in Ω_t grow larger with an increasing size of the problem instance. Due to these three "curses of dimensionality" [12], our MDP model is solvable only for tiny problem instances. Notwithstanding, the MDP model serves as a base for our ADP approach.

4 Solution Approach

Our solution approach is based on ADP, which is a heuristic solution method for MDP models that uses various constructs and algorithmic strategies. Its main idea is to replace the expected next-stage costs in (6) by a Value Function Approximation (VFA), and to update this function via a simulation of the exogenous information. This update procedure is done iteratively, as shown in Fig. 2, with the end result being the approximated values of the solution to the Bellman's equations, and thus a policy π. Certainly, the choice of (i) VFA, (ii) the update procedure, and (iii) the number of iterations, has an influence on the performance, i.e., solution quality and computational time. In the following paragraphs we describe the choices we make and indicate their expected performance.

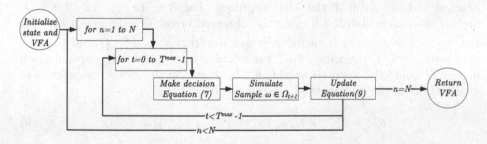

Fig. 2. Overview of the ADP algorithm

In our ADP approach, the expectation of future costs in (6) is replaced by an value function approximation $\overline{V}_t^n(S_t^{x,n})$, where $S_t^{x,n}$ is the so-called post-decision state, i.e., the state after a decision has been made but before the new exogenous information becomes known. As seen in (7), this construct avoids specifying all realizations of the exogenous information Ω_t.

$$V_t^n(S_t^n) = \min_{x_t^\pi \in \mathcal{X}_t} \left(C_t(x_t^\pi) + \overline{V}_t^n(S_t^{x,n}) \right) \tag{7}$$

To avoid the large state space, the optimality equation in (7) is solved for one state at each stage, starting from the initial state S_0. The transition from one state to the next uses a sample from Ω_{t+1}, obtained through a Monte Carlo simulation, and the transition function S^M defined in (4a). This process is performed for the entire planning horizon, and repeated for N iterations, hence the superscript n in the approximate value function and post-decision state.

The general outline of an ADP algorithm can be found in Fig. 4.7, page 141, of the book of [12]. We now focus on two designs (i.e., variations) we propose for that algorithm. Our first design uses a commonly proposed ADP setup. We use *basis functions* for $\overline{V}_t^n(S_t^{x,n})$ and the *non-stationary least squares* method for updating this function. A basis function $\phi_a(S_t^{x,n})$ is a quantitative characteristic of a given feature a of a post-decision state $S_t^{x,n}$ that describes, to some extent, the value of that post-decision state. Examples of features in our problem are the number of freights for a given destination and the number of freights at a given intermodal terminal. Given a set of features $\mathcal{A}$, the approximated next-stage costs in (7) are the result of the product between the basis function $\phi_a(S_t^{x,n})$ and the weight $\theta_{a,t}^n$ for each feature $a \in \mathcal{A}$, as seen in (8).

$$\overline{V}_t^{x,n}(S_t^{x,n}) = \sum_{a \in \mathcal{A}} \theta_{a,t}^n \phi_a(S_t^{x,n}) \tag{8}$$

The weight $\theta_{a,t}^n$ depends on the iteration n because it is updated after each iteration, using observed costs, to improve future cost estimates. We use a Non-stationary Least Squares (NLS) method for updating these weights since it gives more emphasis to the recent observation than to the previous one. This emphasis is necessary at early iterations, where initial conditions might bias the approximation and the result of the ADP approach. The weights $\theta_{a,t}^n$, for all $a \in \mathcal{A}$, are updated each iteration n using the observed error (i.e., difference between the next-stage estimate from the previous iteration $\overline{V}_{t-1}^{n-1}(S_{t-1}^{x,n})$ and the current estimate $\widehat{v}_t^n$), the value of all basis functions $\phi_a(S_t^{x,n})$, the optimization matrix H^n, and the previous weights $\theta_{a,t}^{n-1}$, as seen in (9). For a comprehensive explanation on the NLS method, we refer to [12].

$$\theta_{a,t}^n = \theta_{a,t}^{n-1} - H_n \phi_a(S_t^{x,n}) \left(\overline{V}_{t-1}^{n-1}(S_{t-1}^{x,n}) - \widehat{v}_t^n \right) \tag{9}$$

The first design considers downstream costs only through a one-step estimate. Since estimates can be off, especially in early iterations, it might be beneficial to look ahead more than one step. To do this, our second design builds on the first one and uses two additional constructs. First, we add a valid inequality to the decision space $\mathcal{X}_t$ as follows. If a direct service for a freight between its origin and its destination is cheaper than going from its origin to a given intermodal terminal and subsequently to its destination, we prevent this freight from going to that intermodal terminal when its time-window length allows only a direct service after the intermodal terminal. Second, we add another estimate to $\overline{V}_t^n(S_t^{x,n})$, as seen in (10). In this new approximate value function, $\overline{C}_t^n(S_t^{x,n})$ is an estimate of the downstream cost obtained simulating a fixed rule for the remaining of the horizon, under different demand realizations, and α is a weight to balance the use of basis functions and simulations for $\overline{V}_t^n(S_t^{x,n})$.

$$\overline{V}_t^{x,n}(S_t^{x,n}) = \alpha \sum_{a \in \mathcal{A}} \theta_{a,t}^n \phi_a(S_t^{x,n}) + (1 - \alpha)\overline{C}_t^n(S_t^{x,n}) \tag{10}$$

At last, the output of our two ADP designs are the weights $\theta_{a,t}^N$. The resulting policy π maps state $S_t \in \mathcal{S}$ to decision x_t^π as seen in (11).

$$x_t^\pi = \arg\min \left(C_t(x_t^\pi) + \sum_{a \in \mathcal{A}(S_t^x)} \theta_{a,t}^N \phi_a(S_t^x) \right) \tag{11}$$

5 Numerical Experiments

In this section, we explore the value of our ADP designs through a series of numerical experiments. Using three small instances, we compare the costs achieved by our ADP approach against a benchmark policy and an advance sampling procedure. The benchmark policy mimics a planning approach commonly used in practice. The sampling procedure extends the benchmark policy with a methodology commonly considered in the literature. The section is divided as follows. First, we introduce our experimental setup. Second, we show, analyze, and discuss the results of our experiments.

5.1 Experimental Setup

For the three instances, we use a network containing a single origin, three intermodal terminals, and three destinations over a planning horizon of 15 days. Each day, there are three services between the intermodal terminals, with capacities and durations as shown in Fig. 3. The fixed costs of these services are of $C_{1,2}^F = C_{2,3}^F = 100$ and $C_{1,3}^F = 150$. The variable costs range between 36 and 44, and are equal to the Euclidean distance between the terminals in a plane of 100×50 distance units, as shown to scale in Fig. 3. In addition, every day there is a direct service between the origin and the terminals, between the origin and the destinations, and between the terminals and the destinations; and they all have duration of one day. There are no fixed costs for the direct services, and the variable cost range varies between 241 and 927, and are equal to ten times the Euclidean distance between the two locations they connect. The number of freights that arrives each day varies between $f = \{0, 1, ..., 4\}$, with probability p_f^F as shown in Fig. 3. In the three instances, each freight has destination

$d \in \{4, 5, 6\}$ with probability p_d^D as shown in Fig. 3, and is always released (i.e., $p_0^R = 1$). Each freight has a time-window length $k = \{1, 2, \ldots, 5\}$ with probability p_k^K according to the instances considered. In instances where freights have short time-windows, there are not many feasible options for transportation and almost none for postponement. In instances with large time-windows, the opposite occurs. To test the value of look-ahead decisions, we create instances with different time-window length distributions, as shown in Fig. 3.

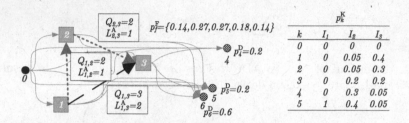

Fig. 3. Network characteristics for the test instances

Using these instances, we test four planning methods: a benchmark heuristic, our two ADP designs (named ADP 1 and ADP 2), and an advance sampling procedure. The set of features $\mathcal{A}$ consists of all state variables and a constant of 1. The weight α for ADP 2 is defined as $\alpha = \max\{25/(25 + n - 1), 0.05\}$ and the sampling method is the same as the advance sampling procedure introduced in the next paragraph. The number of iterations is set to 100 and the NLS parameters used are those recommended by [11]. Although these settings achieved a fast convergence of the ADP algorithm in our tests, the resulting approximate value functions (i.e., policy) is heuristic and not necessarily optimal.

The benchmark heuristic strikes for a balance between using the intermodal services efficiently (consolidate as many freights as possible) and the postponement of freight. It consists of fours steps: (i) define the shortest and second shortest path for each freight to its final destination, without considering fixed costs for services between terminals, (ii) calculate the savings between the shortest and second shortest path and define these as savings of the first intermodal service used in the shortest path, (iii) sort all freights in non-decreasing time-window length, i.e., closest due-day first, and (iv) for each freight in the sorted list, check whether the savings of the first intermodal service of its shortest path are larger than the fixed cost for this service; if so, use this service for the freight, if not, postpone the transport of the freight. Naturally, all capacities, durations, and time-windows must be checked while doing these steps.

The sampling procedure consists of three steps: (i) enumerate all feasible decisions, (ii) for each feasible decision, estimate future costs by sampling, in a Monte Carlo fashion and using common random numbers across the decisions, realizations of the exogenous information for the remainder of the planning horizon, and simulating the use of the benchmark heuristic for making decisions with these samples, and (iii) choose the decision with the lowest sum of direct and estimated future costs. Although heavily computationally intensive (i.e., not applicable to larger instances), this procedure exploits the benefits of looking-ahead in decision making.

The tests are done using ten test states in each instance. To define these states for each instance, we do a simulation of the benchmark heuristic, beginning with an empty state, for a horizon of 15 days. We save the state at the end of the horizon. We replicate this procedure 10,000 times, and choose the ten states that were observed the most. For each of the test states, we simulate each planning method 100 times, using common random numbers across the methods. Note that these 100 simulation replications are different from the 100 iterations of the ADP algorithm. Thus, we test the ADP approach in two phases: (i) learning phase through 100 iterations and (ii) simulation phase of using the resulting policy in (11) for 100 replications.

5.2   Experimental Results and Discussion

First, we analyze Instance I_1. This is the most flexible test instance since all freights have a time-window length of 5 days when they arrive. The results are shown in Table 1. We show the costs for the benchmark heuristic, and the relative savings, as a percentage, of the other planning methods when compared to the benchmark. In addition, we show the number of freights of each test state and the computational time. The computational time (in seconds) is given as the total simulation time for the 100 replications of the 15-day horizon.

Table 1. Results for Instance I_1

State	Total Freights	Benchmark Solution	Time (s)	ADP 1 Solution	Time (s)	ADP 2 Solution	Time (s)	Sampling Solution	Time (s)
1	4	12221	0.92	−13.6 %	29.94	−33.9 %	101.31	−43.3 %	688.29
2	7	14684	0.94	−12.8 %	52.06	−32.7 %	96.67	−39.9 %	1687.18
3	5	13042	0.92	−13.1 %	31.68	−27.5 %	81.46	−41.5 %	827.15
4	6	13863	0.94	−12.3 %	32.99	−25.9 %	81.42	−39.0 %	832.67
5	6	13863	0.91	−12.0 %	108.62	−30.0 %	111.21	−42.3 %	1356.80
6	6	13863	0.94	−10.4 %	102.12	−31.3 %	67.58	−42.9 %	1317.73
7	5	13042	0.94	−12.6 %	40.26	−23.4 %	81.99	−41.5 %	893.59
8	4	12221	0.92	−14.7 %	37.44	−25.0 %	78.41	−38.9 %	547.66
9	2	10579	0.94	−14.9 %	31.72	−29.9 %	45.13	−42.4 %	611.18
10	5	13042	1.01	−11.2 %	30.81	−32.9 %	42.92	−40.6 %	727.28

On average, ADP 1 achieves savings of 12.8 %, ADP 2 of 29.2 %, and the sampling procedure of 41.2 % when compared to the benchmark heuristic. All three methods that explicitly look-ahead in their decisions perform better than the benchmark that does so only implicitly. The sampling method performs the best, at a higher computational expense (more than 10 times the computational time of ADP, and 1000 times the one of the benchmark, on average). For large instances, or even small ones where time is discretized into smaller intervals, this method would not be applicable. ADP 2 performs second best, at a higher computational expense during the learning phase than ADP 1 (965 s instead of 116, on average). However, during the actual decision making for the entire planning horizon, both ADP designs have similar computational time (50 and 79 s, on average, respectively, for I_1). ADP 1 lowest savings indicate that a one-step look-ahead is not sufficient for a good solution. Furthermore, the difference between the two ADP designs suggests that further research that explicitly considers a few stages in advance, such as rolling-horizon procedures within the ADP framework, can improve performance significantly.

The average results across the test states of I_2 and I_3 are shown in Table 2. Note that each instance has its own set of test states, which differs from the other instances. Furthermore, note that I_2 and I_3 have significantly less flexibility than I_1 due to their time-window length, only 40 % and 0.05 % of arriving freights can use any intermodal connection, respectively.

Table 2. Average results for Instance I_2 and I_3

Instance	Benchmark		ADP 1		ADP 2		Sampling	
	Solution	Time (s)	Solution	Time (s)	Solution	Time (s)	Solution	Time (s)
I_2	11078	0.88	−5.2 %	10.52	−9.8 %	13.89	−31.2 %	217.19
I_3	12874	1.01	2.9 %	3.19	0.4 %	2.31	−3.3 %	36.95

The larger savings from all look-ahead methods in I_1 and I_2, compared to I_3, indicate that the more flexibility there is, the better it is to look-ahead when making decisions. In I_2, similar results to I_1 are achieved, but with significantly less cost savings. In I_3, the benchmark heuristic performs better than the ADP approach, and the sampling achieves small savings. In most states of I_3, the only feasible option (time-wise) for freights is to use a direct service via truck. In such a setting, decision making methods that focus on current costs, such as the benchmark heuristic, perform well since there are hardly consolidation opportunities to anticipate for. However, a robust ADP design should be able to learn such a policy, as the sampling method seems to do. In a sensitivity analysis (results not shown), we observed that the number of iterations and the NLS parameters had a small impact on the solution quality, compared to the impact of different approximate value functions (e.g., more basis functions, the sampling method, etc.). In a similar way, the different approximate value functions had a significant difference in computational time during the learning phase, but not during the decision-making phase. Further research on adaptations of the approximating function of future costs within the ADP algorithm, such as aggregates, hierarchical functions and state representatives, is necessary.

6   Conclusions

We developed an MDP model and an ADP algorithm for selecting services and transfers for freights in a synchromodal network. With the MDP model, the optimal balance between transporting and postponing freights, in different locations of the network, over time, and under uncertain demand, can be achieved. With the ADP algorithm, the computational burden of the MDP model is reduced while preserving all of its modeling functionalities.

Through numerical experiments, we explored the value of using look-ahead decisions in our planning problem and reflected on the value and the limitations of our ADP designs. We observed that the more time-window flexibility and number of freights there are, the better the look-ahead methods perform. We also observed that the two methods that look-ahead more than one stage performed better than the standard one-step look-ahead ADP approach. Further research about ADP designs that explicitly consider a few stages in advance (e.g., rolling horizon, sampling, approximate policy iteration) and other, possibly non-linear, value function approximations, are relevant for synchromodal planning.

References

1. Bai, R., Wallace, S.W., Li, J., Chong, A.Y.L.: Stochastic service network design with rerouting. Transp. Res. Part B **60**, 50–65 (2014)
2. Caris, A., Macharis, C., Janssens, G.K.: Decision support in intermodal transport: a new research agenda. Comput. Ind. **64**(2), 105–112 (2013). Decision Support for Intermodal Transport
3. Crainic, T.G., Hewitt, M., Rei, W.: Scenario grouping in a progressive hedging-based meta-heuristic for stochastic network design. Comput. Oper. Res. **43**, 90–99 (2014)
4. Dall'Orto, L.C., Crainic, T.G., Leal, J.E., Powell, W.B.: The single-node dynamic service scheduling and dispatching problem. Eur. J. Oper. Res. **170**(1), 1–23 (2006)
5. Ghane-Ezabadi, M., Vergara, H.A.: Decomposition approach for integrated intermodal logistics network design. Transp. Res. Part E **89**, 53–69 (2016)
6. Li, L., Negenborn, R.R., Schutter, B.D.: Intermodal freight transport planning a receding horizon control approach. Transp. Res. Part C **60**, 77–95 (2015)
7. Lium, A.G., Crainic, T.G., Wallace, S.W.: A study of demand stochasticity in service network design. Transp. Sci. **43**(2), 144–157 (2009)
8. Lo, H.K., An, K., Lin, W.H.: Ferry service network design under demand uncertainty. Transp. Res. Part E **59**, 48–70 (2013)
9. Mes, M.R.K., Iacob, M.E.: Synchromodal transport planning at a logistics service provider. In: Zijm, H., Klumpp, M., Clausen, U., ten Hompel, M. (eds.) Logistics and Supply Chain Innovation: Bridging the Gap Between Theory and Practice, pp. 23–36. Springer, Heidelberg (2016)
10. Nabais, J., Negenborn, R., Bentez, R.C., Botto, M.A.: Achieving transport modal split targets at intermodal freight hubs using a model predictive approach. Transp. Res. Part C **60**, 278–297 (2015)
11. Rivera, A.P., Mes, M.: Dynamic multi-period freight consolidation. In: Corman, F., Voß, S., Negenborn, R.R. (eds.) ICCL 2015. LNCS, vol. 9335, pp. 370–385. Springer, Heidelberg (2015). doi:10.1007/978-3-319-24264-4_26

12. Powell, W.B.: Approximate Dynamic Programming: Solving the Curses of Dimensionality, 2nd edn. Wiley, Hoboken (2011)
13. Riessen, B., Negenborn, R.R., Dekker, R.: Synchromodal container transportation: an overview of current topics and research opportunities. In: Corman, F., Voß, S., Negenborn, R.R. (eds.) ICCL 2015. LNCS, vol. 9335, pp. 386–397. Springer, Heidelberg (2015)
14. SteadieSeifi, M., Dellaert, N., Nuijten, W., Woensel, T.V., Raoufi, R.: Multimodal freight transportation planning: a literature review. Eur. J. Oper. Res. **233**(1), 1–15 (2014)
15. Wieberneit, N.: Service network design for freight transportation: a review. OR Spectrum **30**(1), 77–112 (2008)
16. Zhang, M., Pel, A.: Synchromodal hinterland freight transport: model study for the port of Rotterdam. J. Transp. Geogr. **52**, 1–10 (2016)

A Revenue Management Approach for Network Capacity Allocation of an Intermodal Barge Transportation System

Yunfei Wang[1], Ioana C. Bilegan[1]($\boxtimes$), Teodor Gabriel Crainic[2], and Abdelhakim Artiba[1]

[1] LAMIH UMR CNRS 8201,
Université de Valenciennes et du Hainaut-Cambrésis, 59313 Valenciennes, France
{yunfei.wang,ioana.bilegan,abdelhakim.artiba}@univ-valenciennes.fr
[2] CIRRELT and School of Management, U. du Québec à Montréal,
C.P. 8888, suc. Centre-ville, Montréal H3C 3P8, Canada
teodorgabriel.crainic@cirrelt.net

Abstract. We propose a revenue management (RM) model for the network capacity allocation problem of an intermodal barge transportation system. Accept/reject decisions are made based on a probabilistic mixed integer optimization model maximizing the expected revenue of the carrier over a given time horizon. Probability distribution functions are used to characterize future potential demands. The simulated booking system solves, using a commercial software, the capacity allocation problem for each new transportation request. A conventional model for dynamic capacity allocation considering only the available network capacity and the delivery time constraints is used as alternative when analyzing the results of the proposed model.

Keywords: Revenue management · Network capacity allocation · Intermodal barge transportation · Probabilistic mixed integer model

1 Introduction

Barge transportation offers a competitive alternative for freight transportation, complementing the traditional road and rail modes. Moreover, considered as sustainable, environment-friendly and economical, barge transportation has been identified as instrumental for modal shift and the increased use of intermodality in Europe [3]. Yet, studies targeting barge transportation are scarce, (e.g., [4,6–8,11,14]), the ones considering the intermodal context being even more rare (e.g., [13,15,17,18]). An important and recent review of the scientific literature on multimodal freight transportation planning can be found in [12].

Revenue Management (*RM*), broadly used in passenger transportation to manage trip prices and bookings (e.g., [1]), has been identified as a desirable feature for freight transportation, including barge intermodal services [15]. RM is expected to provide freight carriers with tools to better manage revenues

© Springer International Publishing Switzerland 2016
A. Paias et al. (Eds.): ICCL 2016, LNCS 9855, pp. 243–257, 2016.
DOI: 10.1007/978-3-319-44896-1_16

and enhance service by, in particular, tailoring the service levels and tariffs to particular classes of customers. In [16], the authors study revenue management in synchromodal container transportation to increase the revenue of the transportation providers. In their study, several delivery types are provided by carriers. Each type of delivery is associated with a fare class, characterized by a specific price and a specific due time. In [9], authors propose a cost-plus-pricing strategy to determine the price of delivery types in the context of intermodal *(truck, rail and barge)* freight transportation. The price associated with each delivery type is the sum of the operational cost and the targeted profit margin. The price of a delivery type depends on its urgency as well. Different scenarios, i.e., self-transporting, subcontracting, and a mix of the two are studied, with different operational costs and targeted profit margins. However, in both [9,16], only one type of customers, who sign long-term contracts with the carriers, is considered. Consequently, no accepting or rejecting decision is made during the operational phase. In [10], customers are classified into two categories: contract sale (large shippers, which might be considered regular) customers, and free sale (scattered shippers) customers. A two-stage stochastic optimal model is then proposed to maximize the revenue. In the first stage, the revenue is maximized serving contract sale customers only. In the second stage, the slot capacity after serving contract sale customers is used to serve the scattered shippers customers through a dynamic pricing method for price settling and an inventory control method for slot allocation applied jointly in each period of free sale. The exploration of RM-related issues in freight transportation is still at the very early stages, however, as illustrated by the reviews related to air cargo operations [5], railway transportation [1], and container synchromodal services [15].

We aim to contribute to the field by proposing a RM model to address the network capacity allocation problem of an intermodal barge transportation system. As intermodal barge and rail systems share a number of characteristics, e.g., scheduled services, limited transport capacity (resource) and uncertain future demands, the approach is inspired by the work of [2] where the authors develop a model to dynamically allocate the rail capacity at operational level. In defining the revenue management problem for barge transportation we induce novel features to our modeling, however: we adapt it for the barge transportation space-time network, we enrich it by introducing different categories of customers with the definition of specific treatment for each of them, including particular accept/reject rules. An important feature offered by the new modeling lays in the proposal of a negotiation process based on the optimisation model when dealing with rejected demands, as explained in more details further on. Customers are classified into different categories as follows. Regular customers, who sign long-term contracts with the carriers/providers, must be satisfied and thus all these regular category of demands have to be accepted. On the other hand, the so called spot-market customers, who request transportation less frequently and on an irregular basis, may be rejected if needed. The accept/reject mechanism is settled according to an estimation of the profitability of each new incoming demand, given the availability of service capacities at the time of decision. In order to better consider customer behavior specificities, those spot-market customers are further classified into partially-spot customers, who would accept their requests to be partially accepted, and fully-spot customers, whose requests must be either accepted as a whole or not accepted at all. These acceptance rules are introduced and used in the new RM model (through specific decision variables). Moreover, based on the customer differentiation, and on the associated acceptance rules, different mechanisms are set out in a new negotiation process model which is implemented and used when dealing with rejected demands. At the authors best knowledge, this is the first contribution proposing to introduce RM techniques, e.g., price differentiation and customer classification, at the operational level planning of barge transportation activities.

The application of RM strategies requires a booking system to manage transport requests, and the capability to forecast future demands. In our case, the simulated booking system performs an accept/reject decision for each new transport request, based on the results of the proposed optimization model maximizing the expected revenue of the carrier over a given time horizon. In case of acceptance, the corresponding optimal routing is also provided by the optimization. Probability distribution functions are used to characterize future potential demands for transportation and, thus, the proposed optimization model takes the form of a *probabilistic mixed integer program* (MIP). A commercial solver is used to address this model. Simulation is used to analyze the performance of the proposed optimization model and RM strategies, through comparisons with a conventional dynamic capacity allocation model considering only the available network capacity and the delivery time constraints.

The remainder of this paper is organized as follows. We briefly describe the network capacity allocation problem and the considered RM concepts and strategies for intermodal barge transportation in Sect. 2. The proposed RM model is introduced in Sect. 3. Simulation and numerical results are discussed and analyzed in Sect. 4. We conclude in Sect. 5.

2   Problem Characterization

We first briefly present the general problem of dynamic capacity allocation for barge transportation. The mechanisms of the booking system are then discussed, together with the proposed RM strategies. The associated notation is identified as well.

2.1   Dynamic Capacity Allocation Problem

Consolidation-based carriers, such as those operating barge services, plan and schedule their operations for the "next season" with the goal of jointly maximizing the revenue and satisfying the forecast regular demand, through efficient resource utilization and operations. Transport requests fluctuate greatly during actual operations, however, in terms of origins, destinations, volumes, etc., not to speak of those unforeseen demands the carrier will try to accommodate.

The capability to answer customer expectations of the transport network is consequently continuously changing as well, together with its efficiency and profitability. Setting up some form of advanced booking system is the measure generally adopted to handle this complex situation.

Transport booking requests are traditionally answered on a first-come first-serve (FCFS) basis. Moreover, a transport request is (almost) always accepted provided the network currently has the capability to satisfy both the volume and the delivery time specified by the customer. This has the unwanted consequence that requests coming at a latter time might not be accepted, even though they present the potential to generate a higher revenue, due to a lack of transport capacity, resulting in the loss of additional revenue for the carrier.

RM-based booking systems operate according to different principles. The booking system considered in this paper manages the transport capacity, and the decision to accept or reject a new demand, considering a set of potential future demands characterized by different fare classes. To make the final decision, the acceptance and rejection of the current demand are compared by optimizing the estimated total revenue of all demands, current and potential future ones. Therefore, in our model, a current transport request may be rejected if it appears less profitable compared with the estimated profit of future demands competing for the transport capacity. The resource is then reserved for the future demands, expecting a higher total revenue. On the other hand, when the booking system accepts the current transport request and more than one possible routing exist, a "better" capacity allocation plan can be obtained by considering the future demands. That is, the capacity available in the future might more closely match future demands, increasing the possibility of acceptance and the generation of additional revenue.

We formulate the dynamic capacity allocation problem on a space-time network over a time interval composed of $1, ..., T$ time instants. The nodes of the $G = (N_{IT}, A)$ network are obtained by duplicating the representation of the physical terminals at all time instants, i.e., a node $n(i,t) \in N_{IT}$ specifies the physical terminal i and the time instant t.

A set of already-selected services, each with given schedule, route and capacity, provides transportation among the nodes in N_{IT}. Note that, in this research, we assume that services have already been scheduled at the tactical planning level (i.e., when the Scheduled Service Network Design problem is solved) and are not to be rescheduled at the operational level. The capacities of scheduled services are also fixed since vehicles are already assigned to services and no extra-vehicles are considered to be available upon request. A service $s \in S$ is characterized by its transport capacity $cap(s)$ and set of legs $\eta(s)$. Leg $l \in \eta(s)$ represents a path between two consecutive stops of service s, and is characterized by its origin and destination terminals, $o(l), d(l) \in N_{IT}$, with the respective departure $t_{dep}(l)$ and arrival $t_{avl}(l)$ times. Let $s(l)$ and $cap(l) = cap(s(l))$ identify the service it belongs to and its capacity, and define $cap\_avl(l)$, the residual capacity of leg l after having routed the already accepted demands.

The set of arcs A is then made up of the sets A_L and A_H representing the transport and holding arcs, respectively. Set A_L is composed of all the defined service legs, while A_H arcs link two representations of the same terminal at two consecutive time periods. Holding arcs represent the possibility of demand flows to wait at their respective origins or at intermediate terminals during their journey, to be picked up by services passing by at later periods.

2.2   RM Strategy

Revenue Management groupes together a set of concepts and techniques aimed to better integrate customer behavior knowledge into the optimal capacity allocation models. For instance, different fares are applied to well differentiated products/services and different market segments are identified and used with the overall objective to maximise expected revenue. To define RM strategies for barge transportation systems, we introduce *customer classification* and *price differentiation*.

Customers are classified into three categories according to the business relationship: regular customers (R), who sign long-term contracts with the carrier or whom the carrier trusts; partially-spot customers (P), who contact the carrier infrequently and do not require that all their demand be accepted; fully-spot customers (F), who also require service irregularly but their demand must be accepted as a whole or not at all.

Let $\tilde{k}$ be the current booking request. Let $D(\tilde{k})$ be the set of demands accepted before the arrival of $\tilde{k}$, and $K(\tilde{k})$ the set of forecasted future demands with direct interactions in time with $\tilde{k}$. A transport request $\tilde{d} \in D(\tilde{k}) \cup K(\tilde{k}) \cup \tilde{k}$ is then characterized by the volume to be transported in TEUs, $vol(\tilde{d})$; the origin and destination terminals, $o(\tilde{d})$ and $d(\tilde{d})$, respectively; the time $t_{res}(\tilde{d})$ it is submitted to the booking system; the time $t_{avl}(\tilde{d})$ it becomes available at its origin terminal and the corresponding anticipation time, $\Theta(\tilde{d}) = t_{avl}(\tilde{d}) - t_{res}(\tilde{d})$; the due time (latest delivery time) $t_{out}(\tilde{d})$ and the requested delivery time $\Delta(\tilde{d}) = t_{out}(\tilde{d}) - t_{avl}(\tilde{d})$; the unit tariff $f(\tilde{d})$ according to the fare class of the demand (defined bellow); and the category $cat(\tilde{d})$ of customers (R, P or F). Note that a future demand k is considered to be part of the set of potential future demands $K(\tilde{k})$ when it has "direct interactions" with the current booking request $\tilde{k}$, which is true when the two time conditions are satisfied:

– $t_{res}(k) > t_{res}(\tilde{k})$
– $[t_{avl}(k), t_{out}(k)] \cap [t_{avl}(\tilde{k}), t_{out}(\tilde{k})] \neq \emptyset$.

Let $VMAX(k)$ be the maximum volume a future demand request $k \in K(\tilde{k})$ may take, and $P_k(x)$ the discrete probability distribution function indicating the probability that a given value $0 \leq x \leq VMAX(k)$ occurs.

We define four fare classes for any pair of terminals in the physical network (and the distance separating them) as the combination of $\Theta(\tilde{d})$, early or late booking, and $\Delta(\tilde{d})$, slow or fast delivery requested. A demand with the highest fare class thus corresponds to a late booking and fast delivery request, while a demand with the lowest fare class corresponds to an early booking and slow delivery request.

The proposed RM strategy for barge transportation is then to examine each new transport request, $\tilde{k}$, and decide on its acceptance, and routing through the network for accepted ones, by considering its *feasibility* and *profitability*, given the current status of the network and an estimation of future demands. The former means that currently there is sufficient capacity and time to satisfy $\tilde{k}$. The latter indicates that the expected total revenue given the acceptance of $\tilde{k}$ is at least not worse than the one corresponding to rejecting it, taking into account the potential future demands. The model of Sect. 3 is used to make these decisions.

A rejected request has no influence on the transport network. Similarly, the potential future demands are only used to calculate the expected total revenue, and do not impact the status of the network.

3   The Formulation

We now present the Revenue Management decision model that is to be solved for every arriving request for transportation $\tilde{k}$. The decision variables are:

- $\xi(\tilde{k})$: accept or reject $\tilde{k}$, where $\xi(\tilde{k})$
  - equals 1 when $cat(\tilde{k}) = $ R,
  - varies within $[0, 1]$ when $cat(\tilde{k}) = $ P,
  - takes the value 0 or 1 when $cat(\tilde{k}) = $ F;
- $v(\tilde{k}, a)$: volume of demand $\tilde{k}$ on arc a;
- $maxvol(k)$: maximum volume available on the network (at the decision time) to serve the potential future demand $k \in K(\tilde{k})$;
- $v(k, a)$: volume of the potential future demand $k \in K(\tilde{k})$ on arc a.

Obviously, $\xi(d)$ and $v(d, a)$ variables are fixed on all arcs for the already accepted demands, which we denote d, $d \in D(\tilde{k})$.

The objective function of the model with respect to the current demand $\tilde{k}$ maximizes the sum of its corresponding revenue and the expected revenue computed on the basis of future demand forecasts:

$$\max\ (f(\tilde{k}) \cdot \xi(\tilde{k}) \cdot vol(\tilde{k}) + \phi) \tag{1}$$

where

$$\phi = \sum_{k \in K(\tilde{k})} f(k) \sum_{x=0}^{maxvol(k)} x P_k(x) \tag{2}$$

Following [2], ϕ is linearized by introducing additional binary decision variables y_{kj} for each potential future demand k, where the integer-valued j takes all the values between 1 and $VMAX(k)$. Note that $VMAX(k)$ represents the maximum possible volume of a booking request, which translates mathematically, in terms of probability distribution, as $P_k(j) = 0$ when $j \geq VMAX(k) + 1$.

The binary decision variables y_{kj} are defined to be equal to 1, if no more than volume j of capacity is available on the network to serve the potential future demand k and 0 otherwise. In order to make this definition consistent, for each future demand k, at most one of the variables y_{kj} may take the value 1 (since this will correspond to the maximum capacity available on the network to serve that specific demand). Thus, the objective function becomes:

$$\max \left(f(\tilde{k}) \cdot \xi(\tilde{k}) \cdot vol(\tilde{k}) + \sum_{k \in K(\tilde{k})} f(k) \sum_{1 \leq j \leq VMAX(k)} y_{kj} \sum_{x=0}^{j} (x P_k(x)) \right) \quad (3)$$

since $maxvol(k)$ is defined as follows:

$$maxvol(k) = \sum_{1 \leq j \leq VMAX(k)} j y_{kj} \quad (4)$$

with

$$\sum_{1 \leq j \leq VMAX(k)} y_{kj} \leq 1 \quad (5)$$

and

$$y_{kj} \in \{0, 1\}. \quad (6)$$

Following this definition, note that the optimal value of $maxvol(k)$ is computed (4) as a result of the optimisation problem. Thus, this optimal value is obtained when maximizing the expected revenue corresponding to current demand $\tilde{k}$ on the network, taking into account the entire remaining available capacity and the overall profitability of the whole set of potential future demands on that specific time window.

The constraints of the model are the usual flow conservation relations at nodes and the capacity restrictions imposed by the service network. The latter take the form defined by (7) for each service leg

$$\sum_{k \in K(\tilde{k})} v(k, a) + v(\tilde{k}, a) \leq cap\_avl(a), \quad \forall a \in A_L \quad (7)$$

while the flow conservation constraints for all nodes $n(i, t) \in N_{IT}$ are:

$$\sum_{a \in A^+(n(i,t))} v(\tilde{k}, a) - \sum_{a \in A^-(n(i,t))} v(\tilde{k}, a) = \begin{cases} \xi(\tilde{k}) vol(\tilde{k}) & \text{if}\, (i,t) = o(\tilde{k}) \\ 0 & \text{if}\, (i,t) \neq o(\tilde{k}), (i,t) \neq d(\tilde{k}) \\ -\xi(\tilde{k}) vol(\tilde{k}) & \text{if}\, (i,t) = d(\tilde{k}) \end{cases}$$
$$(8)$$

and

$$\sum_{a \in A^+(n(i,t))} v(k, a) - \sum_{a \in A^-(n(i,t))} v(k, a) = \begin{cases} maxvol(k) & \text{if}\, (i,t) = o(k) \\ 0 & \text{if}\, (i,t) \neq o(k), (i,t) \neq d(k) \\ -maxvol(k) & \text{if}\, (i,t) = d(k) \end{cases}$$
$$(9)$$

where $A^+(n(i,t))$ and $A^-(n(i,t))$ stand for the sets of incoming and outgoing arcs, respectively, of node $n(i,t) \in N_{IT}$.

Finally, the constraints defining the range of the decision variables are:

$$\xi(\tilde{k}) = \begin{cases} 1, & \text{if } cat(\tilde{k}) = R \\ [0,1], & \text{if } cat(\tilde{k}) = P \\ \{0,1\}, & \text{if } cat(\tilde{k}) = F \end{cases} \tag{10}$$

$$v(\tilde{k}, a) \geq 0, \quad \forall a \in A \tag{11}$$

$$v(k, a) \geq 0, \quad \forall k \in K(\tilde{k}), \ \forall a \in A. \tag{12}$$

4   Simulation, Numerical Results and Analysis

To validate the proposed RM model, we use computer simulation. We simulate the sequential arrival of current demands as an iterative process. For each randomly generated demand, we run and solve the optimization problem and use the optimal decision to accept/reject the demand to update accordingly the status of the network in terms of remaining available capacity. Then, a new iteration is performed. The demand forecasts are considered to be known and given at the beginning of the simulation process. Several scenarios are used to test and validate the proposed model. We first set up a scenario with scarce resources and a very limited number of origin-destination (OD) pairs of transport requests. By using this scenario, we analyse the impact of different price ratios applied when different fares are introduced, corresponding to different classes of booking and delivery delays required by the customers. A second scenario, with a more comprehensive problem setting in terms of number of services, number of possible OD pairs of demands is devised. This second scenario is settled to discuss the performance of the RM model with respect to different levels of transportation capacity on the network, as well as with respect to the accuracy of demand forecasts. Based on the second scenario, possible strategies of negotiation when a demand is rejected are equally considered and numerical results analyzed. The remaining of this section is organised as follows. We briefly introduce the scenarios setting for the simulation in Sect. 4.1. We then illustrate and analyze the numerical results in Sect. 4.2.

4.1   Scenarios Setting

For all scenarios, four consecutive terminals, i.e., A, B, C and D, are considered to be located along the inland waterway with travel times for barges between any two consecutive terminals assumed to be the same. As for the service travel times, all the scheduled stops of a service (including at its origin and destination), are assumed to have identical durations as well, these delays corresponding to the time consumption for operations at port (e.g., loading/unloading containers). The maximum capacity of services is identical within one set of experiments but is varied from one scenario to another. The residual capacities of service legs are sequentially updated according to the accepted demands and their optimal routing. Holding arcs of containers at terminals have unlimited capacity.

Let us recall that any current demand $\tilde{k}$ is characterized by its $t_{res}(\tilde{k})$, $vol(\tilde{k})$, $o(\tilde{k})$, $d(\tilde{k})$, $t_{avl}(\tilde{k})$, $t_{out}(\tilde{k})$, $f(\tilde{k})$ and $cat(\tilde{k})$. We discretize the time so that no more than one reservation request $(t_{res}(\tilde{k}))$ may arrive at each time instant during the simulation; $vol(\tilde{k})$ is a discrete random value between 0 and VMAX (the same maximum volume is assumed for any demand) following a given probability distribution function; $vol(\tilde{k}) = 0$ indicates that there is no booking request for the current time instant. The origin-destination pair, thus the values of $o(\tilde{k})$ and $d(\tilde{k})$, are uniformly generated out of the set of possible OD corresponding to a scenario. Both anticipation $\Theta(\tilde{k})$ and delivery time $\Delta(\tilde{k})$ are randomly selected from a predefined pool of possible values, following the uniform distribution; the generation of the latter is equally related to the distance between the $o(\tilde{k})$ and the $d(\tilde{k})$ of the demand. The $t_{avl}(\tilde{k})$ and $t_{out}(\tilde{k})$ are then computed accordingly. Thresholds for the anticipation and delivery time are predefined to split the demands into early/late reservation and slow/fast delivery types, respectively. For a given distance of an OD, a basic fare p is predefined. The unit transportation price (per container) is then defined as $f(\tilde{k}) = p \cdot r_\Theta \cdot r_\Delta$, where r_Θ and r_Δ are the anticipation ratio and the delivery ratio respectively. Their corresponding values for early reservation and slow delivery are both set to 1, the others being integer values (factors) greater than one, corresponding to larger fares charged on high contribution demands requesting higher quality-of-service transportation. Finally, $cat(\tilde{k})$ is randomly generated among R, P and F following the uniform distribution.

For each current demand $\tilde{k}$, the corresponding set of potential future demands is generated following the same generation procedure, except for its volume. Indeed, since the objective function is defined based on the mathematical expectation of the potential revenue of future demands, this computation is performed considering all the possible volumes (from 0 to VMAX), weighted by their probabilities. The summation is bounded, however, by the maximum available capacity (at decision time) on the network to satisfy each specific future demand k ($maxvol(k)$). Following the same idea, note that the categories (i.e., R, P or F) of future demands are not needed either when generating the potential future demands. By doing so, an estimated value of the expected revenue is obtained by simulation and used to make the decision of accepting or rejecting the current demand $\tilde{k}$.

For all the scenarios in the simulation, a FCFS accept/reject policy is conducted as comparison. No potential future demands are considered for the FCFS model. A current demand $\tilde{k}$ is accepted when at least one feasible route exists in the space-time network, without considering the expected revenue and hence, without considering its profitability.

The characteristics of the first scenario are:

– Length of the simulated time horizon is 300 time instants;

- There are 15 identical services defined, starting every 20 time instants, from A to D with an intermediate stop at B;
- 3 different ODs are considered: AB, BD and AD;
- Different experiments are conducted, with different values of the anticipation ratio (r_Θ) for late reservation and the values of the delivery ratio (r_Δ) for fast delivery: 1, 2, 3 and 4.

The characteristics of the second scenario are:

- Length of the simulated time horizon is 600 time instants;
- There is a total of 30 services running on the network, 15 in each direction: from A to D and from D to A; they all stop at all terminals;
- All 12 possible ODs are considered;
- Different experiments are conducted, with different capacities of services: 5, 10 and 20 (TEUs);
- Different experiments are conducted, based on different forecast accuracies: good accuracy, underestimation, overestimation.

4.2   Numerical Results and Analysis

The results obtained when running experiments on the first scenario are illustrated in Fig. 1. Figure 1(a) presents the ratio between the total revenue obtained with the RM model and the total revenue obtained with the FCFS policy, corresponding to different price ratios. Figure 1(b) presents the corresponding ratios of the number of nonprofitable rejected requests over the total number of rejected requests when applying the RM model. On the horizontal axis, r indicates the value of the anticipation ratio (r_Θ) for late reservation and the value of the delivery ratio (r_Δ) for fast delivery; they are considered to have both the same value r. As expected, better revenue is always obtained by applying the RM model when compared with the FCFS policy. When we increase the price ratio r, the difference in profitability of low-fare compared to high-fare demands grows as well. A low-fare demand, which has a feasible routing in the transport network, has then a higher chance to be less profitable compared to a potential future high-fare demand (even if its probability to occur is low) and consequently will be rejected or not fully accepted. Therefore, as shown in Fig. 1(b), when we increase the price ratio r, more demands are rejected because of this economic discrimination (nonprofitability). Consequently, a boost in revenue, as illustrated in Fig. 1(a) is obtained when we increase the anticipation and delivery price ratios.

Note that, even without any price differentiation, the RM model still generates better solutions in terms of total revenue (Fig. 1(a), when r = 1). In fact, the consideration of future demands equally aids in finding the best routing solution when a demand is accepted. This better routing makes room in the space-time network for potentially infeasible future demands, and hence convert them to feasible, which is transformed accordingly into extra revenue.

The ratios between total revenues generated when applying the RM model and when applying the FCFS policy within the second scenario are presented in

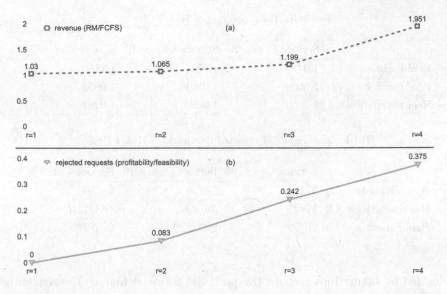

Fig. 1. Effect of price differentiation on revenue (a) and on rejected requests (b)

Table 1. To examine the sensitivity of the RM model to bad forecast accuracy situations, we conduct three different simulations related to the accuracy of the demand forecasts, in terms of volume. In these simulations, if the arrival process of demands to the booking system follows the same probability distribution function as considered in the objective function of the RM model, we say the demand forecast is accurate (Real:Estimate $= 1.0$). Real:Estimate $= 1.5$ indicates the demands are underestimated by a factor of 0.67, while Real:Estimate $= 0.5$ indicates that the demands are overestimated by a factor of 2. The behavior of the RM model with respect to different levels of maximum service capacity is also studied. The values 20, 10 and 5 TEUs for the maximum service capacities are used in three independent sets of experiments.

As expected, the RM model generates higher total revenue than FCFS when the demand forecast is accurate. However, even when demands are not coming as expected, RM model still defeats its competitor. The only exception happens in the simulation when the demands are overestimated and the service capacity is relatively high: the two models generate the same total revenue. The good performance of the RM model is found to overcome the influence of underestimation which implies more booking requests than expected, which can be relatively interpreted as a scarce resource situation. Another observation from Table 1 is that the less network capacity we have, the better the RM model responds. Therefore, the best revenue ratio (1.7196) is obtained when the resource is scarce and the demand forecast is accurate.

The reason why the RM model generates better solutions can be as follows: fully or partially denying demands (due to the different customer categories) create the possibility of saving the precious resource for more profitable (due to higher contribution fares) future demands; to accept a demand, the best routing

Table 1. Total revenue of RM/FCFS

	Service Cap. = 20	Service Cap. = 10	Service Cap. = 5
Real:Estimate = 1.0	1.0483	1.0531	1.7196
Real:Estimate = 1.5	1.0093	1.0391	1.0655
Real:Estimate = 0.5	1	1.0093	1.0282

Table 2. Number of rejected demands of RM/FCFS

	Service Cap. = 20	Service Cap. = 10	Service Cap.=5
Real:Estimate = 0.5	1/1	14/16	59/60
Real:Estimate = 1.0	17/25	76/82	143/151
Real:Estimate = 1.5	70/74	207/220	266/280

is decided by taking into account the potential future demands. Consequently, the better routing of current demand may convert some of the potentially infeasible future demands into feasible demands.

Due to the introduction of RM techniques, less demands are rejected compared with FCFS. As shown in Table 2, the number of rejected demands when applying the RM model, is always less than the corresponding number of rejected demands with the FCFS policy. Given the same level of accuracy of demand forecast, less demands are rejected with higher network capacity. However, the difference between the two competitors is slight. For the RM model, almost one third of the denied transport requests correspond to regular (R) customers.

Therefore, we design another set of simulations including a negotiation phase with the rejected R category customers. Three different strategies, Nego_RM, Nego_FCFS and Nego_PP, are integrated with the proposed RM approach. Once a demand from an R customer is rejected, the negotiation phase is triggered. Both Nego_RM and Nego_FCFS strategies then consider that rejected R demand as a P demand. However, the former tries to fit this demand in the transport network considering estimated future demands (RM model), while the later tries to accept this demand on the transport network in a greedy manner (FCFS model). Instead of changing the category of the demand, the Nego_PP strategy still treats an R customer as regular. In order to transport it, the delivery delay of this demand is extended and a lower unit price is charged (as penalty). For all the tests, a FCFS policy is also carried on as comparison. The effect of different negotiation strategies for rejected R type demands on the total revenue and the percentage of successful negotiation is illustrated in Table 3.

In Table 3, Price Ratio indicates the tested values of both r_Θ late reservation and r_Δ fast delivery. Revenue/FCFS indicates the ratio of total revenue obtained by RM model with (or without) negotiation phase related to FCFS, and Successful Nego shows the percentage of successful negotiation corresponding to each strategy. Even combined with negotiation, RM model still generates

Table 3. Effect of different negotiation strategies for rejected R customers

Price Ratio	Nego. Strategies	Revenue/FCFS	Successful Nego. (%)
$r = 2$	RM	1.1477	0
	Nego_RM	1.1868	15.25
	Nego_ FCFS	1.1849	16.67
	Nego_PP	1.0543	53.52
$r = 3$	RM	1.1493	0
	Nego_RM	1.6227	16.39
	Nego_ FCFS	1.5365	31.88
	Nego_PP	1.2772	54.29
$r = 4$	RM	1.7394	0
	Nego_RM	1.7533	11.11
	Nego_ FCFS	1.7436	16.67
	Nego_PP	1.3500	53.13

better solutions than FCFS. For a given price ratio, Nego_RM always generates slightly better solutions, in terms of total revenue, compared with Nego_FCFS. On the other hand, the latter always has better performance in negotiation than the former. Therefore, carriers can choose the appropriate strategies according to the requirements of their regular customers. In case that R customers have a relative loose constraint on the delivery time, Nego_PP succeeds more than 50 % in the negotiation process for all tested price ratios. One may argue that there exists other possible ways to compensate; we do not claim the proposed negotiation strategies are the best solutions. Instead, we put the emphasis on the fact that with the proposed RM approach, we offer to the carriers a panel of possible ways to simultaneously increase the satisfaction of regular customers and make more revenue. Different negotiation strategies may be adopted based on different types of behavior characterizing regular customers.

5   Conclusions

In this paper, we present a Revenue Management (RM) approach for dynamic capacity allocation of the intermodal barge transportation network. A new model is proposed considering the RM strategies. According to the business relationship, customers are classified into three categories, whose transport requests are accordingly treated differently. A price policy, related to the booking anticipation and delivery type, is also applied to differentiate the products. We conduct a set of experiments to validate the RM approach. Compared with the first-come first-serve (FCFS) based booking strategy, the RM model always generates better total revenue, even with inaccurate demand forecast. Another observation is that facing scarce resource (small transport capacity), the RM model easily outscores its competitor, and this trend grows when resource levels decrease.

We also discuss a set of possible negotiation strategies combined with the proposed RM model and conclude that with slightly lower total revenue the decision support still offers the possibility to better satisfy loyal (regular) customers and generate more revenue compared with FCFS. Encouraged by these preliminary results, we are considering to study how the penalty or compensation for the denied regular demands should be further integrated into the new RM model proposed.

Acknowledgments. We gratefully acknowledge the financial support provided for this project by the i-Trans Association and its innovation platform i-Fret, by the Nord-Pas de Calais Region, France, by the Natural Sciences and Engineering Research Council of Canada through its Discovery grants program, and by Fonds de recherche du Québec through their infrastructure grants.

References

1. Armstrong, A., Meissner, J.: Railway revenue management: overview and models. Technical report, The Department of Management Science, Lancaster University (2010)
2. Bilegan, I.C., Brotcorne, L., Feillet, D., Hayel, Y.: Revenue management for rail container transportation. EURO J. Trans. Logistics **4**(2), 261–283 (2015)
3. European Commission - White Paper: Roadmap to a Single European Transport Area - Towards a competitive and resource-efficient transport system (2011)
4. Fazi, S., Fransoo, J.C., van Woensel, T.: A decision support system tool for the transportation by barge of import containers: a case study. Decis. Support Syst. **79**, 33–45 (2015)
5. Feng, B., Li, Y., Shen, Z.-J.M.: Air cargo operations: literature review and comparison with practices. Transp. Res. Part C Emerg. Technol. **56**, 263–280 (2015)
6. Frémont, A., Franc, P.: Hinterland transportation in Europe: combined transport versus road transport. J. Transp. Geogr. **18**(4), 548–556 (2010)
7. Konings, R.: Opportunities to improve container barge handling in the port of Rotterdam from a transport network perspective. J. Transp. Geogr. **15**(6), 443–454 (2007)
8. Konings, R., Kreutzberger, E., Maraš, V.: Major considerations in developing a hub-and-spoke network to improve the cost performance of container barge transport in the hinterland: the case of the port of Rotterdam. J. Transp. Geogr. **29**, 63–73 (2013)
9. Li, L., Lin, X., Negenborn, R.R., De Schutter, B.: Pricing intermodal freight transport services: a cost-plus-pricing strategy. In: Corman, F., et al. (eds.) ICCL 2015. LNCS, vol. 9335, pp. 541–556. Springer, Heidelberg (2015). doi:10.1007/978-3-319-24264-4_37
10. Liu, D., Yang, H.: Joint slot allocation and dynamic pricing of container sea-rail multimodal transportation. J. Traffic Transp. Eng. **2**(3), 198–208 (2015). (English Edition)
11. Notteboom, T.: Challenges for container river services on the Yangtze River: a case study for Chongqing. Res. Transp. Econ. **35**(1), 41–49 (2012)
12. SteadieSeifi, M., Dellaert, N.P., Nuijten, W., van Woensel, T., Raoufi, R.: Multimodal freight transportation planning: a literature review. Eur. J. Oper. Res. **233**(1), 1–15 (2014)

13. Tavasszy, L.A., Behdani, B., Konings, R.: Intermodality and Synchromodality. Technical report (2015). http://ssrn.com/abstract=2592888
14. Taylor, G.D., Whyte, T.C., DePuy, G.W., Drosos, D.J.: A simulation-based software system for barge dispatching and boat assignment in inland waterways. Simul. Modell. Pract. Theory **13**(7), 550–565 (2005)
15. van Riessen, B., Negenborn, R.R., Dekker, R.: Synchromodal container transportation: an overview of current topics and research opportunities. In: Corman, F., et al. (eds.) ICCL 2015. LNCS, vol. 9335, pp. 386–397. Springer, Heidelberg (2015). doi:10.1007/978-3-319-24264-4_27
16. van Riessen, B., Negenborn, R.R., Dekker, R.: The Cargo Fare Class Mix problem-Revenue Management in Synchromodal Container Transportation. Technical report (2015). doi:10.13140/RG.2.1.4894.9841
17. Ypsilantis, P., Zuidwijk, R.: Joint design and pricing of intermodal port-hinterland network services: Considering economies of scale and service time constraints (No. ERS-2013-011-LIS) ERIM Report Series Research in Management (2013)
18. Zuidwijk, R.: Are we connected? - Ports in Global Networks. ERIM Inaugural Address Series Research in Management. Erasmus Research Institute of Management (2015). ISBN 978-90-5892-435-3

Location and Routing

LORE, A Decision Support Tool for Location, Routing and Location-Routing Problems

Rui Borges Lopes[1]($\boxtimes$), Carlos Ferreira[2], and Beatriz Sousa Santos[3]

[1] DEGEIT/CIDMA, University of Aveiro,
Campus Universitário de Santiago, 3810-193 Aveiro, Portugal
rui.borges@ua.pt
[2] DEGEIT/IEETA, University of Aveiro,
Campus Universitário de Santiago, 3810-193 Aveiro, Portugal
carlosf@ua.pt
[3] DETI/IEETA, University of Aveiro,
Campus Universitário de Santiago, 3810-193 Aveiro, Portugal
bss@ua.pt

Abstract. LOcation Routing Exploration (LORE) is a decision support tool for addressing location, routing and location-routing problems. In this paper the LORE tool will be presented, and its main characteristics addressed. Among the main features of the tool is the ability to support a variety of problems currently being studied in the location and routing literature (due to the proposed data structure), and the graphical user interface (GUI). The data structure will be presented being provided an explanation on how it can support related problems. The GUI main goal is not only to aid the solution-finding process but also to foster greater insight into the problem(s) at hand. To that extent, the GUI, developed to fit the target user's profile and intended tasks, is presented, namely data input and visualization features.

1 Introduction

An efficient logistics system is of the utmost importance for the competitiveness of today's organizations. When designing logistics systems, cost-effectiveness is often the main focus [23, 26], where main cost components concern location of facilities and transportation (distribution from facilities to customers). These are decisions that have an enormous impact on the effectiveness of logistics systems and consequently on the complete supply chain [2]. Making correct choices concerning location and distribution (henceforth named routing) is therefore critical [1]. In such semi-structured decisions, decision support systems (DSS) may play a big role, as they can handle a large number of parameters and relationships and lessen the effect of unknown or changing parameters/relationships [11]. However, the overall complexity of these decisions, and the specifics of each case under study, makes difficult the task of developing an effective decision support tool (DST); despite a relevant and potentially impactful research effort.

In operations research (OR) such logistics decisions have been addressed in a set of well-defined problems. For comprehensive reviews and taxonomies on

© Springer International Publishing Switzerland 2016
A. Paias et al. (Eds.): ICCL 2016, LNCS 9855, pp. 261–274, 2016.
DOI: 10.1007/978-3-319-44896-1_17

these specific problems the reader is referred to [16] for location problems, [7] for vehicle routing problems (VRP), and [15,19] for the integrated location-routing problem (LRP). These have shown to be NP-hard in most scenarios.

DSTs for these problems are typically faced with the lack of knowledge of the models from users (usually decision makers with no such technical expertise). Therefore, having models and algorithms with good performance is often not enough. The exploration of the solution finding process and the solution presentation are equally important. For fostering greater insight, and allowing better judgements and decisions, these tools should be easy to understand, navigate, and interact with.

The development of DSSs (and DSTs) has been fairly active in several areas (for surveys and related concepts see [8,12,25]). Several tools can currently be found addressing VRPs (some of the most recent are [17,22]) and location problems (e.g. [3,20]). Concerning the integrated location-routing approach, only three works have addressed it, namely [4,10,14]. All of these are restricted to specific variants of the problem (e.g. the single-objective capacitated LRP in [14]). Given that the LRP has several variants with a lot of potential real-life applications, new tools must be developed to address (possibly several of) these problems. The applicability of such tools is further increased by the fact that LRPs can be simplified to address, separately, location and routing problems.

The development and availability of such DSTs may help both decision makers and researchers. The former, by allowing obtaining scientifically-supported solutions and easily testing alternative solutions, thus improving the quality of decisions. The latter, by: (a) aiding the process of gathering data; (b) reducing the time to obtain (real-world) instances; (c) enabling visualizing the inner-workings of developed models and algorithms; and (d) enabling improving the functioning of models and algorithms (e.g. helping tuning parameters).

Moreover, such tools may represent a step forward to creating a common decision making process across different organisation levels (location is typically handled at a strategic level, while routing is operational), signalled in [12] as a big research challenge.

This paper presents a decision tool for location, routing and location-routing problems. The tool is able to support several variants of the LRP, having great concerns on usability aspects. The remaining sections are organized as follows. Section 2 addresses the tool architecture, data structure, and supported problems, providing a brief description on how the data structure can support closely related problems. Solving integrated logistics problems is addressed in Sect. 3. In Sect. 4 the graphical user interface (GUI) and its main functionalities concerning data input and visualizations are presented. Finally, concluding remarks and an outlook on future work are given in Sect. 5.

2 LORE Architecture, Data Structure, and Supported Problems

The developed tool, LORE, has an open and modular architecture, allowing functionality to be easily added, updated or removed. The three main components of the proposed architecture are: the data structure, the supported problems, and the user interface. These can be seen in Fig. 1, where interaction with other applications, input and output features, and algorithm integration are also depicted.

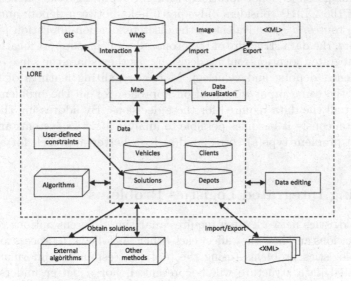

Fig. 1. LORE architecture with its main components

In order to solve instances from various types of LRPs the tool must be able to support several distinct data. Due to the complexity of the data to support, a data structure had to be defined, having the following characteristics: (a) flexible, for easily supporting future developments and file format evolutions, while maintaining compatibility; (b) being able to hierarchically structure all the needed data, making it easier to interpret and maintain; and (c) being able to reflect its structure directly on the files obtained/generated by the tool, facilitating integration of new algorithms and interaction with other applications.

For these reasons, the data structure created for the tool is defined in XML Schema, a standard language for defining an XML document structure. Concerning the XML file format, its characteristics, advantages and disadvantages, the reader is referred to, for example, [27]. Full detail concerning data/file structures of the tool can be found in [13].

Although the proposed tool is mainly directed at supporting location-routing decisions it is also able to support simplifications of the problem, namely: the facility location problem and the VRP. Regarding LRPs, the currently used data structure enables supporting single and multi-objective approaches for (the reader is referred to [15] for further explanation of these LRP variants): round-trip location problem; capacitated LRP (CLRP); location-arc routing problem; plant-cycle location problem; travelling salesman location problem; stochastic LRP; transportation-location problem; many-to-many LRP; and multi-level (or multi-echelon) LRP.

This set of supported problems can be, in some cases, easily adapted to fit other well-known problems. For example, if the CLRP has only one possible depot location it becomes a capacitated VRP (CVRP), or the multi-depot VRP when several possible depot locations with no depot installation costs exist. Likewise, if the CLRP considers only direct links between depots and clients, rather than routes, it is equivalent to the discrete location-allocation problem.

Therefore, the data structure of the proposed tool can support location, routing, and integrated location-routing decisions (as they share the same elements, namely, clients, depots, and vehicles). Moreover, editing features of the GUI (which use the same input/visualization approach for all the problems) allow maintaining all the data required for these decisions. By addressing these decisions simultaneously it becomes possible to analyse logistics systems and determine which problem type(s) correspond(s) to a better approach for a specific scenario.

3   Solving Integrated Logistics Problems

Defining a logistics network often requires analysing different options regarding logistics decisions and how they affect each other. As follows, a process for solving integrated logistics problems (using the tool), corresponding information flow and generated data structure will be presented. For a better understanding, Fig. 2 can be used alongside the description of the process.

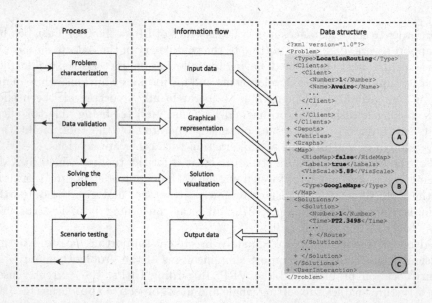

Fig. 2. Solution-finding process, corresponding information flow and data structure

For the correct characterization of the problem several data is required, which can be obtained manually or using geographical tools (e.g. using google maps

API [9]). This corresponds to the input data of the problem, possibly requiring some validation, which is stored after the XML declaration (as seen in Fig. 2, area A).

For data validation, graphical representations may play an important role. Features such as overlapping maps, changing visualizations, etc. often make interpreting information easier for users. To this end, input data must be combined with other visualization-related data. In Fig. 2 we can see an arrow pointing to where this information is obtained in the data structure (area B).

Solutions for the characterized problem can now be obtained. Concerning solution-finding approaches, even though the tool embeds several algorithms for the aforementioned problems, running other algorithms is possible without them being embedded into the tool. By simply obeying to the data structure, algorithms need only to import and export the necessary data files. Note that time required for the DST to obtain solutions is related to the algorithms' ability to solve the problem or the used commercial software (for mixed-integer programming).

Users can afterwards visualize and analyse solutions; corresponding data is added to the last section of the data structure (Fig. 2, area C). All of the obtained data can be exported to an XML file.

The last step of the process, scenario testing, may require significant changes to the original data, possibly to the point where the addressed problem has changed. The following example shows such a decision-making scenario.

Suppose a decision maker, e.g. a goods manufacturer, intends finding the most cost efficient way to distribute products from the production facility to the clients (Fig. 3, left). Often this is handled as a distribution problem and a CVRP solution is sought. However, as the production facility is considerably far from clients, current routing costs are high. A natural analysis would be considering opening other facilities nearer to clients, shifting the analysis to a CLRP scenario, where location costs (costs of opening and operating new facilities) have to be taken into account simultaneously, providing a more integrated view of logistic costs (Fig. 3, centre).

This analysis can go further in depth, testing several scenarios, for example: considering intermediary warehouses between the factory and the clients (becoming a multi-level LRP – Fig. 3, right); or considering additional objectives such as minimizing delivery time. This step-by-step and scenario testing analysis is made possible in the proposed tool, as the different problems are supported and several options for comparing solutions are made available.

4   Graphical User Interface and Main Functionalities

For developing effective interfaces the profile of target users must be taken into account. This was also the case for the proposed tool, where the user (typically a decision maker) will be, in general, someone with: higher education, not necessarily with a background on modelling and optimization; good knowledge of the problem at hand or experience in real-world logistics systems design; at least

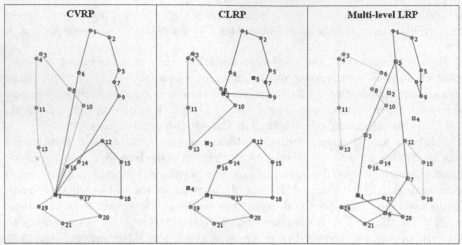

Legend: ○ Client   ■ Production facility   ▫ Warehouse

Fig. 3. Graphical representation of a logistic system analysed as a CVRP (left), CLRP (centre), and multi-level LRP (right). Production facility numbered one is fixed; the remaining production facilities as well as warehouses are being considered for installation. Lines connecting clients, facilities and warehouses represent vehicle routes

reasonable computer literacy; knowledge of (Web) map applications; and who may use the tool infrequently.

For this user profile, the information provided should neither be technical data regarding the used methods nor its validation. Instead, the focus should be on providing a usable interface, where the main usability goal should be easy and efficient access to solutions and ease to learn and remember [6,24]. The profile of the target users, the task they intend to perform using this DST, and usability principles (e.g. consistency, compatibility, familiarity, feedback, robustness, etc.) [6] were taken into consideration during the design of the tool. The tool was developed for Windows operating systems, and implemented in extensible application markup language (XAML) with C# as code-behind.

The main objective behind the development of this tool is to allow obtaining, editing and visualizing data, solving instances of the supported problems and visualizing the corresponding results. To that end, the following main functionalities are provided:

- input/edit data for defining the problem
- interact with web map servers (WMS), for obtaining and visualizing online geographical data
- obtain solutions and visualize them either through numeric or graphical representation
- visually compare different solutions
- allow user input in the solution obtaining process
- save/export data to easily understandable XML files.

The conceptual model of the GUI is organized around a main window, with all functionalities accessible through the toolbar or the menu, in a way easily understandable by users. This conceptual model, based on the information flow and similar map applications, aims allowing an easy and efficient access to solutions, and comprises three main sections (Fig. 4): a toolbar for accessing main functionalities; a left-hand expandable panel for editing/displaying data regarding the problems (with tabs for its elements, namely, Clients, Depots and Vehicles); and a visualization area showing graphical representation of the problems elements and information about the maps.

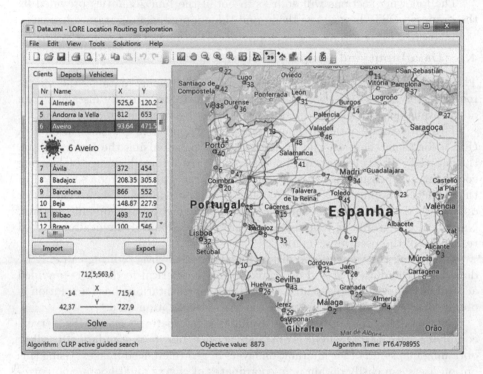

Fig. 4. Graphical user interface of the LORE tool

Buttons in the toolbar enable assessing several functionalities, which are grouped into: standard features (Open, Save, Save as, Print, etc.), map navigation options (Import map, Pan, Zoom out/in, Zoom to fit, Hide map), data visualization options (Objects size, Display labels/images, View required service), and user input options (Fix arc in solution, Import solution). These are also available through the menu bar thus providing greater flexibility and supporting users with different system experience and/or performing different tasks.

The left-hand expandable panel allows editing/displaying data regarding the elements in the problem (clients, depots and vehicles) using a data grid. This panel is most useful when inserting large quantities of data; expanding it enables working with a bigger data grid.

The visualization area, which will be addressed in detail further on, allows seeing the problem elements and information about the maps. Finally, the status bar displays data regarding the used algorithm (name and time needed to obtain the current solution), as well as the objective function(s) value(s) of the currently visualized solution.

The development of the GUI also took into consideration the guidelines defined by Microsoft for Windows desktop applications [18]. Additionally, the GUI was subjected to informal tests of adaptation to real target users; then, a formal usability evaluation was made (evaluation results can be found in [13]).

The following sections will address in detail the functionalities provided by the proposed DST, how to use them, and the adopted visualization solutions.

4.1   Data Input and Graphical Representations

The data allowing defining the problem is the following: data of the clients requiring service; data regarding the depots to install or already installed; data of the available vehicles; and matrix of distances between clients and depots.

This data can be obtained/maintained directly on the map visualization area (Fig. 5) or using the data grid on the left-hand panel. Using the former option the inserted/edited element coordinates are directly obtained/changed (changing coordinates is possible using drag-and-drop of the graphical representation of the element) popping up a form to collect/edit the remaining data. The latter option, the data grid, is most suitable when working with large amounts of data. Numerical and graphical representations are provided and dynamically updated regardless of the used input method.

Concerning the vehicles and distance matrix, data entry/editing can only be done using the data grid and dedicated forms. Numerical feedback is provided accordingly and is complemented with visual representations once a solution is obtained, where routes are drawn in the map visualization area.

Another data input option made available is interacting with WMSs. Servers complying with the OpenGIS Web Map Service Interface standard [21] allow obtaining maps and other information layers in geo-referenced images. Using this option users can easily obtain map coordinates of clients and depots, and corresponding pairwise distances. Additionally, other information can be obtained in map layers, possibly combining different online servers (e.g. road network, satellite imagery, important infrastructures, etc.). The LORE tool currently supports interaction with the OpenGIS standard compliant Demis WMS [5], allowing to pan and zoom any area of the world map and obtain the requested imagery and geographical information (Fig. 6).

Concerning graphical representations, besides the standard ones provided for the different elements involved (circles and squares, respectively for clients and depots, with corresponding labels and images), other representations and the map image can be imported by users. As superimposing elements' representations onto the map may lead to confusions, their colour, opacity and size may be changed. Additionally, users can access other views, such as the service-based view which displays, for each client, a circle with radius directly proportional

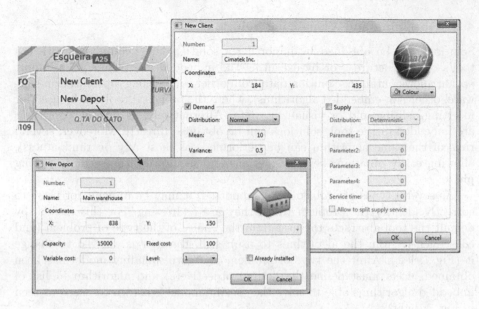

Fig. 5. Data input using the map visualization area

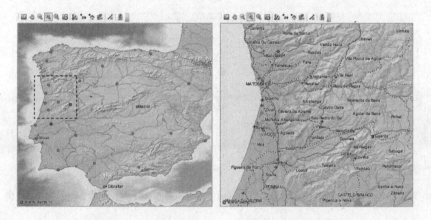

Fig. 6. Obtaining map information from the Demis WMS. The map image on the right was obtained by performing zoom in on the area inside the dashed rectangle of the left-side map image.

to its required service. This view helps users identify clients with higher service values, providing an additional layer of information to the map visualization area.

Finally, for fully evaluating the different elements in the map users can use several navigation options, such as: pan, zoom out/in, and zoom to fit. Note that the graphical representation of vehicle routes is only made available once solutions are obtained, which will be presented as follows.

4.2 Obtaining and Visualizing Solutions

Solutions can be obtained by importing a solution file – complying with the tool's data structure – or by executing the imbedded algorithms. The import option allows obtaining solution data from other sources (e.g. optimization software, other non-embedded algorithms), where the proposed tool can be used for inserting, editing and/or visualizing data. Alternatively, as several algorithms are imbedded in the tool, solutions can be obtained directly. Moreover, several runs of the same algorithm can be performed (as most rely on randomness), allowing easily obtaining several solutions and facilitating the scenario testing phase.

As several types of problems are supported, it may be difficult for users to correctly identify the problem which they are addressing. For this reason, by default the tool abstracts the user from the choice of the type of problem (and consequently from the algorithms to use); still, the user is allowed to change it (Fig. 7, left). After the type of problem and corresponding model has been obtained, users must define the desired objective(s) and algorithm (a list of imbedded algorithms able to solve the specific model is shown to users; as seen in Fig. 7, right).

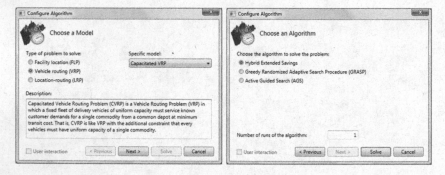

Fig. 7. Choice and configuration of the type of problem (left) and algorithm (right)

After obtaining solutions, an overview of their data, namely algorithm used, time to obtain them, and objective function values, are shown in a control panel (Fig. 8, left); also allowing restoring and comparing previously obtained solutions. For accessing full solution data, a solution data panel is made available to users (Fig. 8, right). This panel shows, for a given solution, the following data: total objective function value, depots to install, vehicles capacity, and route tracing. By using modeless dialog boxes [18], both control and data panels allow easily changing focus between the panel and the main window. This is generally useful as a correct analysis often requires obtaining solutions and comparing them continuously.

Solutions can also be represented graphically in the map visualization area (main window). This can be seen in Fig. 9, left, where vehicle routes linking

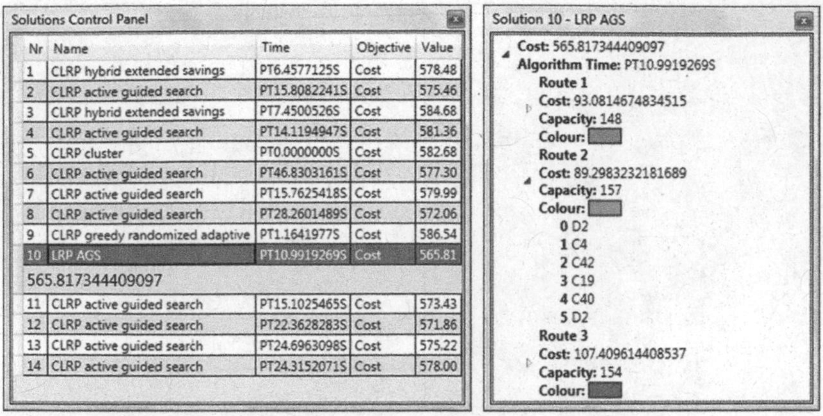

Nr	Name	Time	Objective	Value
1	CLRP hybrid extended savings	PT6.4577125S	Cost	578.48
2	CLRP active guided search	PT15.8082241S	Cost	575.46
3	CLRP hybrid extended savings	PT7.4500526S	Cost	584.68
4	CLRP active guided search	PT14.1194947S	Cost	581.36
5	CLRP cluster	PT0.0000000S	Cost	582.68
6	CLRP active guided search	PT46.8303161S	Cost	577.30
7	CLRP active guided search	PT15.7625418S	Cost	579.99
8	CLRP active guided search	PT28.2601489S	Cost	572.06
9	CLRP greedy randomized adaptive	PT1.1641977S	Cost	586.54
10	LRP AGS	PT10.9919269S	Cost	565.81
	565.817344409097			
11	CLRP active guided search	PT15.1025465S	Cost	573.43
12	CLRP active guided search	PT22.3628283S	Cost	571.86
13	CLRP active guided search	PT24.6963098S	Cost	575.22
14	CLRP active guided search	PT24.3152071S	Cost	578.00

Solution 10 - LRP AGS

Cost: 565.817344409097
Algorithm Time: PT10.9919269S
  Route 1
    Cost: 93.0814674834515
    Capacity: 148
    Colour:
  Route 2
    Cost: 89.2983232181689
    Capacity: 157
    Colour:
      0 D2
      1 C4
      2 C42
      3 C19
      4 C40
      5 D2
  Route 3
    Cost: 107.409614408537
    Capacity: 154
    Colour:

Fig. 8. Solution control panel displaying obtained solutions (left) and solution data panel displaying in tree view all the data of the selected solution (right)

clients and depots are represented using coloured lines; each route with a different colour for easier interpretation. Users can also visually compare different solutions at the same time, as corresponding route links are overlaid with an offset (Fig. 9, right). This comparison may also prove useful in identifying route links that are common to "good" solutions, which can be removed from the problem in order to reduce its size and difficulty. Looking at the solution comparison provided on the right-hand side of Fig. 9, this procedure could be performed, for example, in clients 26, 31, 28, 3, 36 and 35 (top-right), which are linked sequentially in all of the solutions. The following could be done: (1) replace the set of links by a single fixed link between clients 26 and 35 (fixed links are explained in the following paragraph); (2) aggregate into these two clients the required service of the remaining intermediate clients; and (3) remove the intermediate clients from the problem.

Finally, users can capitalize on their experience and/or knowledge of the problem under analysis or even add additional constraints, actively contributing to the solution-finding process. For example, they can use fixed links, i.e., links that must appear in solutions, forcing any newly obtained solution to include them. This can be used when some clients have to be serviced in a predetermined order or when a link must be traversed by a vehicle. Figure 9, left, depicts a fixed link between clients 3 and 20 (graphically represented with a padlock), forcing them to be serviced sequentially.

5   Conclusion

In this paper the LORE tool, a DST developed to address location, routing and location-routing decisions is presented (accessible at: http://lore.web.ua. pt/). The tool's architecture, data structure, supported problems, and GUI are addressed. The data structure is based on XML and allows supporting several

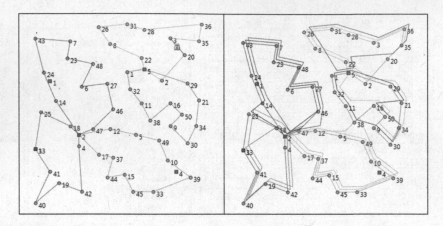

Fig. 9. Solution graphical representation (left) and visually comparing three different solutions (right)

logistics problems, enabling access to online geographic data through WMSs. The tool's GUI and proposed visualizations allow the exploration of the solution-finding process in a way easily understandable by target users.

The profile of target users (who may not have specific knowledge on the used methods) as well as the tasks they have to perform were taken into consideration in the development of visualization and interaction solutions. The users interface' usability was a major concern in the development of the tool, intending practitioners with moderate computer literacy to be able to obtain good solutions to integrated logistics problems without much learning effort.

As future work we identify the incorporation of inventory decisions in the tool, providing new challenges from two points of view: the supported problems (with additional data and increasingly difficult to solve) as well as from a visualization point of view (requiring developing dedicated visualizations, e.g., for depicting and interacting with 3D cargos).

Concluding, the proposed LORE tool, by providing a seamless view of location and routing problems, may improve the insight and judgment of decision makers, possibly helping them make better logistics decisions.

Acknowledgements. This work was supported by Portuguese funds through the CIDMA – Center for Research and Development in Mathematics and Applications, and the Portuguese Foundation for Science and Technology ("FCT – Fundação para a Ciência e a Tecnologia"), within project UID/MAT/04106/2013.

References

1. Ambrosino, D., Scutellà, M.G.: Distribution network design: new problems and related models. Eur. J. Oper. Res. **165**, 610–624 (2005)
2. Bookbinder, J.H.: Global Logistics. Transp. Res. E **41**, 461–466 (2005)

3. Chevalier, P., Thomas, I., Geraets, D., Goetghebeur, E., Janssens, O., Peeters, D., Plastria, F.: Locating fire stations: an integrated approach for Belgium. Socio-Econ. Plann. Sci. **46**, 173–182 (2012)
4. Coutinho-Rodrigues, J., Current, J., Clímaco, J., Ratick, S.: Interactive spatial decision-support system for multiobjective hazardous materials location-routing problems. Transp. Res. Rec. **1602**, 101–109 (1997)
5. Demis: Demis products: Web Map Server (2013). http://www.demis.nl/home/pages/wms/demiswms.htm
6. Dix, A., Finlay, J., Abowd, G., Beale, R.: Human-Computer Interaction. Prentice Hall, New Jersey (2004)
7. Eksioglu, B., Vural, A.V., Reisman, A.: The vehicle routing problem: a taxonomic review. Comput. Ind. Eng. **57**, 1472–1483 (2009)
8. Eom, S.B., Kim, E.B.: A survey of decision support system applications (1995–2001). J. Oper. Res. Soc. **57**, 1264–1278 (2006)
9. Fu, C., Wang, Y., Xu, Y., Li, Q.: The logistics network system based on the Google Maps API. In: International Conference on Logistics Systems and Intelligent Management, pp. 1486–1489 (2010)
10. Gorr, W.L., Johnson, M.P., Roehrig, S.F.: Spatial decision support system for home-delivered services. J. Geogr. Syst. **3**, 181–197 (2001)
11. Hosack, B., Hall, D., Paradice, D., Courtney, J.F.: A look toward the future: decision support systems research is alive and well. J. Assoc. Inf. Syst. **13**, 315–340 (2012)
12. Liu, S., Duffy, A.H.B., Whitfield, R.I., Boyle, I.M.: Integration of decision support systems to improve decision support performance. Knowl. Inf. Syst. **22**, 261–286 (2010)
13. Lopes, R.B.: Location-routing problems of semi-obnoxious facilities: approaches and decision support. Ph.D. thesis. University of Aveiro, Portugal (2011)
14. Lopes, R.B., Barreto, S., Ferreira, C., Santos, B.S.: A decision-support tool for a capacitated location-routing problem. Decis. Support Syst. **46**, 366–375 (2008)
15. Lopes, R.B., Ferreira, C., Santos, B.S., Barreto, S.: A taxonomical analysis, current methods and objectives on location-routing problems. Int. Trans. Oper. Res. **20**, 795–822 (2013)
16. Melo, M.T., Nickel, S., Saldanha-da-Gama, F.: Facility location and supply chain management - a review. Eur. J. Oper. Res. **196**, 401–412 (2009)
17. Mendoza, J.E., Medaglia, A.L., Velasco, N.: An evolutionary-based decision support system for vehicle routing: the case of a public utility. Decis. Support Syst. **46**, 730–742 (2009)
18. Microsoft: Design applications for the Windows desktop (2015). https://dev.windows.com/en-us/desktop/design
19. Nagy, G., Salhi, S.: Location-routing: issues, models and methods. Eur. J. Oper. Res. **177**, 649–672 (2007)
20. Ocalir, E.V., Ercoskun, O.Y., Tur, R.: An integrated model of GIS and fuzzy logic (FMOTS) for location decisions of taxicab stands. Expert Syst. Appl. **37**, 4892–4901 (2010)
21. Open Geospatial Consortium: Web map service (2013). http://www.opengeospatial.org/standards/wms
22. Santos, L., Coutinho-Rodrigues, J., Antunes, C.H.: A web spatial decision support system for vehicle routing using Google Maps. Decis. Support Syst. **51**, 1–9 (2011)
23. Rushton, A., Croucher, P., Baker, P.: The Handbook of Logistics and Distribution Management. Kogan Page, London (2014)

24. Sharp, H., Rogers, Y., Preece, J.: Interaction Design: Beyond Human-Computer Interaction. Wiley, Chichester (2007)
25. Shim, J.P., Warkentin, M., Courtney, J.F., Power, D.J., Sharda, R., Carlsson, C.: Past, present, and future of decision support technology. Decis. Support Syst. **33**, 111–126 (2002)
26. Teo, C.P., Shu, J.: Warehouse-retailer network design problem. Oper. Res. **52**, 396–408 (2004)
27. Wyke, R.A., Leupen, B., Rehman, S.: XML Programming. Microsoft Press, Redmond (2002)

Two Echelon Location Routing Problem with Simultaneous Pickup and Delivery: Mixed Integer Programming Formulations and Comparative Analysis

Ece Arzu Demircan-Yildiz[1](✉), Ismail Karaoglan[2],
and Fulya Altiparmak[1]

[1] Faculty of Engineering, Department of Industrial Engineering,
Gazi University, Ankara, Turkey
{arzudemircan, fulyaal}@gazi.edu.tr
[2] Faculty of Engineering, Department of Industrial Engineering,
Selçuk University, Konya, Turkey
ikaraoglan@selcuk.edu.tr

Abstract. This paper addresses the two-echelon location routing problem with simultaneous pickup and delivery (2E-LRPSPD). The 2E-LRPSPD deals with optimally locating primary and secondary facilities, and integrating goods distribution from depots and collection from customers and secondary depots. To the best of our knowledge there is no previous study on this problem. We propose two mixed integer programming formulations for the 2E-LRPSPD. While the first formulation is a two-index node-based formulation, the second one is a two-index flow-based formulation. Moreover, a family of valid inequalities are adapted from the literature to strengthen the formulations. In order to evaluate the performances of the formulations and valid inequalities, we conduct an experimental study on the instances derived from the literature. The computational results show that the flow-based formulation produces better lower bounds than the node-based formulation on small and medium-size problems.

Keywords: Two-Echelon location routing problem · Simultaneous pickup and delivery · Integer programming

1 Introduction

Globalization makes competitive environment conditions harder. Companies share a significant part of their budget for logistics costs. Therefore, they want to decrease logistic costs by optimizing their distribution network. Location of depots and distribution of goods from depots to customers are the main elements in the design of a distribution system. In most of the studies, it is assumed that customers served directly from depots. In practice, customers may have demand less than truckload, so distribution is done through routes. Determining the location of depots and forming routes from depots to customers are both hard combinatorial problems. These two problems

© Springer International Publishing Switzerland 2016
A. Paias et al. (Eds.): ICCL 2016, LNCS 9855, pp. 275–289, 2016.
DOI: 10.1007/978-3-319-44896-1_18

handled separately for years. In literature, it is shown that the cost efficient design of distribution systems can be obtained by considering location and vehicle routing decisions together. The progress in optimization techniques make possible to integrate these problems and the problem is named as Location-Routing Problem (LRP) in literature [17]. The LRP is the problem of determining the location of facilities and the routes of the vehicles for serving the customers under some constraints such as facility and vehicle capacities, route length, etc. to satisfy demands of all customers and to minimize total cost including routing costs, vehicle fixed costs, facility fixed costs and facility operating costs. The LRP can be applied in food and drink distribution, military equipment location, parcel delivery and telecommunication network design [8]. Comprehensive reviews about the LRP can be found in [4, 11, 12] or [17].

Recently researchers linked logistics, freight distribution and traffic management and generate the idea of city logistics. This notion can be defined as strategical, tactical or operational planning of freight flows in city. Distributing directly from main depots to final customers is not practical so the need for intermediate facilities arises. In this kind of distribution system, main depots serve intermediate depots and intermediate depots serve final customers. One of the problems arising from this distribution system is Two-Echelon Location-Routing Problem (2E-LRP). Figure 1 provides a representation of 2E-LRP. Components of two-echelon freight distribution systems are primary facilities, primary vehicles, secondary facilities, secondary vehicles and customers. Primary facilities are high capacitated facilities and located far from customers. At primary facilities customer demands are loaded on primary vehicles. Each primary vehicle visits one or more secondary facilities. Secondary facilities to be located are low capacitated facilities used for transshipment operations. At this facilities, freights coming from primary facilities on primary vehicles are transferred to low capacitated secondary vehicles. Secondary vehicles are suitable for city transportation operations. Each secondary vehicle visits one or more customers. Customers are end points; each customer is served by exactly one secondary vehicle. At each echelon, routes start and end at same facility [2].

To solve the 2E-LRP mixed integer programming models and a heuristic algorithm based on Tabu Search were developed by Boccia et al. [1]. Nguyen et al. [13]

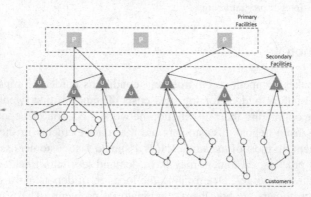

Fig. 1. Two echelon Location-Routing problem representation (Source: [2])

developed a hybrid metaheuristic combining GRASP and evolutionary/iterated local search. Nikbakhsh and Zegordi [16] presented a 4-index mathematical model for two echelon location routing problem with soft time windows, moreover they developed a heuristic algorithm for the problem. Contardo et al. [3] developed a two-index mathematical model and a branch and cut algorithm. They also use adaptive large-neighborhood search to reach better solutions in a short time. Nguyen et al. [14] described four constructive heuristics and two GRASP based metaheuristics. Metaheuristics include a learning process, variable neighborhood descent and path relinking heuristics. Nguyen et al. [15] proposed a multi start iterated local search for the problem and three greedy heuristics to obtain an initial solution. Govindan et al. [5] developed a multi-objective optimization model for 2E-LRP with time windows. They also aimed to reduce costs caused by carbon footprint and greenhouse gas emissions. They designed a method which includes a multi-objective hybrid approach called MHPV. This method is a hybrid of multi-objective particle swarm optimization and adapted multi-objective variable neighborhood search. It is also important to note that two-echelon problems are also seen in telecommunication systems. Some recent studies in this area are given in [10, 19].

In general form of 2E-LRP, customers have only delivery demands. However, in practice, customers can have pickup and delivery demands and they often request that both demands should be met at the same time. In this study we define a variant of the 2E-LRP named as Two Echelon Location-Routing Problem with Simultaneous Pickup and Delivery (2E-LRPSPD). To the best of our knowledge, there is no previous study on the 2E-LRPSPD in the literature. The 2E-LRPSPD applications can be seen in a number of reverse logistics contexts. The beverage industry is one of the application areas. Firms are responsible for both distributing the beverages and collecting the empty bottles for reusing. Bottles are transported from primary facilities to secondary facilities and from secondary facilities to stores, and empty bottles collected while distribution. Another example is the grocery store chain. Products are transported from primary facilities to secondary facilities on pallets and from secondary facilities to stores and empty pallets are returned to secondary facilities. The 2E-LRPSPD deals with determining the location of secondary facilities and the routes of the vehicles at the first echelon for serving the secondary facilities, at the second echelon for customers under some constraints such as facility and vehicle capacities, route length, etc. to satisfy demands of all customers and to minimize the total cost including routing costs, vehicle fixed costs, facility fixed costs and facility operating costs. It should be noted that a variant of this problem, called as the two-echelon multi-products location-routing problem with pickup and delivery (LRP-MPPD-2E), has been studied in [18]. The LRP-MPPD-2E considers multi-product, one or more secondary facilities in the same route and pickup or delivery demands. Thus, the LRP-MPPD-2E differs from the 2E-LRPSPD with these aspects.

By using strong mathematical formulations, efficiency of exact methods such as branch and cut, branch and price can be improved. Besides, strong formulations can be used in matheuristics and yields better results. Therefore, as a first step to solve the 2E-LRPSPD, we propose two polynomial-size Mixed Integer Programming (MIP) formulations. These new formulations have been derived from the formulations developed by [9] for the LRP with Simultaneous Pick-up and Delivery (LRPSPD).

While the first formulation is a node-based formulation, the second one is a flow-based formulation. Moreover, we adapt a family of valid inequalities from the literature to strengthen the formulations. In order to evaluate the performances of the formulations and valid inequalities, we conduct an experimental study on the instances derived from the literature. This study presents the comparative results of performances of mixed integer models. Computational results show that flow-based formulation performs better than node-based formulation in terms of generating tight lower bounds on small and medium-size problems.

The rest of this paper is organized as follows. Problem description and proposed formulations are given in Sect. 2. The adopted valid inequalities presented in Sect. 3. Computational results are reported in Sect. 4. Finally, conclusion and suggestions for the future research directions are discussed in Sect. 5.

2   Problem Description and Mathematical Formulations

This section presents two new mixed integer mathematical formulations for the 2E-LRPSPD. Formulations have been formed based on the formulations developed by [9] for the LRPSPD. The 2E-LRPSPD can be defined formally as follows: Let G = (N, A) be a complete directed network where $N = N_C \cup N_D \cup \{0\}$ is the set of vertices in which N_C represents the customers, N_D represents the secondary facilities and "0" represents the primary facility. While N_1 is the set of vertices in the first echelon ($N_1 = \{0\} \cup N_D$), N_2 is the set of vertices in the second echelon ($N_2 = N_C \cup N_D$). $A = \{(i,j) : i,j \in N\}$ is the set of arcs, and to each arc (i, j) is associated a nonnegative cost (distance) c_{ij} and triangular inequality holds (i.e., $c_{ij} + c_{jk} \geq c_{ik}$). A capacity CD_t and a fixed cost FD_t are associated with each possible secondary facility node $t \in N_D$. At each echelon there is unlimited number of homogeneous vehicles with known capacities (CV_1, CV_2) and fixed operating cost (FV_1, FV_2). In the 2E-LRPSPD, each customer $l \in N_C$ requires a given quantity to be delivered (d_l) and picked-up (p_l). The 2E-LRPSPD consists of locating secondary facilities and finding a set of routes such that;

- At the first echelon each route starts and ends at the primary facility,
- At the second echelon each route starts and ends at the same secondary facility,
- Each secondary facility is visited exactly once by exactly one primary vehicle,
- Each customer is visited exactly once by exactly one secondary vehicle,
- The total vehicle load in any arc does not exceed the capacity of the vehicle,
- The total location, vehicle costs for secondary facilities, and routing costs are minimized.

2.1   Node Based Formulation (M1 Node)

In the M1 node formulation, the additional variables are defined on the nodes of the graph and subtour elimination and vehicle capacity restrictions are modeled using Miller–Tucker–Zemlin (MTZ) constraints. Thus, the M1 node formulation includes lifted version of these constraints given in [6, 7], respectively. In the M1 node,

$$x_{ij} = \begin{cases} 1, & \textit{if a primary vehicle travels directly from node i to node j at first echelon} \\ 0, & \textit{otherwise} \end{cases} \quad (\forall i, j \in N_1)$$

$$h_{lm} = \begin{cases} 1, & \textit{if a secondary vehicle travels directly from node l to node m at second echelon} \\ 0, & \textit{otherwise} \end{cases} \quad (\forall l, m \in N_2)$$

$$a_t = \begin{cases} 1, & \textit{if depot t is opened} \\ 0, & \textit{otherwise} \end{cases} \quad (\forall t \in N_D)$$

$$w_{mt} = \begin{cases} 1, & \textit{if customer m is assigned to secondary facility t} \\ 0, & \textit{otherwise} \end{cases} \quad (\forall m \in N_C, \forall t \in N_D)$$

Additional variables:

U_t: *delivery load on primary vehicle just before having serviced secondary facility t, $\forall t \in N_D$*

V_t: *pickup load on primary vehicle just after having serviced secondary facility t, $\forall t \in N_D$*

U_m: *delivery load on secondary vehicle just before having serviced customer m, $\forall m \in N_C$*

V_m: *pickup load on secondary vehicle just after having serviced customer m, $\forall m \in N_C$*

D_t: *delivery demand of secondary facility t, $\forall t \in N_D$*

P_t: *pickup demand of secondary facility t, $\forall t \in N_D$*

The node-based formulation, M1 node, is as follows:

Formulation (M1 node)

$$Min \sum_{i \in N_1} \sum_{j \in N_1} c_{ij} x_{ij} + \sum_{t \in N_D} FV_1 x_{0t} + \sum_{l \in N_2} \sum_{m \in N_2} c_{lm} h_{lm} + \sum_{t \in N_D} FD_t a_t + \sum_{t \in N_D} \sum_{m \in N_C} FV_2 h_{tm}$$

$$(1)$$

$$\text{s.t.} \sum_{j \in N_1} x_{jt} = a_t \quad \forall t \in N_D \tag{2}$$

$$\sum_{j \in N_1} x_{ji} - \sum_{j \in N_1} x_{ij} = 0 \quad \forall i \in N_1 \tag{3}$$

$$U_j - U_i + CV_1 x_{ij} \leq CV_1 - D_j \quad \forall i, j \in N_D, i \neq j \tag{4}$$

$$D_t \leq U_t \quad \forall t \in N_D \tag{5}$$

$$U_t \leq CV_1 \quad \forall t \in N_D \tag{6}$$

$$D_t = \sum_{m \in N_c} w_{mt} d_m \quad \forall t \in N_D \tag{7}$$

$$\sum_{m \in N_c} w_{mt} d_m \leq CD_t a_t \quad \forall t \in N_D \tag{8}$$

$$V_t - V_e + CV_1 x_{te} \leq CV_1 - P_e \quad \forall t, e \in N_D, t \neq e \tag{9}$$

$$P_t \leq V_t \quad \forall t \in N_D \tag{10}$$

$$V_t \leq CV_1 \quad \forall t \in N_D \tag{11}$$

$$U_t + V_t - D_t \leq CV_1 \quad \forall t \in N_D \tag{12}$$

$$P_t = \sum_{m \in N_c} w_{mt} p_m \quad \forall t \in N_D \tag{13}$$

$$\sum_{m \in N_c} w_{mt} p_m \leq CD_t a_t \quad \forall t \in N_D \tag{14}$$

$$\sum_{m \in N_2} h_{lm} = 1 \quad \forall l \in N_C \tag{15}$$

$$\sum_{m \in N_2} h_{lm} - \sum_{m \in N_2} h_{ml} = 0 \quad \forall l \in N_2 \tag{16}$$

$$\sum_{t \in N_D} w_{mt} = 1 \quad \forall m \in N_C \tag{17}$$

$$h_{mt} \leq w_{mt} \quad \forall t \in N_D, \forall m \in N_c \tag{18}$$

$$h_{tm} \leq w_{mt} \quad \forall t \in N_D, \forall m \in N_c \tag{19}$$

$$h_{lm} + w_{lt} + \sum_{e \in N_D, e \neq t} w_{me} \leq 2 \quad \forall l, m \in N_C, l \neq m, \forall t \in N_D \tag{20}$$

$$U_m - U_l + CV_2 h_{lm} + (CV_2 - d_l - d_m) h_{ml} \leq CV_2 - d_l \quad \forall l, m \in N_C, l \neq m \tag{21}$$

$$V_m - V_l + CV_2 h_{lm} + (CV_2 - p_l - p_m) h_{ml} \leq CV_2 - p_m \quad \forall l, m \in N_C, l \neq m \tag{22}$$

$$d_l + \sum_{m \in N_c, l \neq m} h_{lm} d_m \leq U_l \quad \forall l \in N_C \tag{23}$$

$$U_l \leq CV_2 - (CV_2 - d_l) \sum_t h_{lt} \quad \forall t \in N_D, \forall l \in N_c \tag{24}$$

$$p_l + \sum_{m \in N_C, l \neq m} p_m h_{ml} \leq V_l \quad \forall l \in N_C \tag{25}$$

$$V_l \leq CV_2 - (CV_2 - p_l) \sum_{t \in N_D} h_{tl} \quad \forall l \in N_C \tag{26}$$

$$U_l + V_l - d_l \leq CV_2 \quad \forall l \in N_C \tag{27}$$

$$x_{ij} \in \{0,1\} \quad \forall i,j \in N_1 \tag{28}$$

$$w_{mt} \in \{0,1\} \quad \forall m \in N_D, \forall l \in N_C \tag{29}$$

$$a_t \in \{0,1\} \quad \forall t \in N_D \tag{30}$$

$$h_{lm} \in \{0,1\} \quad \forall l,m \in N_2 \tag{31}$$

$$U_m, V_m, U_t, V_t, D_t, P_t \geq 0 \quad \forall t \in N_D, \forall m \in N_C \tag{32}$$

where preliminary set $h_{lm} = 0$ whenever $\max\{(d_l+d_m),(p_l+p_m),(d_m+p_l)\} > CV_2$, $\forall l,m \in N_C, l \neq m$. This restriction guarantees that any incompatible customer pair whose total demand is greater than the vehicle capacity does not appear in the same route.

Objective function (1) minimizes the total system cost including transportation costs, secondary facility and vehicle fixed costs for both echelons. While constraints (2)–(14) are defined for the first echelon, (15)–(27) are defined for the second echelon. Constraints (2) ensure that each opened secondary depot must be visited exactly once. Constraints (3) guarantee that the number of entering and leaving arcs to each node are equal. Constraints (4) are flow inequalities for delivery demands, eliminate sub tours and guarantee that delivery demand of each secondary facility is satisfied. Constraints (5) and (6) are bounding constraints for U_t. Constraints (7) define D_t, which is equal to total delivery demand of customers that assigned to secondary facility t. Constraints (8) guarantee that the total delivery load on any secondary facility do not exceed the corresponding secondary facility capacity. Constraints (9) are flow inequalities for pickup demands, eliminate sub tours and guarantee that pickup demands of each secondary facility are satisfied. Constraints (10) and (11) are bounding constraints for V_t. Constraints (12) imply that the total load on any arc does not exceed the primary vehicle capacity. Constraints (13) define P_t, which is equal to total pickup demand of customers that assigned to secondary facility t. Constraints (14) guarantee that the total pickup load on any secondary facility do not exceed the corresponding secondary facility capacity. Constraints (15) ensure that each customer must be visited exactly once, constraints (16) guarantee that the number of entering and leaving arcs to each node are equal. Constraints (17) ensure that each customer must be assigned to only one secondary facility. Constraints (18)–(20) forbid the illegal routes which do not start and end at the same depot. Constraints (21) are flow inequalities for delivery demands and eliminate sub tours and guarantee that delivery demand of each customer is satisfied. Constraints (22) are flow inequalities for pickup demands and they eliminate sub tours and guarantee that pickup demand of each customer is satisfied. Constraints (23)–(26) are bounding constraints for the additional variables. Constraints (27) imply that the total load on any arc does not exceed the vehicle capacity. Finally, constraints (28)–(32) are known as integrality constraints.

2.2   Flow Based Formulation (M2 Flow)

In the M2 flow, the additional variables are defined on the arcs of the graph. Definitions of additional variables are given below:

Additional variables:

U_{ij}:   demand to be delivered to sec ondary facilities routed after node i and transported in arc (i, j) if a vehicle travels directly from node i to node j, $\forall i, j \in N_1$, otherwise 0

V_{ij}:   demand to be picked up from sec ondary facilities routed up to node i (including node i) and transported in arc (i, j) if a vehicle travels directly from node i to node $j, \forall i, j \in N_1$, otherwise 0

U_{ml}:   demand to be delivered to customers routed after node m and transported in arc (m, l) if a vehicle travels directly from node m to node l, $\forall m, l \in N_2$, otherwise 0

V_{ml}:   demand to be picked up from customers routed up to node m (including node m) and transported in arc (m, l) if a vehicle travels directly from node m to node l, $\forall m, l \in N_2$, otherwise 0

The flow-based formulation, M2 flow, is as follows:

Formulation (M2 flow)

Min (1),

s.t. (2), (3), (7), (8), (13)–(20) and

$$\sum_{j \in N_1} U_{jt} - \sum_{j \in N_1} U_{tj} = D_t \quad \forall t \in N_D \tag{33}$$

$$\sum_{j \in N_1} V_{tj} - \sum_{j \in N_1} V_{jt} = P_t \quad \forall t \in N_D \tag{34}$$

$$U_{ij} + V_{ij} \leq CV_1 x_{ij} \quad \forall i, j \in N_1, i \neq j \tag{35}$$

$$\sum_{t \in N_D} U_{0t} = \sum_{m \in N_C} d_m \tag{36}$$

$$\sum_{t \in N_D} U_{t0} = 0 \tag{37}$$

$$\sum_{t \in N_D} V_{t0} = \sum_{t \in N_D} p_m \tag{38}$$

$$\sum_{t \in N_D} V_{0t} = 0 \tag{39}$$

$$U_{ij} \leq CV_1 x_{ij} \quad \forall i \in N_D, \forall j \in N_1 \tag{40}$$

$$V_{ij} \leq CV_1 x_{ij}, \quad \forall i \in N_1, \forall j \in N_D \tag{41}$$

$$\sum_{m \in N_2} U_{ml} - \sum_{m \in N_2} U_{lm} = d_l \quad \forall l \in N_C \tag{42}$$

$$\sum_{m \in N_2} V_{lm} - \sum_{m \in N_2} V_{ml} = p_l \quad \forall l \in N_C \tag{43}$$

$$U_{lm} + V_{lm} \leq CV_2 h_{lm} \quad \forall l, m \in N_2, l \neq m \tag{44}$$

$$\sum_{m \in N_C} U_{tm} = \sum_{m \in N_C} w_{mt} d_m \quad \forall t \in N_D \tag{45}$$

$$\sum_{m \in N_C} U_{mt} = 0 \quad \forall t \in N_D \tag{46}$$

$$\sum_{m \in N_C} V_{mt} = \sum_{m \in N_C} w_{tm} p_m \quad \forall t \in N_D \tag{47}$$

$$\sum_{m \in N_C} V_{tm} = 0 \quad \forall t \in N_D \tag{48}$$

$$U_{lm} \leq (CV_2 - d_l) h_{lm} \quad \forall l \in N_C, \forall m \in N_2 \tag{49}$$

$$V_{lm} \leq (CV_2 - p_m) h_{lm} \quad \forall l \in N_2, \forall m \in N_C \tag{50}$$

$$U_{lm} \geq d_m h_{lm} \quad \forall l \in N_2, \forall m \in N_C \tag{51}$$

$$V_{lm} \geq p_l h_{lm} \quad \forall l \in N_C, \forall m \in N_2 \tag{52}$$

$$U_{ij}, V_{ij} \geq 0 \quad \forall i, j \in N_1 \tag{53}$$

$$U_{lm}, V_{lm} \geq 0 \quad \forall l, m \in N_2 \tag{54}$$

where preliminary set $h_{lm} = 0$ whenever $\max\{(d_l + d_m), (p_l + p_m), (d_m + p_l)\} > CV_2$, $\forall l, m \in N_C, l \neq m$ as in the M1 node. Constraints (33) and (34) are flow conservation constraints for secondary facility delivery and pickup demands, respectively, and they both eliminate sub tours. Constraints (35) imply that the total load on any arc does not exceed the vehicle capacity. Constraints (36) ensure that the total delivery load dispatched from primary facility equals to the total delivery demand of customers. Constraints (37) guarantee that the total delivery load returning to the primary facility must be equal to zero. Constraints (38) ensure that the total pick up load entering primary facility equals to the total pickup demand of customers. Constraints (39) guarantee that the total pick up load dispatched from primary facility must be equal to zero. Constraints (40) and (41) are bounding constraints for the additional variables. Constraints (42) and (43) are flow conservation constraints for delivery and pick up demands, respectively, and they both eliminate sub tours. Constraints (44) imply that the total load on any arc does not exceed the vehicle capacity. Constraints (45) ensure that the total delivery load dispatched from each opened secondary facility equals to the total delivery demand of customers, which are assigned to the corresponding secondary facility. Constraints (46) guarantee that the total delivery load returning to the opened secondary facilities must be equal to zero. Constraints (47) ensure that the total pick up load entering each opened secondary facility equals to the total pick up demand of customers, which are assigned to the corresponding secondary facility. Constraints (48) guarantee that the total pick up load dispatched from each opened secondary facility must be equal to zero. Constraints (49)–(52) are bounding constraints for the additional variables. Finally, Constraints (53) and (54) are integrality constraints.

3 Families of Valid Inequalities

In this section, we describe several families of valid inequalities which are used to strengthen the linear relaxation of a mathematical model. In this study, six valid inequalities, which are adopted from [9] developed for LRPSPD, are used to strengthen the formulations. We added these valid inequalities to the formulations introduced in the Sect. 2 in order to strengthen their linear programming relaxation. Three of the valid inequalities are polynomial sized and rest of them are exponential sized.

The first polynomial sized family of valid inequalities (55) and (56) bounds below the number of routes originating from primary facility and secondary facilities, respectively.

$$\sum_{t \in N_D} x_{0t} \geq r_{2E-\text{LRPSPD}}(N_D) \tag{55}$$

$$\sum_{t \in N_D} \sum_{m \in N_C} h_{mt} \geq r_{2E-\text{LRPSPD}}(N_C) \tag{56}$$

where $r_{2E-LRPSPD}(N_D) = \left\lceil \max\left(\sum_{m \in N_C} d_m; \sum_{m \in N_C} p_m \right) / CV_1 \right\rceil$, $r_{2E-LRPSPD}(N_C) = \left\lceil \max\left(\sum_{m \in N_C} d_m; \sum_{m \in N_C} p_m \right) / CV_2 \right\rceil$ and $\lceil \cdot \rceil$ is the smallest integer bigger than $\cdot$.

The following inequality bounds from below the number of opened secondary facilities.

$$\sum_{t \in N_D} a_t \geq a_{\min} \tag{57}$$

where $\alpha_{\min} = \min_{S \subseteq N_0}\{|S| \mid \sum_{k \in S} CD_k \geq \max(d(N_C); p(N_C))\}$ which enforces that the number of opened depots must satisfy the minimum requirement. $a_{\min}$ value can be obtained as follows; sort secondary facilities according to non-increasing order of their capacity, then the first S secondary facility satisfying $\sum_{k\in S} CD_k \geq \max(d(N_C); p(N_C))$ are selected as opened secondary facility set.

Exponential sized inequalities are used for only second echelon. First two exponential-size inequalities are based on the generalized large multi star (GLM) inequalities which have been originally proposed for the VRP.

$$\sum_{l\in S}\sum_{m\in N_C/S} h_{lm} \geq 1/CV_2 \left(\sum_{l\in S} d_l + \sum_{l\in S}\sum_{m\in N_C/S} d_m(h_{lm}+h_{ml}) \right) \quad \forall S\subseteq N_C, S\neq\emptyset \quad (58)$$

$$\sum_{l\in S}\sum_{m\in N_C/S} h_{lm} \geq 1/CV_2 \left(\sum_{l\in S} p_l + \sum_{l\in S}\sum_{m\in N_C/S} p_m(h_{lm}+h_{ml}) \right) \quad \forall S\subseteq N_C, S\neq\emptyset \quad (59)$$

The last exponential-size valid inequality guarantees that the number of vehicles visiting a set of customers is not less than the corresponding lower bound.

$$\sum_{(l,m)\in S} h_{lm} \leq |S| - r_{2A-YSETDARP}(S) \quad \forall S\subseteq N_C, S\geq 2 \tag{60}$$

where $r_{2A-YSETDARP}(S)$ is calculated as in constraint (55) and (56).

The exponential-size constraints are added by using a suitable separation algorithm which works based on creating candidate set for violation of the valid inequality and iteratively adding a single suitable node to the set.

4 Computational Results

This section presents the results from our computational experiments that investigate the effects of valid inequalities on the formulations. Our experimental study consists in solving LP relaxations of the formulations with the state-of-the-art LP/MIP solver GAMS 24.1.3/CPLEX 12 on Intel® Core i7-4770 3.40 GHz equipped with 8 GB RAM computer. Firstly, we give a brief information about the test problems then continue with computational results.

4.1 Test Problems

Since this study is the first considering 2E-LRPSPD, we derive its test problems from 2E-LRP test sets using demand separation approaches proposed by Salhi and Nagy [20]. Two test sets consisting small and medium sized problems are generated for the 2E-LRPSPD. These are derived from [15]. Test sets have 5 or 10 satellites and 25 or 50 customers. Capacity of the first echelon vehicles are 750 or 850 units; second echelon vehicles are 100 or 150 units. Demands follow normal distribution with mean 15 and variance 25. Customer locations follow either a normal distribution or a multi-normal distribution. The distances between nodes are Euclidean distances but for the first

Table 1. Effects of the valid inequalities on the node-based formulation (lower. bound improvement %)

Test Set		(55), (56)	(55), (56), (57)	(55), (56), (57), (58), (59)	All
25-5MN	X	49.10	49.10	54.12	60.19
	Y	46.70	46.70	51.10	57.66
25-5MNb	X	22.57	22.57	24.39	27.77
	Y	23.49	23.49	25.23	28.78
25-5N	X	63.41	63.41	65.80	68.29
	Y	57.96	57.96	59.79	62.09
25-5Nb	X	74.51	74.51	76.14	81.32
	Y	68.20	68.20	69.55	74.78
50-5MN	X	27.65	27.65	28.70	31.84
	Y	28.31	28.31	29.34	32.04
50-5MNb	X	15.59	25.75	26.79	30.83
	Y	15.14	22.54	23.38	27.48
50-5N	X	38.06	48.06	49.73	50.71
	Y	38.04	47.17	49.02	50.76
50-5Nb	X	42.88	51.45	51.50	52.49
	Y	41.23	47.48	47.52	48.21
50-10MN	X	25.56	25.56	26.39	29.33
	Y	25.33	25.33	25.81	27.96
50-10MNb	X	16.63	27.56	27.80	30.48
	Y	16.13	23.69	23.88	27.47
50-10 N	X	13.71	24.96	26.39	28.05
	Y	12.57	20.87	21.75	24.24
50-10Nb	X	21.96	33.24	33.57	34.92
	Y	17.13	27.79	28.05	29.40
Average		33.41	38.06	39.41	42.38

echelon, distances are doubled. Since pickup and delivery demands for the customers are needed, we utilize demand separation approaches of [20]. In Salhi and Nagy's approach, a ratio $r_i = min(x_i/y_i; y_i/x_i)$, is calculated for each customer i. In this equation x_i and y_i are the coordinates of the customers. Delivery and pickup demands are generated as $d_i = r_i * q_i$ and $p_i = q_i - d_i$ respectively where q_i is the original demands of the customers. This type of problem is called as X and another type of problem Y is generated by exchanging the delivery and pickup demands of every other customer. As a result, 24 different test instances are generated considering types of demand separation X and Y.

4.2   Effects of the Valid Inequalities

In order to investigate the effects of valid inequalities on the formulations, lower bound improvement percentage (LBI%) is considered for each instance. The LBI% is the gap between linear programming relaxation objective values (Z_{Or}^{LB}) and (Z_{VI}^{LB}) of the original problem and original problem with valid inequalities, respectively, and it is calculated by Eq. (61).

Table 2. Effects of the valid inequalities on the flow-based formulation (lower bound improvement %)

Test Set		(55), (56)	(55), (56), (57)	(55), (56), (57), (58), (59)	All
25-5MN	X	30.91	30.91	30.91	40.40
	Y	29.76	29.76	29.76	43.90
25-5MNb	X	22.14	22.14	22.14	26.38
	Y	23.23	23.23	23.23	27.25
25-5N	X	37.29	37.29	37.29	41.65
	Y	35.36	35.36	35.36	40.48
25-5Nb	X	45.99	45.99	45.99	58.07
	Y	36.96	36.96	36.96	49.07
50-5MN	X	11.71	11.71	11.71	17.02
	Y	11.41	11.41	11.41	17.48
50-5MNb	X	6.54	11.55	11.55	18.30
	Y	6.05	9.83	9.83	16.16
50-5N	X	14.16	20.32	20.32	25.30
	Y	14.12	19.77	19.77	26.01
50-5Nb	X	13.29	20.07	20.07	24.81
	Y	9.33	14.49	14.49	19.47
50-10MN	X	10.94	10.94	10.94	14.70
	Y	10.54	10.54	10.54	14.17
50-10MNb	X	6.20	12.65	12.65	17.37
	Y	4.89	9.88	9.88	14.46
50-10N	X	6.90	8.80	8.80	13.70
	Y	6.68	7.85	7.85	12.47
50-10Nb	X	9.69	20.41	20.41	29.64
	Y	7.76	15.75	15.75	24.74
Average		17.16	19.90	19.90	26.38

$$LBI\% = 100 * \left(\frac{Z_{VI}^{LB} - Z_{Or}^{LB}}{Z_{Or}^{LB}} \right) \tag{61}$$

In Tables 1 and 2, effects of the valid inequalities on node- and flow- based formulations are presented. The first column in the tables shows the name of test set. The rest of the columns show the lower bound improvement obtained by solving the LP relaxations of the mathematical model with the valid inequalities written on captions.

As seen on tables, valid inequalities have significant effects on both formulations to obtain tight bounds. Successive inclusion of the valid inequalities improves lower bounds for M1 node by 42.38 % and M2 flow by 26.38 % on the average. Observing the tables, we conclude that introducing inequality (55) and (56) improves lower bounds by 33.41 % for M1 node, by 17.16 % for M2 flow. Inequality (57) yields 4.65 % lower bound improvement for M1 node, 2.74 % for M2 flow. It is also interesting to note that inequality (58) and inequality (59) leads to a slight improvement on the lower bounds 1.35 % for M1 node and no improvement for M2 flow. When we compare the effects of valid inequalities it can be said that inclusion of the inequality (60) gives better lower bound improvements for both of the formulations. It is seen from the tables that LBI%s on M2 flow are lower than those of M1 node. The reason behind this is that original M2 flow produces better lower bounds than M1 node. This result is also consistent with the literature. As a result, flow-based formulation can be used to develop new exact solution procedures such as branch and cut, etc.

5 Conclusion

In this study two-echelon location routing problem with simultaneous pickup and delivery, 2E-LRPSPD, is proposed. The problem includes pickup and delivery activities at each echelon. Moreover, secondary facilities and all vehicles are capacitated. As a first step to solve the 2E-LRPSPD, two mixed integer mathematical formulations are proposed for the problem; one is node based the other is flow based.

Six valid inequalities adapted from literature and used to reach strong bounds. While three of the valid inequalities is polynomial sized, others are exponential sized. Computational experiments have been conducted to evaluate the effects of valid inequalities in terms of lower bound improvement. The results show that the valid inequalities improve the lower bounds for both formulations. However, their impact on M1 node is more significant and also M2 flow produces better lower bounds than M1 node.

For further researches there are several directions. New valid inequalities can be developed for tighter lower bounds and exact algorithms such as branch and cut can be developed to obtain optimal or near-optimal solutions.

References

1. Boccia, M., Crainic, T.G., Sforza, A., Sterle, C.: A metaheuristic for a two echelon Location-Routing problem. In: Festa, P. (ed.) SEA 2010. LNCS, vol. 6049, pp. 288–301. Springer, Heidelberg (2010)
2. Boccia, M., Crainic, T.G., Sforzá, A., Sterle, C.: Location-Routing Models for Designing a Two-Echelon Freight Distribution System. Technical report 2011- 06, CIRRELT, Montréal (2011)
3. Contardo, C., Hemmelmayr, V., Crainic, T.G.: Lower and upper bounds for the two-echelon capacitated Location-Routing problem. Comput. Oper. Res. **39**, 3185–3199 (2012)

4. Drexl, M., Schneider, M.: A survey of Location Routing Problem. Technical report LM-2013-03 (2013)
5. Govindan, K., Jafarian, A., Khodaverdi, R., Devika, K.: Two echelon multiple vehicle Location-Routing problem with time windows for optimization of sustainable supply chain network of perishable food. Int. J. Prod. Econ. **152**, 9–28 (2014)
6. Kara, I.: Two Indexed Polynomial Size Formulations for Vehicle Routing Problems. Technical report 2008/01. Baskent University, Ankara/Turkey (2008)
7. Kara, I., Laporte, G., Bektas, T.: A note on the lifted miller–tucker–zemlin subtour elimination constraints for the capacitated vehicle routing problem. Eur. J. Oper. Research. **158**, 793–795 (2004)
8. Karaoglan, I., Altıparmak, F., Kara, I., Dengiz, B.: A branch and cut algorithm for the Location-Routing problem with simultaneous pickup and delivery. Eur. J. Oper. Res. **211**, 318–332 (2011)
9. Karaoglan, I., Altiparmak, F., Kara, I., Dengiz, B.: The Location-Routing problem with simultaneous pickup and delivery: formulations and a heuristic approach. Omega **40**, 465–477 (2012)
10. Karasan, O., Mahjoub, A.R., Ozkok, O., Yaman, H.: Survivability in hierarchical telecommunications networks under dual homing. INFORMS J. Comput. **26**, 1–15 (2014)
11. Min, H., Jayaraman, V., Srivastava, R.: Combined Location-Routing problems: a synthesis and future research directions. Eur. J. Oper. Res. **108**, 1–15 (1998)
12. Nagy, G., Salhi, S.: Location-Routing: issues, models and methods. Eur. J. Oper. Res. **177**, 649–672 (2007)
13. Nguyen, V.-P., Prins, C., Prodhon, C.: A multi-start evolutionary local search for the two-echelon location routing problem. In: Blesa, M.J., Blum, C., Raidl, G., Roli, A., Sampels, M. (eds.) HM 2010. LNCS, vol. 6373, pp. 88–102. Springer, Heidelberg (2010)
14. Nguyen, V.P., Prins, C., Prodhon, C.: A multi start iterative local search with tabu list and path relinking for the two-echelon location routing problem. Eng. Appl. Artif. Intell. **25**, 56–71 (2012)
15. Nguyen, V.P., Prins, C., Prodhon, C.: Solving the two-echelon location routing problem by a GRASP reinforced by a learning process and path relinking. Eur. J. Oper. Res. **216**, 113–126 (2012)
16. Nikbakhsh, E., Zegordi, S.: A heuristic algorithm and a lower bound for the two-echelon Location-Routing problem with soft time window constraints. Sci. Iranica Trans. E Ind. Eng. **17**, 36–47 (2010)
17. Prodhon, C., Prins, C.: A survey on recent research on Location-Routing problems. Eur. J. Oper. Res. **238**, 1–17 (2014)
18. Rahmani, Y., Cherif-Khettaf, W.R., Oulamara, A.: The two-echelon multi-products Location-Routing problem with pickup and delivery: formulation and heuristic approaches. Int. J. Prod. Res. **54**(4), 999–1019 (2016)
19. Rodríguez-Martín, I., Salazar-González, J.-J., Yaman, H.: A branch-and-cut algorithm for two-level survivable network design problems. Comput. Oper. Res. **67**, 102–112 (2016)
20. Salhi, S., Nagy, G.: A cluster insertion heuristic for single and multiple depot vehicle routing problems with backhauling. J. Oper. Res. Soc. **50**, 1034–1042 (1999)

Vehicle Routing for Fleets
with Electric- and Combustion-Powered Vehicles

Herbert Kopfer and Kristian Schopka[✉]

Chair of Logistics, University of Bremen,
Wilhelm-Herbst-Str. 5, 28359 Bremen, Germany
{kopfer,schopka}@uni-bremen.de
http://www.logistik.uni-bremen.de

Abstract. Optimal transportation plans for fleets with electric-powered vehicles (EPVs) differ substantially from plans generated for fleets with combustion-powered vehicles (CPVs). The main reasons for this difference are the reduced range and payload of EPVs (compared to CPVs) as well as their increased efficiency. In this paper, transportation plans for CPVs and EPVs which must not be recharged during route fulfillment are analyzed by computational experiments. The advantages of CPVs with respect to totally driven distances, number of used vehicles and the ability to generate feasible plans are opposed to the advantages of EPVs with respect to CO_2 emissions. Additionally it is shown that the specific drawbacks of CPVs and EPVs can be mitigated by exploiting the flexibility of a fleet which is composed of both, EPVs and CPVs.

Keywords: Vehicle routing · Electric-powered vehicles versus combustion-powered vehicles · Mixed vehicle fleet · Energy consumption · Reduction of CO_2 emissions · Adaptive large neighborhood search

1 Motivation and Problem Description

The usage of electric-powered vehicles (EPVs) for cargo transportation brings about new challenges for research on transportation planning [8]. One of the challenges which are frequently accepted by the research community is the small range (operating distance) of EPVs, which is caused by the limited battery capacity. The scarce energy capacity of EPVs either allows only short vehicle routes, or alternatively and in contrast to combustion-powered vehicles (CPVs), detours to recharging stations become necessary, see [12]. Furthermore, the payload of EPVs is reduced due to the high weight of the batteries. Compared to CPVs of the same size (with respect to gross weight), an increased number of EPVs is needed for fulfilling a given set of transportation tasks. Consequently, the proportion between fixed and variable costs is changing. That is why research on the fleet size and the utilization of mixed vehicle fleets require new specific investigations, e.g. [3]. Altogether, new tour planning methods considering the specific characteristics of EPVs are required.

© Springer International Publishing Switzerland 2016
A. Paias et al. (Eds.): ICCL 2016, LNCS 9855, pp. 290–305, 2016.
DOI: 10.1007/978-3-319-44896-1_19

Few trucking companies have recently started using EPVs (see e.g. [19]). Of course, they do not replace all CPVs of their fleet by EPVs. In fact, they use EPVs tentatively for getting experience in applying electric power for cargo transport on roads. That is why EPVs usually are not used in fleets consisting exclusively of EPVs. They mostly are part of a mixed fleet composed of vehicles with electric traction and conventional, i.e. combustion-powered, vehicles. Furthermore, EPVs nowadays are almost exclusively used for local traffic on short-distance routes. Apart from some exceptions, trucking companies operate EPVs in that way that they avoid recharging during their routes. Exceptions refer to planning situations where EPVs can be recharged during the service time at customer locations. However, this requires precise agreements and cooperation between the trucking companies and the operators of customer locations. Detours to charging stations are avoided since the extra traveling distance and, even more important, the loss of time would be very costly. The usage of recharging stations is excluded in our paper since for local transport recharging on tour would be economically useless due to the driver wages which have to be paid for the time when drivers and vehicles are idle.

Out of the above reasons and in contrast to most research on vehicle routing for EPVs, we assume that recharging will only be done at the depot of the trucking company. That is why the tour lengths of routes planned for EPVs have to be adapted to the maximum range which can be driven by an EPV without recharging. Moreover, it might even happen that there is no feasible transportation plan for fulfilling a given set of transportation tasks with a homogeneous fleet of EPVs since some distances between customer locations are simply too long for EPVs. Since we are considering routes which have to be completed by one driver within one day, the tour length is additionally limited for any vehicle type by the maximum permissible daily driving time prescribed by EC-regulations.

EPVs are more energy-efficient than CPVs. However, one of the major drawbacks of EPVs is that their capabilities are more restrictive than those of CPVs; e.g. EPVs have a lower range and a lower payload. Consequently, using EPVs instead of CPVs leads to a reduction of the solution space for routing and scheduling. This means that the solution quality may decrease, and e.g. in case of distance minimization, the total travel distance of the vehicles will increase. However, the amount of increase of travel distances is not known in advance without knowing the characteristics of the deployed vehicles and transportation tasks at hand. Anyway, increased travel distances of EPVs will in turn cause increased energy consumption. That is why this paper is focusing on the following research questions:

1. What is the effect of the reduced range and payload of EPVs (compared to CPVs) on the travel distances and on the feasibility of transportation plans?
2. What is the amount of energy reduction or emission reduction reachable by using EPVs instead of using CPVs?
3. Can the typical strengths of EPVs (low energy consumption) and CPVs (high range and payload) be exploited by a fleet which is composed of both, EPVs and CPVs?

For investigating Question 1, transportation plans for test instances with short transportation distances are considered and the traveling distances obtained by these transportation plans are opposed for CPVs on the one hand and EPVs on the other hand. Then, the transportation distances are stepwise stretched or compressed in order to explore the impact of traveling distances on transportation plans; and the demands regarding transportation tasks are also modified in order to see the impact of capacity limitations of the vehicles.

For answering Question 2, transportation plans for CPVs and EPVs are compared with respect to the average values for energy consumption and CO_2 emissions. For CPVs, it is widely accepted that the following Eq. (1) is a good and reasonably simplified approximation for the expected energy consumption of a truck k carrying payload of weight q_{ij} from a location i to a location j with d_{ij} representing the travel distance for the non-stop travel between i to j [5, 6, 17].

$$F_k = a_k \cdot d_{ij} + b_k \cdot q_{ij} \cdot d_{ij} \tag{1}$$

In Eq. (1), a_k denotes the energy consumption of a CPV k per 100 km while b_k denotes the vehicle specific energy consumption per ton payload and 100 km. In this paper, Eq. (1) is also applied for estimating the expected energy consumption for EPVs. Of course, the values for a_k and b_k substantially differ for CPVs and EPVs. Since EPVs make use of recuperation of energy whenever it is possible, the difference between energy consumptions of EPVs and CPVs is strongly sensitive to the type of use of EPVs.

Nevertheless, for an averaged prediction of the energy consumption which has to restrict to ex-ante parameters of vehicle operation, Eq. (1) can be applied to EPVs in the same way as to CPVs. For comparing the emissions of CPVs and EPVs, the generated problem instances which have been solved for answering Question 1 are reconsidered and evaluated with respect of the energy consumption of vehicles. Question 3 will be investigated by allowing fleets with both, EPVs and CPVs, to be used for tour fulfillment.

Light-Duty and Medium-Duty trucks are frequently used in distribution logistics, and within this class of trucks, vehicles with 7.5 tons gross weight and those with 18 tons gross weight are very popular and widely-used. The truck market has offered many products for these vehicles types. Moreover, there are manufacturing companies which offer EPVs of 7.5 tons gross weight (e.g. [20]) and of 18 tons gross weight (e.g. [21]). Table 1 shows the specific characteristics of CPVs and EPVs of a size of 7.5 tons gross weight and 18 tons gross weight (c.f. [18, 21, 22]). The energy consumption declared by the manufacturers for EPVs is adjusted to two different modes of usage: city traffic and overland traffic. The lower value for energy consumption in Table 1 refers to city traffic while the higher value refers to overland traffic. For the EPV with 18 tons gross weight, the manufacturer only announces values for the weight and energy consumption of a chassis without platform. In Table 1, it is assumed that a platform with a weight of 4 tons is supplemented to the chassis (with a weight of 5 tons). The values for payload and energy consumption are adapted accordingly.

The remainder of the paper is structured as follows. Section 2 introduces the vehicle routing problem with time windows and limitations for energy

Table 1. Characteristics of CPVs and EPVs

Vehicle type → Practical example	CPV-7.5 to UPS-P80	EPV-7.5 to UPS-P80E	CPV-18 to IVECO Stralis	EPV-18 to E-FORCE
Traction				
→Engine	Diesel	Electric	Diesel	Electric
→Energy content	70 l	62 kWh	200 l	2 × 120 kWh
→Maximal range	450 km	130 km	1,200 km	350 km
Weights				
→Empty weight	3.5 to	4 to	9 to	12 to
→Payload	4 to	3.5 to	9 to	6 to
Energy consumption (per 100 km)				
→ Empty vehicle	13 l	40–44 kWh	18 l	73.3–80 kWh
→ Loaded vehicle	16.2 l	60–63 kWh	24 l	90–95 kWh

consumption (VRPTW-EC). To generate near optimal transportation plans for the VRPTW-EC an Adaptive Large Neighborhood Search (ALNS) is used. The ALNS is presented in Sect. 3. Section 4 presents the results of computational experiments and derives answers for the research questions 1 to 3. Finally the paper closes with a summary of the findings.

2 Mathematical Model

The mathematical formulation for the VRPTW-EC is built by extending the traditional VRP-formulation (see [2]). The main extensions are:

- the implementation of time windows for customers
- the implementation of tour length restrictions (regarding traveled time and energy consumption)
- the consideration of different types of vehicles (regarding capacity, tour length restrictions and energy consumption)

The VRPTW-EC is described by the following mathematical model (c.f. [16]):

Indices:

i, j locations: $i, j \in I$ where 0 and $n + 1$ represent the depot, $I = \{0, ..., n + 1\}$
k vehicles: $k \in K$ where k describes the vehicle parameters, $K = \{1, .., m\}$

Parameters:

d_{ij} travel distance between locations i and j
t_{ij} time for traveling from location i to j ($t_{ij} = d_{ij}/v$ where v represents the average traveling speed)
α_j time window starting time of customer j
β_j time window ending time of customer j

s_j service time of customer j
q_j demand of customer j
Q_k capacity of vehicle k
T_k maximum tour length of vehicle k (regarding travel time)
a_k energy consumption of the empty vehicle k per kilometer
b_k energy consumption for the load of vehicle k per ton and kilometer
E_k maximum energy content for vehicle k (regarding liters of diesel or kWh)

Variables:

q_{ijk} cargo of vehicle k traveling between locations i and j
t_j service starting time at location j
y_{jk} $=1$ if customer j is served by vehicle k,
      $=0$ otherwise
x_{ijk} $=1$ if vehicle k serves location j immediately after serving location i,
      $=0$ otherwise

$$minimize \quad z = \sum_{k \in K} \sum_{(i,j) \in I \times I} d_{ij} \cdot x_{ijk}, \tag{2}$$

$$subject\ to: \quad \sum_{j \in I \setminus \{0\}} x_{0jk} = 1, \qquad \forall k \in K, \quad (3)$$

$$\sum_{i \in I \setminus \{n+1\}} x_{i,n+1,k} = 1, \qquad \forall k \in K, \quad (4)$$

$$\sum_{i \in I} x_{ihk} - \sum_{j \in I} x_{hjk} = 0, \qquad \forall k \in K, h \in I \setminus \{0, n+1\}, \quad (5)$$

$$\sum_{k \in K} y_{jk} = 1, \qquad \forall j \in I \setminus \{0, n+1\}, \quad (6)$$

$$\sum_{j \in I} q_j \cdot y_{jk} \leq Q_k, \qquad \forall k \in K, \quad (7)$$

$$t_i + s_i + t_{ij} - T_k \cdot (1 - x_{ijk}) \leq t_j, \qquad \forall k \in K, (i,j) \in I \times I, \quad (8)$$

$$\alpha_i \leq t_i \leq \beta_i, \qquad \forall i \in I, \quad (9)$$

$$\sum_{i \in I} q_{ijk} - \sum_{i \in I \setminus \{0, n+1\}} q_{jik} = q_j \cdot y_{jk}, \quad \forall k \in K, j \in I \setminus \{0, n+1\} \quad (10)$$

$$q_{ijk} - Q_k \cdot x_{ijk} \leq 0, \qquad \forall k \in K, (i,j) \in I \times I \quad (11)$$

$$\sum_{(i,j) \in I \times I} t_{ij} \cdot x_{ijk} \leq T_k, \qquad \forall k \in K, \quad (12)$$

$$\sum_{(i,j) \in I \times I} d_{ij} \cdot (a_k \cdot x_{ijk} + b_k \cdot q_{ijk}) \leq E_k, \qquad \forall k \in K, \quad (13)$$

$$q_{ijk} \geq 0, \qquad \forall k \in K, (i,j) \in I \times I \quad (14)$$

$$t_i \geq 0, \qquad \forall i \in I, \quad (15)$$

$$x_{ijk} \in \{0, 1\}, \qquad \forall k \in K, (i,j) \in I \times I, \quad (16)$$

$$y_{jk} \in \{0, 1\}, \qquad \forall k \in K, j \in I. \quad (17)$$

The Objective (2) minimizes the tour length. Constraints (3), (4) and (5) are the flow constraints. Whereas constraints (3) require that each vehicle has to leave the starting depot 0, constraints (4) dictate that all vehicles have to reach the duplicated depot $n + 1$ at the end of the tours. Constraints (5) observe that each customer is reached and left by the same vehicle. Constraints (6) ensure that all customers are assigned to one vehicle which means that y_{jk} is equal to the value obtained by summarizing x_{ijk} for all customers i. The amount of demand must not exceed the vehicles' capacity (constraints (7)). Constraints (8) are an adaption of the sub-tour elimination restrictions described in [7] and set the service starting time for all nodes. The time windows are restricted by constraints (9). Constraints (10) are responsible for balancing the flow of goods. These equations allow the determination of the amount of cargo flow on each edge. Constraints (11) inhibit any transportation on unused edges. Otherwise it would be possible that the demanded quantities take paths differing from those of the vehicles. Since we consider daily planning for distribution logistics, the maximum tour length is restricted due to the maximum operation times of drivers. Whereas the constraints (12) limit the tour length regarding the travel time, constraints (13) restrict the amount of energy available for tours. The transport of negative payload is excluded by constraints (14) and negative times are excluded by constraints (15). Finally, constraints (16) and (17) define the domains of the decision variables.

3   Solution Method

To solve the VRPTW-EC we propose a modified ALNS. The ALNS was introduced by Ropke and Pisinger (see [9,11]). It proposes improving an initial solution (i.e. transportation plan) by a ruin and recreate strategy (c.f. [13]). In an iterative approach a feasible transportation plan is destroyed by a removal operator and repaired by an insertion operator until a certain stop criterion is met (e.g. maximal number of iterations). To investigate large solution spaces, an ALNS uses several removal and insertion operators that reshuffle up to 40 % of all transportation tasks per iteration. Thereby an adaptive procedure guides the selection of the removal and insertion operators. To deal with local optima, simulated annealing (SA) is used, where better solutions are always accepted and worse solutions are accepted with a predefined probability [4].

3.1   Procedure of ALNS

Algorithm 1 visualizes the procedure of an ALNS. The procedure of the ALNS starts with the generation of an initial transportation plan s (line 1). Typically, this initial transportation plan results from a construction heuristic. In our case, the initial transportation plan is generated by a savings algorithm (c.f. [1]), where customers are merged to vehicle routes based on savings of travel distances.

The initial transportation plan s is stored as the actual best known solution $sBest$ (line 2); and the start temperature of the SA is determined (line 3).

Algorithm 1. Procedure of ALNS

---

1   *Generation of initial transportation plan s;*
2   *sBest := s;*
3   $T := T_0;$
4   **for** $i \leftarrow 0 \rightarrow it_{max}$ **do**
5 | $s' \leftarrow s;$
6 | *Choose a random value for q in the range* $[q_1, q_2];$
7 | *Choose a removal and an insertion operator by a roulette wheel selection;*
8 | *Remove q transportation tasks from s' by removal operator;*
9 | *Reinsert removed transportation tasks in s' by insertion operator;*
10 | **if** $f_{s'} < f_{sBest}$ **then**
11 | | $sBest \leftarrow s';$
12 | **end**
13 | **if** $random[0,1] < e^{-\frac{f_s - f_{s'}}{T}}$ **then**
14 | | $s \leftarrow s';$
15 | **end**
16 | $T := T \cdot \varsigma;$
17 | *Adjust probabilities for roulette wheel selection;*
18 **end**
19 **return** *sBest;*

Afterward, the improvement heuristic is applied in an iterative approach (lines 4–18) until a certain number of iterations it_{max} is reached. In each iteration the ALNS modifies the initial solution s, so that a new neighbor solution s' is developed. Thereby, customers are removed from the current transportation plan and reinserted into the remaining transportation plan. To increase the diversity of the improvement heuristic a randomly chosen number q of transportation tasks in the range $[q_1, q_2]$ is reshuffled in each iteration (line 6). Simultaneously, a removal operator and an insertion operator are chosen randomly by a roulette wheel selection, where the probability to select an operator depends on its performance in earlier iterations (line 7). Whereas the well-known operators worst removal, random removal, and shaw removal [14] as well as new sequence removal are available, the used insertion operators are different versions of the regret-k heuristics [10] with and without a noise factor (c.f. [11]). The removal operators remove q transportation tasks from the initial transportation plan (line 8); and the insertion operators reinsert those transportation tasks in the transportation plan (line 9).

A neighborhood solution s' is accepted as new best solution, if its objective value $f_{s'}$ improves the objective value of the best known solution f_{sBest} (line 10–12). To avoid stucking in local optima, an SA supervises the accepting of a neighborhood solution s' as new initial solution s, where a solution with a higher objective value is accepted always as new initial solution and a worse solution is accepted with a probability (line 13–15). Furthermore, in each iteration the temperature T is reduced by a cooling rate $\varsigma = (0, 1)$ (line 16), and the probabilities for the roulette wheel selection are adjusted (line 17; c.f. [11]). Finally, the best transportation plan is returned (line 19).

3.2 Modifications to ALNS

The modifications made to the ALNS refer to the adaptation of removal operators. The shaw removal was originally provided for the pick-up and delivery problem, where the idea is preferably to remove similar transportation tasks. To suit the VRPTW-EC, the shaw removal is slightly modified. Our version of the shaw removal rates the similarity $\gamma(ij)$ of a transportation task i to a randomly chosen transportation task $j \neq i$ based on Eq. (18). Thereby, the features distance between the transportation tasks d_{ij}, the similarity of the time windows ($|\alpha_i - \alpha_j|, |\beta_i - \beta_j|$) and the demands ($|q_i - q_j|$) are considered. All terms of Eq. (18) are normalized to values between $(0, 1]$; i.e. the terms are divided by the specific maximal values. Furthermore, the individual terms are extended by weights δ_1, δ_2, and δ_3. To increase the flexibility, the weights for the individual function terms are randomly re-chosen in the range $[0, 10]$ for each using of the shaw removal.

$$\gamma(ij) = \delta_1 \cdot \left(\frac{d_{ij}}{d_{max}} \right) + \delta_2 \cdot \left(\frac{|\alpha_i - \alpha_j| + |\beta_i - \beta_j|}{\alpha_{max} + \beta_{max}} \right) + \delta_3 \cdot \left(\frac{|q_i - q_j|}{q_{max}} \right) \quad (18)$$

Since the problem described by the VRPTW-EC has the special feature to consider heterogeneous fleets of vehicles, removal operators that force the use of different vehicles are worth investigating. That is why we introduced the sequence removal. It removes connected parts of tours from transportation plans, in order to enable the assignment of these parts to small vehicles. Overall, we propose three versions of the sequence removal, where one of the following strategies is randomly chosen for each application of the sequence removal:

- remove all transportation tasks of a random tour
- remove all transportation tasks after a random edge of a random tour
- remove all transportation tasks after the edge with the highest distance of a random tour

Regardless of which version of the sequence removal is used the procedure is repeated until at least q transportation tasks are removed from the initial transportation plan.

4   Computational Experiments

The effects of using either EPVs or CPVs for vehicle routing are demonstrated for vehicles of different size. Based on the vehicle characteristics shown in Table 1, the experiments presented in this section are performed for vehicles with 7.5 tons gross weight and for vehicles with 18 tons gross weight. CPVs and EPVs behave differently with respect to the energy needed to fulfill a set of transportation tasks. In case of EPVs the energy consumption needed for traveling strongly depends on the type of application. Especially, it is to a high degree dependent on the traffic and road conditions relevant for fulfilling transportation tasks, and most typical for EPVs, the average travel efficiency (i.e. the energy consumption per travel distance) in urban traffic deviates a lot from the average efficiency reachable for overland traffic. Actually, the efficiency of EPVs in overland traffic is much lower than the efficiency in city traffic while for CPVs the difference between city and overland traffic is not generally significant. That is why we differentiate between three types of vehicle usage: CPV (VC), EPV in city traffic (VE_C), and EPV in overland traffic (VE_O). Each type of vehicle usage is considered for vehicles of 7.5 tons gross weight and 18 tons gross weight. Altogether we consider six types of vehicle utilization in Table 2: $VC(7.5), VE_C(7.5), VE_O(7.5), VC(18), VE_C(18), VE_O(18)$.

Table 2 shows the values for the parameters a_k (energy consumption of the empty vehicle k per kilometer) and b_k (energy consumption for the load of vehicle k per ton and kilometer) for the above six types of vehicle utilization. These parameter values are derived from Table 1 by taking the energy consumption per 100 Km for the empty vehicle and the loaded vehicles as basis. In case of EPVs, the declaration for average energy consumption announced by the manufacturers of these vehicles varies considerably between a lower bound and an upper bound. That is why we take the values declared for the lower bound as the value for VE_C, and the declared upper bound as the value for VE_O. Note that, although the energy consumption of EPVs in overland traffic is always higher than the energy consumption in city traffic, the value of the proportionality factor b_k (i.e. the increase of consumption per ton and km) is lower for overland traffic than for city traffic. This is caused by the values announced by the manufacturers for the average lower and upper bounds for fuel consumption and the values derived for empty and full vehicles Additionally to the parameters for energy consumption, Table 2 shows for all six vehicle types the values for the parameters E_k (energy content for vehicle k regarding tank volume or battery capacity) and T_k (maximum tour length for vehicle k in km). The duration of daily tours is restricted by the EC-regulations for maximum driving times and by the regulations for working hours. That is why an upper limit for the sum of driving times and service times is statutory for daily trips of vehicles. We include the limitation on tour durations by restricting the maximum possible tour length (sum of traveled distances). Since we assume that smaller vehicles usually handle local tours with many stops and larger vehicles will execute larger tours with less stops, we fix the maximum tour length to 450 km for 7.5-ton-vehicles and to 500 km for 18-ton-vehicles. For EPVs the maximum tour length is additionally limited due to their limited battery capacity.

The generation of test instances is based on the adaptation of the well-known Solomon instances [15]. In order to adjust the customers' demands to the capacity of the used vehicles and to adjust the tour lengths to the maximal range of the vehicles, a demand-factor and a length-factor are introduced. The demand-factor linearly and uniformly increases the demands of all customers occurring in

Table 2. Considered vehicle types

	$VC(7.5)$	$VE_C(7.5)$	$VE_O(7.5)$	$VC(18)$	$VE_C(18)$	$VE_O(18)$
a_k	0.13	0.4	0.44	0.18	0.73	0.8
b_k	0.8×10^{-5}	0.571×10^{-5}	0.543×10^{-5}	0.667×10^{-5}	0.278×10^{-5}	0.25×10^{-5}
E_k	70	62	62	200	240	240
T_k	450	450	450	500	500	500

Table 3. Characteristics of test sets

	S-1	S-2	S-3	S-4	S-5	S-6	S-7	S-8	S-9
Demand-factor	20	20	20	30	30	30	50	50	50
Length-factor	0.5	1.0	2.0	2.0	3.0	4.0	2.0	3.0	4.0
Vehicle size	7.5 to	7.5 to	7.5 to	18 to	18 to	18 to	18 to	18 to	18 to

the original Solomon instances. The length-factor linearly stretches all distances between any location pair. Additionally, the durations of the time windows of the Solomon instances are stretched according to the length-factor applied to the traveling distances. The values of the demand- and the length-factor are modified within a reasonable scope in order to investigate the effects of varying distances and weights on differently sized CPVs and EPVs. Altogether, nine test sets S-1 to S-9 have been generated (see Table 3).

In our computational experiments, the nine test sets of Table 3 are solved for each of the following scenarios for vehicle utilization:

- (A) homogeneous fleet of CPVs
- (B) homogeneous fleet of EPVs (city traffic)
- (C) homogeneous fleet of EPVs (overland traffic)
- (D) fleet of CPVs and EPVs (city traffic)
- (E) fleet of CPVs and EPVs (overland traffic)

The scenarios (D) and (E) are implemented by using a homogeneous fleet of CPVs for solving the test sets S-1 to S-9 and subsequently replacing CPVs in the obtained solutions by EPVs whenever it is possible. A CPV can be replaced by an EPV if the tour assigned to that CPV is not too long for the range of the EPV respectively its payload is not exceeded. Furthermore, the test sets S-2, S-4, and S-7 are solved by considering various heterogeneous fleets of CPVs and EPVs.

All instances were solved by the ALNS described in Sect. 3 with a maximum of 50,000 iterations. The ALNS was implemented in a C++-application and computed on a Windows 7 PC (i7-2600 processor with 3.4 GHz, 16 GB RAM). The results obtained for the utilization scenarios (A), (B), and (C) are presented in Table 4.

To establish comparability among the energy consumption of CPVs and EPVs, both, diesel consumption and electricity consumption, are converted into the resulting values for Tank to Wheel (T2W) emissions and Well to Wheel (W2W) emissions. Whereas, the T2W rates the CO_2 emissions of the energy consumed by the vehicle, the W2W also rates the CO_2 emissions of the energy production. For CPVs applies that one liter diesel accords with 2.629 kg CO_2 emissions for T2W respectively 3.168 kg CO_2 emissions for W2W [18]. Simultaneously, one kWh equates 0.542 kg CO_2 emissions for T2W and 0.57 kg CO_2 emissions for W2W [23].

The entries in Table 4 show that the test sets with the lowest of the provided length-factors (0.5 in test set S1, 2.0 in test set S-4, and 2.0 in test set S-7) per fixed demand-factor and fixed vehicle size could always be solved for all three scenarios (A), (B) and (C). In case of vehicles with 7.5 tons gross weight and a demand-factor of 20 (i.e. test set S-2), all three scenarios are also solvable for a length factor with the value 1.0. All other test sets are only solvable for scenario (A), i.e. for using CPVs. Averaged over all test sets which are solvable for all scenarios, the number of used vehicles increases by 17 % respectively 18 % in case that CPVs are replaced by EPVs in city traffic respectively overland traffic. Moreover, the total travel distance increases by 10.0 % respectively 10.8 %. On the opposite side, the amount of T2W emissions decreases by 13 % respectively by 6 % if the values of [18,23] are used for calculating the T2W-values for CPVs and EPVs. However, for one of the test sets (S-7) the total amount of emissions even increases if for overland transport CPVs are replaced by EPVs. The average values for distance decrease and emission increase in Table 4 (i.e. 13 % respectively 6 %) have to be opposed to the fact that, according to the values of [18,23], replacing a travel distance of an empty 7.5 tons respectively 18 tons CPV by a travel distance of a corresponding EPV would imply an emission reduction 33.4 % respectively 12.2 %.

Table 5 shows the results for mixed vehicle fleets in case of city traffic (scenario (D)). In scenario (D), the solutions of scenario (A) are modified by replacing CPVs by EPVs as much as possible. For each test set we consider the situation that 0, 2, 4, or an unlimited number (∞) of EPVs are available for replacing CPVs. The quotient (u/a) in Table 5 denotes the number u of actually used EPVs divided by the number a of available EPVs.

In contrast to the results of the scenarios (B) and (C) with homogeneous electric-powered fleets (see Table 4), all test sets of Table 5 can be solved by using the mixed fleets considered in Table 5 since there are always enough CPVs available in the scenarios shown in Table 5. Increasing the number of available EPVs has the effect that an increased number of EPVs actually are used. However, averaged over all test cases, only one-third of the available EPVs are deployed since in all other cases the generated routes are too energy-consumptive for EPVs. Anyway, using mixed fleets according to Table 5 for fulfilling the routes which have been generated for a homogeneous fleet of CPVs, has the advantage that on the one hand all test sets can be solved successfully and on the other hand the CO_2 emissions can be reduced compared to a pure CPV-fleet.

Table 4. Results of test sets for scenarios (A), (B), (C)

Test sets	Scenario	Solvable	Vehicle (num)	Length (km)	Energy consumption (l)	(kWh)	T2W (kg)	W2W (kg)
S-1	(A)	Yes	10.61	533.54	76.22	—	200.39	239.19
	(B)	Yes	11.41	561.77	—	271.77	147.30	154.91
	(C)	Yes	11.41	562.53	—	292.64	158.61	166.81
S-2	(A)	Yes	10.66	1,068.20	160.93	—	423.09	505.00
	(B)	Yes	11.78	1,141.86	—	548.77	297.43	312.80
	(C)	Yes	12.13	1,173.51	—	602.06	326.32	343.17
S-3	(A)	Yes	11.34	2,228.96	316.00	—	830.75	991.60
	(B)	No	—	—	—	—	—	—
	(C)	No	—	—	—	—	—	—
S-4	(A)	Yes	9.36	2,019.45	402.70	—	1,058.69	1,263.66
	(B)	Yes	10.77	2,137.87	—	1,709.16	926.37	974.22
	(C)	Yes	10.86	2,150.40	—	1,840.14	997.36	1,048.88
S-5	(A)	Yes	9.64	3,037.05	601.97	—	1,582.57	1,888.97
	(B)	No	—	—	—	—	—	—
	(C)	No	—	—	—	—	—	—
S-6	(A)	Yes	10.75	4,315.00	844.26	—	2,219.56	2,649.28
	(B)	No	—	—	—	—	—	—
	(C)	No	—	—	—	—	—	—
S-7	(A)	Yes	11.30	2,229.15	457.31	—	1,202.27	1,435.04
	(B)	Yes	14.95	2,595.36	—	2,106.52	1,141.73	1,200.72
	(C)	Yes	14.95	2,596.40	—	2,251.06	1,220.75	1,283.10
S-8	(A)	Yes	11.36	3,338.90	684.59	—	1,799.78	2,148.24
	(B)	No	—	—	—	—	—	—
	(C)	No	—	—	—	—	—	—
S-9	(A)	Yes	11.70	4,605.03	937.19	—	2,463.89	2,940.90
	(B)	No	—	—	—	—	—	—
	(C)	No	—	—	—	—	—	—

If the number of available EPVs which are available for substituting CPVs is unrestricted (i.e. $a = \infty$ in Table 5), then the total T2W emissions for all considered test sets are reduced by 3.2 % compared to the strict usage of CPVs only. The values shown in Table 5 refer to the usage of EPVs in city traffic. In case of overland traffic (scenario (E)) the averaged values of the columns of Table 5 deviate in the following way: the average number of used EPVs (u) is decreasing by 8.4 %; and the value for T2W emissions is increasing by 0.9 %.

Since the objective of all vehicle routing experiments in this paper is given by the minimization of traveling distances, the objective values and the optimal solutions do not depend on the fact whether CPVs or EPVs are used. However, since CPVs are more flexible with respect to range and payload, there will be many routes which are only executable by CPVs. That is why mixed fleets should be investigated more intensively. Table 6 shows the results of additional experiments on mixed fleets for the test sets S-2, S-4 and S-7. The additional experiments are restricted to the above test sets since these test sets are the only ones of Table 4 which can always be solved for the homogeneous scenarios (B) and (C); i.e. an arbitrary combination of CPVs and EPVs will always be able to fulfill all given transportation tasks of the test instances occurring in these

Table 5. Results of test sets for scenario (D)

Test sets	EPVs (u/a)	Energy consumption		T2W		W2W	
		(l)	(kWh)	(kg)	(%)	(kg)	(%)
S-1	0/0	76.22	—	200.39	—	239.19	—
	1.84/2	61.74	49.47	189.14	(−5.66)	221.95	(−7.27)
	3.07/4	53.50	77.43	182.62	(−8.77)	212.03	(−11.24)
	5.77/∞	39.86	120.46	170.08	(−13.92)	193.74	(−17.57)
S-2	0/0	160.93	—	423.09	—	505.00	—
	1.71/2	135.72	81.59	401.02	(−5.30)	472.39	(−6.56)
	2.84/4	121.17	128.64	388.27	(−8.22)	453.55	(−10.19)
	5.02/∞	101.40	186.91	367.90	(−12.37)	424.75	(−15.13)
S-3	0 / 0	316.00	—	830.75	—	991.60	—
	1.07/2	300.94	49.72	818.13	(−1.50)	972.70	(−1.88)
	1.27/4	299.00	55.94	816.38	(−1.67)	970.14	(−2.09)
	1.32/∞	298.47	57.58	815.89	(−1.72)	969.43	(−2.15)
S-4	0/0	402.70	—	1,058.69	—	1,263.66	—
	1.43/2	342.45	245.92	1,033.58	(−2.32)	1,214.77	(−3.79)
	2.48/4	299.53	421.08	1,015.69	(−3.92)	1,179.95	(−6.39)
	5.96/∞	202.22	896.12	963.13	(−8.07)	1,088.35	(−12.61)
S-5	0 / 0	601.97	—	1,582.57	—	1,888.97	—
	1.36/2	536.23	286.23	1,555.13	(−1.72)	1,835.58	(−2.81)
	2.30/4	495.61	433.98	1,538.17	(−2.75)	1,802.58	(−4.48)
	3.60/∞	457.84	588.02	1,522.36	(−3.64)	1,771.87	(−5.94)
S-6	0/ 0	844.26	—	2,219.56	—	2,649.28	—
	1.18/2	791.42	215.50	2,197.45	(−1.00)	2,606.32	(−1.62)
	1.64/4	773.71	287.75	2,190.04	(−1.32)	2,591.91	(−2.15)
	1.86/∞	767.50	313.06	2,187.43	(−1.41)	2,586.86	(−2.29)
S-7	0/0	457.31	—	1,202.27	—	1,435.04	—
	1.11/2	423.32	138.78	1,188.13	(−1.11)	1,407.48	(−1.81)
	1.66/4	406.35	208.04	1,181.06	(−1.62)	1,393.72	(−2.65)
	2.68/∞	381.73	308.53	1,170.78	(−2.29)	1,373.17	(−3.74)
S-8	0/0	684.59	—	1,799.78	—	2,148.24	—
	1.14/2	641.22	176.99	1,781.71	(−0.95)	2,113.04	(−1.55)
	1.63/4	621.23	258.58	1,773.36	(−1.36)	2,096.81	(−2.21)
	2.21/∞	604.10	328.44	1,766.20	(−1.67)	2,082.88	(−2.72)
S-9	0/0	937.19	—	2,463.87	—	2,940.90	—
	0.7/2	910.35	109.50	2,452.66	(−0.43)	2,919.09	(−0.69)
	0.88/4	904.05	135.20	2,450.02	(−0.52)	2,913.97	(−0.84)
	1.0/∞	900.80	148.44	2,448.66	(−0.56)	2,911.32	(−0.91)

Table 6. Results for a heterogeneous fleet of CPVs and EPVs

Test sets	CPVs avail.	CPVs (num)	EPVs (num)	Length (km)	T2W		W2W	
					(kg)	(%)	(kg)	(%)
S-2	20	10.66	0.00	1,068.20	423.09	—	505.00	—
	10	9.16	1.55	1,068.45	405.11	(−4.25)	478.39	(−5.27)
	9	8.68	2.05	1,066.89	398.49	(−5.81)	468.93	(−7.14)
	8	7.89	2.88	1,070.69	390.54	(−7.69)	456.83	(−9.54)
	7	6.91	3.88	1,072.97	377.67	(−10.74)	437.65	(−13.34)
	6	5.96	4.86	1,077.60	368.63	(−12.87)	423.75	(−16.09)
	5	4.98	5.88	1,079.41	356.88	(−15.45)	406.26	(−19.55)
S-4	20	9.36	0.00	2,019.45	1,058.69	—	1,263.66	—
	10	7.88	1.61	2,022.40	1,037.96	(−1.96)	1,222.35	(−3.27)
	9	7.46	1.95	2,024.94	1,031.59	(−2.56)	1,208.80	(−4.34)
	8	7.02	2.36	2,023.13	1,025.40	(−3.14)	1,197.87	(−5.21)
	7	6.50	2.95	2,019.73	1,013.83	(−4.24)	1,177.26	(−6.84)
	6	5.77	3.61	2,022.29	1,005.94	(−4.98)	1,160.62	(−8.15)
	5	4.91	4.68	2,033.29	995.16	(−6.00)	1,136.52	(−10.06)
S-7	20	11.30	0.00	2,229.15	1,202.27	—	1,435.04	—
	10	9.77	1.59	2,229.13	1,181.42	(−1.73)	1,394.66	(−2.81)
	9	8.96	2.55	2,245.63	1,176.26	(−2.16)	1,379.22	(−3.89)
	8	8.00	3.88	2,271.42	1,172.01	(−2.52)	1,362.87	(−5.03)
	7	7.00	5.09	2,302.29	1,163.77	(−3.20)	1,337.30	(−6.81)
	6	6.00	6.63	2,331.64	1,158.40	(−3.65)	1,317.84	(−8.17)
	5	5.00	7.79	2,364.04	1,153.14	(−4.09)	1,296.70	(−9.64)

test sets. In contrast to Table 5, where the number a (available EPVs for the test cases of Table 4) is introduced and stepwise increased, Table 6 shows the effects of decreasing the limit of available CPVs on the test cases of Table 4. In this case the vehicle routing algorithm is forced to use EPVs due to the lack of available CPVs. Like in Table 5, the first line for each scenario in Table 6 is equal to the first line of that same scenario in Table 4 since there are enough CPVs available for generating the same solutions as for Scenario (A). As shown in Table 6, stepwise decreasing the number of available CPVs has the effect that the total travel distances are increasing while the emissions are decreasing. In case of city traffic a limitation to five CPVs implies an increment of travel distances by 1.0 %, 0.7 %, 6.0 % and a decline of emissions by 15.5 %, 6.0 %, 4.1 % for test sets S-2, S-4, S-7 respectively. The values of Table 6 can be opposed to corresponding values for homogeneous electric-powered fleets for city traffic (Scenario (B) of Table 4). For Scenario (B) the growth of travel distances compared to a pure fleet of CPVs (Scenario (A)) is 9.8 %, 5.8 %, and 16.4 % and the reduction of emissions is 29.7 %, 12.5 %, and 5.0 %. This clearly shows the potential of a mixed fleet to reduce the emissions tremendously while the travel distances are only increasing slightly. In case of overland traffic, the results for using mixed fleets for the test sets S-2, S-4 and S-7 are similar to the results for city traffic. Compared to city traffic, the overland travel distances increase by 0.1 % and the T2W emissions increase by 1.5 %.

5   Conclusion

The main contributions of our paper are (i) the comparison of EPVs and CPVs (ii) by considering not only the reduced range but also the reduced payload of EPVs and (iii) analyzing the benefits of mixed fleets consisting of EPVs and CPVs. The analysis of the experiments presented in this paper clearly measures, demonstrates and contrasts the specific strengths of CPVs and EPVs. Moreover it could be shown that the drawbacks of CPVs and EPVs can be mitigated by deploying a mixed fleet consisting of electric-powered as well as combustion-powered trucks.

References

1. Clarke, G., Wright, W.: Scheduling of vehicles from a central depot to a number of delivery points. Oper. Res. **12**(4), 568–581 (1964)
2. Dantzig, G.B., Ramser, J.H.: The truck dispatching problem. Manage. Sci. **6**(1), 80–91 (1959)
3. Hiermann, G., Puchinger, J., Ropke, S., Hartl, R.F.: The electric fleet size and mix vehicle routing problem with time windows and recharging stations. Eur. J. Oper. Res. **252**, 995–1018 (2016)
4. Kirkpatrick, S., Gelatt, C.D., Vecchi, M.P.: Optimization by simmulated annealing. Science **220**(4598), 671–680 (1983)
5. Kopfer, H.W., Kopfer, H.: Emissions minimization vehicle routing problem in dependence of different vehicle classes. In: Kreowski, H.-J., Scholz-Reiter, B., Thoben, K.-D. (eds.) Dynamics in Logistics, pp. 49–58. Springer (2013)
6. Kopfer, H.W., Schönberger, J., Kopfer, H.: Reducing greenhouse gas emissions of a heterogeneous vehicle fleet. Flex. Serv. Manuf. J. **26**(1–2), 221–248 (2014)
7. Miller, C.E., Tucker, A.W., Zemlin, R.A.: Integer programming formulation of traveling salesman problems. J. ACM **7**(4), 326–329 (1960)
8. Pelletier, S., Jabali, O., Laporte, G.: Goods distribution with electric vehicles: review and research perspectives. cirrelt.ca [PDF] (2014)
9. Pisinger, D., Ropke, S.: A general heuristic for vehicle routing problems. Comput. Oper. Res. **34**(8), 2403–2435 (2007)
10. Potvin, J.-Y., Rousseau, J.-M.: A parallel route building algorithm for the vehicle routing and scheduling problem with time windows. Eur. J. Oper. Res. **66**(3), 331–340 (1993)
11. Ropke, S., Pisinger, D.: An adaptive large neighborhood search heuristic for the pickup and delivery problem with time windows. Transp. Sci. **40**(4), 455–472 (2006)
12. Schneider, M., Stenger, A., Goeke, D.: The electric vehicle-routing problem with time windows and recharging stations. Transp. Sci. **48**(4), 500–520 (2014)
13. Schrimpf, G., Schneider, J., Stamm-Wilbrandt, H., Dueck, G.: Record breaking optimization results using the ruin and recreate principle. J. Comput. Phys. **159**(2), 139–171 (2000)
14. Shaw, P.: Using constraint programming and local search methods to solve vehicle routing problems. In: Maher, M.J., Puget, J.-F. (eds.) CP 1998. LNCS, vol. 1520, pp. 417–443. Springer, Heidelberg (1998)
15. Solomon, M.M.: Algorithms for the vehicle routing and scheduling problems with time window constraints. Oper. Res. **35**(2), 254–265 (1987)

16. Vornhusen, B., Kopfer, H.: Emission vehicle routing problem with split delivery and a heterogeneous vehicle fleet. Comput. Logistics **9335**, 76–90 (2015)
17. Xiao, Y., Zhao, Q., Kaku, I., Xu, Y.: Development of a fuel consumption optimization model for the capacitated vehicle routing problem. Comput. Oper. Res. **39**(7), 1419–1431 (2012)
18. O.V.: So ermitteln Sie den CO_2-Fußabdruck. Verkehrs Rundschau 51-52/2010. Verlag Heinrich Vogel
19. O.V.: Wie Machen sich Ihre Elektro-LKW in der Praxis? Verkehrs Rundschau 46/2015. Verlag Heinrich Vogel
20. http://www.electric-trucks.de/umruestung/lkw-7-5t.html. Accessed 11 Apr 2016
21. http://eforce.ch/wp/wp-content/uploads/2013/06/E_FORCE_Fact_Sheet_E_2015.pdf. Accessed 11 Apr 2016
22. http://efa-s.de/Eigene%20Dateien/UPS%20Datenblatt%20englisch.pdf. Accessed 11 Apr 2016
23. https://www.ffe.de/download/wissen/186_Basisdaten_Energietraeger/Basisdaten_von_Energietraegern_2010.pdf. Accessed 11 Apr 2016

The Bi-Objective k-Dissimilar Vehicle Routing Problem

Sandra Zajac$^{(\boxtimes)}$

Logistics Management Department, Helmut-Schmidt-University,
Holstenhofweg 85, 22043 Hamburg, Germany
sandra.zajac@hsu-hh.de

Abstract. This paper deals with the k-dissimilar vehicle routing problem in which a set of k dissimilar alternatives for a Capacitated Vehicle Routing Problem (CVRP) has to be determined for a single instance. The tradeoff between minimizing the longest routing alternative and maximizing the minimum dissimilarity between two routing alternatives is investigated. Since short vehicle routings tend to be similar to each other, a conflict of objectives arises. The developed heuristic approach approximates the Pareto set with respect to this tradeoff using a dissimilarity metric based on a grid. The method is tested on benchmark instances of the CVRP and findings are reported.

Keywords: Bi-objective · k-dissimilar vehicle routing problem · Pareto set approximation

1 Introduction

In the k-dissimilar Vehicle Routing Problem (kd-VRP) k distinct vehicle routing alternatives (abbreviated as *routings*) need to be determined for a single instance of the capacitated vehicle routing problem. The CVRP is a well-studied problem in which all customers are visited exactly once, all vehicles begin and end at the depot, and the capacity limit of each vehicle is respected. In other words, an alternative X_k to the kd-VRP is a set which contains k distinct routing alternatives x_i with $i = 1, \ldots, k$. The kd-VRP has several practical applications, i.e. in the context of congested networks [1,10] and transporting dangerous goods [1,6,13] or within the cash-in-transit sector [18]. In the latter application, significant amounts of money need to be delivered or picked up from a set of customers. As a result, a serious risk of robbery arises. A potential approach to decrease this risk is to generate spatially dissimilar vehicle routing alternatives. By periodically changing the routes to dissimilar ones, the unpredictability of the actually driven routes can be increased which in turn can reduce the risk of robbery.

In the CVRP, solution quality is typically measured as the total distance travelled by all vehicles. Comparably, an alternative to the kd-VRP, denoted as a set of k routings or a k-routing alternative, is evaluated by the distance of the longest routing in the set [18]. Typically, short vehicle routing alternatives are

© Springer International Publishing Switzerland 2016
A. Paias et al. (Eds.): ICCL 2016, LNCS 9855, pp. 306–320, 2016.
DOI: 10.1007/978-3-319-44896-1_20

similar to each other. As a result, there is a conflict of objectives – the kd-VRP is inherently a bi-objective problem. Thus, (1) the *minimization of the distance of the longest routing* and (2) the *maximization of the lowest dissimilarity between two routing alternatives* in the set X_k is considered.

This contribution presents a heuristic approach to approximate the Pareto set of the kd-VRP. To the best of our knowledge, the generation of the Pareto set for the bi-objective kd-VRP has not been studied before in literature. The remainder of the paper is organized as follows: First, Sect. 2 gives a short literature overview on the kd-VRP and related problems while Sect. 3 presents and discusses selected dissimilarity metrics before the used metric is introduced. After a brief problem description in Sect. 4, Sect. 5 explains the suggested solution approach for the bi-objective kd-VRP. Finally, computational results for the data set of Christofides et al. [3] of the CVRP are reported and analysed in Sect. 6. A short summary concludes the paper in Sect. 7.

2 Literature Review

The kd-VRP is a rather recent problem which was formally introduced by Talarico et al. [18]. The authors consider the CVRP to be a subproblem of the kd-VRP where k dissimilar routings need to be selected. The aim is to minimize the cost of the worst routing alternative in the set of k routings while satisfying a similarity threshold. An initial routing alternative is improved for a given number of times by local search. Then, if the routing alternative satisfies a similarity threshold, it is accepted into the current k-routing alternative. Otherwise, the iterative penalty method (IPM), introduced in [9], is applied to increase the costs of all edges which the best found routing alternative shares with the already included routing alternatives. The procedure continues until the current set contains k routing alternatives which satisfy the similarity constraint and then restarts for a given number of iterations.

Results showed that this method can quickly generate an acceptable k-routing alternative. However, routing alternatives are not saved during the process and need to be recalculated over again. It is therefore possible that the algorithm gets stuck in a local optimum with respect to the k-routing alternative. Another approach is to determine a candidate set beforehand from which k dissimilar routing alternatives are extracted. In this case, the kd-VRP is seen as a subset selection problem [1]. Obviously, special attention needs to be paid to the inclusion of both short and dissimilar routing alternatives since these crucially influence the quality of the obtained k routings. This idea has been studied for the closely related k-dissimilar path problem (kd-PP) [1,6,10]. Here, a set of k distinct paths from a given origin to a destination node has to be determined [1,6,9,10,12,13]. To ensure the quality of the candidate set, both an algorithm to generate a certain number of shortest paths (solving the k shortest path problem [19]) as well as the IPM method may be applied [1,13]. To the best of our knowledge, only Martí et al. [13] treated the maximization of the dissimilarity between two paths explicitly as an additional second objective in the

kd-PP. More precisely, the authors examine the tradeoff between minimizing the average path costs and maximizing the average dissimilarity between a pair of paths in a k-paths alternative. A greedy randomized adaptive search procedure approximates the efficient frontier and the authors study it with some measures in multi-objective optimization.

Other problems related to the kd-VRP include the *disjoint path problem* in which a number of edge-disjoint or vertex-disjoint paths is sought [17]. This problem is extended into the temporal dimension in the *m-peripatetic vehicle routing problem* [14]. These alternative routings, however, might be unacceptably costly and overachieve what is required by the decision maker. The kd-VRP therefore can be seen as a generalization of these problems allowing for some but not total dissimilarity between routing alternatives. Finally, a complementary problem to the kd-VRP is the *k-similar vehicle routing problem* in which a number of k routings need to be found that are close to a given baseline routing alternative [16].

3 Dissimilarity Metrics

For the kd-VRP, a metric needs to be defined which measures the dissimilarity between routing alternatives. Typically, it is standardized between 0 (*completely similar alternatives*) and 1 (*completely dissimilar alternatives*). An obvious approach is to either use the number or the length/costs of the shared edges between two routing alternatives [1,10,18]. Let $r_{x_i}^\iota$ ($r_{x_j}^\gamma$) be the ιth (γth) route of routing alternative x_i (x_j) with $\iota = 1, \ldots, I$ and $\gamma = 1, \ldots, \Gamma$. Talarico et al. [18] define an edge-based dissimilarity metric $\delta(x_i, x_j)$ for the kd-VRP as follows:

$$\delta(x_i, x_j) = 1 - \max_{\substack{\iota=1,\ldots,I, \\ \gamma=1,\ldots,\Gamma}} \frac{1}{2} \left[\frac{c^{sh}(r_{x_i}^\iota, r_{x_j}^\gamma)}{c(r_{x_i}^\iota)} + \frac{c^{sh}(r_{x_i}^\iota, r_{x_j}^\gamma)}{c(r_{x_j}^\gamma)} \right] \quad (1)$$

where $c^{sh}(r_{x_i}^\iota, r_{x_j}^\gamma)$ represents the length of the edges shared between the two routes, while $c(r_{x_i}^\iota)$ and $c(r_{x_j}^\gamma)$ are the respective total route costs. Thus, the metric sets the dissimilarity of two routing alternatives x_i and x_j to be the minimum found dissimilarity value comparing every route of x_i to every route of x_j. Note that this formulation strongly discourages identical routes. Consider the case where a customer is located far away from a cluster of customers and/or has a high demand. It might be very uneconomical if not infeasible to approach this customer together with other customers in a single trip. The dissimilarity between many short routing alternatives will be 0 and dissimilarities of other route pairs are disregarded. Moreover, edge-based dissimilarity metrics can generate alternatives which are not spatially dispersed [13] as the following example demonstrates. Let the vertices A, B and C lie on a straight line in the given order. Now assume that a route in one routing alternative contains edge $A - B$ and $B - C$ while a route in another routing alternative uses edge $A - C$ and $C - B$. If these two routes are compared, an edge-based dissimilarity metric

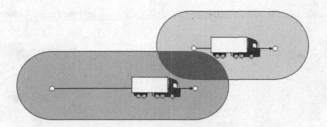

Fig. 1. Determination and intersections of two buffer zones.

yields 1 since no edges are shared. Thus, it does not take the spatial proximity between $A - B - C$ and $A - C - B$ into account.

Of course, spatially dissimilar routing alternatives are not relevant in all practical contexts. If the purpose of generating dissimilar solutions is to, for instance, increase reliability in a telecommunications network, it is indeed irrelevant if the used links are spatially close to each other. However, in the context of cash-in-transit operations, there is a high chance that robbers observe a certain geographical area which urges to take spatially close edges into account. In literature, several dissimilarity metrics have been developed which incorporate spatial information [6,12,13]. Our metric is based on the intuitive spatial dissimilarity metric of Dell'Olmo et al. [6]. The authors generate k dissimilar paths in the context of hazardous goods transportation. The dissimilarity of the alternative paths helps in distributing the associated risk fairly on the impacted population. For a dissimilarity metric, the concept of a *buffer zone* is introduced which is determined by moving a circle of a predetermined radius w along the path whose center is the vehicle itself (see Fig. 1). Obviously, the metric heavily depends on w. In the case of hazardous material transportation, w can be set as the average impact area in which the population is put at risk in case of an accident. More generally, w is a problem input parameter and depends on the decision maker's definition of spatial similarity. Note that this metric implicitly includes the case of common edges between two routing alternatives.

In this paper, the computation of the intersection area of buffer zones is facilitated by introducing a grid with a size of $n \times n$ grid units. In order to get a good approximation of the overlapping buffer zones, n has to be set high enough. However, the higher the n, the more computation time is necessary. Let u_1^v and u_2^v be the coordinates of location v in the Euclidean plane. Let further $u_1^{min}(u_2^{min})$ and $u_1^{max}(u_2^{max})$ be the minimum and maximum of all coordinates of the locations in a given data set. Each grid unit is unambiguously identified by a horizontal and a vertical index η and θ and denoted $g(\eta, \theta)$. Then, a *direct* grid unit is determined by:

$$g(\eta, \theta) = g\left(\left\lfloor \left(\frac{u_1^v - u_1^{min}}{u_1^{max} - u_1^{min}} \right) \right\rfloor \cdot n, \left\lfloor \left(\frac{u_2^v - u_2^{min}}{u_2^{max} - u_2^{min}} \right) \right\rfloor \cdot n \right) \qquad (2)$$

Here, a location may lie on a border of multiple grid units. In that case, multiple direct grid units are associated. In addition, the location is linked to all those

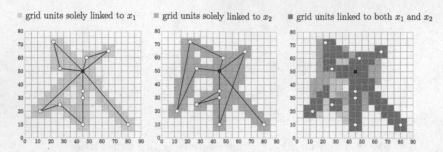

Fig. 2. Associated grid units with routing alternatives x_1 and x_2 as well as shared grid units between x_1 and x_2 from left to right.

grid units which lie within its buffer zone with radius w. Let $n^{sh}(x_i, x_j)$ be the total number of shared grid units between the routing alternatives x_i and x_j. Let further $n(x_i)$ and $n(x_j)$ be the total number of grid units of the respective routing alternative. The dissimilarity between two routings is defined by:

$$\delta(x_i, x_j) = 1 - \frac{1}{2}\left[\frac{n^{sh}(x_i, x_j)}{n(x_i)} + \frac{n^{sh}(x_i, x_j)}{n(x_j)}\right] \tag{3}$$

Figure 2 illustrates the approach. First, for each routing alternative $x_i \in X_k$ the associated grid units are identified. Then, the number of common grid units is determined and the dissimilarity can be computed. In this example, there are 99 and 111 grid units linked to x_1 and x_2, respectively. With 84 common grid units the dissimilarity calculation yields $\delta(x_1, x_2) = 1 - \frac{1}{2} \cdot \left(\frac{84}{99} + \frac{84}{111}\right) = 0.19738$.

4   Problem Description

A graph $G = (V, E)$ is given with V as the set of vertices with demand D_v for each vertex $v \in V$ and E the set of edges with associated lengths c_e for $e \in E$. Let Q further be the vehicle's capacity. The lth k-routing alternative X_{kl} is feasible if all contained routing alternatives are feasible. In other words, they belong to the set of feasible routing alternatives Ω, so $x_i \in \Omega \ \forall x_i \in X_{kl}$. Further, X_{kl} needs to contain exactly k distinct routings (see e.g. [11] for a mathematical formulation of the CVRP). The objective is to find an approximation $\hat{P}$ of the true Pareto set which contains Pareto optimal k-routing alternatives with respect to maximum distance $F_1(X_{kl})$ and minimum dissimilarity $F_2(X_{kl})$. X_{kl}^* is called efficient or non-dominated if there is no other X_{km} such that $F_1(X_{kl}^*) > F_1(X_{km})$ while $F_2(X_{kl}^*) \leq F_2(X_{km})$ or $F_1(X_{kl}^*) \geq F_1(X_{km})$ while $F_2(X_{kl}^*) < F_2(X_{km})$. Moreover, $k > 1$ is required since the kd-VRP reduces to a CVRP for $k = 1$ which leaves $F_2(X_{kj})$ as a meaningless objective. More specifically, $F_1(X_{kl})$ is determined as follows:

$$F_1(X_{kl}) = \max_{x_i \in X_{kl}} \frac{c(x_i) - \zeta}{\zeta} \quad \text{where } c(x_i) = \sum_{e \in x_i} c_e \ \forall x_i \in X_{kl} \tag{4}$$

We assume that the decision maker will only accept a k-routing alternative if the difference between the distance of the longest routing in X_{kl} to the distance ζ of the best found routing alternative in the given instance is within reasonable limits. Based on Eq. 3, the second objective $F_2(X_{kl})$ is computed as the minimum dissimilarity value found comparing all routings x_i and x_j in X_{kl}:

$$F_2(X_{kl}) = \min_{x_i, x_j \in X_{kl}, i \neq j} \delta(x_i, x_j) \tag{5}$$

The bi-objective kd-VRP can then be formulated as:

$$
\begin{aligned}
\text{(bi-objective } k\text{d-VRP)} \quad & \min F_1(X_{kl}) \\
& \max F_2(X_{kl}) \\
& \text{s.t. } x_i \subset \Omega \quad \forall i \in \{1, \ldots, k\}
\end{aligned}
\tag{6}
$$

5 Solution Approach

5.1 Generating the Candidate Set

The candidate set CS needs to contain both short as well as dissimilar routing alternatives in order to get a good approximation of the Pareto set. First, the focus lies on the length of the routing alternatives. An initial routing alternative x_i is generated by the Savings approach [4] which is improved by a variable neighbourhood descent (VND). To decrease the distance inside a route, the intra-tour operators 2-Opt [5] and 3-Opt [2] are used. The inter-tour operators 2-Exchange [15] and 3-Exchange [8] swap two and three customers, respectively, between two different tours. Moreover, the inter-tour operator Relocate [15] repositions a customer from one route to another. All moves are only accepted if an improvement regarding the distance of the routing alternative has been detected. The generated routing x_i is included into CS if its distance deviation from ζ is smaller or equal to α_1. If it is smaller than ζ, the list L_ζ which contains all routing alternatives with length ζ is updated. Additionally, routing alternatives need to be removed from CS if their distance deviations to the updated ζ now exceed α_1. In that way, only high-qualitative routing alternatives are admitted to CS in the first step which, however, may be very similar to each other. The procedure restarts from a perturbed solution in order to escape local optima until a maximum number of iterations is met. Specifically, a randomly chosen routing $x_i \in L_\zeta$ is perturbed by removing $q\%$ routes. In any case, at least two routes are removed in order to break up clusters of customers. Then, a new trip is opened. Starting from a base node, which is initially the depot, its NN nearest neighbours are identified which have been previously removed and whose (individual) inclusion in the currently considered trip satisfies the capacity constraint. If the NN-candidate list is not empty, a customer is randomly chosen out of it, added to the trip and becomes the next base node. Otherwise, a new trip is opened. This procedure repeats until all customers are assigned.

Since it is likely that the routing alternatives found so far are rather similar to each other, the focus is now laid upon finding dissimilar routings to them as

---

Algorithm 1. Get dissimilar routing alternatives

---
    input: The α_1 shortest routing alternatives
1 **repeat**
2 | Reset C^{Pen} to C
3 | **repeat**
4 | | $x_i \leftarrow$ Perturb
5 | | $x_i \leftarrow$ VND
6 | | **if** $c(x_i) < \zeta$ *or else* $(\emptyset\delta(CS,x_i) \geq \emptyset\delta(CS)$ *and also* $c(x_i) < \alpha_2)$ **then**
7 | | | Add x_i to CS
8 | | | **if** $c(x_i) \leq \zeta$ **then** $L_\zeta \leftarrow$ Update, $\zeta \leftarrow c(x_i)$
9 | | | Exit loop
10 | | **else**
11 | | | $C^{Pen} \leftarrow$ Penalize with β
12 | | **end**
13 | **until** *maximum number of penalizations met*
14 **until** *maximum number of iterations met*

---

shown in the pseudo code of Algorithm 1. After applying the perturbation move and VND, it is again checked if the current routing alternative x_i is accepted into CS, that is if its distance is shorter than ζ. If this does not hold, it is admitted if its distance deviation to ζ is not higher than α_2. Additionally, the average dissimilarity between all routing alternatives in CS must not decrease when x_i is included. α_2 is used to prevent excessively long routings in CS. The restriction helps to focus on the relevant part of the Pareto front and facilitates the selection decision due to the relative smaller size of the Pareto set. Obviously, the higher the α_2, the more the true Pareto front becomes covered. Moreover, if α_2 is set to (positive) infinity, the distance of a routing alternative has no influence on the acceptance in this stage of the algorithm. If the routing alternative is not accepted, a penalized distance matrix C^{Pen} – which builds on the original distance matrix C – is updated by using a penalization function based on the iterative penalty method [9]. Let $c(e)$ be the current length of edge e, $n^{imp}(e)$ be the number of impacted grid units of e, $n(e)$ be the number of total linked grid units of e and β be the penalization factor. Then, the length $c(e)$ is updated to $c^*(e)$ according to:

$$c^*(e) = c(e) \cdot \left[1 + \beta \cdot \frac{n^{imp}(e)}{n(e)}\right] \tag{7}$$

Thereby those grid units are considered as "impacted" that x_i shares with all routing alternatives in CS. The search continues with a perturbation move and with VND in which C^{Pen} is used. This guides the algorithm to routing alternatives which raise the average dissimilarity in the candidate set. C^{Pen} is reset to C after maximum Pen_{max} penalization moves. The described procedure repeats for a number of iterations and then returns the final candidate set.

Algorithm 2. Extracting an approximation of P

---

input: Candidate set CS

1 **repeat**
2   Generate initial k-routing alternative X_{kl} from RCL^s and RCL^d
3      $X_{kl} \leftarrow$ Swap(X_{kl}, RA), no deterioration in objectives, prefer distance
4      $\hat{P} \leftarrow$ Update
5      $X_{kl} \leftarrow$ Swap(X_{kl}, RA), no deterioration in objectives, prefer dissimilarity
6      $\hat{P} \leftarrow$ Update
7   randomly choose sequence $F_1 \rightarrow F_2$ or $F_2 \rightarrow F_1$
8   **repeat**
9          $X_{kl} \leftarrow$ Swap(X_{kl}, RCL), improve first chosen objective
10          $\hat{P} \leftarrow$ Update
11          $X_{kl} \leftarrow$ Swap(X_{kl}, RCL), improve second chosen objective
12          $\hat{P} \leftarrow$ Update
13   **until** *no further improvements found*
14 **until** *maximum number of iterations met*

5.2 Determining an Approximation of the Pareto Set

The candidate set is now used to obtain the approximated Pareto set $\hat{P}$ as described in the pseudo code of Algorithm 2. The first routing alternative to be included in the k-routing alternative X_{kl} is chosen pursuing $F_1(X_{kl})$. Then, it is randomly chosen if the focus lies on $F_1(X_{kl})$ or $F_2(X_{kl})$ until X_{kl} contains k routing alternatives. If $F_1(X_{kl})$ is minimized, a solution x_i is randomly chosen from a restricted candidate list RCL^s containing the r shortest alternatives in CS. When pursuing $F_2(X_{kl})$, a routing alternative from RCL^d is included which consists of the r routing alternatives exhibiting the highest dissimilarities to $x_i \in X_{kl}$ in the worst case.

Now routing alternatives are swapped between X_{kl} and CS$\backslash X_{kl}$ until it is not possible anymore to improve $F_1(X_{kl})$ without deteriorating $F_2(X_{kl})$ and vice versa. Then, the focus of the exchanges first lies on decreasing the longest distance in X_{kl}. When again no further improving swaps are possible, it is checked if the k-routing alternative can be included into the Pareto set. This is possible if it is not already contained in $\hat{P}$ and if a dominance check is passed – that is if it is not dominated by any other k-routing alternative in $\hat{P}$. If another k-routing alternative becomes dominated by X_{kl}, it is removed. The maximum distance in the k-routing alternative decreases if the excluded routing is the longest and solely the longest in the set and the current routing alternative is shorter than $F_1(X_{kl})$. Simultaneously, the minimum dissimilarity of this routing alternative to the remaining routing alternatives in X_{kl} is not allowed to be smaller than $F_2(X_{kl})$. The same effort towards a Pareto optimal k-routing alternative is subsequently done with a focus on dissimilarity. In order to improve $F_2(X_{kl})$, one of those routing alternatives has to be excluded from X_{kl}, which was part of the routing pair with lowest dissimilarity in X_{kl} and thus was determining $F_2(X_{kl})$. The minimum dissimilarity in the k-routing alternative will increase if (1) the remaining dissimilarity is truly higher than $F_2(X_{kl})$ and (2) the minimum dissimilarity of the current routing alternative to the remaining routing alternatives in X_{kl} also exceeds $F_2(X_{kl})$. Moreover, the distance of the included routing alternative has to be maximum $F_1(X_{kl})$. In both cases, a single swap may not be enough to improve the objective function values. In order to allow improvements "into the right direction" while avoiding cycling, it is prohibited to consider the last swap partners for a new exchange.

In the next step, it is checked if routing alternatives can be exchanged between X_{kl} and RCL^s or X_{kl} and RCL^d so that $F_1(X_{kl})$ decreases disregarding the consequences for $F_2(X_{kl})$ and vice versa. Thereby, it is randomly chosen which objective is followed first. In order to reduce the longest distance in the k-routing alternative, a random routing alternative is chosen from $RCL^s \setminus X_{kl}$. This routing is swapped with a routing which is currently the longest one in the set and results in the highest increase in the dissimilarity objective. After each exchange, the inclusion in $\hat{P}$ is checked until no further improving swaps regarding distance are possible. While pursuing the dissimilarity objective, first RCL^d is identified for each potentially to be excluded routing alternative. Then, it is tested if those routing alternatives have a dissimilarity higher than $F_2(X_{kl})$. If so, a swap is made and $\hat{P}$ is updated. The separate optimization of the respective objectives continues until no further improvements can be made. The algorithm then restarts from a newly constructed k-routing alternative for a number of iterations and returns $\hat{P}$.

6   Experimental Investigation

The solution approach has been coded in Visual Basic .NET and was tested on the instances CMT1-CMT5 and CMT11-CMT12 of Christofides et al. which include between 50 and 199 customers [3]. Two types of instances need to be distinguished: While the customers' locations in CMT1-CMT5 follow a random distribution, customers in CMT11-CMT12 appear in clusters. Moreover, the depot in CMT11 is not located in the geographical centre of all locations. First, the effects of the problem input parameters on the solution of the problem are discussed. Secondly, the impact of the heuristic parameters on solution quality is investigated for $k = 3$ and the best heuristic parameter configuration is determined. To evaluate the solutions, the hypervolume indicator [20, 21] is used which shows how well the Pareto front is covered. Following [7], the objective function values are normalized so that the hypervolumes assume values between 0 and 1 with 1 being the best possible coverage. The reference point is chosen in such a way that each k-routing alternative in the approximated Pareto set contributes to the hypervolume. Lastly, the results for all instances and varying k are presented.

6.1   Impact of Problem Input Parameters

The problem input parameters comprise the number of routing alternatives k, the size of the grid matrix $n \times n$ and the similarity range w. The higher the k, the more k-routing alternatives can be extracted from a given size of CS. More specifically, there are $\binom{|CS|}{k}$ distinct subsets which contain k routing alternatives. Taking $|CS| = 100$ as an example, there are 4,950 subsets with $k = 2$ elements, 161,700 subsets with $k = 3$ elements, 3,921,225 subsets with $k = 4$ elements and already 75,287,520 subsets with $k = 5$ elements. However, it is difficult to predict the number of *Pareto optimal* k-routing alternatives. The evaluation of a routing alternative with respect to dissimilarity always depends on the routing alternatives to which it is compared which makes it problematic to estimate bounds for the kd-VRP. The higher the n, the more differences in terms of dissimilarity can be identified between pairs of routing alternatives. However, this is also linked to a higher number of grid units per edge on average which leads to a higher computational burden. For the computational study, $n = 100$ is chosen which is equivalent to 10,000 grid units in total. The total number of grid units is reasonably high while allowing to test for different parameter configurations. w depends on the decision maker's definition of spatial similarity. The smaller the w, the more the dissimilarity metric resembles an edge-based one which means that the less other non-common edges are considered as (partly) similar. However, for a high w many edges could be regarded as completely similar to each other.

6.2   Impact of Heuristic Parameters

Table 1 gives an overview of the tested heuristic parameters of a full factorial experiment for $k = 3, w = 1, n = 100$ and $\alpha_2 = 0.3$. Here, α_2 can be seen as a problem input parameter since it represents the permitted upper bound on the distance of a routing alternative. For the perturbation move, based on [18], $q = 40\%$ and $NN = 5$ is assumed. Further 5,000 iterations each are allocated for determining short routing alternatives, dissimilar routing alternatives and an approximation of the Pareto set.

Table 1. Tested heuristic parameters

Parameter	Values	No. of values	Best setting
α_1	0.1, 0.2, 0.3	3	**0.2**
β	0.1, 0.3, 0.5	3	**0.5**
Pen_{max}	10, 20, 30	3	**20**
r	20, 50, 100	3	**20**

α_1 ensures a high quality in CS in terms of distance in the beginning of the algorithm. The idea is that by searching for routing alternatives which are dissimilar to *short* ones also *shorter* k-routing alternatives can be found. Thus, longer routing alternatives are only accepted into CS if a dissimilarity constraint is satisfied to avoid including longer routing alternatives which are too similar to already included ones. The smaller the α_1, the shorter and more similar the routing alternatives will tend to be on average after this procedure. Hence, the average dissimilarity in the candidate set, and thus the acceptance requirement, might be initially lower. Another result is a lower number of routing alternatives in CS after this stage of the algorithm. The computational study confirmed these theoretical considerations and revealed an increase in the hypervolume by 2.42% from $\alpha_1 = 0.1$ to $\alpha_1 = 0.2$ which then remained stable. A higher α_1 is accompanied by a rise in computation time. More specifically, the computation time increases by 62 min between $\alpha_1 = 0.1$ and $\alpha_1 = 0.2$ and by 11 min between $\alpha_1 = 0.2$ and $\alpha_1 = 0.3$. This can be explained by a steady rise in the total number of routing alternatives in CS from 3,359 ($\alpha_1 = 0.1$) to 5,851 ($\alpha_1 = 0.3$). Moreover, a higher α_1 increases the number of accepted short routing alternatives in the first procedure while decreasing the number of dissimilar routing alternatives in the second one. This can be traced back to the higher average dissimilarity in CS for larger α_1 which also evokes an increase in the number of average penalization moves from 2.7 to 3.5 as well as in the number of maximum penalization moves per accepted routing alternative from 17.7 to 18.5.

In order to obtain dissimilar routing alternatives in CS, a penalization is applied as described in Sect. 5.1. Clearly, the design of the penalization function is difficult and leads to various discussions, especially about the magnitude of β [1]. A low β will tend to change the current routing alternative only marginally and therefore generate more similar routing alternatives. A high β could lead faster to dissimilar routing alternatives which however might not meet the α_2-requirement. The lower the β, the more penalization moves could be necessary in order to find a routing alternative which satisfies the dissimilarity requirement. This in turn leads to a smaller number of alternatives in CS. On the contrary, the quality of CS might be improved with respect to dissimilarity. Generally, the higher the Pen_{max}, the stronger an incentive is given to the algorithm to search deeper for dissimilar alternative routings. Thus, Pen_{max} can be seen as the *intensification duration* while β could be called *intensification strength*. Moreover, the more penalization repetitions are applied, the more C^{Pen} may differ from C so that the perturbation does not yield a routing alternative nearby a local optimum with respect to C^{Pen} anymore. Additionally, the routing alternatives could change so much during the course of penalization moves that C^{Pen} does not reflect the shared grid units between the current routing alternative and the routing alternatives in CS in a reasonable way any longer.

The experiments showed that the maximum hypervolume was found for $Pen_{max} = 20$ while the lowest was determined for $Pen_{max} = 10$. There is no clear relationship between the choice of β and Pen_{max}. The results identified $\beta = 0.3$ as the best option assuming $Pen_{max} = 10$, $\beta = 0.5$ for $Pen_{max} = 20$ and $\beta = 0.1$ for $Pen_{max} = 30$ which shows the discussed interdependencies between β and Pen_{max}. It has to be noted that for $Pen_{max} = 30$ and $\beta = 0.1$, only around 4 routing alternatives were accepted after 20 penalization moves or more while 28 were accepted for penalization moves between 10 and 20 and the majority, 1, 710 routing alternatives, were already admitted applying 10 penalization moves or less. For $\beta = 0.5$, the average number of performed penalization repetitions per accepted routing alternative were around 2.9 for $Pen_{max} = 10$, 3.27 for $Pen_{max} = 20$ and 3.22 for $Pen_{max} = 30$ with each maximum $10, 18.17$ and 21.11 average penalization moves. This means that a low number of penalization moves often is enough to increase the average dissimilarity in CS for the given parameter configuration, possibly due to an easier acceptance of new routing alternatives in the beginning when the average dissimilarity in CS is still low. In other words, the actually applied penalization moves increase in the course of the procedure. Taking a randomly selected run for CMT2 as an example, on average 0.85 penalization moves were used for the first 1,000 accepted routing alternatives into CS, 1.63 moves for the next 1,000, and 2.15 for the last 164.

During the extraction of $\hat{P}$, the restricted candidate sets RCL^s and RCL^d of size r are used. The restricted candidate sets help to focus on promising swap partners that are routing alternatives with a low distance or a high dissimilarity. The larger the r, the longer but more dissimilar the RCL^s will tend to be while the opposite applies to RCL^d. Moreover, this leads to a more strongly randomized approach. While RCL^s is a static set once CS is determined, the composition of RCL^d always depends on to which routing alternatives it is compared and thus needs to be recalculated frequently. The experiments revealed $r = 20$ as the best choice with respect to hypervolume. Thus, it is worthwhile to focus on the shortest/most dissimilar routing alternatives. In fact, increasing r leads to a steady decrease in the hypervolume of 0.8124 to 0.8094 and to 0.804.

6.3   Results for Various Instances and Varying k

In this subsection, the results for the best configuration for $k = 3$ averaged over all instances are presented. Figure 3 shows the shortest k-routing alternatives found for CMT3 and CMT12 in a run using the best configuration. These instances both contain 101 nodes in total but differ strongly in structure.

While in CMT3 the routing alternatives do not seem to vary at the first glance, for CMT12 it can be observed that the routing alternatives differ primarily in long edges. On the one hand, this could be explained by a w which is set "too high" with respect to the small distances between customers within a cluster. Since many edges within the cluster are regarded as similar to each other, the algorithm does not have an incentive to change those: It is not rewarded by a higher dissimilarity but possibly penalized by an increased distance instead. On the other hand, it has to be noted that short edges are also always associated with a lower number of grid units and therefore have a lower impact on the total dissimilarity of one routing alternative to another. In other words, by using the grid metric the algorithm clearly prefers changing long edges which are connected with a higher number of grid units. In the context of cash-in-transit operations, larger edges are often associated with a longer time spent traversing an edge. This in turn is linked to a higher robbery risk so the grid metric is suitable in this context. Nevertheless, if using different edges within a cluster is desired, w could be set smaller. This, however, contradicts our understanding of w as a problem input parameter. Besides, (positive) weights on the grid units

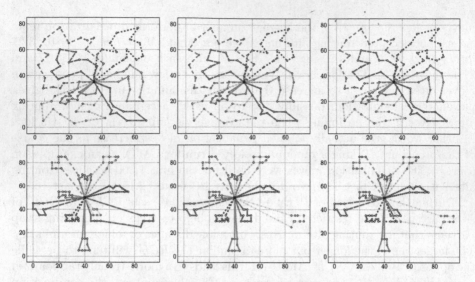

Fig. 3. The shortest k-routing alternatives for CMT3 (top) and CMT12 (bottom).

located in clusters could be imposed. Lastly, note that the routing alternatives are considered as dissimilar to each other although they contain some identical routes.

Using the best configuration found for $k = 3$ on the basis of the hypervolume indicator, Table 2 finally shows the average hypervolume, the average number of k-routing alternatives in $\hat{P}$, the average computation time in minutes as well as the best and average deviations of the shortest k-routing alternative to the respective best known CVRP alternatives for the given instances for varying k. Taking the hypervolume as an indicator, the algorithm successfully achieved a high coverage of the true Pareto front in all instances. As assumed, an increase in the number of found Pareto optimal k-routing alternatives can be observed for increasing k. However, no relation can be detected to the hypervolumes of the instance, to the gaps of the shortest k-routing alternatives to the best known solutions as well as to the running time. Generally, we do not notice a rise of $|\hat{P}|$ but of the computation time for instances with a higher number of nodes for a specific k. This can be explained by a higher number of edges and thus more possibilities to find different routing alternatives. More specifically, 67% of the computation time averaged over all instances is needed to determine the candidate set from which only 3 % are used to obtain short routing alternatives and 97 % are attributed to increasing the average dissimilarity in CS. Going from CMT1 to CMT5 a rise in the gaps is observed which is partially due to the growing problem size. However, although CMT11 contains more nodes than CMT12, there is consistently a higher gap for CMT12. This again shows that the structure of the underlying instances clearly plays a role in the solution of the kd-VRP.

Table 2. Results of the benchmark instances for varying k [3].

Instance (no. of nodes)	CMT1 (51)	CMT2 (76)	CMT3 (101)	CMT4 (151)	CMT5 (200)	CMT11 (121)	CMT12 (101)
k=2							
Average hypervolume	0.78456	0.82795	0.79428	0.79808	0.78898	0.87667	0.78768
Average of $|\hat{P}|$	27	29	25	22	27	40	28
Average running time [in mins]	34	101	118	179	253	91	58
Percentage best gap	0	1.62	3.61	8.37	9.13	0	1.02
Percentage average gap	0.47	2.84	4.48	9.55	10.11	0.25	1.28
k=3							
Average hypervolume	0.81048	0.87099	0.83036	0.79544	0.84325	0.88545	0.77912
Average of $|\hat{P}|$	56	48	52	50	53	98	52
Average running time [in mins]	51	114	130	198	263	72	65
Percentage best gap	0.06	2.22	3.88	8.43	9.67	0.23	1.29
Percentage average gap	0.51	3.12	4.84	9.96	10.3	0.29	1.65
k=4							
Average hypervolume	0.83655	0.82017	0.79475	0.79835	0.85556	0.84745	0.76792
Average of $|\hat{P}|$	103	63	82	69	66	213	80
Average running time [in mins]	53	144	146	195	264	77	81
Percentage best gap	0.06	2.35	4.2	9.33	9.53	0.08	1.49
Percentage average gap	0.51	3.37	5.00	10.09	10.31	0.23	1.9
k=5							
Average hypervolume	0.79105	0.82463	0.82273	0.81627	0.87211	0.84897	0.75907
Average of $|\hat{P}|$	135	90	110	90	79	269	110
Average running time [in mins]	41	154	164	252	278	127	101
Percentage best gap	0.25	1.91	4.47	9.45	10.48	0.1	1.68
Percentage average gap	1.29	3.24	5.46	10.43	10.77	0.27	2.6

7   Conclusions

This paper deals with the bi-objective version of the k-dissimilar vehicle routing problem in which k distinct vehicle routing alternatives need to be determined. The objectives comprise minimizing the distance of the longest routing alternative and maximizing the lowest dissimilarity between two routing alternatives in a set of k routing alternatives. Our contributions to this problem are manifold. First, a way to simplify the spatial dissimilarity metric of Dell'Olmo et al. [6] is presented. Further, an approach to approximate the Pareto set of Pareto optimal k-routing alternatives is proposed with respect to the two criteria which, to the best of our knowledge, has not been investigated before in literature. Moreover, the impact of the problem input parameters as well as of the heuristic parameters on the benchmark instances of Christofides et al. [3] is studied. The obtained results are promising and reveal that the proposed algorithm is able to obtain a good coverage of the Pareto set. Future research needs to focus on the analysis of the interdependencies in the kd-VRP and on the development of strategies to further increase the quality of the candidate set.

References

1. Akgün, V., Erkut, E., Batta, R.: On finding dissimilar paths. Eur. J. Oper. Res. **121**(2), 232–246 (2000)
2. Bock, F.: An algorithm for solving 'Traveling Salesman' and related network optimization problems. Technical report, 14th National Meeting of the Operations Research Society of America (ORSA), St Louis (1958)
3. Christofides, N.: Combinatorial optimization. Wiley, Chichester and New York (1979)
4. Clarke, G., Wright, J.W.: Scheduling of vehicles from a central depot to a number of delivery points. Oper. Res. **12**(4), 568–581 (1964)
5. Croes, G.A.: A method for solving traveling salesman problems. Oper. Res. **6**, 791–812 (1958)
6. Dell'Olmo, P., Gentili, M., Scozzari, A.: On finding dissimilar Pareto-optimal paths. Eur. J. Oper. Res. **162**(1), 70–82 (2005)
7. Geiger, M.J.: Fast approximation heuristics for multi-objective vehicle routing problems. In: Chio, C., et al. (eds.) EvoApplications 2010, Part II. LNCS, vol. 6025, pp. 441–450. Springer, Heidelberg (2010)
8. Glover, F.: Ejection chains, reference structures and alternating path methods for traveling salesman problems. Discrete Appl. Math. **65**(1–3), 223–253 (1996)
9. Johnson, P., Joy, D., Clarke, D.: HIGHWAY 3.01, an enhancement routing model: program, description, methodology and revised user's manual. Technical report, Oak Ridge National Laboratories, Washington, D.C. (1992)
10. Kuby, M., Zhongyi, X., Xiaodong, X.: A minimax method for finding the k best "differentiated" paths. Geogr. Anal. **29**(4), 298–313 (1997)
11. Laporte, G.: The vehicle routing problem: an overview of exact and approximate algorithms. Eur. J. Oper. Res. **59**(3), 345–358 (1992)
12. Lombard, K., Church, R.L.: The gateway shortest path problem: generating alternative routes for a corridor location problem. Geogr. Syst. **1**, 25–45 (1993)
13. Martí, R., González Velarde, J.L., Duarte, A.: Heuristics for the bi-objective path dissimilarity problem. Comput. Oper. Res. **36**(11), 2905–2912 (2009)
14. Ngueveu, S.U., Prins, C., Wolfler Calvo, R.: A hybrid tabu search for the m-peripatetic vehicle routing problem. In: Maniezzo, V., Stützle, T., Voß, S. (eds.) Matheuristics. Annals of Information Systems, vol. 10, pp. 253–266. Springer, Boston (2010)
15. Savelsbergh, M.W.P.: The vehicle routing problem with time windows: minimizing route duration. INFORMS J. Comput. **4**, 146–154 (1992)
16. Sörensen, K.: Route stability in vehicle routing decisions: a bi-objective approach using metaheuristics. CEJOR **14**(2), 193–207 (2006)
17. Suurballe, J.W.: Disjoint paths in a network. Networks **4**(2), 125–145 (1974)
18. Talarico, L., Sörensen, K., Springael, J.: The k-dissimilar vehicle routing problem. Eur. J. Oper. Res. **244**(1), 129–140 (2015)
19. Yen, J.Y.: Finding the k shortest loopless paths in a network. Manage. Sci. **17**(11), 712–716 (1971)
20. Zitzler, E., Thiele, L.: Multiobjective evolutionary algorithms: a comparative case study and the strength Pareto approach. IEEE Trans. Evol. Comput. **3**(4), 257–271 (1999)
21. Zitzler, E., Thiele, L.: Multiobjective optimization using evolutionary algorithms - a comparative case study. In: Eiben, A.E., Bäck, T., Schoenauer, M., Schwefel, H.-P. (eds.) PPSN 1998. LNCS, vol. 1498, pp. 292–301. Springer, Heidelberg (1998)

A Branch-and-Price Algorithm for the Vehicle Routing Problem with 2-Dimensional Loading Constraints

Telmo Pinto[✉], Cláudio Alves, and José Valério de Carvalho

Departamento de Produção e Sistemas, Escola de Engenharia,
Universidade do Minho, 4710-057 Braga, Portugal
{telmo,claudio,vc}@dps.uminho.pt

Abstract. In this paper, we describe a branch-and-price algorithm for the capacitated vehicle routing problem with 2-dimensional loading constraints and a virtually unlimited number of vehicles. The column generation subproblem is solved heuristically through variable neighborhood search. Branch-and-price is used when it is not possible to add more attractive columns to the current restricted master problem, and the solution remains fractional. In order to accelerate the convergence of the algorithm, a family of valid dual inequalities is presented. Computational results are provided to evaluate the performance of the algorithm and to compare the different branching strategies proposed.

Keywords: Vehicle routing · Loading constraints · Branch-and-price · Computational study

1 Introduction

In the recent years, the number of contributions related to vehicle routing problems with loading constraints has increased significantly. These problems combine the well-known Capacitated Vehicle Routing Problem (CVRP) with the 2- or 3-dimensional bin packing problem (2L-CVRP and 3L-CVRP, respectively).

The 2L-CVRP addressed in this paper can be defined in a complete directed graph composed by one depot and a set of customers. The demand of each customer is composed by two-dimensional and rectangular items, with distinct height and width. We consider a homogeneous and virtually unlimited fleet. Each vehicle has a two-dimensional rectangular loading surface. The objective of the 2L-CVRP consists in finding a set of routes that minimize the transportation costs, while satisfying the following constraints:

This work has been supported by COMPETE: POCI-01-0145-FEDER-007043 and FCT – Fundação para a Ciência e a Tecnologia within the Project Scope: UID/CEC/00319/2013, and through the grant SFRH/BD/73584/2010 (funded by QREN-POPH-Typology 4.1- co-funded by the European Social Fund).

© Springer International Publishing Switzerland 2016
A. Paias et al. (Eds.): ICCL 2016, LNCS 9855, pp. 321–336, 2016.
DOI: 10.1007/978-3-319-44896-1_21

(C1) each route starts and it ends at the depot;

(C2) each customer has to be visited exactly once;

(C3) items have a fixed orientation, and thus, they cannot be rotated in the loading area;

(C4) items must fit in the loading area, without overlapping;

(C5) (*sequential constraints*) when visiting a given customer, unloading their items must be performed in a straight movement, while keeping the edges of items parallel to the edges of the loading area, without rearranging items from other customers.

The first exact method described in the literature for the 2L-CVRP is due to Iori *et al.* [6]. The authors proposed a branch-and-cut approach for the 2L-CVRP. Initially, the integer programming model is solved without considering loading or capacity-cut constraints. In what concerns the capacity-cut constraints, separation procedures are then applied. These procedures consist in heuristic methods for the minimum-cut problem that are used to find violated inequalities. When an integer solution is obtained, the feasibility of the packing is verified through a branch-and-bound algorithm.

There are several column generation based approaches for different variants of the vehicle routing problem. In contrast, approaches relying on column generation for the 2L-CVRP remain very rare. To the best of our knowledge, the first column generation formulation for the 2L-CVRP was presented in [1]. The authors proposed a branch-and-cut-and-price algorithm whose subproblem deals only with area and capacity constraints. For this purpose, an elementary shortest path problem is solved by considering the area and the capacity as resources. Then, valid inequalities are added to the master problem in order to ensure the loading feasibility of the routes.

Another column generation approach for the 2L-CVRP was suggested in [11]. Two general approaches were developed. In the first approach, each column that is inserted corresponds to a feasible solution according to the loading constraints. When no more columns can be added to the restricted master problem, branch-and-bound is used in order to obtain an integer solution. In the second approach, the packing feasibility of the routes is checked only after column generation and branch-and-bound have been applied. If there are routes that violate the loading constraints, the corresponding columns are removed from the restricted master problem. For both approaches, and in order to solve the subproblem, four heuristics are successively applied in order to derive one solution with negative reduced cost. If they fail, the label correcting algorithm [3] is used instead.

For the 3L-CVRP, a column generation algorithm was proposed in [9]. Two methods were described to solve the pricing subproblem. The first one consists in relaxing the loading constraints, and hence in solving an elementary shortest path problem with resource constraints related to the volume and capacity of the vehicle. For this purpose, the authors resort to a label correcting algorithm proposed in [3]. If a given route is not feasible, then customers are successively removed until a valid solution is found or until the reduced cost becomes positive. The second method relies on a greedy heuristic method, which aims to generate a list of feasible routes corresponding to a negative reduced cost, even though there is not any route corresponding to the minimum reduced cost. The procedure consists in creating, for each node, a list of customers that are linked to that node. These lists are ordered by the increasing order of cost of the arcs. For each customer linked to the depot, a route will be iteratively built by adding the nearest neighbor, and ensuring that loading constraints are satisfied, until reaching the depot.

Junqueira *et al.* [7] proposed the first formulation for the 3L-CVRP based on an extension of the time-dependent formulation for the Travelling Salesman Problem. Additional constraints are considered such as vertical load stability, multi-drop situations and load bearing. These constraints arise frequently in real-world situations. To evaluate the performance of their approach, the authors conducted a set of computational experiments on randomly generated instances. They concluded that their approach was able to solve satisfactorily medium-size instances of the problem, but that it found serious difficulties for large-size instances.

In [5], the authors describe an exact method for the 2L- and 3L-CVRP based on the branch-and-cut approach proposed by Iori *et al.* in [6]. Again, a relaxed version of the integer programming model for these problems is solved at an initial stage. Concerning the routing component, multiple separation procedures are applied right after obtaining the solution of the relaxed version, including capacity inequalities, framed capacity inequalities, multistar inequalities, among others. Moreover, when no more cuts are found, separation procedures concerning the packing are applied. These procedures consist in eliminating the routes that are not satisfying the loading constraints. Two main strategies are applied. The first strategy is applied right after reaching an integer solution provided by the branch-and-bound, by verifying the feasibility of each route included in the solution. On the contrary, the second strategy does not require the execution of the branch-and-bound, since it relies on a procedure to find infeasible routes from non-integer solutions.

The lack of column generation approaches for the 2L-CVRP strongly motivated the work presented in this paper. We suggest a branch-and-price algorithm for this problem with a variable neighborhood search approach to solve the subproblem. We aim to contribute with new features such as different partition strategies of the branching tree. We also suggest a family of valid cuts that may accelerate the convergence of the algorithm.

This paper is organized as follows. In Sect. 2, we present a column generation model for the 2L-CVRP and we define the pricing subproblem. The overall approach of the branch-and-price algorithm is described in Sect. 3. The dual inequalities developed for this problem are presented in Sect. 4, while several branching rules are described in Sect. 5. In Sect. 6, computational results of this approach are presented and discussed. Finally, some conclusions are drawn in Sect. 7.

2 Integer Programming Formulations for the 2L-CVRP

2.1 A Compact Formulation

In this section, we describe a compact integer programming formulation for the 2L-CVRP proposed originally by Iori *et al.* in [6]. This formulation will be used in the sequel to define our reformulated column generation model. Let $G = (V, A)$ be a complete directed graph where V represents a set of $n + 1$ nodes, and A the set of arcs. The set V includes the depot (denoted by 0) and a set N of n customers. We assume that the fleet is homogeneous with a virtually unlimited number of vehicles. Additionally, let σ represent the bijection which defines the order by which the customers are visited, and $\Sigma(S)$ the collection of sequences σ in which (S,σ) is a feasible route. The set of arcs in a route (S,σ) is defined by $A(S, \sigma)$. The formulation has binary variables x_{ij}, which takes the value 1 if the arc (i, j) is used by one vehicle, and 0 otherwise. To travel through an arc (i, j), there is a cost c_{ij}. Additionally, let $\delta^+(i)$ be the set of customers j adjacent to i such that $(i, j) \in A$, and $\delta^-(i)$ the set of customers j adjacent to i such that $(j, i) \in A$. The formulation of Iori *et al.* [6] states as follows.

$$\min \sum_{(i,j)\in A} c_{ij}x_{ij} \tag{1}$$

$$\text{subject to } \sum_{j\in\delta^+(i)} x_{ij} = 1, \forall i \in N, \tag{2}$$

$$\sum_{j\in\delta^+(i)} x_{ij} - \sum_{j\in\delta^-(i)} x_{ji} = 0, \forall i \in V, \tag{3}$$

$$\sum_{(i,j)\in A(S,\sigma)} x_{ij} \leq |S| - 1 \quad \forall(S,\sigma) \quad \text{such that} \quad \sigma \notin \Sigma(S), \tag{4}$$

$$x_{ij} \in \{0,1\}, \forall(i,j) \in A. \tag{5}$$

Constraints (2) ensure that each customer is visited exactly once. Flow conservation is represented through the constraints (3). The constraints (4) are named by the authors as the *infeasible path constraints*. They ensure the loading feasibility of the route considering the constraints (C3) to (C5) referred to above, since all the infeasible routes are forbidden in the solution.

2.2 A Column Generation Model

Master Problem. A column generation model for the 2L-CVRP can be obtained from (1)–(5) by applying a Dantzig-Wolfe decomposition [2] in which the constraints (2) remain in the master problem, while the others define the pricing subproblem. Note that the convexity constraints are omitted since the fleet is homogeneous and virtually infinite. Let Ω be the set of all the feasible routes, *i.e.* the set of all the extreme points. The columns (or decision variables) of the master problem are denoted by λ_r, with $r \in \Omega$. Hence, a variable λ_r taking the value 1 means that the corresponding route is part of the solution.

Each route r has an associated cost c_r, and it can be described by a vector $(a_{1r}, a_{2r}, \ldots, a_{nr})^T$ where each coefficient a_{ir} takes value 1 if customer i $(i \in N)$ is visited in route r $(r \in \Omega)$, and 0 otherwise. The resulting reformulated model is a set partitioning problem which is defined as follows.

$$\min \sum_{r \in \Omega} c_r \lambda_r \tag{6}$$

$$\text{subject to} \sum_{r \in \Omega} a_{ir} \lambda_r = 1, \forall i \in N, \tag{7}$$

$$\lambda_r \in \{0, 1\}, \forall r \in \Omega. \tag{8}$$

Pricing Subproblem. The pricing subproblem defined through the constraints (3) and (4) of (1)–(5) corresponds to an Elementary Shortest Path Problem with Resource and Sequential Constraints (ESPPRSC). The ESPPRSC consists in finding a shortest path without cycles that starts and ends at the depot such that the 2-dimensional loads of the visited customers fit in the vehicle in such a way that the sequential constraints described in Sect. 1 are satisfied. The costs of the arcs in the underlying graph depend on the dual values associated to a solution of the Linear Programming (LP) relaxation of (6)–(8). In each iteration of the algorithm, the costs of the arcs in the subproblem will be updated. Therefore, finding the shortest path corresponds to find the route with the minimum reduced cost.

Let π_i $(i \in N)$ be the dual variables associated to each constraint of type (7). The expression of the reduced cost c'_r for a given route $r \in \Omega$ is given by: $c'_r = c_r - \sum_{i \in N} \pi_i a_{ir}$.

To solve the subproblem, we resort to the Variable Neighborhood Search (VNS) algorithm for the ESPPRSC, described in [10]. To the best of our knowledge, this algorithm was the first approach for the ESPPRSC, and it relies on constructive procedures to generate feasible solutions. These methods consist in different strategies to place an item while satisfying the sequential constraints, using bottom-left and level packing approaches. A VNS algorithm is used in order to search for improved solutions, and it explores different neighborhood structures, which are divided in routing and in packing neighborhoods. Several variants were tested through the combination of the distinct constructive strategies with the VNS algorithm.

3   Outline of the Algorithm

Generally, the master problem is initialized with a restricted set of decision variables. For this reason, in the literature it is usual to denominate the master problem as Restricted Master Problem (RMP). The RMP is initialized with a subset of columns, which correspond to a subset of valid routes. In order to build this subset, three strategies are used. The first strategy consists in the generation of single customer routes. One route is created for each customer, and only that

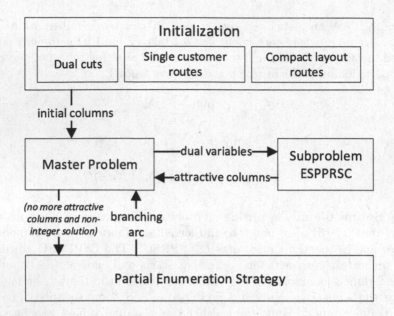

Fig. 1. Outline of the algorithm

customer is visited. The second strategy relies on the insertion of dual valid inequalities to be presented in Sect. 4. Finally, the third strategy consists in the use of a meta-heuristic to derive routes with a high percentage of used space in the vehicle. In this sense, we resort to the VNS for the ESPPRSC [10] that is also used to solve the subproblem, as referred to above. In order to generate routes with a compact layout, the costs of all arcs are set at -1. The solution provided by the VNS algorithm will consist in a route with a desirable compact layout and the corresponding column will be added to the RMP. Then, the arcs of the inserted route will take a very high cost, and the process is repeated according to a parameter n_{init}. An artificial variable was also added to the initial subset of columns.

After the RMP initialization, dual information is provided to the subproblem, which will seek for attractive columns. If there is any attractive column, then it will be added to the RMP. The procedure is repeated until no more attractive columns are found by the subproblem. If an integer solution is found, the algorithm stops, returning the obtained solution. Otherwise, a branch-and-bound procedure is performed within a partial enumeration algorithm (Sect. 5.3), using branching rules to be presented in Sects. 5.1 and 5.2. The overall approach is outlined in Fig. 1.

4   Stabilization Strategies

Despite the effectiveness of column generation algorithms, they usually exhibit a slow convergence rate with solutions that improve only very slightly at the last iterations of the procedure. This phenomenon is also known as long tail convergence. Some strategies are commonly used to improve the convergence. One of the most promising consists in restricting the dual space by enforcing the so-called *dual cuts*. In this section, we explore a family of cuts for the particular case of the 2L-CVRP. Our cuts are based on the fact that a route corresponds to a sequence of visits, and hence it should be possible to replace a customer $i \in N$ by another customer $j \in N$ $(i \neq j)$ in the position of the route provided that:

(D1) the number of items of customer j is less than or equal to the number of items of customer i;

(D2) the area of one item of customer i can be used to place at most one item of customer j, without exceeding the height and width of the former item;

(D3) all the items of customer j can be placed in the vehicle satisfying the previous condition.

From a primal standpoint, the idea behind these three conditions is that the loading area of the vehicle, which is occupied with items of customer i, can be used to place the items of customer j. The primal interpretation of the associated dual cuts is that a customer i satisfying the above conditions can be replaced by a customer j in any feasible route without breaking the feasibility of the resulting route. However, since this replacement can take place in any feasible route that is in the RMP, one does not know a priori what will be the associated cost. To ensure that the computed cost cope with all the possible situations, and hence that the related dual cut is feasible, we compute the cost of the resulting route by considering the worst possible case. Let $\bar{c}_{ij}$ be the cost difference between the two less costly arcs that are incident to i and the two higher costly arcs that are incident to j. Let i_1 and i_2 be, respectively, the first and the second nearest customers to customer i. Let j_1 and j_2 be, respectively, the first and second customer which are more far from j. Thus, $\bar{c}_{ij} = c_{j_1,j} + c_{j_2,j} - c_{i_1,i} - c_{i_2,i}$. The following proposition shows that the corresponding dual cut is indeed a valid dual inequality.

Proposition 1. Let π_i and π_j be the dual variables of constraints (7) of the RMP associated to customers i and j, respectively. If the customers i and j satisfy the conditions (D1)–(D3) referred to above, the following inequalities are valid dual cuts for the 2L-CVRP:

$$-\pi_i + \pi_j \leq \bar{c}_{ij}, \quad \forall i, j \in N, i \neq j.$$

Proof. The proof is based on the results obtained by Macedo *et al.* [8] for the vehicle routing problem with different service constraints. It starts by establishing valid conditions in the dual space, and then it demonstrates, by contradiction, that the validity conditions are not obeyed for a cut that is invalid in the dual space.

Let Ω be the set of columns corresponding to the routes. Then,

$$\sum_{m \in N} a_{mr} \leq c_r, \forall r \in \Omega. \tag{9}$$

In the optimal solution, customer i is associated to exactly one route. Let $A_r = (a_{1r}, \ldots, 1, \ldots, 0, \ldots, a_{mr})^T$ with a unit coefficient in row i. This route has a reduced cost equal to zero. Therefore, according to the reduced cost expression, $c_r = \sum_{m \in N} \pi_m a_{mr}$. Let s be another route such that $A_s = (a_{1s}, \ldots, 0, \ldots, 1, \ldots, a_{ms})^T$, i.e., $a_{is} = 0$ and $a_{js} = 1$, and all the other coefficients equal to the ones in A_r. Then, $c_s - c_r \le \bar{c}_{ij}$. If there is a cut which is not valid, then, $-\pi_i + \pi_j > \bar{c}_{ij}$. Thus, $-\pi_i + \pi_j > c_s - c_r$. Consequently, $-\pi_i + \pi_j > c_s - \sum_{m \in N} \pi_m a_{mr}$. Since $-\pi_i + \pi_j = -\sum_{m \in N} \pi_m a_{mr} + \sum_{m \in N} \pi_m a_{ms}$, then, $\sum_{m \in N} a_{ms} > c_s$, not satisfying (9). $\square$

From the primal standpoint, each dual inequality can be interpreted as the use of the space left by items of customer i to place the items of customer j. It is worth noting that applying this procedure gives rise to a route which is necessarily feasible: all the packing constraints are obeyed since the placed items fit within the space of the removed items. Consequently, the unloading sequence of other items remains unchanged and the sequential constraints are satisfied.

5   Branch-and-Price

In order to derive an integer solution, it can be necessary to combine the branch-and-bound approach with the column generation algorithm. At the root of the branching tree, the LP relaxation of the reformulated model is provided. Thus, branching constraints are introduced. At nodes from lower levels of the branching tree, new columns may be needed, as many as required to solve the LP relaxation of that node. This integrated method is denominated by branch-and-price. The branching constraints are usually based on the original problem, preventing deadlock situations that could arise if branching is performed in the decision variables of the RMP.

5.1   Branching Rules Based on a Single Variable

In the following, we present the branching strategies based on single arcs. Each arc is in fact a variable of the original formulation. Therefore, the structure of the pricing subproblem is not affected by the new branching constraints that appear in the RMP, and hence, its complexity remains unchanged.

(**BB1.1**) Among all the arcs of the solution, the one that has the highest fractional flow is selected to branch on, i.e.,

$$(i', j') = \arg \max_{(i,j) \in A} \{ x_{ij} \mid x_{ij} \ne 0, x_{ij} \ne 1 \}. \tag{10}$$

This rule aims to explore the branching tree guided by the solution provided by the LP relaxation of the RMP.

(**BB1.2**) Among all arcs with fractional flow, the one that has the lowest cost is selected,

$$(i', j') = \arg \min_{(i,j) \in A} \{ c_{ij} \mid x_{ij} \ne 0, x_{ij} \ne 1 \}. \tag{11}$$

This rule aims to fix the arcs by the increasing order of cost.

(BB1.3) Among all routes of the LP solution, the one that visits more customers is selected; from the set of arcs traversed by this route, the arc that has the highest fractional flow is selected. The selected route will have expectably a layout with good quality since it includes a high number of customers. Since the loading component is the most critical in the 2L-CVRP, the aim is to fix the flow on the arcs belonging to these type of routes.

(BB1.4) Among all arcs that are incident to the depot, the one that has the highest fractional flow is selected. If there are no arcs satisfying this condition, then rule $(BB1.1)$ is applied. This rule aims to fix the values of the arcs that leaves the depot, *i.e.* the origin of the flow.

5.2   Branching Rules Based on Sets of Variables

Using the branching rules based on a single variable may lead to a branching tree with high depth. Alternatively, one may branch on the flow of a subset of arcs instead. In these cases, a set of original variables is selected for branching. The sum of their flows is used to define the branch, with an expectably greater impact in the solution. In the sequel, we describe the rules used to select those arcs.

(BB2.1) Among the set of routes of the solution, the one that has the highest fractional value is selected. The sum of the flow in the arcs traversed by this route is computed. Let r be the selected route and P_r be the sequence of arcs traversed in route r. In one branch it is imposed that $\sum_{(i,j)\in P_r} x_{ij} \geq \left\lceil \sum_{(i,j)\in P_r} x_{ij} \right\rceil$, while in the other branch the following constraint is applied: $\sum_{(i,j)\in P_r} x_{ij} \leq \left\lfloor \sum_{(i,j)\in P_r} x_{ij} \right\rfloor$. Guided by the solution provided by the LP relaxation of the RMP, this rule aims to explore the branching tree by fixing the sum of the flow of the arcs belonging to routes with highest fractional value.

(BB2.2) Among the set of arcs of the solution, a subset of arcs with the highest flow is selected. Let $A' \subset A$ be that subset, whose cardinality is a parameter $(m_{arcs} = |A'|)$. Then a binary branching is performed by imposing in one branch that $\sum_{(i,j)\in A'} x_{ij} \geq \left\lceil \sum_{(i,j)\in A'} x_{ij} \right\rceil$, while in the other branch it is provided that $\sum_{(i,j)\in A'} x_{ij} \leq \left\lfloor \sum_{(i,j)\in A'} x_{ij} \right\rfloor$.

(BB2.3) Among the set of arcs of the solution, a subset of arcs with the lowest flow is selected. Then, the branching is performed with the same branching constraints presented in rule $(BB2.2)$.

(BB2.4) Among the set of routes of the solution, the one that has more visited customers is selected. The branching is performed with the same branching constraints presented in rule $(BB2.1)$.

5.3   Combining the Branching Rules for Partial Enumeration

Taking into account the set of branching rules, it is necessary to define how to apply and combine them, and, in this sense, which strategies are used to explore the nodes of the branching tree. All of them rely on a depth-first search strategy for choosing the node of the branching tree to explore. Whenever it is not possible to dive down a given node, the search continues at the upper level of the branching tree. This happens when the LP relaxation of the RMP associated to the node is infeasible. It is worth noting that it is not possible to leave unexplored a node when the value of the LP relaxation of the RMP is greater than the value of the incumbent solution. This is due to the fact that the solution provided by the RMP relies on column generation based heuristic. In the following, we describe the three strategies implemented.

(Single rule) Branch-and-price is performed using only one branching rule. This means that in a given node, whenever there are no attractive columns and the solutions remains fractional, the search space is divided into two distinct search spaces according to the selected branching rule. With this strategy, a different branching tree is derived for each branching rule.

(Random strategy) At a given node of the branching tree, if the solution remains fractional, branching is performed by selecting randomly one of the rules described above. This strategy ensures a greater diversity of the divided search spaces at each node of the branching tree.

(Sequential strategy) In this strategy, the branching rules are explored by the order they were presented, $i.e.$, according to a sequence from $(BB1.1)$ to $(BB2.4)$. Each branching rule is used by n_{max} iterations, as long as there is no improvement of the incumbent solution. When n_{max} is reached, the following branching rule is selected. Once the last branching rule $(BB2.4)$ is used after n_{max} iterations without improvement of the incumbent solution, the process is repeated from the first branching rule $(BB1.1)$.

6   Computational Results

To evaluate and compare the performance of the different enumeration algorithms presented in Sect. 5.3, we conducted a set of preliminary computational experiments on 25 instances of the 2L-CVRP proposed in [4,6]. This set is described in Table 1, where m represents the number of customers while it corresponds to the number of items. The name and the class of each instance is also provided. Note that the number of the class corresponds to the maximum number of items for each customer. The instances of class 1 are considered as pure CVRP instances, since each customer demands a single item with height and width equal to one unit. The height and the width of each vehicle for all instances are, respectively, 40 and 20 units. The algorithms were coded in C++, and the tests were run on an Intel Xeon Processor E5-1620 v3 with 3.50 GHz and 64 GB of RAM.

6.1   Preliminary Computational Experiments

In the preliminary tests, we imposed a time limit of 300 s in the LP relaxation of the RMP, and a time limit of 1800 s in the branch-and-price. The parameters n_{init}, m_{arcs} and n_{max} are set at 50, 10 and 10, respectively.

Table 1. Set of instances

Instance	Name	Class	m	it	Instance	Name	Class	m	it
1	E016-03m	1	15	15	14	E051-05e	4	50	134
2	E016-03m	2	15	24	15	E051-05e	5	50	157
3	E016-03m	3	15	31	16	E076-08s	1	75	75
4	E016-03m	4	15	37	17	E076-08s	2	75	112
5	E016-03m	5	15	45	18	E076-08s	3	75	154
6	E026-08m	1	25	25	19	E076-08s	4	75	198
7	E026-08m	2	25	40	20	E076-08s	5	75	236
8	E026-08m	3	25	61	21	E151-12b	1	150	150
9	E026-08m	4	25	63	22	E151-12b	2	150	225
10	E026-08m	5	25	91	23	E151-12b	3	150	298
11	E051-05e	1	50	50	24	E151-12b	4	150	366
12	E051-05e	2	50	82	25	E151-12b	5	150	433
13	E051-05e	3	50	103					

In Table 2, we report on the average results for the 10 strategies described in Sect. 5.3, namely the Single Rule (SR), the Random Strategy (RS) and the Sequential Strategy (SS). There is always an integer incumbent solution, which is initialized with a single customer route for each customer. The meaning of the columns in Table 2 is the following:

- $Inst$: number of the instance according to Table 1;
- I_{OPT}: number of the instances (according to column $Inst$) in which the algorithm was able to achieve solutions that are better than the initial incumbent;
- sp_{LP}: average number of subproblems solved before branching;
- $cols_{LP}$: average number of generated columns during the LP relaxation of the RMP;
- sp_{BB}: average number of subproblems solved in the branch-and-price;
- $cols_{BB}$: average number of generated columns in the branch-and-price;
- nod_{BB}: average number of branching nodes generated during branch-and-price, excluding the root;
- z_{LP} average cost of the LP solution;
- z_{OPT} value of the best solution achieved.

The obtained results show that strategies based only on one rule (SR) lead to cost value in the LP solution similar to the ones obtained with random and sequential schemes. Considering the values obtained with branch-and-price, the strategies SR ($BB1.2$) and SR ($BB2.4$) provide better average values. Not surprisingly, these strategies are also the ones providing a higher number of instances

Table 2. Computational results for the preliminary set of experiments

	$Inst$	I_{OPT}	sp_{LP}	$cols_{LP}$	sp_{BB}	$cols_{BB}$	nod_{BB}	z_{LP}	z_{OPT}
SR (BB1.1)	1 to 5	1; 2; 4; 5	46	44	74	64	10	281,09	343
	6 to 10	6; 8	63	61	111	101	10	530,64	976
	11 to 15	11; 15	71	69	171	164	6	1016,76	2000
	16 to 20	16	82	80	243	240	3	1523,21	3015
	21 to 25	21	81	79	422	421	1	3737,07	5998
	avg.		*69*	*67*	*204*	*198*	*6*	*1417,75*	*2466*
SR (BB1.2)	1 to 5	1; 2; 3; 4; 5	40	38	101	91	11	282,47	298
	6 to 10	6; 7; 8; 9; 10	62	60	80	74	6	535,88	549
	11 to 15	11	75	73	187	184	3	977,48	2001
	16 to 20	16	82	80	250	248	2	1511,51	3012
	21 to 25	21	81	79	424	423	1	3705,37	5997
	avg.		*68*	*66*	*208*	*204*	*5*	*1402,54*	*2371*
SR (BB1.3)	1 to 5	1; 2	45	43	31	9	22	277,21	461
	6 to 10	6	63	61	63	42	20	530,04	1129
	11 to 15	11	75	73	150	142	8	986,43	2006
	16 to 20	16	82	80	235	233	2	1547,96	3008
	21 to 25	21	82	80	418	417	1	3722,53	5997
	avg.		*69*	*67*	*179*	*169*	*11*	*1412,83*	*2520*
SR (BB1.4)	1 to 5	1; 2; 3; 4; 5	44	42	23	19	4	278,87	278
	6 to 10	6; 8; 9; 10	62	60	99	91	8	541,77	663
	11 to 15	11	73	71	166	160	6	1023,62	2001
	16 to 20	16	82	80	237	234	3	1501,04	3011
	21 to 25	21	81	79	421	420	1	3749,97	5997
	avg.		*69*	*67*	*189*	*185*	*4*	*1419,05*	*2390*
SR (BB2.1)	1 to 5	1; 2; 3; 4; 5	47	45	49	43	6	277,67	282
	6 to 10	6; 7; 8; 10	65	63	118	110	8	533,56	695
	11 to 15	11	77	75	196	191	5	999,07	2006
	16 to 20	16	83	81	232	228	3	1529,20	3010
	21 to 25	21	82	80	405	404	1	3773,60	5998
	avg.		*71*	*69*	*200*	*195*	*5*	*1422,62*	*2398*
SR (BB2.2)	1 to 5	1; 2; 4; 5	44	42	70	62	7	279,99	343
	6 to 10	6	59	57	126	121	5	530,78	1127
	11 to 15	11	74	72	199	197	3	1000,01	2007
	16 to 20	16	82	80	269	267	2	1523,10	3012
	21 to 25	21	82	80	417	417	1	3722,49	5996
	avg.		*68*	*66*	*216*	*213*	*4*	*1411,27*	*2497*

(Continued)

Table 2. (*Continued*)

	Inst	I_{OPT}	sp_{LP}	$cols_{LP}$	sp_{BB}	$cols_{BB}$	nod_{BB}	z_{LP}	z_{OPT}
SR (BB2.3)	1 to 5	1; 2; 4	46	44	72	68	4	280,50	404
	6 to 10	6	59	57	145	141	4	544,71	1132
	11 to 15	11	75	73	208	205	2	987,18	2001
	16 to 20	16	83	81	263	262	1	1518,59	3014
	21 to 25	21	81	79	425	424	1	3729,47	5997
	avg.		69	67	222	220	2	1412,09	2510
SR (BB2.4)	1 to 5	1; 2; 3; 4; 5	46	44	83	74	10	283,91	299
	6 to 10	6; 7; 8; 9; 10	64	62	116	106	10	531,53	549
	11 to 15	11	77	75	178	175	3	999,46	2001
	16 to 20	16	82	80	255	253	2	1534,11	3012
	21 to 25	21	81	79	425	425	1	3737,81	5998
	avg.		70	68	211	206	5	1417,36	2372
RS	1 to 5	1; 2; 4	47	45	68	63	4	277,82	403
	6 to 10	6; 9	62	60	133	128	6	524,79	972
	11 to 15	11	74	72	189	185	3	985,05	2008
	16 to 20	16	81	79	250	248	2	1513,53	3012
	21 to 25	21	81	79	430	429	1	3742,99	5996
	avg.		69	67	214	211	3	1408,83	2478
SS	1 to 5	1; 2; 3; 4; 5	45	43	76	67	9	283,12	285
	6 to 10	6	62	60	119	109	9	541,35	1130
	11 to 15	11	75	73	167	160	7	977,43	2004
	16 to 20	16	82	80	243	241	3	1528,39	3012
	21 to 25	21	82	80	419	418	1	3798,95	5998
	avg.		69	67	205	1969	6	1425,81	2486

where the best solution is better than the initial incumbent (instances 1–11, 16, and 21). The number of generated columns tends to be greater for instances with a higher number of customers. In these instances, it is more difficult to achieve a solution better than the incumbent. Therefore, the branching continues giving rise to larger branching trees. However, within strategy SR ($BB1.1$), it was possible to update the incumbent for instance 15, which has 50 customers and more than 150 items. The strategy SR ($BB1.3$) leads to the worst average cost values. Indeed, with the exception of the pure CVRP instances, the algorithm was able to update the initial incumbent only for instance 2. Similar results were found by strategy SR ($BB2.3$). Finally, results concerning the random strategy and sequential strategy (RS and SS) lead to similar results.

6.2 Second Set of Computational Experiments

Considering the preliminary results, we conducted a second set of computational experiments. For this purpose, we considered three subset of instances.

Table 3. Computational results for the second set of experiments

Inst	I_{OPT}	sp_{LP}	$cols_{LP}$	sp_{BB}	$cols_{BB}$	nod_{BB}	z_{LP}	z_{opt}	t_{PP}	t_{LP}	t_{BB}	t_{tot}
SR (BB1.1) 1 to 5	1; 2; 3; 4; 5	49	47	108	97	11	278,36	283	21,61	360,82	1534,44	1916,87
11 to 15	11	111	109	239	222	18	894,22	2001	3,01	409,93	2890,93	3303,87
21 to 25	21	122	120	591	589	2	3270,95	5996	3,13	402,20	2891,86	3297,18
SR (BB1.2) 1 to 5	1; 2; 3; 4; 5	50	48	150	133	17	276,36	303	25,82	380,61	2165,32	2571,75
11 to 15	11; 14	105	103	303	292	11	931,07	1747	3,02	393,55	2883,09	3279,66
21 to 25	21	121	119	602	601	2	3349,72	5997	3,18	411,43	2886,13	3300,74
SR (BB1.3) 1 to 5	1; 2	49	47	56	14	42	277,21	462	21,02	375,80	2169,47	2566,29
11 to 15	11	104	102	178	147	31	939,24	2004	3,01	409,28	2890,60	3302,89
21 to 25	21	121	119	581	579	2	3317,72	5997	3,24	410,02	2886,63	3299,89
SR (BB1.4) 1 to 5	1; 2; 3; 4; 5	54	52	98	85	13	275,19	276	23,42	394,44	1455,20	1873,06
11 to 15	11	107	105	248	231	17	919,09	2001	3,01	404,42	2898,24	3305,66
21 to 25	21	121	119	566	563	3	3307,61	5996	3,16	412,72	2891,09	3306,97
SR (BB2.1) 1 to 5	1; 2; 3; 4; 5	54	52	122	97	24	277,37	296	28,22	389,62	2272,17	2690,01
11 to 15	11; 13	105	103	319	310	9	929,87	1725	3,01	399,04	2894,71	3296,76
21 to 25	21	122	120	576	573	2	3311,13	5997	3,17	406,80	2889,34	3299,31
SR (BB2.2) 1 to 5	1; 2; 3; 4	51	49	102	91	12	274,38	340	22,88	393,84	1448,23	1864,96
11 to 15	11	103	101	337	329	8	954,47	2004	3,04	396,50	2883,56	3283,10
21 to 25	21	120	118	585	582	2	3311,88	5995	3,28	399,12	2883,19	3285,59
SR (BB2.3) 1 to 5	1; 2	54	52	150	132	18	276,07	460	24,09	410,09	2166,04	2600,21
11 to 15	11	102	100	344	340	4	948,25	2008	3,03	403,75	2882,79	3289,57
21 to 25	21	121	119	692	691	1	3288,20	5997	3,34	415,03	2882,39	3300,75
SR (BB2.4) 1 to 5	1; 2; 3; 4; 5	52	50	122	94	28	275,97	288	24,69	406,49	2384,65	2815,83
11 to 15	11; 12; 13; 14; 15	105	103	267	256	12	931,50	975	3,01	393,40	2885,91	3282,33
21 to 25	21	120	118	630	628	2	3319,67	5995	3,31	393,80	2882,73	3279,84
RS 1 to 5	1; 2; 3; 4; 5	52	50	152	138	14	274,01	282	14,30	395,22	1975,90	2385,42
11 to 15	11; 13; 14	104	102	320	311	8	938,33	1498	3,02	417,63	2888,29	3308,94
21 to 25	21	120	118	592	590	2	3415,39	5998	3,16	392,40	2892,54	3288,10
SS 1 to 5	1; 2; 3; 4; 5	55	53	81	72	9	274,72	278	21,04	422,14	1187,09	1630,27
11 to 15	11; 14	103	101	218	208	10	927,68	1776	3,02	408,62	2169,25	2580,90
21 to 25	21	120	118	578	576	2	3272,76	5995	3,15	386,84	2884,05	3274,05

We selected the instances with 15, 50 and 150 customers, in order to build a set of instances with different sizes. Additionally, the time limit for the LP relaxation was increased to 450 s, and the branch-and-price duration was set at a maximum of 3600 s. The values of the remaining parameters were not modified. In Table 3, we present the set of computational experiments for the second set of experiments. In this table, we use the same columns defined in Sect. 6.1, and the additional notation:

- t_{PP}: average computing time for the initialization of the RMP (in seconds);
- t_{LP}: average computing time for the LP relaxation (in seconds);
- t_{BB}: average computing time for the branch-and-price phase (in seconds);
- t_{tot}: average total computing time (in seconds).

The obtained results for strategy SR ($BB1.1$) show an average improvement in the cost of the best solution achieved for instances 1 to 5 (roughly 17 %), when compared with the preliminary tests. For the remaining instances, the values are very close to those obtained in the preliminary tests for the same strategy. Similar improvements were found within strategy SR ($BB1.2$) for instances 11 to 15, reaching an average improvement of roughly 12,69 %. The values for strategy SR ($BB1.3$) are very similar to those obtained in the preliminary phase. The strategy SR ($BB2.1$) presents the worst average values concerning instances with 15 customers, but presents important improvements for the instances with 50 customers (roughly 14 %). The strategy SR ($BB2.3$) leads to an average improvement of 12,17 % when considering 15 customers. For instances with a greater number of customers, the average improvement is less significant.

7 Conclusions

In this work, a branch-and-price approach for the capacitated vehicle routing problem with 2-dimensional loading constraints is presented. The master problem relies on a set partitioning formulation, while the subproblem corresponds to an elementary shortest path problem with loading constraints. The overall approach includes the generation of valid dual inequalities in order to accelerate the convergence. Different branching strategies were implemented and tested. We conducted an extensive set of computational experiments using benchmark instances from the literature. The obtained results provided solutions which are clearly better than the initial incumbent for small size instances. However, for instances with a greater number of customers, the algorithm tends to have more difficulty in finding integer solutions with acceptable values.

References

1. Cordeau, J., Iori, M., Ropke, S., Vigo, D.: Branch-and-cut-and-price for the capacitated vehicle routing problem with two-dimensional loading constraints. In: ROUTE 2007, Jekyll Island (2007)
2. Dantzig, G.B., Wolfe, P.: Decomposition principle for linear programs. Oper. Res. 8(1), 101–111 (1960)
3. Feillet, D., Dejax, P., Gendreau, M., Gueguen, C.: An exact algorithm for the elementary shortest path problem with resource constraints: application to some vehicle routing problems. Networks 44(3), 216–229 (2004)
4. Gendreau, M., Iori, M., Laporte, G., Martello, S.: A Tabu search heuristic for the vehicle routing problem with two-dimensional loading constraints. Networks 51(1), 4–18 (2008)
5. Hokama, P., Miyazawa, F., Xavier, E.: A branch-and-cut approach for the vehicle routing problem with loading constraints. Expert Syst. Appl. 47, 1–13 (2016)
6. Iori, M., Salazar-Gonzalez, J.-J., Vigo, D.: An exact approach for the vehicle routing problem with two-dimensional loading constraints. Transp. Sci. 41(2), 253–264 (2007)
7. Junqueira, L., Oliveira, J., Carravilla, M.A., Morabito, R.: An optimization model for the vehicle routing problem with practical three-dimensional loading constraints. Int. Trans. Oper. Res. 20(5), 645–666 (2013)
8. Macedo, R., Alves, C., Valério de Carvalho, J.: Exact algorithms for vehicle routing problems with different service constraints. In: CTW09, France (2009)
9. Mahvash, B., Awasthi, A., Chauhan, S.: A column generation based heuristic for the capacitated vehicle routing problem with three-dimensional loading constraints. In: 15th IFAC Symposium on Information Control Problems in Manufacturing, vol. 48(3), pp. 448–453 (2015)
10. Pinto, T., Alves, C., de Carvalho, J.V.: Variable neighborhood search for the elementary shortest path problem with loading constraints. In: Gervasi, O., Murgante, B., Misra, S., Gavrilova, M.L., Rocha, A.M.A.C., Torre, C., Taniar, D., Apduhan, B.O. (eds.) ICCSA 2015. LNCS, vol. 9156, pp. 474–489. Springer, Heidelberg (2015)
11. Souza, V.: Algoritmos para o problema de roteamento de veículos capacitado com restrições de carregamento bidimensional. Master's thesis, Universidade Federal de Minas Gerais, Belo Horizonte, Brasil (2013)

The Static Bicycle Repositioning Problem - Literature Survey and New Formulation

Hans Martin Espegren, Johannes Kristianslund,
Henrik Andersson[✉], and Kjetil Fagerholt

Department of Industrial Economics and Technology Management,
Norwegian University of Science and Technology, Trondheim, Norway
henrik.andersson@iot.ntnu.no

Abstract. This paper considers the static bicycle repositioning problem (SBRP), which deals with optimally re-balancing bike sharing systems (BSS) overnight, i.e. using service vehicles to move bikes from (nearly) full stations to (nearly) empty stations. An exhaustive literature survey comparing existing models is presented, and a new and improved mathematical formulation for the SBRP is proposed. The model is tested on a number of instances generated based on data from a real BSS.

1 Introduction

As urbanization proceeds throughout the world, public decision makers are looking for effective, affordable, and environmentally friendly means of transportation. Bike sharing fulfills these criteria for short distance traveling within city centres, and consequently bike sharing is getting increased attention from both governments and the public. Currently there are 948 cities with an active Bike Sharing System (BSS) and 273 with a system under planning or construction [10]. Figure 1 shows the expansion of bike sharing over the recent years, expressed as number of cities in the world with a public BSS. For an extensive review of the historical development of BSSs, the reader is referred to [9,24,35].

Bike sharing is a public system for automatic or semi-automatic lending of bicycles for use within a restricted time period and area. A bike can be lent at one station and delivered at another. Note that during the night most non-automatic systems are either closed or in limited use. For the system to function well, it is crucial that there are bikes available at a station when someone wants to pick up a bike and that there are free slots available when someone wants to return one. To achieve this, most BSSs use service vehicles to re-balance the system, i.e. to move bikes from (nearly) full stations to (nearly) empty stations. This paper studies the logistics of the service vehicles used to re-balance the system overnight.

The planning problems arising from BSSs are divided into three levels in accordance with [37]; a strategic, a tactical, and an operational level, as illustrated in Fig. 2. The strategic level contains problems that arise when designing the system, e.g. determining the optimal number of bikes and locations of stations. On the tactical level the objective is to find an optimal distribution of

© Springer International Publishing Switzerland 2016
A. Paias et al. (Eds.): ICCL 2016, LNCS 9855, pp. 337–351, 2016.
DOI: 10.1007/978-3-319-44896-1_22

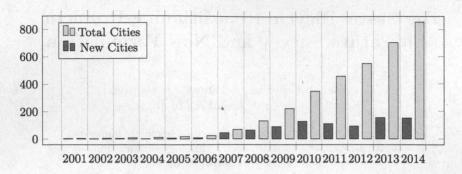

Fig. 1. Worldwide development in number of cities with a public BSS, 2000–2014 [10]

bikes between the stations at a specific time, while finding optimal routes for the service vehicles to re-balance the system is the objective at the operational level.

It is common to divide the operational level in two: static and dynamic problems. In line with [31], the problems are named *static bicycle repositioning problem* (SBRP) and *dynamic bicycle repositioning problem* (DBRP). The SBRP is typically used for overnight balancing, when the demand forecast for the operating period is not considered; the problem is static and deterministic. To describe the SBRP we introduce the concept of states, i.e. a distribution of bikes throughout the system, expressed as a specific number of bikes at each station. The *optimal state* is the desired distribution of bikes at the end of the planning period, i.e. early in the morning, while the *initial state* is the distribution at the beginning of the planning period, i.e. late in the evening. After solving the model, we get the *final state*. The difference between the final state and optimal state is called deviation. All stations and vehicles have restricted capacities, and the fleet of service vehicles may be either homogeneous or heterogeneous. For every vehicle, a complete route and the number of bikes to pick up or deliver at each station must be decided. Hence the SBRP can be classified as a *static many-to-many one-commodity pickup and delivery problem with selective pickups and selective deliveries*, in accordance with [3]. The DBRP is on the other hand used for intraday re-balancing, as the demand during the operating time is taken into account. Hence, the DBRP is both dynamic and stochastic.

In this paper we focus on the SBRP. In the literature survey, we identify a need for a new formulation of the problem including more real-life aspects

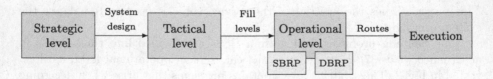

Fig. 2. Planning levels of BSS optimization

important for system planners. Our contributions are (1) to present an exhaustive literature survey on the SBRP, including a systematic comparison of the existing models, and (2) to propose a new mathematical model of the problem that captures more real-life aspects. We also propose symmetry-breaking constraints and valid inequalities to tighten the formulation. The model is tested on a number of test instances based on data from a real BSS.

Section 2 provides the literature survey on the SBRP, while a new mathematical model for the SBRP is introduced in Sect. 3. A computational study is presented in Sect. 4 and concluding remarks are given in Sect. 5.

2   Literature Survey

In this literature survey we focus on the static bicycle repositioning problem (SBRP). For studies on the strategic level, we refer to [16,23,33] that determine the number of stations and their locations, and to [15] that finds the optimal number of bikes in the system and the number of slots at each station. At the tactical level we can refer to [30,34,38] for analyses of the placement of bikes, while [20] studies the detection of broken bikes in the system. There are also a number of studies regarding the DBRP, see for example [1,4,5,7,21,26,27,32,39]. An overview of planning problems arising in shared mobility systems, for example a bike-sharing system, is given in [22].

The SBRP was first studied in [2]. They describe the system using graph theory. The objective is to move bikes along the arcs so each station is perfectly re-balanced at minimal cost. One of the main findings is that the SBRP is NP-hard. In [6], the work from [2] is continued. An optimization model is presented, but shows to be hard to solve, so they relax the problem by removing the sequential dimension and solve it using a branch-and-cut (B&C) algorithm.

In [31], two different mixed integer programming formulations are introduced; an arc-indexed and a time-indexed. The objective is to minimize a weighted sum of the stations' penalty costs for deviations and the operating cost. The authors conclude that the arc-indexed model provides the best results for most instances, but the time-indexed formulation is easier to adapt to the DBRP. Valid inequalities and dominance rules are proposed to strengthen the formulations.

The arc-indexed formulation from [31] is enhanced in [14,19], both proposing methods for solving larger instances. In [19], the formulation is simplified by allowing only one vehicle, stating that a station is either a pickup or delivery station and assuming that each station only can be visited once. The objective is to minimize a penalty function depending on the number of bikes at each station. The authors present a construction heuristic used to generate an initial solution followed by a tabu search. On the other hand, the model is expanded in [14] by using a three-step algorithm. In the first step, stations are clustered using a saving heuristic. In the second step, vehicles are assigned to clusters, while the routes for each vehicle are determined in the third step.

The SBRP is represented using a complete directed graph in [28,29]. Further, several metaheuristics are presented and tested. The authors conclude that

Variable Neighborhood Search (VNS) yields the best results on instances of moderate size, while a PILOT/GRASP hybrid turns out to be superior on large instances. A neighborhood search is also used in [17]. Two formulations for the SBRP are also developed; a routing model and a step model, both incorporated in a Large Neighborhood Search (LNS). The routing model uses an arc-indexed formulation, while the step model allocates all station visits to routes.

In [34], the SBRP is solved in combination with the tactical level problem of finding the optimal states. The routes from the SBRP must satisfy the service level requirements from an inventory problem. The objective is to minimize the maximal route length, hence it is formulated as a makespan problem. To solve the model the authors propose a cluster first route second heuristic.

Four possible formulations of the SBRP are tested and discussed in [8]. To handle the exponential number of subtour eliminating constraints, a B&C algorithm is proposed in addition to both valid inequalities and separation procedures. The authors conclude that the subtour elimination and separation techniques proposed by [18] for the 1-PDTSP give the best computational results.

A decomposition method is introduced in [36], consisting of a request generation algorithm and a *bike request scheduling problem* (BRSP). The request generation algorithm uses various data to generate repositioning requests. A request includes the location and number of bikes to be picked up or delivered, a time window and an importance weight. The BRSP determines which requests to execute and assigns them to vehicles. The objective is to minimize the total weight of rejected requests.

The objective of the SBRP-model in [27] is to maximize the number of rebalanced stations, only allowing pickup and delivery of full truckloads of bikes. The authors use a heuristic that solves the one-vehicle problem for each vehicle.

In [13], the SBRP is decomposed using a Benders decomposition scheme. The subproblem determines the pickup and delivery quantities along a fixed route of station visits, while the master problem finds new routes visiting all stations with too few or too many bikes. In a later study, [12], the authors use insights from [13] to solve the SBRP formulation from [6]. Whilst [6] could only find heuristic solutions for realistically sized instances, the method from [12] yields optimal solutions.

Table 1 shows a comparison of the main characteristics of the SBRP models in the studies surveyed above, as well as some key information about the solution methods. Note that the mathematical model proposed in Sect. 3 is also included in the table. The numbers in the top row correspond to the numbers in Table 2.

From the table it becomes evident that half of the studies solve the problem with only one service vehicle, even though most problems of realistic size use several. Note that many articles use clustering algorithms. By assigning each cluster to a vehicle, the SBRP could be solved once for each vehicle. Among the studies allowing multiple vehicles, two assume the fleet to be homogeneous. Half of the studies allow multiple visits to a station, while the other half does not. When the deviation between the optimal and initial state is larger than the vehicle capacity, allowing multiple visits to each station seems most reasonable.

Table 1. Comparison of SBRP Articles. The numbers in the table header are explained in Table 2

Parameter	1	2	3	4	5	6	7	8	9	10	11	12	13	14
Multiple vehicles	No	No	Yes	Yes	Yes	No	No	Yes	Yes	No	No	Yes	Yes	Yes
Heterogeneous fleet	n/a	n/a	Yes	Yes	Yes	n/a	n/a	No	Yes	n/a	n/a	No	Yes	Yes
One vehicle can visit a station multiple times	Yes	Yes	No/Yes two mod.	Yes	Yes	No	No	No	Yes	No	Yes	No	No	Yes
Several vehicles can visit the same station	n/a	n/a	Yes	Yes	Yes	n/a	n/a	No	Yes	n/a	n/a	No	No	Yes
Modeling loading/unloading	No cost for l/unl.	No cost for l/unl.	Depends on quantity	Average time for station	No cost for l/unl.	Depends on quantity	No cost for l/unl.	Time for each request	Average time for station	Depends on quantity	No cost for l/unl.	Average time for station	Depends on quantity	Depends on quantity
Selective pickup/delivery	Yes	Yes	Yes	Yes	Yes	No	Yes	Yes	Yes	No	Yes	No	Yes	Yes
Stations used as temporal inventories	No	Yes	Yes	No	Yes	No	No	No	No	No	Yes	No	Yes	No
Allows non-perfect rebalancing	No	No	Yes	No	No	Yes	No	Yes	Yes	No	No	Yes	Yes	Yes
Objective function	Min. cost	Min. cost	Min. dev. and cost	Min. dev & operations	Min. longest route	Min. penalty func.	Min. cost	Min. rejected requests	Min. dev. and cost	Min. dev. and cost	Min. cost	Max. rebal. nodes	Min. dev. and cost	Min. dev. and time
Subtour elimination	Many new var. & cons.	Many new var. & cons.	MTZ / Time	Heuristics	Time	MTZ	MTZ, Sep. cut	Time	Time / Route	Separation & cut	Separation & cut	A variant of MTZ	MTZ	Strengthened MTZ
Solution method	n/a	B&C & Tabu search	Heuristics & exact	PILOT, GRASP, VNS	Cluster first route second	Tabu search	Exact: B&C	n/a	LNS	Exact: Benders decomp.	Exact: Benders cut	Heuristics & exact	Cluster first route second	Exact
Size of solvable instances	n/a	1v., 100st.	1v., 60st.	21v., 700st.	5v., 135st.	1v., 400st.	1v., 50st.	n/a	6v., 240st.	1v., 50st.	1v., 60st.	5v., 100st.	3v., 200st.	2v., 15st.
Based on article (table header as reference)	n/a	1	n/a	n/a	n/a	3	n/a	n/a	4	n/a	2 & 10	n/a	3	n/a

Table 2. Articles overview for Table 1

1	Benchimol et al. [2]	8	Sörensen and Dilip [36]
2	Chemla et al. [6]	9	Gaspero et al. [17]
3	Raviv et al. [31]	10	Erdoğan et al. [13]
4	Rainer-Harbach et al. [28,29]	11	Erdoğan et al. [12]
5	Schuijbroek et al. [34]	12	O'Mahony and Shmoys [27]
6	Ho and Szeto [19]	13	Forma et al. [14]
7	Dell'Amico et al. [8]	14	Espegren et al. (this study)

Five studies assume that there is no time usage or cost associated with the loading and unloading operations at the stations, three use an average time and five studies let the time usage depend on the number of bikes handled. Note that none of the studies take traffic congestion into account, but presume the driving time between two stations to be constant. Just one study, [27], allows only full truckloads.

The studies by [2,6,8,12,13,34] minimize the time and/or cost associated with repositioning the bikes. In these studies, the solutions are only valid if the number of deviations is zero, i.e. the system is perfectly re-balanced. The remaining studies use objective functions that in various ways minimize the number of deviations.

All but two studies [2,36] include computational experiments on either theoretical or real instances. The majority use some kind of heuristics to solve the instances. All studies that use exact methods fail to find the optimal solution when the problem size increases and only yield upper and lower bounds. Since the problems include binary and/or integer variables, a common approach is to use B&C algorithms. The cuts can be generated using inequalities from [18] or using Benders decomposition [12]. Popular heuristics are tabu search and VNS/LNS. In [14] the problem is decomposed, and one part is solved by a heuristic and another part using exact methods.

The studies using a time-variable do not need subtour eliminating constraints. Among the remaining articles, the Miller-Tucker-Zemlin (MTZ) formulation [25] is widely used to avoid subtours, while three studies, [8,12,13], eliminate subtours using separation algorithms and cuts.

3 Mathematical Formulation

In this section, we propose a new mathematical model for the SBRP. The objective of the model is to minimize a weighted combination of the total deviation in the number of bikes at each station from the optimal state at the time limit and the time used. We assume a heterogeneous fleet of service vehicles that start and finish their routes empty at the depot. Several vehicles can visit the same station and a single vehicle can visit the same station several times. We presume

Table 3. Notation used in the mathematical formulation

Sets	
$\mathcal{N}$	Set of stations, indexed by i, j
$\mathcal{V}$	Set of vehicles, indexed by v
$\mathcal{M}_i$	Set of possible visits at station i, indexed by m, n
Parameters	
T_{ij}^D	Driving time between stations i and j
T^P	Time used for parking a vehicle
T^H	Handling time used for loading or unloading a bike
$\overline{T}$	Time limit for operation of service vehicles
Q_v	Capacity of vehicle v
J_i	1 if station i is a pickup station, and -1 if it is a delivery station
α	Weight on deviations in the objective function relative to time usage
$\overline{A}$	Maximum number of station visits for a vehicle
I_i	Initial state, number of bikes at station i
O_i	Optimal state, number of bikes at station i
Variables	
x_{imjnv}	1 if vehicle v is driving directly from station visit (i, m) to station visit (j, n), 0 otherwise
f_{ijv}	Total number of bikes carried by vehicle v between stations i and j
q_{iv}	Number of bikes either picked up or delivered at station i by vehicle v
y_i	Final state, number of bikes at station i
u_{imv}	The sequence number in which station visit (i, m) is made by vehicle v

the driving time between stations to be constant and independent of the hour. In addition to the driving time, each vehicle uses a fixed parking time at each station visit. Time used to load and unload bikes at a station is proportional to the number of bikes handled plus a given parking time. All stations are defined as either *pickup stations* or *delivery stations* depending on their initial state relative to their optimal state. It is not possible to pick up bicycles at a delivery station or deliver them at a pickup station.

Each station $i \in \mathcal{N}$ has a set of possible visits $\mathcal{M}_i$. Note that the depot is included in this set. Our formulation uses arc flow variables x_{imjnv}, $i \in \mathcal{N}$, $m \in \mathcal{M}_i$, $j \in \mathcal{N}$, $n \in \mathcal{M}_j$, $v \in \mathcal{V}$ indicating whether vehicle v drives from station visit (i,m) to station visit (j,n) or not, where m and n are the station visit numbers. The entire notation is presented in Table 3.

$$\min \quad \alpha \sum_{i \in \mathcal{N}} J_i(y_i - O_i)$$

$$+ (1-\alpha)\left[\sum_{i \in \mathcal{N}}\sum_{m \in \mathcal{M}_i}\sum_{j \in \mathcal{N}}\sum_{n \in \mathcal{M}_j}\sum_{v \in \mathcal{V}}\left(T_{ij}^D + T^P\right)x_{imjnv} + \sum_{i \in \mathcal{N}}\sum_{v \in \mathcal{V}}T^H q_{iv}\right] \quad (1)$$

subject to:

$$\sum_{j \in \mathcal{N}}\sum_{n \in \mathcal{M}_j} x_{dvjnv} = 1 \qquad\qquad v \in \mathcal{V} \quad (2)$$

$$\sum_{i \in \mathcal{N}} \sum_{m \in \mathcal{M}_i} x_{imd(v+|\mathcal{V}|)v} = 1 \qquad v \in \mathcal{V} \quad (3)$$

$$\sum_{j \in \mathcal{N}} \sum_{n \in \mathcal{M}_j} x_{jnimv} - \sum_{j \in \mathcal{N}} \sum_{n \in \mathcal{M}_j} x_{imjnv} = 0 \qquad i \in \mathcal{N} \backslash \{d\}, m \in \mathcal{M}_i, v \in \mathcal{V} \quad (4)$$

$$\sum_{j \in \mathcal{N}} \sum_{n \in \mathcal{M}_j} \sum_{v \in \mathcal{V}} x_{imjnv} \leq 1 \qquad i \in \mathcal{N}, m \in \mathcal{M}_i \quad (5)$$

$$\sum_{j \in \mathcal{N}} f_{jiv} + J_i q_{iv} - \sum_{j \in \mathcal{N}} f_{ijv} = 0 \qquad i \in \mathcal{N}, v \in \mathcal{V} \quad (6)$$

$$y_i + \sum_{v \in \mathcal{V}} J_i q_{iv} = I_i \qquad i \in \mathcal{N} \quad (7)$$

$$\sum_{v \in \mathcal{V}} q_{iv} - J_i(I_i - O_i) \leq 0 \qquad i \in \mathcal{N} \quad (8)$$

$$f_{ijv} - \sum_{m \in \mathcal{M}_i} \sum_{n \in \mathcal{M}_j} Q_v x_{imjnv} \leq 0 \qquad i, j \in \mathcal{N}, v \in \mathcal{V} \quad (9)$$

$$\sum_{j \in \mathcal{N}} f_{djv} = 0 \qquad v \in \mathcal{V} \quad (10)$$

$$\sum_{i \in \mathcal{N}} f_{idv} = 0 \qquad v \in \mathcal{V} \quad (11)$$

$$\sum_{i \in \mathcal{N}} \sum_{m \in \mathcal{M}_i} \sum_{j \in \mathcal{N}} \sum_{n \in \mathcal{M}_j} (T_{ij}^D + T^P) x_{imjnv} + \sum_{i \in \mathcal{N}} T^H q_{iv} \leq \overline{T} \qquad v \in \mathcal{V} \quad (12)$$

$$u_{imv} - u_{jnv} + (\overline{A} - 1)x_{imjnv} + (\overline{A} - 3)x_{jnimv} \leq \overline{A} - 2$$
$$i, j \in \mathcal{N}, m \in \mathcal{M}_i, n \in \mathcal{M}_j, v \in \mathcal{V} \quad (13)$$

$$x_{imjnv} \in \{0,1\} \qquad i, j \in \mathcal{N}, m \in \mathcal{M}_i, n \in \mathcal{M}_j, v \in \mathcal{V} \quad (14)$$
$$f_{ijv} \geq 0, \text{integer} \qquad i, j \in \mathcal{N}, v \in \mathcal{V} \quad (15)$$
$$q_{iv} \geq 0, \text{integer} \qquad i \in \mathcal{N}, v \in \mathcal{V} \quad (16)$$
$$y_i \geq 0, \text{integer} \qquad i \in \mathcal{N} \quad (17)$$
$$u_{imv} \geq 0, \text{integer} \qquad i \in \mathcal{N}, m \in \mathcal{M}_i, v \in \mathcal{V} \quad (18)$$

The objective function (1) consists of two terms that are to be minimized. The first term is the deviation in number of bikes between the final state, y_i, and the optimal state, O_i, for all stations. Having too many and too few bikes are equally penalized. The second term is the total time used to obtain the final state. Total time corresponds to the sum of driving time, T_{ij}^D, parking time, T^P, and handling time, T^H. By setting α slightly below one, the most effective routes minimizing the deviation are found.

Constraints (2) and (3) force the vehicles to start and end at the depot, d. Symmetry at the depot is handled by stating that vehicle v uses visit numbers v and $v + |\mathcal{V}|$ when leaving and arriving at the depot, respectively. Constraints (4) ensure that a vehicle that enters a station visit, leaves the same station visit, while constraints (5) make sure all station visits happen at most once.

The loading and unloading constraints (6) ensure that the flow of bikes into station i, f_{jiv}, equals the flow out of the station, f_{ijv}, plus the net pickup, q_{iv}. Since the problem is static, only the total net pickup is considered. Constraints (7) and (8) assign values to the final state, y_i. In addition, constraints (8) give an upper bound on the net pickup at station i by vehicle v, q_{iv}.

The vehicle capacity constraints (9) make sure that a vehicle never carries more bikes along an arc than the vehicle's capacity multiplied by the number of times the arc is traversed. Constraints (10) and (11) state that the service vehicles must be empty when leaving and returning to the depot. Capacity constraints for the stations are handled implicitly. The total time spent for each vehicle is limited to $\overline{T}$ by constraints (12).

Subtours are handled in constraints (13), similar to the MTZ constraints [25], but with a strengthening proposed in [11]. Various methods for eliminating subtours have been tested, and these constraints showed to perform best.

Symmetry breaking constraints remove solutions that are mathematically different, but practically identical, while adding valid inequalities is a way of improving the solution of the linear relaxation. Various symmetry breaking constraints and valid inequalities have been tested, and the ones presented here are those found most effective.

$$\sum_{j\in\mathcal{N}} \sum_{n\in\mathcal{M}_j} \sum_{v\in\mathcal{V}} \left(x_{imjnv} - x_{i(m-1)jnv}\right) \leq 0 \qquad i \in \mathcal{N}\backslash\{d\}, m \in \mathcal{M}_i\backslash\{1\} \qquad (19)$$

$$\sum_{i\in\mathcal{N}} \sum_{m\in\mathcal{M}_i} \sum_{j\in\mathcal{N}} \sum_{n\in\mathcal{M}_j} \left(T_{ij}^D + T^P\right) \left(x_{imjnv} - x_{imjn(v+1)}\right)$$
$$+ \sum_{i\in\mathcal{N}} T^H \left(q_{iv} - q_{i(v+1)v}\right) \geq 0 \qquad v \in \mathcal{V} \backslash \{|\mathcal{V}|\} \ \Big| \ Q_v = Q_{(v+1)} \qquad (20)$$

Constraints (19) reduce symmetry by handling the station visits, so that they appear in the right sequence. By introducing constraints (20), symmetry that occurs when using a homogeneous fleet of service vehicles is reduced.

$$\sum_{v\in\mathcal{V}} q_{iv} - |(I_i - O_i)| \sum_{m\in\mathcal{M}_i} \sum_{j\in\mathcal{N}} \sum_{n\in\mathcal{M}_j} \sum_{v\in\mathcal{V}} x_{imjnv} \leq 0 \qquad\qquad i \in \mathcal{N} \quad (21)$$

$$\sum_{v\in\mathcal{V}} \sum_{m\in\mathcal{M}_i} \sum_{n\in\mathcal{M}_j} x_{imjnv} + \sum_{v\in\mathcal{V}} \sum_{m\in\mathcal{M}_i} \sum_{n\in\mathcal{M}_j} x_{jnimv} \leq 1 \quad i,j \in \mathcal{N} \ \Big| J_i = J_j \quad (22)$$

Constraints (21) force the x_{imjnv}-variables to take values closer to one or zero in the linear relaxation. For instance, for a station to be perfectly rebalanced, the sum over the x_{imjnv}-variables associated with that station must equal one.

In [6] it is shown that the arcs between two stations of similar type need not be traversed more than once, resulting in constraints (22).

Table 1 includes a comparison of this mathematical model with the models in previous studies.

4   Computational Study

The mathematical model presented in Sect. 3 has been implemented in Xpress-IVE 1.24.06 using the Mosel programming language. The computational experiments have been executed on a computer with Intel Core i7-3770 3.40 GHz processor, 16 GB of RAM and running Windows 7.

4.1   Test Instances

Based on the BSS in Oslo, Norway, six test areas (geographical regions) have been identified. Details about the areas can be found in Table 4. The areas have an estimated optimal state for each station and a driving time matrix, T_{ij}^D. A parking time, T^P, set to one minute, is added for each station, while the handling time for each bike, T^H, is set to 30 s. All areas have two service vehicles. For each area, three instances are created by varying the initial states, while all other parameters are unchanged. Note that we assume perfect re-balancing for the third instance in each area, making the instances easier to solve because of a simpler structure.

Table 4. Test areas

Area	$|\mathcal{N}|$	Avg. driving time	$\overline{T}$	$|\mathcal{V}|$	Cap. $v = 1$	Cap. $v = 2$
1	6	2 min	16 min	2	10	10
2	8	6 min	30 min	2	10	15
3	10	6 min	40 min	2	12	12
4	12	5 min	30 min	2	10	10
5	14	7 min	45 min	2	12	12

4.2   Computational Results

Various parameters in the model affect the computational time; the time limit, $\overline{T}$, the number of stations, $|\mathcal{N}|$, the maximum possible number of visits to each station, $|\mathcal{M}_i|$, and the number of service vehicles, $|\mathcal{V}|$. Among these, the time limit and the maximum possible number of visits are studied here.

Figure 3 shows that the computational time peaks when the time limit is set so that the total deviation is slightly above zero. By only changing the time limit,

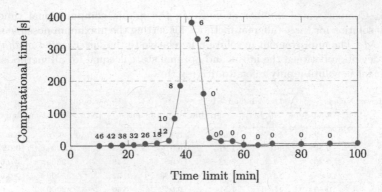

Fig. 3. The computational time depicted for different time limits, $\overline{T}$, for instance 4.1, i.e. the first instance from area 4. The numbers beside the markers indicate the total deviation between the initial and optimal state in the solution.

the computational time varies from less than one second to more than 35 min. The same pattern is seen for all instances.

The use of station visit numbers, $m, n \in \mathcal{M}_i$, is a new approach for the SBRP, allowing multiple station visits without a time-index. Though this formulation has some advantages, both the solution and the computational time depend on the value of $|\mathcal{M}_i|$, i.e. the maximum possible number of visits to each station. Each possible station visit (i, m) could be considered a distinct node in the graph. Hence, adding one element to the set $\mathcal{M}_i$ for one station i is equivalent to adding a node to the graph.

Consequences of using different values for $|\mathcal{M}_i|$ are illustrated in Table 5. The *lower bound method* is the smallest number of visits to each station to allow perfect re-balancing, defined as: $|\mathcal{M}_i| = \left\lceil \frac{|I_i - O_i|}{\min_{v \in \mathcal{V}} C_v^{\mathcal{V}}} \right\rceil$. The *lower bound +1 method* allows one more visit to each station than the *lower bound method*. The *upper bound method* is defined as $|\mathcal{M}_i| = |I_i - O_i|$. For all our test instances the total number of deviations at the stations were the same for every method, independent of $|\mathcal{M}_i|$, hence only improvement in driving time is recorded in the table. Consequently, the *lower bound method* is recommended as it yields near optimal solutions with much less computational effort.

Depending on the input parameters, the mathematical model from Sect. 3 can be solved to optimality for instances of about 15 stations. Combined with some form of clustering, this could be enough to solve many realistically sized instances.

4.3 Comparison with Rules of Thumb

Today, in the Oslo BSS, the operators utilize their experience and common sense to decide the routes and the pickup and delivery quantities. Here, two greedy rules of thumb are created to imitate the operators behavior. The first rule of thumb states that the service vehicle should visit the nearest pickup and delivery

Table 5. Comparison of number of nodes in the graph, computational times, and quality of solution for three different methods for setting the maximum possible number of visits, $\mathcal{M}_i$. The improvement in solution is relative to the *lower bound method*. Note that the deviation between the initial and optimal state is equal for all methods, hence improvement in solution only refers to driving time.

Instance	Lower bound		Lower bound +1			Upper bound		
	$\sum_{i \in \mathcal{N}} |\mathcal{M}_i|$	Comp.time	$\sum_{i \in \mathcal{N}} |\mathcal{M}_i|$	Comp.time	Imprv.in sol.	$\sum_{i \in \mathcal{N}} |\mathcal{M}_i|$	Comp.time	Imprv.in sol.
1.1	6	0.19 s	12	5.60 s	0.0 %	24	139.70 s	0.0 %
1.2	8	0.34 s	14	1.91 s	0.0 %	38	47.40 s	0.0 %
1.3	8	0.20 s	14	0.23 s	0.0 %	48	>3000 s	≥0.0 %
2.1	8	0.64 s	16	697.00 s	0.0 %	32	>3000 s	≥0.0 %
2.2	9	0.44 s	17	1.51 s	0.0 %	46	>3000 s	≥0.0 %
2.3	10	0.62 s	18	7.81 s	3.6 %	48	462.00 s	3.6 %
3.1	10	1.25 s	20	279.50 s	0.0 %	56	>3000 s	≥0.0 %
3.2	12	7.00 s	22	281.00 s	0.0 %	64	>3000 s	≥0.0 %
3.3	12	1.25 s	22	74.70 s	0.0 %	58	>3000 s	≥0.0 %
4.1	12	8.40 s	24	>3000 s	≥0.0 %	52	>3000 s	≥0.0 %
4.2	15	17.00 s	27	2089.00 s	0.0 %	74	>3000 s	≥0.0 %
4.3	12	0.40 s	24	20.30 s	3.3 %	62	286.50 s	3.3 %
5.1	14	69.00 s	28	>3000 s	≥0.0 %	70	>3000 s	≥0.0 %
5.2	16	15.30 s	30	2708.00 s	0.0 %	86	>3000 s	≥0.0 %
5.3	16	1.07 s	30	57.70 s	7.7 %	106	>3000 s	≥7.7 %
Average	n/a	8.21 s	n/a	>814.95 s	≥1.6 %	n/a	>2262.00 s	≥1.6 %

stations in sequence, unless it is able to meet the demand at two subsequent stations of the same type. The vehicle should serve the entire demand of bikes at the stations, but is restricted by its capacity and the time limit for re-balancing. The second rule of thumb works quite similar, but the vehicle always goes to the station with the largest deviation.

A comparison is made between the results obtained with these rules of thumb and the ones obtained by solving the model from Sect. 3. The comparison is only made for instances 2.1 and 3.1, and to simplify only one vehicle is used. With regard to deviations, the SBRP-model finds solutions that are between 20.0 and 56.6 % better than the two rules of thumb. A characteristic for the optimal solution is that it has less slack in the time restriction than the rules of thumb.

4.4 Practical Use of the Model

Six of the 13 articles listed in Table 1 minimize time usage or cost, given that the system will be perfectly re-balanced. By assuming zero deviation, several simplifications can be made, and the computational time will decrease significantly, as indicated in Fig. 3.

It is possible to utilize intervals, rather than a fixed number, to describe the optimal state. This provides more flexibility to the model, presumably making it harder to solve, but it may be more realistic. An alternative to use intervals, is to punish large deviations relatively more than small, for example by punishing the square of the deviation.

In addition to serving as a tool for operational planning, the SBRP-model could be used to support both strategic and tactical decisions. Analyzing changes in parameter values can be done by re-solving the problem for different values. By increasing the time limit for re-balancing operations, the number of deviations could go down. The operator may use this information to decide whether to expand the time limit or not. To support the decision of whether to acquire or dispose a service vehicle, the SBRP-model may be used to quantify the effect. Increased vehicle capacity leads, as expected, to a reduced objective value. At a certain point, the objective value reaches its lowest point, where the total deviation is zero or the time limit restricts the objective value from decreasing further. To compare a change in the objective value with the cost of changing a parameter, the system operator is referred to a cost-benefit analysis.

5   Concluding Remarks

As the SBRP is a relatively novel problem, a review of the research made on the topic is missing in the literature. An extensive literature survey, consisting of the review and systematic comparison of 13 studies, has therefore been conducted. As can be seen from Table 1, many studies make assumptions that are unrealistic for most practical problems. We have proposed a new mathematical model for the SBRP that makes fewer assumptions and allows more possibilities than many existing models. For instance, this model allows a heterogeneous fleet, multiple visits to each station, and non-perfect re-balancing.

Since we have focused on the modeling and not on solution algorithms in this study, we are only able to solve relatively small instances. The model should, however, provide a good starting point for proposing more advanced solution methods, for instance as an important part of a clustering algorithm for solving realistically sized instances.

References

1. Angeloudis, P., Hu, J., Bell, M.G.: A strategic repositioning algorithm for bicycle-sharing schemes. Transportmetrica A Transp. Sci. **10**(8), 759–774 (2014)
2. Benchimol, M., Benchimol, P., Chappert, B., De La Taille, A., Laroche, F., Meunier, F., Robinet, L.: Balancing the stations of a self service "bike hire" system. RAIRO Oper. Res. **45**(1), 37–61 (2011)
3. Berbeglia, G., Cordeau, J.F., Gribkovskaia, I., Laporte, G.: Static pickup and delivery problems: a classification scheme and survey. Top **15**(1), 1–31 (2007)
4. Brinkmann, J., Ulmer, M.W., Mattfeld, D.C.: Short-term strategies for stochastic inventory routing in bike sharing systems. Transp. Res. Procedia **10**, 364–373 (2015)
5. Caggiani, L., Ottomanelli, M.: A modular soft computing based method for vehicles repositioning in bike-sharing systems. Procedia Soc. Behav. Sci. **54**, 675–684 (2012)
6. Chemla, D., Meunier, F., Calvo, R.W.: Bike sharing systems: solving the static rebalancing problem. Discrete Optim. **10**(2), 120–146 (2013)

7. Contardo, C., Morency, C., Rousseau, L.M.: Balancing a dynamic public bike-sharing system. Technical report CIRRELT-2012-09, Universitè de Montrèal, Montrèal, Canada (2012). http://claudio.contardo.org/wp-content/uploads/2011/09/CIRRELT-2012-09.pdf
8. Dell'Amico, M., Hadjicostantinou, E., Iori, M., Novellani, S.: The bike sharing rebalancing problem: mathematical formulations and benchmark instances. Omega **45**, 7–19 (2014)
9. DeMaio, P.: Bike-sharing: history, impacts, models of provision, and future. J. Public Transp. **12**(4), 3 (2009)
10. DeMaio, P., Meddin, R.: The bike-sharing world map (2015). www.bikesharingmap.com. Accessed 06 Oct 2015
11. Desrochers, M., Laporte, G.: Improvements and extensions to the Miller-Tucker-Zemlin subtour elimination constraints. Oper. Res. Lett. **10**(1), 27–36 (1991)
12. Erdoğan, G., Battarra, M., Calvo, R.: An exact algorithm for the static rebalancing problem arising in bicycle sharing systems. Eur. J. Oper. Res. **245**(3), 667–679 (2015)
13. Erdoğan, G., Laporte, G., Calvo, R.W.: The static bicycle relocation problem with demand intervals. Eur. J. Oper. Res. **238**(2), 451–457 (2014)
14. Forma, I.A., Raviv, T., Tzur, M.: A 3-step math heuristic for the static repositioning problem in bike-sharing systems. Transp. Res. Part B Methodol. **71**, 230–247 (2015)
15. Fricker, C., Gast, N.: Incentives and redistribution in homogeneous bike-sharing systems with stations of finite capacity. EURO J. Transp. Logistics **3**, 1–31 (2014)
16. García-Palomares, J.C., Gutiérrez, J., Latorre, M.: Optimizing the location of stations in bike-sharing programs: a GIS approach. Appl. Geogr. **35**(1), 235–246 (2012)
17. Gaspero, L., Rendl, A., Urli, T.: Balancing bike sharing systems with constraint programming. Constraints **21**(2), 318–348 (2016)
18. Hernández-Pérez, H., Salazar-González, J.J.: The one-commodity pickup-and-delivery traveling salesman problem: Inequalities and algorithms. Networks **50**(4), 258–272 (2007)
19. Ho, S.C., Szeto, W.: Solving a static repositioning problem in bike-sharing systems using iterated tabu search. Transp. Res. Part E: Logistics and Transp. Rev. **69**, 180–198 (2014)
20. Kaspi, M., Raviv, T., Tzur, M.: Detection of unusable bicycles in bike-sharing systems (2015). http://www.eng.tau.ac.il/talraviv/Publications/DetectionUnusableBicycles.pdf, working paper. Tel-Aviv University. Accessed 08 Nov 2015
21. Kloimüllner, C., Papazek, P., Hu, B., Raidl, G.R.: Balancing bicycle sharing systems: an approach for the dynamic case. In: Blum, C., Ochoa, G. (eds.) EvoCOP 2014. LNCS, vol. 8600, pp. 73–84. Springer, Heidelberg (2014)
22. Laporte, G., Meunier, F., Calvo, W.R.: Shared mobility systems. 4OR **13**(4), 341–360 (2015)
23. Lin, J.R., Yang, T.H.: Strategic design of public bicycle sharing systems with service level constraints. Transp. Res. Part E Logistics Transp. Rev. **47**(2), 284–294 (2011)
24. Midgley, P.: Bicycle-sharing schemes: enhancing sustainable mobility in urban areas. In: 19th Session of the Commission on Sustainable Development, 02 May 2011. United Nations, Department of Economic and Social Affairs, Background Paper No. 8, May 2011

25. Miller, C.E., Tucker, A.W., Zemlin, R.A.: Integer programming formulation of traveling salesman problems. J. ACM (JACM) **7**(4), 326–329 (1960)
26. Nair, R., Miller-Hooks, E., Hampshire, R.C., Bušić, A.: Large-scale vehicle sharing systems: analysis of Vélib'. Int. J. Sustain. Transp. **7**(1), 85–106 (2013)
27. O'Mahony, E., Shmoys, D.B.: Data analysis and optimization for (citi) bike sharing. In: Twenty-Ninth AAAI Conference on Artificial Intelligence, 25 January 2015. Association for the Advancement of Artificial Intelligence, January 2015
28. Rainer-Harbach, M., Papazek, P., Hu, B., Raidl, G.R.: Balancing bicycle sharing systems: a variable neighborhood search approach. In: Middendorf, M., Blum, C. (eds.) EvoCOP 2013. LNCS, vol. 7832, pp. 121–132. Springer, Heidelberg (2013)
29. Rainer-Harbach, M., Papazek, P., Raidl, G.R., Hu, B., Kloimüllner, C.: PILOT, GRASP, and VNS approaches for the static balancing of bicycle sharing systems. J. Global Optim. **63**(3), 597–629 (2015)
30. Raviv, T., Kolka, O.: Optimal inventory management of a bike-sharing station. IIE Trans. **45**(10), 1077–1093 (2013)
31. Raviv, T., Tzur, M., Forma, I.A.: Static repositioning in a bike-sharing system: models and solution approaches. EURO J. Transp. Logistics **2**(3), 187–229 (2013)
32. Regue, R., Recker, W.: Proactive vehicle routing with inferred demand to solve the bikesharing rebalancing problem. Transp. Res. Part E: Logistics Transp. Rev. **72**, 192–209 (2014)
33. Romero, J.P., Ibeas, A., Moura, J.L., Benavente, J., Alonso, B.: A simulation-optimization approach to design efficient systems of bike-sharing. Procedia Soc. Behav. Sci. **54**, 646–655 (2012)
34. Schuijbroek, J., Hampshire, R., van Hoeve, W.J.: Inventory rebalancing and vehicle routing in bike sharing systems (2013). http://repository.cmu.edu/cgi/viewcontent.cgi?article=2490&context=tepper, working paper. Tepper School of Business. Accessed Feb 2013–01 Dec 2015
35. Shaheen, S., Guzman, S., Zhang, H.: Bikesharing in Europe, the Americas, and Asia: past, present, and future. Transp. Res. Rec. J. Transp. Res. Board **2143**, 159–167 (2010)
36. Sörensen, K., Dilip, D.: The (city) bike request scheduling problem-a novel approach to solve the city bike repositioning problem. In: Toklu, Y.C., Bekdas, G. (eds.) Metaheuristics and Engineering, Workshop of the EURO Working Group, vol. 15, pp. 157–161. Bilecik Şeyh Edebali University (2014)
37. Vogel, P., Ehmke, J.F., Mattfeld, D.C.: Service network design of bike sharing systems (2015). https://www.tu-braunschweig.de/Medien-DB/winfo/publications/service_network_design_of_bike_sharing_systems.pdf, working paper. Technische Unversität Braunschweig. Accessed 24 Mar 2015–24 Sep 2015
38. Vogel, P., Greiser, T., Mattfeld, D.C.: Understanding bike-sharing systems using data mining: exploring activity patterns. Procedia Soc. Behav. Sci. **20**, 514–523 (2011)
39. Vogel, P., Neumann Saavedra, B.A., Mattfeld, D.C.: A hybrid metaheuristic to solve the resource allocation problem in bike sharing systems. In: Blesa, M.J., Blum, C., Voß, S. (eds.) HM 2014. LNCS, vol. 8457, pp. 16–29. Springer, Heidelberg (2014)

Service Network Design of Bike Sharing Systems with Resource Constraints

Bruno Albert Neumann-Saavedra[1(✉)], Teodor Gabriel Crainic[2,3],
Bernard Gendron[3,5], Dirk Christian Mattfeld[1], and Michael Römer[4]

[1] Decision Support Group, University of Braunschweig,
Mühlenpfordtstraße 23, 38106 Braunschweig, Germany
{b.neumann-saavedra,d.mattfeld}@tu-braunschweig.de
[2] Department of Management and Technology,
Université du Québec à Montréal, Station Centre-Ville, P.O. Box 8888,
Montréal H3C 3P8, Canada
[3] Interuniversity Research Centre on Enterprise Networks,
Logistics and Transportation (CIRRELT), Université du Québec à Montréal,
Station Centre-ville, Montréal, Québec H3C 3P8, Canada
teodorgabriel.crainic@cirrelt.net, bernard.gendron@cirrelt.ca
[4] Institute of Business Information Systems and Operations Research,
Martin Luther University, Halle-Wittenberg,
Universitätsring 3, 06108 Halle (Saale), Germany
michael.roemer@wiwi.uni-halle.de
[5] Department of Computer Science and Operations Research,
Université de Montréal, Station Centre-Ville, P.O. Box 6128,
Montréal H3C 3J7, Canada

Abstract. Station-based bike sharing systems provide an inexpensive
and flexible supplement to public transportation systems. However, due
to spatial and temporal demand variation, stations tend to run full or
empty over the course of a day. In order to establish a high service level,
that is, a high percentage of users being able to perform their desired
trips, it is therefore necessary to redistribute bikes among stations to
ensure suitable time-of-day fill levels. As available resources are scarce,
the tactical planning level aims to determine efficient master tours periodically executed by redistribution vehicles. We present a service network
design formulation for the bike sharing redistribution problem taking into
account trip-based user demand and explicitly considering service times
for bike pick-up and delivery. We solve the problem using a two-stage
MILP-based heuristic and present computational results for small real-
world instances. In addition, we evaluate the performance of the master
tours for multiple demand scenarios.

Keywords: Bike sharing systems · Bike redistribution · Tactical planning · Service network design · Master tours

© Springer International Publishing Switzerland 2016
A. Paias et al. (Eds.): ICCL 2016, LNCS 9855, pp. 352–366, 2016.
DOI: 10.1007/978-3-319-44896-1_23

1   Introduction

Station-based bike sharing systems (BSS) enhance the public transportation system in several cities by offering bike rentals. After registration, users can perform trips between any pair of stations scattered in the service area. Bike rentals are usually free of charge for the first (half) hour, additional driving time incurs fees. Thus, BSS have become a valid and inexpensive approach for the "last mile" between the metro/bus station and the final destination. For a review of the history of BSS, see [1].

The percentage of users who can successfully perform desired trips, defining the service level, is an important measure for the reliability of a BSS. For a high reliability, a sufficient number of bikes and free bike racks need to be provided at stations within the day. Still, given spatial and temporal demand variation, together with different trip purposes such as commuting, leisure and tourism, ensuring a high service level is a challenging task [2]. For instance, stations near to working areas run full in the morning peak hour and empty in the afternoon peak hour. Full and empty stations may negatively affect the service level since users cannot return or rental bikes at them, respectively. To ensure availability of bikes and free bike racks when demanded, bikes need to be redistributed among stations. Resources such as vehicles, fuel and drivers are available to realize the necessary redistribution operations. Unlimited resources would fulfill user demand by setting up many redistribution operations with few bikes involved e.g., see [3]. However, given that due to the offered free-of-charge user trips, the revenues produced by BSS are limited, the resources available for redistribution operations are scarce. In fact, redistribution operations incur the most significant operational costs, putting on risk the bike sharing's profitability [4].

Information systems provide real-time status of BSS, including fill levels, user trips, and weather conditions. In addition, external information systems can be used for supporting the operation of vehicles, see e.g. [5,6]. Although future user demand is unknown, it is possible to obtain estimates through the analysis of historical trip data, see e.g. [2]. Outputs of such analyses are used to anticipate at which time of day the rental or return rate is critical at particular stations. Although user demand varies between days, days with similar characteristics, e.g. commute activitiy during workdays in a summer season exhibit very similar demand patterns. Given these recurring patterns, it makes sense to think about a "redistribution master plan" indicating how the redistribution vehicles should be regularly operated and forming the backbone for the operational redistribution planning.

In recent years, shared mobility systems have attracted a considerable amount of research regarding e.g. the location of stations, fill level at stations, user incentives, as well as the car/bike redistributions (for a review, see [7]). The BSS redistribution problem is related to the traditional inventory routing problem [8] since at stations, inventory decisions regarding the fill levels are made. A challenging feature of BSS is that bikes can be moved several times by both users and distribution vehicles. In the majority of related articles, however, it is assumed that repositioning only occurs during the night when user demand and traffic are considered as negligible; see for example [9–11].

Contrastingly, publications dealing with intra-day bike redistribution are still scarce. Most of these publications assume perfect knowledge of the user demand and consider the redistribution decisions in terms of bike flows through a time space network. They differ, however, in the way of handling user demand and in the considered objective functions. The approach presented in [12] assumes that nodes of the time space network can be partitioned into rental and return nodes, avoiding that both situations occur simultaneously. In other words, the user demand is not defined in terms of bike flows, but is associated at the nodes of the time space network as a rental or return request. Bikes are artificially added or removed when demand is not fulfilled, leading to an imbalance of the number of bikes in the system. Redistribution costs for operating vehicles are not considered in this approach. In [13], a multi-objective approach is proposed. User demand at stations is represented in terms of a expected accumulated demand over time. The expected unfulfilled demand is counted and penalized. A mismatch between initial and final fill levels for the given time horizon is also penalized. However, the initial fill level is not an output of the approach but selected arbitrarily. In [14], a cluster-first route-second approach is proposed, classifying stations according to user demand into pick-up or delivery stations. In [3], time-dependent origin-destination matrices are proposed for the resource allocation problem. The approach yields station-to-station redistribution decisions without considering the fact that these need to be performed by vehicles in a connected tour. In all papers described above, the service times for (un)loading bikes from the vehicle are neglected or assumed to be constant without regard to the number of (un)loaded bikes. To sum up, in the current literature, we identify a lack of properly representing critical issues such as time-dependent bike fill levels, service times incurred by redistribution decisions and user demand for the (intra-day) BSS redistribution problem in an optimization-based decision support system.

In this paper, we consider the intra-day BSS redistribution problem at a tactical planning level. At this planning level, the aim is to efficiently use the limited resources in order to yield a high expected service level for characteristic user demand patterns, e.g. for a working day in a given season. Redistribution operations are scheduled in master tours periodically operated by the redistribution vehicles. It is assumed that master tours are adjusted in an operational planning level based on the real-time BSS status by adapting the number of redistributed bicycles and/or by locally changing the route of the vehicle. The BSS redistribution problem can be addressed by service network design formulations [15] maximizing the service level while taking both vehicle fleet and monetary budget limitations into account. Outputs are the time-dependent fill level at stations and the necessary master tours to achieve these targeted fill levels.

We make the following contributions: First, we present a mixed-integer linear programming (MILP) formulation for the service network design of BSS. The MILP integrates the service level, the time-dependent fill levels, the master tours, the redistribution decisions, and the resources used for redistribution purpose. Second, based on a "small" real-world BSS, we conduct computational experiments to test different settings of available resources. Finally, we evaluate the quality of the master tours under different demand realizations and point to future research opportunities.

2 Problem Description and Model

The tactical BSS redistribution problem to be considered in this paper can be viewed as a special variant of a service network design problem. In this section, we first describe the key elements of this problem: The network underlying the BSS, the representation of fill levels, the tours conducted by the redistribution vehicle, the forecast of user demands as well as the service level and the costs incurred by the redistribution. This description, along with the introduced notation, forms the basis for the mathematical formulation of the problem as a mixed-integer linear program presented at the end of this section.

2.1 The Network

The BSS infrastructure is defined on the set $\mathcal{N}'$ of physical nodes, i.e., the bike stations, and links connecting them, where the vehicles and users are allowed to drive. Each station $i \in \mathcal{N}'$ has a capacity of c_i bike racks. The vehicles are parked at the depot $\{0\} \in \mathcal{N}'$ considered as a station with big capacity and no bike demand. A total number of b' bikes are distributed among all stations. Theft of bikes, as well as damage of bikes or racks at stations, are neglected. It is supposed that the redistribution vehicles do not realize intermediate stops in order to simply represent them in terms of the corresponding vehicle paths. Figure 1 illustrates a small BSS infrastructure with three bike stations, two bikes allocated at each station, and the depot where a redistribution vehicle is parked. The solid line represents vehicle paths whereas the dashed lines are potential user trajectories between stations.

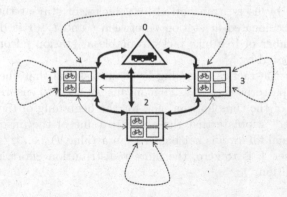

Fig. 1. A small BSS infrastructure.

Let $\mathscr{T}$ be the target time horizon, e.g., a day, discretized into $\mathscr{T} = \{t\} = \{0, ..., T_{MAX}\}$ chronologically indexed time points; two adjacent time points represent one time period. We create a time space network represented by the graph $\mathscr{G} = (\mathscr{N}, \mathscr{A}_U \cup \mathscr{A}_V \cup \mathscr{A}_H)$. Each node $(i,t) \in \mathscr{N}$ represents a physical node $i \in \mathscr{N}'$ and a time point $t \in \mathscr{T}$. Each node (i,t) has a successor, i.e., the next time realization of the physical node, defined as $(i, t+1)$, if $t < T_{MAX}$.

The arc set $\mathscr{A}_U$ contains the arcs $e_U = ((i,t),(j,\bar{t})), \bar{t} = t + \Delta_{ij}^U, \forall i,j \in \mathscr{N}' \setminus \{0\}, \forall t, \bar{t} \in \mathscr{T} \mid \bar{t} > t$, where Δ_{ij}^U is the number of periods a that a user requires to drive from station i to station j. Each arc e_U of the set $\mathscr{A}_U$ models the possibility that users realize trips, renting a bike from station i at time t and returning it at station j at time $\bar{t}$. The arc set $\mathscr{A}_V$ contains the arcs $e_V = ((i,t),(j,\bar{t})), \bar{t} = t + \Delta_{ij}^V, \forall i,j \in \mathscr{N}', \forall t, \bar{t} \in \mathscr{T} \mid \bar{t} > t$, where Δ_{ij}^V is the required number of periods that a vehicle needs to drive from station i to j. Each arc e_V of the set $\mathscr{A}_V$ models the possibility that a redistribution vehicle drives from physical node i at time t arriving at physical node j and, in the case that a bike station is located there, serving it until time $\bar{t}$. If the physical node j is the depot, the vehicle park there until time $\bar{t}$. Finally, the arc set $\mathscr{A}_H$ contains the arcs $e_H = ((i,t),(i,t+1)), \forall i \in \mathscr{N}', \forall t, \bar{t} \in \mathscr{T} \mid \bar{t} > t$. The arc set $\mathscr{A}_H$ models holding arcs, i.e., the possibility that a vehicle, loaded or not, stays in a physical node from time t to time $\bar{t}$. Holding arcs allow the vehicle to stay at a station for additional time in order to service the station with more bikes, if necessary. The union of both sets $\mathscr{A}_V \cup \mathscr{A}_H$ is referred to the set of vehicle arcs. The three type of arc sets allow bike movements through the time-dependent network. Thus, in the case that bikes are "moved" by one of these arcs, these bikes are not available for new purposes from the departure node (i,t), appearing instantaneously at the destination node $(j,\bar{t})$.

2.2   The Time-Dependent Fill Levels

Let I_i^t be the number of bikes at physical node i and time point t including both the bikes allocated at the station located in i and plus the load of the vehicles parked in the physical node i at time point t. Immediately after t, bikes can either be rented by users, transported by vehicles, or stay at the station. The number of bikes allocated at station i between t and $t+1$ is denoted by β_i^t, whereas the number of free bike racks available at station i from time t until time $t+1$ is denoted by γ_i^t.

Dealing with the tactical planning level, we assume that the user demand exhibits similar patterns each day. That means we need to ensure a suitable fill level at the end of the time horizon, i.e., for the beginning of the new day. For that, we explicitly stipulate that the absolute value of the mismatch between the initial and final fill level is not bigger than a value Ψ, i.e., $|I_i^0 - I_i^{T_{MAX}}| \leq \Psi$. Clearly, the closer Ψ is to zero, the more redistribution effort is necessary to satisfy this condition.

2.3   The Vehicle Routing and Bike Redistribution Decisions

The size of the vehicle fleet available during the time horizon is denoted by $v \in \mathbb{Z}^+$ bounded by a maximal vehicle fleet size V_{MAX}. Each vehicle can transport a maximal lot size of l bikes. Let $y_{ij}^{t\bar{t}} \in \mathbb{Z}^+$ be a variable capturing the number of vehicles which implement the corresponding vehicle arc in $\mathscr{A}_V \cup \mathscr{A}_H$. When a vehicle arc is implemented, the driver can handle, i.e., pick up or deliver, a maximal number of $\delta_{ij}^{t\bar{t}} \in \mathbb{Z}^+$ bikes at station j until time $\bar{t}$. Note that $\delta_{ij}^{t\bar{t}}$ depends on the time left after the driving time of the vehicle. The number of picked up or delivered bikes at station j until time $\bar{t}$ is denoted by $\rho_j^{\bar{t}} \in \mathbb{Z}^+$ or $\sigma_j^{\bar{t}} \in \mathbb{Z}^+$, respectively. Holding arcs allow the bike handling at stations during several time periods if it is required. $x_{ij}^{t\bar{t}} \in \mathbb{R}^+, \forall ((i,t),(j,\bar{t})) \in \mathscr{A}_V \cup \mathscr{A}_H$ represents the total load of the vehicle implementing the corresponding vehicle arc e_V, i.e., the vehicle bike flows. In order to avoid symmetries in the optimization model, the presented formulation operates with a set of aggregated vehicles. Note that assumption is only suitable when the master tours are implemented by a homogeneous vehicle fleet.

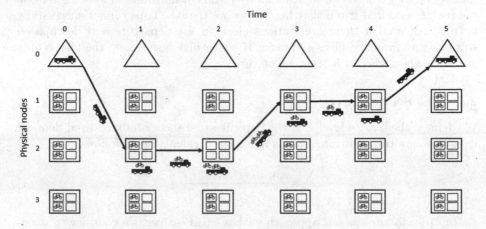

Fig. 2. Time-space network. One redistribution vehicle operating.

A time-space diagram is showed in Fig. 2 based on the BSS infrastructure presented above. The vertical axis represents the stations (and the depot), whereas the horizontal axis represents the time horizon, discretized into 6 time points. At each node (i, t) the the number of bikes on it, i.e., I_i^t, is illustrated. The solid lines represents all the vehicle arcs which describe the master tour operated by the vehicle. Let suppose that the driver can handle only one bike per time period. Thus, the vehicle starts from the depot at time point 0, arriving at station 2, and picking up one bike until time point 1. For loading one additional bike at the vehicle, the driver has to stay at the station one additional time period, i.e., a holding arc is implemented at station 2 between time points 1 and 2. Thus, at time point 2, two bikes are still on the physical node 2, but now the load of the vehicle, whereas the station is actually empty. At time point 2, the vehicle drives from station 2 to station 1, handling one bike from the load of the vehicle to the station. To deliver the second bike at the station, a holding arc is implemented again. Now, the loaded vehicle drives from station 2 to station 1, and the delivering process begins. Finally, the vehicle returns to the depot. Note that for the sake of clarity, Fig. 2 does not illustrate user trips through the network.

2.4   The Representation of the User Demand

We assume that the demand can be defined in terms of time-dependent origin-destination matrices representing expected user bike flows. Let $\zeta_{ij}^{t\bar{t}} \in \mathbb{Z}^+, \forall e_U \in \mathscr{A}_U$ be the number of expected user bike flows for the corresponding arc e_U. The decision variable $f_{ij}^{t\bar{t}} \in \mathbb{Z}^+, \forall e_U \in \mathscr{A}_U$. represents the user bike flows actually met. An expected user bike flow is only met if there is at least one bike at the departure station i and time t and at least one free bike rack at the destination station j and time point $\bar{t}$. Otherwise, the expected user bike flow is not realized.

Note that this demand representation has some limitations: It is assumed that users know the status at stations by means of information systems and do not realize a desired trip if they become aware that the trips cannot successfully be realized, even if there are stations close to the departure and destination stations with available bikes and racks. If a user bike flow is met, the bike is only available again when it is returned at time $\bar{t}$.

2.5   The Service Level

We defined the service level λ as the percentage of successfully realized demand trips during a time horizon. The service level is calculated as follows:

$$\lambda = \frac{\sum_{((i,t),(j,\bar{t})) \in \mathscr{A}_U} f_{ij}^{t\bar{t}}}{\sum_{((i,t),(j,\bar{t})) \in \mathscr{A}_U} \zeta_{ij}^{t\bar{t}}} \tag{1}$$

In order to address out approach with a MILP solver, we consider to maximize the successful user trips. The coefficient $\phi_{ij}^{t\bar{t}}$ may be considered in order to prioritize particular spatial and temporal demand (see Eq. 2).

$$max \sum_{((i,t),(j,\bar{t})) \in \mathscr{A}_U} \phi_{ij}^{t\bar{t}} \cdot f_{ij}^{t\bar{t}} \tag{2}$$

2.6   The Redistribution Costs

Regarding the operational expenses ω, a cost F is associated with each redistribution vehicle used, a fixed cost $k_{ij}^{t\bar{t}}$ is incurred if each a vehicle implements an arc in $\mathscr{A}_V \cup \mathscr{A}_H$ (except the holding arcs when the vehicle stays in the depot) and a variable cost q_i^t is incurred per picked up or delivered bike at the node (i,t). Operational expenses are limited by a maximal budget L. The total operational expenses are calculated as Eq. 3.

$$\omega = F \cdot v + \sum_{((i,t),(j,\bar{t})) \in \mathscr{A}_V \cup \mathscr{A}_H} k_{ij}^{t\bar{t}} \cdot y_{ij}^{t\bar{t}} + \sum_{(i,t) \in \mathscr{N} \mid i \neq \{0,T_{MAX}\}} q_i^t \cdot \left(\rho_i^t + \sigma_i^t \right) \qquad (3)$$

2.7 The Model

With the notation introduced above, the optimization model reads as follows:

$$\max \quad z = \sum_{((i,t),(j,\bar{t})) \in \mathscr{A}_U} \phi_{ij}^{t\bar{t}} \cdot f_{ij}^{t\bar{t}} \qquad (4)$$

subject to

$$f_{ij}^{t\bar{t}} \leq \zeta_{ij}^{t\bar{t}}, \quad \forall ((i,t),(j,\bar{t})) \in \mathscr{A}_U \qquad (5)$$

$$\sum_{i \in \mathscr{N}'} I_i^0 = b' \qquad (6)$$

$$I_i^{t+1} = I_i^t - \sum_{\substack{((i,t),(j,\bar{t})) \\ \in \mathscr{A}_U}} f_{ij}^{t\bar{t}} + \sum_{\substack{((j,\bar{t}),(i,t+1)) \\ \in \mathscr{A}_U}} f_{ji}^{\bar{t},t+1}$$
$$- \sum_{\substack{((i,t),(j,\bar{t})) \\ \in \mathscr{A}_V \cup \mathscr{A}_H}} x_{ij}^{t\bar{t}} + \sum_{\substack{((j,\bar{t}),(i,t+1)) \\ \in \mathscr{A}_V \cup \mathscr{A}_H}} x_{ji}^{\bar{t},t+1}, \quad \forall i \in \mathscr{N}', t < T_{MAX} \qquad (7)$$

$$I_i^t - \sum_{\substack{((i,t),(j,\bar{t})) \\ \in \mathscr{A}_U}} f_{ij}^{t\bar{t}} - \sum_{\substack{((i,t),(j,\bar{t})) \\ \in \mathscr{A}_V \cup \mathscr{A}_H}} x_{ij}^{t\bar{t}} = \beta_i^t, \quad \forall i \in \mathscr{N}', t < T_{MAX} \qquad (8)$$

$$c_i - \beta_i^t - \sum_{\substack{((j,\bar{t}),(i,t+1)) \\ \in \mathscr{A}_U}} f_{ji}^{\bar{t},t+1} - \sum_{\substack{((j,\bar{t}),(i,t+1)) \\ \in \mathscr{A}_V \cup \mathscr{A}_H}} x_{ji}^{\bar{t},t+1} = \gamma_i^t, \quad \forall i \in \mathscr{N}', t < T_{MAX} \qquad (9)$$

$$x_{ij}^{t\bar{t}} \leq l \cdot y_{ij}^{t\bar{t}}, \quad \forall ((i,t),(j,\bar{t})) \in \mathscr{A}_V \cup \mathscr{A}_H \qquad (10)$$

$$\sum_{\substack{((i,t),(j,\bar{t})) \\ \in \mathscr{A}_V \cup \mathscr{A}_H}} y_{ij}^{t\bar{t}} = \sum_{\substack{((j,\bar{t}),(i,t)) \\ \in \mathscr{A}_V \cup \mathscr{A}_H}} y_{ji}^{\bar{t}t}, \quad \forall (i,t) \in \mathscr{N}, t \neq \{0,T_{MAX}\} \qquad (11)$$

$$v \leq V_{MAX} \qquad (12)$$

$$\sum_{\substack{((0,0),(j,\bar{t})) \\ \in \mathscr{A}_V \cup \mathscr{A}_H}} y_{0j}^{0\bar{t}} = \sum_{\substack{((j,\bar{t}),(0,T_{MAX})) \\ \in \mathscr{A}_V \cup \mathscr{A}_H}} y_{j0}^{\bar{t}T_{MAX}} = v \qquad (13)$$

$$\sum_{\substack{((0,0),(j,\bar{t})) \\ \in \mathscr{A}_V \cup \mathscr{A}_H}} x_{0j}^{0\bar{t}} = \sum_{\substack{((j,\bar{t}),(0,T_{MAX})) \\ \in \mathscr{A}_V \cup \mathscr{A}_H}} x_{j0}^{\bar{t}T_{MAX}} = 0 \qquad (14)$$

$$\rho_i^t - \sigma_i^t = \sum_{\substack{((i,t),(j,\bar{t})) \\ \in \mathscr{A}_V \cup \mathscr{A}_H}} x_{ij}^{t\bar{t}} - \sum_{\substack{((j,\bar{t}),(i,t)) \\ \in \mathscr{A}_V \cup \mathscr{A}_H}} x_{ji}^{\bar{t}t}, \quad \forall (i,t) \in \mathscr{N}, t \neq \{0,T_{MAX}\} \qquad (15)$$

$$\rho_i^t + \sigma_i^t \leq \sum_{((j,\bar{t}),(i,t)) \in \mathscr{A}_V \cup \mathscr{A}_H} \delta_{ji}^{\bar{t}t} \cdot y_{ji}^{\bar{t}t}, \quad \forall (i,t) \in \mathscr{N}, t \neq \{0, T_{MAX}\} \tag{16}$$

$$F \cdot v + \sum_{\substack{((i,t),(j,\bar{t})) \\ \in \mathscr{A}_V \cup \mathscr{A}_H}} k_{ij}^{t\bar{t}} \cdot y_{ij}^{t\bar{t}} + \sum_{\substack{(i,t) \in \mathscr{N} | \\ i \neq \{0, T_{MAX}\}}} q_i^t \cdot (\rho_i^t + \sigma_i^t) \leq L \tag{17}$$

$$I_i^{T_{MAX}} - \Psi \leq I_i^0 \leq I_i^{T_{MAX}} + \Psi, \quad \forall i \in \mathscr{N}' \tag{18}$$

$$I_i^t \in \mathbb{Z}^+, \forall (i,t) \in \mathscr{N}, \quad \beta_i^t, \gamma_i^t, \rho_i^t, \sigma_i^t \in \mathbb{Z}^+ \quad \forall (i,t) \in \mathscr{N}, t \neq \{0, T_{MAX}\} \tag{19}$$

$$y_{ij}^{t\bar{t}} \in \mathbb{Z}^+, x_{ij}^{t\bar{t}} \geq 0, \forall ((i,t),(j,\bar{t})) \in \mathscr{A}_V \cup \mathscr{A}_H \tag{20}$$

$$v \in \mathbb{Z}^+ \tag{21}$$

As explained above, the objective function (4) maximizes the service level. Constraints (5) ensure that the number of realized user trips are not higher than the expected trips from the demand data. At the beginning of the target time horizon, all bikes are allocated at the stations (6). Constraints (7) model the bike flow conservation taking into account the total number of bikes allocated at each station, user trips and bike relocation activities. The number of allocated bikes and available free bike racks at a station immediately after a time point is defined by Eqs. (8) and (9). Equation (10) limit the load of the vehicles. The design-balanced constraints, that is, the vehicle flow constraints, are presented in (11). Equation (12) limits the size of the redistribution vehicle fleet. The master tours needs to start at end from the depot (13) with no bikes on the load (14). Equation (15) relate the number of picked-up and delivered bikes to the number of incoming and outgoing of bikes due relocation activities. Equation (16) restrict the handle time that a driver has to pick up or deliver bikes at a station until a time point. Constraint (17) models the limitation of the total relocation costs to the provided budget. Similar fill levels are expected at the beginning and end of the time horizon (18). Finally, all variables are non-negative, whereas the decision of implementing vehicle arcs, as well as the size of the vehicle fleet, are represented as integer variables (19, 20, 21).

3   Computational Experiments

This section presents computational experiments conducted to test our service network design formulation based on a "small" real-world BSS. Section 3.1 describe the input data, Sect. 3.2 presents the selected strategies to tackle our BSS instance, whereas results are reported on Sect. 3.3.

3.1   Input Data

We use the data of the San Francisco's BSS "Bay Area" to generate instances. Although Bay Area covers more cities, we only consider the data of San Francisco's service area. As we are interested in days with similar user demand patterns, we only consider the bike trips recorded during the summer season 2015, i.e., between May and September, excluding weekends. The bike sharing's infrastructure, as well as the recorded user trips, are presented and described on its website http://www.bayareabikeshare.com/ and summarized in Table 1.

Table 1. San Francisco's Bay Area: instance description

Bike sharing system	San Francisco's Bay Area
Number of stations	35
Min - Max - Avg. bike racks per station	15 - 27 - 19
Year period	01 May - 31 Sep
Avg. trips per day	824

Analyzing the selected trip data, there are around 824 user trips per day out of which most happen in the morning and afternoon peak hours. In general, the user trips follow the activity patterns observed in [2]. To obtain a suitable user bike flow input for our service network design formulation, we aggregate the user trip data from multiple days to obtain the demand rate for each time-dependent origin-destination pair corresponding to the user bike flows utilized in the model. As the mean trip duration is around 12 min, we decided to split the time horizon into 15-min time intervals. We assume that every user bike flow only takes one time period.

Figure 3 illustrates the rental and return activity at two Bay Area's bike stations. On the left, the San Francisco Caltrain 2 (330 Townsend), a station next to the train station, presents a high rental activity in the morning peak

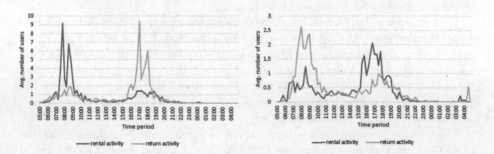

Fig. 3. Rental and return activity of two Bay Area's bike stations. On the left, the San Francisco Caltrain 2 (330 Townsend). On the right, the Townsend at 7th.

hour and a high return activity in the afternoon peak hour. On the right, the Townsend at 7th, a station located near to work places and shopping centers, presents the opposite behavior: A high return activity is observed in the morning peak hour and rental activity in the afternoon peak hour. Both stations exhibit typical commute activity observed in most BSS. Note, however, that the user activity at the Caltrain 2 station is clearly higher than at the Townsend at 7th.

After aggregating the data set, we obtain real-valued time-dependent user bike flows. For a suitable input for out service network design formulation, we need to generate integer user bike flows based on the real-valued ones. Assuming a Poisson distribution on the real-valued user bike flows, we generate 100 demand realizations with integer bike user flows. To obtain the master tours, we run our MILP with only one of the demand realizations. After that, we evaluate the quality of the master tours for all demand realizations by fixing the vehicle movements decisions of this solution and solve the resulting residual formulation once for each demand realization.

In addition, we use the following parameters: Regarding the redistribution vehicles, having a vehicle available during the time horizon costs 25 €/day. Based on the input data used in [15], each vehicle movement costs 0.5 €/km, whereas the bike handling costs are 2 €/bike between 8 and 17 h, otherwise 3.5 €/bike. The vehicle speed is 1 m/s, and the service time is 1 min/bike. 665 bikes are distributed among stations at the beginning of the time horizon. All user bike flows are weighted with the coefficient $\phi_{ij}^{t\bar{t}} = 1, \forall((i,t),(j,\bar{t}) \in \mathscr{A}_U$. Finally, $\Psi = 5$ is considered as the allowed mismatch between the initial and final fill levels.

3.2 Solution Strategy

Even for small instances, solving the service network design formulation with standard MILP solvers is not possible within a reasonable amount of computation time. We propose the following approaches to speed-up the solution. First, we follow the "Two-phase solution method" proposed in [9]: In a first step, the integrality constraints for the fill level and bike flow variables are relaxed in order to obtain vehicle tours with fractional bike flows. In the second step, the vehicle tour decisions are fixed and the rest of the problem is solved again, now considering integer fill levels and bike flows.

We test with different number of vehicles by fixing v to 1, 2, or 3. In this first phase, the monetary budget is considered as unlimited. In the second phase, we aim at finding the minimal redistribution costs to obtain the optimal service level from the first phase. Note that it is possible that there exist solutions yielding the same service level with a fewer use of resources. To check that, we fix the optimal service level by introducing an additional constraint and select the left hand side of Eq. 3 as objective function.

The service network design formulation is implemented in Java using the ILOG Concert Technology to access CPLEX 12.5. An Intel Xeon X7559 CPU at 2 GHz processor with 80 RAM was used to run the experiments. All experiments were run for a maximal running-time of 10 h per objective function.

3.3 Results

Table 2 shows the results for the Bay Area instance for different numbers of available vehicles. With one vehicle, a service level λ of 97.90 % is obtained, meaning a 7.73 % improvement comparing with a solution where no vehicles are used. Nevertheless, considering additional vehicles does not increase the service level significantly. For a second vehicle, only a 0.58 % improvement is achieved in comparison to the one-vehicle solution. With three vehicles, the expected user bike flows are almost completely fulfilled. For the service level objective, the remaining MIP gap after reaching the time limit is always under 2.5 %.

Table 2. Computational results after 10 h running time per objective

	Objective		MIP gap	
v	λ	ω (€)	λ	ω
0	90.17 %	0.00	-	-
1	97.90 %	293.46	2.39 %	15.73 %
2	98.48 %	306.23	1.54 %	1.62 %
3	99.65 %	403.71	0.35 %	3.04 %

The redistribution cost ω obtained after solving for the cost objective with a fixed service level from the first phase increases with the number of vehicles. Interestingly, the second vehicle incurs only 12.77€ more cost than the one-vehicle solution, whereas the redistribution cost increases considerably for the third vehicle. Note, however, that the results for the cost objective suffer from a high variation in the remaining MIP gap. In particular for the one-vehicle case, the solution quality may be improved considerably – the lower bound after the time limit is 247.31€.

Figure 4 illustrates the number of available bikes $\beta_{i,t}$ throughout the day for the two San Francisco stations discussed above, when one vehicle is used. The San Francisco Caltrain 2 station on the left almost runs full before the morning peak hour. As expected, a lot of bike rentals means that the stations is almost empty during the midday – this is not particularly critical since only few rentals are expected in that time. Moreover, a low fill level is desired before the afternoon peak hour to enable several bike returns. A significant decrease of the fill level is observed around 18:00 since bikes are removed from the station by a vehicle. This avoids that the station runs full, allowing more bike returns later on. Finally, low activity is observed during the night. The Townsend at 7th displayed on the right exhibits a completely different pattern. It begins with a low fill level, running almost full after the morning peak hour due to a large number of bike returns. In the afternoon peak hour, there is a high decrease of the fill level due to the large number of rentals. Around 17:00, bikes are delivered to the station to facilitate additional bike rentals during the evening and to maintain proper fill levels for the next day.

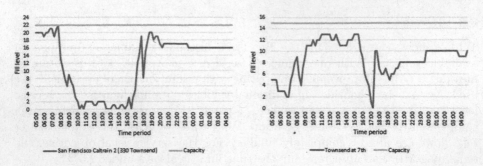

Fig. 4. Available number of bikes within the day for the San Francisco Caltrain 2 (330 Townsend) (on the left) and the Townsend at 7th (on the right).

To evaluate the quality of the master tour obtained for a single vehicle and for a single of set of demand realizations in presence of different demand scenarios, we fix the master tour and solve the remaining bike flow problem for different demand scenarios. The results are depicted in Fig. 5 by means of box-plots for the service level and redistribution costs obtained. The average service level is 95.23 %, with a standard deviation of 1.53 %. In fact, for most demand realizations, the service level lies between 94.00 % and 96.00 %. In fewer cases, the service level can range between 91 % and 98 %. A notch is used to show the 95.00 % confidence interval. Regarding the redistribution costs, the mean is 218.33€, with a standard deviation of 44.78€. Most of the redistribution costs are between 175.00€ and 250.00€.

4   Discussion

For the small instances employed in our experiments, using a single redistribution vehicle already leads to a high service level. In fact, given a comparably small number of stations with comparably few bike rentals allows serving a high percentage of stations during the day with a single vehicle. Depending on the BSS infrastructure and daily rentals, however, more vehicles can have a more significant impact on achieving a higher service level. Moreover, considering the redistribution costs is critical to evaluate the quality of the solutions. For instance, the amount of redistribution costs associated with a given vehicle gives an indication on its utilization which may help to decide if the extra vehicle is actually necessary. We also observe that good fill level decisions consider the final fill level at stations, i.e., the initial fill level for the next time horizon. For instance, a station with several rental request each morning should dispose with a suitable number of bikes before the morning peak hours. This condition needs to be modeled explicitly in the service network design formulation.

Regarding the solution process, no optimal solution was found after the given running time. As for most service network design formulations, the design-balanced constraints necessary to set up the master tours are challenging for a

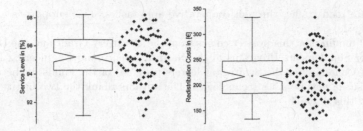

Fig. 5. Box plots of service level and redistribution costs under different demand realizations with fixed vehicle movements.

standard MILP solver [16]. In fact, even solving the linear programming relaxation is very time-consuming and moreover only yields a weak lower bound for the optimal integer solution. Instances from bigger BSS with of hundreds of stations are not tractable using the MILP-based solution approach presented above. Alternative solution approaches are necessary to tackle bigger instances in an acceptable running-time. Heuristic search techniques should contribute to select a reduced but promising set of vehicle arcs to set up master tours.

Finally, our experiments show that the master tours are effective under different demand scenarios with similar characteristics for the selected BSS instance. Thus, master tours can support short-term operational redistribution decisions dealing with real-time fill levels and user demand as discussed by [5].

5   Conclusions

In this paper, we present a novel service network design formulation for the bike sharing redistribution problem. The model aims at obtaining master tours for the redistribution vehicles and bike redistribution operations in order to establish time-of-day-dependent station fill levels maximizing the service level. Our model uses a trip-based representation of user demand and explicitly considers the time needed for bike pick-up and delivery operations. The decision maker can evaluate the benefits of using different numbers of redistribution resources in order to make an informed trade-off between redistribution costs and service level. For example, our computational experiments show that for certain numbers of vehicles, an additional vehicle does not significantly improve the service level.

Taking a tactical planning perspective, we assume perfect knowledge of the user bike flows for the whole time horizon, i.e., a "deterministic" case. In our experiments presented in this paper, evaluated the performance of these master tours for multiple demand scenarios. In future work, we consider to explicitly model demand variations in our service network design formulation to obtain more robust master tour decisions. In addition, we aim at developing solution approaches to be able to tackle instances with a large number of stations.

Acknowledgments. This research has been supported by the German Research Foundation (DFG) through the Research Training Group SocialCars (GRK 1931). The focus of the SocialCars Research Training Group is on significantly improving the city's future road traffic, through cooperative approaches. This support is gratefully acknowledged.

Partial funding for this project comes from the Discovery Grant and the Discovery Accelerator Supplements Programs of the Natural Science and Engineering Research Council of Canada, and the Strategic Clusters program of the Fonds québécois de la recherche sur la nature et les technologies. The authors thank the two institutions for supporting this research.

References

1. DeMaio, P.: Bike-sharing: history, impacts, models of provision, and future. J. Publ. Transp. **12**(4), 3 (2009)
2. O'Brien, O., Cheshire, J., Batty, M.: Mining bicycle sharing data for generating insights into sustainable transport systems. J. Transp. Geogr. **34**, 262–273 (2014)
3. Vogel, P., Neumann-Saavedra, B.A., Mattfeld, D.C.: A hybrid metaheuristic to solve the resource allocation problem in bike sharing systems. In: Blesa, M.J., Blum, C., Voß, S. (eds.) HM 2014. LNCS, vol. 8457, pp. 16–29. Springer, Heidelberg (2014)
4. Büttner, J., Petersen, T.: Optimising Bike Sharing in European Cities-A Handbook. Intelligent Energy Europe, European Commission (2011)
5. Brinkmann, J., Ulmer, M.W., Mattfeld, D.C.: Short-term strategies for stochastic inventory routing in bike sharing systems. Transp. Res. Procedia **10**, 364–373 (2015)
6. Brinkmann, J., Ulmer, M. W., Mattfeld, D.C.: Inventory routing for bike sharing systems. Working Paper, 12 January 2015
7. Laporte, G., Meunier, F., Calvo, R.W.: Shared mobility systems. 4OR **13**(4), 341–360 (2015)
8. Coelho, L.C., Cordeau, J.F., Laporte, G.: Thirty years of inventory routing. Transp. Sci. **48**(1), 1–19 (2013)
9. Raviv, T., Tzur, M., Forma, I.A.: Static repositioning in a bike-sharing system: models and solution approaches. EURO J. Transp. Logistics **2**(3), 187–229 (2013)
10. Rainer-Harbach, M., Papazek, P., Raidl, G.R., Hu, B., Kloimüllner, C.: PILOT, GRASP, and VNS approaches for the static balancing of bicycle sharing systems. J. Global Optim. **63**(3), 597–629 (2015)
11. Dell'Amico, M., Hadjicostantinou, E., Iori, M., Novellani, S.: The bike sharing rebalancing problem: mathematical formulations and benchmark instances. Omega **45**, 7–19 (2014)
12. Contardo, C., Morency, C., Rousseau, L.M.: Balancing a dynamic public bike-sharing system, vol. 4. CIRRELT (2012)
13. Kloimüllner, C., Papazek, P., Hu, B., Raidl, G.R.: Balancing bicycle sharing systems: an approach for the dynamic case. In: Blum, C., Ochoa, G. (eds.) EvoCOP 2014. LNCS, vol. 8600, pp. 73–84. Springer, Heidelberg (2014)
14. Kloimüllner, C., Papazek, P., Hu, B., Raidl, G.R.: A cluster-first route-second approach for balancing bicycle sharing systems. In: Moreno-Díaz, R., Pichler, F., Quesada-Arencibia, A. (eds.) EUROCAST 2015. LNCS, vol. 9520, pp. 439–446. Springer, Heidelberg (2015)
15. Neumann-Saavedra, B.A., Vogel, P., Mattfeld, D.C.: Anticipatory service network design of bike sharing systems. Transp. Res. Procedia **10**, 355–363 (2015)
16. Andersen, J., Crainic, T.G., Christiansen, M.: Service network design with asset management: formulations and comparative analyses. Transp. Res. Part C Emerg. Technol. **17**(2), 197–207 (2009)

(General) Logistics and Supply Chain Management

An Agent-Based Simulation Framework to Evaluate Urban Logistics Schemes

Wouter van Heeswijk$^{(\boxtimes)}$, Martijn Mes, and Marco Schutten

Department of Industrial Engineering and Business Information Systems,
University of Twente, P.O. Box 217, 7500 AE Enschede, The Netherlands
{w.j.a.vanheeswijk,m.r.k.mes,m.schutten}@utwente.nl

Abstract. Inefficient urban freight transport has a negative impact on both livability in cities and profit margins in the supply chain. Urban logistics schemes, consisting of governmental policies and company initiatives, attempt to address these problems. However, successful schemes are difficult to realize due to the divergent objectives of the agents involved in urban logistics. Traditional optimization techniques fall short when evaluating schemes, as they do not capture the required change in behavior of autonomous agents. To properly evaluate schemes, we develop an agent-based simulation framework that assesses the interaction between five types of autonomous agents. Compared to existing studies in this field, we contribute by (i) explicitly including company-driven initiatives, and (ii) adopting a supply chain-wide perspective. We illustrate the working of our framework by testing a number of schemes on a virtual network.

Keywords: Urban logistics · Agent-based simulation · Logistics schemes

1 Introduction

The need to organize urban freight transport in an efficient manner is becoming increasingly important. Projections indicate a strong growth in the population of urban areas (both relatively and in an absolute sense) [21], resulting into a larger demand for goods. Other trends affecting urban freight transport are e-commerce, just-in-time approaches at retailers, higher dispersion of delivery locations, and increased service levels (e.g., shorter lead times, narrow delivery slots) [2,5]. As a result, shippers and carriers need to deal simultaneously with increasing shipment frequencies and decreasing order volumes, making it difficult for individual agents to transport goods efficiently [7]. As a result, trucks are often forced to carry low volumes and make inefficient delivery tours. This inefficiency contributes to external costs such as congestion, emissions, and noise hindrance, thereby negatively affecting the quality of life in urban areas. Furthermore, it reduces the profitability of the agents in the supply chain. In response to these developments, there is a strong interest in city logistics initiatives. Such initiatives, commonly called schemes, consist of one or more forms of company-driven change and governmental policies, with the aim to improve efficiency

© Springer International Publishing Switzerland 2016
A. Paias et al. (Eds.): ICCL 2016, LNCS 9855, pp. 369–383, 2016.
DOI: 10.1007/978-3-319-44896-1_24

and/or reduce external costs [3]. Urban consolidation centers (UCCs) have a central role in most schemes, facilitating order bundling and efficient last-mile distribution. In Fig. 1, we give an example of the typical network setting that we consider. Since agents that handle large volumes often have access to the economies of scale and expertise to optimize their transport processes, our focus is on agents that handle small volumes, who are affected the most by the aforementioned trends.

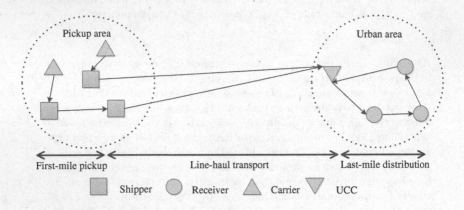

Fig. 1. Example of a network with a UCC facilitating last-mile distribution

Despite the eminent need for better organizing urban logistics, the vast majority of schemes fail after a short life-span [8]. A key reason for this is that the involved agents typically have divergent objectives, making it difficult to find solutions to which all agents are willing to commit [4]. Administrators often attempt to generate commitment by providing financial incentives in the form of subsidies [22]. However, such solutions are often not sustainable once the subsidies are halted. Another problem is that schemes are often implemented with little preliminary analysis, thereby not adequately evaluating their system-wide impact [16]. Finally, studies often focus solely on the processes within the city boundaries, while last-mile distribution accounts for a small part of the supply chain. As such, they ignore the impact of upstream decisions. Of particular importance is the allocation of slack in the chain; holding freight early in the supply chain may improve vehicle fill rates, but reduces flexibility for the UCC in last-mile distribution. In our framework, we explicitly address these aspects.

A key success factor for urban logistics schemes is the right combination of company involvement and governmental policies [8]. Agents must be willing to permanently change their behavior, without requiring an ongoing external cash flow. Traditional optimization techniques may be used to find viable system-wide solutions, yet these are not guaranteed to be stable when depending on multiple decision makers. Furthermore, it is difficult to evaluate the impact of combining multiple measures into a scheme. Agent-based simulation studies are suitable to evaluate such schemes, as they are capable of monitoring and altering the behavior of autonomous agents under conditions that can be flexibly adjusted [20]. With this study, we provide an agent-based simulation framework to evaluate the effectiveness of urban logistics schemes that include both governmental policies and company-driven initiatives.

2 Literature Review

For recent literature reviews on urban logistics, we refer to Anand *et al.* [2] and Bektaş *et al.* [4]. These reviews state that most studies focus on describing and evaluating existing initiatives, rather than optimizing. Only few papers adopt an operations research perspective [10]; these papers generally address (i) the positioning of UCCs and (ii) solution methods to one-echelon or two-echelon routing problems. Most urban logistics initiatives are characterized by the use of UCCs. Inbound trucks no longer need to enter the city center, but instead unload at a UCC, which is typically located at the edge of an urban area. Subsequently, goods can be bundled at the UCC, such that efficient tours can be made for the last-mile distribution. Furthermore, environment-friendly vehicles can be dispatched for last-mile distribution. Particularly for independent low-volume, high-frequency deliveries, UCCs could substantially improve performance.

Browne *et al.* [8] provide an elaborate overview of real-life UCC projects, and report that only few initiatives were able to remain in operation for multiple years. A key success factor is the involvement of commercial parties that share a common objective. UCCs yield the best results when involving a sufficiently large number of small, independent shippers and retailers, where low-volume, high-frequency shipments are the norm. Government administrators are typically required to cover the capital expenses of the UCC. Furthermore, gains from policies could (partially) cover operational expenses. However, UCCs that heavily rely on subsidies are unlikely to succeed in the long run, as profit margins in logistics are too small to absorb a subsidy cut. Generally accepted financial models do not exist for UCCs [1]; it is often not clear how the costs of the UCC should be distributed among the administrator, receivers and carriers.

Quak [16] distinguishes four classes of initiatives in urban logistics. First, he considers improvements within the context of existing operations, in which he distinguishes between (i) governmental policies and (ii) company-driven initiatives. Second, he considers improvements that require changing the context of urban logistics, which he divides in (iii) physical infrastructure initiatives (including UCCs) and (iv) transport-reorganizing initiatives. Our present work is primarily focused on the first two classes, as they can be captured by the decision-making role of agents. Evaluating the latter two classes within our framework can be done by using various network configurations as input.

We discuss the aforementioned classes of initiatives, starting with governmental policies. To achieve norms on external costs, administrators encourage or enforce the desired behavior of agents in the supply chain by implementing policies. Common policies are vehicle access restrictions, time access restrictions, enforcing a minimum load factor, and road pricing [18]. Such policies typically favor small vehicles, e.g., heavy trucks face stricter time windows and higher costs than delivery vans. Individually, policies are often not enough to achieve the intended change. Agents should have viable alternatives to change their behavior, otherwise policies may even have results that oppose the intended effect [18]. For example, restrictive access times may increase the number of transport movements, forcing carriers to deploy additional vehicles.

Next, we describe the concept of company-driven change. Companies aim to increase transport efficiency mainly for economic reasons, but also because external costs become increasingly important for them. Forms of company-driven changes are, e.g., joint transportation by a coalition of carriers, deliveries outside normal delivery hours, or using the UCC as the delivery address [3]. The latter can be initiated by the receiver or by the carrier. For the carrier, cost savings (the costs of last-mile distribution are disproportionally high [11]) and legislative restrictions are the main reasons to use a UCC. For receivers, poor accessibility by truck and lower receiving costs (due to bundled deliveries) are reasons to consider delivery via the UCC [24].

Collaboration is notoriously difficult to realize in urban logistics. As the objectives of the agents in urban logistics are often divergent [4], system-wide optimization yields little practical insights. Techniques such as multi-criteria, multi-actor evaluation may yield more insights into the alignment of individual agents' objectives and feasible solutions [13]. However, such an evaluation does not guarantee commitment of the individual agents. Tanaguchi *et al.* [20] state that agent-based simulation is the most applicable method to study the behavior of and interaction between the various agents for urban logistics schemes. Agent-based simulation is not fit to study detailed interactions [4], yet is suitable to deduce generic insights on system performance. We mention some notable agent-based simulation studies in the field of urban logistics. Tamagawa *et al.* [19] perform an agent-based simulation, in which they heuristically solve a VRP and iteratively update the actions of the agents. They test the effects of road pricing and truck bans. Van Duin *et al.* [22] focus on the financial model and environmental impact of UCCs, taking into account UCC service fees, road pricing, and subsidies. Wangapisit *et al.* [25] evaluate the use of consolidation centers by imposing parking constraints and providing subsidies to carriers.

The contribution of our evaluation framework is twofold. First, we take into account the transport process outside the city. As last-mile distribution accounts for only part of the transport process, a narrow perspective does not properly assess the decisions made by shippers and carriers. Second, we explicitly include various forms of cooperation between companies, while existing studies tend to have a strong focus on testing governmental policies. As practice shows that successful schemes require both policies and commitment from companies, a framework including both aspects is essential for proper evaluation of these schemes.

3   Framework Design

In this section, we outline the design of our agent-based simulation framework. We start by describing the roles of the agent types in Sect. 3.1. In Sect. 3.2, we formally define the state of the system, based on which we define the objective functions for each agent type and the corresponding performance indicators in Sect. 3.3. In Sect. 3.4, we discuss various policies for operational decision-making (e.g., dispatching, routing) during the simulation. Finally, Sect. 3.5 assesses the use of scenario analysis to incorporate tactical and strategic decisions (e.g., coalition forming, governmental policies) into the framework.

3.1 Agent Types

We design our agent-based simulation framework such that it can simultaneously evaluate company-driven initiatives and governmental policies. We focus on supply chains for a single city; extension of the framework to multiple cities is relatively straightforward. In such a context, harmonization of local policies and consolidation on the line haul are noteworthy challenges [16]. In our simulation, decisions are made at discrete moments in time. Five types of agents are distinguished: receivers, shippers, carriers, the UCC operator, and the administrator. We proceed to briefly describe their roles; Fig. 2 summarizes the array of actions, monetary flows and information flows between the agents. We note that the real-life counterparts of the agents are not necessarily rational decisionmakers, particularly when large changes in behavior are required. However, the simulation results yield insights into the behavioral effects of real-life agents, as such providing directions for change.

The **receivers** have a demand that is subject to some (stochastic) process, and they may order from multiple suppliers at a single decision moment. They order at fixed decision moments (e.g., twice per week); we assume that their ordering pattern already takes into account factors such as internal consolidation, storage costs, and stockouts. When ordering, receivers specify a delivery windows. Receivers can opt to select the UCC as their fixed delivery address. The **shippers** act on incoming orders, and hire carriers to transport orders. As carriers charge relatively less for higher volumes, shippers have an incentive to bundle multiple orders before shipping. However, the shippers should dispatch the orders in time, such that the carrier is able to meet the delivery windows. Line-haul **carriers** pick up goods at the shippers, and transport them either directly to the receivers or to the UCC. They may outsource the last-mile distribution to the UCC when this yields a financial benefit or is enforced by regulation. The carrier uses a price function based on volume and line-haul distance (i.e., the distance between cities, ignoring distance variations due to routing) that reflects economies of scale. In the typical setting we study, a dispatched truck will visit multiple cities during a single tour, yet we focus on a single city only. Consequently, the load destined for the city is generally much less than the truck's capacity. The **UCC** receives incoming goods, and is responsible for the last-mile distribution. At the UCC, orders from various carriers can be bundled, and may be temporarily held to account for future consolidation opportunities. Finally, the **administrator** can implement governmental policies to influence the behavior of agents. Since such policies are typically implemented for a longer time, we do this on a scenario basis. The financial gains stemming

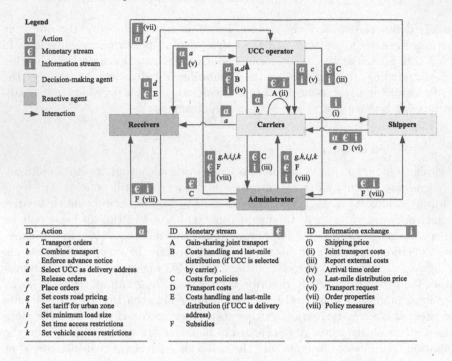

Fig. 2. Actions and interactions for all agent types

from these policies may be redistributed to subsidize agents; to keep the scheme sustainable we do not allow for external cash flows.

3.2   System State

In this section, we provide the notation required to define the state of the system and the actions of agents. Let $\mathcal{T} = \{0, 1, \ldots, T\}$ be the set of discrete decision moments upon which agents can make decisions. Typically, the time between two decision moments will correspond to several hours, e.g., one decision moment in the morning, one in the afternoon, and one in the evening.

Let $\mathcal{C}$ be the set of carriers, $\mathcal{R}$ the set of receivers, and $\mathcal{S}$ the set of shippers. We assume a single UCC. The network is comprised by a vertex set $\mathcal{V}$ and a set of arcs $\mathcal{A}$. Vertex set $\mathcal{V}$ is defined as $\mathcal{V} = \mathcal{V}^R \cup \mathcal{V}^S \cup \mathcal{V}^C \cup \mathcal{V}^H$, i.e., the set consists of subsets of locations of receivers, shippers, carriers and the UCC. As we have a single UCC, we have $\mathcal{V}^H = \{v^{ucc}\}$. A vertex in $\mathcal{V}^C$ indicates the starting point of a carrier, i.e., its home depot. Every arc $a \in \mathcal{A}$ connects a vertex pair (v_a, v'_a). Let $\mathcal{F} = \{\frac{1}{y}, \frac{2}{y}, \ldots, 1\}$ (with integer $y > 1$) be the set of possible order volumes, expressed in terms of the capacity of the smallest vehicle (e.g., a delivery van). Based on the UCC dispatching problem defined by Van Heeswijk et al. [23], we define an order as a request to ship a certain load, with an *order type* being a unique combination of the delivery window $[t^e, t^l]$, the current position of the order $v \in \mathcal{V}$, (which indicates the agent responsible for handling the order at the current decision moment t), the receiver $r \in \mathcal{R}$, the carrier $c \in \mathcal{C} \cup \mathcal{H}$ (the UCC can be a carrier from the perspective of the receiver), the shipper $s \in \mathcal{S}$, the order volume $f \in \mathcal{F}$, and an indicator $\gamma \in \{0, 1\}$ that specifies whether delivery takes place via the UCC ($\gamma = 1$ sets the UCC as the delivery address for the carrier). The indicator γ can be specified either by the receiver (as a tactical decision) or by the carrier (as an operational decision); the agent specifying the index might incur a subsidy for this. We use $I_{t,t^e,t^l,v,r,c,s,f,\gamma}$ to denote the number of orders of a specific type. Not all indices are required by every agent for decision-making. For instance, the receiver will not specify which carrier delivers the order; this index is left blank until specified by the shipper. Furthermore, decisions may also transform order types, e.g., when the carrier decides to deliver via the UCC. The generic notation is applicable to all agents. We denote the number of orders per order type in the system at time t as $I_t = [I_{t,t^e,t^l,v,r,c,s,f,\gamma}]_{\forall t^e,t^l,v,r,c,s,f,\gamma}$. In some form, every agent is faced with a dispatch decision based on I_t. Using generic notation, we denote the number of orders per order type dispatched at time t as

$$x_t = [x_{t,t^e,t^l,v,r,c,s,f,\gamma}]_{\forall t^e,t^l,v,r,c,s,f,\gamma} \ ,$$

subject to

$$x_{t,t^e,t^l,v,r,c,s,f,\gamma} \leq I_{t,t^e,t^l,v,r,c,s,f,\gamma} \qquad \forall t^e,t^l,v,r,c,s,f,\gamma,$$
$$x_{t,t^e,t^l,v,r,c,s,f,\gamma} \in \mathbb{N} \qquad \forall t^e,t^l,v,r,c,s,f,\gamma.$$

Both shippers and the UCC decide on the set of orders to dispatch at decision moment t, we denote these actions as $x_{t,v^s,s}^{shp}$ and $x_{t,v^{ucc}}^{ucc}$ respectively. The order of a receiver (based on the demand at time t) is described by $x_{t,v^r,r}$, while the shipment of the carrier is given by $x_{t,v^c,c}$.

We proceed with the notation required to denote routes. Let $\mathcal{Q}_c$ denote the set of vehicles operated by carrier c. A vehicle $q \in \mathcal{Q}_c$ has a vehicle capacity $\psi_{c,q} \in \mathbb{R}_{\geq 1}$, a line-haul travel speed $\tau_{c,q}^{lh} \in \mathbb{R}_{>0}$, and a last-mile travel speed $\tau_{c,q}^{lm} \in \mathbb{R}_{>0}$. To ease the notation, we assume that all routes starting at t are completed at $t+1$. For the same reason, we do not explicitly include the pickup tour. We denote a route started by vehicle q of carrier c at time t as $\delta_{t,c,q}^{car} = \{\delta_{t,c,q}^{car,lh}, \delta_{t,c,q}^{car,lm}\}$, with the components referring to line-haul transport (lh) and last-mile distribution (lm) respectively. This distinction is used to assign distinct properties (e.g., fuel usage, road pricing, driver wage) to the associated travel distances d^{lh} and d^{lm}. We let $\Delta_{t,c}^{car}$ denote the set of routes for carrier c at decision moment t, and use Δ_t^{ucc} to describe the set of routes for the UCC. The UCC only has to deal with last-mile distribution, such that $\delta_{t,q}^{ucc} = \{\delta_{t,q}^{ucc,lm}\}$. We use $\Delta_t = [\Delta_{t,c}^{car}, \Delta_t^{ucc}]_{\forall c}$ to denote all routes starting at time t.

The system state at t is given by $[I_t, \Delta_t]$; this description provides all information required for decision making and computing the performance indicators.

3.3 Objective Functions and Key Performance Indicators

In this section, we provide the objective functions and Key Performance Indicators (KPIs) of the agents. We start by introducing some notation required to describe the price- and cost functions. For a variety of parameters and variables, we use the superscript hd to refer to costs for handling operations (e.g., (un)loading by the driver), rc for receiving (e.g., lost work time, allocating goods), sp for shipping (e.g., lost work time, loading operations), and sb for income from subsidies. In our description, we restrict ourselves to subsidies for using the UCC. Price functions P describe the income of agents and cost functions C describe their expenses. The used order volumes depend on the context of the function. For example, the volume transported by carrier c' at time t to the UCC is given by $f_{t,v^{c'},c',\gamma|\gamma=1} = \sum_{\forall t^e,t^l,r,s,f} x_{t,t^e,t^l,v^{c'},r,c',s,f,1} \cdot f$. Other volumes are computed in a similar manner, using the corresponding subscripts.

For the carriers and UCCs, handling costs depend on the subsets of locations visited. A shipment may involve subsets of shippers $\mathcal{S}' \subseteq \mathcal{S}$ and receivers $\mathcal{R}' \subseteq \mathcal{R} \cup \mathcal{H}$, this information is embedded in the route description. Note that the UCC is a receiver from the perspective of the carrier. The symbol α – with the appropriate sub- and superscripts – refers to a fixed price- or cost component; similarly, the symbol β refers to a variable price- or cost component. In Table 1, we provide price- and cost functions for corresponding to the agent's actions; for notational convenience we formulate all functions linearly. For the same purpose, we assume that carriers use homogenous fleets. Definitions are kept at a generic level; we define the objective functions of the actors and illustrating the main cost- and price components, without introducing excessive notational complexity.

Having defined the price- and cost functions, we now introduce the objective functions for the agents. The outcomes of these objective functions serve as KPIs for the agents. Although agents aim to optimize over the full planning horizon, they make periodic decisions based on incomplete information.

The objective of the shipper is to minimize the sum of transportation- and shipping costs. Shippers can influence these costs by selecting the set of orders to ship at every decision moment (denoted by $x^{shp}_{t,v^s,s}$), and by selecting the cheapest carrier $c \in \mathcal{C}$ for the shipment.

$$\min \sum_{t \in \mathcal{T}} \left(C^{shp,tr}_{t,s}(f_{t,v^s,c,s}, d^{lh}) + C^{shp,sp}_{t,s}(f_{t,v^s,c,s}) \right).$$

The objective of the UCC is to maximize profit, which is determined by the price charged by the UCC, subsidy income, receiving costs, and transport costs. To influence their profit, they select a subset of orders to dispatch $x^{ucc}_{t,v^{ucc}}$, and a corresponding route set Δ^{ucc}_t:

$$\max \sum_{t \in \mathcal{T}} \left(P^{ucc,sb}_t(f_{t,v^{ucc}}) + P^{ucc,rec,tr}_t(f_{t,v^r,r,\gamma|\gamma=1}) + P^{ucc,car,tr}_t(f_{t,v^c,c,\gamma|\gamma=1}) \right.$$
$$\left. - C^{ucc,rc}_t(f_{t,v^{ucc}}) - C^{ucc,tr}_t(f_{t,v^{ucc}}, d^{lm}, \mathcal{R}') \right).$$

Carriers attempt to maximize profit (determined by the transport price, subsidy income, transport costs, and outsourcing costs) by selecting the route set $\Delta^{car}_{t,c}$ that minimizes costs at every decision moment. In addition, carriers can

Table 1. Price and cost functions for all decision-making agents

Function		Notes
Receiver *(rec)*		
$P_{t,r}^{rec,sb}\big(f_{t,v^r,r,\gamma\mid\gamma=1}\big)$	$= \alpha_r^{rec,sb} + \beta_r^{rec,sb} \cdot f_{t,v^r,r,\gamma\mid\gamma=1}$	Income subsidies (if r selects UCC)
$C_{t,r}^{rec,rc}\big(f_{t,v^r,r,c}\big)$	$= \alpha_r^{rec,rc} + \beta_r^{rec,rc} \cdot f_{t,v^r,r,c}$	Costs receiving shipment
$C_{t,r}^{rec,lm}\big(f_{t,v^r,r,\gamma\mid\gamma=1}\big)$	$= P_t^{ucc,tr}\big(f_{t,v^r,r,\gamma\mid\gamma=1}\big)$	Costs outsourcing UCC
Shipper *(shp)*		
$C_{t,s}^{shp,tr}\big(f_{t,v^s,c,s}, d^{lh}\big)$	$= P_{t,c}^{tr}\big(f_{t,v^s,c,s}, d^{lh}\big)$	Costs transportation
$C_{t,s}^{shp,sp}\big(f_{t,v^s,c,s}\big)$	$= \alpha_s^{shp,sp} + \beta_s^{shp,sp} \cdot f_{t,v^s,c,s}$	Costs shipping
Carrier *(car)*		
$P_{t,c}^{car,sb}\big(f_{t,v^c,c,\gamma\mid\gamma=1}\big)$	$= \alpha_c^{car,sb} + \beta_c^{car,sb} \cdot f_{t,v^c,c,\gamma\mid\gamma=1}$	Income subsidies (if c selects UCC)
$P_{t,c}^{car,tr}\big(f_{t,v^c,c}, d^{lh}\big)$	$= \alpha_c^{car,tr} + \beta_c^{car,tr} \cdot f_{t,v^c,c} \cdot d^{lh}$	Price shipping
$C_{t,c}^{car,tr}\big(d^{lh}, d^{lm}, \mathcal{S}', \mathcal{R}'\big)$	$= \alpha_c^{car,tr} + \beta_c^{car,lh} \cdot d^{lh} + \beta_c^{car,lm} \cdot d^{lm} + \beta_c^{car,hd} \cdot \lvert \mathcal{S}' \cup \mathcal{R}' \rvert$	Costs full transport
$C_{t,c}^{car,lm}\big(f_{t,v^c,c}, d^{lh}, \mathcal{S}'\big)$	$= \alpha_c^{car,lm} + \beta_c^{car,lh} \cdot d^{lh} + \beta_c^{hd} \cdot \lvert \mathcal{S}' \rvert + P_t^{ucc,tr}\big(f_{t,v^c,c}\big)$	Costs outsourcing UCC
UCC *(ucc)*		
$P_t^{ucc,sb}\big(f_{t,v^{ucc}}\big)$	$= \alpha^{ucc,sb} + \beta^{ucc,sb} \cdot f_{t,v^{ucc}}$	Income subsidies
$P_t^{ucc,rec,tr}\big(f_{t,v^r,r,\gamma\mid\gamma=1}\big)$	$= \beta^{ucc,rec,tr} \cdot f_{t,v^r,r,\gamma\mid\gamma=1}$	Price distribution (if r selects UCC)
$P_t^{ucc,car,tr}\big(f_{t,v^c,c,\gamma\mid\gamma=1}\big)$	$= \beta^{ucc,car,tr} \cdot f_{t,v^c,c,\gamma\mid\gamma=1}$	Price distribution (if c selects UCC)
$C_t^{ucc,rc}\big(f_{t,v^{ucc}}\big)$	$= \alpha^{ucc,rc} + \beta^{ucc,rc} \cdot f_{t,v^{ucc}}$	Costs receiving
$C_t^{ucc,tr}\big(f_{t,v^{ucc}}, d^{lm}, \mathcal{R}'\big)$	$= \beta^{ucc,lm} \cdot f_{t,v^{ucc}} \cdot d^{lm} + \beta^{ucc,hd} \cdot \lvert \mathcal{R}' \rvert$	Costs distribution

choose whether they perform the full transport themselves, or they can decide to outsource last-mile transport to the UCC. For the latter decision, the carriers compare the costs of outsourcing (minus the subsidy income) to performing the last-mile distribution itself, selecting the cheapest solution. Their objective function is given by

$$\max \sum_{t \in \mathcal{T}} \bigg(P_{t,c}^{car,tr}(f_{t,v^c,c}, d^{lh}) - \min\bigg(C_{t,c}^{car,tr}(d^{lh}, d^{lm}, \mathcal{S}', \mathcal{R}'),$$

$$\Big(C_{t,c}^{car,lm}(f_{t,v^c,c}, d^{lh}, \mathcal{S}') - P_{t,c}^{car,sb}\big(f_{t,v^c,c,\gamma\mid\gamma=1}\big) \Big) \bigg) \bigg).$$

For the receivers and the administrator, we do not explicitly define an objective function, as these agents do not make operational decisions in our framework. The performance of the receiver is measured as the sum of receiving costs. These depend on the tactical decision whether delivery takes place via the UCC. If the receiver does not mandate delivery via the UCC, its costs are given by

$$\sum_{t \in \mathcal{T}} \sum_{c \in \mathcal{C} \cup \mathcal{H}} C_{t,r}^{rec,rc}(f_{t,v^r,r,c}).$$

If the receiver mandates deliveries via the UCC, the receiver pays the UCC for last-mile delivery, but incur lower receiving costs due to receiving bundled orders from only one carrier. The costs for the receiver are then given by:

$$\sum_{t \in \mathcal{T}} C_{t,r}^{rec,rc}(f_{t,v^r,r}) + C_{t,r}^{rec,lm}(f_{t,v^r,r}) - P_{t,r}^{rec,sb}(f_{t,v^r,r}).$$

The performance of the administrator is measured with the following KPIs: (i) the number of vehicles per type that enter the urban area, (ii) the total distance covered within the urban area per vehicle type, (iii) the income from policies minus the provided subsidies, and (iv) the emission levels for CO_2, SO_2, NO_x, and particulate matter (PM). The first two KPIs indirectly capture effects such as noise hindrance and the contribution to road congestion. The third KPI should be a nonnegative number for a financially sustainable scheme.

3.4   Decision-Making Policies

All agents aim to optimize their own objective functions. In our dynamic environment, the corresponding operational decision problems are subject to incomplete information. Exact solution methods for stochastic models usually require an unfeasibly large computational effort, which is why we typically resort to heuristic solutions in agent-based simulation. Various policies can be used to tackle the operational decision problems. The specific policies to be used in the simulation are selected based on the instance, and are chosen as simulation settings. For an overview of the possible decisions per agent type, we refer to Fig. 2.

Both shippers and the UCC are faced with the decision when to dispatch accumulated orders. Minkoff [14] describes this problem class as the Delivery Dispatching Problem (DDP). Typical solutions for the DDP are fixed policies based on (i) a threshold on accumulated volume and (ii) the elapsed service time. In our simulation, the dispatching decision is more complicated, as orders are subject to distinct delivery windows, and subsets of orders are periodically dispatched. Orders may be held in inventory for a limited time, anticipating future order arrivals for better consolidation opportunities. Dispatch decisions can be significantly improved when taking into account expected future costs [23]. For this DDP variant, methods such as scenario sampling or stochastic modeling are suitable methods to estimate future costs.

Carriers, as well as the UCC, are required to solve a vehicle routing problem (VRP). An abundant amount of studies has been performed on many variants of the VRP. We refer to Cattaruzza et al. [9] and Kim et al. [12] for recent overviews of VRP solution methods in urban logistics; these methods pay particular attention to aspects such as regulations, emissions, and delivery windows.

As we split the decision problems into a periodic dispatch decision and a vehicle routing problem, solution methods for the static VRP can be applied. To establish credibility of the simulation model with the stakeholders involved, it is sensible to incorporate algorithms similar to the ones used in practice.

3.5 Scenario Analysis

To embed tactical and strategic decisions – requiring commitment on the longer term – into our framework we make use of scenario analysis: measures are given as input to the simulation. In our discussion of scenario analysis, we again refer to the classification of Quak [16]. Governmental policies are typically described by forms of road pricing, parking fees, zone access, and time access restrictions. Such policies are incorporated in the framework by (i) setting constraints as network input, (ii) defining conditional costs and conditions for transport via the urban network, and (iii) specifying allocation rules for possible redistribution in the form of subsidies. Next, we discuss company-driven initiatives. To evaluate measures such as adjusting the fleet or selecting the UCC as the delivery address by the receiver, the characteristics of the agent can be adjusted. Cooperation initiatives are incorporated into the framework as follows. First, the members of the coalition should be specified. Second, the action space of the coalition needs to be defined, including rules for the allocation of tasks to agents. Third, a single objective function must be specified for the coalition. Stable solutions require that the coalitional profit is at least equal to the sum of individual profits of the coalition members. Fourth – as coalitions require rational agents that are willing to cooperate – an appropriate gain-sharing mechanism should be incorporated. Such mechanisms can drawn from the field of cooperative game theory; a comprehensible overview is provided by Osborne & Rubinstein [15].

Finally, physical infrastructure- and transport-reorganizing initiatives are incorporated by modifying the network and may entail, e.g., positioning the UCC or including special transport lanes for licensed vehicles. It is important that the applied routing algorithms properly take into account such restrictions.

The reliability of the simulation results depends on the scenario input data, which may be subject to high variability. For a complete simulation study, we would propose to first establish a reliable range for each parameter, and subsequently apply a fractional factorial design. Such a design only uses the values corresponding to the range bounds, thereby (i) focusing on the main (interaction) effects of measures, and (ii) providing high-level sensitivity analysis. Afterward, more detailed analysis can focus on promising schemes.

4   Computational Study

To briefly illustrate the working of our framework, we test a few urban logistics schemes. We implemented the framework as a discrete-event simulation model in Delphi XE6. We represent the city by a virtual 10×10 km grid, with 1 UCC located at the edge of the grid, 3 carriers, 10 shippers, and 20 receivers (agents of the same type are identical). Network properties are chosen to sufficiently reflect flexibility and diversity. The line-haul distance between shippers and receivers is 100 km. We consider a planning horizon with 500 decision moments, and perform 5 replications per scenario. A warmup period of 10 time units ensures reaching a steady state. At every decision moment, receivers have a demand between 0 and 5 orders, with order sizes ranging between 0.05 and 0.20 of the capacity of a delivery van. The earliest delivery time varies between 0 and 2 time units; the length of the delivery window varies between 1 and 4 time units. Order properties are generated stochastically, and are subject to uniform distributions.

In Table 2, we show the used vehicle properties. Vehicle capacities and average emission values are obtained from Boer *et al.* [6], using capacities for voluminous goods and 2020 engine standards. The UCC uses large vans (> 2 ton), the line-haul carriers deploy medium-sized trucks (10–20 ton). For the delivery van, we deduce costs per hour and vehicle speeds from Roca-Riu *et al.* [17]. We multiply these costs with 1.5 for medium-sized trucks. We set the transport price charged by the carrier to a fixed shipment fee of €35 and a variable cost of €1.5 per km. The UCC charges a volume-based price of €100 per van-load, and incurs receiving costs of €20 for every incoming truck. For receivers and shippers, we set receiving- and shipping costs at €5 per vehicle, respectively.

Table 2. Vehicle properties for carriers (truck) and UCC (delivery van)

Vehicle type	Large van > 2 ton	Truck 10–20 ton
Capacity (ton)	1.2	8
Speed line-haul (km/hour)	50	50
Speed urban area (km/hour)	25	25
Handling costs (€/receiver)	7.9	7.9
Costs line-haul (€/km)	0.83	1.24
Costs urban (€/km)	1.35	2.03
CO_2 (g/km)	299.5	943
SO_2 (mg/km)	2.3	7.2
NO_x (g/km)	0.55	3.1
$PM_{2.5}$ (mg/km)	42	56

We now describe the used decision methods. Shippers only dispatch the set of accumulated orders when it contains an urgent order, and holds the shipment otherwise. To obtain the expected future costs for the UCC, we use a one-step lookahead policy. We sample 5 random order arrivals, for which we compute the expected future costs per action. We select the dispatch action that minimizes the sum of direct costs and lookahead costs. Finally, to solve the routing problems of the carriers and the UCC, we use the cheapest insertion algorithm. Tactical decisions include selection of the UCC by the receiver, forming a carrier coalition, setting parking costs, and subsidizing the UCC.

Table 3. Performance of all agent types under various urban logistics schemes.

Scheme	Measures					Net income($\times 10^3$ €)					External costs
	A	B	C	D	E	Receiver	Shipper	Carrier	UCC	Admin	Admin
1	No	No	No	No	No	−0.6	−12.9	32.9	0.0	0.0	o
2	Yes	No	No	No	No	−0.4	−12.9	40.0	**−24.9**	0.0	++
3	No	Yes	No	No	No	**−2.1**	−12.9	50.8	**−24.2**	0.0	++
4	No	No	Yes	No	No	−0.2	−12.9	67.1	0.0	0.0	+
5	Yes	No	No	Yes	Yes	−0.4	−12.9	40.2	5.0	**−28.2**	++
6	Yes	No	Yes	No	No	−0.3	−12.9	68.5	**−11.5**	0.0	+
7	Yes	No	Yes	Yes	No	−0.4	−12.9	67.9	**−12.0**	1.3	+
8	Yes	No	Yes	Yes	Yes	−0.4	−12.9	68.0	0.3	3.0	+

We test the following measures: (A) carriers may deliver via the UCC (operational decision), (B) receivers mandate delivery via the UCC (scenario input), (C) carriers form a coalition (scenario input), using the Shapley value as a gain-sharing mechanism, (D) parking costs (€3 per stop, only for trucks), and (E) volume-based subsidy to the UCC (€70 per full van-load). Based on these measures, we compose and test eight urban logistics schemes. With these schemes, we aim to show how both individual and combined measures affect system performance. In Table 3, we show the results of the agent types for all schemes, stating the financial performance and an indicator for the external costs. Agents that are negatively affected by a scheme (compared to Scheme 1) are marked in bold. The results underline the difficulty to find feasible schemes. Individual measures often fail to generate the required commitment from all agents. The funding of the UCC is particularly complex. The correct balance between subsidies and policy income must be found; if carriers mostly deliver via the UCC, the income stemming from parking costs may be insufficient to support the UCC. For the tested instance, the existence of the carrier coalition is required to obtain sufficient income from parking costs. We highlight the results of Scheme 8, which significantly cuts emissions (CO_2 by 47.5 %, SO_2 by 47.4 %, NO_x by 53.1 %, and PM by 30.2 %), reduces the number of trucks in the city center by 60 %, and reduce the overall urban transport distance (by both trucks and vans) by 20 %. Although many measures have the potential to reduce external costs, the challenge remains to combine them into a feasible scheme.

5   Conclusion

Although the need for improving urban freight transport is widely recognized, existing initiatives often fail due to a lack of commitment by the actors involved. In this study, we designed an agent-based simulation framework to evaluate a wide array of urban logistics schemes. We defined the roles of five agent types, and described their actions, monetary streams, and information streams. For every agent type, we specified KPIs to measure the system performance. To reflect the practice of urban logistics – where we must align the interests of multiple actors – every agent is an autonomous decision maker. As such, we assess the behavior and performance of every agent type. Agents rationally optimize their operational decisions during the simulation, whereas tactical and strategical decisions are embedded by means of scenario analysis.

As practice indicates that schemes combining both governmental policies and company-driven initiatives yield the best results, we designed the framework such that both aspects are well represented. The urban consolidation center (UCC) has a key role in our framework, as it facilitates both consolidation and the deployment of designated delivery vehicles against lower (external) costs. Furthermore, we included governmental policies such as road pricing, zone access and parking costs; gains stemming from these measures can be used to subsidize agents in a closed-loop scheme. To define company-driven initiatives, we described collaboration between carriers, as well as various kinds of interaction between the companies and the UCC. Another distinctive feature of our framework is that we explicitly took into account the effect of line-haul transport on the last-mile distribution, rather than focusing only on the last mile. With our simulation framework, we can measure the impact of schemes on financial performance and external costs, and verify whether autonomous actors could commit to such a scheme in the long run.

References

1. Allen, J., Browne, M., Woodburn, A., Leonardi, J.: The role of urban consolidation centres in sustainable freight transport. Transp. Rev. **32**(4), 473–490 (2012)
2. Anand, N., Quak, H., van Duin, R., Tavasszy, L.: City logistics modeling efforts: trends and gaps - a review. Procedia Soc. Behav. Sci. **39**, 101–115 (2012)
3. Anderson, S., Allen, J., Browne, M.: Urban logistics - how can it meet policy makers sustainability objectives? J. Transp. Geogr. **13**(1), 71–81 (2005)
4. Bektaş, T., Crainic, T.G., Van Woensel, T.: From managing urban freight to smart city logistics networks. CIRRELT 2015–2017 (2015)
5. Benjelloun, A., Crainic, T.G.: Trends, challenges, and perspectives in city logistics. In: Transportation and Land Use Interaction, Proceedings TRANSLU, vol. 8, pp. 269–284 (2008)
6. Boer, E., Otten, M.B.J., Essen, H.: Comparison of various transport modes on a EU scale with the STREAM database. CE Delft (2011)
7. Boerkamps, J., van Binsbergen, A.: Goodtrip - a new approach for modelling and evaluating urban goods distribution. In: Taniguchi, E., R.G., T. (eds.) City Logistics I, pp. 175–186. ARRB Group Limited, Melbourne (1999)
8. Browne, M., Sweet, M., Woodburn, A., Allen, J.: Urban freight consolidation centres. Transport Studies Group 10 (2005)
9. Cattaruzza, D., Absi, N., Feillet, D., González-Feliu, J.: Vehicle routing problems for city logistics. EURO J. Transp. Logistics, 1–29 (2015)
10. Crainic, T.G., Ricciardi, N., Storchi, G.: Models for evaluating and planning city logistics systems. Transp. Sci. **43**(4), 432–454 (2009)
11. Gevaers, R., Van de Voorde, E., Vanelslander, T.: Characteristics and typology of last-mile logistics from an innovation perspective in an urban context. In: Macharis, C., Melo, S. (eds.) City Distribution and Urban Freight Transport: Multiple Perspectives, pp. 56–71. Edward Elger, Cheltenham (2011)

12. Kim, G., Ong, Y.S., Heng, C.K., Tan, P.S., Zhang, N.A.: City vehicle routing problem (city VRP): a review. IEEE Trans. Intell. Transp. Syst. **16**(4), 1654–1666 (2015)
13. Macharis, C., Milan, L., Verlinde, S.: A stakeholder-based multicriteria evaluation framework for city distribution. Res. Transp. Bus. Manage. **11**, 75–84 (2014)
14. Minkoff, A.S.: A Markov decision model and decomposition heuristic for dynamic vehicle dispatching. Oper. Res. **41**(1), 77–90 (1993)
15. Osborne, M.J., Rubinstein, A.: A Course in Game Theory. MIT Press, Cambridge (1994)
16. Quak, H.: Urban freight transport: the challenge of sustainability. In: Macharis, C., Melo, S. (eds.) City Distribution and Urban Freight Transport: Multiple Perspectives, pp. 37–56. Edward Elger, Cheltenham (2011)
17. Roca-Riu, M., Estrada, M., Fernández, E.: An evaluation of urban consolidation centers through continuous analysis with non-equal market share companies. Transp. Res. Procedia **12**, 370–382 (2016)
18. Russo, F., Comi, A.: A classification of city logistics measures and connected impacts. Procedia Soc. Behav. Sci. **2**(3), 6355–6365 (2010)
19. Tamagawa, D., Taniguchi, E., Yamada, T.: Evaluating city logistics measures using a multi-agent model. Procedia Soc. Behav. Sci. **2**(3), 6002–6012 (2010)
20. Taniguchi, E., Thompson, R.G., Yamada, T.: Concepts and visions for urban transport and logistics relating to human security. In: Taniguchi, E., Fwa, T.F., Thompson, R.G. (eds.) Urban Transportation and Logistics: Health, Safety, and Security Concerns, pp. 1–30. CRC Press, Boca Raton (2014)
21. United Nations: Worlds population increasingly urban with more than half living in urban areas (2014). https://www.un.org/development/desa/en/news/population/world-urbanization-prospects.html. Accessed 22 Mar 2016
22. Van Duin, R.J., van Kolck, A., Anand, N., Taniguchi, E.: Towards an agent-based modelling approach for the evaluation of dynamic usage of urban distribution centres. Procedia Soc. Behav. Sci. **39**, 333–348 (2012)
23. Van Heeswijk, W.J.A., Mes, M.R., Schutten, M.J.: An approximate dynamic programming approach to urban freight distribution with batch arrivals. In: Corman, F., Voß, S., Negenborn, R.R. (eds.) ICCL 2015. LNCS, vol. 9335, pp. 61–75. Springer, Switzerland (2015)
24. Van Rooijen, T., Quak, H.: Local impacts of a new urban consolidation centre-the case of Binnenstadservice. nl. Procedia Soc. Behav. Sci. **2**(3), 5967–5979 (2010)
25. Wangapisit, O., Taniguchi, E., Teo, J.S., Qureshi, A.G.: Multi-agent systems modelling for evaluating joint delivery systems. Procedia Soc. Behav. Sci. **125**, 472–483 (2014)

Continuous-Time Formulation for Oil Products Transportation Scheduling

Hossein Mostafaei[1,2] and Pedro M. Castro[1(✉)]

[1] Centro de Matemática Aplicações Fundamentais e Investigação Operacional,
Faculdade de Ciências, Universidade de Lisboa, 1749-016 Lisbon, Portugal
{hmostafaei, pmcastro}@fc.ul.pt
[2] Department of Applied Mathematics,
Azarbaijan Shahid Madani University, Tabriz, Iran

Abstract. This paper presents a novel Mixed Integer Linear Programming (MILP) model for the operational planning of an oil transportation system characterized by a straight multiproduct pipeline with dual purpose terminals that could represent facility input or output. It is based on a continuous representation in both time and volume scales and is capable of meeting all operational constraints related to product sequencing, mass balances and pipeline loading/unloading operations. Contrary to previous approaches, the model allows an intermediate node and the previous segment to simultaneously inject material in the pipeline. Computational results and data are reported.

Keywords: Transportation · MILP · Pipeline networks · Continuous representation

1 Introduction

Compared with other transportation modes (rail, road tankers and coastal vessels), liquid pipelines provide an economic mode of transportation for refined petroleum products when large quantities have to be moved over large distances. Pipelines must always be full, meaning that a volume of material must be pushed into a segment in order to pump out the same amount at the other extremity, not necessarily of the same product. The main goal of pipeline scheduling is to ensure that oil products will be available to the customer at the right time, preferably at the lowest cost. This paper is concerned with a pipeline system that must distribute a number of petroleum products from multiple refineries to several distribution centers.

Research on the operational planning of pipeline networks has used mixed integer linear programming (MILP) or non-linear programming (MINLP) and consider the time representation as either discrete or continuous. Discrete approaches divide the planning horizon into time intervals of equal and fixed duration [5, 11], whereas the continuous representation relaxes such assumption by determining interval length as part of the optimization, [1, 3, 4, 6–8, 10, 12]. Cafaro et al. [2] presented a two-level approach based on continuous time MILP for detailed scheduling of real world pipeline system with dual purpose stations. The model is able to handle simultaneous injections and deliveries during any pumping operation. Mostafaei et al. [9] developed a single level MILP formulation to solve the problem. The approach meets the same targets

© Springer International Publishing Switzerland 2016
A. Paias et al. (Eds.): ICCL 2016, LNCS 9855, pp. 384–396, 2016.
DOI: 10.1007/978-3-319-44896-1_25

with a reduced number of pumping operations and a lower makespan. Both approaches assume that at any time, each segment of the pipeline can receive material from either the previous segment or the tank farm at the segment origin. To overcome this limitation and address more realistic pipeline operations, this paper introduces a monolithic MILP framework for operational scheduling that is capable of handling interacting pumping runs, in which a pipeline segment can simultaneously receive product from its upstream segment and the dual purpose station at its origin.

The remainder of the paper is structured as follows: Following the problem statement in Sect. 2, we present, in Sect. 3, a novel MILP formulation for scheduling oil products distribution through a multi-source pipeline network. The validity of the proposed model is tested using three case studies, leading to the results in Sect. 4. Finally, we give the conclusions in Sect. 5.

2 Problem Statement

This paper takes into account a real world pipeline system. Figure 1 depicts a schematic representation of the pipeline configuration. The straight pipeline system consists of a set of segments with single or dual purpose stations in between. Refineries act as input nodes that send product batches to the pipeline that are destined to reach the output terminals. The goal is to determine the size and sequence of the new batches to inject in order to minimize unmet product demand at the output terminals and the number of pumping runs. The time horizon is fixed and the following restrictions apply: (1) pipeline segments are always full, (2) a pumping operation involves at most one batch injection and removal at each node and (3) pipeline segments operate in single flow direction, from left to right in the diagrams, with the flow rate belonging to a given acceptable range.

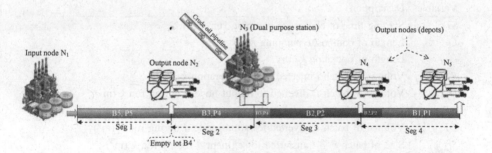

Fig. 1. Straight pipeline system with multiple intermediate nodes

3 Mathematical Formulation

The proposed model can be regarded as a generalization of the mathematical model recently introduced by Mostafaei et al. [9] for the scheduling of multi-source pipeline systems. The model involves six major sets: (a) composite pumping runs K (b) pipeline segments $d \in D$ with segment d connecting nodes N_d and N_{d+1} (c) product batches $I = \{i_1, i_2, \ldots\}$ traveling inside the pipeline during the planning horizon; (d) new batches I^{new} to be injected ($I^{new} \subseteq I$); (e) product batches $I_d \subseteq I$ ($I_d = I_d^{old} \cup I_d^{new}$) to passing segment d, with I_d^{old} indicating the batches initially inside segment d and I_d^{new} denoting the batches to be transferred to segment d within the planning horizon; (f) oil products $P = \{p_1, p_2, \ldots p_{|P|}\}$. The parameters and decision variables are shown in Tables 1 and 2.

Table 1. List of parameters

Parameter	Description
$h_{\max}$	Horizon length (measured in hours)
ST	Starting time of the first composite run (h)
$vs_{d,\min}/vs_{d,\max}$	Minimum/ maximum flow rate in the segment d (m³/h)
$vd_{d,\min}/vd_{d,\max}$	Minimum/maximum injection rate at the input node d (m³/h)
$vp_{p,d}$	Maximum delivery rate of product p to output terminal d (m³/h)
V_d	Volume of segment d (m³)
$R_{d,\min}/R_{d,\max}$	Minimum/maximum batch sizes injected from the input node d (m³)
$S_{d,\max}$	Minimum batch size transferred to segment d (m³)
$D_{d,\min}/D_{d,\max}$	Minimum/maximum batch sizes diverted to the output node d (m³)
$IW_{i,d}$	Size of old batch i in segment d (m³)
$Dem_{p,d}$	Demand of product p at output terminal d (m³)
$Q_{p,d}$	Inventory of product p at input terminal d (m³)
cb	Unit backorder cost ($/m³)
fc	Fixed cost for performing a pumping run ($/run)

Table 2. List of variables

Variables	Description
ST_k	Starting time of composite pumping run k (h)
L_k	Length of composite pumping run k (h)
$L_{k,d}$	Length of operation k_d (h)
$R_{i,k,d}$	Volume of batch i injected during operation k_d (m³)
$D_{i,k,d}$	Volume of batch i_d diverted to output node d during run k (m³)
$RP_{i,p,k,d}$	Volume of batch i containing product p injected during operation k_d (m³)
$DP_{i,p,k,d}$	Volume of batch i_p diverted to output node d during run k (m³)
$S_{i,k,d}$	Size of batch i_{d-1} transferred to segment d during run k (m³)
$W_{i,k,d}$	Size of batch i_d at the end of composite run k (m³)
$F_{i,k,d}$	Upper coordinate of batch i_d at the end of composite run k (m³)
$B_{p,d}$	Unsatisfied demand of product p at output terminal d (m³)
$w_{i,k,d}$	1 if a portion of batch i is injected during operation k_d; 0 otherwise
z_k	1 if pipeline is active during composite run k; otherwise 0
$x_{i,k,d}$	1 if batch i_d is diverted to output terminal d through run k; 0 otherwise
$u_{i,k,d}$	1 if batch i_{d-1} is transferred to segment d through run k; 0 otherwise
$v_{k,d}$	1 if segment d is active through run k; 0 otherwise
$y_{i,p}$	1 if batch i conveys product p; 0 otherwise

Pipeline Loading from Input Nodes. Binary variable $w_{i,k,d}$ is equal to 1 if pumping run k performed at input node d (input operation k_d) injects batch i into segment d. Eq. (1) states that at most one batch can be injected by a pumping run. Let non-negative continuous variable $F_{i,k,d}$ give the upper coordinate of batch i in segment d (batch i_d) at the end of run k. Batch i_d can receive product from input node d only if the lower coordinate of i (upper coordinate of $i+1$) at the end of the previous run k with respect to segment d is equal to zero, i.e. $F_{i+1,k-1,d} = 0$, see Eq. (2). Furthermore, its upper coordinate must have reached the end of the previous segment, $F_{i,k-1,d-1} = V_{d-1}$, leading to Eq. (3). The volume of batch i injected into the pipeline ($R_{i,k,d}$) must be within given lower and upper bounds, Eq. (4). Similarly, the duration of input operation k_d, given by continuous variable $L_{k,d}$, must be within a range calculated dividing the injected volume ($R_{i,k,d}$) by the minimum and maximum processing rates in the segment, see Eq. (5).

$$\sum_{i \in I_d} w_{i,k,d} \leq 1, \quad \forall k \in K, d \in D, \tag{1}$$

$$F_{i+1,k-1,d} \leq V_d(1 - w_{i,k,d}), \quad \forall i \in I_d, k \in K, d \in D, \tag{2}$$

$$F_{i,k-1,d-1} \geq V_{d-1} w_{i,k,d}, \quad \forall i \in I_d, k \in K, d \in D, \tag{3}$$

$$R_{d,\min} w_{i,k,d} \leq R_{i,k,d} \leq R_{d,\max} w_{i,k,d}, \quad \forall i \in I_d, k \in K, d \in D, \tag{4}$$

$$\sum_{i \in I_d} \frac{R_{i,k,d}}{vd_{d,\max}} \leq L_{k,d} \leq \sum_{i \in I_d} \frac{R_{i,k,d}}{vd_{d,\min}}, \quad \forall k \in K, d \in D. \tag{5}$$

Each batch consists of at most a single product p, imposed by Eq. (6). If new batch i is injected into the pipeline during the time horizon, it will convey a product and vice versa, Eq. (7). The continuous variable $RP_{i,p,k,d}$, indicating the volume of product p contained in batch i pumped during input operation k_d, will be equal the initial size of batch i, Eqs. (8–9). Besides, the total volume of product p pumped from an input terminal d cannot be greater than $Q_{p,d}$, a known datum denoting the inventory level of product p at input terminal d, Eq. (10).

$$\sum_{p \in P} y_{i,p} \leq 1, \quad \forall i \in I, \tag{6}$$

$$\sum_{p \in P} y_{i,p} \leq \sum_{d \in D} \sum_{k \in K} w_{i,k,d} \leq |K| \sum_{p \in P} y_{i,p}, \quad \forall i \in I^{new}, \tag{7}$$

$$\sum_{k \in K} RP_{i,p,k,d} \leq |K| R_{d,\max} y_{i,p}, \quad \forall i \in I_d, p \in P, d \in D, \tag{8}$$

$$\sum_{p \in P} RP_{i,p,k,d} = R_{i,k,d}, \quad \forall i \in I_d, k \in K, d \in D, \tag{9}$$

$$\sum_{i \in I_d} \sum_{k \in K} RP_{i,p,k,d} \leq Q_{p,d}, \quad \forall p \in P, d \in D. \tag{10}$$

Pipeline Unloading to Output Nodes. Being binary variable $x_{i,k,d}$ equal to 1 if pumping run k directs batch i_d into depot d, Eq. (11) allows for at most one batch discharged during composite run k. Discharge to depot d can happen only if the upper coordinate at time ST_k satisfies $F_{i,k-1,d} = V_d$. It is translated into Eq. (12). Equation (13) then limits the amount discharged $D_{i,k,d}$ to the given range of values. If batch i_d conveys product p, the size of product p contained in batch i_d discharged to depot d ($DP_{i,p,k,d}$) will be equal to $D_{i,k,d}$; otherwise $DP_{i,p,k,d}$ is set to zero, Eq. (15). To meet demand during the scheduling horizon, the size of batches containing product p diverted into depot d should be as large as $Dem_{p,d}$, known data standing for total demand of depot d_p. The unsatisfied demand $B_{p,d}$ in Eq. (16) is penalized in the objective function.

$$\sum_{i \in I_d} x_{i,k,d} \leq 1, \quad \forall k \in K, d \in D, \tag{11}$$

$$F_{i,k-1,d} \geq V_d x_{i,k,d}, \quad \forall i \in I_d, k \in K, d \in D, \tag{12}$$

$$D_{d,\min} x_{i,k,d} \leq D_{i,k,d} \leq D_{d,\max} x_{i,k,d}, \quad \forall i \in I_d, k \in K, d \in D, \tag{13}$$

$$\sum_{p \in P} DP_{i,p,k,d} = D_{i,k,d}, \quad \forall i \in I_d, k \in K, d \in D, \tag{14}$$

$$\sum_{k \in K} DP_{i,p,k,d} \leq |K| D_{d,\max} y_{i,p}, \quad \forall i \in I_d, p \in P, d \in D, \tag{15}$$

$$\sum_{i \in I_d} \sum_{k \in K} DP_{i,p,k,d} + B_{p,d} \geq Dem_{p,d}, \quad \forall p \in P, d \in D. \tag{16}$$

On the other hand, due to operation rules, some oil products cannot be discharged to certain depots at full pressure and so:

$$\sum_{i \in I_d} DP_{i,p,k,d} \leq vp_{p,d} L_k, \quad \forall p \in P, k \in K, d \in D. \tag{17}$$

Moving Material from Segment d–1 to d. Binary variable $u_{i,k,d}$ is equal to 1 if pumping run k inputs batch i_{d-1} into segment d. As before, at most one batch can enter segment d during run k, Eq. (18). During the execution of composite run k, a portion of batch i_{d-1} can be transferred into segment d only if its upper coordinate at time ST_k touches the end of segment $d - 1$, Eqs. (19)–(20). Constraint (21) acts as an upper bound on the material simultaneously transferred from batch i_d to segment $d + 1$ and output terminal d.

$$\sum_{i \in I_{d-1}} u_{i,k,d} \leq 1, \quad \forall k \in K, d \in D(d \geq 2), \tag{18}$$

$$F_{i,k-1,d-1} \geq V_{d-1} u_{i,k,d}, \quad \forall i \in I_{d-1}, k \in K, d \in D(d \geq 2), \tag{19}$$

$$D_{d,\min} u_{i,k,d} \leq S_{i,k,d} \leq S_{d,\max} u_{i,k,d}, \quad \forall i \in I_{d-1}, k \in K, d \in D(d \geq 2), \tag{20}$$

$$S_{i,k,d+1} + D_{i,k,d} \leq W_{i,k-1,d} + R_{i,k,d} + S_{i,k,d}, \quad \forall i \in I_d, k \in K, d \in D. \tag{21}$$

Interacting Pumping Operations. Interacting pumping operations between the input node d (at the start of segment d) and segment $d - 1$, also feeding d, are possible only if the same batch is involved, see Eq. (22).

$$\sum_{i' \in I_{d-1}, i' > i} u_{i',k,d} + w_{i,k,d} \leq 1, \quad \forall i \in I_d, k \in K, d \in D(d \geq 2). \tag{22}$$

No material can be transferred from batch $i'(i' > i)$ to segment $d + 1$ when a pumping run belonging to composite run k discharges some materials from batch i_d to depot d. Thus,

$$\sum_{i' \in I_d, i' > i} u_{i',k,d+1} + x_{i,k,d} \leq 1, \quad \forall i \in I_d, k \in K, d \in D. \tag{23}$$

Timing Constraints. Let L_k give the length of composite run k. If run k is executed at the input node located at the start of segment d, then the two duration variables must have the same values:

$$L_{k,d} \leq L_k \leq L_{k,d} + h_{\max}(1 - \sum_{i \in I_d} w_{i,k,d}), \quad \forall k \in K, d \in D. \tag{24}$$

The duration of all runs must be lower than the planning horizon ($h_{\max}$) :

$$\sum_{k \in K} L_k \leq h_{\max}. \tag{25}$$

The starting time of composite run k must be greater than the starting time of the previous run plus its duration:

$$ST_k - ST_{k-1} \geq L_{k-1}, \quad \forall k \in K(k \geq 2). \tag{26}$$

$$ST_k = ST, \quad k = first(K). \tag{27}$$

Tracking Batch Size and Location. $W_{i,k,d}$ is the size of batch i_d at the end of composite pumping run k. Its value is given by Eqs. (28)–(29):

$$W_{i,k,d} = W_{i,k-1,d} + R_{i,k,d} + S_{i,k,d} - D_{i,k,d} - S_{i,k,d+1}, \quad \forall i \in I_d, k \in K, d \in D, \quad (28)$$

$$W_{i,k,d} = IW_{i,d}, \quad \forall i \in I_d^{old}, d \in D, k = first(K). \quad (29)$$

The upper coordinate of batch i_d at time ST_{k+1} is the volume between the origin of segment d and the interface between batches i_d and $(i+1)_d$:

$$F_{i,k,d} = \sum_{i' \geq i, i' \in I_d} W_{i',k,d} \quad \forall i \in I_d, k \in K, d \in D. \quad (30)$$

Mass Balances. Since pipeline segments are always full, the total volume of products entering segment d due to run k must be equal to the amount leaving the segment.

$$\sum_{i \in I_{d-1}} S_{i,k,d} + \sum_{i \in I_d} R_{i,k,d} = \sum_{i \in I_d} D_{i,k,d} + \sum_{i \in I_d} S_{i,k,d+1}, \quad \forall k \in K, d \in D. \quad (31)$$

Flow Rate Limitation. Binary variable $v_{k,d}$ is equal to 1 if there is a flow motion in segment d during run k and its value satisfies the following Eqs:

$$\sum_{i \in I_d} w_{i,k,d} \leq v_{k,d}, \quad \forall k \in K, d \in D, \quad (32)$$

$$\sum_{i \in I_d} x_{i,k,d} \leq v_{k,d}, \quad \forall k \in K, d \in D, \quad (33)$$

$$v_{k,d} \leq v_{k,d-1} + \sum_{i \in I_d} w_{i,k,d}, \quad \forall k \in K, d \in D(d \geq 2), \quad (34)$$

$$\sum_{i \in I_{d-1}} u_{i,k,d} \leq v_{k,d}, \quad \forall k \in K, d \in D(d \geq 2). \quad (35)$$

Due to operational rules, flow rate in an active segment is kept in the feasible range, where $vs_{d,\min}$ and $vs_{d,\max}$ are the minimum and maximum rates in segment d, respectively:

$$vs_{d,\min} L_k - S_{\max,d}(1 - v_{k,d}) \leq \sum_{i \in I_d} R_{i,k,d} + \sum_{i \in I_{d-1}} S_{i,k,d} \leq vs_{d,\max} L_k, \quad \forall k \in K, d \in D.$$

$$(36)$$

Objective Function. The objective function is to meet product demand at the depots while keeping the number of pumping runs at a minimum:

$$\min z = \sum_{d \in D} \sum_{p \in P} cb \times B_{p,d} + \sum_{k \in K} fc \times z_k, \tag{37}$$

where the binary variable z_k satisfies the following Eqs:

$$z_k \geq \sum_{i \in I_d} w_{i,k,d}, \quad \forall k \in K, d \in D. \tag{38}$$

$$z_{k-1} \geq z_k, \quad \forall k \in K(k \geq 2). \tag{39}$$

4 Results and Discussion

Three examples are solved to illustrate the capabilities of the new continuous-time formulation for the short-term scheduling of multi-source pipeline systems, one of them involving an industrial case study. All MILP problems were solved by GAMS/CPLEX 12.6 in parallel deterministic mode (using up to 4 threads) on an Intel i5-4210U (2.7 GHz) CPU with 6 GB of RAM running Windows 7 (64-bit).

Remark: To determine the optimal number of pumping operations, we start with a few injections and then increase the number one by one. The procedure is repeated until no better optimum is discovered.

Example 1. This example is similar to one presented by Mostafaei et al. [9], in which a pipeline connects three input nodes (N1–N3) to three depots (N2–N4). The first line of Fig. 2 depicts pipeline topography and its initial state at time $ST = 0$ h. Product supplies and demands at pipeline terminals are listed in Table 3. The horizon length is 168 h and the flow rate at every pipeline segment should not surpass 1.4 volumetric units per hour (v.u/h). Besides, the following values for parameters are used: $R_{d,\min} = D_{d,\min} = 10$, $R_{d,\max} = D_{d,\max} = S_{d,\max} = 40$, $cb = 200$ and $fc = 100$.

The optimal operational schedule for Example 1 is presented in Fig. 2 and was found in 3.23 CPUs. Shown in Fig. 2 are: batch sizes inside the segments, size of batch injections at input nodes (arrows pointing down), size of batches transferred to depots (upward-pointing arrows), and volume transferred between segments in interacting pumping runs (horizontal colored arrows). Composite runs *k1* and *k4* feature interacting pumping runs. Through composite run *k1* (see the second line of Fig. 2) 40 v.u of product P4 and 10 v.u of product P1 are simultaneously injected into the pipeline from input nodes N1 and N3, respectively, and at the same time 10 v.u of product P1 owing to the pumping operation at node N1, is entering segment N3–N4. On the other hand, 30 v.u of product P4 and 20 v.u of product P1 are simultaneously transferred into the output depots N2 and N4 respectively. Through the careful coordination among input and output operations, product demands at depots are fully satisfied within 121.41 h,

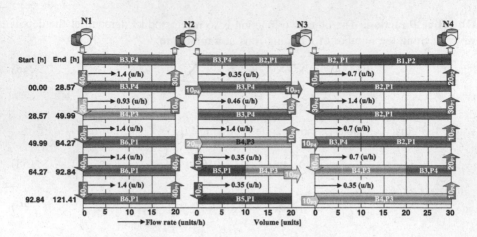

Fig. 2. Pipeline schedule for Example 1.

Table 3. Product supplies and demands for Example 1.

Product	Supplies (v.u)			Demands (v.u)		
	N1	N2	N3	N2	N3	N4
P1	100	-	40	80	-	60
P2	-	20	-	-	-	20
P3	20	-	10	-	-	-
P4	40	-	-	40	20	10

almost 2 days short of the planning horizon. The model includes 1568 constraints and 1241 variables, of which 227 are binary.

Example 2. Example 2 is a real world case study [9] and concerns the scheduling of an Iranian oil products pipeline with a length of 345 km connecting two inputs (N1, N3) to three output terminals (N2, N3, N4). The pipeline can be divided in three segments with node N3 being a dual purpose node (see the top of Fig. 3). The acceptable flow rate ranges, given in (m^3/h), are the following: [80, 400] for segments N1–N2 and N2–N3 and [80, 320] for segment N3–N4. The maximum unloading rate for products P3 and P4 at depot N2 is 200 m^3/h. Product supply and demand for a planning horizon of four days are given in Table 4. Each composite run has a fixed cost of \$1200, while backorder costs 200 \$/m3. Other data can be found in [9].

The optimal pipeline schedule allowing for interacting pumping runs is shown in Fig. 3 and was found in just 3.127 CPUs (see Table 5). The first line of Fig. 3 shows the pipeline situation at the starting time of the planning horizon i.e. at time $ST = 0$ h, while the next lines represent the pipeline status at the end of the composite runs. The pipeline schedule consists of 8 pumping runs from the two input nodes that are arranged in 4 composite runs ($|K| = 4$). Composite runs $k2$, $k3$ and $k4$ feature interacting pumping runs, in which the last segment is fed by both dual purpose node N3

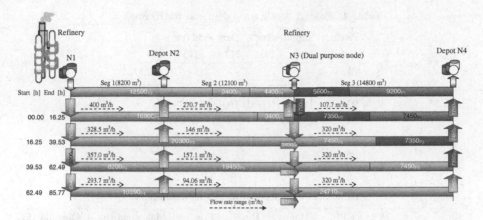

Fig. 3. Best pipeline scheduling for Example 2 using proposed model.

and segment N2–N3. Pipeline segments are kept active and demands are fully satisfied within 85.77 h, 10.23 h below the planning horizon length.

To show the improvements based on both operational performance and computational cost, Example 2 has been also solved using the MILP model recently introduced by Mostafaei et al. [9] that is not capable of handling interacting runs. The best pipeline schedule with non-interacting runs is given in Fig. 4. It includes 7 composite and 14 output operations at input nodes. The model size and the optimal operation cost for example 2 are listed in Table 5. The results confirm that the proposed MILP model finds a better schedule, improves all key performance indicators and leads to much better pipeline operation.

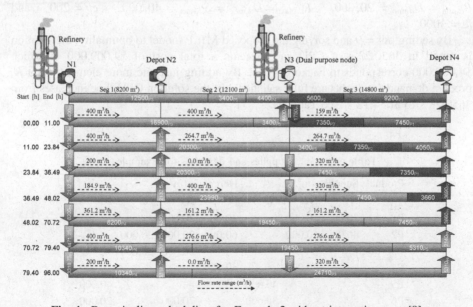

Fig. 4. Best pipeline scheduling for Example 2 without interacting runs [9].

Table 4. Product supplies and demands for Example 2.

Product	Supplies (m³)		Demands (m³)		
	N1	N3	N2	N3	N4
P1	-	-	-	-	9,200
P2	-	3,000	-	-	7,350
P3	14,200	9,000	10,940	-	-
P4	15,100	-	4,650	4,400	-
P5	5,000	4,500	-	-	7,450
P6	-	-	-	-	-

Table 5. Computational results for Example 2.

Case	$|K|$	CPU (s)	Cont. vars	Bin. vars	Eqs	Makespan (h)	Obj. fun ($)
Mostafaei et al. [12]	7	12.36	1478	242	1,677	96.00	8,400
Proposed model	4	3.127	866	155	993	85.77	4,800

Example 3. This example is considered in Cafaro et al. [2] and concerns the scheduling of an oil products pipeline with a length of 900 km connecting three inputs (N1, N2, N3) to four output terminals (N3, N4, N5, N6). Cafaro et al. [2] considered a horizon length of 700 h, but here we reduce the time horizon to 250 h. Product supply and demand is given in Table 6. The flow rate in every active segment should be kept between 400 and 800 m³/h. Besides, the following values for parameters are used: $R_{d,min} = D_{d,min} = 20,000$, $R_{d,max} = D_{d,max} = S_{d,max} = 40,000$, $cb = 200$ and $fc = 1000$.

By setting $|K| = 9$ and solving the proposed MILP model to optimality, the solution is found in 3650.23 s of CPU and presents a total cost of $4,009,000 of which $4,000,000 corresponds to backorder cost. By adding just one more element to set K, product demands at depots are fully satisfied, but the solution CPU time increases from 3650.23 s to 8654.12 s (see Table 7).

Table 6. Product supplies and demands for Example 3.

Product	Supplies (m³)			Demands (m³)			
	N1	N2	N3	N3	N4	N5	N6
P1	20,000	60,000	-	40,000	20,000	-	-
P2	40,000	60,000	-	60,000	20,000	20,000	-
P3	-	-	-	-	20,000	20,000	-
P4	-	40,000	-	40,000	-	-	20,000
P5	-	-	40,000	-	-	-	40,000
P6	-	-	80,000	-	20,000	-	20,000

Table 7. Computational results for Example 3.

Case	$|K|$	CPU (s)	Cont. vars	Bin. vars	Eqs	Backorder (%)	Obj. fun ($)
Proposed model	9	3,650.23	4688	905	7,625	5.8	4,009,000
Proposed model	10	8,654.12	5196	966	8,413	0	10,000

5   Conclusion

A monolithic continuous-time MILP model for the scheduling of multi-product pipeline networks was developed. It can be applied to straight pipeline networks featuring multiple input and output terminals, including dual-purpose stations. Contrary to previous approaches, the model is capable of handling interacting pumping runs, significantly reducing the number of pumping operations and the makespan. The model was successfully applied to a real world case study.

Acknowledgment. Financial support from the Iranian Ministry of Science and Technology and Fundação para a Ciência e Tecnologia through the Investigador FCT 2013 program and project UID/MAT/04561/2013.

References

1. Cafaro, D.C., Cerda, J.: Optimal scheduling of multiproduct pipeline systems using a non-discrete MILP formulation. Comput. Chem. Eng. **28**, 2053–2068 (2004)
2. Cafaro, V.G., Cafaro, D.C., Mendez, C.A., Cerda, J.: Optimization model for the detailed scheduling of multi-source pipelines. Comput. Ind. Eng. **88**, 395–409 (2015)
3. Castro, P.M.: Optimal scheduling of pipeline systems with a resource-task network continuous-time formulation. Ind. Eng. Chem. Res. **49**, 11491–11505 (2010)
4. Ghaffari-Hadigheh, A., Mostafaei, H.: On the scheduling of real world multiproduct pipelines with simultaneous delivery. Optim. Eng. **16**, 571–604 (2015)
5. Hane, C.A., Ratliff, H.D.: Sequencing inputs to multi-commodity pipelines. Ann. Oper. Res. **57**, 73–101 (1995)
6. Mostafaei, H., Alipouri, Y., Shokri, J.: A mixed-integer linear programming for scheduling a multi-product pipeline with dual-purpose terminals. Comput. Appl. Math. **34**, 979–1007 (2015)
7. Mostafaei, H., Alipouri, Y., Zadahmad, M.: A mathematical model for scheduling of real-world tree-structured multi-product pipeline system. Math. Methods Oper. Res. **81**, 53–81 (2015)
8. Mostafaei, H., Castro, P.M., Ghaffari-Hadigheh, A.: A novel monolithic MILP framework for lot-sizing and scheduling of multiproduct tree-like pipeline networks. Ind. Eng. Chem. Res. **54**, 9202–9221 (2015)
9. Mostafaei, H., Castro, P.M., Ghaffari-Hadigheh, A.: Short-term scheduling of multiple source pipelines with simultaneous injections and deliveries. Comput. Oper. Res. **73**, 27–42 (2016)

10. Mostafaei, H., Ghaffari-Hadigheh, A.: A general modeling framework for the long-term scheduling of multiproduct pipelines with delivery constraints. Ind. Eng. Chem. Res. **53**, 7029–7042 (2014)
11. Rejowski, R., Pinto, J.M.: Scheduling of a multiproduct pipeline system. Comput. Chem. Eng. **27**, 1229–1246 (2003)
12. Zaghian, A., Mostafaei, H.: An MILP model for scheduling the operation of a refined petroleum products distribution system. Oper. Res. (2015). doi:10.1007/s12351-015-0212-y

Impact of Collaborative Decision Making
in Optimized Air Traffic Control:
A Game Theoretical Approach

Manish Tripathy[1,2], Marcella Samà[3], Francesco Corman[1(✉)],
and Gabriel Lodewijks[1]

[1] Transport Engineering and Logistics,
Delft University of Technology, Delft, The Netherlands
F.Corman@tudelft.nl
[2] Fuqua School of Business, Duke University, Durham, NC, USA
[3] Department of Engineering, Roma Tre University, Rome, Italy

Abstract. Air traffic is growing, putting increasing stress to airports and air traffic control. The introduction of optimized approaches, based on mathematical optimization paradigms for planning and real time control, can be a possible solution to this issues. We investigate the practical setting of an advanced optimization algorithm in a real-life setting of a major airport where traffic is diverse, belonging to multiple companies. We compare to the incumbent practice (based on First Come First Served) in order to determine a gap with optimized solutions computed by advanced algorithms. Those are based on a job shop scheduling model and solved by a commercial solver.

This paper analyses the benefit for the involved operators of such approaches by associating a monetary cost/benefit to operations. Cooperative game theory tools have been used in the analysis. In particular, we use the Shapley value to determine the fair distribution of the costs based on the marginal improvement that the optimization of the traffic belonging to any airline brought to the system. The main conclusions of this study are the determination of the superior performance in terms of minimising the delay experienced by the whole airport, which reaches more than 25 %. The benefit allocation gives share of benefits more insightful than a simple proportional approaches based on share of traffic, or share of delay. The practical implications of the analysis with regard to variety in benefits as well as possible implementations by the different operators and companies are also analysed.

Keywords: Air traffic control · Collaborative decision making · Game theory · Aircraft scheduling problem

1 Introduction

The growth of aviation industry has continued unabated through the last decade, almost doubling its revenue from 369 billion USD to 746 billion USD as of 2014. However, with limited scope of expanding the infrastructure and high level of competition, the margins of profit have been very thin, almost less than 3 % (IATA 2015; Clayton and

© Springer International Publishing Switzerland 2016
A. Paias et al. (Eds.): ICCL 2016, LNCS 9855, pp. 397–410, 2016.
DOI: 10.1007/978-3-319-44896-1_26

Hilz 2015). To increase overall profitability, it is necessary to improve the operational efficiency of the aviation operation, while balancing competition and cooperation amongst the airlines. Those ideas lead to the concept of Collaborative Decision Making (CDM): sharing information between all stakeholders and Air Traffic Control (ATC), to take better decisions at system level. CDM implies and necessitates fairness.

Within the issues raised in CDM, this paper addresses the evaluation of an advanced optimization algorithm to solve the aircraft scheduling problem at a major European Airport, Schiphol (AMS). This is a crucial theoretical step in view of the current design and specifications for CDM. In fact, the long term implications of CDM in terms of actual improvements, possible setups, and impact of design choices are being partially investigated now before the design and implementation of such systems. A further contribution is the analysis of the output to derive implications on possible collaborations of the stakeholders (airlines), and their impact on the performance of the system. More in detail, instances have been created using real traffic data from the Terminal Control Area (TCA) of Schiphol. Updated schedules compatible with safety regulations of departing and arriving aircraft within the AMS-TCA are computed by modelling the problem using the Mixed Integer Linear Programming (MILP) formulation of (Samà et al. 2013, 2014) and using IBM ILOG CPLEX MIP 12.0 to solve it. The gap between the optimized solution and the commonly applied First-Come-First-Served (FCFS) solution identifies the surplus for the system. Since a lot of stakeholders are involved in the airport operation, we evaluated whether the said algorithm could be universally acceptable by all the airlines, as globally optimal and fair, or not. A game theoretical study was setup based on a cooperative game between the airlines; concept such as core and Shapley value identify a mechanism for the allocation of the benefits and its economical and performance implications. This paper quickly goes through a short literature review, model definition, and a description of the computational experiences, ending with the extension of those ideas for a further research.

2   Scientific Literature and Stakeholders Analysis

Due to the limited capacity in air traffic networks and the difficulties and high costs building new airport resources often requires, aviation authorities seek better methods to improve operational efficiency during daily air traffic operations (Ball et al. 2007). Currently, the order in which multiple aircraft use common airport resources and their timing is often decided according to the FCFS principle (see Samà et al. 2014 for an overview of different objective functions and a review of the practice). In the literature, when dealing with a single airport, different aspect of its management are considered: some works deal with airport ground movements, spanning from the ground delay program (Ball et al. 2010b) to the taxiway planning (Clare and Richards 2011); others focus on the management of landing and taking-off procedures (Bennell et al. 2011). In particular, when dealing with the Aircraft Scheduling Problem (ASP), different approaches have been considered to solve it, ranging from applications of queuing theory (Bäuerle et al. 2007) to travelling salesman (Luenberger 1988) to heuristics and exact approaches (D'Ariano et al. 2015; Samà et al. 2016). This paper considers the problem modelled as a job shop scheduling problem (Beasley et al. 2000; Carr et al. 1998) since it is able to represent many of the constraints which characterize the ASP, allowing a microscopic model able to incorporate the finer information compliant with safety regulations. In particular, we consider the problem of scheduling landing and taking-off aircraft both when using air (holding circles, air segments, common glide path) and ground resources (runways, taxiways).

The management of air traffic operations interests a variety of stakeholders, namely airlines, ATC, airports. Fairness, i.e. avoiding any systematic advantage to any player, is an important aspect in ATC since the benefits that each player/stakeholder gets depend on a variety of factors and always commensurate with the investments each player makes to the whole cause. The study of fairness in air traffic operations has a long tradition, starting from the seminal papers of (Bertsimas and Gupta 2009, 2015; Bertsimas et al. 2011). Allowing for more collaboration (Soomer and Franx 2008) proposed taking the airlines preference as a parameter in the optimization algorithm to ensure a more inherent fairness. This might lead to the situation that any algorithm used is perceived as fair since the airline decide which aircraft to prioritise, but this assumes a high volume of operations for each airline, whereas, in reality this was not the case.

Game theoretical approaches have been proposed by (Skowron and Rzadca 2014) and used for analysing fairness in a collaborative environment of resource allocation. The concept of cooperative game theory has been used in the aviation industry, although for a differently framed problem, focusing on the role of runways as bottle-necks (Littlechild and Owen 1973). We also resort to cooperative game theory, particularly the Shapley value is used to find the unique imputation of the collective global surplus (Shapley 1953). This is a procedure which assigns a unique distribution (among the players) of a total surplus generated by the coalition of all players. This means that every player contributes to a common fund to utilize common resources, and eventually, depending on the marginal contribution each player makes to the group as a whole, they each receive the benefits.

We quickly review in what follows the stakeholders and their interrelation. Those findings are based on study of policy papers and interviews, and the application of two tools from research methodology literature in order to characterise the test case and evaluation of the same. The first one is stakeholders' analysis which involved enumerating all the involved stakeholders and their respective interests. This step was qualitative in nature and was fairly high level interpretation of interests of various players. The following list illustrates the primary stakeholders and their respective interest along with their involvement in the modelling and analysis of this paper.

1. ATC – It is considered the problem owner and ATC is interested in running smooth and safe operations and in identifying the motivation for a coalition and consensus in policy, owing to CDM and importance of fairness.
2. Airline Companies – They are affected the most by the used policy, with direct impact on their revenue stream; thus they are the most interested in the inherent fairness of the policy as well as the resulting social optimal scenario.
3. Infrastructure manager– The primary objective of the infrastructure manager – in our case, Schiphol group, is to ensure smooth and efficient operation in order to maintain the attractiveness of Schiphol as a hub resulting in improved revenue stream.

4. National Civil Aviation Authorities – The civil aviation authorities are not affected directly or operationally by the proposed policy, however they want to maintain the attractiveness of national airports, including Schiphol, and hence want a social optimal solution.
5. Passengers – The interest of the passengers can be considered as a combination of all the above mentioned factors. Although they are a financial contributor to the system and are affected most by the operational variation, they don't have much voice in the policy formulation part. However, since government is a major player in aviation sector, it can be assumed that the socially optimal solution would benefit them as well.

The proposed policy has to primarily ensure the smooth, efficient and safe operation a airport and conditional on the above standards being met, come up with scheduling policies that is socially optimal i.e. fair to all the affected stakeholders in terms of revenue stream. This is a result of the fact that the objectives of different stakeholders are not perfectly aligned with each other.

The second qualitative analysis tool used in this paper is the XLRM framework. The XLRM framework structures the analysis around key uncertainties, options, metrics and models. This is a useful analytical tool because it represents, at a glance, the whole process flow of the project. By identifying, the above mentioned parameters, it is easier to execute and evaluate any process. Also, it is helpful while negotiating the decision strategy with the stakeholders. The XLRM model can be described having the following properties:

1. Exogenous (X) Uncertainties – These are a set of factors which affect the ability to achieve a certain objective.
2. Response (R) Packages/Policy Levers – Management strategies available to the agents which can be used to achieve the defined objective.
3. Models – Models to produce metrics of performance (M) for each strategy (L) in the face of ensembles of uncertainties (X).
4. Performance Metrics – These are the outputs of interest which reflect the decision maker's goals.

The 4 concepts can be schematically reported as follows:

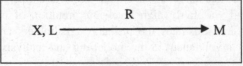

A final scheme summarizing the two objectives is reported in Fig. 1.

3 Methodology

The ATC's objective is to ensure the efficient operation of the airport while adhering to the defined security and safety standards. So, the ATC always looks for the global optimal solution irrespective of its impact on the other agents (FAA). This also translates to the airport being an efficient node in the network of neighbouring airports.

EXOGENOUS UNCERTAINTIES	RESPONSE PACKAGES
1. Delays due to weather, accident or some other issue. 2. Schedule agreements between airlines and Schiphol group 3. Perception or alignment of objectives of different actors 4. Fair distribution of the decision from ATC	1. Minimise delay globally 2. Minimise delay locally 3. Use another advance algorithm instead of FCFS 4. Prioritise KLM in the algorithm 5. Prioritise other airline in the algorithm 6. Implement Fair Distribution through Shapley Value 7. Implement financial compensation through utility redistribution
MODELS	PERFORMANCE METRICS
1. Advanced Optimisation Algorithm using alternative graph formulation with modifications. 2. B&B, FCFS, TABU Search, CPLEX 3. Game Theoretic Analysis 4. Financial Framework	1. Delay for each aircraft translating to delay for each airline 2. Financial output with respect to the operational costs – landing, delay, noise charges 3. Distribution of the cost amongst the airlines – Shapley Value 4. Redistribution of the costs amongst the airlines – Financial Framework

Fig. 1. Stakeholder analysis at Schiphol airport, based on Lempert (2012)

The airline's objective is to minimize delay and maximize flexibility while the airport's objective is to maximize its revenue. These objectives are not exactly aligned with each other. As mentioned above, the first step to negate the non-alignment and improve efficiency globally is the CDM practice (CDM/FAA 2015). Since information sharing is the underlying principle supporting CDM, this sets the stage for necessitating fairness in the system; an agent sharing information for the global benefit would expect the system to be fair and beneficial to it and pay the cost of the information.

In this paper we model the ASP using the MILP formulation of (Samà et al. 2014), which is based on the alternative graph model (Mascis and Pacciarelli 2002), a generalization of the disjunctive graph formulation for job shop scheduling problems (Roy and Sussman 1964). Each job represents a single aircraft and each operation the traversing of a TCA resource (air segments, holding circles, runways, taxiways) by an aircraft. The sequencing of aircraft operations is modelled using fixed constraints. Holding and scheduling decisions are modelled using pairs of alternative (or disjunctive) constraints. To each pair of alternative constraints is associated a binary variable x_{kjhi}. Holding decisions state if a certain number of holding circles are to be performed. A scheduling decision states the order in which two aircraft use a common resource. The objective function considered in this work is the minimization of the average delay regarding operations of specific interest. In particular, delays are computed for all aircraft at runways and for landing aircraft also at the TCA entrance.

Let F and A be the set of fixed and alternative constraints, t_i the starting time of operation i, with $i = 1, ..., m$. We also introduce two special operations, identified by 0 and *, and which represent the start and end of the schedule. This latter is used to compute the final delay of each aircraft, and thus the total objective function. Moreover, w_{ij} is the minimum time separation between the start time of operations i and j,

d_k and z_k the due date time and the delay associated to an operation k, the ASP is introduced:

$$\min \frac{1}{|K|} \sum_{K=1}^{|K|} z_k$$

s.t.
$$t_v - t_u \geq w_{uv} \quad \forall (u, v) \in F$$
$$\left.\begin{array}{l} t_j - t_k + M(1 - x_{kjhi}) \geq w_{kj} \\ t_i - t_h + M x_{kjhi} \geq w_{hi} \end{array}\right\} \quad \forall((k, j), (h, i)) \in A$$
$$z_k - t_k \geq - d_k \quad \forall (k, *) \in F$$
$$z_k \geq 0$$
$$x_{kjhi} \in \{0, 1\}$$

Once a feasible solution for the ASP has been computed, it has to be evaluated in terms of the benefits it is able to bring to the overall system. Such benefits have then to be proportionally distributed to all the players involved.

From this point of view, the application of advanced automatic scheduling approaches will generate a surplus for the system, which corresponds to a decrease in delays penalties and costs. The next question then is how this surplus for the all system can be translated in a surplus for each single participant and stakeholder in the system. This is a typical problem in supply chain, and organization of complex systems, where parties have a partially cooperative behaviour. This might result in reluctance in giving advantages to competitors, and interest in having private advantage, while the advantages are related to some form of collaboration with a competitor (Von Neumann and Morgenstern 1953).

The interaction of all players related to operations in ATC and TCA can be modelled as a cooperative game with the stakeholders having various strategies and objectives, and can, together, decide whether to implement any system or not. We model this scenario from the point of ATC, with ATC dispensing the decision with respect to scheduling and the airlines, as they stand to expect changes in operational finance, as the players. A game, in the context of Game Theory, is a scenario where all the involved actors have strategic interests in a particular outcome. Each of the players has their individual objective which they want to fulfil, by choosing a set of strategies, but are bound by some operational constraints. The result has some quantitative outcome (profit or loss). The goal is to determine the most profitable strategies. In cooperative games, players can determine together a strategy, which will bring bigger benefits. The problem is then how to redistribute the benefit among all players. The value of a group of player is determined by the gap between the status quo (in this case the FCFS solution) and the optimized solution where some players are together. The more players are joining this coalition, the larger the benefits. In other words; the players joining the coalition can benefit from the optimization results, while those not joining the coalition are following the orders and times as provided by the FCFS algorithm. The problem is then who is "accountable" or "responsible" for the improved service performance and related benefits. To ensure a fair outcome with regard to the benefits achieved, the concept of core in game theory is important. The ratio of expenditure incurred by the airlines must be commensurate with the ratio of the decisions going in their favour in an aggregated manner i.e. the savings in delay due to algorithm. This corresponds to computing the Shapley Value $\phi_p(v)$ of each player p in the game (Shapley 1953), defined mathematically as

$$\phi_p(v) = \sum_{S \subseteq N\{p\}} \frac{|S|!(n - |S| - 1)!}{n!} (v(S \cup \{p\}) - v(S))$$

where S represents the subset of players, n the number of players and v the value of the coalition, i.e. the benefits for the system in terms of delays. The Shapley Value has a set of desirable properties, making a game design desirable, like efficiency, symmetry, linearity, and zero players, which ensure t is the fairest manner of redistributing the surplus from the coalition. Using the Shapley value in a financial framework ensures redistribution of benefits to players with unequal size and importance, while minimizing the cost of the airlines in any specific time horizon.

4 Test Case

This study was conducted at Amsterdam Schiphol Airport. First, traffic data of arrivals and departures within the AMS-TCA has been collected from public sources. The TCA has been divided into various sections, with an associated traversing time, according to

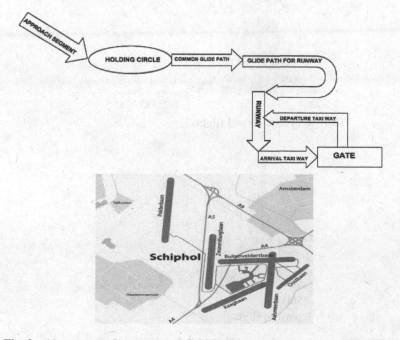

Fig. 2. Airport operations (top) and Schiphol airport (bottom, source: Wikipedia)

the published safety regulations. Four different classes of aircraft are considered, for the purposes of minimal safe separation according to safety regulations. We considered three hours of operations on an average day of traffic: this translates into 226 airplanes (117 departing, 109 arriving) and 42 companies, of which five are considered explicitly as players, having more than five flights in the considered time window. The general scheme of resources and operations is reported in Fig. 2 (top), while Fig. 2 (bottom) reports a map of the airport, with the five runways and the terminal building.

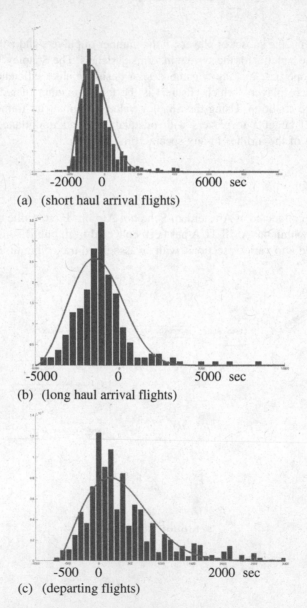

(a) (short haul arrival flights)

(b) (long haul arrival flights)

(c) (departing flights)

Fig. 3. Recorded statistics and probability distributions used for traffic.

A set of delayed instances has been further generated, by considering a deviation between actual times of arrival/departure and the plan. This is calculated based on realized operations over five days of operations, and fitted to three different Three-parameter Weibull probability distributions: long haul flight arrival, short haul flight arrivals, and departures. Figure 3(a–c) reports the three distributions for short haul arrivals, long haul arrivals and departing flights respectively, over the variation in entrance time (expressed in seconds) reported on the x-axis.

Those distributions generate a set of 10 instances of variations in arrival/departure times for all airplanes in the network. On average the traffic is 140 s ahead of schedule, with 48 % of the planes delayed. The average delay is 547 s, and the maximum considered reaches up to 3000 s. The traffic at the airport is analysed by considering individually each of the five major companies, selected based on their traffic share, while for the remaining 37 it is assumed they can be considered as a unified conglomerate. The share of traffic handled by those six players is reported graphically in Fig. 4. It is remarkable how the majority of the traffic belongs to a single company. The main message depicted in the picture is that the distribution of traffic is *diverse* across players, ranging from only 2 % to 50 %; this diversity should be taken into account while redistributing the benefits.

Traffic share

■1 ■2 ■3 ■4 ■5 ■6

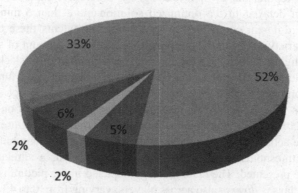

Fig. 4. Share of companies with regard to traffic.

The operations at the airport have then been modelled using the MILP formulation presented in Sect. 3 and solved using alternatively the FCFS rule and the IBM ILOG CPLEX MIP 12.0 solver, with a computation time up to 5 min for any instance.

5 Results

Table 1 reports the performance gap between the solution computed using the FCFS rule and the optimized solution found by CPLEX. Column 1 shows the solving approach considered, Column 2 the value of the objective function of the solution found, i.e. the average delay for the air traffic, expressed in seconds, Column 3 the approximate economic value connected to those performances, approximate by a fixed value of delay cost per minute. It relates to a cost, the lower the better. In this paper, this value has been fixed at 100 EUR per minute per aircraft (Ball et al. 2010a). Each row presents average values on the 10 instances studied. On each solution, the delays for each airline are computed as the total delays of the aircraft belonging to that company. The savings realized due to the proposed system results in a global surplus of savings for the system, with a reduction in terms of delays going well beyond 25 %. The game theoretical study is targeting how this benefit can be redistributed to the stakeholders.

Table 1. Gap between FCFS and optimized operations

Solving approach	Average delay (sec)	Approx Economic value (EUR)
FCFS	43.04	16211
CPLEX	31.42	11834

Figure 5 analyses for each company its share of severely delayed traffic. More precisely, Fig. 5 reports the division among the different companies of the aircraft which have been delayed in the optimized solution more than 5 min. It is already evident how the different companies suffer to different extents these delays. This is provoked by a variety of effects. Those include the different amount of short haul/long haul/departing flights, which have different delay distributions, slack in planning, capacity available at the time at which operations are planned, and further stochastic effects. Some companies, namely company number 3 and 5, are not suffering at all from large delays while company number 2, despite a traffic share of only 5 %, counts more than 40 % of the all traffic delayed more than 5 min. The picture gives a rough impression of the actual delays, as much traffic is delayed, by an amount smaller/larger than the 5 min thresholds. Once a threshold is determined, a similar analysis and pictures could be presented. The main message depicted in the picture is again that the distribution of delays is *diverse* also across players, varying from 0 to 43 %. Again, this diversity should be taken into account while redistributing the benefits.

Table 2 reports the performance obtained in redistributing the benefits from the ASP (optimized) solution to the players considered using the Shapley Value. Columns 2–7 reports for each company the results for the performance indicator of each row. In particular, Row 1 states the company the values refer to; Row 2 the average delay suffered by the company aircraft in the optimized solutions, expressed in seconds. Row 3 reports the computed benefit/cost associated to each company, based on the Shapley value of the cooperative game. In particular, the values reported identify the benefit

Traffic delayed more than 5 minutes

■1 ■2 ■3 ■4 ■5 ■6

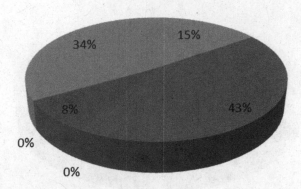

Fig. 5. Companies operating the traffic delayed more than 5 min.

Table 2. Performances, analysed per company

Company	1	2	3	4	5	6
Average delay (sec)	28.7	39.5	4	34.6	12.1	38.3
Benefit allocation (EUR)	1184	605	507	473	473	1144

(savings) which can be realized due to the proposed system being implemented by monetizing the delays resulting in a global surplus of savings for the system.

We also report graphically the share of benefits based on the Shapley allocation in Fig. 6. The main goal of this figure is to provide a direct comparison between the share of flights, share of delays, and the share of benefits. The division of benefits is more equilibrated than the share of flights (Fig. 3) as well as delayed traffic (Fig. 4). This is one principal advantage of the complex framework here developed.

6 Practical Implications and Possible Implementation

The practical implications of the proposed framework target a few directions, here summarized.

Collaborative decision making

Providing data for collaborative decision making, together with smart algorithms, might allow a reduction in delays at airport level going beyond 25 %, and limited adjustments in operational setup. The adaptation of published algorithms to additional airport with varying traffic is proven at least at the level of a laboratory experiments, provided that operations can be described by discrete operations.

Shapley allocation

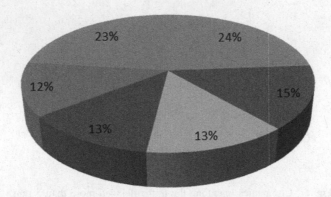

Fig. 6. Division of the benefits associated to the Shapley value, per company.

Stakeholder power and equity/fairness of operations

The computational experiments practically underline the discrepancy between share of traffic, delays and benefits from the introduction of an optimized traffic control approach. A complex scheme to redistribute the benefits, based on game theoretical approach is thus necessary. The determination of the power of the stakeholders based on a single operational descriptor might not be a complete assessment of the impact of the stakeholder on operations (capacity usage and delay propagation), as well as the impact of operations on the stakeholders (delays suffered)

Perspective development at airports

The implementation of an advanced mechanism and implementation needs support from many stakeholders, which include the companies (which face less delays) as well as the airport system, which can use more efficiently the available capacity, as well as traffic controllers, which can benefit from optimized solutions computed within a small computation time. The benefits identified by the game theoretical analysis here can be translated to economic benefits for each of those categories. An integrated optimization of operations, analysed by a similar game theoretical approach, can determine the power and economic benefits to be associated to collaborative decision making.

7   Conclusion

The application of an optimized approach to solve the air traffic control (ATC) problem in at a major airport Terminal control area (TCA) shows a potential superior performance in terms of minimizing the delay experienced by the whole airport. The gap between FCFS and the optimized algorithm reach up to 25 %, in terms of average delay, at system level. While looking for system optimum performance, the performance of individual airlines depends on a variety of factors, which include at least the amount of traffic, its organization in peak or off-peak moments, and the amount of slack in the planning, the delays experienced currently. This complexity justified the application of a game theoretical framework to determine the redistribution of the extra benefits throughout all players, which turned out to be more equilibrated than what the share of traffic or share of delays might have suggested in first instance. The implications of the development of collaborative decision making are also pointed out. It is possible to study in detail the financial agreements between the airlines and Schiphol to align the actual financial transactions with the benefits coming from the usage of advanced scheduling approaches, based on collaborative decision making principles. In general, it is possible to identify dominant players whose individual (local) performance affects the global performance, and subsets of companies which together would have enough power to pull all other operators towards support of advanced ATC approaches.

Future research should investigate a variety of directions which have been only identified in this preliminary study. A larger scale assessment should include more airports, more traffic, longer time horizons and more possibility for rescheduling and rerouting of aircraft. All those developments would result in heavy computational burden which would require developments of advanced algorithms. The possibility of representing explicitly the different objectives of the stakeholders in some (decomposed) optimization problem would include some game theoretical aspect already in the optimization problem, for an integrated perspective, otherwise a larger study of more players and coalitions could clarify the benefit of a variety of minor players which are now aggregated. The game theoretical approach could be further developed by proving under specific assumption the convexity and existence of a core, for abstract and practical cases, and its implications towards the allocation and the economic benefits of the parties. Moreover, the concept of fairness and optimality in traffic management is pertinent to a variety of other fields, such as railway systems (Corman et al. 2015) and currently approached via priorities, which are straightforward extensions of FCFS principles (see for instance Corman et al. 2011). Thus large possibilities for improvement would be available in that sense.

References

Ball, M.O., Barnhart, C., Nemhauser, G., Odoni, A.: Air transportation: irregular operations and control. In: Handbooks in Operations Research and Management Science, vol. 14, no. 1, pp. 1–68 (2007)

Ball, M.O., Barnhart, C., Dresner, M., Hansen, M., Neels, K.: Total Delay Impact Study. NEXTOR (2010a)

Ball, M.O., Hoffman, R., Mukherjee, A.: Ground delay program planning under uncertainty based on the ration-by-distance principle. Transp. Sci. 44(1), 1–14 (2010b)

Bäuerle, N., Engelhardt-Funke, O., Kolonko, M.: On the waiting time of arriving aircraft and the capacity of airports with one or two runways. Eur. J. Oper. Res. 177(2), 1180–1196 (2007)

Beasley, J., Krishnamoorty, M., Sharaiha, Y., Abramson, D.: Scheduling aircraft landing - the static case. Transp. Sci. 34(2), 180–197 (2000)

Bennell, J.A., Mesgarpour, M., Potts, C.N.: Airport runway scheduling. 4OR – Q. J. Oper. Res. **4** (2), 115–138 (2011)

Bertsimas, D., Gupta, S.: Fairness in air traffic flow management. In: INFORMS Meeting, CA, USA (2009)

Bertsimas, D., Gupta, S.: Fairness and collaboration in network air traffic flow management: an optimization approach. Transp. Sci. **50**(1), 57–76 (2015)

Bertsimas, D., Farias, V., Trichakis, N.: The price of fairness. Oper. Res. **59**(1), 17–31 (2011)

Carr, G., Erzberger, H., Neuman, F.: Airline arrival prioritization in sequencing and scheduling. In: 2nd USA/EUROPE Air Traffic Management R&D Seminar, pp. 1–11 (1998)

CDM/FAA: Improving Air Traffic Management Together (2015). http://cdm.fly.faa.gov/

Clayton, E., Hilz, A.: 2015 Aviation Trends - Efficiency & Attitudes, Strategy& (2015). http://www.strategyand.pwc.com/perspectives/2015-aviation-trends

Corman, F., D'Ariano, A., Hansen, I.A., Pacciarelli, D.: Optimal multi-class rescheduling of railway traffic. J. Rail Trans. Plann. Manag. **1**(1), 14–24 (2011)

Corman, F., D'ariano, A., Pacciarelli, D., Pranzo, M.: Dispatching and coordination in multi-area railway traffic management. Comput. Oper. Res. **44**, 146–160 (2015)

D'Ariano, A., Pacciarelli, D., Pistelli, M., Pranzo, M.: Real-time scheduling of aircraft arrivals and departures in a terminal maneuvering area. Networks **65**(3), 212–227 (2015)

FAA. Federal Aviation Administration (n.d.). https://www.faa.gov/air_traffic/

Gröflin, H., Klinkert, A.: Scheduling with generalized disjunctive graphs: feasibility issues. In: XV Conference on European Chapter on Combinatorial Optimization (2002)

IATA: Annual review (2015)

Lempert, R.: RAND - Infrastructure, Safety and Environment. RAND Corporation (2012)

Littlechild, S., Owen, G.: A simple expression for the Shapley value in a special case. Manag. Sci. **20**(3), 370–372 (1973)

Luenberger, R.A.: A traveling-salesman-based approach to aircraft scheduling in the terminal area. NASA Technical report 100062 (1988)

Mascis, A., Pacciarelli, D.: Job shop scheduling with blocking and no-wait constraints. Eur. J. Oper. Res. **143**(3), 498–517 (2002)

Mason, S.J., Oey, K.: Scheduling complex job shops using disjunctive graphs: a cycle elimination procedure. Int. J. Prod. Res. **41**(5), 981–994 (2003)

Roy, S., Sussman, B.: Les Problèmes d'ordonnancement avec contraintes disjonctives. Note DS n.9 bis, SEMA, Montrouge (1964)

Samà, M., D'Ariano, A., D'Ariano, P., Pacciarelli, D.: Optimal aircraft scheduling and routing at a terminal control area during disturbances. Transp. Res. Part C **47**(1), 61–85 (2014)

Samà, M.A., D'Ariano, A., D'Ariano, P., Pacciarelli, D.: Scheduling models for optimal aircraft traffic control at busy airports: tardiness, priorities, equity and violations considerations. Omega (2016). doi:10.1016/j.omega.2016.04.003

Samà, M., D'Ariano, A., Pacciarelli, D.: Rolling horizon approach for aircraft scheduling in the terminal control area of busy airports. Transp. Res. Part E **60**(1), 140–155 (2013)

Shapley, L.S.: A value for n-person games. Ann. Math. Stud. **28**, 307–317 (1953)

Skowron, P., Rzadca, K.: Fair share is not enough: measuring fairness in scheduling with cooperative game theory. In: Wyrzykowski, R., Dongarra, J., Karczewski, K., Waśniewski, J. (eds.) PPAM 2013, Part II. LNCS, vol. 8385, pp. 38–48. Springer, Heidelberg (2014)

Soomer, M.J., Franx, G.J.: Scheduling aircraft landings using airlines' preferences. Eur. J. Oper. Res. **190**(1), 277–291 (2008)

Von Neumann, J., Morgenstern, O.: Theory of Games and Economic Behavior. Princeton University Press, Princeton (1953)

Impact of Dwell Time on Vertical Transportation Through Discrete Simulation in SIMIO

Marcelo Henriques, António A.C. Vieira, Luís M.S. Dias[✉],
Guilherme A.B. Pereira, and José A. Oliveira

University of Minho, Campus Gualtar, 4710-057 Braga, Portugal
marcelo@nhenriques.com,
{antonio.vieira,lsd,gui,zan}@dps.uminho.pt

Abstract. This work has the objective of simulating an elevator system, using SIMIO software. Firstly, two different approaches, and its implementation, will be explained and compared: Vehicle vs. Entity. After selecting the Entity-approach, due to its more flexible processes and the limitations of the Vehicle-approach, it will be used to conduct the simulation experiments. The purpose is to evaluate the impact of dwell time - time in which the elevator remains stopped, allowing for clients to enter and exit - in the performance of the system. That will be achieved analysing the impact on the total time - spent by clients from placing a call until reaching its destination - number of clients inside the system and waiting for the elevator, waiting time, elevator occupation and number of elevator movements. The analysis of the results indicates that, for the properties defined, the best time for the elevator to stay with its doors open is around 10 seconds.

Keywords: Elevator · Lift · Management systems · Intelligent objects · Modelling · SIMIO · 3D simulation · Case study

1 Introduction

The most typical objective of an elevator system is to move people and cargo in a vertical way. In the elevator industry, changing the entire elevator system - or simply the algorithm - has high costs associated and can imply system inoperability for some time. The heart of any elevator system is its elevator management system, which decides what will be the next elevator movement through its algorithm, based on various inputs. A simple algorithm for only one elevator, as in the studied case, can be described as follows (Setchi 2010):

- Move in a certain direction, up or down, stopping at all floors where there are calls or destinations;
- Change its direction when there are no calls or destinations at floors beyond the current floor in the current direction, or when it reaches the last floor, changing from going down to going up when it reaches the bottom floor, or changing from going up to going down when it reaches the upper floor;
- Stop, in case there are no calls or destinations in the system.

© Springer International Publishing Switzerland 2016
A. Paias et al. (Eds.): ICCL 2016, LNCS 9855, pp. 411–426, 2016.
DOI: 10.1007/978-3-319-44896-1_27

One of the main advantages of simulating a system is the possibility to change it in a virtual way and measure the consequences, before physically changing it, with all the investments involved. These measurements allow management to take decisions based on data. Decision making based on simulation data will help management deciding what system to implement, or elevator companies deciding what parameters should be defined. One of these parameters is the dwell time, which is the time that the elevator remains stopped, with its doors open to allow clients to enter or exit it.

This paper describes a simulation model of an elevator system, developed in the discrete event simulation tool SIMIO; Pegden (2007). The basis of this work was a hospital located on the north of Portugal. Two different approaches were addressed and compared. Afterwards, one of the approaches was used to conduct simulation experiments and analyse the obtained data.

The remainder of this paper is organized as follows: First, in Sect. 2, a literature review will be presented, addressing the selected simulation tool for this problem. Afterwards, in Sect. 3, two different approaches for modelling the system in question will be presented. The analysis of the obtained results on one of the approaches will be discussed and lastly, in Sect. 5 the main conclusions will be withdrawn, along with some future work.

2 Literature Review

Most recent models of elevator group management systems (e.g. Destination Dispatch) had, in their genesis, tests and data retrieved from using computing simulation. One simulation tool that outstands in the elevator industry is the software Elevate® (Barney and Al-Sharif 2015), which allows to simulate and analyse elevator traffic, with support for different configurations and applications, e.g. two floor elevators, an elevator system with different speeds and different attending floors ("About Elevate" 2016). This software runs on Windows™ and was developed by the London-based company Peters Research. Another innovation by this company is the software Elevate Live™, which allows checking the status of the elevator management system in real time ("About Elevate Live" 2016).

This software is not the only simulation tool used in the elevator industry, but it is one of the most referred and promoted. But, taking into account the will to share information, the intellectual property protection and the maintenance of market advantage, companies of this industry tend to not reveal which tools are used.

But the need and use of simulation in this field is real (Barney and Al-Sharif 2015; Hakonen and Siikonen 2009; Zhang and Zong 2014), because elevator models can reach high levels of complexity. Taking, for instance, the Shanghai Tower, where hundreds of elevators travel vertically, with certain restrictions and different purposes, the level of complexity associated to this system becomes obvious.

The number of simulation tools is very large. Thus, its comparison is important. However, most scientific works related to this subject "analyse only a small set of tools and usually evaluating several parameters separately avoiding to make a final judgement due to the subjective nature of such task" (Dias et al. 2007).

Hlupic and Paul (1999) compared a set of simulation tools, distinguishing between users of software for educational purpose and users in industry. In his turn, Hlupic (2000) developed "a survey of academic and industrial users on the use of simulation software, which was carried out in order to discover how the users are satisfied with the simulation software they use and how this software could be further improved". Dias et al. (2007) and Pereira et al. (2011) comparing a set of tools based on popularity on the internet, scientific publications, WSC (Winter Simulation Conference), social networks and other sources, claim: "Popularity should never be used alone otherwise new tools, better than existing ones would never get market place, and this is a generic risk, not a simulation particularity" (Dias et al. 2007); however, a positive correlation may exist between popularity and quality, since the best tools have a greater chance of being more popular. According to the authors, the most popular tool is ARENA, Kelton et al. (2009), and the good classification of SIMIO is noteworthy. Based on these results, Vieira et al. (2014) compared both tools taking into consideration several factors. This latter paper is also a good source of information for researcher and practitioners, since it compares SIMIO with the most popular tool (ARENA), giving some basic examples.

SIMIO has two main levels for modelling. The simpler one, called 'Facility', is suitable for practitioners without computer science background, where one can create models in a building-block approach over a physical layout, providing a realistic 3D animation. The second level, called 'Process', enables the creation of detailed behaviour using logical flow charts to specify virtually anything.

Processes, once created, can be used anywhere in the 'Facility' level. Moreover, processes can be "attached" to Entities (objects) to enabling them to react actively and autonomously. This behaviour pushes SIMIO "living" objects to agents. It is controversial to consider SIMIO objects as intelligent, once such term has a connotation to support logical programming and self-learning ability.

Another relevant capability is the support for object class hierarchy, allowing the extension of existing objects rather than creating from scratch.

SIMIO was the chosen tool for this project. It is based on intelligent objects (Sturrock and Pegden 2010; Pegden 2007; Pegden and Sturrock 2011). These "are built by modellers and then may be used in multiple modelling projects. Objects can be stored in libraries and easily shared" (Pegden 2013). Unlike other object-oriented systems, in SIMIO there is no need to write any programming code, since the process of creating a new object is completely graphic (Pegden and Sturrock 2011; Pegden 2007; Sturrock and Pegden 2010). The activity of building an object in SIMIO is identical to the activity of building a model. In fact, there is no difference between an object and a model (Pegden 2007; Pegden and Sturrock 2011). A vehicle, a customer or any other agent of a system are examples of possible objects and, combining several of these, one can represent the components of the system in analysis. Thus, a SIMIO model looks like the real system (Pegden and Sturrock 2011; Pegden 2007). This can be very useful, particularly while presenting the results to someone unfamiliar to simulation.

In SIMIO, the model logic and animation are built in a single step (Pegden and Sturrock 2011; Pegden 2007). This makes the modulation process very intuitive (Pegden and Sturrock 2011). Moreover, the animation can also be useful to reflect the changing state of the object (Pegden 2007). In addition to the usual 2D animation, SIMIO also supports 3D animation as a natural part of the modelling process (Sturrock and Pegden 2010). To switch between them the user only needs to press a specific key (Sturrock and Pegden 2010). Moreover, SIMIO provides a direct link to Google Warehouse (Pegden and Sturrock 2011).

SIMIO offers two basic modes for executing models: interactive and experimental. In the first it is possible to watch the animated model, which is useful for building and validating the model. In the second, it is possible to define properties of the model that can be changed (Sturrock and Pegden 2010).

3 Comparison of Different Implementation Approaches

To elucidate the need of building the two approaches and its comparison, it is beneficial to explain them individually, their common points and the disadvantages and advantages of each approach. This matter will be addressed in the present chapter.

The use of a SIMIO standard object to transport entities has the advantage of being already developed, and thus the user only needs to place it and edit some properties. However, to model more complex situations can become a hard task. The use of an entity to overcome this situation implies a higher initial effort. Nonetheless, once this has been surpassed, the user will be able to model its own transportation logic. The choice that has to be made, between using the standard Vehicle object, or an Entity, is not an obvious one. In this sense, this chapter will analyse both alternatives.

The model facility has some equal parts between the two approaches implemented, as their objective is common: simulate an elevator. Both facilities are composed by seven floors, named from floor 1 to floor 7. Each floor has its own source, creating entity clients through a random exponential expression. The ground floor has a separate property than the upper floors, allowing different scenarios simulation, like: up-peak, down-peak and mixed movements, common on elevator passenger traffic (Barney and Al-Sharif 2015). Each source is linked to a series of central nodes by a path, guiding clients to the place where they will wait for the elevator to pick them up. Once a client is sent out of the elevator to its destination floor, it will be transferred to a node linked by a path to a final sink, where each client is destroyed.

3.1 Vehicle Approach

The Vehicle approach consists of using the Vehicle object from the standard SIMIO library. Among other properties, the user can specify load capacity, unload time and task selection methods; however, trying to shift the Vehicle from its standard behaviour can be a complex task. This approach has two sides, one based on processes and another based on parameters. Both are used to model client and elevator behaviour.

To start, client behaviour has to be modelled. In this sense, a destination node, representing his or her destination floor, is randomly assigned to each client. This destination node is chosen from a list, which is individual to each node. These options are selected inside the source parameters.

Afterwards, all clients will travel through a Path object that will take them to a TransferNode, where they will wait for the elevator. It should be stressed that the 'Allow Passing' property of these Paths, must be set to false, in order to ensure that no overtaking occurs and that a queue of waiting clients is formed. Moreover, the 'Ride On Transport' property of each TransferNode must be set to true to obligate clients to wait for the Vehicle and seize it. In this approach, the node where the clients wait for the elevator is the same where the elevator travels, to ensure that the Vehicle can pick the waiting clients.

The major benefit of this approach consists on the automatic transfer of clients from the waiting node to the elevator, since the native Vehicle object was designed specifically for this purpose: transporting people or goods. The transfer steps, responsible for transferring the clients onto the Vehicle, are defined within the Vehicle model, being hidden from the common user. A downside of this aspect is the inability to see and change the processes that allow such automated actions to a more suitable one, according to the needs of the specific system intended to implement.

Contrary to the nodes for clients, which have only one direction: pointing towards the Vehicle, the destination nodes could not be modelled as nodes mutually travelled by clients and the elevator itself, otherwise, the elevator would leave its natural vertical path and enter the final path to the sinks. If the nodes were separated by networks other difficulties would arise, namely transferring the clients out of the elevator, when the automated transfers would not occur, thus needing the same process step and a separate node to transfer the client to as implemented. To overcome this, the central nodes - where clients wait for the elevator - and the out nodes - where clients reach their final path to destination - are physically separated. To make the final transfer from the central nodes to the out nodes, a process was created to each central node, being triggered whenever a client enters that specific central node. Such process is illustrated below in Fig. 1.

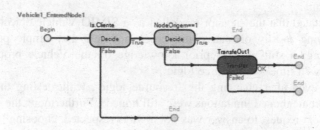

Fig. 1. Process to transfer clients out of the elevator

The first Decide step protects the process from being executed by the Vehicle, as the Vehicle also crosses the central nodes. The following Decide step verifies if the client entered on the current floor. In an affirmative result, the process ends and the client continues waiting for the elevator; if the result is False - meaning that the current node is its destination, since it was transferred out of the vehicle - the Transfer step will transfer the client from the central node to the correspondent out node. Finally, the out node is connected through a path to a sink, responsible for destroying the client.

The Vehicle object, in its default state, displays some difficulties answering elevator calls. When the vehicle is in movement, it answers firstly the destination of those inside its ride, ignoring calls from clients that are waiting on floors that the vehicle passes through. The vehicle only lets clients enter its ride in two occasions: when it stops to leave out a client inside its own ride, or when its ride is empty and starts receiving seize requests from clients waiting, first answering the oldest request, instead of the nearest.

To bypass the aforementioned difficulties and adapt the Vehicle to the current objective, some properties of the Vehicle can be edited, namely:

- Initial Ride Capacity: Specifies the capacity of the elevator;
- Task Selection Strategy: Defines the strategy to select the next task;
- Dwell Time: Defines the time the vehicle will wait, whenever it has to load/unload clients;
- Routing Type: Specifies how the vehicle will decide its next movement, either following a fixed route, or a route based on client demand. The first option sets the Vehicle to a predefined route, e.g. a milk run, whilst the later regulates the Vehicle depending on client requests.

When this last property is set on 'on demand', it is possible to manipulate two more properties inside 'resource logic': 'ranking rule' and 'dynamic selection rule'. These two properties are responsible for ordering the requests when they are placed, and allow to dynamically select the next call to answer, respectively.

As such, the selected expression for the property 'ranking rule' is the origin of the client, which orders the queue based on the originated floor; and the property 'dynamic selection rule' is set to 'DirectDistanceTo.Object(Candidate.Object)'. 'Candidate' refers to the client which is requesting a pick-up, and the main expression returns the distance between the Vehicle and the client. As this later expression is dynamic, it is independent of the previous expression and resulting queue. This decision occurs in the moment when the Vehicle is available to be seized. These expressions are native SIMIO functions.

It can be stated that the elevator modelled as a SIMIO Vehicle object is simple to conceive, relying mostly on native properties and few and simple process steps. Notwithstanding, it still requires prior knowledge on the Vehicle properties being edited, e.g. 'dwell time' or 'resource logic'.

However, even after changing the 'resource logic', while testing the simulation model, the aforementioned limitations were still noticed. Furthermore, the dynamic rule to select the next request to answer was not always respected, choosing to answer the request of the client that was waiting the longest, even if the floor difference was between the top and bottom floor, also ignoring all clients in the middle.

Another way to order client requests and Vehicle decision is through priority. That is, a priority level has to be given to each client that performs a request to the Vehicle, e.g. going from high priority to the closest client, and lowest priority to the client that is further away from the elevator. This strategy would require a dynamic calculation of the priority level each time the elevator moves, as the distance from the elevator to the client changes with each movement. This strategy could be implemented through the same properties under 'resource logic', facing the same issues as the strategy applied and mentioned above; or it could be implemented through robust and complex processes, erasing the major advantage of a Vehicle approach: simplicity.

As concluding remarks, a Vehicle approach is simple, but it is very limited and does not fulfil all the needs and requirements of an elevator system, even through new processes it was not possible to change the Vehicle route in the way intended, as it has its own 'logic' behind it. Furthermore, if a change in the algorithm of the elevator system is needed, the change is very limited and unpredictable, as all the Vehicle built-in processes are hidden from the common user. All these limitations would decrease the number of applications which the model could be used to simulate and experiment, and even the importance of itself. All these limitations and factors contributed to the selection of the elevator as an entity, as it would be further demonstrated.

3.2 Entity Approach

Opting for this approach will imply the construction of a SIMIO object, similar to the Vehicle one, from scratch. This approach implies that all actions are modelled in a detailed way. Thus, this section is divided in processes executed by the client and by the elevator.

1. Client Processes

Each client, after being created in the source, runs on the entrance path and, upon arrival at the central node of its floor of origin, will execute the process in Fig. 2.

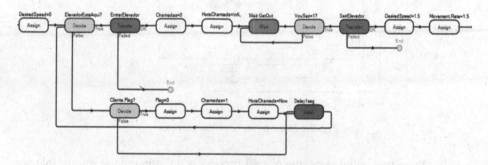

Fig. 2. Process executed by clients

This process is responsible for ensuring that each client waits for the elevator, calls the elevator, enters it when the elevator is on the same floor as the client, and the client gets out of the elevator onto the last path into the sink of the destination floor. Upon executing this process, the client will be stopped, in order to obligate him or her to wait for the elevator to answer the call that will be placed. This is achieved by setting the speed property to zero. Thereafter each client will verify if the elevator is positioned at the same floor he or she is. While waiting for the elevator, the client will change two data structures of the model: one array representing the number of calls on each floor, and another array that records the time on which calls are made. Both indexes correspond to the floor where the call was placed.

When the elevator is in the same floor as the client, it stops and opens its doors, the client is transferred from the central node to a ride station inside the entity and both aforementioned arrays are reinitialized and updated. While inside the elevator the client is kept in a step of the process, waiting to arrive at its floor destination. It is ensured the client leaves the elevator at the right floor by checking a variable of the entity - that stores the *id* of the destination floor - and comparing it with the index of the floor at which the elevator currently is.

2. Elevator Processes

The approach in question consists of modelling the elevator as an entity, but, apart from giving it the behaviour of a typical elevator - the algorithm - it is necessary to create the object and place it in the right location. To this end, the two first steps of the process represented on Fig. 3 do that.

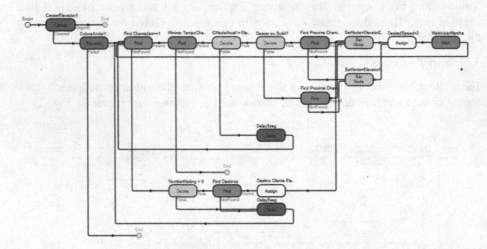

Fig. 3. Main process of the elevator

After those two initial steps, the overall process is an infinite loop responsible for the management system of the elevator, meaning that these steps are responsible for deciding the next elevator movement and will be run for the entire period of the simulation in a closed perpetual loop. Note that the next destination of the elevator will always avoid making direction changes, thus giving priority to floors with calls in the same direction it is traveling. First, the elevator verifies if there are calls registered on the system, through the array mentioned above. If there are no calls registered, the elevator will decide its next destination based on the destination of each client riding it. If there are calls, the elevator then analyses the time in which they were made, thus giving priority to clients that made the calls sooner. After having decided on the next destination, the elevator will be kept on a wait step until its doors are closed and thus it is ready to initiate its trip. To ensure the elevator stops at all floors which have calls

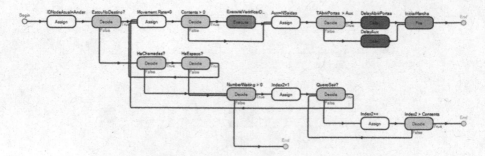

Fig. 4. Process executed by the elevator whenever it arrives to a new floor

registered or a client wanting to exit, the process represented in Fig. 4 is executed, whenever the elevator arrives at a given node that represents a floor.

In this process, the elevator will firstly analyse if it has arrived on the floor which was assigned to it as a destination. If the node in question is not its destination floor, the elevator will then analyse if there are calls on that node - ensuring that it still has capacity to hold additional clients - or if any client inside it wants to exit at that node. If the current node is the elevator destination, has a call placed, or is the destination of a client inside the elevator, the next steps will ensure that the elevator stops, and will model the time that the elevator is kept with its doors open (dwell time), allowing for clients to exit or to enter the elevator. Afterwards, an event will be fired to indicate that the elevator can resume its trip, allowing the process represented in Fig. 3 to continue its loop. In this regard, communication between these two processes is necessary and ensured, since both processes are executed in parallel.

3.3   Final Remarks

The complexity of the model using an Entity as an elevator is evidenced by the size of the developed processes and by their relation, where a process executes another process. Moreover, a process can trigger an event which was holding a token in another process, ensuring the communication among entity clients, entity elevator and processes.

The behaviour of an elevator was modelled with success and its behaviour was taken farther than what was achieved in the approach using the SIMIO Vehicle. In this sense, the approach chosen to conduct simulation experiments was the Entity approach. Figure 5 shows the elevator modelled as an entity in SIMIO. The animation in 3D represents an advantage when interacting with the model and/or showing it to others.

4   Results

Once the model was developed and validated, data was retrieved from it, in order to get relevant information that would lead to conclusions about the developed model. One of the major benefits of using SIMIO is the possibility of conducting simulation

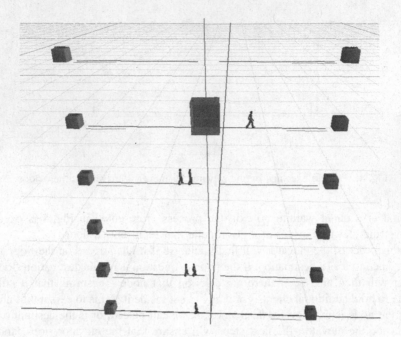

Fig. 5. 3D view of the model during its runtime

experiments on a model. A simulation experiment allows for executing a set of scenarios with different values for the model properties, and the impact of those changes on the model KPIs (Key Performance Indicators). In the present model, dwell time is the main model property in study, being changed from 1 to 20 seconds. Other properties were implemented and can be analysed in future studies, such as: capacity of the elevator and different arrival rates of clients per floor.

The dwell time is crucial to the total time of a client (waiting time plus travel time) because if it is increased, it increases the probability of clients entering the elevator at a floor, thus diminishing client waiting time on the current floor; but will also increase the waiting time of clients on other floors. If this time is decreased, the probability of clients entering the elevator at each stop decreases and the elevator will move more, thus decreasing the waiting time on other floors. A balance between these two possibilities needs to be found. In order to have a good representation of the impact of this property on all KPIs, the value will vary from 1 to 20 seconds. To note that a value of dwell time with a good performance on a specific KPI, e.g. average client total time, at up-peak time can have a bad performance on a mixed or down-peak movement of clients, as calls can be placed in a more focused area of the building, e.g. the ground floor, or can be spread across all floors. The main focus was, therefore, to analyse the impact of dwell time in the system performance, namely the following established KPI:

- Average <u>total time</u> in the system, per client: sum of waiting time and travel time for the clients;
- Average elevator <u>occupation</u> (or load): number of clients riding the elevator;

- Elevator <u>movements</u>: number of movements executed by the elevator in the simulation runtime;
- Average <u>number of clients in the system</u>: sum of clients waiting for the elevator with the ones already riding it;
- Average <u>number of clients waiting</u>: number of clients that are waiting for the elevator on all floors;
- Average <u>waiting time</u> per client;

In order to ensure that the results do not contain irrelevant data, as a result of the time needed for the system to achieve a "full-operating status", it is very important to define an accurate warm-up period. In this context, a warm-up period of 3600 seconds was defined because, on the several tests conducted, it was found that from this time on, the KPI values achieved a more stable status. Furthermore, 10 replications were used to ensure that different random number seeds are used. The simulation time in the experiments was 24 hours.

Figure 6 represents the evolution of the average total time in system per client, as a function of dwell time. Dwell time is displayed in seconds, in all graphics, while average total time is in minutes.

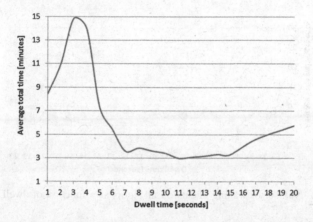

Fig. 6. Total time in system per client as a function of dwell time

For dwell time of 1 to 4 seconds, an increase of the average total time per client was observed, due to less time that the clients have to enter the elevator. The lower average total time values are seen in the 10 to 15 seconds band, rounding 3 minutes between the 11 and 15 seconds of dwell time. After this value, an ascend curve is seen due to the increase of time in which the elevator is stopped at the same floor, thus not traveling to attend other calls, increasing waiting time on other floors.

Average waiting time is a performance measure which affects the average total time and is responsible for the perception of the system quality on clients using it. Figure 7 presents the obtained results for the evolution of the average waiting time per client as a function of the dwell time.

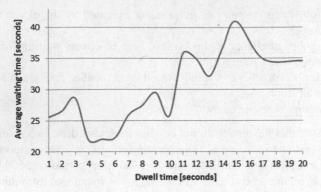

Fig. 7. Waiting time per client as a function of dwell time

The lower values are located on **4 to 6 seconds** of dwell time, and the maximum is reached in 15 seconds. The graphic in Fig. 8 shows variation of the average **number** of **waiting clients** on all floors.

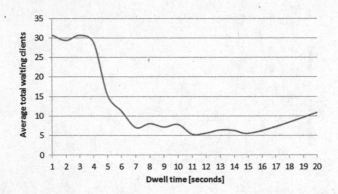

Fig. 8. Number of waiting clients on all floors as a function of dwell time

A dwell time of 1 to 5 seconds results in the highest values on clients waiting for the elevator, and from 20 seconds onwards, the curve returns to an ascending state. It is in the 7 to 18 seconds band that the average number of waiting clients remains below 10. The lowest values of this KPI are reached on the **11 to 16 s** band, where values close to an average of 5 to 6 clients waiting are shown.

Figure 9 shows the evolution of the **total** number of **clients** in the system as a function of the elevator dwell time. As previously stated, the values of this KPI should be the result of the sum of the total number of clients waiting with the load of the elevator. As can be seen, the values indicated by the above graph match the sum of the average number of clients riding the elevator (average occupation) and the average number of clients waiting.

The KPIs analysed until this point focus more on the side of the user of the elevator. However, other perspectives, as the **power consumption** of an elevator, do not

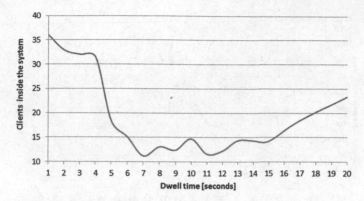

Fig. 9. Number of clients inside the system as a function of dwell time

necessarily react in the same way to a change of the dwell time of an elevator. In this sense, the consumption of the elevator was also analysed. The power consumption of an elevator system is very important, especially considering many of those systems are free of charge. There are two factors influencing this expense: number of movements and elevator occupation. The smaller the movements, the less energy will be consumed. But elevator occupation is not linear, meaning it is related to the difference in weight between the elevator cabin (including the weight carried) and counterweight, which each one is placed on each end of the cables of an elevator system. The weight difference between these two masses is the momentum the elevator engine has to provide, as in every movement one of these masses is going down, and with its gravitational force helps reducing the amount of torque the engine has to provide in order to move the cables and hoist the other mass. The weight of the cabin and the counterweight depend on the system installed, client demand and other design decisions. So, it is not possible to directly relate these two factors without knowing the system itself, but it seems correct to say that the closer it is to 40 % of the cabin maximum load, the less power will be consumed. This claim comes from the general calculation method of counterweights in the elevator industry, essential for reducing the engine effort to hoist the cabin and to maintain traction on all the cables (McCain 2007).

Figure 10 shows the number of elevator movements and its average load as functions of the dwell time. It is difficult to say the exact point on which the system will be more efficient. But it is possible to refer a band on which the system will be more efficient. That band probably lays between 8 to 15 seconds, due to less movements - which are less than 1/3 of the highest value registered, with a low dwell time - and the load on the elevator reaches up to 30 to 40 % of its maximum load. For this decision, it was considered that the counter-weight of the elevator is calculated for an elevator with 40 % of its load – situation in which it consumes less energy to perform its movements.

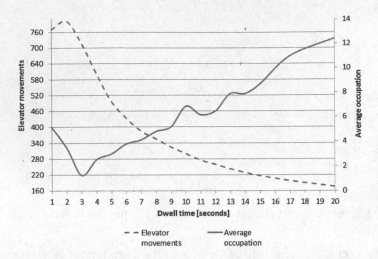

Fig. 10. Number of elevator movements and its average occupation as functions of dwell time

5   Conclusions

An **elevator** system was modelled in **SIMIO** - a recently developed discrete simulation tool. The simulation model was based on a hospital located in the north of Portugal. The tool was chosen due to its similarities to ARENA - the most used simulation tool worldwide - since they were developed by the same authors. Moreover, it fully supports 3D animation, which results in very appealing simulation models, which also contributes to a better understanding of the system in its execution.

Two implementation approaches to model the elevator behaviour were considered. First, the entity was modelled using a SIMIO built-in object, whose purpose is to transport entities from one location to another. This approach enabled a fast basic-modelling of the system, since the standard behaviour is already defined by the transporter. However, it proved to be complex to model different strategies for the elevator. Moreover, different problems with this approach were identified, for instance the elevator would always give priority to customers on board rather than stopping to allow new entrances on the way. Possible workarounds to this problem would require mathematical expressions and as such, modelling different behaviours in the vehicle would be very complex. On the other hand, modelling the elevator as an entity was very challenging, since all the behaviour had to be developed from scratch. Nevertheless, when its modelling was finished, it proved to be more flexible than the first approach, since it could be easily added different strategies to the elevator. In this sense, the model with the elevator modelled as an entity was the one used to conduct simulation experiments. One of the great advantages of using this approach is that it allows different strategies of the elevator to be incorporated. To the study in question, the only strategy modelled was to give priority to the closest floors with clients with higher waiting times. Different strategies, such as the milk run strategy could easily be implemented.

In this analysis phase, the only parameter analysed was the **dwell time**, which is the time that the elevator keeps its doors opened to allow new entrances. In future studies, other properties, such as different arrival rates of clients to the elevator, or the capacity of the elevator, could be analysed. To evaluate the performance of the system, the following Key Performance Indicators (**KPI**) were defined: average total time; average occupation; number of elevator movements; average of waiting clients on all floors and average waiting time.

In the beginning of this study, the authors thought the optimum value for the dwell time was around 5 seconds. However, the final analysis of the multiple KPI, indicates that the option would be to use a dwell time of around **10** seconds. It was found that within this time frame of dwell time a balance between all the KPI could be achieved. Different goals of the management system, may lead to the adoptions of other dwell times.

By re-using previously defined SIMIO objects in other models, this elevator model could be used on other **future research**. For instance, in multiple elevators, where ETD (Estimated Time to Destination) or other algorithms could be implemented. Furthermore, the power consumption of the elevator could also be quantified.

Acknowledgements. This work has been supported by FCT – Fundação para a Ciência eTecnologia in the scope of the project: UID/CEC/00319/2013 and by COMPETE: POCI-01-0145-FEDER-007043.

References

About Elevate (n.d.). https://www.peters-research.com/index.php/elevate/elevate-elevate-express. Accessed 23 Jan 2016

About Elevate Live (n.d.). https://www.peters-research.com/index.php/elevate-live/more-about-elevate-live. Accessed 23 Jan 2016

Barney, G., Al-Sharif, L.: Elevator Traffic Handbook: Theory and Practice, 2nd edn. Routledge, New York (2015)

Dias, L., Pereira, G., Rodrigues, G.: A shortlist of the most popular discrete simulation tools. Simul. News Eur. **17**, 33–36 (2007)

Hakonen, H., Siikonen, M.-L.: Elevator Traffic Simulation Procedure. Lift Report (2009)

Hlupic, V., Paul, R.: Guidelines for selection of manufacturing simulation software. IIE Trans. **31**, 21–29 (1999)

Hlupic, V.: Simulation software: an operational research society survey of academic and industrial users. In: Proceedings of the Winter Simulation Conference, vol. 2, pp. 1676–1683 (2000)

Kelton, W.D., Sadowski, R., Zupick, N.: Simulation with Arena, 5th edn. McGraw-Hill Education, New York (2009)

McCain, Z.: Elevators 101, 2nd edn. Elevator World Inc., Masdar (2007)

Pegden, C.D.: SIMIO: a new simulation system based on intelligent objects. In: Simulation Winter Conference, pp. 2293–2300, 9–12 December 2007

Pegden, C.D., Sturrock, D.T.: Introduction to SIMIO. In: Proceedings - Winter Simulation Conference, Phoenix, AZ, pp. 29–38 (2011)

Pegden, C.D.: Intelligent objects: the future of simulation (2013). http://www.simio.com/resources/white-papers/Intelligen-objects/

Pereira, G.B., Dias, L.S., Vik, P., Oliveira, J.: Discrete simulation tools ranking – a commercial software packages comparison based on popularity. In: ISC 2011 – 9th Industrial Simulation Conference, Venice, Italy, pp. 5–11, 6–8 June 2011

Setchi, R.: Knowledge-based and intelligent information and engineering systems. In: Setchi, R., Jordanov, I. (eds.) Knowledge-Based and Intelligent Information and Engineering Systems, vol. 1, pp. 133–134. Springer Science & Business Media, Cardiff (2010)

Sturrock, D.T., Pegden, C.D.: Recent innovations in SIMIO. In: Proceedings - Winter Simulation Conference, Baltimore, MD, pp. 21–31 (2010)

Vieira, A., Dias, L.S., Pereira, G.B., Oliveira, J.A.: Comparison of SIMIO and ARENA simulation tools. In: 12th Annual Industrial Simulation Conference, ISC 2014, EUROSIS, Skovde, Sweden, pp. 5–13, 11–13 June 2014

Zhang, J., Zong, Q.: Energy-saving-oriented group-elevator dispatching strategy for multi-traffic patterns. Build. Serv. Eng. Res. Technol. **35**(5), 543–568 (2014). http://doi.org/10.1177/0143624414526723

Improving Order Picking Efficiency by Analyzing Combinations of Storage, Batching, Zoning, and Routing Policies

Teun van Gils[1]([⊠]), Kris Braekers[1,2], Katrien Ramaekers[1], Benoît Depaire[1], and An Caris[1]

[1] Hasselt University, Agoralaan Building D, 3590 Diepenbeek, Belgium
{teun.vangils,kris.braekers,katrien.ramaekers,benoit.depaire,
an.caris}@uhasselt.be
[2] Research Foundation Flanders (FWO), Egmontstraat 5, 1000 Brussels, Belgium

Abstract. In order to differentiate from competitors in terms of customer service, warehouses accept late orders while providing delivery in a quick and timely way. This trend leads to a reduced time to pick an order. The objective of this research is to simulate and evaluate the interaction between several storage, batching, zone picking and routing policies in order to reduce the order picker travel distance. The value of integrating these four operation policy decisions is proven by a real-life case study. A full factorial ANOVA provides insight into the interactions between storage, batching, zoning, and routing policies. The results of the study clearly indicate that warehouses can achieve significant benefits by considering storage, batching, zone picking, and routing policies simultaneously. Awareness of the influence of an individual policy decision on the overall warehouse performance is required to manage warehouse operations, resulting in enhanced customer service.

Keywords: Order picking · Storage · Order batching · Zone picking · Routing · Warehouse policies interactions

1 Introduction

As customer markets globalize, supply chains are increasingly depending on efficient and effective logistical systems to distribute products across a large geographical area. Warehouses are important parts of supply chains, and therefore warehouse operations need to work in an efficient and effective way. A warehouse can be defined as a facility where activities of receiving, storage, order picking, and shipping are performed [9].

Order picking management, in particular organizing efficient and flexible order picking systems, has been identified as an important and complex planning operation. In order to differentiate from competitors in terms of customer service, warehouses accept late orders from customers while providing delivery in a quick and timely way. By accepting late orders, the remaining time to pick

© Springer International Publishing Switzerland 2016
A. Paias et al. (Eds.): ICCL 2016, LNCS 9855, pp. 427–442, 2016.
DOI: 10.1007/978-3-319-44896-1_28

an order is reduced. Furthermore, the order behavior of customers has changed from ordering few and large orders to many orders consisting of only a limited number of order lines [6]. The changed order behavior can be ascribed to upcoming e-commerce markets and forces warehouses to handle a larger number of orders, while order picking time has shortened.

Four operational policy decisions can be distinguished with respect to order picking: storage location assignment, order batching, zone picking, and routing. In this paper several policies for each decision are considered and potential interactions between these decisions are investigated in order to manage order picking operations more efficiently. While the number of publications dealing with one specific order picking policy decision is extensive [6, 9], only a limited number of researchers examine different decisions simultaneously (e.g. [12, 13, 15, 17]), even though the efficiency of different order picking policy decisions seems to be interdependent [9]. The effect of zoning in combination with other order picking decisions, such as storage, routing and batching, has received especially little research attention. Therefore, the study's main objective is to analyze storage, batching, zoning, and routing in order to minimize the distance traveled by order pickers, with particular emphasis on the relation between these four order picking decisions. To the best of our knowledge, this study is the first to analyze the interaction of the four main operational order picking policy decisions (i.e. storage, batching, zoning, and routing).

The main contribution of this paper is the integration of storage, order batching, zone picking, and routing in order to improve order picking activities of a real-life warehouse. Furthermore, insights into the interactions between the four operational policy decisions are provided by performing a full factorial analysis of variance (ANOVA). It determines the impact of storage location assignment, order batching, zone picking, and routing on the distance traveled by order pickers, as well as the relation between each of the four order picking policy decisions.

The remainder of the paper is organized as follows. Section 2 is devoted to describe the context of the problem. In Sect. 3, the case study and the assumptions linked to the case are described. Subsequently, the experimental design is presented in Sect. 4, followed by the empirical results of the real-life case in Sect. 5. Managerial implications of this study are discussed in Sect. 6. Finally, Sect. 7 is devoted to the concluding remarks and future research directions.

2   Problem Context

Order picking as a warehouse function arises because goods are received in large volumes and customers order small volumes of different products. Each customer order is composed of one or more order lines, with every order line representing a single stock keeping unit (SKU) [6]. In order to manage order picking operations, warehouse managers are confronted with four operational decisions, in particular storage location assignment, order batching, zone picking, and routing.

The storage location assignment problem can be defined as determining the physical location at which incoming products are stored. One way to obtain a more efficient order picking process is to allocate fast moving products to storage locations closely located to the depot, rather than randomly assigning SKUs to storage locations. As traveling in a warehouse is often the dominant factor in order picker's activities, the travel distance reduction resulting from turnover based storage location assignment policies, will contribute to a more efficient order picking process. A turnover based storage assignment policy defines product classes by some measure of demand frequency of the product. Within-aisle storage, where all products in a pick aisle belong to the same class, across-aisle storage, where each product class is located across several pick aisles, diagonal storage, where product classes are located with respect to the depot, and perimeter storage where product classes are located around the perimeter of the warehouse are frequently used policies to locate the product classes in the order picking area [17].

Furthermore, batch picking, instead of picking each order separately, allows warehouses to handle a larger number of orders in shorter time windows. By picking multiple orders in a single picking tour, the order picker travel distance per order will be reduced. The order batching problem is concerned with deciding on rules defining which orders to combine on a pick list in order to minimize the order picker travel distance. The most straightforward algorithm for creating pick lists is a priority rule based algorithm, in which orders are prioritized and assigned to pick lists based on their priority (e.g. first-come-first-served (FCFS)). Seed algorithms generate batches by selecting an initial seed order (e.g. select the smallest order), after which unassigned customer orders are added to the seed order according to an order congruency rule (e.g. add an order such that the number of additional pick locations is minimal). Three other order batching heuristics can be distinguished: savings algorithms, data mining approaches, and metaheuristics. The reader is referred to [11] for an extensive overview of order batching algorithms.

Another practice of moving to a more efficient order picking process is dividing a warehouse into different smaller areas, being order picking zones. In contrast to strict order picking, in which order pickers are allowed to retrieve SKUs in the entire order picking area, each order picker is assigned to a single zone and responsible for picking all SKUs of an order belonging to this zone. As a consequence each order picker travels in a pre-specified part of the warehouse and thus travel time will be reduced. The assignment of items to different zones is mainly based on physical properties of products such as size and weight. Other allocation policies that may be considered are based on product demand properties, such as customer type and order frequency. If order integrity is violated (i.e. customer orders are split into separate pick lists), additional sorting activities are required to consolidate orders after retrieving the SKUs [14].

Finally, the purpose of considering routing policies is to sequence the items on the pick list in order to reduce the order picker travel distance. The problem of routing order pickers in a warehouse is mainly solved by using heuristics. The routing problem cannot be solved to optimality for every warehouse layout within reasonable computation times. A growing number of picking aisles, or larger pick lists result in fast increasing computing times. Furthermore, optimal routes may seem illogical to order pickers, resulting in deviations from the specified optimal routes. As an alternative to the optimal route, several more straightforward routing heuristics are proposed in the literature, including aisle-by-aisle, traversal or S-shape, return, midpoint, and largest gap. The aisle-by-aisle routing policy is the most straightforward routing method, where order pickers visit every pick aisle containing at least one pick location through the entire length. Traversal routes are closely related to aisle-by-aisle routes. Order pickers only traverse every subaisle (i.e. the part of a pick aisle that is within one warehouse block) containing at least one pick location through the entire length. Another straightforward routing policy is the return strategy, where order pickers enter and leave each aisle containing at least one pick location from the same end. A midpoint routing policy extends the return strategy by requiring the order picker to return if he reaches the aisle midpoint. At the midpoint, the order picker returns and leaves the aisle from the same end as he entered the aisle. The largest gap strategy is similar to the midpoint strategy except that a picker enters an aisle only as far as the start of the largest gap within an aisle, instead of the midpoint. The largest gap is defined as the maximum distance between any two adjacent pick locations within a single aisle, or the maximum distance between an aisle end and a pick location [16, 18].

Previous research has focused on either storage, batching, zoning, or routing. The number of studies analyzing interactions between these operational warehouse policies are limited. Several simulation studies analyze combinations of two operational order picking policies (e.g. storage–routing [16, 17], zoning–batching [21], and routing–batching [3, 4, 20]), while [2, 12, 13, 15] investigate the combination of storage, batching, and routing policies. This paper differs from previous studies by analyzing the four main operational policy decisions simultaneously.

3   Case Study

In order to analyze the effect of integrating storage, batching, zoning, and routing, real-life data are used. The case study is based on a large warehouse located in Belgium. The warehouse stores approximately 90.000 SKUs on a surface of 30.000 m². In accordance with the large majority of order picking systems in Western Europe, the warehouse is fully manually operated. Automated picking systems are only useful in case of valuable, small and delicate products [6]. These kind of products are limited in the warehouse under consideration.

Strict order picking is currently applied in combination with random storage location assignment. Customer orders are transformed into pick lists according to the FCFS rule. Order pickers follow the aisle-by-aisle routing policy to retrieve all items on the pick list. The policy combination of random storage, FCFS batching, strict order picking, and aisle-by-aisle routing is used as benchmark in order to evaluate other storage, batching, zoning, and routing policies. As discussed before, choosing the optimal combination of different order picking policies is crucial for warehouse managers in order to minimize the distance traveled by order pickers and consequently reduce the order throughput time.

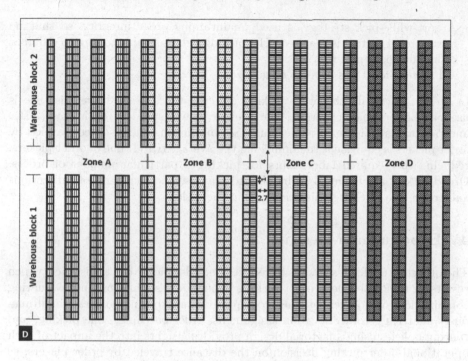

Fig. 1. Warehouse layout

The warehouse under consideration is shown in Fig. 1. The traditional multiple-block warehouse layout is frequently used in practice [17], making results of the study easily transferable to other warehouses. Furthermore, cross aisles have proven to result in significant efficiency benefits [18]. Besides traditional warehouse layouts with parallel pick aisles and straight middle aisles, alternative warehouse layouts, such as fishbone designs, can improve the order picking performance in case of a small number of items on the pick list [1]. As the batch capacity is limited to 26 orders in our problem setting, the fishbone design will likely be outperformed by the traditional warehouse layout. The warehouse in the simulation experiment has the following properties:

- The order picking area is divided into two warehouse blocks, each consisting of 16 picking aisles. The picking aisles are two-sided and wide enough for two-way travel. However, crossing the aisle is required in order to pick items from both sides of the same aisle, as the aisle width is 2.7 m. The dimensions of the aisles, as well as the warehouse block configuration and the zone configuration (in case zone picking is applied) are shown on Fig. 1.
- Order picking is completed manually using a picking vehicle with a capacity of 26 orders.
- Each picking tour starts and ends at the decentralized depot. The depot is marked as D in the bottom left corner of Fig. 1.

- A sort-while-pick strategy is used, maintaining order integrity, so that no downstream sorting is required. The picking vehicle is able to sort 26 different orders during a pick tour.
- All storage locations have an equal size.

In order to evaluate the order picking policies, the average travel distance is used as performance criterion. The average travel speed in both cross aisles and pick aisles is assumed to be equal. So, minimizing the distance traveled by order pickers is equivalent to minimizing the average travel time of order pickers, reducing the required labor hours for picking a particular number of orders. Order pickers are assumed to be able to traverse the aisles in both directions and to be able to change direction within the aisles.

4   Experimental Design

The objective of this research is to reduce the order picker travel distance, which results in a more efficient order picking process, by simulating and evaluating combinations of storage, batching, zone picking, and routing policies. Simultaneously analyzing storage location assignment, order batching, zone picking, and routing policies using a factorial design provides insights into the impact of each operational order picking decision on the distance traveled by order pickers, as well as into the relation between the operational order picking decisions. In the experiments of this paper five different storage location assignment policies, two order batching policies, five zone picking policies, as well as five routing policies are analyzed. The four factors and their associated factor levels are summarized in Table 1. The baseline scenario of this experiment is indicated in italic.

Besides randomly assigning SKUs to storage locations, four turnover based storage location assignment policies are simulated, in particular across-aisle assignment, within-aisle assignment, diagonal assignment and assigning SKUs across the perimeter of the order picking area. Within each product class, in case of turnover based storage location assignment, each SKU is randomly assigned to only one storage location.

The currently used FCFS batching policy actually results in a random creation of pick lists in terms of travel distance, as FCFS batching does not take the location of SKUs in the order picking area into account. A seed order batching

Table 1. Experimental factor setting

Factor	Factor levels (number of levels)
Storage (S)	*Random*; across-aisle; within aisle; diagonal; perimeter (5)
Batching (B)	*FCFS*; seed (2)
Zone picking (Z)	*Strict*; 2 zones (CT); 2 zones (PF); 4 zones (CT); 4 zones (PF) (5)
Routing (R)	*Aisle-by-aisle*; traversal; return; largest gap; optimal (5)

CT = storage zone assignment based on customer type
PF = storage zone assignement based on pick frequency

algorithm is used as an alternative to create batches. The order that requires the smallest number of picking aisles to visit, is selected as seed order. Next, the order that minimizes the number of additional aisles to visit in the route is added to the pick list. This algorithm is repeated until the batch contains 26 orders. Subsequently a new seed order is selected. The combination of this seed order selection rule and this accompanying order selection rule have yielded good results for different storage location assignment and routing policies [12, 13].

Strict order picking is compared to four zone picking policies. Both the number of zones as well as the storage zone assignment policy should be determined in case of zone picking. In the simulation experiments, the warehouse is divided into either two or four order picking zones, and SKUs are assigned to order picking zones based on customer type (CT) or pick frequency (PF). This results in four additional zone picking policies.

In addition to the aisle-by-aisle routing heuristic, the travel distance for return, traversal, largest gap, and the optimal route is computed. As the routing problem cannot be solved to optimality for a multiple-block warehouse in reasonable computing times, the Lin-Kernighan-Helsgaun (LKH) heuristic for the traveling salesman problem (TSP) is used to approximate the optimal route [10]. The LKH heuristic has shown to provide excellent results, both in a general TSP context, and in the context of routing order pickers in a warehouse. Theys et al. [19] reported an average optimality gap of 0.1 % for different warehouse settings.

To sum up, the simulation experiment consists of 250 possible combinations of policies (i.e. five storage location assignment policies × two batching policies × five zone picking policies × five routing policies). To reduce the stochastic effect from order generation, 30 replications per policy combination are performed, resulting in 7,500 observations. During each replication, all combinations of storage, batching, zoning and routing are tested on the same 1,690 randomly generated orders. Order sizes follow an exponential distribution with mean of 2.65 order lines. This factorial setting results in a $5 \times 2 \times 5 \times 5$ full factorial design.

The results of the simulation experiments are analyzed by a full factorial ANOVA. The assumptions under which the ANOVA F statistic is reliable, are independent observations, homogeneity of variance, as well as normally distributed observations. For each replication, all combinations of storage, batching, routing and zoning are simulated on the same randomly generated orders in order to stress the effects of policy decisions. Consequently, the 7,500 observations are not independently and a repeated measures ANOVA with storage, batching, routing, and zoning as within-subjects factors is required to analyze the main and interaction effects of the policy decisions [5]. Since the homogeneity assumption is violated, the F-test Type I error rate increases. The Greenhouse-Geisser (G-G) correction of the degrees of freedom is used to compensate for the increased F-test type I error rate. The G-G adjustment is the most conservative correction to compensate for the violation of sphericity [5, 8]. In order to ensure the last ANOVA assumption (i.e. normality), the experimental design is balanced. The F statistic is quite robust to violations of normality when group sizes are equal [5]. In the simulation experiments in this paper, a balanced $5 \times 2 \times 5 \times 5$ full factorial repeated measures ANOVA, with storage, batching, zoning, and routing as the within-subjects factors, is used to prove the value of studying the four operation policy decisions in an integrated manner.

5   Empirical Results

First, results of the repeated measures ANOVA are discussed in Sect. 5.1. Subsequently, the impact of each individual operational order picking policy decision, as well as the interaction effects between policy decisions are analyzed in Sects. 5.2 and 5.3 respectively.

5.1   ANOVA Results

In order to get a first insight into the results of the simulation experiments, the route lengths of the different factor combinations are analyzed by a $5 \times 2 \times 5 \times 5$ full factorial repeated measures ANOVA on average travel distance. The results of the repeated measures ANOVA are shown in Table 2. The first three columns show the sum of squares, the G-G degrees of freedom and the resulting mean square for the main and interactions effects, as well as for the residuals. The last two columns are devoted to the F statistic and the p-value for testing the statistical significance of storage, batching, zoning, and routing, as well as all interactions between the four operational policy decisions.

Table 2 indicates that the main effects of storage location assignment, order batching, zoning and routing are statistically significant. This means that there is a significant difference between the five storage location policies, the two order batching policies, the five zoning policies, as well as the five different routing policies on the average distance traveled by order pickers, respectively. The decision on which storage, which batching, which zoning, and which routing policy to use does influence the average route length.

Furthermore, Table 2 shows that all factors in the simulation experiment are significantly interacting with each other. All of the six two-way interactions, all three-way interactions, as well as the four-way interaction between storage, batching, zoning and routing are statistically significantly different form zero. As three out of the four factors in the experiment contain five levels, the 30 replications give rise to a large number of observations. Null hypotheses are much easier rejected with a large number of factor levels and a large number of observations because of a greater probability that one of the factor levels is interacting with another factor level [7]. However, the ANOVA shows strong statistically effects, both for the main effects and the interaction effects. Given the significance of the effects, the main and interaction effects are examined in more detail in the next sections.

Table 2. $5 \times 2 \times 5 \times 5$ full factorial repeated measures ANOVA on average travel distance

	Sum of squares	df	Mean square	F	p-value
Main effects					
Storage (S)	26,895,933,301	2.91	9,237,614,573	13,853.95	0.000
Batching (B)	181,937,289,935	1.00	181,937,289,935	284,683.12	0.000
Zoning (Z)	358,908,254,822	2.57	139,604,086,655	60,486.02	0.000
Routing (R)	79,222,871,786	2.18	36,318,042,321	229,618.82	0.000
Two way interaction					
S × B	11,070,135	3.27	3,383,774	11.14	0.000
S × Z	16,831,331,146	7.61	2,211,840,545	3,526.56	0.000
S × R	8,595,751,592	7.03	1,222,476,423	11,468.01	0.000
B × Z	16,416,356,030	2.91	5,634,479,183	9,634.53	0.000
B × R	5,391,003,315	2.74	1,966,180,751	47,170.76	0.000
Z × R	12,905,574,845	6.00	2,152,147,805	18,137.89	0.000
Three way interaction					
S × B × Z	621,242,209	8.43	73,716,968	179.82	0.000
S × B × R	505,815,157	8.47	59,717,570	1,132.60	0.000
S × Z × R	6,383,449,026	13.79	463,008,935	2,894.19	0.000
B × Z × R	703,844,710	6.98	100,770,162	1,642.05	0.000
Four way interaction					
S × B × Z × R	478,689,655	15.11	31,682,633	330.12	0.000
Residuals					
Between subjects	330,171,235	29.00	11,385,215		
Within S	56,300,343	84.44	666,786		
Within B	18,533,524	29.00	639,087		
Within Z	172,078,430	74.56	2,308,039		
Within R	10,005,553	63.26	158,167		
Within S × B	28,813,836	94.87	303,705		
Within S × Z	138,409,444	220.68	627,196		
Within S × R	21,736,707	203.91	106,599		
Within B × Z	49,413,333	84.49	584,821		
Within B × R	3,314,322	79.51	41,682		
Within Z × R	20,634,248	173.90	118,655		
Within S × B × Z	100,189,592	244.39	409,950		
Within S × B × R	12,951,295	245.63	52,726		
Within S × Z × R	63,962,727	399.82	159,979		
Within B × Z × R	12,430,509	202.55	61,369		
Within S × B × Z × R	42,053,031	438.16	95,977		
Total	716,889,475,792	7,499.00			

5.2   Main Effect of Storage, Batching, Routing and Zone Picking

Table 3 summarizes the average route length in meters for each operational policy decision over all combinations with other policies, as well as the relative difference between each order picking policy and the average best performing policy within each operational decision area. Additionally, the statistical significance of all levels of the different experimental factors are analyzed using a Bonferroni t-test. The Bonferroni method seems to be the most robust technique in terms of power and control of the Type I error rate for evaluating multiple hypotheses [7]. The test results are summarized in Table 4. If two order picking policies are listed in the same subset in Table 4, differences fail to be statistically significant. The simulation results of storage location assignment policies, order batching policies, routing policies and zoning policies are discussed independently below.

The within-aisle storage location assignment policy is on average the best performing method for assigning SKUs to individual storage locations, followed by the diagonal and across-aisle storage policy. Except for the perimeter storage location assignment policy, all turnover based storage policies (i.e. within-aisle, across-aisle, and diagonal) are able to outperform the random assignment of SKUs to storage locations. These three turnover based storage policies are in the three top subsets in Table 4 and result in statistically significantly shorter travel distances compared to the random and perimeter storage location assignment policy. Random and respectively perimeter assignments yield on average 14.3 %

Table 3. Average travel distance for each operational order picking policy (in meter)

	Storage	Mean	Batching	Mean	Zoning	Mean	Routing	Mean
[1]	Within-aisle	25,831.1	Seed	23,016.4	4 zones (CT)	19,916.0	Optimal	22,814.0
	Diagonal	26,220.9	FCFS	32,866.9	4 zones (PF)	24,577.2	Traversal	26,945.9
Gap over [1] (%)		*1.5*		*30.0*		*19.0*		*15.3*
	Across-aisle	27,283.4	**Mean 27,941.6**		2 zones (CT)	25,355.3	Largest gap	27,035.7
Gap over [1] (%)		*5.3*				*21.5*		*15.6*
	Random	30,142.2			2 zones (PF)	29,489.9	Return	31,405.2
Gap over [1] (%)		*14.3*				*32.5*		*27.4*
	Perimeter	30,230.6			Strict	40,369.7	Aisle-by-aisle	31,507.4
Gap over [1] (%)		*14.6*				*50.7*		*27.6*
	Mean 27,941.6				**Mean 27,941.6**		**Mean 27,941.6**	

Table 4. Post hoc multiple Bonferroni t-test for each operational policy decision on average travel distance (familywise error rate = 0.01)

Storage	Batching	Zoning	Routing
Within-aisle	Seed	4 zones (CT)	Optimal
Diagonal	FCFS	4 zones (PF)	Traversal
Across-aisle		2 zones (CT)	Largest gap
Random		2 zones (PF)	Return
Perimeter		Strict	Aisle-by-aisle

and 14.6 % larger route lengths compared to the best performing method. These two storage policies form a single subset in the Bonferroni t-test, indicating that the average travel distance is on average not statistically significantly different.

Two subsets are composed by evaluating the two batching policies (Table 4), giving evidence that the mean route length is statistically significantly different for each order batching policy. Simulations show that the seed order batching policy on average results in 30 % shorter route lengths compared to FCFS batching (Table 3). This result is rather obvious as the seed rules take the product locations of each order into account in composing pick lists, while FCFS batching results in a random composition of pick lists in terms of travel distances.

The policy of dividing the warehouse into order picking zones outperforms the strict order picking policy. The average travel distance halves when changing from strict order picking to the best performing zone picking policy, i.e. the customer type storage zone assignment in which the order picking area is divided into four order picking zones. All sixteen picking aisles can be visited in a single pick tour in case of strict order picking, while a maximum of either eight or four aisles should be entered if the warehouse is respectively divided into two or four order picking zones. So each order picker only traverses a small part of the order picking area in order to retrieve all items on the pick list.

Tables 3 and 4 show that the optimal routing policy results in the smallest average distance traveled by order pickers. The optimal routing procedure is in the top performing subset as items on the pick list are sequenced in order to minimize the route length. The optimality gap for the four routing heuristics (i.e. traversal, largest gap, return, and aisle-by-aisle) is on average 15.3 %, 15.6 %, 27.4 %, and 27.6 % respectively. The results of the simulation experiments show statistically significant differences between all routing policies. However, the average route length difference between traversal and largest gap, as well as the mean difference between return and aisle-by-aisle are rather limited. Return and aisle-by-aisle routes are the most straightforward and worst performing routing heuristics. The traversal routing policy outperforms the aisle-by-aisle heuristic, because the traversal routing policy allows order pickers to leave an aisle in the middle cross-aisle, which results in shorter routes. The largest gap heuristic extends the return routing policy by requiring the order picker to return as he reaches the largest gap within an aisle. Consequently, largest gap routes outperform routes in which the order picker always returns to the middle cross-aisle.

5.3   Interaction Effects

The results of the simulation experiments are graphically illustrated in Fig. 2, disaggregated into combinations of storage location assignment policies, order batching policies, zoning policies, and routing policies. The interaction plot shows all two-way interactions between the four operational order picking policies. The lines on the graph illustrate the average travel distance for a particular order picking policy combination. The three graphs in the first column show the average travel distance in function of the different storage location assignment policies per batching, zoning and routing policy in the respective first, second and third graph of the first column. The graphs in the three remaining columns illustrate the average route length in function of the different batching, zoning and routing policies in an equivalent way. Most lines on the graphs converge and some even cross. For example, the lines of the aisle-by-aisle routing heuristic and the return policy are crossing on the graph illustrating the interaction between batching and routing, while the return, traversal, and largest gap routing heuristic converge when changing from the FCFS to the seed batching policy. The converging and crossing lines are in accordance with the results of the ANOVA in Table 2, indicating that there are strong interactions between the different operational order picking decisions.

The significant interactions between the different order picking policies originate from the fact that some combinations of warehouse policies yield excellent performances (e.g. perimeter storage assignment in combination with largest gap routing), while other combinations result in large average travel distances (e.g. FCFS batching in combination with return routing). From Fig. 2, the combination of the perimeter storage policy and the largest gap routing policy is an example of a well performing combination. Since fast moving SKUs are stored along the periphery of the warehouse blocks and the largest gap routes tend to follow the periphery of the warehouse, this combination of order picking policies outperforms other combinations of routing heuristics and perimeter storage location assignment. Aisle-by-aisle, traversal, as well as return routes show a strong increase in travel distance in combination with the perimeter storage compared to other storage location assignment policies.

Combinations of the straightforward routing policies (i.e. aisle-by-aisle and return) with FCFS batching appear to be inefficient. FCFS batching, which in fact results in a random creation of batches, generates pick lists with SKUs located in a large number of aisles and SKUs are diffused within each aisle. Aisle-by-aisle routes can work efficiently only if the number of aisles to be visited is minimized, while return routes aim to minimize the travel distance within a pick aisle. This results in a large travel distance when combining FCFS batching with either the aisle-by-aisle or return routing policy. The average route length difference between FCFS and seed batching is much larger when combined with aisle-by-aisle and return routing compared to other routing methods.

In addition to some excellent performing and some inefficient combinations, the statistically significant interaction can be further explained by the fact that shifting from a bad performing factor level to a good performing level within the same factor results in much smaller performance benefits when other order picking policies are already efficiently performed compared to the situation in which other order picking policies on average result in large travel distances. For example the effect of different storage location assignment policies is not consistent over all levels of zoning. By dividing the warehouse into order picking zones, the effect of shifting to a more efficient storage policy on the route length is reduced compared to the strict order picking policy. The reason for this significant interaction term can be found in the smaller area that is crossed by order pickers to retrieve all items on the pick list in case of two or four order picking

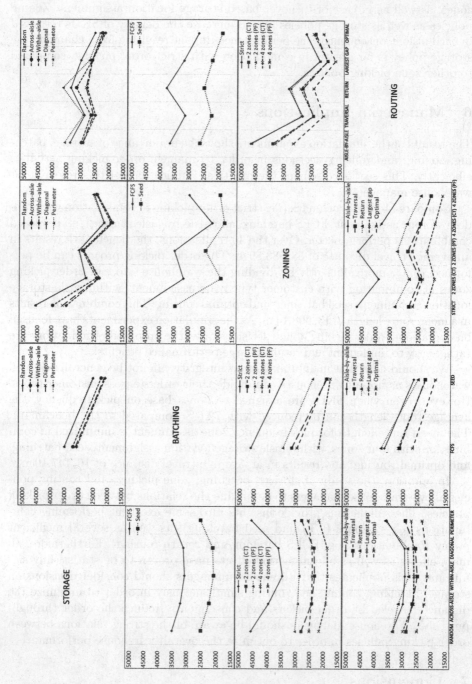

Fig. 2. Average travel distance in meter for each combination of storage, batching, zoning and routing policy

zones, as well as in case of turnover based storage location assignment. Zoning policies as well as storage policies aim to increase the density of SKUs retrieved in each aisle. Consequently, the performance impact resulting from changing the storage policy is far greater in combination with strict order picking, compared to other zone picking policies.

6   Managerial Implications

The results of the simulation experiments show the importance of storage, batching, zoning, and routing decisions in order to manage order picking activities efficiently. This section discusses the practical implications of this research for warehouse managers.

Compared to the benchmark (i.e. strict order picking in combination with random storage assignment, FCFS batching, and aisle-by-aisle routing), all proposed combinations perform better. Over the 30 replications, the benchmark results in an average travel distance of $58,983.89$ m. The order picking process can be performed 76.9% more efficiently by dividing the warehouse into four order picking zones in combination with customer type zone assignment, within-aisle storage location assignment, seed batching, and optimal routing. This combination results in a mean route length of $13,608.14$ m. As the simulation experiments have focused on operational order picking policy decisions only, the proposed combinations are rather easy to implement and result in large performance benefits.

We should note that maintaining order integrity can not be generalized to all warehouses as not all warehouses can divide their orders across customer types. However, even when SKUs are assigned to zones base on pick frequency, the average route length can be reduced with 72.6% compared to the benchmark. The mean route length for pick frequency zone assignment is minimized in combination with four zones, within-aisle storage location assignment, seed batching, and optimal routing, and results in an average travel distance of $16,147.10$ m.

In addition, the study of storage, batching, zone picking, and routing policies allows warehouse managers to determine the relations between order picking policies. The simulations provide insights into some excellent performing combinations (e.g. 2 zones (CT) and seed batching), as well as several inefficient policy combinations (e.g. FCFS batching and return routing). Furthermore, all main effects as well as all interaction effects have proven to be statistically significant. This implicates that warehouse managers should consider decisions on storage, batching, zoning, and routing simultaneously in order to minimize the distance traveled by order pickers and consequently reduce the order throughput time. Warehouse managers should be aware of the strong relations between order picking policies in order to optimize the overall warehouse performance.

7   Conclusions

The delivery of e-commerce markets forces warehouses to handle a growing number of orders in shorter time windows. Awareness of the influence of an individual warehouse operation on the overall warehouse performance is required to manage warehouse operations, resulting in enhanced customer service.

In this paper, the relation between storage, batching, zone picking, and routing policies is studied for the first time. The results of the study clearly indicate that warehouses can achieve significant benefits by considering storage, batching, zone picking, and routing policies simultaneously. The combination of within-aisle storage, seed batching, zone picking (4 zones and customer type zone assignment), and the optimal route results in the lowest route length. As traveling is the dominant factor in order picking operations, the order picking process can be performed more efficiently. As a result, warehouse managers can either reduce the number of order pickers or reduce the customer order throughput time.

The simulation results of our study contribute to both practitioners and academic research. The evaluation of an extensive range of order picking policies helps warehouse managers to reduce the order throughput time. The simulated order picking policies can be easily implemented and immediately result in significant performance benefits. This paper is limited to the four main order picking policy decisions. However in future research, these order picking policies could be enlarged to other operational decisions, such as workforce planning decisions and alternative zone configurations. Furthermore, simulating other warehouse layouts may allow us to achieve higher practical and managerial relevance. Enlarging the simulation experiment will provide insight into more warehouse policy interactions, helping warehouse managers to further reduce the order throughput time, which can result in faster deliveries.

Acknowledgments. This work is supported by the Interuniversity Attraction Poles Programme initiated by the Belgian Science Policy Office (research project COMEX, Combinatorial Optimization: Metaheuristics & Exact Methods).

References

1. Çelik, M., Süral, H.: Order picking under random and turnover-based storage policies in fishbone aisle warehouses. IIE Trans. **46**(3), 283–300 (2014)
2. Chen, C.M., Gong, Y., de Koster, R.B., van Nunen, J.A.: A flexible evaluative framework for order picking systems. Prod. Oper. Manag. **19**(1), 70–82 (2010)
3. Chen, T.L., Cheng, C.Y., Chen, Y.Y., Chan, L.K.: An efficient hybrid algorithm for integrated order batching, sequencing and routing problem. Int. J. Prod. Econ. **159**, 158–167 (2015)
4. Cheng, C.Y., Chen, Y.Y., Chen, T.L., Yoo, J.J.W.: Using a hybrid approach based on the particle swarm optimization and ant colony optimization to solve a joint order batching and picker routing problem. Int. J. Prod. Econ. **170**(Part C), 805–814 (2015)
5. Cohen, B.H., Welkowitz, J., Lea, R.B.: Introductory Statistics for the Behavioral Sciences, 7th edn. Wiley, Hoboken (2011)
6. De Koster, R.B.M., Le-Duc, T., Roodbergen, K.J.: Design and control of warehouse order picking: a literature review. Eur. J. Oper. Res. **182**(2), 481–501 (2007)
7. Field, A.: Discovering Statistics Using IBM SPSS Statistics. SAGE, London (2013)

8. Geisser, S., Greenhouse, S.W.: An extension of box's results on the use of the f distribution in multivariate analysis. Ann. Math. Stat. **29**(3), 885–891 (1958)
9. Gu, J., Goetschalckx, M., McGinnis, L.F.: Research on warehouse operation: a comprehensive review. Eur. J. Oper. Res. **177**(1), 1–21 (2007)
10. Helsgaun, K.: An effective implementation of the Lin-Kernighan traveling salesman heuristic. Eur. J. Oper. Res. **126**(1), 106–130 (2000)
11. Henn, S.: Algorithms for on-line order batching in an order picking warehouse. Comput. Oper. Res. **39**(11), 2549–2563 (2012)
12. Ho, Y.C., Tseng, Y.Y.: A study on order-batching methods of order-picking in a distribution centre with two cross-aisles. Int. J. Prod. Res. **44**(17), 3391–3417 (2006)
13. Ho, Y.C., Su, T.S., Shi, Z.B.: Order-batching methods for an order-picking warehouse with two cross aisles. Comput. Ind. Eng. **55**(2), 321–347 (2008)
14. Jane, C.C., Laih, Y.W.: A clustering algorithm for item assignment in a synchronized zone order picking system. Eur. J. Oper. Res. **166**(2), 489–496 (2005)
15. Petersen, C.G., Aase, G.: A comparison of picking, storage, and routing policies in manual order picking. Int. J. Prod. Econ. **92**(1), 11–19 (2004)
16. Petersen, C.G., Schmenner, R.W.: An evaluation of routing and volume-based storage policies in an order picking operation. Decis. Sci. **30**(2), 481–501 (1999)
17. Roodbergen, K.J.: Storage assignment for order picking in multiple-block warehouses. In: Manzini, R. (ed.) Warehousing in the Global Supply Chain, pp. 139–155. Springer, London (2012)
18. Roodbergen, K.J., de Koster, R.B.M.: Routing methods for warehouses with multiple cross aisles. Int. J. Prod. Res. **39**(9), 1865–1883 (2001)
19. Theys, C., Bräysy, O., Dullaert, W., Raa, B.: Using a TSP heuristic for routing order pickers in warehouses. Eur. J. Oper. Res. **200**(3), 755–763 (2010)
20. Won, J., Olafsson, S.: Joint order batching and order picking in warehouse operations. Int. J. Prod. Res. **43**(7), 1427–1442 (2005)
21. Yu, M., de Koster, R.B.M.: The impact of order batching and picking area zoning on order picking system performance. Eur. J. Oper. Res. **198**(2), 480–490 (2009)

Improving Production Logistics Through Materials Flow Control and Lot Splitting

Catarina Gomes[1], Andreia Ribeiro[1], João Freitas[1], Luís Dias[1], Guilherme Pereira[1], António Vieira[1], Nuno O. Fernandes[2(✉)], and Sílvio Carmo-Silva[1]

[1] Department of Production and Systems, University of Minho, Campus de Gualtar, 4710-057 Braga, Portugal
catarinafrlgomes@gmail.com,
andreia.queiroz.ribeiro@gmail.com,
jtp_1993@hotmail.com,
{lsd,gui,antonio.vieira,scarmo}@dps.uminho.pt
[2] Instituto Politécnico de Castelo Branco, Av. Empresário, 6000-767 Castelo Branco, Portugal
nogf@ipcb.pt

Abstract. Competitive advantage of make-to-order manufacturing companies is highly dependent on their capability to offer short delivery times and on time delivery. This calls for effective production and materials flow control – a core part of production logistics. This paper applies discrete simulation to study the delivery performance of a make-to-order manufacturing system configured as a general flow shop, when operated under two card-based material flow control mechanisms: CONWIP and GKS. The influence of two lot splitting strategies on the performance of these mechanisms is also evaluated. Results show that GKS clearly outperforms CONWIP and that splitting strategies have a positive impact on the performance of both mechanisms. GKS also showed to be particularly robust to the variation of the number of production authorisation cards used. This, together with the fact that the card-based mechanisms require little data handling and simplify production control, makes GKS attractive for practical application in make-to-order companies.

Keywords: CONWIP · GKS · Lot splitting · MTO · Simulation

1 Introduction

Production and materials flow control are important functions of production logistics. Production logistics fundamentally pursues high delivery capability and reliability with minimum logistic and production costs [12]. Delivery capability expresses the degree to which a company can commit itself to customer desired delivery dates. Delivery reliability, on the other hand, expresses the extent to which the order due dates are met. To achieve this, production and materials flow control must organize and manage the entire production and material flow, from the acquisition of raw materials to the delivery of end products to customers, ensuring that each machine or workstation of the production system is fed with the right jobs at the right time.

© Springer International Publishing Switzerland 2016
A. Paias et al. (Eds.): ICCL 2016, LNCS 9855, pp. 443–453, 2016.
DOI: 10.1007/978-3-319-44896-1_29

Card-based materials flow control mechanisms such as the Generic Kanban Systems (GKS) [4] and CONstant Work-In-Process (CONWIP) [14] can be simple and yet effective means of controlling production and materials flow. Such mechanisms have been proposed as alternatives to the Toyota Kanban system (TKS), which do not typically apply to the make-to-order (MTO) and high-variability production: the former as a way of applying Kanbans (i.e. production authorization cards) to control production and materials flow in dynamic environments; the latter as a simplified alternative to TKS for the MTO production.

Chang and Yih [4] compared these mechanisms in a pure flow shop. GKS was shown to be more flexible in that by manipulating the number of kanbans at each workstation the performance of GKS could be improved beyond that achieved by CONWIP. To the best of our knowledge no study was carried out on the influence of lot splitting on the performance of these two material flow control mechanisms, neither were them evaluated for manufacturing systems more suited to satisfy demand under MTO. Thus, this research work gives a contribution to fill this research gap, using discrete event simulation to model and analyse the performance of a general flow shop under MTO production, when operated by these two card-based materials flow control mechanisms. In particular, the following research questions are addressed:

1. How materials flow control mechanisms perform in the context of make-to-order and general flow shops?
2. How lot splitting impacts the performance of these mechanisms?

Lot splitting allows accelerating the flow of work by splitting job lots into sublots. The basic idea is not to process the whole job at one workstation and then move them to the next, but to move smaller quantities (sublots) to the next workstation as soon as they are completed. This may result in the overlapping of operations, shortening throughput times and thus improved logistic performance, as pointed out by Jacobs and Bragg [9] and Wagner and Ragatz [15], among others. It also reduces the amount of storage space as well as the capacity of material handling equipment required. Chang and Chiu [3] and Cheng et al. [5] make comprehensive literature reviews on lot streaming, i.e. lot splitting for operations overlapping.

The remainder of the paper is organized as follows. In Sect. 2, we present the simulation study carried out, including the simulation model, the experimental set-up and the performance measures considered. In Sect. 3, we discuss the results of the simulation study, and finally, in Sect. 4 of the paper, we summarize key results and managerial implications.

2   Simulation Study

A discrete event computer simulation model was developed using Arena® software to model the system under study and carry out experimentation towards answering the above research questions.

2.1   Simulation Model

In this study, we consider a six-stage general flow shop (GFS) manufacturing system with one workstation in each processing stage. The GFS is seen as a more realistic model of the flow structure of job shops than pure job shop [6, 13]. A representation of the GFS used in the study is shown in Fig. 1, while Table 1 summarises the characteristics of the simulation model.

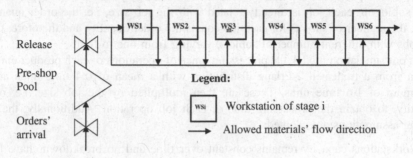

Fig. 1. The material flow structure of a general flow shop with six workstations (adapted from [2])

Table 1. Job and shop characteristics

Shop configuration	General flow shop; no re-entrant flows
No. of workstations	6
Workstation capacities	All equal and constant over time
Workstation utilisation	90 %
Inter-arrival times	Exponentially distributed; mean = 0.647 time units
No. of operations per job	Discrete uniformly distributed [1, 6] operations
Job or order size (quantity)	Discrete uniformly distributed [1, 4] units
Unit processing times	2-Erlang, mean of 0,4 time units; truncated at 1.6 time units
Set-up time	Sequence independent, included in the processing times

As customer orders arrive to the manufacturing system, their operation times and due dates are established. It is assumed that all orders are accepted and enough raw materials inventory is always available. Orders' inter-arrival times follow an exponential distribution with mean 0.647 time units. The inter-arrival times when combined with the orders routings and operations times will result in an average utilisation of 90 % at all workstations. This is adopted in our model once it is a utilization level that usually is aimed at in practice and it allows having a good insight on the performance behaviour of the production control mechanisms tested.

Market driven due dates are set by adding a uniformly distributed time allowance to order arrival time. In this study, the allowance varies between 35 and 55 time units. The minimum value was set to cover a minimum shop floor throughput time corresponding to a planned operation lead time of 5 time units plus an allowance for the pool waiting time. The maximum value was chosen in order to get a good perception of the relative performance of the control strategies on tardy jobs. This leads to approximately 18 % of orders being tardy under immediate release if lot splitting is not applied. To reflect the environment where customers demand unique or small quantities of products, the order quantity is randomly generated according to a discrete uniform distribution between one and four product units.

Customer orders, here also referred as jobs, can be split into sublots of equal size, which can be processed separately in the manufacturing system. The number of possible sublots in each job is directly related with the job size, i.e. the order quantity. Thus, the number of sublots for each job equals the order quantity and therefore, there are jobs with different number of sublots, varying from one to four.

In our simulation model, the processing times of operations of each product unit are drawn from a truncated 2-Erlang distribution with a mean of 0.4 time units and a maximum of 1.6 time units. These are then multiplied by the job size, i.e. order quantity, to obtain the processing time of each job operation. Additionally, the following assumptions are adopted:

- Workstations capacity remains constant over time and no breakdowns have been modelled.
- Set-up times are assumed to be sequence-independent and included in the operation processing times.
- Distances and transportation times between workstations and between production stages are assumed to be negligible.
- Information of production control events and production control cards are transmitted instantly.

The simulation model presented here was kept simple and the values of system parameters were set to ensure easy and correct interpretation of the effects of the experimental factors as a contribution for the understanding of the performance behaviour of material flow control mechanisms when applied to the widely used in practice general flow shop manufacturing system configuration.

2.2 Materials Flow Control: Order Release and Dispatching

Materials flow control, an important part of production logistics, addresses two main production control functions: order release and priority dispatching. Order release determines the time and the orders to be released to the system, authorizing production to start. Release decisions are usually based on the orders' urgency and on their influence on the current shop floor situation [8]. Priority dispatching selects the job or the sublot to be processed next at a workstation that becomes free, from those waiting in workstations' queues.

In the manufacturing system considered, an arriving order immediately flows into a pre-shop pool, waiting its release to the system, i.e. to shop floor, for processing. This means that orders are not immediately released to the system as they arrive. Rather, they wait until release required conditions are met. The controlled release, associated to the use of a pre-shop pool, is expected to reduce the level of work-in-process (WIP) in the system and allow better control over the flow of work or materials through the system. Orders in the pool are sequenced for release according to their urgency, i.e., a planned release date (Eq. 1), and are released under the control of two possible card-based materials flow control mechanism: CONWIP (CONstant-Work-In-Process) and GKS (Generic Kanban System).

$$\tau_j = d_j - \sum_{k \in R_j} b_k \qquad (1)$$

Where:

τ_j is the planned release date of job j;

d_j is the due date of job j;

b_k is the lead time at workstation k;

R_j is the set of workstations in the routing of job j.

Lead times at each workstation are fixed at 5 time units based on the throughput times observed in preliminary simulation runs of this study;

In both CONWIP and GKS mechanisms the cards, which are used for authorizing production, are not part or product number specific and therefore can be acquired, for production and materials flow control purposes, by any job in the pre-shop pool waiting release. CONWIP cards are all identical, i.e. of the same type, but GKS cards are not: they are workstation specific.

Cards for each sublot of a job are attached to the job at release. Detached cards from jobs are sent back to the pre-shop pool, where they can be attached to new production job when released into the system. CONWIP cards, as many as the number of sublots, are attached to the job at release and detached when the job (or a sublot, when lot splitting is performed), completes processing at its last production stage. GKS works in different way. Since GKS cards are associated to each workstation, then GKS cards from each workstation in the routing of the job are attached to the job at release and detached, and sent back for new releases, when the job or each one of the sublots, depending on the splitting policy used (see Sect. 2.3), completes its operation at the corresponding workstation.

The role of priority dispatching is a very moderate one when order release control is applied, because the choice among jobs is limited due to short queues [1]. Thus, in this study, shop floor dispatching is based on the *first-come-first-served* (FCFS) priority-dispatching rule that supports the natural flow of the orders through the shop, stabilizing operation throughput times.

2.3   Control Policy - Lot Splitting

Regarding lot splitting three alternative policies are analysed to determine whether splitting should be considered or not and when, i.e. before or after release to the shop for processing:

- Policy P0: The job (or order) is not split, and thus released to the shop floor and processed as a whole.

- Policy P1: The job (or order) is split before release and split sublots are released in an independent manner to the shop floor.
- Policy P2: The job (or order) is released as a whole and then split in sublots on the shop floor for independent processing.

2.4   Experimental Design and Performance Measures

The experimental factors and simulated levels of the study are summarised in Table 2. Two material flow control mechanisms, namely CONWIP and GKS, are applied to release jobs from the pre-shop pool to the shop floor. Both were tested at five card counts, i.e. number of production authorisation cards, and for the three lot-splitting policies referred above. Thus, 30 simulation cases are tested (2 release mechanisms × 5 card counts × 3 lot splitting policies). Each test case runs 100 replicates. The time horizon for a simulation case is 13 000 time units and only data of the last 10 000 time units are collected, i.e., a warm-up period of 3 000 time units is considered.

Table 2.   Experimental factors and levels

Experimental factor	Levels		
Material flow control mechanisms	CONWIP		GKS
Lot splitting policies	P0	P1	P2
Number of production authorisation cards	5 levels of WIP restriction		

The number of production authorisation cards is an experimental factor in our study. CONWIP uses a single-type production authorisation card. GKS, on the other hand, requires one card type per workstation. We define the number of cards per workstation to be different in GKS. The number of cards at workstations two to six equals those of workstation one multiplied by the workstation number. We adopt this on the assumption that cards for downstream workstations of the GFS are likely to remain longer in the system than for upstream workstations and because we have a balanced GFS with identical workstation throughput times.

Concerning system performance, two types of criteria are used: (1) the ability to deliver orders (jobs) on time, and (2) the ability to provide short delivery times. To measure performance with regard to the former, the percentage of tardy jobs and the standard deviation of lateness are recorded. To measure performance with regard to the latter, the shop throughput time and the total throughput time are used. The shop throughput time refers to the time that elapses between job release and job completion. The total throughput time is the shop throughput time plus the job delay in the pre-shop pool. Note that a job is not completed until all the lots that belong to it are fully processed. Thus we can define the synchronization time of a job as the time that elapses between the completion of the first and last lot of the job.

3   Simulation Results and Discussion

Here we present and discuss the results of the simulation study described in the previous section. Section 3.1 studies the impact of the CONWIP and GKS mechanisms under lot splitting policy P1. A detailed analysis of results under the three policies, P0 to P2, is given in Sect. 3.2.

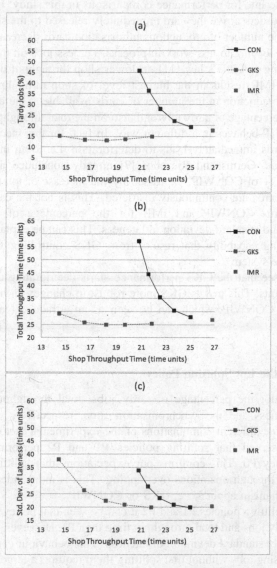

Fig. 2. Release results of release methods for: (a) percentage of tardy jobs; (b) total throughput time; (c) standard deviation of lateness.

3.1   Impact of Release Methods on Performance

Figure 2(a)–(c) plot the percentage of tardy jobs, total throughput time, and the standard deviation of lateness, respectively, against the shop throughput time for the two material flow control mechanisms. By comparing plotted curves, we can determine their performance differences for different values of card counts. A marker on a curve is the result of simulating a release method at a specific card count. Five card counts have been simulated.

Additionally, we also collect and show results for immediate release (IMR) as it was used as a base line for performance comparisons in this study. Immediate release means that when orders arrive they are immediately released to the shop floor without any restriction. The number of production authorisation cards decrease along the curve from right to left, leading to less work-in-process, i.e. less jobs on the shop floor, and therefore, according to Little's law [11], to lower shop throughput time.

As expected, IMR results in the highest level of shop throughput time. Accompanying an initial reduction in the number of cards available at the pre-shop pool is a reduction in the percentage of tardy jobs and also on the total throughput time for GKS. However, CONWIP behaves in a different way. In fact, for this mechanism, reducing the number of cards immediately leads to deterioration, i.e. to an increase of all performance measures. Germs and Riezebos [7] already concluded about the lack of balancing capability of CONWIP, expressed by the increase of total throughput time when CONWIP cards are continuously restricted. This is not the case in GKS. GKS clearly outperforms CONWIP and IMR for the percentage of tardy jobs, total throughput time and standard deviation of lateness. This can be explained by the better workload balancing capability that results from GKS controlling workload in each workstation of the system.

We can also see that the GKS performance starts deteriorating only for very low levels of card counts. This makes GKS more robust to changes in the number of card comparatively to CONWIP, which can be seen as an attractive feature for practical application.

3.2   Impact of the Lot Splitting Policy

Figure 3(a)–(d) plot the percentage of tardy jobs, total throughput time, standard deviation of lateness and the synchronisation time, respectively, against the shop throughput time for different combinations of the experimental factors.

It can be observed that splitting policies P1 and P2 perform better than the non-splitting Policy P0. This confirms our expectations that splitting jobs decrease throughput times through operations overlapping. This is independent of the material flow control mechanism applied, i.e. GKS or CONWIP.

Comparing splitting policies P1 and P2 it can be seen that policy P2 leads to better percentage of tardy jobs and total throughput time than P1. However, this is obtained at the cost of a higher standard deviation of lateness. This behaviour can be explained by the fact that releasing jobs without first splitting them requires a larger number of cards to be available at release. This means that larger jobs have a less streamlined release

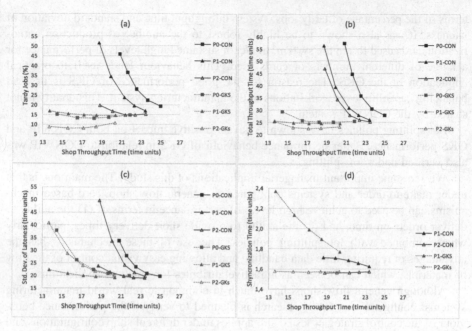

Fig. 3. Performance results for the impact of the splitting policy for: (a) percentage of tardy jobs; (b) total throughput time; (c) standard deviation of lateness and (d) synchronization time.

than smaller jobs, i.e. sometimes they can be release in due time and sometimes they cannot, due to the shortage of cards. This tends increase the standard deviation of lateness. This problem is mitigated by policy P1 that splits jobs before release. In this case, a single card per sublot is required, not the whole set of cards for a job, therefore facilitating the release of large jobs. However, this creates another problem, as we can see from Fig. 3(d): once lots are released independently they have to wait for each other after processing, to gather for the sublots of each job, increasing therefore the synchronization delay. This problem is more expressive under GKS than under CONWIP. This behaviour of the synchronization delay is the main reason why policy P1 performs worse than P2 in terms of tardy jobs and job throughput time. One explanation for the severe effects of policy P1, on the synchronization delay under GKS is the need to have available the right cards from the right workstations required by the sublot routing. This tends to make the time interval for the release of all lots of the same job to be highly extended in relation to the case of policy P2, which releases the whole job at the same point in time.

4   Conclusions and Managerial Implications

This study on production logistics compares two card-based material flow control mechanisms GKS and CONWIP when applied to a make-to-order manufacturing system configured as a general flow shop. GKS was shown to outperform CONWIP in terms of the percentage of tardy jobs, system throughput time and standard deviation of lateness. It was also shown to be highly robust to the number of production authorization cards used to run the system. In fact, it sustained high levels of performance for a range of different numbers of cards used. This behaviour lends itself to practical application of the GKS. The reason for the good performance of GKS is its load balancing capability over workstations of the manufacturing system. This quality is not shared by the CONWIP system.

Lot splitting policies have shown to have a positive impact on both CONWIP and GKS performance. Better performance behaviour of GKS in relation to CONWIP was also verified under lot splitting.

We see some important managerial implications of this study. The main one is that under make-to-order and systems configured as general flow shop, card-based mechanisms can be used to achieve high levels of performance in terms of (1) the ability to deliver orders on time, and (2) the ability to provide short delivery times, particularly when combined with lot splitting policies. The use of these mechanisms has the advantages of requiring little data handling and allowing easy visual control of the flow of materials, which can be seen as attractive attributes for practical applications.

Although general flow shops have much in common to real world manufacturing systems' configurations, future research is planned to verify if the performance behaviour of the control strategies tested still applies under different shop configurations and manufacturing settings, e.g. considering set-up times since these have been proved to have an impact on throughput times as batch sizes change [10].

Acknowledgements. This study had the financial support of COMPETE: POCI-01-0145-FEDER-007043 and FCT – Fundação para a Ciência e Tecnologia within the Project Scope: UID/CEC/00319/2013

References

1. Bechte, W.: Load-oriented manufacturing control, just-in-time production for job shops. Prod. Planning Control **5**(3), 292–307 (1994)
2. Carmo-Silva, S., Alves, A.C.: A framework for understanding cellular manufacturing. In: Ferreira, J.J.P. (ed.) E-Manufacturing: Business Paradigms and Supporting Technologies, pp. 163–172. Springer, New York (2004)
3. Chang, J.H., Chiu, H.N.: A comprehensive review of lot streaming. Int. J. Prod. Res. **43**(8), 1515–1536 (2005)
4. Chang, T.M., Yih, Y.: Generic Kanban systems for dynamic environments. Int. J. Prod. Res. **32**(4), 889–902 (1994)
5. Cheng, M., Mukherjee, N.J., Sarin, S.C.: A review of lot streaming. Int. J. Prod. Res. **51**(23–24), 7023–7046 (2013)
6. Enns, S.T.: An integrated system for controlling shop loading and work flow. Int. J. Prod. Res. **33**(10), 2801–2820 (1995)
7. Germs, R., Riezebos, J.: Workload balancing capability of pull systems in MTO production. Int. J. Prod. Res. **48**(8), 2345–2360 (2010)

8. Henrich, P., Land, M., Gaalman, G.J.C.: Exploring applicability of the workload control concept. Int. J. Prod. Econ. **90**(2), 187–198 (2004)
9. Jacobs, F.R., Bragg, D.J.: Repetitive lots: flow time reductions through sequencing and dynamic batch sizing. Decis. Sci. **19**(1), 281–294 (1988)
10. Karmarkar, U.S.: Lot sizes, lead times and in-process inventories. Manage. Sci. **33**(3), 409–418 (1987)
11. Little, J.: A proof of the theorem L = λW. Oper. Res. **9**(3), 383–387 (1961)
12. Nyhuis, P., Wiendahl, H.-P.: Fundamentals of Production Logistics: Theory Tools and Applications. Springer, Heidelberg (2009)
13. Oosterman, B., Land, M.J., Gaalman, G.J.C.: The influence of shop characteristics on workload control. Int. J. Prod. Econ. **68**(1), 107–119 (2000)
14. Spearman, M., Woodruff, D.L., Hopp, W.J.: CONWIP: a pull alternative to Kanban. Int. J. Prod. Res. **28**(5), 879–894 (1990)
15. Wagner, B.J., Ragatz, G.L.: The impact of lot splitting on due date performance. J. Oper. Manage. **12**(1), 13–25 (1994)

Author Index

Printed in the United States
By Bookmasters